Here in its first English translation is the first part of *La Philosophie moderne*, originally published as the second volume of Émile Bréhier's *Histoire de la philosophie*.

Bréhier traces and illustrates the pervasive themes of the seventeenth century — the grandeur and the wretchedness of man, faith and reason, the concepts of "body" and "soul," the search for order in science and politics, absolutism and freedom. He examines the work of the moralists and political writers — Pascal, Nicole, La Rochefoucauld, and Hobbes; of the innovators and synthesizers—Descartes, whose seminal thinking dominated the century, Francis Bacon, Spinoza, Malebranche, Leibniz, and Locke; and of those who associated themselves with Cartesianism, Spinozism, anti-Spinozism, and Malebranchism.

Also discussed are the doctrine of occasional causes, innatism, German philosophy before Leibniz, the contributions of Bayle and Fontenelle, and late seventeenth-century English philosophy as represented by the rationalism inspired by Cambridge Platonism, by the rationalism of Samuel Clarke, and by critical rationalism.

Originally published in 1938 as Histoire de la philosophie:
La Philosophie moderne. I: Le dix-septième siècle.
© *1938, Presses Universitaires de France*

*The present bibliography has been revised and enlarged to
include recent publications. These have been
supplied by the translator and others.*

*Library of Congress Catalog Card Number: 63-20912
The University of Chicago Press, Chicago & London
The University of Toronto Press, Toronto 5, Canada
Translation © 1966 by The University of Chicago
All rights reserved. Published 1966
Printed in the United States of America*

THE HISTORY OF PHILOSOPHY

Volume 4 :

THE SEVENTEENTH CENTURY

BY ÉMILE BRÉHIER

TRANSLATED BY WADE BASKIN

THE UNIVERSITY OF CHICAGO PRESS

CHICAGO AND LONDON

CONTENTS

THE HISTORY OF PHILOSOPHY

THE SEVENTEENTH CENTURY

GENERAL CHARACTERISTICS OF
THE SEVENTEENTH CENTURY

1 *The Conception of Human Nature:*
Authority and Absolutism

NO CENTURY has exhibited less confidence than the
seventeenth century in the spontaneous forces of unbridled nature.
Where could we find a more wretched portrait of natural man—
the hapless victim of conflicting passions—than that provided by
political thinkers and moralists of the seventeenth century? On this
point Hobbes agreed with La Rochefoucauld and La Rochefoucauld
with the Jansenist Nicole: Hobbes held that men in the state of
nature were sinister beasts of prey that could be subdued only by
an absolute ruler, and the Jansenists were unwilling to admit that
any charitable or altruistic impulse in men given, through sin, to
concupiscence could have its source outside divine grace.

The seventeenth century was also the century of the Counter-
reformation and of absolutism. The Counterreformation eradicated
the pagan elements of the Renaissance and brought into full bloom
a Catholicism aware of its obligation to offer guidance to the minds
and souls of men. The Jesuit Society, which had more than two
hundred schools in France, provided educators, spiritual directors,
and missionaries. Thomism as formulated by the Jesuit Suarez was
universally taught and finally supplanted the doctrine of Melanch-

I

thon, even in the universities of Protestant countries. The Counter-reformation was instigated in Rome and drew its support from private efforts. The French royalty itself was Gallican and the English royalty was Anglican. Still, the rulers of France did not shrink from using violent means to assure religious unity, and the final blow came when the revocation of the Edict of Nantes simply did away with Protestantism.

The absolutism of the king was not the power of a strong individual to exact obedience from his subjects through personal prestige or by violent means; it was a social phenomenon which endured—independently of the person who exercised it—even during long minorities when omnipotent ministers exercised it in the name of the prince. This social phenomenon, of divine origin, imposed duties even more than it imposed rights, and the king, who is absolute by divine right but who is first subjugated to his task by election of God, is the exact opposite of the Renaissance tyrant.

Thus harsh measures were accepted and tolerated in religion and in politics by people who understood their necessity as well as their benefits. Rigid rules constituted not thraldom but support, and without them man would fall, disjointed and uncertain, like Montaigne in his *Essays*. Ceremony was his guide in social relations just as ritual was his guide in church.

There were instances of resistance, however, and they were frequent. In England, absolutism grounded on divine right twice collided with the common will and succumbed; in France, religious unity was established only at the price of periods of persecution. Throughout the seventeenth century Holland served as a refuge for the persecuted from all countries—the Jews from Spain and Portugal, the Socinians from Poland, and later the Protestants from France—but it was a precarious refuge where their lives were often endangered. The Catholic religion was itself threatened in France, its adopted country, by the quarrel of the Jansenists and the Molinists and, at the end of the century, by the stir raised by Mme Guynon's mysticism. Behind these known facts lay hidden an intellectual ferment which was translated into thousands of incidents, books, or lampoons now forgotten. Declarations in support of freedom and tolerance did not begin in the eighteenth century; they were heard continually throughout the seventeenth century, especially in England and in Holland, and the century drew to a close with a bitter debate between Bossuet, who supported the divine right of kings, and Jurieu, the Protestant statesman who defended the sovereignty of the people.

On closer examination, however, we find that these protestations and debates bear the mark of the century: they were not penned by individualists concerned only with promoting their private opinions.

Here we should note that one of the most characteristic productions of the century was the *De jure belli ac pacis* (1625) of Hugo Grotius (1583–1645), the author of the doctrine of natural law, who claimed he had discovered universal laws binding on all men even when they resort to the use of force. Not individuals but impersonal reason determines whether a war is just or unjust, whether a prince has the right to impose a religion on his subjects, and what is the legitimate scope of his authority. Where Machiavelli saw conflicts between individual forces that could be resolved only through violence, Grotius saw clearly defined relations based on law. Natural law is a rule of reason that commands or prohibits an action depending on whether such action is in harmony or disharmony with the nature of rational beings. The rule is in no way arbitrary and could not be changed by God himself. Natural law is joined to positive law, which is established either by God (in matters of positive religion) or by the sovereign (in matters of civil legislation); the one great rule of positive law is not to contradict natural law. By the same token, within these limits, it is the law of nature to respect positive law. Consequently, Grotius' system leads generally to the conclusion that the established powers must be respected. For example, it does not recognize the right of the people to resist their sovereign; indeed, the reason why the people formed a nation and accepted a sovereign was that the individuals were too weak to subsist alone. Moreover, there was nothing to prevent them from giving their sovereign absolute control over their lives—the control a master has over his slaves. The tendency of his argument is obviously to justify rationally certain positive laws—the laws of warfare, punishment, property, and sovereignty. Law exists not for the purpose of making men independent of each other but for the purpose of uniting them. Although Grotius pleaded for tolerance toward all positive religions, he drew the line when it came to atheists and to those who denied the immortality of the soul: natural religion is as binding as natural law.

The question of tolerance was posed in the same spirit. In England, for example, pleas for tolerance were of two kinds: either they were made by men who thought that they were rediscovering reason through a natural religion comprehensive enough to unite all churches and bring an end to dissension, or they were directed toward freedom of interpretation of the Bible, "the only religion of the Protestants," according to Chillingworth. Associated with pleas of the first kind were men like Herbert of Cherbury, who in his *De veritate* (1628) advocated a means of ending religious controversies and "the stubbornness with which wretched men embrace all the opinions of the doctors, or reject them wholesale, as if they do not know how to choose." [1] The choice was to be made by separating common notions—which were primitive, independent, universal, necessary, and certain—from all adventitious beliefs. These common notions constituted a veritable credo which predicated a sovereign power that must be worshiped and which taught that worship consisted mainly in a virtuous life, that vices must be expiated through repentance, and that vices would be punished after death just as virtue would be rewarded—a natural religion that established universal peace, though not without a trenchant criticism of the illusion of "private revelations" and especially of the notion that divine grace, individually bestowed, was necessary for salvation. At the end of the century Locke still clung to the same notions.

Associated with pleas of the second kind were men who preserved the spirit of free thought inherited from the Reformation.

---

[1] 1639 edition, p. 52.

But, according to its defenders, free thought had the sole function of eradicating gradually, through independent criticism, everything Bossuet called "private opinions" and "variations," with the result that it was but another means of arriving at "catholicity" though the route chosen was different from that of authority. Freedom of thought together with the conflicts that it implied seemed to Milton (*Areopagitica,* written in 1644, after Cromwell's victory) to be the prerequisite of a truth that must be won by continuous progress; if the waters of truth "flow not in a perpetual progression, they sicken into a muddy pool of conformity and tradition." Truth, of course, "turns herself into all shapes except her own, and perhaps tunes her voice according to the time," but this is not an instance of skepticism: "Truth is strong next to the Almighty." [2]

Whereas tolerance was linked to a strong religious sentiment, which united men, the skepticism of the freethinkers led to religious intolerance—another path to unity. The disciples of Machiavelli championed a state religion. Hobbes provides us with a good example, and James Harington in his *Commonwealth of Oceana* (1656) describes a state church that would be controlled by the clergy in the universities. Conversely, it was against a religious background that there emerged in England the idea of a secular state, completely independent of religion; at the beginning of the century the Anabaptists proclaimed that a national church to which all belonged from birth contradicted faith, a personal gift of the Holy Spirit, and they preached revolt against intolerant princes.[3]

Despite all these conflicts, advocates of a natural religion and revelation, defenders of tolerance, and apologists of a state religion had a common goal: unity capable of binding individuals together and keeping them together.

Socinianism, the movement that spread from Poland to Holland and England after the end of the sixteenth century, also rejected everything in religion subject to controversy and dissension. Named

[2] Quoted by Denis Saurat, *Milton et le matérialisme chrétien en Angleterre* (Paris, 1928), p. 206. [English follows the *Areopagitica.*—Trans.]

[3] Freund, *Die Idee der Toleranz im England der grossen Revolution* (Halle, 1927), pp. 224–25.

after Faustus Socinus (Sozzini), an Italian who fled to Poland in 1579, it was like a revival of Arianism. The Socinians denied the Trinity, the divinity of Christ, and the sacramental value of the Eucharist and infant baptism; furthermore, they denied the theory of atonement according to which divine justice could be fulfilled only through the suffering of God's own son. Thus they simplified religion by eliminating all its mysteries and its supernatural side— not because they refused to base religion on the revelation of Scripture but because "they think that they are not excluding reason but rather including it when they state that the Holy Scripture is sufficient for salvation." And to the rationality of beliefs was joined their plea for tolerance, which they posited as the necessary condition of social stability: "With the severance of the bond that unites under the same law all those who hold different opinions concerning divine things," they wrote to the states of Holland (1614), "comes the collapse and retrogression of everything."

The Arminians or Remonstrants, who broke with Calvinism after the Synod of Dort (1618–19), tried in the same way to eradicate from the theory of grace every element of mystery, everything incompatible with human notions of justice. Arminius (1560–1609) denied the "absolute decree" of God who, according to Calvin, predestines the salvation of the souls he elects; and he argued against Gomarus (1563–1641) that each man was responsible for whatever sanctions he might incur.

Using a different approach, the Catholics also were diligently seeking unity. They found it only in divinely inspired authority, in the unbroken tradition and discipline of the Church (whereas the other sects under discussion grounded their search on reason). The debate about grace, which pitted Jansenists against Molinists after 1640, was a debate between theologians who accused one another of being unfaithful to tradition or of breaching discipline. Their conflict focused attention on the Christian life itself rather than on theoretical discussions.

In addition, the Jesuits adhered to the policy of transferring the debate from the domain of doctrine and dogma to that of discipline.

They had Port Royal condemned not for supporting a particular dogma concerning grace but for resisting the authority of the pope and of the king. Richelieu kept St. Cyran in prison in the fortress of Vincennes after 1638, at the instigation of the Jesuits, because St. Cyran had defended the rights of the secular hierarchy.

The main incident of the struggle hinged on the question of the limits of spiritual authority. In 1649 the syndic of the faculty, Father Cornet, presented five propositions concerning efficacious grace to the faculty, hoping to have them condemn the doctrine advanced by Jansen and his supporters, but without naming its author. These five propositions were condemned by Pope Innocent X in 1653. But his decision—although it was accepted without protest by Arnauld and his friends—did not satisfy the Jesuits, who wished to go even further and have the five propositions identified as extracts from Jansen's *Augustinus*. Thus, to the question of law, "Are these five propositions heretical?" was added the question of fact, "Are they Jansen's?" The validity of the law could be established only on the basis of authority, but the validity of facts could be established only by experience. Consequently, in 1654 a convocation of bishops decided that the five propositions were in the *Augustinus,* not because they found them there but because the bull of 1653 seemed to attribute them to Jansen. In 1655 Pope Alexander VII renewed the condemnation by treating those who did not believe that the propositions were Jansen's as "children of iniquity." A formulary was drawn up setting down both the law and the facts; it was to be signed by all clerics and members of religious orders in France. In 1665 a new bull prescribed the signing of the formulary and prohibited any accompanying restriction. The nuns of Port Royal kept protesting that, although they submitted completely to the pope with respect to the law, they could not affirm the existence of a fact that they were not in a position to verify independently.

With respect to the heart of the dispute, the theory of grace, the aim of the Port-royalists (gratuitously called Jansenists) was to direct man's attention to his utter helplessness when isolated and separated from the universal source of all being. Man can learn what he is and what he can accomplish only through revelation, and the power of his will to pursue the good is realized fully only under the influence of efficacious grace. The theory of efficacious grace brings out clearly the deep-rooted hostility between the naturalistic humanism of the Renaissance, which claimed to find in the wonders of antiquity proof of the power of human nature, and the conditions governing the Christian life. But the new emphasis was opportune, for we must note that Jansenism left intact and even enhanced whatever was vital and fruitful in the intellectual current that had issued from the sixteenth century. Nicole said of geometry: "Its object is not linked in any way to concupiscence." [4] Thus there is a whole sphere of knowledge—knowledge of things in the material world, astronomy, physics—where selfish interests have no part and where the light of nature, undimmed by sin, allows man to discover the truth for himself. Arnauld went even further and conceded that a society, whatever its nature, could not exist without observing the maxims of justice which are rooted in a natural law and of which man has innate knowledge. The Jansenists, still hostile in this respect to Scholasticism, accepted every particle of Renaissance innatism; they were, in their own way, true humanists.

Truths revealed by the light of nature and conduct inspired by it, however, cannot justify us in the eyes of God and save us. In 1641 Arnauld refuted the book of La Mothe le Vayer, *On the Virtue of the Pagans,* in which the author marshaled telling examples from antiquity to prove the futility of salvation through Christ.[5] Pagan virtues are sterile and illusory, Arnauld replied, if we seek out their cause: ambition, vanity, the search for inner satisfaction—in short, the fundamental sin that consists in believing in our own self-sufficiency. This is true because nothing more closely resembles the effects of charity than the effects of self-love. "In states where [charity] cannot enter because true religion is excluded, a man can live as peacefully, as securely, and as comfortably as if

[4] Quoted by J. Laporte, *La Doctrine de la Grâce chez Arnauld,* p. 111, n. 74.
[5] *Ibid.,* p. 137.

he were in a republic of saints." [6] This is because self-love "imitates the main actions of charity" and produces "human decency," humility, kindness, moderation. The Jansenists adopted the same views as La Rochefoucauld, whose celebrated *Maxims* were written in 1665. We recall what he said about himself: "I am not very sensitive to pity, and I wish I were completely insensitive to it. Still, I would do my best to comfort a person in distress, and I also believe that one ought even to go so far as to express much compassion for his suffering . . . but I also hold that one must be satisfied with expressing compassion without actually feeling it." [7] What better commentary could there be on Jansenist views!

If the Jansenists were right, there is no morality, no virtue other than Christian morality and Christian virtue. These must be separated from worldly life, which has its own rules; they find no support in nature or society. They are possible only through a sort of transmutation of our will under the influence of divine grace—an irresistible influence, yet one that does not destroy, but rather fortifies, free will if it is true that God and the soul, instead of being two complementary realities external to each other, fuse and interpenetrate under the influence of grace.

II *The Conception of External Nature: Galileo, Gassendi, and Atomism*

Thus man's idea of his own nature took on a new form. The individualistic ardor of the Renaissance subsided and gave way to the belief that the individual must be guided by order and unity— unity grounded on reason or on authority. Man's image of external nature had undergone a similar change: the vital, exuberant spontaneity that men like Bruno saw in nature gave way to the rigid rules of mechanism; only faint traces of Renaissance animism remained, still represented by Campanella. Not only was life withheld

---

[6] P. Nicole, *Essais de morale,* in *Œuvres philosophiques et morales de Nicole,* ed. C. Jourdain (Paris, 1845), p. 181.
[7] Autobiographical sketch printed in 1658.

from nature; Descartes even withheld it, so to speak, from the living being which he made into a simple machine. Aristotle's substantial forms were condemned even in the universities. At Leiden, even before 1618, men were wondering about the nature of beings "really distinct from matter and yet material, whether a part of matter changes into form, whether form pre-exists in matter, as a bench pre-exists in the plank from which it is made." [8]

Prevalent everywhere was a mechanistic conception that eliminated from nature any semblance of vital spontaneity. The tendency was dominant in Galileo, Hobbes, and Descartes as well as in more obscure philosophers like Gassendi, Basson, and Bérigard, who revived the teachings of Democritus and Epicurus.

Galileo (1564–1642) was not actually the author of a theory of universal mechanics, but he laid the groundwork for such a theory by creating a physico-mathematical science of nature that would accommodate diverse phenomena. He did not say what things were, but he proved that mathematics with its triangles, circles, and geometric figures was the sole language capable of deciphering the book of nature. He was more interested in the method of deciphering nature than in studying the nature of living beings; the "compositive" or synthetic method draws together under a single mathematical formula a great number of observed facts— the formulas that he discovered concerning the laws of gravitation, for instance—and the "resolutive" or analytic method makes it possible for us to deduce from these laws a great number of separate facts. For the first time we find a clear, pure idea of natural law as a functional relation; henceforth the progress of mathematics would keep pace with that of physics, and this would impose on the philosopher a new manner of posing the problem of the relation between the mind, the author of mathematics, and nature, which the mind interprets through mathematics. Furthermore, the new methods were possible only by virtue of the exact measurement of individual phenomena, and the numerical data provided by experiment were the only data that applied to the discovery of

---

[8] Quoted in Bayle's *Dictionary*, art. *Heidanus*.

laws. Galileo therefore was led to consider that which can be measured as the only true reality. Thus we see in him a revival of the ideas of Democritus: sensible qualities, such as color and smell, are not in things, for we can imagine things without these qualities; sound and heat, apart from the mind, are but modes of motion. Galileo was inclined for the same reason to favor the corpuscular theory of matter although he did not accept it as proved. He also supported the theory of Copernicus and tried to find experimental proofs of the theory; and we recall that he was forced by the Inquisition to renounce his opinion before the Holy Office (1632). We see, then, that Galileo treated universal mechanics as a technical discovery and not as a necessity grounded in the nature of mind and of things; that is why he allowed many traces of the old elements to subsist in his thought: Aristotle's distinction between natural and violent motion, for example, and the spontaneous tendency of the stars to move in circles (which implicitly denies the principle of inertia, the basis of universal mechanics).[9]

The atomistic and anti-Aristotelian movement which emerged in France at the beginning of the seventeeth century and which in fact issued from the atomism of the Renaissance showed the same tendency. Sebastian Basson, in a book which even has an aggressive title (*Philosophiae naturalis adversus Aristotelem libri XII, in quibus abstrusa veterum physiologia restauratur, et Aristotelis errores solidis rationibus refelluntur*), offers us an image of the universe based on elementary particles of a different nature: they are surfaces as in the *Timaeus,* not corpuscles as in Democritus. These atoms, aggregated in the form of bodies, do not exist in a void but are immersed in a fluid, continuous ether—the medium through which the divine power is transmitted. The hypothesis of continuous ether obviously discouraged acceptance of the notion of physical mechanics.

Claude Bérigard (1578–1663), a French professor in Padua, published in the *Circulus Pisanus* (1643) a series of commentaries

---

[9] On the last point, cf. A. Koyré, *Galilée et la loi d'inertie* (Paris, 1939), pp. 45–78.

on Aristotelian physics in which he contrasted the latter with the corpuscular physics of Anaxagoras. He conceived of an infinite number of qualitatively different corpuscles. Like Descartes, and in contrast to Democritus, he accepted the plenum and explained motion as a continuous ring of bodies each of which immediately replaced the preceding one (Anaxagoras' system of physics was of course annular). The *Democritus reviviscens* (1646) of Jean Magnien, a French professor in Pavia, posited atoms that were indivisible and yet capable of changing their shape. Here he was guided by Epicurus' theory of *minima,* according to which the atom was not simple but composed of very small particles which, in their relative arrangement, produced the shape of the atom. Magnien added to the hypothesis the notion that the inner arrangement might change even though the number of minima remained identical in a particular atom. That he, too, was reluctant to accept universal mechanics is demonstrated by the fact that he searched for the moving cause of atoms in sympathetic attraction or in the tendency of atoms to join together to produce a body with a determinate essence. It is strange that not one of these atomists saw collision as the cause of motion; Basson's ether, Bérigard's vortex, Magnien's sympathetic attraction all show how indistinct was the idea of universal mechanism when Descartes gave it a new formulation.

Nearer to Lucretius and at the same time more closely linked to the intellectual trend of the time was the atomism of Pierre Gassendi (1592–1655), whose detailed explanations of natural phenomena long rivaled those of Descartes. Gassendi, provost of the cathedral at Digne, championed astronomical observation and the system of Copernicus. He corresponded with Galileo, to whom he wrote during his trial at the Holy Office: "I am deeply disturbed by the fate that awaits you, O you greatest glory of the century; if the Holy See decides something contrary to your belief, endure it as befits a sage. May you at least live secure in the knowledge that you have sought after truth." From Epicureanism he accepted the sensualist theory of knowledge. He censured Descartes for his innatism and especially for the idea of God he professed to have, since God remains incomprehensible to a mind enslaved by sensible images. To Herbert of Cherbury he objected that investigation into the inner nature of things results from intemperance in our desire to know, and that human knowledge ought to be restricted to whatever is indispensable to life—that is, to the external qualities that fall under the senses; only the creator of things can know their nature.[10] His atomism bears no trace of originality; it is the atomism of Lucretius and of Epicurus' *Letters*—invisible atoms of different shapes, falling through the void. Only two traits identify him: Gassendi makes gravity—the principle of motion inherent in the atom, "a propensity to motion, unengendered, innate, impossible to lose"—something given to the atom by God. All atoms move through the void at the same speed, and collisions between them have the effect of changing their direction, not their motion. That is diametrically opposed to the principles of Cartesian mechanics, which makes velocity following collision dependent not only on the velocity of the colliding bodies but also on their mass. In any case it follows that no body is at rest; apparent rest hides very rapid but very slight internal motions. The second distinctive trait is that the universe is considered as a completely integrated, regular whole, which cannot be the result of a fortuitous concourse of atoms but can be explained only by an omnipotent God. Superimposed on Epicureanism, then, is a theology that introduces finality. Gassendi even superimposed a spiritualistic theory upon Epicurus' materialistic theory of the soul which he accepted in its entirely: the effective, vegetative, and sensitive soul is, in effect, merely a very subtle and tenuous body, and sensation, for example, is adequately explained by the impression made on this substance by the *idola* emitted by each body; but above the soul that perishes with the body is an immaterial substance capable of self-reflection, of reason, and of freedom.

A similar combination of mechanistic and spiritualistic theories, so unfaithful to the authentic spirit of Epicurus, was characteristic of the period. Nature was abandoned, turned over to its own

---

[10] *Opera,* III, 413.

mechanism; it was forsaken by the mind that had studied it, penetrated it, and found in it no support. The consequences were more apparent in Descartes and in Hobbes.

III   *The Organization of Intellectual Life:
Academies and Scientific Gatherings*

The aspirations of the century were translated into profound disgust for the sectarian struggles that had inflamed the Renaissance. Meditating upon the texts of Plato or Plotinus was no longer the rule. La Mothe le Vayer considered one of the most important results of his "Christian Skepticism" to be the joint dismissal of Plato and Aristotle, both of whom contradict theology, thus leaving "the soul of the Christian Skeptic like a field that has been cleared and rid of bad plants." [11] Distaste for sectarianism was matched by a marked reaction against the study of Greek. Except at Port Royal the course of studies did not include Greek because of the pagan spirit associated with it. Comenius (1592–1670), the great Moravian teacher, did not include Greek in his plan of studies, nor did he see fit to include dangerous Latin authors. "With the exception of Seneca, Epictetus, Plato, and other such virtuous and honorable masters, he would like to see other pagan authors banished from Christian schools." [12] Reduced, or almost reduced, to Latin, studies of the ancients were intended solely to shape literary taste, to contribute, by means of spirited statements, to moral training, and to give students practice in using the current scientific language. That is what Descartes retained from his classical studies under the Jesuits—in other words, nothing that might be of any use in educating him as a philosopher. The contempt with which philosophers viewed erudition reached its limit with Malebranche, and at the end of the century Locke eliminated Greek from his plan of education.

On account of its sectarian particularism, therefore, Greco-Latin

---

[11] *Prose chagrine,* in *Œuvres complètes* (Dresden, 1756), V, 299–318.
[12] Anna Heyberger, *Jean Amos Comenius* (Paris, 1928), p. 146.

antiquity posed as great a danger to science as to faith. Philosophy has as the object of its search true universality. Its exemplar is found in mathematical and experimental techniques developed without reference to any known philosophy. Cavalieri, Fermat, and Harvey, and a century earlier Ambroise Paré and Bernard Palissy, were independent of the philosophers of their time just as Archimedes, Apollonius, and Hero of Alexandria were independent of their Stoic contemporaries. It is obvious that nothing contributed less to intellectual progress in mathematics and the natural sciences than the theories of the mind elaborated during the Middle Ages and the practice of dialectic, which was intended to reveal agreement or disagreement between opinions.

In exposition, philosophy was stripped of all its technical apparatus. Discourses, essays, meditations, conversations, dialogues— all were literary forms borrowed from Christian or pagan antiquity and revived by sixteenth-century humanists. Direct and unencumbered by scholarly discussion, these forms found favor with seventeenth-century thinkers. Descartes wanted people to read his *Principles* for the first time just as they would read a novel. Like Montaigne, Bacon (a great admirer of Machiavelli) wrote *Essays* in which he set down fully his experience as a man of the court and as a man of the world.

The same generality was manifested even in the lives of the great philosophers, who were anything but academics: Bacon, a courtier who expended so much energy in upholding in judicial practice the doctrine of royal prerogative of James I; Descartes, a French gentleman who lived in seclusion; Hobbes, secretary of a great English lord and a frequent traveler on the Continent; Spinoza, a Jew who had been expelled from the synagogue and who earned his living by polishing lenses; Malebranche, an Oratorian; Leibniz, minister of a petty German prince, whose mind was always filled with vast political projects; and Locke, a good, liberal, middle-class Englishman.

Outside and remote from the universities new intellectual circles were formed, private ones at first, like the society of scholars and philosophers who gathered around Father Mersenne, a member of the Minim Order and a friend and correspondent of Descartes. Pascal said of Mersenne: "He was responsible for several outstanding discoveries which probably would never have been made if he had not stimulated other scholars." [13] Then came the Academy of Sciences (1658), offshoot of private gatherings which began with Montmor in 1636 and were attended by Roberval, Gassendi, and the two Pascals.[14] There was a similar development in Italy: the Lincei Academy, founded in 1603, welcomed Galileo in 1616; and the Cimento, founded in Florence in 1657, maintained relations with the Parisian Academy and communicated to it the results of some of its studies.[15] In England the Royal Society of London drew together, after 1645, all those interested in "philosophical matters, physics, anatomy, geometry, astronomy, navigation, magnetism, chemistry, mechanics, experiments with nature." Their rules stated that "the society will not subscribe to any hypothesis, any system, any doctrine concerning the principles of natural philosophy, proposed or mentioned by any philosopher, ancient or modern." More than anything else, they refused to risk passing off their private thoughts as common notions; experience alone must decide.[16] Finally, in the last year of the century Leibniz founded a society in Berlin that later became the Academy of Science.

The voluminous correspondence of men like Descartes and Leibniz (their letters were often veritable treatises) bears witness to the vigor of intellectual exchanges. But in the second half of the century there also came into being a press devoted to scientific news: in France, the *Journal des Savants* (1644) and the *Nouvelles de la République des Lettres,* a review which was founded by Bayle (1684) and which later (1687–1709) became the *Histoire des Ou-*

---

[13] This activity is revealed in the *Correspondance du P. Mersenne.* The first two volumes (letters from 1617 to 1630) were published by Mme Paul Tannery (Paris, 1933; Beauchesne, 1937). Publication of the remaining volumes has been assured by C. de Waard, in collaboration with Lenoble and Rochot. Volume V (1635) appeared in 1959.

[14] Alfred Maury, *Les Académies d'autrefois* (Paris, 1864).

[15] A. Maugain, *Étude sur l'évolution intellectuelle de l'Italie* (Paris, 1909).

[16] P. Florian, "De Bacon à Newton," *Revue de Philosophie,* 1914.

vrages des Savants, edited by Protestants. Finally, in Leipzig, Leibniz founded the *Acta eruditorum* (1682).

Nothing from the past compares with this tenacious, continuous, collective quest for a universal and yet human truth. The thirty years between 1620 and 1650 were decisive years in the history of the movement: Bacon published the *Novum organum* (1620) and the *De dignitate et augmentis scientiarum* (1623); Galileo wrote his *Dialogo* (1632) and his *Discorsi* (1638); Descartes published the *Discourse on the Method* (1637), *Meditations* (1641), and *Principles* (1644); the philosophy of law and political philosophy were taken up by Grotius (*De jure belli ac pacis,* 1625) and by Hobbes (*De cive,* 1642). All these works indicate that the humanistic phase of the Renaissance—which had always, to some degree, confused erudition and philosophy—had definitely ended. An emergent rationalism set itself to consider human reason not from the standpoint of its divine origin but from the standpoint of its positive activity.

Would reason be the principle of order, of organization, sought by all during the seventeenth century? Would it be capable, if "properly managed," of advancing human knowledge and even, beyond that, of introducing a social bond between all men? This question accounts for the enduring interest of that new upsurge of intellectual activity.

BIBLIOGRAPHY

Useful Translations and Anthologies

The English Philosophers from Bacon to Mill. Edited by Edwin A. Burth. New York, 1939.
The European Philosophers from Descartes to Nietzsche. Edited by Monroe C. Beardsley. New York, 1960.
Philosophers Speak for Themselves. Edited by T. V. Smith and Marjorie Grene. New ed. 4 vols. Chicago, 1957. Vol. III, *From Descartes to Locke.*
Philosophic Classics. Edited by Walter Kaufmann. 2 vols. Englewood Cliffs, N.J., 1961. Vol. II, *Bacon to Kant.*
The Philosophy of the Sixteenth and Seventeenth Centuries. Edited by Richard H. Popkin. New York, 1966.

Histories and Studies of Seventeenth Century Thought

Burtt, E. A. *The Metaphysical Foundations of Modern Physical Science.* 2d ed. New York, 1955.
Butterfield, Herbert. *The Origins of Modern Science.* Rev. ed. New York, 1962.
Butterfield, Herbert, et al. *A Short History of Science.* Garden City, N.Y., 1959.
Cassirer, Ernst. *The Problem of Knowledge.* Translated by William H. Woglom and Charles W. Hendel. New Haven, Conn., 1950.
Clark, G. N. *The Seventeenth Century.* 2d ed. Oxford, 1947.
Copleston, Frederick C. *A History of Philosophy.* 7 vols. London, 1946–62. Vol. IV, *Descartes to Leibniz;* Vol. V, *Hobbes to Hume.*
Crombie, A. C. *Augustine to Galileo: The History of Science, A.D. 400–1650.* London, 1952.
Dampier, W. C. *A History of Science and Its Relations with Philosophy and Religion.* 4th ed. Cambridge, 1949.
Dibon, Paul. *La philosophie néerlandaise au siècle d'or.* Amsterdam, 1954.
Dunning, W. A. *A History of Political Theories from Luther to Montesquieu.* New York, 1905.
Flint, R. *Philosophy of History in Europe.* London, 1874.
Gilson, Etienne, and Thomas Langan. *Modern Philosophy from Descartes to Kant.* New York, 1963.
Hall, A. R. *The Scientific Revolution, 1500–1800.* 2d ed. London, 1962.

Hazard, P. *The European Mind, 1680–1715*. Translated by J. L. May. London, 1953.

Höffding, H. *A History of Modern Philosophy*. Translated by B. E. Meyer. 2 vols. New York, 1950.

Laporte, J. *Études d'histoire de la philosophie française au XVIIe siècle*. Paris, 1951.

Lovejoy, Arthur O. *The Great Chain of Being*. Reprint: Cambridge, Mass., 1948.

Popkin, Richard H. *The History of Scepticism from Erasmus to Descartes*. New York, 1964.

Randall, John H. *The Career of Philosophy from the Middle Ages to the Enlightenment*. New York, 1962.

Sabine, G. H. *A History of Political Theory*. Rev. ed. New York, 1950.

Strong, E. W. *Procedures and Metaphysics: A Study in the Philosophy of Mathematical and Physical Science in the Sixteenth and Seventeenth Centuries*. Berkeley, Calif., 1936.

Überweg, F. *Grundriss der Geschichte der Philosophie*. 12th ed. 5 vols. Berlin, 1923. Vol. III, *Die Philosophie der Neuzeit bis zum Ende des XVIII Jahrhunderts*, edited by M. Frischeisen-Köhler and W. Moog.

Wightman, W. P. D. *The Growth of Scientific Ideas*. New Haven, Conn., 1951.

Willey, Basil. *The Seventeenth Century Background*. London, 1934.

Wolf, A. *A History of Science, Technology and Philosophy in the Sixteenth and Seventeenth Centuries*. 2d ed., revised by D. McKie. London, 1950.

A Critical History of Western Philosophy. Edited by D. J. O'Conner. New York, 1964.

I

Texts

Bodin, Jean. *Œuvres philosophiques*. Edited and translated by P. Mesnard. Paris, 1951.

Studies

Busson, H. *La pensée religieuse française de Charron à Pascal*. Paris, 1933.

Laporte, J. *La doctrine de Port-Royal*. 2 vols. Paris, 1923–52.

Mesnard, P. *L'essor de la philosophie politique au XVIe siècle*. Paris, 1936.

Moreau-Reibel, J. *Jean Bodin et le droit public comparé dans ses rapports avec la philosophie de l'histoire*. Paris, 1933.

———. *Le droit de société interhumaine et le jus gentium . . . jusqu'à Grotius*. Paris, 1950.

Pintard, R. *Le libertinage érudit dans la première moitié du XVIIe siècle*. Paris, 1943.

Polin, R. "Économique et politique au XVIᵉ siècle: L'Oceana de James Harrington," *Revue française de science politique,* 1952, pp. 24–41.
Reynolds, B. *Proponents of Limited Monarchy in Sixteenth Century France: Francis Hotman and Jean Bodin.* New York, 1931.

II

Texts

Gassendi, Pierre. *Opera omnia.* Edited by H. L. Habert de Montmort. 6 vols. Lyons, 1658–75.
———. *Dissertations en forme de paradoxes contre les Aristotéliciens.* Edited and translated by B. Rochot. Paris, 1959.
———. *Disquisitio metaphysica.* Edited and translated by B. Rochet. Paris, 1962.

Studies

Brent, G. S. *The Philosophy of Gassendi.* New York, 1908.
Koyré, A. *Études galiléennes.* 3 vols. Paris, 1939.
Rochot, B. "Gassendi et la logique de Descartes," *Revue philosophique,* 1955.

III

Text

Mersenne, Marin. *Correspondance.* Edited by Mme P. Tannery, C. de Waard, R. Lenoble, and B. Rochot. 5 vols. Paris, 1933–59.

Studies

Lenoble, R. *Mersenne; ou, La naissance du mécanisme.* Paris, 1943.
———. "Les origines de la pensée scientifique moderne," in *Histoire de la science,* edited by M. Daumas. Paris, 1957. Pp. 369–534.
History of Science. Edited by R. Taton. Translated by A. J. Pomerans. 3 vols. New York, 1964. Vol. II, *The Beginnings of Modern Science from 1450 to 1800.*

FRANCIS BACON AND
EXPERIMENTAL PHILOSOPHY

1 The Life and Works of Bacon

FRANCIS BACON (1561–1626) was the son of Sir Nicholas Bacon, Lord Keeper of the Great Seal, who prepared him for a career as a statesman. Elected to the House of Commons in 1584, he later became learned counsel to the Crown; during the reign of James I he was appointed to the highest judicial offices. His education was that of a jurist. Licensed in 1582, he began teaching at the school of law in London in 1589; in 1599 he edited his *Maxims of the Law,* which was to serve as a basis for the codification of English laws. Ambitious, scheming, adept at changing sides whenever this was to his advantage and at flattering the absolutist pretentions of James I, he rose gradually through the ranks, becoming Solicitor General in 1607, Attorney General in 1613, Lord Keeper in 1617, and Grand Chancellor in 1618. He was created Baron Verulam in 1618 and Viscount St. Albans in 1621. He always defended the royal prerogative. He was responsible for the condemnation of Talbot, a member of the Irish Parliament, who had approved Suarez' ideas on the legitimacy of tyrannicide. In the matter of ecclesiastical commendams he established the principle that judges must suspend judgment and confer with the king whenever the king believes that his power is at issue in a pending suit. It was the meeting of Parliament in 1621 that brought about his downfall. Accused by the House of Commons of bribery and corrupt dealings in chancery suits, he admitted that he had indeed received gifts from parties involved in pending litigation. The House of Lords sentenced him to a fine of 40,000 pounds and prohibited him from ever discharging any public office, from sitting in Parliament, and from living close to the Court. Old, sick, and dishonored, he tried in vain to win reinstatement. He died five years later.

In spite of such an active career, Bacon was forever concerned with the advancement of learning. His works, considered as a whole, have a unified character. It was undoubtedly early in his career that he conceived the comprehensive work outlined in the preface of the *Novum organum* (1620) and later called the *Instauratio magna,* for in a letter written in 1625 he stated that he had prepared a treatise on the subject forty years earlier. The treatise, entitled *Temporis partus maximus (The Greatest Parturition of Time),* may be identical with the *Temporis partus masculus sive de interpretatione naturae,* a short posthumous treatise containing a plan almost identical to that found in the preface to the *Novum organum.* In any case, the last plan contains six divisions: (1) "Partiones scientarum" (Classification of the Sciences); (2) "Novum organum sive indicia de interpretatione naturae"; (3) "Phenomena universi sive historia naturalis et experimentalis ad condendam philosophiam"; (4) "Scala intellectus sive filum labyrinthi"; (5) "Prodromi sivi anticipationes philosophiae secundae"; (6) "Philosophia secunda sive scientia activa." The realization of his plan called for a series of treatises which, starting from the actual state of learning, with all its lacunae (I), first discussed the new organon designed to replace that of Aristotle (II), then described the investigation of facts (III), passed on to the investigation of laws (IV), and returned to the actions and knowledge that allowed us to control nature (V and VI). The treatises that we possess are like the *disjecta membra* of a vast undertaking which could never be realized, as Bacon was the first to admit, by a single man. We cite most of them by classifying them according to the plan of the *Instauratio* (though they were not written in that order). According to his own admission, only the first part of the projected work was completed: the *De dignitate et augmentis scientiarum libri IX,* published in 1623. This treatise was a Latin translation, with many additions, of the *Advancement of Learning,* published in 1605. His papers also contained other outlines of the same subject: the *Valerius terminus,* written about 1603 and published in 1736, and the *Descriptio globi intellectualis,* written around 1612 and published in 1653. The *Novum organum sive indicia vera de interpretatione naturae,* published in 1620, corresponds to the second part. The third part, whose aim is indicated in a tract published after the *Novum organum,* the *Parasceve ad historiam naturalem et experimentalem,* is treated in the *Historia naturalis et experimentalis ad condendam philosophiam sive Phaenomena universi,* published in 1622. This work announced a number of monographs, some of which were written or outlined after the Chancellor's downfall: the *Historia vitae et mortis,* published in 1623; the *Historia densi et rari* (1658); the *Historia ventorum* (1622); and the *Sylva sylvarum,* a collection of materials published in 1627. To the fourth part belong the *Filum labyrinthi sive inquisitio legitima de motu,* composed in 1608 and published in 1653; the *Topica inquisitionis de luce et lumine* (1653); and the *Inquisitio de magnete* (1658). To the fifth part (*Prodromi sive anticipationes philosophiae secundae,* published in 1653) belong three works published in 1653: the *De fluxu et refluxu maris,* written in 1616; the *Thema caeli,* written in 1612; and the *Cogitationes de natura rerum,* written between 1600 and 1604. Finally, second philosophy is the subject of the *Cogitata et visa de interpretatione naturae sive de scientia operativa* and of the third book of the *Temporis partus masculus,* published in 1653.

Even treatises that are not integral parts of his great work relate to it: the *Redargutio philosophiarum,* published in 1736; and especially the *New Atlantis,* a plan for organizing scientific research, published in 1627. To these must be added his literary works, the

Essays (1597), which were enlarged with each new edition (1612 and 1625), and a great number of historical and legal works.

Through his writing he was the herald of a new spirit, a trumpeter whose mission was to awaken and to initiate a new movement that would transform human life by assuring man's domination over nature. He had the zeal of an initiator and a vivid imagination that engraved precepts in unforgettable characters; but he also had the systematic mind of a legislator or an administrator, prudence that bordered on fastidiousness, and the desire to apportion to each individual (the observer, the experimenter, the discoverer of laws) a limited and precise role in the secular work that he was initiating.

II *The Baconian Ideal: Understanding and Experimental Science*

Bacon considered the existing state of the sciences and of the intellectual world. He saw around him (he ignored or failed to recognize the works of the great minds of his era, notably those of Galileo) rigidity, stagnation, and complacency—early symptoms of the end; and he tried to determine how learning could be revitalized and advanced. What was his criticism of the sciences of his era? "Their hasty, premature reduction to arts and to methods; after which learning progresses but little or not at all. So long as learning is dispersed in the form of aphorisms and observations, it keeps increasing; once it has been imprisoned in its methods, however, it can be polished and refined by usage, but its mass cannot be increased." [1] "Methods," then, are but more or less artificial expository procedures that solidify learning in its existing state. Learning comes into its own, according to the procedure adopted by Bacon himself in the *Novum organum,* only when it finds free expression in the absence of any preconceived plan. Bacon was so apprehensive about rigidity that he was even afraid of certainty. "In speculations," he said, "whoever begins with certainty

[1] *De augmentis,* I, 41.

will end with doubt; whoever begins with doubt and patiently entertains it for a while will end with certainty." [2] This seems to be the methodical doubt of Descartes but is, in fact, the opposite; for Descartes really "began" with certainty implied by doubt, the certainty of the *Cogito,* and this certainty led him to other certainties. Bacon held that certainty was not the beginning but the end that concluded any investigation.

All of Bacon's criticisms derive from his primary criticism of the humanists who saw in the sciences nothing more than a theme for literary development; his criticism of the Scholastics who by "imprisoning their minds in Aristotle just as they imprison their bodies in their cells," solidify dogmas (*rigor dogmatum*); his criticism of all those for whom learning is something already completed, something from the past; his criticism of the specialists who renounce first philosophy, take refuge in their discipline, and imagine that their favorite field of learning contains the whole of reality (like the Pythagorean geometers and Cabalists, who, like Robert Fludd, saw numbers everywhere). Whatever classifies, whatever solidifies is bad.

Hence his distrust of the very instrument of classification, the *intellectus* or understanding. Left to itself (*permissus sibi*) the intellect can only produce one distinction after another, as was evidenced by disputes among "intellectualists" in which the subtlety of matter ruled out anything other than sterile intellectual exercises.[3]

The only intellect ever recognized by Bacon is the abstract and classifying intellect that the Arabs and St. Thomas discovered in Aristotle. He knew nothing of the intellect that Descartes found at work in mathematical discovery. According to him, then, it is not through an inner reform of the understanding that learning can ever become tractable and fruitful. On this point Bacon is perfectly clear: the ideas in the human understanding do not have and will never have anything to do with the divine ideas according to which the Creator made the universe. "There is a vast difference

---

[2] *Novum organum,* I, aphorism 45.
[3] *Novum organum,* I, aphorism 19; *De augmentis,* I, 43.

between the images in our minds and the ideas in the divine mind, between our vain opinions and the true characters that God has imprinted in his creatures." [4] Between human intellect and truth there is no natural kinship. Intellect is like a distorting mirror; without metaphor, it is constrained to see everywhere equality, uniformity, analogy. Here Bacon could justly invoke the most celebrated metaphysical speculations of the Renaissance—the speculations of Paracelsus or of Giordano Bruno.

If the subtlety of the mind cannot equal the subtlety of nature, it is to nature itself that we must turn in order to acquire knowledge of it. Experience is the true teacher. Francis Bacon is linked to the tradition of experimental natural science which, since Aristotle, had always had a rather obvious place in Western thought, and which appeared in the Middle Ages in the work of Roger Bacon. This natural science had two aspects. On one hand were the *Historiae* or collections of natural facts, such as Aristotle's *History of Animals* and especially Pliny's *Natural History*—a compilation which embraces all the kingdoms of nature and which was for centuries a source of inspiration for those who sought a more concrete and vivid image of the world than that of the philosophers. Alongside the *Historiae* were the operative techniques, tainted by all sorts of superstitions, which supposedly forced nature to obey the designs of man—natural magic which controlled nature's caprices and alchemy which changed base metals into gold. These sciences, like astrology, were all grounded on a representation of the universe derived from Stoicism and from Neo-Platonism: the representation of mysterious sympathies or antipathies whose secret could be revealed to us only by experience. The histories, like the operative techniques, appealed strongly to men of the sixteenth century. Notwithstanding all the superstitions that they carried with them, they had the concrete, progressive character that Bacon sought in science, and they gave man hope of controlling nature provided that he would obey it (*natura non vincitur nisi parendo*)—that is, provided that he would learn the laws of nature. Bacon did not fail to recog-

---

[4] *Novum organum*, I, aphorism 23.

nize in these sciences many elements of credulity and imposture, but he gave his unqualified approval to their aims—to investigate "the influence of things above on things below," as in astrology; "to divert natural philosophy from myriad forms of speculation and focus attention on the importance of operative techniques," as in natural magic; "to separate and extract the heterogenous parts of bodies that are hidden and intermixed, to purify them of their impurities," as in chemistry. All these ends are worthy of his approval,[5] and the means employed, absurd as they often were, nevertheless resulted in fruitful discoveries.

The *Instauratio magna* does not rank among contributions to mathematics or mathematical physics, where advances were the distinctive trait of the seventeenth century. Here Bacon abandoned the sciences of argumentation and concentrated on organizing rationally the tangled mass of assertions about nature, of operational procedures, and of practical techniques that constituted the experimental sciences.

III The Division of the Sciences

We turn now to the first task of the *Instauratio,* the one that is resolved in the *De dignitate et augmentis scientiarum*. It is a classification of the sciences intended not so much to introduce order into those that existed as to indicate those that were still lacking. The most general division is the division into *History,* or science of the memory, *Poetry,* or science of the imagination, and *Philosophy,* or science of reason. History and Philosophy each have two distinct objects, nature and man. History is therefore subdivided into natural history and civil history, and philosophy into philosophy of nature and philosophy of man.

Natural history is, in turn, divided into *historia generationum, praetergenerationum, artium.* This is the division that Pliny the

---

[5] *De augmentis,* III, 5 (ed. Spedding, p. 574), on the transmutation of metals. Spinoza (ed. Van Vloten, II, 330), Malebranche (*Entretiens sur la métaphysique,* X, 12), and Leibniz (*New Essays,* III, 9, 22) consider this a perfectly legitimate and soluble problem.

Elder made. As in Pliny's second book, the "history of generations" relates to celestial phenomena, to meteors, and finally to masses composed of the same element, the sea and rivers, the earth, volcanic phenomena. After this come the "history of monsters" and the "history of the arts" through which man changes the course of nature. These are the two subjects of Pliny's seventh book (the part included between Books II and VII is devoted to geography). Bacon deserves credit, not for bringing the study of abnormal conditions and the arts into natural history, but for stating that such study constitutes an indispensable part of natural science and is not merely an appendage of curious facts. Monsters and technics bring to light forces that were less obvious in natural generation— *natura omnia regit*. In the arts, for instance, man can create no force which is not in nature; he can only place bodies closer to each other or farther apart and in this way create new conditions for the interplay of natural forces. The new spirit justifies Bacon's decision to number among the sciences that are still lacking (*desiderata*) the two new subdivisions of natural history (Vol. II, chap. i).

As for civil history, its subdivisions correspond to the historical literary types which were prevalent in Bacon's time and which were rooted in the past. They are ecclesiastical history, initiated by Eusebius of Caesarea, and civil history proper, which he subdivides according to the documents on which it is based: memoirs (*fastes*), antiquities, ancient stories such as the *Judaic Antiquities* of Josephus, true and complete historical accounts such as biographies, chronicles of a reign, or the narration of particular events. Bacon outlines a vast scheme of scholarly investigation and adds "literary history," which is primarily the history of advances in technics and the sciences. This was the program adopted universally by scholars throughout the seventeenth century.

After civil history come the divisions of philosophy. Here, too, the divisions are traditional, but their spirit is new. "I desire to deviate as little as possible from the opinions and manners of speaking of the ancients," said Bacon (Vol. III, chap. iv, sec. i). God, nature, and man (or, as he says—reminding us of the perspectivists of the Middle Ages—luminous source, its refracted ray, its reflected ray) are the three objects of the three great philosophical sciences. This is Aristotle's division into theology, or first philosophy, physics, and moral philosophy. But the spirit is quite different: in Aristotle, first philosophy, or metaphysics, was, at the same time, science of axioms, science of causes or principles of every substance, sensible or intelligible, and science of God. We rediscover all these elements in Bacon, but their arrangement is completely different. *First philosophy* refers to the science of axioms, *metaphysics* to the science of causes, and *theology* to the science of God.

First philosophy, or the science of axioms, is the common trunk of the three branches—the sciences of God, of nature, and of man. According to Bacon, the "axioms" are adages sufficiently universal to apply equally to divine things, to natural things, and to human things. For instance, "Whatever can best preserve the order of things (*conservativum formae*) is also the most powerful"; whence, in physics, the horror of the void which preserves the terrestrial mass; in politics, the pre-eminence of the conservative forces of the state over private interests; and in theology, the pre-eminence of the virtue of charity, which unites all men. In short, Bacon asks that these universal notions be treated "according to the laws of nature rather than of discourse—physically, and not logically." Adages about rarity and quantity, for example, should help us understand why one product, such as gold, is rare, and another, such as iron, plentiful.

Theology becomes the first of the philosophical sciences. After it comes the *science of nature,* which is subdivided into *metaphysics,* or the science of formal and final causes, and *special physics,* or the science of efficient and material causes. We recall that medieval followers of Aristotle considered knowledge of forms, or the true differences of things, as inaccessible to the human mind. Thus, what Bacon sought to create, under the name of metaphysics, was a new science, a science intimately related to the study of nature. Later we shall examine this new science in detail.

The third and last of the philosophical sciences, the *science of man,* is subdivided according to the human faculties into the science of the intellect, or *logic,* the science of the will, or *ethics,* and, finally, the science of men living together in societies. Thus Bacon separated the science of societies from morality.

Baconian *logic* is but the description of the natural progress of science. First, there is *invention* or discovery of truths, accomplished only through experience (*experientia litterata,* or experiences that are set down in writing), and induction, the particular object of the *Novum organum.* After invention comes judgment of proposed truths, for which the principal instrument is the Aristotelian syllogism. Its function is precise but limited: to reduce proposed truths to universal principles. Logic is useful also in refuting sophisms; it prevents the incorrect use of general words with multiple meanings used in every discussion—for instance, "little" and "much," "like" and "different"; and it brings to light the "idols" of the human mind—that is, its reasons for making mistakes.

The contrast between Baconian ethics and classical ethics is no less striking than that between Baconian physics and Aristotelian physics. Bacon censured the ancients for offering no practical means of attaining their proposed goal, for speculating about the supreme good without knowing about the future life in which Christianity teaches us to seek the supreme good, and, in particular, for failing to subordinate the good of the individual to the good of the society to which he belongs. It was because of such ignorance that Aristotle falsely stated that the speculative life is superior to the active life; that throughout antiquity the sovereign good was sought in the tranquility of the individual soul, without reference to the common good; and that an Epictetus taught that the sage should find in himself the principle of his happiness—an outgrowth of ancient individualism with its emphasis on achieving a tranquil life, free from external concerns, and its choice of serenity rather than magnanimity, passive enjoyment rather than active good manifested through works. Bacon's ethics, like his science, was more operative than speculative. He preferred the tyrant Machiavelli, with his love of power for its own sake, to the Stoic sage with his inert and joyless virtues; he preferred a true treatise on the passions, based on materials taken from historians, to Theophrastus' *Characters*. Finally, he completed the science of man with politics, which is distinct from ethics, and which is chiefly a doctrine of the state and of power.

Along with History and Philosophy, Bacon recognized a third science, Poetry, the science of the imagination. We recall the ardor with which Renaissance men returned to the interpretation of myths and fables—the basis for a science of enigmas and images. Descartes himself, as a young man, paid some attention to such whimsical notions. They are the subject of the *De sapientia veterum*, in which Bacon finds in the fable of Cupid the idea of the original motion of the atom and of the action of atoms on each other across distances; in the song of Orpheus, the prototype of natural philosophy, which has as its aim the restoration and renovation of corruptible things. It is this whole collection of fables, interpreted in the context of the great reformation of the sciences, that Bacon calls poetry.

But, at bottom the three sciences of history, poetry, and philosophy are only three successive advances of the mind in the formation of the sciences: history, the accumulation of materials; poetry, the first, wholly chimerical use of materials—a kind of dream of science beyond which the ancients failed to progress; and philosophy, the solid construction of reason. This is how things appeared to Bacon whenever he was thinking not of all the sciences listed in the *De augmentis,* but only of the one that truly engrossed him, the science of nature.

IV *The Novum Organum*

A new instrument was needed to effect the development of the new sciences systematized by Bacon, and it was to be created by the *Novum organum.* Is the difference between the *Novum organum* and the *De augmentis* the same as the difference between a systematic plan of the sciences and a universal, over-all method of promoting them? No. In reality, the content of the *Novum organum* coincides exactly with certain parts of the *De augmentis*. If we remove from the work everything that relates to history and to poetry, from the chapters on philosophy everything that relates to theology, and from science of man everything that has to do with ethics and politics, there remains the program of the science of nature and logic. Now the *Novum organum* is precisely that and nothing else: it is a program of the sciences of nature together with the part of logic that relates to them. The errors treated in the theory of idols concern only man's conception of nature; and the organum, or tool, that aids reason as a compass aids the hand, pertains exclusively to the science of nature.

The description of idols, or mistakes made by the mind as it follows its natural flight, stands at the beginning of the *Novum organum* and is, therefore, an opportune prelude to our understanding of the necessity of the new instrument. There are four kinds of idols. *Idola tribus* ("idols of the tribe"), are natural fallacies reflecting laziness and inertia. We generalize solely on the basis of affirmative instances and thus create superstitions, such as astrology, because we fail to take into account instances where predictions have been wrong. We desire to see realized in nature the notions which, by virtue of their simplicity and uniformity, best fit our minds. This accounts for the birth of ancient astronomy, which denied the stars any trajectory other than a circular one, and to the whole pseudo-science of the Cabala (revived in England in the time of Bacon by Robert Fludd), which imagines non-existing realities in order to have them correspond to our numerical combinations. As we base our conception of the activity of nature on human activity, so alchemists discovered sympathies and antipathies among things as well as among men. *Idola specus* ("idols of the cave") relate to the inertia of the habits and training which imprison the mind, as in Plato's cave. *Idola fori* ("idols of the market place") are the words that influence our conception of reality. If we wish to classify things, common language, with its ready-made classification, interferes. Furthermore, many words have indistinct meanings and many have no counterpart in reality (as when we speak of chance or of the heavenly spheres). *Idola theatri* ("idols of the theater") are traceable to certain exotic philosophical theories—those of Aristotle, "the worst of the Sophists," and Plato, "the jester, the bombastic poet, the impassioned theologian." Bacon was no less critical of the empiricists, who collected facts as an ant collects provisions, and of the rationalists, who constructed their spider-web theories without benefit of experience. Idols, then, are not sophisms or errors of reasoning but vicious mental dispositions which, like some kind of original sin, make us disregard nature.

Bacon's aim, strictly speaking, is not knowledge, but power over nature, operational science. Knowledge, however, is a means, and its rules are determined by the end it is supposed to serve. Bacon enunciated his aim in these words: "To create one or several new natures and to introduce them into a particular body." [6] Here "nature" means specific properties such as density and rarity, heat and cold, heaviness and lightness, volatility and stability—in short, the pairs of properties listed in the fourth book of Aristotle's *Meteorology* and used as a model by all the physicists. The operational technique, particularly that of the alchemists, consists in engendering one or more properties in a body that does not already possess them, in changing it from cold to hot, from stable to volatile, and so forth. Bacon thinks, like Aristotle, that each of these natures is the manifestation of a certain *form* or essence that produces it. If we are masters of forms, we shall then be masters of properties. But we cannot be masters of forms until we have knowledge of them.

Here the positive task of the *Novuum organum* becomes apparent: to provide knowledge of the forms which engender natures. Aristotle failed to solve this problem (and his failure was perpetuated by Thomism) because the differences that enable us to

[6] *Novum organum*, II, aphorism 1.

determine a genus and to define a specific essence are not "true differences." [7] Now true differences are precisely what Bacon credits himself with grasping: "form," "true difference," "thing in itself" (*ipsissima res*), "nature-engendered nature," "source of emanation," determination of the "pure act," "law"—many such expressions clearly indicate Bacon's intention. Furthermore, one means by which Aristotle determined essence and law was induction; Bacon employs the same kind of reasoning for the same purpose.

The *Novum organum* then has the same external design as the ancient one—knowledge of forms or essences, beginning with facts, through induction. But Bacon claimed to succeed where Aristotle failed; moreover, he makes knowledge of forms the prelude to a practical operation rather than the satisfaction of a speculative need. How is this possible?

The study of forms was compared by Bacon to the work of the alchemist who through a series of operations separates the pure matter he is looking for from the forms with which it is mixed. When we are seeking a form, we find through observation that its nature is inextricably mixed with a mass of other natures; the form is there, but we can obtain it only by separating it from everything which is not it. Induction is a process of elimination.

How is observation to be conducted in order to effect the desired elimination? That is the question with which Bacon was primarily concerned. He never asked himself what constitutes good observation, *when observation alone is being considered,* or what critical precautions are to be taken; on this point he made only vague, superficial remarks. He tended in practice to gather facts indiscriminately, and for this he was severely censured by professional scientists like Liebig. What mattered most to him was to multiply and to diversify experiences in order to prevent the mind from becoming rigid and immobile. This accounts for the procedures associated with Pan's hunt (*venatio Panis*), the pursuit of observations in which the sagacity of the hunter plays the dominant role just as in the ancient fable the sagacity of Pan enabled him to find Ceres.

[7] See É. Bréhier, *The Hellenic Age*, trans. J. Thomas (Chicago, 1963), p. 179.

Experiences must be varied (*variatio*)—for instance, by grafting forest trees in the same way as fruit trees, by observing how the force of attraction of rubbed amber varies when the substance is warmed, or by changing the quantity of substances used in an experiment; they must be repeated (*repetitio*)—for instance, by distilling new spirit of wine from wine that had already undergone distillation; they must be extended (*extensio*)—for instance, by observing certain precautions and, while keeping water and wine apart in the same receptacle, trying to separate the heavier parts of the wine from the lighter parts. They must also be transferred (*translatio*) from nature to art, as in the case of the rainbow artificially produced in a waterfall; inverted (*inversio*)—for instance, by observing that heat is propagated by means of an ascending motion and then determining whether cold is propagated by means of a descending motion; suppressed (*compulsio*)—for instance, by determining whether certain bodies placed between a magnet and a piece of iron will suppress magnetic attraction; applied (*applicatio*)—that is, they must be used to disclose useful properties (for example, to determine the salubrity of the air in different places or in different seasons by the rate of putrefaction). Finally, several experiences must be combined (*copulatio*), following the example of Drebbel who, in 1620, lowered the freezing point of water by mixing ice and saltpeter. There remain accidents (*sortes*) of experimentation, which result from changing the conditions slightly—for instance, producing combustion, which ordinarily takes place in the open air, inside a closed vessel.[8]

These eight experimental procedures do not indicate the means of producing a given result, for we can never know in advance what will result from variation, repetition, and so forth. For example, under the rubric *variatio* Bacon proposes to determine whether the velocity of heavy falling objects will increase when their weight is increased; and (apparently ignoring Galileo's celebrated experiments) he maintains that one must not assume a priori that the answer will be either affirmative or negative. Pan's hunt does not

[8] *De augmentis*, V, 2, secs. 8–14.

yield fertile (*fructifera*) observations since we are unable to forsee whether the outcome will measure up to our expectation, but such observations are illuminating (*luctifera*) since they expose the falsity of presumed relations and lay the basis for elimination.

Still more obviously linked to the aim of induction is the division of experiences into the three tables: presence, absence, and degrees. To the "table of presence" or "essence" he consigns, along with all their circumstances, experiences involving the production of the nature whose form is sought; to the "table of absence" or "declination," those in which this same nature is absent; to the "table of degrees" or "comparison," those in which nature varies. It is understood, in addition, that the table of presence will also include the experiences in which a nature exists in subjects that differ to the utmost degree; and the table of absence will contain experiences that are as similar as possible to those included in the table of presence.

Induction consists wholly and exclusively in inspecting the three tables. Comparison will suffice to eliminate from the form sought, spontaneously and with almost mechanical certainty, a great number of phenomena which accompany nature. It will obviously be necessary to eliminate all phenomena not found in every experience in the table of presence; then among the remaining phenomena, all those present in the experiences in the table of absence; finally, all those in the table of degrees that are invariable, in contrast to nature, which varies. The form sought will of necessity be in the residue that persists "once the rejections and exclusions have been made in the appropriate manner." Suppose that the form of heat is to be determined. Bacon specifies twenty-seven cases in which heat is produced; thirty-two, similar to the first group, in which it is not produced—for example, the fact that the sun warms the earth (presence) in contrast to the fact that the sun does not melt perpetual snow (absence); and forty-one in which it varies. The residue that persists after elimination is the vibrating motion which produces the effect observed in a flame or in boiling water. Bacon defines it in this way: an expansive motion which goes upward, which affects not the whole body but its smallest parts, and which is repelled in such a manner that it becomes intermittent and vibratory.

The difference between this operation and Aristotle's induction, which consists of simple enumeration, is obvious. Aristotle enumerated every case in which a certain circumstance (the absence of gall) accompanied the phenomenon (longevity) whose cause he was seeking. He therefore restricted himself to the cases assigned by Bacon to the table of presence. The utilization of negative experiences in this domain was truly Bacon's discovery.

v *Form: Bacon's Mechanism*

One of the conditions governing the success of Bacon's induction is that form be not the mysterious thing sought by Aristotle but an element observable in the world about us—something that can be perceived by the senses or by instruments that assist the senses, such as the microscope. A form is not inferred but is made the object of obervation; induction only enables us to narrow more and more the field of observation surrounding the form.

We should add that in all problems of this type for which Bacon outlined a solution, the residue is always, as in the case of heat, a certain constant mechanical arrangement of matter. If we investigate the form of the whiteness that appears in snow, in foaming water, or in pulverized glass, we see that in every case there is "a mixture of two transparent bodies, together with a certain simple, uniform arrangement of their optical parts." [9] Furthermore, in a passage that Descartes reproduced almost word for word in his *Rules,* he sees the "form" of colors in a certain geometric arrangement of lines. We see that induction has the effect of eliminating, in order to identify the form, every qualitative or sensible element in our experience. We can therefore say that in a sense Bacon was

---

[9] *De augmentis,* III, 4, sec. 11.

a mechanist, for he ascribed the essence of each thing in nature to a permanent geometric and mechanical structure. It is true that there have been attempts to separate form from what Bacon called the "latent schematism"—that is, the intimate constitution of bodies that escapes us because of the smallness of their elements—and make it a superaddition to a mechanical structure or schematism, which then would be the material condition of the form and not its substance. But Bacon explicitly identifies them. Besides, when he speaks of latent progress (*progressus latens*)—that is, of insensible operations through which a body acquires its properties—he still has reference to a mechanical process. Hidden structures and motions (*occultos schematismos et motus*)—these are the true objects of physics.[10] Thus his thought has its place in the great mechanistic tradition that took shape in the seventeenth century. If there remained in his thinking any trace of the Aristotelian concept of form, would he have treated the investigation of final causes, which to Aristotle was inseparable from the investigation of form, as a "sterile virgin"?

But Bacon's is a mechanism of a particular type. It appears first as something unexpected, as a simple result of induction. The mechanical structure is what remains after "rejection and exclusion." In addition, he posited many forms, many mechanical structures as inexplicable absolutes. Whereas structures were the things to be explained in the case of Descartes and Gassendi, they were to Bacon the things that explained. Thus, in his view, mathematics did not have the dominant role assigned to it by Descartes; Bacon distrusted mathematics, especially after he saw the results of a mathematical conception of nature in the case of his contemporary, the Cabalist Robert Fludd, who had no objection when his calculations arrived at the most arbitrary combinations of figures and numbers in nature; and he wanted mathematics to remain the "handmaid" of physics—that is, to be limited to providing him with a language for his measurements.

[10] *Novum organum,* II, aphorisms 6, 39; *De augmentis,* III, 4, sec. 11. Cf. Lalande, *Quid de mathematica senserit Baconius* (Paris, 1899), p. 38.

VI Experimental Proof

Let us return to the organon. Bacon tells us that induction allows us to narrow the field in which a form is to be sought. But if induction indicates the exclusions we are to make, it obviously cannot indicate the moment of completion of the process. New facts could force us to make new exclusions. The result of the process of induction is provisional; it is a first vintage (*vindemiatio prima*).

Just how to reach a definitive result is something that Bacon promises to explain in his discussion of the "more powerful auxiliaries" provided by reason.[11] He draws up a list of nine such "auxiliaries," but discusses only the first, which he calls the "prerogatives of facts" (*praerogativae instantiarum*); he lists twenty-seven types of "privileged facts." How are we to interpret this expression? Why are these facts not included in the preparatory tables associated with induction? Take the "solitary instances," that is, experiences in which the nature under investigation is manifested without any of the circumstances that ordinarily accompany it (for example, producing colors by sending light through a prism). This fact belongs in the table of presence, and the same is true of *instantiae migrantes,* instances where a nature is suddenly manifested (the whiteness of foaming water). The *instantiae ostensivae et clandestinae,* instances where a nature is maximal or minimal, belong to the table of degrees; the *instantiae monodicae et deviantes,* where a particular nature appears under exceptional conditions (a magnet among minerals, monsters), belong to the table of presence; the *instantiae divortii* which reveal to us two separate natures that are ordinarily paired (for example low density and heat—air has low density without being warm) belong in the table of absence. Not even the famous crucial facts (*instantiae crucis*) fail to find a place in the tables. When we hesitate between two forms to explain a particular nature, the crucial facts must show "that the union between one of these forms and the nature is stable and indissoluble,

[11] *Novum organum,* II, aphorisms 21 *et seq.*

whereas that of the other is variable" (Aphorism 36). How are we
to interpret this formula? It is easy for us to understand how facts
in the table of absence conclusively demonstrate such variability
(this is an *instantia divortii*), but it is hard for us to understand
how a stable, indissoluble union could be demonstrated according
to Baconian logic. We can continue to narrow the field of investigation but can never say that we have reached the limit. For instance, in Bacon's view we can show that the form or cause of
gravity is the earth's attraction of heavy objects if we observe that
the pendulum of a clock moves faster when brought near the
earth's center; but this is clearly a simple fact to be added to the
table of presence, and it will be probable only so long as it is not
contradicted by another fact. Never does Bacon offer decisive proof
of affirmations; only negations are proved. Thus the "prerogatives
of facts" add nothing at all to the new instrument created by Bacon,
and when he includes among them *instantiae lampadis*—simple
means of extending our information either through instruments
that aid the senses, such as the microscope or the telescope, or
through signs, such as the pulse in sickness—we see that he is
much more attentive to the means of gathering materials than to
their possible utilization.

VII *The Last Parts of the "Instauratio Magna"*

The *Novum organum* then is merely a description of one phase
in the constitution of the sciences of nature. The last four parts of
the *Instauratio* were supposed to make natural science a reality—
from the very first step, the *Historia,* to the last, operative science.
The third part concerns the *Historia,* and this is the work that
engrossed Bacon particularly toward the end of his life, from 1624
to 1626. Aided by his secretary Rawley, he stuffed into the *Sylva
sylvarum* all the odd facts he could find in books of travel, physics,
chemistry, or medicine. His authorities are not the best: he borrowed freely from Paracelsus; he took recipes for the fabrication of
gold from the alchemists. He found better guides, however, in

Gilbert's works on magnetism and in Drebbel's experiments with thermometry. The *Sylva* is a general history. Bacon stipulated that a particular history must be written about each "nature," and he himself drew up some of them, the *Historia vitae et mortis,* for instance, which was often directed against Harvey, who through decisive experiments had just demonstrated the circulation of the blood. Not very careful in the matter of direct observation, he committed the same error as Roger Bacon; in his *Historia* he relied on traditional statements of presumed experience (transmitted by Pliny) rather than on experience itself.

The fourth part of the *Instauratio*—the *Scala intellectus*—was supposed to resume and to apply the theme of the *Novum organum*. Its title, the ladder of the intellect, refers to the need for not leaping from particular observations to general axioms, but, instead, for moving gradually, through intermediate axioms, to the general ones.

The fifth part, supported by general axioms, prepares the ground for the operative science realized in the sixth part and designed to give man mastery over nature. But even as he advances toward this goal, his fragmentary work becomes increasingly vague and sketchy. He understood that his aim could not be realized through blind empiricism but only at the price of an intellectual revolution of which he was the self-proclaimed herald, that he must not consider returning to the field of action until the revolution could be carried out. He understood that scientific work must be a collective endeavor shared by a great number of investigators, and he devoted one of his last works, the *New Atlantis,* to the description of a scientific republic in which each individual is assigned a task. First come the factual investigators: the *mercatores lucis* who go to foreign lands to investigate strange observations, the *depraedatores* who strip the ancient books, the *venatores* who discover the secrets of the artisans, and the *fossores* or pioneers who initiate new experiments. Then come those who assign the facts to the three tables, the *divisores;* then those who extract provisional laws; then those who devise experiments to prove the provisional laws; and finally those who carry out experiments under their direction. Even here, in his imaginary republic, Bacon was still remote from the operational science for which everything else was made.

VIII *Experimental Philosophy in England*

Voltaire in his *Philosophical Letters* rendered an opinion on Bacon that must have been fairly general in England at the beginning of the eighteenth century: "The most singular and the best of his works is today the least read and the most useless. I mean his *Novum scientarum organon*. It is the scaffold with which the new philosophy has been built, and now that the new edifice has been constructed, at least partially, the scaffold is no longer of any use. Chancellor Bacon still did not know nature, but he knew all the roads that lead to nature." The fact is that there was in England, beginning about 1650, remarkable progress in what was called the new philosophy, experimental philosophy, or effective philosophy— that is, in the whole field of experimental natural science. The Royal Society of London, founded around 1645 and officially recognized in 1662, the work of the physicist Robert Boyle (1627-1691), and especially the work of Newton (1642-1727) mark the stages in the new development. The collective work of the Royal Society—an endeavor to catalogue natural phenomena— was a unique attempt to realize the first requirement set by Baconian science: a *History*. Glanvill in his *Scepsis scientifica* (1665) sees "in the New Atlantis the prophetic project of the Royal Society." The same man clearly expresses the spirit of the Society by showing in his work the uncertainty of our knowledge about every matter dealt with by Cartesian philosophy—the union of mind and body, the nature and origin of mind, the origin of living bodies, ignorance of causes ("we cannot know," he said, earlier than Hume, "that one thing is the cause of another, if it is not the cause of what we expect it to be; even this path is not infallible"). But Glanvill called attention to the vast number of discoveries engendered by the practical and experimental part of philosophy, by the "new philosophy which he intends to make the subject of his treatise." Every demonstration must be experimental; this was the essential precept of the Society which was henceforth to seek to achieve only provisional results, since "it is probable that the experiments of future ages will not agree with those of the present, but on the contrary will oppose and contradict them." Hooke, the secretary of the Society and an admirer of "the incomparable Verulam," censured "those who wish to transcribe only their own thoughts and therefore risk making general statements about things that are peculiar to them." Until the time of Newton, Boyle was the most eminent member of the Society. He was especially interested in chemistry and in the theory of matter. He favored the corpuscular theory and mechanism, and he deduced the "secondary qualities" from the primary qualities of extension and impenetrability. But his theory of mechanics was that of an English experimental philosopher; in discussing Descartes' mechanics he used the very terms employed by Hooke: "The mechanical explanation that Descartes gives of qualities depends so much on his *private* views of a subtle matter, of globules of the second element, and other similar things, and he has interwoven these notions so closely with the rest of his hypothesis that we can rarely put it to use unless we adopt his whole philosophy." Descartes' theory, too systematic and personal, stifled the free flow of ideas, which must be responsive to experience. The starting point of Boyle's mechanics was experimental; it was the mathematical theory of machines, a theory "that permits the application of pure mathematics to the production or modification of motions in bodies."

BIBLIOGRAPHY

I to VII

Texts

Bacon, Francis. *The Works of Francis Bacon*. Edited by James Spedding, R. L.
Ellis, and D. D. Heath. 7 vols. London, 1857–59.
———. *The Letters and Life of Francis Bacon*. Edited by James Spedding. 7
vols. London, 1861–74.
———. *The Philosophical Works of Francis Bacon*. Edited by J. M. Robert-
son. London, 1905.
———. *Selected Writings*. Edited by H. G. Dick. New York, 1955.
———. *The Advancement of Learning*. Edited by G. W. Kitchin. London,
1934.
———. *Essays*. Edited by J. M. McNeill. London, 1959.
———. *The New Organon and Related Writings*. Edited by F. H. Anderson.
Indianapolis, Ind., 1960.

Studies

Adam, C. *La philosophie de F. Bacon*. Paris, 1890.
Anderson, F. H. *The Philosophy of Francis Bacon*. Chicago, 1948.
———. *Francis Bacon: His Career and His Thought*. Los Angeles, 1962.
Bevan, B. *The Real Francis Bacon*. London, 1960.
Bowen, C. D. *Francis Bacon: The Temper of a Man*. Boston, 1963.
Broad, C. D. *The Philosophy of Francis Bacon*. Cambridge, 1926.
Brochard, V. "La philosophie de Bacon," *Études de philosophie ancienne et
de philosophie moderne*. Paris, 1912. Pp. 303–13.
Crowther, J. G. *Francis Bacon*. London, 1960.
Church, R. W. *Bacon*. London, 1884.
Eiseley, L. C. *Francis Bacon and the Modern Dilemma*. Lincoln, Neb., 1962.
Farrington, B. *Francis Bacon: Philosopher of Industrial Science*. New ed.
New York, 1961.
Gibson, R. W. *Francis Bacon: A Bibliography of His Works and of Baconiana
to the Year 1750*. Oxford, 1950.
Green, A. W. *Sir Francis Bacon, His Life and Works*. New York, 1948.
Jameson, T. H. *Bacon*. New York, 1954.

Janet, P. *Baco Verulamis alchemicis philosophis quid debuerit.* Angers, 1889.
Lalande, A. *Quid de mathematica vel rationali vel naturali senserit Baconius Verulamius.* Paris, 1899.
———. *Les théories de l'induction.* Paris, 1929.
———. "Sur quelques textes de Bacon *et* de Descartes," *Revue de métaphysique et de morale,* XIX (1911), 296–311.
Levi, A. *Il pensiero de Francesco Bacone.* Turin, 1925.
Von Liebig, J. *Über Francis Bacon von Verulam.* Munich, 1863.
De Maistre, J. *Œuvres complètes.* New ed. 14 vols. Lyons, 1884–86. Vols. VIII and IX, *Examen de la philosophie de Bacon.*
Rossi, P. *Francesco Bacone; della magia alla scienza.* Bari, 1957.
Schuhl, P. M. *La pensée de Lord Bacon.* Paris, 1949.
Sortais, G. *La philosophie moderne depuis Bacon jusqu'à Leibniz.* 3 vols. Paris, 1920–29. Vol. I, *Bacon.*
Steegmuller, F. *Sir Francis Bacon: The First Modern Mind.* New York, 1930.
Sturt, M. *Francis Bacon.* New York, 1932.
Williams, C. *Bacon.* London, 1933.

VIII

Texts

Robert Boyle. *Opera omnia.* Venice, 1697.
———. *The English Works.* Edited by T. Birch. 5 vols. London, 1774.

Studies

Florian, P. "De Bacon à Newton," *Revue de philosophie,* 1914.
Masson, F. *Robert Boyle: A Biography.* Edinburgh, 1914.
Sprat, T. *The History of the Royal Society of London.* London, 1667.

DESCARTES AND CARTESIANISM

I Life and Works

RENÉ DESCARTES (1596–1650) descended from a prominent family in Touraine. His grandfather, Pierre Descartes, fought in the religious wars. His father Joachim, who became a counselor to the *parlement* of Britanny in 1586, married Jeanne Brochard, daughter of the lieutenant-general of Poitiers. They had three children; Pierre, who succeeded his father, was the oldest, and René was the youngest. From 1604 to 1612 he studied at the college of La Flèche, founded by Henry IV and directed by the Jesuits. There during his last three years he received training in philosophy which consisted of expositions, summaries, or commentaries on the works of Aristotle: the *Organon* in the first year, the books on physics in the second year, the *Metaphysics* and *On the Soul* in the third year. This training was intended to prepare him, according to tradition, for theology. During his second year he also studied Father Clavius' recent treatise on mathematics and algebra. In 1616 he passed his examinations in law at Poitiers. Like many of the gentry of his time he was freed from any material concern by his modest fortune. In Holland, then allied with France against Spain, he enlisted in the army of Maurice of Nassau, Prince of Orange. There he struck up a friendship with Isaac Beeckman, a doctor of medicine at the University of Caen. Beeckman, born in 1588, noted

46

in his journal that he and Descartes were both interested in mathematical or physicomathematical problems. Released from his commitment to the Protestant prince in 1619, Descartes turned to the army assembled against the king by the Catholic duke, Maximilian of Bavaria. At Frankfurt he attended the coronation of Emperor Ferdinand. On November 10, 1619, in a German village near Ulm, "filled with enthusiasm," according to his own statement, he discovered "the basic principles of a marvelous science."[1] His statement undoubtedly refers to a universal method capable of introducing unity into the sciences. At that time Descartes was passing through a period of mystical exaltations. He was affiliated—perhaps through the agency of Faulhaber, a mathematician in Ulm—with the Rosicrucians, a society that prescribed the free practice of medicine among its members. The titles of the manuscripts of this period, of which only a few lines remain, are significant: the *Experimenta* deals with sensible things, the *Parnassus* with the realm of the muses and the *Olympica,* with divine things. Further, it was during this period that he had a prophetic dream in which he read, in a collection of Latin poets which he used as a student, this line from Ausonius: "Quod vitae sectabor iter?" He interpreted the line as the sign of his philosophical vocation.

From 1619 to 1628 Descartes traveled. From 1623 to 1625 he was in Italy, where he took part in the pilgrimage to the Holy House of Loretto, which he had vowed at the time of his dream to visit.[2] From 1626 to 1628 he remained in Paris, studying mathematics and dioptrics. It was probably in Paris that he wrote the unfinished treatise, *Regulae ad directionem ingenii,* which was published in 1701, Rules 12 and 13 of which are translated into French in the *Logic of Port Royal* (Part IV, chap. ii, 1664). During the same period, Cardinal Bérulle, founder of the Oratory, encouraged him to pursue philosophical studies in order to serve the cause of religion against the free-thinkers.

---

[1] *Œuvres de Descartes,* ed. Adam-Tannery (hereafter identified as AT), X, 179.

[2] There is some doubt as to whether he actually carried out his vow; see Maxime Leroy, *Descartes, le philosophe au masque,* I, 107–18

Toward the end of 1628, Descartes retired to Holland in search of solitude. Except for a trip to France in 1644, he remained there until 1649, although he changed his residence several times. Between 1628 and 1629 he wrote a "short treatise on metaphysics," on the existence of God and of our souls, designed to lay the foundations of his physics. In 1629 he turned his attention to physics. It was then that he wrote the treatise *On the World.* His progress on the treatise can be traced in his correspondence until 1633. His reflections on the phenomenon of parhelions, observed in Rome in 1629, led him to an orderly explanation of all natural phenomena—the formation of the planets, gravity, tides—and finally to his explanation of man and the human body. Then came the event that was to change his plans: Galileo was condemned by the Holy Office for upholding the principle that the earth moves. "This came as such a shock to me," he wrote to Mersenne on July 22, 1622, "that I have almost resolved to burn all my papers, or at least not to let anyone see them. I confess that if [the principle of the earth's motion] is false, then all the foundations of my philosophy are also false, for this principle is obviously demonstrated by them and is so closely linked to every part of my treatise that I could not remove it without invalidating all the rest." The treatise remained among Descartes' papers and was not published until 1677.

He did not, however, abandon the idea of making his physics known, and in 1637 he published a *Discourse on Method;* the *Dioptric;* the *Meteors;* and the *Geometry.* The three essays and the *Discourse* that precedes them are intended, according to his statement, merely "to chart the course and to determine the depth of the water." The *Dioptric,* which he had already completed in 1635, actually contained a report on studies made in 1629 of a glass-cutting machine; a chapter on refraction, written in 1632; and the elaboration of the corresponding chapter on vision in the treatise *On the World. Meteors* was composed in the summer of 1635, and the *Geometry* in 1636, while *Meteors* was being printed. The original title of the work was "Plan of a universal science that can raise our nature to its highest degree of perfection; in particular, Dioptric, Meteors and Geometry, in which the most curious matters that the author could select are explained in such a manner that even those who have not studied can understand them." Descartes later gave it a new title: *Discourse on a Method of Properly Guiding Reason in the Search for Truth in the Sciences; Also, Dioptric, Meteors and Geometry, Which Are Essays in this Method.*

In 1641 Descartes published in Latin the *Meditationes de prima philosophia in quibus Dei existentia et animae immortalitas demonstrantur,* which he had completed in 1640. He took every precaution to have the theologians look with favor on his *Meditations on First Philosophy.* According to his letter to Mersenne, it contained all the foundations of his physics. He first submitted the work to Caterus, a young Dutch theologian; then, late in 1640, he sent it, together with Caterus' objections and his replies (first objections), to Mersenne. His intention was to have Mersenne bring the treatise to the attention of the theologians "in order to have their judgment and to learn from them what should be changed, corrected, or added before it is published." It was preceded by a letter to the theologians of the Sorbonne, whose approbation he sought by stressing the definitive character of his demonstrations against the ungodly. Mersenne then collected the objections of different theologians (second objections), Hobbes (third objections), Arnauld (fourth objections), Gassendi (fifth objections), and other theologians and philosophers (sixth objections). The treatise was published, followed by the objections and by Descartes' replies, and since it was erroneously assumed that the work would have the approbation of the Sorbonne, on the bottom of the cover was printed *"cum approbatione doctorum."* This notice disappeared from the edition of 1642, and the title was modified (*Animae a corpore distinctio* replaced *Animae immortalitas*). This edition also contained, in the reply to Arnauld, a passage on the Eucharist which Mersenne had suppressed in the first edition, and the objections of the Jesuit Bourdin (seventh objections). Finally, Descartes' *Correspondence* made public other objections—from an anonymous person nicknamed Hyperaspistes and from the Oratorian Gibieuf. A French translation of the first edition, revised in part by Descartes, appeared in 1647; the second edition (1661) also contained the seven objections.

Descartes' persistent effort to have his ideas widely accepted was based on something much greater than personal ambition; it was an awareness of the profound significance of his work, the "true generosity that causes a man to rate himself as high as he legitimately can." In 1642 he manifested to Huyghens his intention to publish *On the World* in Latin and to entitle it *Summa philosophiae* "in order that it may be more easily introduced into the conversation of educated people who now condemn it." His summation was actually the *Principia philosophiae,* which appeared in 1644 and for which he tried to obtain the approval of his former Jesuit masters, who were in the best position to disseminate a philosophy different from Aristotle's. The French translation by Abbé Picot, published in 1647, was preceded by a letter to the translator designed to reveal the over-all plan of Descartes' philosophy.

From this moment on, ethical questions seem to have commanded Descartes' attention. His correspondence with Princess Elizabeth, daughter of Frederick, the titular king of Bohemia, who had found refuge in Holland, provided him with an opportunity to elaborate his ideas on the highest good and culminated in the treatise *On the Passions,* his last work, published in 1649.

His long stay in Holland was often disturbed by polemics. The *Discourse* of 1637, communicated to the learned men of his time by Mersenne, the great reporter of scientific developments, brought down upon him Morin's and Hobbes's criticism of the *Dioptric.* The *Geometry* was the cause of bitter disputes with the French mathematicians Fermat and Roberval, who caused it to be looked upon unsympathetically by those associated with the young Pascal. More than once in the challenges that he made or answered, Descartes had the opportunity to show the fertility of his method as well as his own virtuosity, and he found an ardent disciple in

Florimond de Beaune, whose commentary on the *Geometry* was published in 1649, along with Schoot's Latin translation of the work.

In Holland, ministers and members of the teaching profession saw that the success of Descartes' philosophy posed a threat to their teachings, and they fought violently for Aristotle. The polemic began at the Academy of Utrecht between Regius, a professor of medicine, and Gisbert Voet, a theologian. Regius, one of Descartes' admirers, "even gives private lessons in physics and in a few months makes his disciples capable of heaping ridicule on the old philosophy." Troubles increased until March 17, 1642, when the Senate of Utrecht prohibited the teaching of the new philosophy, "first because it is new, next because it turns our youth away from the old, wholesome philosophy, and finally because it teaches various false and absurd opinions." From this moment on, Descartes personally defended himself against personal attacks. He was completely exonerated at the University of Groningen in 1645, but in spite of his repeated protestations, the Utrecht magistrates did not consent to review their sentence declaring his letter to Voet defamatory. Besides, he was no longer supported by Regius, who misunderstood his philosophy and whose theses on the soul he was forced to attack in 1647. The next attack on Descartes came from the University of Leyden during the same year. Revius, the theologian, accused him of blasphemy, a crime punishable under the law. To defend himself, Descartes was obliged to appeal to the ambassador of France.

His stay in Holland was interrupted only by three short trips to France, in 1644, 1647, and 1648. On his second trip he met the young Pascal and suggested to him, according to a report written later, the notion of conducting experiments with quicksilver and a vacuum. It was also on his second trip that Mazarin granted him a pension which was never paid. His third trip coincided with the parliamentary Fronde and the Day of Barricades. He never liked Paris. The air there, he said, "makes me dream instead of thinking philosophical thoughts. There I see so many people who are wrong in their opinions and in their calculations that it seems to me that there is a universal sickness" (AT, V, 133).

In September, 1649, he left Holland and traveled to Stockholm. He died there on February 11, 1650.

II *The Method and Universal Mathematics*

In the preface to the French edition of the *Principles* (1647) Descartes, wishing to present his doctrine according to the traditional outline of philosophy, divided it into Logic, Metaphysics, and Physics. His logic, however, is not traditional but is "that which teaches us to use reason wisely to discover truths of which we are ignorant; and because usage plays an important part, it is good for us to devote much time to practicing the rules that apply to simple, easy questions, such as those of mathematics."

We can easily find the last two parts of Descartes' philosophy: metaphysics is explained in the fourth part of the *Discourse,* in the *Meditations,* and in the first book of the *Principles;* physics is explained in the *Dioptric* and *Meteors,* in the treatise *On the World,* in the fifth and sixth parts of the *Discourse,* and in the last three books of the *Principles.* We are hard put, however, to find the logic of which Descartes speaks. He wrote no *Organon* comparable to the *Analytics* or to the *Novum organum* of Bacon. The second part of the *Discourse,* which contains the rules of the method, does not go beyond generalities, and the *Rules,* probably written before 1629, are unfinished. There remains the *Geometry* which, according to Descartes, "demonstrates the method." Furthermore, it demonstrates the method not by explaining it but by using it to solve problems, and we are wrong to treat it purely and simply as a mathematical procedure. We are not to study mathematics in and for itself in order to find the properties of "sterile numbers and imaginary figures," but in order to accustom the mind to procedures that can and ought to be extended to objects important in an entirely different sense. Descartes always treated mathematics as a product of his method, not as the method itself. "I am convinced," he said, "that this method has already been perceived by superior minds guided solely by nature. For in an undefinable, divine part of the human consciousness, the first seeds of useful thoughts have been deposited, so that often, no matter how neglected and repressed they may be as a result of prejudicial studies, they yield their fruits spontaneously; this we see in the easiest sciences, arithmetic and geometry."

Historically, it is hard to determine whether the prodigious strides marked by his mathematical discoveries—beginning with his association with Beeckman (1619) and culminating in the theory of equations advanced in the *Geometry* (1637) and in his letters on the problem of tangents (1638)—precede or follow the discovery of a universal method "for the orderly direction of his thoughts" in any matter whatsoever.

One thing is certain: "practice" in the method was to be based not on "vulgar mathematics" but on what since Aristotle had been classed as "pure mathematics" which studied numbers and dimensions and "applied mathematics" such as astronomy, music, and optics. Descartes was first drawn to applied mathematics. In 1619 he studied the acceleration of falling objects, musical chords, pressure exerted by liquids on the bottom of a container, and, later, the laws of refraction. His investigations tended at that time, like those of Kepler and Galileo, toward the mathematical expression of the laws of nature. But his thought subsequently took an entirely different course, in the direction of a universal mathematics. Rejecting the subject matter of vulgar mathematics—numbers, figures, stars, sounds—this universal mathematics was concerned only with *order and measure*: order, by which the understanding of one term is the necessary result of understanding another; and measure, by which objects are related to one another through some shared trait.

What is this universal mathematics that a philosopher must learn in order to train himself in the method? The fundamental idea is expressed at the end of the *Geometry:* "In the matter of mathematical progressions, after we have grasped the first two or three terms, it is not hard to find the others." A progression consists essentially of a series of terms arranged in such a manner that the following term depends on the preceding one. *Order,* in this case, allows us not only to put each term in the right place but also to discover, on the basis of the place assigned to them, the values of the unknown terms; it has an inventive, creative capacity. To be sure, Descartes was not the first to realize that method consists in order; no idea had been more commonplace since Ramus. But whereas earlier logicians treated order as a more or less arbitrary arrangement of previously discovered terms (I, 774), Descartes showed that a progression manifests a type of order which does not depend on an arbitrary judgment but is inherent in the nature of the terms and makes possible their discovery.

In a mathematical problem, unknown quantities whose values are to be determined are always linked to known quantities through relations implicitly defined in the statement of a problem. For instance, Pappus' problem, solved in the first book of the *Geometry,* may be stated most simply in this way: given three straight lines on a plane, to find a point from which straight lines can be drawn on them, resulting in equal angles so that the product of the first two angles is equal to the square of the third. Then, "without taking into account any difference between known and unknown lines, we must study the difficulty according to *order,* which shows in the most natural way how each depends on the others, until we find a means of expressing the same quantity in two ways—in other words, an equation. And we must find such an equation for each of the unknown lines that we assumed" (VI, 372). Having brought to light the "natural" order, we can determine the value of the unknown line by solving the equation. Thus the inventive capacity of order is truly demonstrated by the expedient of equations.

Universal mathematics, therefore, had to surmount several technical difficulties. In the first place, it was necessary to free algebra from all the geometric representations to which it was linked. And it is not surprising that Descartes began the *Geometry* by showing that if a and b represent straight lines, $a \times b$ or a^2 represents not a rectangle or a square but another line that is to a as b is to unity. In the same way, a quotient and a root represent straight lines; as a rule, the results of operations are always straight lines. In the second place, it was necessary to investigate more thoroughly the methods of solving equations independently, without relating symbols to any geometric quantity. This is the subject of the first half of the third book of the *Geometry*. Finally, it was necessary to show the fertility of his method in the solution of geometric problems, such as the construction of co-ordinates—that is, lines whose points all exhibit a given property. The result was the creation of analytic geometry, to which Descartes' work in mathematics is often (wrongly) reduced. Thanks to the expedient of co-ordinates, any point on a line can be determined if we know the constant relation between two indeterminate straight lines whose points of intersection supply each of the points of the curve. It follows that any problem depends on the discovery of a relation between straight lines—a relation which, as we have seen, can be expressed algebraically. Knowledge of qualities or properties of curves is therefore amenable to algebraic calculation.

Such is the universal mathematics whose procedures have today become part and parcel of science. But this mathematics is not the method; it is but the application of the method to the simplest objects. Above universal mathematics, and at the same time engendering it, Descartes' method is the knowledge which the intellect acquires of its own nature and, consequently, of the conditions under which it is exercised. Wisdom consists in this: "in each situation in life, the intellect will first show the will what it must do" (*Rules,* xii). To accomplish this, the mind must increase its insights, not "in order to resolve a particular academic difficulty" but "in order to prepare itself to make true, solid judgments about all objects presented to it." Now among the cognitive faculties—intellect, imagination, sense, and memory—"intelligence alone can perceive truth" (*Rules,* xii). This intellectual knowledge alone should be the primary concern of the wise man. "It surprises me"

says Descartes, "that most men study with the greatest care properties of plants, transmutations of metals, and the like, while only a
very small number concern themselves with the intellect and with
the universal science of which we are speaking." Nevertheless,
many philosophers of the past had meditated on the nature of the
intellect; but Descartes studied the intellect neither in order to
determine its place in the metaphysical scale of beings (like a Neo-
Platonist) nor in order to discover the mechanism of the formation
of ideas through sensations (like the Peripatetics). These two questions reappeared in the eighteenth and nineteenth centuries, and
Condillac censured Descartes for knowing neither the origin of our
ideas nor how they are generated. They did not concern Descartes,
and the *intellectus* was to him not a reality to be explained but a
point of departure and a fulcrum. The sciences are distinguished
from one another not by their objects but as distinct forms or
aspects of an intellect eternally identical to itself (*Rules,* i).

We must first apprehend pure intellect by isolating it "from the
variable testimony of the senses and the deceptive judgments of the
imagination." In this way we identify its two essential faculties—
intuition, "conception of a pure and attentive mind, so easy and so
distinct that we have absolutely no doubt about what we understand," and deduction through which we understand a truth as
being the consequence of another truth of which we are convinced.

Descartes borrowed his vocabulary from traditional philosophy,
and he did not try to hide this fact. He also stated that he did
not "worry much about the meanings attached by the different
schools to these expressions" (*Rules,* iii). In the language of
Aristotle, the word "intuition" signifies at the same time knowledge of terms prior to their synthesis by judgment, knowledge of
the unity that connects the different elements of a concept, and
knowledge of something present as being present. In the first two
instances, it is intuition that arrives at the elements from which
judgments are formed. Similarly, Cartesian intuition has as its
object first the "simple natures" of which everything is composed.
"It is often easier to examine several natures joined together,"

remarks Descartes *(Rules,* xii), "than to separate one of them from the others. For example, I can have knowledge of a triangle even though I may never have noticed that my knowledge contains knowledge of angles, lines, and so forth, and this still does not prevent our saying that the nature of the triangle is composed of all these natures and that they are better known than the triangle since they are what we understand in the triangle." But first we should note that these simple natures—extension, motion, figure— are not concepts of which judgments are composed but realities which, when combined, produce other realities. It follows that their simplicity is not the simplicity of an abstraction, and that a term does not become simpler as it becomes more abstract. The reverse is true. For instance, the abstract surface of a body is defined as the limit of the body; although it implies the notion of body, it is less simple than this notion. To the intellect, simple natures are ultimate, irreducible terms, so clear that they can be grasped only intuitively but not explained or reduced to something more distinct. There is "no logical definition" of those "things which are very simple and which can be recognized naturally—shape, size, place, time, and the like" (AT, II, 597).

Intuition, according to Descartes, apprehends not only notions but also undeniable truths such as: "I exist," "I think," "a globe has but one surface." It should be understood that a simple nature, existence, or thought is first apprehended in a subject to which it is attributed and from which it can be separated only through a process of abstraction. Number, for example, is only in the thing that is counted, and the "follies" of the Pythagoreans, who ascribed miraculous properties to numbers, would have been impossible if they had not conceived numbers as being distinct from the things that are counted *(Rules,* xiv). The first step toward understanding, therefore, is not the concept from which we fabricate propositions but intuitive knowledge of certain truths, the certainty of which will be extended by degrees to their dependent truths.

Finally, we perceive through intuition not only truths but also the link between one truth and another immediately dependent on it (for example, between $1 + 3 = 4$, $2 + 2 = 4$ on the one hand and $1 + 3 = 2 + 2$ on the other); and what we call common notions (for example, "two things equal to a third thing are equal to one another") are revealed immediately by the intuition of these relations.

Such is the threefold nature of intuition, the "natural light" or "intellectual instinct" by which we acquire knowledge that is "much more detailed than one might think and sufficient to demonstrate countless propositions" (AT, VIII, 599).

This demonstration is accomplished by means of the second intellectual operation, deduction, by which "we understand all the things that are the consequence of certain other things" (*Rules,* iii). Cartesian deduction is quite different from the traditional syllogism. The syllogism is a relation between concepts, deduction a relation between truths; the relation between the three terms of the syllogism is determined by complicated rules that can be applied mechanically to reveal whether the syllogism is conclusive, whereas deduction is known by intuition—through evidence such that "it can be omitted if not perceived but cannot be impaired by the mind least suited to logical reasoning." The syllogism is characterized by fixed relations between fixed concepts, and these relations exist even when they are not perceived; deduction is "the continuous and uninterrupted motion of thought that perceives things, one after the other, with absolute clearness" (AT, X, 369). It follows that there is a place in Cartesian deduction only for propositions that are certain, whereas the syllogism accommodates propositions that are merely probable.

All these differences are easily explained if we understand clearly that Cartesian deduction is typified by the comparison of two quantities by means of a unit of measurement. "Any knowledge that is not acquired through intuition pure and simple is acquired through comparison of two or more objects. In any process of reasoning, it is only through comparison that we acquire exact knowledge of the truth. If there is in a magnet a type of being unlike anything ever perceived by our minds, we can never hope to acquire knowledge of it through reasoning" (*Rules,* xiv). The nature of an unknown thing is determined by its relations with known things. The unknown quantity in an equation is nothing in itself apart from its relations with the known quantities, and it draws its nature entirely from these relations; the same applies to any truth known through deduction. The object is not (as in Aristotelian logic) to determine whether an attribute belongs to a subject whose nature is known, but rather to determine the very nature of the subject, just as a term in a progression is determined wholly by the principle of the progression that engenders it. Cartesian deduction is a solution to the problem of the determination of essences—a problem which baffled the Peripatetics.

Intuition and deduction are not method. Method indicates "how we must *use* intuition to avoid falling into error contrary to truth and how deduction should operate in such a manner that we may arrive at knowledge of all things" (*Rules,* iv). To demonstrate a proposition, mathematicians choose from among the certain propositions placed at their disposal by intuition and deduction those immediately applicable, with the result that the convergence of those propositions produces a new truth. Descartes' reason for censuring the mathematicians is that they do not tell us how they have arrived at their choice, which seems to result from a "stroke of luck" (*Rules,* iv). The whole problem of method is to provide rules for making the right choice: "Method consists wholly in the order and arrangement of the things the mind should turn toward in order to discover a truth" (*Rules,* v). What we must learn is not to see or deduce truth but infallibly to choose the propositions that bear on the problem at hand. We arrive at this result by an exercise described by Descartes in his sixth rule. It includes three steps: "We must first collect indiscriminately all truths that present themselves, then gradually determine whether we can deduce from them other truths, and from the latter still others, and so on." Thus I deduce one number from the other in a continuous progression by always doubling the preceding number. "That done, we must reflect attentively on the truths that we have discovered and examine carefully why we were able to discover some of them more easily than others, and which truths they are." Thus, in the preceding progression, I easily discover the following term by doubling the preceding one, but it is harder for me to discover the proportional mean to intercalate between the extremes 3 and 12, for here it is necessary for me to deduce from the proportion that exists between 3 and 12 another proportion that will allow me to determine the geometric mean. Finally (this is the third step) "it follows that we shall then know, when we approach a particular question, the appropriate manner in which to begin our study." Thus, according to the *Rules,* method consists mainly in providing the mind with various schemes that will enable us to know, when faced with a new problem, on which truths and on how many truths the solution depends. And the object is not to "store them in the memory [like the rules of the syllogism] but to shape the mind in such a way that it will discover them immediately whenever the need arises." The discovery of order is not accomplished through the mechanical application of a rule but through the strengthening of the mind by exercising its spontaneous faculties of deduction.

It follows that method must train us to distinguish between things of which our knowledge depends on nothing else and things of which our knowledge is always conditional; between what is *absolute* and what is *relative*. Furthermore, the two notions depend on the nature of the problem under consideration. In a geometric progression, the absolute is the principle that allows us to determine all of the terms; in the measurement of a body, the absolute is the unit of volume; in the measurement of a volume, the unit of length. In general, the absolute is the ultimate condition of the solution of a problem.

Does method consist entirely in order? At first glance, *enumeration,* dealt with in the seventh rule, seems to be less a rule of discovery than a practical means of enlarging the scope of intuition. We recall that deduction is an uninterrupted motion, like a chain of truths. After apprehending intuitively the bond that unites one truth and the next, we can (this is the process of enumeration) "rapidly survey the different links so that we seem to be apprehending them at a single glance, barely helped by memory." Successive intuitive revelations tend to change into a single, instantaneous revelation in which we apprehend the bond between the first truth and the last in one intuitive glance. But enumeration seems also to designate a slightly different operation: "If it were necessary," said Descartes, "to study separately each of the things which relate to the goal we have set ourselves, no man's lifetime would be sufficient for the task, either because they are too numerous or because the same things would reappear too often." Enumeration is a methodical choice that excludes everything not necessary to the solution of the problem at hand, and it eliminates in particular the examination of countless individual cases by reducing things to definite classes, just as we might reduce all conical sections to classes according to whether the plane that cuts the cone is perpendicular to its axis, parallel, or oblique.

"It is to be noted," wrote Descartes to Mersenne, "that I do not follow the order of materials but only of reasons" (AT, III, 260). That is the distinctive trait of the Cartesian method; for the real order of production he substitutes the order that legitimatizes our affirmations concerning things. This accounts for the four famous precepts of the *Discourse,* the meaning of which is now clear: "The first of these was never to accept as true anything that I did not clearly perceive to be so, and to accept in my judgments nothing more than what was presented to my mind so clearly and distinctly that I could have no reason to doubt it." This precept excludes any source of knowledge other than the natural light of intelligence; the clarity of an idea is the very presence of the idea to the attentive mind; distinctiveness is knowledge of what the idea contains in itself—knowledge such that it cannot be confused with another idea. What constitutes method is certainly not natural light, for neither intuition nor deduction can be learned; but it is possible for us to learn to employ nothing else. "The second was to divide up each of the difficulties that I was going to examine into as many parts as possible and as might be required to resolve them in the best manner. The third was to think in an orderly fashion, beginning with the objects which were simplest and easiest to understand, and gradually, by degrees, reaching upward toward more complex knowledge, even assuming an order among things that follow no natural sequence." These are the two rules of *order;* the first prescribes the identification of the simple natures and the *absolute* of a problem (study of the equations of the problem); the second refers quite clearly to the formation of schemes of increasing complexity known to us from the *Rules* (composition of equations). "And the last was always to make enumerations so complete and reviews so general that I was certain that nothing had been omitted." It is through *enumeration* that everything necessary and sufficient to resolve a question is studied methodically. For as we see clearly in the words added to the Latin translation of the *Discourse* (*tam in quaerendis mediis quam in difficultatibus percurrendis*), the important thing is not to retain demonstrations in the memory once they have been accomplished, but to discover everything necessary to their accomplishment.

III *Metaphysics*

Descartes wrote to Mersenne on April 15, 1630: "I believe that all those to whom God has given the use of reason are obliged to employ it principally for the purpose of acquiring knowledge of him and of themselves. That is why I undertook my studies, and I must tell you that I would never have been able to discover the foundations of physics if I had not searched for them in this way." Thus, according to Descartes, metaphysics, which is knowledge of God and of one's self, fulfills several requirements. It is a Christian's obligation to use reason to combat the negations of freethinkers; furthermore, metaphysics is the first question necessitated by methodical order; finally, physics cannot achieve certainty unless it draws support from metaphysics.

The first of these three reasons reveals Descartes' participation in the campaign against the free-thinkers. We recall that before he retired to Holland, Descartes was asked by Cardinal Bérulle to support the cause of religion, and that the *Meditations,* considered in this light, belong to the tradition of the rationalistic apologetics that originated in the sixteenth century. Descartes wanted to do his part and stated repeatedly that he supported "God's cause" (AT, III, 240). He sought the approbation of the theologians at the Sorbonne and asked Mersenne to submit the *Meditations* only to theologians. It is clear that his metaphysics had a place in the religious movement of his time, and we need only note the use to which it was put by the philosopher-theologians of the second half of the century—Bossuet, Arnauld, and Malebranche.

But that is merely an external aspect of Descartes' thought. Most important is the place it has in his system; to Descartes the knowledge of God provided by metaphysics was not an end but a means. He thought the goal he had set for himself—"to make true, valid judgments concerning all the objects that present themselves"— could not be attained without first seeking the foundation of certainty in God himself. What was at stake was certainty, the certainty of mathematics and physics which underlie all of the arts that collectively constitute the happiness of man—mechanics, medicine, and ethics. "I will tell you privately," he wrote to Mersenne, "that these six meditations contain the complete foundations of my physics, but this must not be told to others." Never did Descartes arbitrarily introduce the least trace of a specifically Christian or Catholic dogma into the fabric of his doctrine. He affirmed his faith not as a philosopher but as a citizen of a country associated with a religion in which God had graciously caused him to be born. His attachment to religion, obviously sincere, quite naturally implied the conviction that no philosophical truth can be incompatible with the truth of revealed dogmas (which is the generally held concept of the relations between faith and reason in Thomism); therefore, when theologians criticized his theory of matter and stated that it was not consonant with the dogma of transubstanti-ation, Descartes took pains to show that the two are compatible. Thus we see that religious considerations intervene only indirectly and accidentally, and that the Cartesian vision of the universe is essentially independent of dogma.

The eminent role of metaphysics must have come to the attention of Descartes early in life. While writing the *Rules* he announced that he would "one day" demonstrate some of the truths of faith— in all probability the existence of God and the immortality of the soul. In 1628, still not certain of his physics, he composed a "short treatise on metaphysics." The unfinished dialogue *On the Search for Truth,* probably written in Stockholm during the last year of his life, also begins with the rational soul and its creator, which makes it possible for us to deduce "what is most certain concerning other creatures" (AT, X, 505). During the intervening years he was always preoccupied by the same thought: the *Discourse* (1637), the *Meditations,* the *Principles*—of which the first part, an exposition of metaphysics, is entitled "Principles of Human Knowledge"—all agree on the point that no certainty is possible unless based on the existence of God.

It is hard for us to imagine how paradoxical this thesis must have seemed to Descartes' contemporaries. In Scholasticism the affirmation of the existence of God owes its certainty wholly to the certainty of sensible things which lead us back to God as from an effect to a cause; inversely, Neo-Platonism begins with intuition of the divine principle and goes from God—the first cause, to things—the effects of this cause. Descartes was apparently confronted with two alternatives, but his chain of reasoning pro-vided an escape. The first two steps of his metaphysics point up the impossibility of either course: methodical doubt, by showing that there is no certainty in sensible things or even in mathe-matical things, prevents us from going from things to God, and the theory of eternal truths prohibits our deriving the essence of things from God as the model.

IV Metaphysics: The Theory of Eternal Truths

Let us first consider the theory which Descartes expounded in his letters as early as 1630 but did not take up again in his published works. According to the Platonic thesis which suffused the Middle Ages and the Renaissance, the essence of a created thing participates in the divine essence, so that there is no knowledge other than that of the divine essence. Degraded, confused, and inadequate as it applies to created things, such knowledge will be perfected, as nearly as it can be in a created being, only in the illuminative vision. It also follows that God is the creator of existences but not of essences, which merely participate in his eternal essence. Descartes held that the essences of created things, no less than their existences, were created by God: "The mathematical truths that you call eternal truths were established by God and depend wholly on him, as do all other creatures. To say that such truths are independent of him is in effect to speak of God as if he were Jupiter or Saturn and to subjugate him to the Styx and to fate" (April 15, 1630). The possible and the good are not rules to which the will of God, in creating things, submits, for this would limit his omnipotence; possible only are "the things that God willed to be truly possible" and "the reason for their goodness depends on the fact that he saw fit to create them" (May 1644). Why such an attachment, then, to the freedom of God to which the Oratorian Gibieuf, a friend of Descartes, devoted a work published in 1630? Because, in the finite understanding of man, this theory alone is compatible with a perfect knowledge of essences. "There is no particular one [of these eternal truths] that we cannot understand if our minds are disposed to consider it. In contrast, we cannot understand the greatness of God even though we are familiar with it" (April 16, 1630). By positing between God and the essences of finite things a bond of creature to creator and not a bond of participation, Descartes ruled out the possibility of any metaphysics or physics that might aspire rationally to deduce the forms of being and of knowledge from their first cause; and he was able to make God the guarantee rather than the model of our understanding. In other words, according to the general precept of his method, he no longer followed the order of God's production of things but "the order of reasons," which shows how one certainty can engender another, how certainty of the existence of God is for us the principle of any other certainty.

v *Metaphysics: Doubt and the Cogito*

In the three published expositions of his metaphysics (the fourth part of the *Discourse,* the *Meditations,* and the first book of the *Principles*), Descartes always followed the same order: doubt concerning the existence of material things and the certainty of mathematics; the unshakeable certainty of "I think, therefore I am"; the demonstration of the existence of God; the guarantee that this existence provides for judgments grounded on clear and distinct ideas; and the resulting certainties concerning the essence of the soul, which is thought, the essence of the body, which is size, and the existence of material things. Thus metaphysics goes from doubt to certainty, or rather from an initial certain judgment implied in doubt itself, the *Cogito,* to a growing succession of certain judgments, for only certainty can engender certainty.

Since the third century B.C. the followers of Plato and the Skeptics had accumulated reasons for doubting sensible things. Descartes took up these reasons. In the illusions of the senses and in dreams we believe things to be true that we later judge to be false—sufficient reason to distrust the senses that have once deceived us. But if his arguments were the same as those of the Skeptics, his intentions were quite different. He gave the reason for his doubt in his reply to the sensationalist Hobbes: "I used [reasons for doubting] partly for the purpose of training readers' minds to consider intellectual things and to separate them from corporeal things, for which they have always seemed to me to be an absolute necessity." In the *Summary of Meditations* he stated that "doubt provides us with an easy means of accustoming our minds to detach themselves from the senses," and that such detachment is the necessary condition of certainty.

Doubt concerning material things, therefore, is methodical doubt, an *ascesis* comparable to the effort made by Plato's prisoner to turn toward the light, and Descartes utilized skepticism to achieve, in the nothingness of the sensible world, an awareness of the spiritual reality. Theologians who criticized Descartes on this point were not mistaken, and objections to his methodical doubt were raised not by theologians but by sensationalists—Hobbes and Gassendi.

Cartesian doubt goes much further in one sense than does skeptical doubt. For once Descartes had established even the slightest reason for doubting, he did not hesitate to posit other reasons that amplified it and carried it to the utmost degree, proceeding here (he remarked to Gassendi) like those who "assume that false things are true in order to cast more light on the truth"—the geometers, for instance, who "add new lines to given figures." This makes possible the "hyperbolic doubt" that has to do with mathematical propositions. Such doubt, truly extraordinary since it causes us to hold as uncertain knowledge considered the most certain of all, is made possible by the hypothesis of an omnipotent "evil spirit" whose hypothetical power is such that it can introduce error "whenever I add two and three or count the sides of a square or make a decision about something even simpler." Thus the hypothesis of the evil spirit casts doubt on knowledge classed as intuitive in the *Rules*. But how is the very possibility of such doubt conceivable apart from Descartes' God who has decreed the eternal truths through his omnipotence? If we posit, instead of God whose existence is still unknown to us, a spirit that has the same power but is "evil," this spirit will be capable of changing the truths of things at the very instant we perceive them, and thus of causing us to make mistakes.

In another sense, however, Cartesian doubt fails to go as far as skeptical doubt. It does not go beyond "notions so simple that,

by themselves, they provide no knowledge of anything that exists"
(*Principles,* I, 10), such as the notions of consciousness or existence,
or common notions—for instance, the principle that there must be
at least as much reality in the total efficient cause as there is in its
effect. Furthermore, it differs by nature from skeptical doubt, for
whereas the skeptic persists in his doubting, Descartes would have
us consider as patently false all propositions that give us the slightest
reason to doubt. Thus he leaves no middle ground between certainty and the absence of certainty.

Such doubt would lead nowhere if Descartes, like his predecessors,
considered only its objects, for whether they are intelligible or sensible, they are all objects of knowledge. Like Plato's prisoner, he
cannot turn toward a world of realities where there is no doubt. But
he considers uncertainty independently, as thought—my thought;
in this sense my doubt, which is my thought, is linked to the
existence of the self that thinks; I cannot perceive that I think
without seeing with certainty that I am: *Cogito ergo sum.* If I came
to doubt this relation, my doubt would again entail my affirmation,
and every reason for doubting that I have managed to adduce—
doubt about sensible things, the existence of an evil spirit—are but
new reasons for repeating my affirmation. The certainty of my
existence as thought is the necessary condition of my doubt. Thus
Descartes arrives at an initial judgment of existence by abandoning
the vain pursuit of objects and substituting reflection on the very
thing that pursues them.

The function of the *Cogito,* according to Descartes, is twofold;
it provides the paradigm of a certain proposition, and it establishes
the radical distinction between mind and body. The *Cogito* is
certain because I perceive clearly and distinctly the relation between
my thought and my existence. Therefore I can consider as true
everything which I perceive with the same evidence. My conviction
is grounded on a relation, a deduction, a progression from one
notion to another, from the notion of my thought to that of my
existence. I am not searching for an identity like the one that the
ancient metaphysicists from Parmenides to Plotinus tried to estab-

lish between thought and being—an identity based on an attempt
to attain to the total reality of the universe within the confines
of thought. The total apprehension of reality that Plotinus achieved
through the intuitive act of a soul co-extensive with all reality
must not be sought in the *Cogito*. Descartes warns us that the
Cogito is not "an illumination of the mind through which it sees
in a divine light the things that God sees fit to reveal to it by
means of a direct impression of divine lucidity on our understanding" (AT, V, 133); it is at most "a proof of the capacity of
our soul to receive intuitive knowledge from God." Above all else,
it shows that the mind can have complete, total knowledge of a
particular object in the absence of total certainty with respect to
the whole of reality. This is a necessary condition of the application
of method. The human mind is so limited that it can perceive
distinctly only a very small number of objects at the same time,
and certainty must be instantaneous in order to be effective. If the
mind could have no certainty about anything without having
certainty about everything, as many metaphysicists still believed
after Descartes, then certain knowledge would be impossible.

It is only in this sense that the *Cogito* typifies all other certainties
that might be attained. But it does not follow that other certainties
ought to be attained by the same path—that is, through self-reflection. Through reflection on his thought Descartes found no existence
other than the existence of his own thought, and from this he could
not deduce the existence of God or of matter. The *Cogito* has nothing to do with any type of idealism that seeks progressively to define
all forms of reality as conditions of the reflection of the self upon
itself.

The second function of the *Cogito* in the system is to establish
the distinction upon which the whole of Cartesian physics is based
—the distinction between mind and body. I know myself only as a
thinking being and uniquely as such. It is true that I still cannot
know through the *Cogito* alone whether I am not also a substance,
a subtle fire, or something entirely different; I know myself as a
thinking being, but I still do not know whether I am only a

thinking being. I can nevertheless be certain of my being as a being that thinks, senses, and wills without knowing anything about the existence of bodies. A distinction must be made between the mechanism of these acts, which probably implies corporeal conditions of which I am totally ignorant, and the fact that we "perceive them immediately by ourselves," a common characteristic which makes "not only hearing, willing, and imagining but also sensing the same thing as thinking" (*Principles,* I, 9). It would be a mistake to try to define the operation of the mind in terms of the object to which it relates. Thus it is assumed that bodies are known by sensation; but if I try to determine how I know a piece of wax which is at first fragrant, hard, and cold but later loses all these qualities on being heated, or how I know its flexibility, which is the capacity to receive an infinite number of changes of figure, I perceive clearly that I must rely neither on my senses (since all of its sensible qualities change from one state to another) nor on my imagination (which is unable to apprehend an infinite number of figures), but "only on mental inspection." It follows that the action of the mind is not defined by its object or limited by it and that *bodies are not known through sensation.* This affirmation is of great significance. Descartes denied that there is one corporeal reality, or object of the senses, and another intelligible reality, or object of the intellect or understanding, as medieval thought with all its inherent Platonism had conceived it. The understanding is not defined from without by its objects but from within by its inner need for clarity and distinction.

When theologians became acquainted with Descartes' *Cogito,* Arnauld was quick to note that St. Augustine had said the same thing. Indeed, St. Augustine used the idea *"Si fallor, sum"* to escape from pessimism; furthermore, in the *De trinitate* he used it to demonstrate that the soul is spiritual and distinct from the body. He used it also to reveal the image of the divine Trinity in the soul. In all probability Descartes was acquainted with St. Augustine's texts. But in St. Augustine the *Cogito* did not terminate a doubt comparable to the methodical doubt of Descartes and did not initiate a study like physics. If he came under St. Augustine's influence, consciously or unconsciously, Descartes used his ideas as he would use one of Euclid's theorems in a demonstration in his *Geometry*. What matters is not a truth so simple and so readily accessible as this one, but the use to which it was put. As Pascal noted in this context, we must "explore how an idea is accommodated in its author." Augustine seized its immediate consequences —the acquisition of certainty and the spirituality of the soul. He failed to see in it the "remarkable series of consequences" that made it "the firm and constant principle of a whole system of physics."[3]

VI *Metaphysics: The Existence of God*

The certainty of the *Cogito* is limited to the existence of our own thought. At first glance Descartes seems to have followed strictly in the path of the Skeptics when, after reducing all our knowledge to the ideas that are in us, he defined an idea as a simple mode of thought, thought being to ideas as "a piece of wax" is to "the different figures that it can receive." Hence an idea is "everything conceived immediately by the mind," that is, desire or fear ("because I conceive that I desire or fear at the same time I desire or fear, I give my desire and fear a place among my ideas") as well as the idea of a triangle or a tree. In this sense ideas, in their formal or essential reality, are all equal and imply nothing other than my thought. This is the solipsism of the Skeptic which reduces all things to the modes of being of the self, making no distinction between an emotion and the notion of an object.

It was by choosing a completely different path that Descartes emerged from doubt. Doubt is an act of the will through which we retract the judgments that we have spontaneously made concerning things. Our act leaves unaltered the ideas by which we represent these things to ourselves; our beliefs have changed but not our notions. Doubt is not intended to accustom us not to feel or perceive or relate ideas; it is intended to accustom us not to

[3] *De l'esprit géométrique,* ed. Brunschvicg, p. 192.

believe that the objects of these sensations, perceptions, and relations exist.

Our ideas (in the language of philosophy, inherited from Plato, "ideas" meant "forms of divine understanding" and models of things) continue, however, to be representations or images of things. They have an "objective reality" which is the being of the thing represented, in so far as this being is in the mind. There are on the one hand ideas that represent "true, immutable natures," such as those utilized by geometers—the idea of a triangle or of extension, for instance; and on the other, ideas that cannot be said to represent either a positive nature or a privation—ideas like heat or cold.

Thus we find that there is a qualitative difference between our own ideas—a difference which is decisive and which rules out the "suspension" of the Skeptics. We should note that ideas of the second class are so vivid and forceful that they compel us, before doubting, to believe they exist. Now these are the ideas (for example, the idea of heat or of cold—the bases of Peripatetic physics) that Descartes rigorously excluded from his physics; he conceded the right to existence only to ideas of the first class. The distinction between the two types of ideas, therefore, is one of the moments (and perhaps the main one) in the vast seesaw movement by which Descartes was to transform physics—until then the science of sensible, obscure, fleeting qualities—into a science which thereafter would deal only with true, immutable natures. But in this very distinction we also discover one of the great difficulties of his system: at this point in his exposition Descartes could not justly attribute to these natures a higher value by referring to their future employment and fertility in physics, but only by considering them independently before he used them as the point of departure for the methodical elaboration of the system. It is all too obvious that Descartes knew that they could be so used at the time he was meditating on metaphysics, but it is also obvious that he wanted to prove the value of his principles independently of their application. He was probably fully aware that the explicative fertility of a principle was sufficient to confer on it "moral certainty" and that, apart from any metaphysics, mechanical principles would have this type of certainty if they served to explain a great number of natural phenomena; but it is only by "relying on metaphysics" that one can give them "something more than moral certainty" (*Principles,* IV, art. 205). That is why Descartes decided, even before emerging from doubt, to make a distinction between true, immutable natures (he cited the familiar example of the objects of mathematics) and all the disorder and confusion associated with the objects of the senses, all the arbitrariness and irregularity associated with the objects of the imagination.

Descartes' *innatism* is merely the formulation of this separation. Innatism means that there are ideas which the intellect draws from its own resources and uses to initiate thought; it asserts the independence and the interiority of the succession of methodically connected thoughts in contrast to the arbitrary succession of the impressions of the senses and the imagination. Innatism is not the strange doctrine that Locke tried to refute—the doctrine of an inner awareness, actual and constant, of every principle of our knowledge. The innatism of ideas consists in the disposition and, so to speak, the vocation of the understanding for conceiving them; they are innate in us just as gout and gravel are hereditary in certain families. Like Plato's reminiscence, innatism means the independence of the intellect in its investigations. It is concerned not so much with the question of origin (obviated, as we have seen, by the conditions of the problem) as with the question of value.

But what are the true, immutable natures which have their objective reality in the mind? Thanks to the *ascesis* of methodical doubt, thanks also to mathematics and to the manner in which the muddled ideas of the senses, such as the idea of heat, are eliminated, Descartes accepted only the objects of pure understanding—objects of a facile, even a common or vulgar type of knowledge, like the knowledge of number, thought, motion, extension. Essences are no longer grasped with great difficulty and always incompletely even after much labor, as in Aristotelian logic, but are apprehended immediately as points of departure.

It was the contemplation of objective reality that led Descartes to the existence of God. Not all ideas are equal with respect to their objects; there is more perfection in some than in others—in the idea of an angel, for instance, than in the idea of a man. The question of determining how ideas are comparable from this stand-point is hard to resolve. What mattered to Descartes was that such a comparison necessarily implies the idea of an absolutely perfect being, the standard on which all comparisons are based. The "true idea" was secretly present when metaphysical medita-tion began, "for how would it be possible for me to know that I doubt and that I desire—that is, that I lack something and that I am not wholly perfect—if I did not have within me an idea of a being more perfect than mine to serve as a basis for comparison and reveal to me the defects in my own nature?" Thus the idea of perfect and infinite is not only a "very clear and very distinct idea," inasmuch as it contains more objective reality than any other, but it is also the first and the clearest of all ideas, and it is in relation to it that I conceive finite and limited beings. We cannot say, then, with the theologians of the second and the fourth objections, that this idea was fabricated by a mind that arbitrarily augments the perfections it conceives of and combines them into a fictitious being.

Hence a first argument to prove the existence of God. Descartes drew support from the following enunciation of the principle of causality: "There is at least as much reality in a cause as in an effect." Here we recognize the old Aristotelian maxim, "A potential being can become actual being only under the influence of an actual being." An effect can have no perfection except that which is provided by its cause; this formulation makes sense only if the cause is conceived as an actual being and the effect as residing in a potential being that comes under its influence (by itself brass cannot become a statue). Descartes applied the principle to ideas in our minds, considered as an effect: "There is at least as much formal reality in the cause of an idea as there is objective reality in the idea itself." The idea of a new horological mechanism could not spring up indiscriminately but was possible only in the mind of a talented and well trained artisan. It follows that all we need in order to find out whether our ideas represent and require a "formal" reality different from our thought—that is, the existence of a being outside our thought—is to determine whether we ourselves have enough reality or perfection to be the authors of these ideas. Now it is obvious that we, imperfect beings that we are, cannot be the author of the idea of the perfect being; only the perfect being has enough reality to produce it in us and must therefore exist with the infinite perfections conceived by us.

Descartes' proof received further confirmation from the following line of argument: I am an imperfect being and I have the idea of a perfect being; it follows that I cannot conceive of myself as the author of my being, for if I had the power to create myself, I would have the power a fortiori to give myself all the perfections of which I conceive; for the same reason I can eliminate causes which would be less perfect than God (since they would have given themselves every possible perfection) and also my parents, who are responsible only for my body; therefore, I am created by the perfect being. His proof appears to be similar to the proof *a contingentia mundi,* which begins with any kind of finite effect and traces it back to the first cause, but it is actually quite different, since Descartes begins with a finite mind possessed of the idea of the first cause.

Thus two existences have been established: that of myself as a thinking being and that of God outside me. The point worth noting, the reason for Descartes' radical originality in spite of the alien material he employed, is this: it is possible for us to establish the existence of things only when we have a clear and distinct idea of them—for instance, thought or the perfect being. A methodical axiom of Aristotelianism was that existence must be proved before investigating essence, in order to avoid pursuing mere chimeras, like the stag-goat. This implies that we can make a judgment of existence before we know the nature of the thing whose existence we are affirming—an attitude wholly in keeping with the common-sense approach that forces us to accept for the very same reason many obscure and ill-defined notions. Against this, methodical doubt rules out the existence for the human mind of anything that is the object of an obscure, muddled idea. Certain judgments of existence can be made only if their subjects are clear and distinct ideas. Descartes was able to dispense with existence and posit essence because he had a means, not accessible to Aristotle, of separating "true natures" from the chimeras of the imagination. By conceding existence only to objects of clear ideas, we arrive at a reality where thought is in a realm of its own and can engage in its methodical flight without fear of being submerged by an ocean of alien realities inaccessible to the mind.

Descartes' intention is manifested in the means by which he effected his intention—proof of the existence of God. We recall that hyperbolic doubt revealed the evil spirit as a being capable of introducing error even into clear and distinct thought, with the result that thought was never master of its own domain. But demonstration of the existence of God destroys the strength of such doubt. Knowledge of that true nature represented by the idea of a perfect being shows us that the evil spirit was a chimera of our imagination, for an omnipotent being has all the other perfections at the same time and could not be malicious or deceptive. The existence of this benevolent being, therefore, is our guarantee that we cannot be deceived about things that we have once perceived clearly and distinctly. If "an atheist cannot be a geometer" it is because he lacks this guarantee of certainty. If we make mistakes the fault lies not in our understanding but in our will. Our understanding is finite—that is, it has obscure, confused ideas alongside clear and distinct ideas. Our will is finite—that is, we have full freedom to adhere or not to adhere to the conjunctions of ideas presented to us by our understanding. Judgment is not knowledge of a relation but rather assent through an act of the will. We are free to act in such a manner that only the light of our understanding will determine the consent of our will; methodical doubt proves this precept and is merely its application.

This marks a veritable turning point in philosophical thought. That truth perceived through human understanding had its foundation in divine understanding was a familiar precept of Thomism: "Uncreated truth and divine understanding are neither measured nor produced, but they measure and produce a double truth, one in things and the other in the soul." No matter how blurred, our notions are still images of the intelligible reasons of things as they exist in God; our knowledge, authenticated because it is a reflection of divine understanding, is therefore turned naturally toward its origin, and our true vocation is in the eternal life in which this reflection will become a direct vision. Against this, according to Descartes, intellectual knowledge is not in the least degree a participation in divine understanding, and it is well for us to recall here that in his thinking the essences which are the object of human understanding are creatures of God. In consequence God is the guarantee of our knowledge, not through an attribute relating to his understanding but through attributes relating to his creative power, omnipotence, and goodness. The vocation of human understanding is not to consummate the vision of essences in the eternal life. Clear and distinct knowledge, which was the object or goal when these essences were viewed as reflections of those that existed in divine understanding, became a point of departure for the mind in search of its combinations and effects. Descartes looked forward toward the methodical analysis of things rather than backward at their transcendent origin. The natural destiny of human understanding had no supernatural destiny as its complement, and the thought of the dazzling vision promised to the elect did not in any way obscure the perfect clarity of human knowledge, which proceeds not from obscurity to clarity but from clarity to clarity. Descartes, who established a close relation between knowledge and God, and even went so far as to say that an atheist could not be a geometer, at the same time radically separated knowledge from any theological design by putting it wholly on the plane of human understanding, which has a certainty authenticated by God.

But was Descartes justified in using this means to emerge from doubt? A number of his contemporaries took issue with him on this point. They discovered that he had been caught in a vicious circle, for the existence of God could be demonstrated only by relying on the evidence of clear and distinct ideas, yet such evidence depended on prior demonstration of his existence. Descartes answered the objection by saying that there are two types of certainty, the certainty of axioms, which are grasped directly and which are not subject to doubt, and the certainty of acquired knowledge, which consists of conclusions that depend on a long chain of reasoning. As we proceed we are able to grasp successively each of the propositions that make up the links in the chain and to see its relation to the preceding link. Having reached the conclusion, however, we recall that we clearly perceived the first propositions even though we can no longer perceive them now. In short, divine authentication is useless in the case of axioms and necessary only for acquired knowledge.

Descartes' reply is itself somewhat perplexing. First, if proof of the existence of God depends on a rather long and complicated chain of reasoning, the vicious circle persists. Furthermore, Descartes seems to have extended doubt far beyond the results assumed in his reply. When he said that the simplest operations, such as counting the sides of a square, were subject to doubt, he was certainly not limiting doubt to the conclusions drawn from a chain of reasoning. Finally, even if these two difficulties were removed, Descartes still could not have meant, as it is sometimes stated, that God authenticates memory, for nothing would prevent memory from being fallible, from leading us to believe that we had perceived an obvious truth when there was none; the fidelity of memory depends solely on our attention.

As far as the first point is concerned, Descartes thought he had found a clear, axiomatic proof of the existence of God: the one customarily called the *ontological proof,* expounded for the first time in the *Discourse* and for the last time in the *Meditations;* the existence of God is deduced from the notion of God, just as a property of a triangle is deduced from the definition of this figure. Once we understand that God is the being possessed of every perfection, we see that God possesses existence since existence is a perfection. Existence is a perfection: it implies a positive power in the thing that exists or in whatever has conferred existence upon this thing. But God reveals himself to us through the idea that we have of him as an infinite power. To say that he does not exist is to say that there is in him some power which is not realized, that he is therefore not absolutely perfect, which is contradictory. From this viewpoint God is the ground of his own being (*causa sui*), a power that produces its own existence. This is the proof to which Descartes referred when he said he did not believe "that the human mind could know anything with greater evidence and certainty." Thus the first difficulty vanishes if proof of the existence of God acquires the certainty of an axiom.

But the second difficulty remains, since hyperbolic doubt seems to extend even to axioms. Here it is necessary for us to note one distinction that Descartes clearly established in his reply to Regius, who had objected that divine authentication was not necessary for axioms of clear and self-evident truth. Descartes stated in his reply (May 22, 1640): "I agree with this too, *so long as they are clearly understood.*" It is therefore not possible for us to doubt a truth whenever we perceive it clearly. So long as we are unfamiliar with the nature of God, however, we cannot conclude that the same proposition will appear to us again with equal clearness even if it is an axiom. What guarantees the goodness and the immutability of God is the constancy of positive proof throughout time. It follows that we need only recall having clearly perceived a proposition (provided of course that our memory is faithful) in order to be sure that it is true. Certainty derives from an instantaneous vision, and successive instants are in themselves independent of each other. We therefore could not conclude that one moment's truth will endure until the next moment if we did not have divine immutability to link together a host of successive instants.[4]

VII *Metaphysics: Soul and Body*

Descartes had a good reason for stressing the necessity of raising doubts "on even the slightest metaphysical pretext": at stake was the certainty of his physics, which was a web of paradoxes to his contemporaries. The result of Descartes' theology was this: clear and distinct ideas of human understanding are the measure of things and indicate to us the natures of which they are composed; and the criticism constantly leveled against him was that man did not have the right to make thought, as Gassendi phrased it, "the rule of the truth of things." Thus Descartes was depicted by his adversaries as a new Protagoras who did not draw support from anything solid or lasting.

He answered Gassendi confidently: "Yes, the thought of any individual—that is, his perception of a thing—must be the standard of its truth; in other words, to be sound, all his judgments must conform to his perception."

I can have a clear and distinct idea of myself as a thinking being and can conceive this thinking being without introducing any notion of my body. According to the rule, then, I have the right to say that my soul is a thinking substance wholly distinct from my body. But Arnauld raised an objection: because I am able to acquire some knowledge of myself without knowing anything about my body, can I be certain that I am not making a mistake when I exclude the body from the essence of my soul? I can be certain, for to attribute materiality to the soul is to confer on it an attribute that contributes nothing to our knowledge of it; consequently there is no reason to do so. The spirituality of the soul and

[4] Cf. Jean Wahl, *Du rôle de l'idée de l'instant dans la philosophie de Descartes* (Paris, 1920).

the distinction between soul and body then are rational truths and are derived from their notions.

A body, in turn, is distinct from a soul and contains in its substance only that which by itself can constitute the object of a clear and distinct idea apart from any other idea: for instance, three-dimensional extension, the object of geometers. Since I am able to conceive it as existing independently, it must be the material substance that physicists have long sought. Obviously, therefore, I should make it a rule to attribute to it only those properties that imply extension, and to refuse to attribute to it any quality—heaviness, lightness, heat, cold—of which the mind has but a confused and indistinct notion, and which does not seem to us to be a mode of extension.

Regius objected, of course, that we can conceive thinking substance only as thinking substance and are under no compulsion whatsoever to attribute extension to the same substance, but that nothing prevents us from doing so "since these attributes—thought and extension—are not contradictory but merely different." Descartes could answer the objection (which Spinoza seems to have adumbrated in his doctrine) only by showing that thought and extension are both essential attributes and that a substance can have but one such attribute. "If attributes that constitute the natures of things are different and the notion of one attribute is not contained in the other, we cannot say that they fit the same subject, since this would mean that the same subject could have two different natures." But how can an attribute be said to constitute the nature of a thing? The explanation is that the attribute is "the common reason that includes" everything that might be said about a substance—here, for instance, that the body is susceptible to figure and to motion.

There is in the dualism of Descartes something completely new. Of course Peripateticism recognized thought apart from the body, and the corpuscular physics of Democritus advanced mechanical explanations in which mind played no part. In the first place, however, the word "thought" did not mean the same thing to Aristotle and to Descartes. "By the word 'think,' I mean everything that occurs within us in such a way that we perceive it immediately by ourselves; that is why not only hearing, willing, and imagining but also sensing is the same thing here as thinking." In Aristotle the thinking intellect was separated from the active or sensitive functions for which the body was indispensable. But methodical doubt proved that the act of sensing or willing in no way implied the existence of the body. Therefore it is the whole mind that is spiritual and rational in all its functions, to the degree that "it must always think."

As for Democritus, he was not satisfied merely to refrain from introducing a spiritual soul into his explanation of things; in his theory of mechanics he denied outright the existence of this soul. Democritus and Epicurus rejected because of their system what Descartes excluded because of his method. We should add that the point of departure for Descartes' corpuscular physics was not obscure ideas of atoms and the void but the clear idea of extension.

We are certain that the thinking substance exists, that it is distinct from the body, and that God exists, but we do not know whether bodies exist outside us even though we are familiar with their essence, which is extension. The existence of a body is not evident; it is not contained in our idea of the body, and this idea is not so perfect that it could not have been produced by us. There remains our strong natural inclination to believe in its existence although doubt showed that our inclination did not entail assent and could be offset by equally compelling, opposing reasons. Still, the situation is no longer the same after we know God. This perfect being could not have wished for our natural inclination to mislead us, and his goodness therefore is one more guarantee for us. Such is the Cartesian proof of the existence of bodies. It is rather disconcerting inasmuch as it attributes to nature, to propensity, to inclination, a property that would seem to belong only to clear and distinct ideas. To appreciate its significance we must remember that we have within us a faculty—imagination—whose existence is not in any

way necessary to the thinking being as such. Distinct from understanding, it perceives its objects as being present only through "a
particular mental contention" that is of no use in intellection. We
can apprehend intellectually a myriagon as easily as a pentagon
and know with certainty, for example, the sum of the angles of
each figure; but our image of the first is quite indistinct, whereas
we can easily imagine the second. Universal mathematics served
by and large to disentangle mathematical thought and the imagining of figures. Thus the imagination always appears as something
essentially alien to the mind, as an intrusive, obfuscating element
that can be explained only through a force outside the mind. Consequently, no matter how paradoxical it may seem, affirmation of
the existence of external things is grounded on the presence within
us of confused and indistinct ideas that contribute nothing to the
clear and distinct idea of extension which constitutes the essence
of these same things.

VIII *Physics*

If we wished to examine Descartes' physics from the standpoint
of his positive contribution to the history of this science, we would
need to separate from metaphysics, in which he chose to place
them, a number of discoveries that do not belong there—that is,
discoveries made before 1627, when he was trying to find support
for his physics in metaphysics. The law of the velocity of falling
bodies that he expounded to Beeckman as early as 1619 is a mathematical investigation that assumes the law of inertia (the conservation of acquired motion in a moving object) and has nothing to do
with the cause of gravity which he explained at a later date. As
early as 1626 he had discovered the law of the equality of the sine
of the angle of incidence and the sine of the angle of refraction—
the starting point of formulas for the fabrication of lenses—through
an experiment which he described quite independently of the presumed demonstration that he offered later (1637) in the *Dioptric*.
In October, 1637, he wrote for Huyghens an "explanation of en-

gines that will enable the operator, by applying a small force, to lift a heavy burden." This short treatise on machines, in which he defined the effect of a force (action or work) solely by the displacement that it produced in a unit of mass and without taking into account the speed of its motion, introduced general notions which he never employed in his physics.

Such investigations led to the discovery of natural laws that could be expressed mathematically, like those of Kepler and Galileo; based solely on experience and mathematical techniques (in 1619 Descartes used the method of indivisibles devised by the physicist Cavalieri to express the law of falling bodies), they implied no hypothesis concerning the constitution of matter. This orientation toward mathematical expression of the laws of nature disappeared in the definitive version of Descartes' physics; in the last two books of the *Principles* we find no mathematical formulas but, instead, a description of mechanical combinations capable of producing the effects observed through experience. Descartes was apparently convinced that the prodigious complexity of causes prevented him from arriving at effects that could be expressed in simple formulas, for he did not pursue his investigations of the law of falling bodies, and he challenged the validity of the law of the isochronism of oscillations of the pendulum. The result was a strange anomaly: Descartes, the inventor of analytical geometry, which later became the indispensable instrument of physicists, found not the slightest use for it in his physics.

One contrast, admirably elucidated by Pierre Boutroux,[5] is worth noting. Kepler, who introduced aesthetic considerations into his vision of the universe, and Galileo, whose conception of the principle of inertia remained vague, discovered exact laws that make possible a rigid prediction of phenomena; Descartes, whose chief concern was the exactness and precision of principles such as those expounded in the second book of his *Principles of Philosophy*, finally managed to describe (in the third and fourth books) mechanisms which would provide a rough explanation of things but

[5] *Revue de Métaphysique* (November, 1921).

would make possible no prediction. We now turn our attention to those principles.

The essence of matter is extension. It follows that matter is infinitely small and infinitely large (that is, we must reject both the indivisible atoms of Democritus and the finite world of Aristotle), and that it is one (that is, we must reject any distinction between the matter of celestial things and the matter of the elements). A body is but a limited portion of extension, and one body can differ from another only through its shape and position. When one body is presumed to be at rest and the position of a second body in relation to the first is never the same at different moments, the second body is said to be in motion. Moreover, each body is impenetrable, and this means that two bodies cannot be in the same place.

The physical problem consisted in reducing all the effects and properties of bodies known to us by experience to a combination of bodies which have prescribed shapes and relative positions and which are animated by certain motions—a combination similar to that observable in mechanical artifices invented by man. Descartes modeled the intimate constitution of natural bodies on just such artifices. "The example of several bodies constructed by human artifice has been of great use to me in this matter," he said, speaking of his mechanical explanations; "for I recognize no difference between the machines constructed by artisans and the different bodies composed by nature alone, except that the effects of machines depend only on the arrangement of certain tubes or springs or other instruments which, since they must be proportionate to the hands of their makers, are always so big that their shapes and movements can be seen, whereas the tubes or springs that cause the effects of natural bodies are ordinarily too small to be perceived by our senses. And we can be certain that all the rules of mechanics pertain to metaphysics, with the result that all artificial things are also natural" (*Principles*, IV, 203).

Mechanics was known to the ancients only as the totality of the processes that allowed man to produce "violent" motions—for example, to lift weights by means of a lever or a windlass; thus it existed only on the human scale. In contrast, physics was the study of "natural" motions, such as falling—that is, a spontaneous motion which in the absence of any obstacle directs a spontaneous motion toward its natural place, the center of the world. In an infinite world, however, there was no longer a center, no longer a natural place, and consequently no longer a means of separating natural motions from violent motions. By the same token there was an obvious necessity for a law of inertia; by itself a body is incapable of changing its state of rest or of motion. If it is at rest, it will remain at rest indefinitely, and if in motion it will continue to move indefinitely with a rectilinear and uniform motion unless its state is changed by collision with an external body. Impact is the only cause of a change of state, and this cause is eminently mechanical. Mechanical structure, therefore, is wholly independent of the size of the scale, and we must picture it to ourselves on the invisible scale by analogy with mechanisms known to us on the visible scale through experience.

This analogy was responsible in the eyes of Descartes' contemporaries for the real difficulty of his physics. "In nature," Morin wrote to him, "can be found many effects that have no equal, such as those relating to the magnet. And if I told you what I know about celestial influences, they would again be something wholly different, for they act in a manner that defies comparison with anything other than God himself" (AT, II, 411). Descartes was thinking of physicists with just such views when he wrote in his *Rules* (1628) of those who were convinced that for each new effect they "must search for a new species of beings unknown to them previously."

Descartes' mechanics is one of impact, impact being the only action capable of modifying the state of a body. It must be added that the colliding action is instantaneous, that is, it modifies the state of the body that is struck at the very instant the impact occurs. Descartes' physics recognizes only instantaneous actions. And just as methodical doubt eliminated any type of certainty other than that of immediate perception, his physics eliminates any force which would require duration in order to unfold the effects of its action. The action of light is instantaneous and is transmitted from the luminous body to the eye just as an impulse is transmitted from one end of a rigid stick to the other. The point is so important to Descartes that he makes the extreme statement (AT, I, 308) that his "whole philosophy would be radically destroyed if the experience of the senses showed any delay at all." (The velocity of light was not demonstrated by Roemer until 1675.) The slightest delay would in effect imply a discontinuity and a void in the interval between light and the eye.

How are such instants, each powerless to prolong itself in another, linked together? By a law of permanence based on the immutability and constancy of God, a law that corresponds in physics to the divine attribute of perfect veracity in the theory of knowledge. It is the famous law of the quantitative conservation of motion. At every instant in time the quantity of motion imparted by God to the universe at the initial instant remains identical; the quantity of motion of a body is the product of its mass (calculated according to the geometric dimensions of the body) and its velocity. The state of the universe at a particular instant is therefore equivalent to the state of the universe at just any other instant. Thus all difficulties inherent in change are eliminated.

The only remaining modifications are modifications that are themselves instantaneous, due to impact. The seven laws of impact are dominated by the principle that the quantity of motion is the same after as before impact. They show how the quantity of motion is divided between two bodies following their collision and how their direction changes.

If two bodies (assumed to be completely impenetrable) are equal and moving at the same speed, each rebounds after impact with the same speed and in the opposite direction. If one of the bodies is larger and both have the same velocity, the larger body continues in the same direction and at the same velocity while the smaller one maintains the same velocity and moves in the opposite direction. If both are equal, and one of them is moving more rapidly than the other, the slower object rebounds while the faster one maintains its direction; furthermore, both assume the same velocity, the faster imparting half of its excess velocity to the slower. If one body is larger than the other and is at rest, the smaller body rebounds and maintains its motion while the larger one remains motionless. If under the same conditions the smaller one is at rest, the larger one continues to move in the same direction, carrying along with it the smaller one, to which it transfers a part of its motion. If they are equal and one is at rest while the other is in motion, the body in motion rebounds but loses one-fourth of its motion, which it imparts to the other body. If both bodies are going in the same direction and one is moving faster than the other, at the moment of impact two possibilities arise: if the quantity of motion of the slower body is greater than that of the faster one, the faster body rebounds but maintains its motion; in the opposite case, the faster body carries the slower one along with it, imparting to it a part of its motion.

These "laws of nature," though inexact, apply to an ideal case. They are based on the assumption that the two bodies under consideration are absolutely impenetrable, a fiction that Descartes admittedly accepted only "in order that things may fall under mathematical examination." Another fiction is that such bodies are not subject to any influence emanating from adjacent bodies, for this is impossible in the plenum. Whereas Newton's law of attraction (which was considered the paradigm of a natural law in the eighteenth century) issued from experience and led to the prediction and discovery of phenomena, the laws of impact were derived from reason and could not be used deductively. No human understanding can predict every impact to which adjacent bodies will subject a particular body at a given instant or, consequently, its speed and direction at the next instant. Just as human artifice cannot reproduce natural mechanisms because of their complexity, so "one can indeed make a machine that will remain in the air like a bird, *metaphysice loquendo* (for as I see it even birds are such machines) but not *physice* or *moraliter loquendo,* for this would necessitate such delicate and at the same time such strong springs that they could not be fabricated by a man" (AT, III, 163). Similarly, we can say that everything is accomplished through collision but we cannot explain all the details.

Descartes' conception of the nature of matter involves the necessity of vortexes. In the plenum the only possible motion is in effect a vortical motion; when one body relinquishes its place to the body pursuing it, the second body must take the place of another body, the latter of a third body, and so on until the last body, which will immediately have to occupy the place vacated by the first body. Descartes compared the circular motion of one of the bodies that make up the vortex to that of a stone in a sling: the stone would move at each instant in a straight line at a tangent to its trajectory if not held back by a strap; similarly, the body in a vortex must constantly be pressed toward its axis by adjacent bodies that oppose its rectilinear motion at a tangent to its trajectory.

Our solar system, with its planets, issues from a vortex which has its axis in the sun. Descartes described its genesis in this way: if we suppose that the matter of the vortex was formed at the outset by almost equal bodies, then it is necessary for these moving bodies constantly to find something to oppose their motion, with the result that their angles are rounded off and they become spheres. The scrapings of these spheres engenders a fine matter or *first element* capable through its tenuousness and agitation of filling up all the interstices between the spheres and of assuming every possible shape. The spheres themselves constitute the *second element.* As it slips through the spheres of the second element, fine matter tends always to escape from the center of the vortex and to move toward its periphery. Light is merely the force of the fine matter that we feel when it presses against our eyes. Since no void is possible, the first element that escapes from its axis is immediately replaced by other corpuscles of the first element. The first element then produces light, and the second element produces the matter of the heavens.

The particles of the first element, set in the interstices of the spheres of the second, are shaped like a curvilinear triangle with concavities or flutings. If these particles are halted in their motion, their flutings will mesh, gradually forming a rough, crusty matter, as we see in sunspots and in solid planets such as the earth: this is the *third element,* made up of multiform particles, some of them forked, others long, others almost round. In short, they exhibit as many differences among themselves as Democritus' atoms, and they play the same role; it was through the conjunction of particles with determinate shapes that Descartes explained the diverse bodies seen on the earth. With his subtle matter, his liquid heavens, and his solid matter with its parts to which he can give whatever shape he wishes, Descartes hoped to construct mechanisms to explain all terrestrial phenomena: heaviness, light, heat, tides, the chemical composition of bodies, magnetism. We shall not attempt to follow his detailed explanations.

We must try to grasp the spirit of what his adversaries called the "fiction of the vortexes." The most notable point is that, in order to explain the present state of the universe, he began with a state of affairs (the division of matter into corpuscles of equal size) which he chose as arbitrarily as geometers choose their hypotheses.

"It matters little," he said, "how I reach the assumption that matter was arranged in the beginning, for it is scarcely possible for us to imagine an arrangement that did not change continuously, as we can prove according to these laws, in such a manner that it would finally constitute a world quite like this one, since these laws cause matter successively to assume all shapes" (*Principles,* III, art. 45).

In this way Descartes freed physics from the obsession of the Hellenic cosmos, that is, from the image of a certain privileged state of things that satisfies our aesthetic needs and can be produced and maintained only through the action of a supreme intelligence—an obsession from which even physicists like Kepler and Galileo were not exempt. There is no such thing as a privileged state since all states are equivalent; nor is there a place in physics for the investigation of final causes or for the consideration of the best possible state. "Even if we posited the chaos of the poets, we could always demonstrate that through them [the laws of nature] this confusion must gradually return to the order that now exists in the world."

The physicist could divest himself of the stable concept of the cosmos only by imagining a theory which was too capacious for experience and which went beyond the explication of what is given. For instance, from principles we can deduce an infinite number of effects wholly different from those actually realized, just as a watchmaker, using the same methods, can contrive movements quite distinct from those actually imagined.

But the absence of conformity is precisely what makes experience indispensable in the Cartesian system of physics. We can indeed state a priori that the universe is composed of a unique, divisible matter animated by circular movements, and that motion is preserved. "But we were unable in the same way to determine the size of the parts into which this matter is divided, or the speed at which they move, or the circles that they describe; for since God might have ordained these things in countless ways, it is through experience alone and not through the power of reason that we can know which of these ways he has chosen" (*Principles,* III, 46). The physicist with his principles therefore would not have the slightest chance of falling upon the combination actually realized (since there are innumerable similar combinations), and he must "anticipate causes through effects."

In each instance experience indicates the particular problem that principles are supposed to provide the means for resolving. There can be no cosmology unless we begin, like astrologers, by describing exactly what we see in the heavens; no theory of the magnet before we have enunciated in detail the properties discovered by such experimenters as Gilbert. From this point of view theory goes hand in hand with experience, as Descartes clearly stated in his *Rules:*

"The physicist cannot answer the question, 'What is the magnet?' but only the question, 'What is the magnet in the light of the experiments conducted by Gilbert?'"

Thus it is important for experiments to be as numerous and as precise as possible. Descartes liked always to join experience with reasoning. He began, as we have seen, with problems of applied mathematics—music, barology, dioptrics. He held Bacon in high esteem and concluded that there was "nothing more to be said" after he had given the rules for carrying out useful experiments. "A history of celestial phenomena following the method of Verulamius," he wrote in 1632, "without the introduction of reason or hypotheses, would be more useful to the public than it might at first seem to be, and it would relieve me of much difficulty." Thus Descartes always promoted experimentation; at the end of the *Discourse* he asks rulers to subsidize the vast expenditures required for experiments necessary for the advancement of the sciences. After he retired to Egmond, Descartes himself was deeply interested in anatomical research and practiced dissections. In short, he was a rationalist who never disavowed the contempt manifested in the *Rules* for astronomers who studied the nature of the heavens without having observed their motions, who studied mechanics apart from physics, and who neglected experiment, thinking that they could extract truth from their brains.

But here a distinction must be made. There is a world of difference between precise experiments involving measurement and calculation—long practiced by astronomers and exemplified by Galileo and Pascal—and experiences which simply recount the immediate perceptions of the senses and which are exact only qualitatively. Those of the first type suggest numerical laws concerning the specific phenomenon under study and provide a basis for predictions that can be confirmed or invalidated by new experiments. Those of the second type, since they are descriptive, can lead only to theories which are themselves descriptive, which are not stated mathematically, and which in consequence provide no basis for prediction. Only experiments of the second type were used by Descartes in his physics, at least in the *Principles*. His descriptions of the heavens, tides, and the magnet contain no precise mathematical data.[6] More-over, the mechanical structures that he imagined in order to explain diverse phenomena are simply "rough" descriptions, as Pascal said, and do not give detailed dimensions and relations to provide a basis for mathematical deduction. For instance, his attempt to explain tides through lunar pressure did not allow him to indicate the exact nature of the phenomenon.

That was not his aim. His disdain for experiments involving exact measurements had the same deep-rooted causes as his lack of interest in the investigation of laws which could be expressed mathematically. Such experiments were useless in a world like his; the simplicity of mathematical laws is possible only in a universe in which causes, such as gravity and universal gravitation, act in limited numbers and always in the same manner; experience involving measurement, laws expressed mathematically, and physics of central forces go together. The mechanism of impact, with its infinite complication, jeopardizes any attempt to reduce nature to mathematical form.

Whenever Descartes ceased to be the theoretician of the *Principles,* however, he adhered to the tradition that led by way of Roberval, Pascal, and Huyghens to Newton—he used mathematics to determine certain effects numerically and called on experience to check the results. For instance, in his correspondence with Mersenne and Cavendish concerning the discovery of a simple pendulum isochronous with a compound pendulum, even after he had determined mathematically the length of a simple pendulum (by using methods of integration that transcended the limits he had prescribed in the *Geometry*), he still felt constrained to answer objections arising from experiences which, according to Cavendish, showed that his results were inaccurate. Furthermore, he specified that such experiments must be subject to precise measurements and

---

[6] Or, rather, if they are precise they are inexact; for instance, he assumed that astronomical distances were much less than they actually are. Cf. P. Busco, *Les cosmogonies modernes* (Paris, 1924), p. 20 (note).

gave the following rule, which is actually that of a true experimenter: "I believe that in the examination of experiences the greatest skill is required for choosing those which are least dependent on diverse causes and which have the most easily discovered true causes" (AT, IV, 392). The rule is apt but strictly inapplicable to a universe like his, where everything depends on innumerable causes.

The scientist constantly overshadowed the theoretician in Descartes. This was not true, however, in the works intended for the public. Here experience always retained the role that we have indicated.

IX *Physiology*

The treatise *On the World,* written between 1629 and 1632, concluded with some chapters on man, a sample of which appears in the fifth part of the *Discourse,* in his discussion of the motions of the heart. In 1648 Descartes wrote a description of the human body (published by Clerselier in 1664) entitled *On the Formation of the Foetus.* Here Descartes expanded his mechanics to make it include the functions of the body, "the digestion of food, the beating of the pulse, the distribution of the five senses" (AT, XI, 221). "I am now anatomizing the heads of different animals," he wrote to Mersenne, "in order to explain imagination and memory" (AT, I, 263). That the bodies of animals and men are comparable to machines or automatons is a notion which is found frequently in Greek philosophy, even in Plato and Aristotle, and which left its vestiges throughout the Middle Ages. Yet the idea that the body is a machine is linked traditionally to another idea—to the idea that the body is an instrument for a soul that uses it as a mechanic would do. We find nothing like this in Descartes, whose machine is constructed and made to function in accordance with the universal laws of nature, with the result that there is no need, to use the same image, for a particular mechanic. Hence the possibility of the famous theory of animal-machines, which eliminates any governing soul in the aniaml. This theory, made possible by the universal mechanism, derived from something more than his conception of the soul as a thinking substance distinct from the body: by withdrawing any vital, animal function from the soul and making it pure thought, capable of self-reflection, Descartes in effect eliminated every motive for attributing souls to animals.

Descartes' physiology rests entirely on the experimental discovery that Harvey had just made of the circulation of the blood. Nutritive juices are converted into blood in the liver and carried to the right auricle of the heart through the vena cava, then to the lungs through the pulmonary vein, then to the left auricle through the pulmonary artery, and finally throughout the body by the aorta and all its branches. But if Descartes agreed with Harvey on the circulatory movement of the blood, he differed completely with him on the cause of circulation. Harvey looked upon the heart as a propeller which, by contracting, drove blood into the arteries, and which, by expanding, drew blood from the veins; the movement of the heart (systolic and diastolic) caused the circulation of the blood. Descartes, clinging to the ancient Aristotelian concept, looked upon the heart as a source of heat capable of dilating the blood that entered its cavities; the blood, when dilated, in turn dilated the cavity of the heart that enclosed it, until it found an outlet through the pulmonary vein when it was in the right cavity, and through the aorta when it was in the left cavity; thus the movement of the heart was no longer the cause of the circulation of the blood but the result, passively sustained, of the dilation of the blood produced by its heat. Thus Descartes, in opposition to Harvey and contrary to the facts, reversed the true order of the motions of the heart, for he assumed that it dilated in the systole (when the blood escaped through the aorta) and that it contracted in the diastole (when blood came in through the vena cava).

His mistake was not accidental but was tied in with his whole physiological system. After criticizing Harvey, Descartes goes so far as to say: "It is very important for us to know the true cause of the motion of the heart, for without this knowledge we can know nothing relating to the theory of medicine" (AT, XI, 245). His mistake was, in effect, responsible for the revival of the traditional theory of animal spirits and for the establishment of a link between all of the functions known today as relational functions and the circulation of the blood. For "the most agitated and active parts of the blood are carried to the brain through the arteries that come by the straightest line from the heart, and they make up a very subtle air or wind called *animal spirits;* these, by dilating the brain, prepare it to receive impressions of external objects and also impressions of the soul—that is, they prepare it to be the organ or seat of common sense, imagination, and memory. Then this same air or these same spirits flow from the brain through the nerves into all the muscles and prepare the nerves to serve as organs of the external senses; and by distending the muscles variously, they impart motion to every member" (AT, XI, 227). All of these effects depend on the heart's heat, "which is like the main spring and the cause of all the motions" of the body.

According to Descartes, the body is composed of a system of canals and cavities through which the blood circulates, undergoing various modifications, all of them dependent on its heat. These cavities or tubes are simple containers which function no less actively than similar organs might function in an artificial machine and which passively receive the effects of the dilation of the blood or spirits. The cause of these effects is the heart's own heat.

It was in this sphere that lack of experience was most acutely felt. "Descartes was too familiar with the lacunae in our present knowledge of the history of man," wrote the anatomist Steno a short time later, "to undertake to explain his true composition. Thus he does not attempt to do it in his treatise on man, but he does try to explain the workings of a machine that performs all the actions of which men are capable." And addressing the Cartesians who went further than the master, he added: "Those who undertake to demonstrate that Descartes' man is made like other men will learn through the study of anatomy that their undertaking cannot be successful." [7]

x *Ethics*

Wisdom, the goal of philosophy, is attained when "intelligence first shows the will the choice that it should make." But there is a conflict between the urgency of moral wisdom, since action admits no delay, and the exigencies of method and of order, which teach us that "perfect knowledge of all the other sciences necessarily precedes knowledge of moral science." This is the conflict supposedly resolved in the "provisional morality," which Descartes (according to his statement in the *Discourse*) drew up in 1618, after he had become aware of the vanity of the sciences, "in order that I should not remain irresolute in my actions even though reason might oblige me to be irresolute in my judgments."

The moral maxims of Descartes, enunciated in the third part of the *Discourse,* are nevertheless imbued with rational considerations: "The first was to obey the laws and customs of my country, holding fast to the religion in which God graciously caused me to be instructed from childhood, and basing my conduct in all other matters on the most moderate and least extreme opinions which were commonly accepted in practice by the most intelligent of those with whom I had to live." Here Descartes recommended social conformity because it is "most profitable" to pattern our conduct according to those with whom we must live, and moderation because the most moderate opinions are "most appropriate in practice." "My second maxim was to be as firm and resolute as possible in my actions, and to follow the most dubious opinions, once I had made up my mind, with no less constancy than if they had been absolutely certain." Such constancy, having no roots in the certainty of opinion, is nevertheless rooted deep in a "very certain truth," for inconstancy in conduct, which derives from

[7] N. Steno, *Discourse on the anatomie of the Brain,* in *Opera Philosophica* (Copenhagen, 1910), II, 7.

instability of opinions, does not promote contentment of mind but is forever producing remorse and repentance. "My third maxim was to try always to master myself rather than fortune, to change my desires rather than the order of the world; and generally to accustom myself to believe that nothing is wholly in our power except our thoughts, so that after we have done our best with respect to the things that are outside us, everything we fail to accomplish is absolutely impossible so far as we are concerned." This attitude suffices to eliminate desires that cannot be satisfied and "thus to make me content."

Provisional morality, therefore, is the art of living happily in spite of the doubt which persists in our judgments of things but which in no way affects the conditions of our happiness. Social conformity, constancy of the will, moderation of desires—these standards reflecting a wisdom easily traceable in origin to ancient paganism were the very ones identified, independently of the clash and conflict between speculative opinions, by moralists like Du Vair, Montaigne, and Charron. The provisional elements of his moral philosophy were not identical to these standards. They reappeared in the same form when Descartes, after constructing his metaphysics and his physics, treated moral questions systematically in his letters to Princess Elizabeth, his correspondence with Chanut, and his treatise on the passions. In speculative matters their veracity remained independent of doubt and of certainty, but in the definitive statement of his moral philosophy Descartes based his precepts on a rational, analytical conception of man.

In the study of man as in everything else, Descartes followed the "order of reason" rather than the "order of matter"; consequently his notion of man was fashioned from clear and distinct elements which he discovered one after the other as deduction progressed. Metaphysics, knowledge of the distinction between soul and body, knowledge of the union of soul and body—every advance in knowledge was matched by the entry of a new element into the notion that man was fashioning of himself.

Man was first defined as a thinking and spiritual substance. But to Descartes sensation, passion, and will are modes of thought just as intellectual notions were. Passions and sensations not only did not imply a new feeling soul superadded to the intellectual soul but were merely aspects of the thinking faculty. In thought itself Descartes distinguishes two groups of modes—passions and actions. The word "passion" designates in a general way everything given to consciousness without any action on its part: the clear and distinct notions of understanding (extension and thought, first axioms) as well as true sensations and passions (desire, anger). The word "action" designates only the free will that enables us to judge or to abstain from judging, that is, to give or withhold our assent to the associations of ideas that are presented to us by the imagination, understanding, or the senses. Human knowledge is limited and finite, but the human will is "infinite" like the will of God—that is, it is free to give or to withhold assent.

The whole of Cartesian philosophy assumes this infinite will, the freedom of which is proved to us by a strong inner feeling. The first steps of the philosopher—his firm, constant resolution to adhere only to positive proofs, methodical doubt which results from this resolution—these are the fruits of an initiative of will. In philosophy there is no separation between extension of knowledge and nurture of judgment. But judgment, subjecting itself to the understanding, leads to the "highest good considered by natural reason without the light of faith," which is "the acquisition of knowledge of truth through first causes—that is, wisdom."

Physics, in turn, adds to man's knowledge by giving him a clear and distinct idea of his body and of the world to which he belongs. Here man is merely a machine obedient to the general laws of nature, and the concept of thinking substance does not intervene. The mechanism of the animal spirits which travel from the heart to the brain and are spread through the nerves to the muscles, where they produce motion, is the same in nature as the mechanism of any fluid whatsoever. But knowledge of this unlimited world and of the universal mechanism of which our body is an infinitesimal part inclines us to judge rationally events of the outer world and accidents that befall us. It destroys the false idea of a world that has its end in man: "For if we imagine that beyond the heavens there is nothing but imaginary spaces, and that the fulness of the heavens exists only for the benefit of the earth and the earth for man, the result is that we are inclined to think this earth is our principal abode, this life our best life . . . and beginning to show an impertinent presumption, we aspire to be in God's council and with him assume charge of the conduct of the world, all of which gives rise to an infinite number of vain concerns and vexations." Descartes' denial of anthropomorphic finality is in no way a denial of divine providence. Nothing is less incompatible than elimination of the study of final causes in physics and belief in the providence of God over the mechanism which he has created and which he preserves. "Everything is directed by divine providence" and "we ought to think that everything that happens to us is necessary and inexorable, so that it would be wrong for us to wish for it to happen any other way." This is a resurgence of Stoic fate and the resignation that it entails, but now it is tempered by reason and divested of the false notion of a finality favorable to man.

Metaphysics has recourse to notions of pure understanding to acquaint us with the soul and its maker, and physics with the help of imagination gives us a clear and distinct idea of the body. But we need only practice "suspension of the senses" to realize that man is something other than a soul and a body, that he is also a soul joined to a body, and that fusion is so complete that the human composite is an independent entity. This union consists in an interaction: the action of the body on the soul in sensation and passion, the action of the soul on the body in voluntary acts. If the relation of action to passion merits the name of union, it is because the relation is natural and totally unknown to the soul; in experiencing passion, the soul is totally unaware of the mechanism of animal spirits that has produced it; in exercising the will, it knows nothing of the complicated mechanism by which it moves an arm or a leg; such relations were instituted by nature. Furthermore, these relations have a special mode of intelligibility—finality. Descartes had excluded finality from physics, but it reigns supreme in the union of soul and body—a union decreed by nature for the conservation of our being—and it enters explicitly into the definition of the passions. The passions are defined as being dependent on corporeal causes "whose effects are felt as in the mind itself and which generally cannot be related to an immediate cause"; moreover, they are fully understood only in light of their utility, which consists "in the fact that they fortify thoughts and cause them to endure." It is well that the mind "preserves them, for otherwise they might be effaced." The same natural finality is seen again in the corporeal movements that spontaneously execute voluntary decisions: for instance, the pupillary reflex depends on will, "for although the subject is ordinarily unaware of its performance, his ability to see clearly is nonetheless dependent upon and a consequence to the will; and movements that enable the lips and tongue to pronounce words are called voluntary movements because they are a consequence of the will to speak, notwithstanding our ignorance of the manner in which they must be executed in pronouncing each letter" (AT, VI, 107).

The notion of the union of soul and body, sharply criticized by Spinoza, Malebranche, and Leibniz but considered by Descartes as being as "primitive" and legitimate as the notions of extension and thought, provides a clearer understanding of his view of intelligibility. God is not deceptive; any error originates in us, from the manner in which we employ notions outside the sphere of their proper application. Physics has been falsified because it has made use of sensible qualities, forces, substantial forms, finality; but these notions are not illusory in themselves (as Spinoza later believed); and if they are related to the union of soul and body, their veracity will be brought to light. Sensible qualities serve to warn the soul of the dangers of the body. The notion of a force or a substantial form which represents for us a spiritual being acting within an extended form is true as soon as we apply it to the union of soul and body. The natural finality contained in this union even makes it impossible for our desires or our natural needs to deceive us, except by accident. For instance, a dropsical person may still experience thirst, even though it is dangerous for him to drink, because the relation between a certain motion of his spirits and his feeling of thirst—a relation normally useful and indispensable to an organism—continues to exert its effects.

Man, as a soul united to a body, is subjected to the sensations and passions that come to him from his body, but he is to a certain degree the master of his corporeal movements. On the other hand, man's happiness and unhappiness depend solely upon his passions. "The philosophy I cultivate," said Descartes, "is not so barbaric or so ferocious that it rejects the enjoyment of the passions; on the contrary, it is to this alone that I attribute all the sweetness and happiness in life."

It is important for the moralist first to have knowledge of the nature and utility of each passion, then measurement of the influence passions have on will, and the influence will has on passions.

Passions are "affections or emotions which are related specifically to the soul itself [they are distinguished in this way from sensations, which are related to objects outside the soul] and which are engendered, continued, and augmented by a particular motion of the animal spirits." The study of this motion, unknown to the mind that senses its effects, is part of the physics of the body. Descartes tried to determine the particular motion of spirits that corresponded to each passion and the reason for its continuation through the organic modifications known as expression of the emotions—angry outbursts, tears, depression.

The motions of animal spirits generally have their source in the impression of an external object on the senses, or at least in the image of the object. Passion is essentially the attitude passively assumed by the will, under the influence of the motion of spirits, with respect to eternal objects. Thus the first of the passions—the necessary condition of all other passions—is *wonder,* which in Descartes is but one form of spontaneous attention. Thanks to wonder, an object is somehow brought into the foreground because of its novelty in relation to the others. Then comes *love* in which the will is disposed to unite with an object, and *hatred* which disposes the will to evade the object. *Joy* and *sadness* imply prior love and hatred, since one of them derives from the satisfaction of such passions and the other from failure to realize their satisfaction. All other passions are but variations or combinations of these five primitive passions.

By their nature passions predispose our will, before reason intervenes in any way, to welcome new knowledge (wonder), to seek out what is useful (love), and to flee from danger (hatred). But such dispositions also contain judgments concerning good and evil, and such judgments are true so long as passions remain within their natural limits. Of course "the utility of any passion derives solely from the fact that it fortifies thoughts and, fortunately for us, causes them to be preserved in the mind," but Descartes added: ". . . just as any evil that they can cause also derives from the fact that they fortify and preserve these thoughts to a greater degree than is necessary." The finality of passions, which depends on the union of soul and body, is only general and imperfect: not everything we love is good, not everything we hate is bad. These judgments are largely determined by accidental circumstances. First, physical circumstances, such as the constitution of the brain, can produce vast differences in the capacity of each of us to be affected by objects; secondly, the same object can be neutral and can arouse either love or hatred, depending on personal experiences; finally, accidental associations, by transferring our passion to objects associated with the primary object, can cause us to love or fear things in a manner which we would least expect and which is least advantageous to us.

But it is precisely this imperfection in the finality of the passions that will provide a foothold for the will and give it sovereign power. In the first place man can influence the conditions that govern the flow of spirits in the brain—through medicine, through hygiene, through alimentation—and such physical therapeutics are not negligible. But there are also intellectual therapeutics. The body exerts its influence on the mind, according to Descartes, through a particular organ—the pineal gland. This little organ, located at the base of the brain, was selected as the "seat of the soul," first because it is located on the axis of the body and is one of the few assymetrical parts of the brain, and secondly because Descartes inferred from its structure and location that it could be shaken by the slightest disturbance in the flow of animal spirits moving upward from the heart or sense organs into the "cavities" of the brain or descending from the brain into the muscles. The mind acts through the pineal gland on the motion of the spirits. According to the principles of Cartesian physics, the mind cannot be a moving force—that is, it cannot add even the slightest quantity of motion to the constant quantity of motion in the universe. Without violating the law of its conservation, however, the mind can change the direction of motion. It uses force without adding anything to it, just as a horseman guides his steed without contributing to its impulsion. Thus it can change the direction of motion of the pineal gland and in this way influence the flow of spirits to the brain and muscles. We must bear in mind, however, that the motion of the gland is voluntary only in the sense that the pupillary reflex is voluntary. The will is unaware of it and is not linked directly to it; but the will provokes modifications in the flow of spirits by willing a particular motion, and these modifications produce the desired muscular contraction in accordance with natural laws governing the union of soul and body.

Thus the will has only an indirect influence on the motion of the animal spirits and consequently on the passions, but its influence when appropriately exercised is unlimited, either because it fixes the attention of the mind on objects opposed to those which produce the passions we wish to destroy, or because it makes the body assume attitudes incompatible with bad passions, or because it takes advantage of associations of ideas and makes a passion change its object by a voluntary transfer. Through the mechanism of habit we can cause an object to produce an effect diametrically opposed to the one it produces naturally, just as we can train a dog to set or point in the presence of game which, spontaneously, he would pursue. In this way only "licit" passions—joys and desires that do not present things as being better and more desirable than they are—are allowed to subsist.

The consequences of this progressive, orderly inspection of man's nature have still not been exhausted. "According to the rule of reason," said Descartes, "each pleasure ought to be measured by the magnitude of the perfection that produces it." It follows that the highest good is knowledge of truth and that the sole virtue is a firm and constant resolution to subordinate the will to the light of our understanding. For our good can be only in "that which somehow appertains to us and is such that we must have it in order to achieve perfection," and the only such thing in us is our free will. It follows that the rational exercise of the will must produce the greatest pleasure if the rule of reason is used, and that such pleasure must be independent of the passion which issues from the body and bears the same name, since its dependence upon the body would introduce an element of imperfection. Therefore "the soul has its own pleasures," and, in a general way, it has passions which do not depend on the body—love and joy—"the causes of which are clearly known to us." These are the passions which the Stoics, under the name of εὐπάθειαι, attributed to the wise man; they are the seat of consummate bliss.

It is from a clear and distinct idea of human nature that the passions which constitute our beatitude must issue. Each of us sees himself clearly not only as a being endowed with a free will and as a soul united with a body but also as a part of a whole without which we could not survive. "Each of us is a part of the universe, and more especially a part of the earth, the state, the group, the family to which one is joined by his dwelling place, his oath, his birth; and he must always prefer the interests of the whole to which he belongs over those of his person in particular." This rational consideration, when it is perfectly clear to us, is accompanied by an "intellectual love" for the whole to which we owe our perfections—a love that links us to the whole voluntarily, as sensible love linked us to our bodies. Love for the whole is not charity distributed equally and indifferently to everyone; it is a rational love which enables us to estimate our worth in relation to the whole and which increases as our worth decreases. We sacrifice ourselves only for that which is worth more than we—for our country, for instance, but not for wealth.

The exact estimation of our worth is the fruit of *generosity*, a passion which is but one aspect of the search for truth when we are the object of the search. Knowing that human knowledge is severely limited, the generous man realizes that his worth depends not on the superiority of his intelligence but solely on his will and on the firmness with which the will always chooses whatever seems best to his intelligence. He therefore has neither misplaced humility nor scorn for other men, for he knows that each of them has a free will which is infinite and capable of equal virtue.

But he knows that God, among all other beings, is the one upon whom he is most completely dependent. Not only is our being created and preserved by God, but our free acts themselves are dependent upon his will. "Before he sent us into this world, he knew exactly what every inclination of our wills would be; he knew that our free wills would make us decide on a particular thing; and he willed it thus." In the whole consisting of God and ourselves, we count for so little that our love for him should be as great as possible. Furthermore, our love is intellectual and rational; it is born of natural illumination and independent of faith or grace; and it acts in such a way that, "surrendering ourselves utterly to our wills, we divest ourselves of our own interests and have no passion other than that of doing what we believe to be pleasing to him."

Cartesian philosophy, based on method, is essentially the cultivation of judgment. It is an unflinching will to adhere to ideas only by reason of their clarity and distinctiveness. "The most important thing that I try to teach in my *Meditations* is the formation of distinct ideas of the things about which judgments are to be made." The fundamental intention of mathematics, metaphysics, and physics is not to augment our knowledge of quantities, of God, or of nature, but to fortify judgment. Since judgment is an act of the free will, it follows that from the very beginning philosophy embraces this attitude of the will, which constitutes virtue.

XI *Cartesianism in the Seventeenth Century*

Cartesianism was a fashionable philosophy. Physics, especially, aroused enthusiasm. In his celebrated novel, Cyrano de Bergerac described sunspots in terms of Descartes' hypothesis, and in *Les Femmes savantes,* the following exchange takes place:

BÉLISE

I can take small bodies in my stride, but the void seems hard to endure, and I find subtle matter much more palatable.

TRISSOTIN

Descartes' theory of magnetism makes sense to me.

ARMANDE

I like his vortexes.

PHILAMINTE

And I his falling worlds.

Theologians and Peripatetics saw their vested interests imperiled and managed to convince the king and even the *parlement* that the public good was at stake. Descartes' doctrine was prohibited, not by a spiritual power enunciating the truth, as in the case of St. Thomas Aquinas and Siger of Brabant, but by a temporal power charged with the administration of public affairs. There is an outward, anecdotal side to the history of Cartesianism. It may be amusing, as when Boileau, warned that the *parlement* of Paris was on the point of passing a decree prohibiting the teaching of any philosophy other than that of Aristotle, prevented its passage by writing his famous *Arrêt burlesque;* but it may also be tragic, as when the debate was complicated by conflicts between Jesuits, Jansenists, and Oratorians, all of whom insisted on directing the education of youth. The Jesuits were generally hostile to Descartes and clung to their traditional courses; the Jansenists, like Arnauld and Nicole, showed their liking for Descartes by introducing whole passages from the *Rules* into their *Logic;* and the Oratorians, many of whom Descartes had numbered among his friends from the very beginning, were favorably disposed toward him by the resemblance they saw between his spiritualism and St. Augustine's. This complicated affair culminated in pamphlets such as Father Daniel's *Le Voyage du monde de Descartes,* in the heresy of M. de La Ville (Father Valois), and in a formulary brutally imposed by the Jesuits on Oratorian professors (1678), who were forced to state that they believed in substantial forms, in real accidents, and in the void.

But these noisy episodes do not constitute the true history of Cartesianism. What matters to us is the slow, silent process of assimilation through which mental habits, gradually modified through meditation on Cartesian truths, were once again harmonized.

The philosophy of Descartes spread throughout Europe. First to Holland: Daniel Lipstorp (*Specimina philosophiae cartesianae,* 1653); Jean de Raey (*Clavis philosophiae naturalis,* 1654); Adrien Heerebord, who published his first work, *Parallelismus aristotelicae et cartesianae philosophiae,* in 1643; Geulincx; and Chr. Wittich, whose *Annotations to the Meditations* (1688) was followed by *Antispinoza* (1690). In England, Antoine le Grand, a Frenchman, spread the ideas of Descartes and defended him in his handbooks (*Institutiones philosophiae,* London, 1672 and 1678), against Samuel Parker. In Germany, there were Clauberg and Balthasar Bekker, author of a *De philosophia cartesiana admonitio candida* (1691); and in France, Rohault, Sylvain Régis, Cordemoy, La Forge, and Malebranche.

Of course Cartesianism did not progress in the direction intended by its founder, and while it advanced principles which he thought to be sufficiently established, it made little progress in physics and especially in medicine, which required for its development difficult and costly experiments that an individual could not conduct at his own expense. On this point Leibniz was harsh in his criticism of the sterility of Descartes' disciples. The only physicist whom the Cartesians could cite by way of rebuttal was Jacques Rohault (1620–1675) and his investigations of capillarity. In his *Treatise on Physics* (1671), based on lectures that he gave in Paris over a period of several years, he advocated a science inspired by Cartesianism to replace Aristotle's treatises, which the universities were still teaching under the name of physics. Rohault's physics, divided into four parts according to the Cartesian order—natural bodies and their properties, the system of the world, the nature of the earth and of terrestrial bodies, and animated bodies—stresses the role of experience, which is especially useful in verifying suppositions. When we formulate a hypothesis concerning the nature of a subject, "if what we believe about its nature is verifiable, then by arranging it in a certain manner we must of necessity reveal a new effect which we had not yet imagined; and to test our reasoning we do whatever we had thought capable of causing the subject to produce this effect" (Preface).

But the imprint and continuing influence of Cartesian thinking was manifested much more clearly in metaphysical principles, the nature of ideas, the value of knowledge, and the union of soul and body. Having lost any right to refer to the sensible, the Cartesian had to discern through intrinsic qualities what constitutes the true value of objects of the mind—*ideas*—and what keeps us from confusing ideas with fictions. For just as Descartes, in the name of clear ideas, censured the Peripatetics for attributing reality to sensible qualities, his adversaries in their turn pretended that he was substituting a figment of his imagination, an invention of his mind, for the real world. Such was the preoccupation of Geulincx.

XII *Geulincx*

Arnold Geulincx (1625–1669) studied at the University of Louvain, where he later taught for six years. Forced for obscure reasons to give up his post, he became a Protestant and sought refuge in Leiden, where he gave private lessons after 1663. His works, among them a *Metaphysica vera* and a *Metaphysica ad mentem peripateticam,* appeared belatedly after his death (1691–1698, after Malebranche's works).

The central idea of all his investigations was to escape from "the inclination of the human mind to base the modes of its own thoughts on known things." Aristotle was the exemplar of those who succumbed, Descartes the model for those who sought to resist. One of the first mistakes of the Peripatetics was to imagine corporeal agents capable of producing in us a great variety of sensations and ideas; for I simply acknowledge on the one hand that I am, on the other that I have many different modes of thought; I am also a simple being, since I remain the same in spite of such diversity; since I am a simple being, I cannot produce in myself this diversity, which therefore has its source in an external agent. But is the agent to be found in bodies, as Aristotle maintained? No, for it is "quite obvious that there is no action unless there is consciousness in the agent. Prejudice convinces me that fire produces heat; but when I follow my "natural instinct," I see clearly that I cannot be the author of an action of which I am not conscious and of which I do not know the mode of production; consequently I know that the body, which lacks consciousness, cannot act, and that the cause of modes of thought can only be a thinking being outside me. But every thinking being is simple like me and can therefore produce diverse effects only through the intervention of something capable of diverse changes that give rise to diverse objects of thought—through the intervention of extension and bodies. "Bodies then act as instruments and not as causes." They act as the instruments of an ineffable cause—God who can create more things than I can conceive. This is one form of the occasionalist thesis advanced by Malebranche.[8]

Geulincx went much further in his reasoning. Descartes learned to consider bodies as being intelligible and attributed to them exten-

---

[8] *Metaphysica vera,* ed. Land, pp. 150–51, 153, 268 (note).

sion, infinitely divisible, impenetrable, and endowed with diverse other properties. But these properties are intelligible and therefore cannot belong to brute bodies as such; they must have been introduced by a mind. God put into matter not only motion but all its other properties.

We see the tendency of his reasoning. If we follow his train of thought to the end, we must conclude that the mind can conceive and know nothing about a thing except what has been introduced into the thing by the mind. But if Geulincx was firm about the principle, he was much less sure about the consequences that he drew from its application. Sometimes he viewed the mind's contribution to things as an obstacle to the acquisition of knowledge of things as they are in themselves (*ut sunt in se*)—for instance, when qualities conceal from us their physical reality. Similarly, when Aristotle said that things were beings and that he was describing their modes, genera, and species, he was not speaking of things but of human considerations which had no more reality than left or right or the rules of grammar and which, like these, could constitute a discipline (*doctrina*). For example, "being is nothing but a mode of thinking through which we apprehend something on which we have decided to state an opinion," and the same is true of parts and wholes, of unity and plurality. But human wisdom would then have severe limitations; it would reach only things which we ourselves have produced: "such is our consciousness of love, hatred, affirmation, negation, and all our other actions," in other words, immediate psychological data.

Wisdom sometimes is defined as knowledge derived from ideas ("ideas" are radically distinct from "human considerations and thoughts"), yet an idea is not simply an image of a thing in itself (as we saw in the example of the body) but an addition of the mind. The distinguishing mark of an idea—the idea of extension, for instance—is this: because it derives from the divine mind, it acquires the character of a rule or law, something not found in human modes of thinking.[9] In any case, nothing is more instruc-

[9] *Metaphysica ad mentem peripateticam,* ed. Land, II, 199; 191 (note).

tive than the fluctuation in the reasoning of Geulincx who, finding
the thing-in-itself only in immediate consciousness, tried to provide
science with an object by tracing a line of demarcation, never quite
distinct, between thoughts that have their source in us and true
ideas.

XIII *Clauberg*

Johann Clauberg (1622–1665), a Westphalian who wrote two of
his philosophical treatises in German (noteworthy in view of the
practice of his contemporaries), taught first at Herborn (1650), then
at Duisburg (1652). An erudite Cartesian, he was familiar with
Renaissance Platonism, with Marsilio Ficino, Plotinus, and Plato.
The essential characteristic of his work, which has not received the
attention it deserves, is his attempt to relate Cartesianism to the
Platonic tradition. Nothing is more singular in this respect than his
teaching concerning the theologian Conrad Berg. According to
Clauberg, in his unpublished writings Berg defended a theory of
ideas "similar in every way to Descartes' theory," and almost identical to Plato's: ideas are "species" of the absolute Being, have more
perfection than the things they represent in proportion as they are
spiritual, and are "something inanimate." Berg was even familiar
with the proof of the existence of God through the idea of God,
for this proof is at bottom only one aspect and one application of
the principle that led Plato to infer the existence of ideal models
from sensible things: things are natural signs of spiritual realities;
similarly, the idea of God is "the natural sign of the divine reality." [10] It was his Christian Platonism, suffused with an awareness
of the dignity of the soul, that led Clauberg to deny that any corporeal modification could produce a modification in the soul, since
an effect could not be more noble than its cause. It follows, he
said (using a Stoic expression), that "the motions of our bodies are
only procatarctic causes that provide the mind, as well as the prin-

[10] *De cognitione,* exercise xvi, pp. 619–20.

ciple cause, with an occasion (*menti occasionem dant*) for it to call forth ideas that are always potential (*semper virtute*) at a particular time." This thesis clearly reveals its Platonic origin.

XIV *Digby*

Sir Kenelm Digby (1603–1665), who lived for many years in Paris, tried to construct a corpuscular physics as remote from Gassendi's as from Descartes'. To construct the corpuscles of his dynamic physics he fused three forces: condensation, rarefaction, and weight. His system reveals his hostility to the thesis of the identity of extension and matter. But it also shows that on many points his thinking parallels that of Geulincx. "Aristotle's axiom that there is nothing in the understanding which was not previously in the senses falls so far short of being true in a strict sense," he says in his *Demonstratio immortalitatis animae rationalis* (1664, p. 216), "that we ought rather to say the opposite: there is nothing in the understanding that was first in the senses." With respect to sensible things, when we speak of existence, relations—for instance, parts and wholes, cause and effect, number, the continuum, or substances—we are making statements about their properties that cannot pass for our inner images of things. "The things behind the relations we are making statements about can be depicted and drawn in appropriate colors, but how can we depict their relations and have an *image* of half, or of cause and effect?" What is there in common between a pile made up of ten objects and the ideal signification of the number ten? And (according to terms reminiscent of Geulincx) why do we attribute substantiality to the notions we formulate, if not "because substance—that is, a self-subsistent thing circumscribed by its own limits—provides the mind with a convenient, solid basis to which it can attach itself and on which it can somehow depend?" These characteristics call attention to the way in which the exigencies of our minds are reflected in the notions which we have of things.

xv   *La Forge*

In the preface of his *Treatise on the Mind of Man, Its Faculties and Functions and Its Union with the Body, according to the Principles of René Descartes* (1666), Louis de la Forge tried, like Clauberg, to show that Descartes' ideas are in harmony, not only with St. Augustine's but also with those of Marsilio Ficino and the other Platonists. One of the main results of his meditation was that he cast light on the manner in which a Cartesian was to interpret the action of bodies on one another and the interaction of body and soul. He had to struggle not only against materialists who, imagining that any action would have to be modeled on action through contact, declared that a soul could not act on a body unless the soul itself was corporeal, but also against certain Cartesians who viewed the constant quantity of motion that God introduced into the universe as a real quality: materialism and dynamism are both inimical to clear ideas, and for identical reasons. Indeed, if we consider the clear and distinct idea of body—extension—we find in it no notion of a moving force. The "action" of one body on another, if we consider only bodies, is unintelligible, and the materialists erred in deducing from it an argument against the spirituality of mind since "it is neither harder [nor easier] to understand how a mind can act on a body and move it than to understand how one body pushes another" (p. 254). The only moving force is God, the universal cause of all the motions in the world. Consequently we can say that one motion is the particular cause of another motion or that the soul is the particular cause of a corporeal motion only if we mean that it "directs and obliges the first cause to apply its force and its moving power to bodies in whose absence it would not have acted, according to the manner in which it has resolved to govern itself with bodies and minds—for bodies according to the laws of motion . . . and for minds according to the extension of the power which it has elected to accord to the will."

XVI Gérard de Cordemoy

Gérard de Cordemoy, counselor to the king and reader to the grand dauphin, followed the same course in his own reflections. Like La Forge, he published his first work in 1666: *Ten Discourses on the Separation and the Union of Body and Soul*. He had formulated his ideas on the subject seven or eight years earlier (p. 72), and had discussed it with several friends. We see that what was later called occasionalism was in the ascendancy and appealed strongly to most Cartesians. Cordemoy offered a clear formulation of this thesis in his fourth discourse ("The First Cause of Motion"): "What we really mean when we say that some bodies move others is that all bodies are impenetrable and cannot always be moved, at least at the same speed, and that consequently, when they come together, they provide the mind that moved the first with an occasion to move the second." The interaction of body and soul is conceived in the same way. "A soul moves a body when, because it wishes this to happen, whatever was already moving the body actually moves it in the direction desired by the soul." From such considerations Cordemoy drew conclusions, some of which are rather surprising. Since there is no intrinsic relation between what is commonly called cause and effect deriving from the nature of these terms, we can imagine, between a soul and a body or between one soul and another, modes of relation quite different from actual modes; for instance, it is possible for the mind, separated from the body, to imagine all bodies, without union with one precluding, as it now does, union with another. We can also imagine minds which, to communicate thoughts, need only will their communication, for a thought can, after all, occasion another thought even more easily than a motion; furthermore, inspiration, which discloses new thoughts to us whose cause we cannot grasp, can probably be traced to the influence upon us of minds unknown to us (*Discourse on Words*, pp. 75–79). It is obvious that Cordemoy's Cartesianism tends toward the sort of disconnected vision of the universe which caused Leibniz to censure the occasionalists and which almost anticipated Hume's vision—a conclusion wholly consonant with the type of atomism that he substituted in physics for the master's continuous matter. Finally, he concluded from his thesis, as Malebranche also concluded, that belief in the existence of bodies can be guaranteed only by faith.

XVII *Sylvain Régis and Huet*

Descartes made it known that his metaphysics was too strong to suit the tastes of many. The history of Platonism proves that idealism based solely on spiritual realities, unless tempered by the rigorous discipline, self-control, and generosity typified by Descartes, is in danger of becoming visionary. The fault lies not in Descartes but in the weak minds of those who tried to interpret idealism. In his *System of Philosophy* (1690) Sylvain Régis (1632–1707)— one of the most celebrated popularizers of Cartesianism in Toulouse (1665), Montpellier (1671), and Paris—expounded a bland variety of Cartesianism which eliminated that danger. He put an end to speculative excesses in the doctrine by considering all realities— even innate ideas and clear and distinct ideas—as simple images of non-spiritual realities. These ideas derive all their value from their reference to non-spiritual realities, with which their existence begins and ends; furthermore, the same principle applies even more forcefully to truths grounded on such ideas. "Numerical, geometric, and metaphysical truths can be eternal neither according to their matter nor according to their form—not on the basis of their matter because this is nothing other than the substances that God has produced, and not on the basis of their form because this is nothing other than the operation through which mind considers substances in a certain way, and the mind's operation cannot be eternal." This Cartesian then accepted Aristotle's axiom, "there is nothing in the understanding that has not been in the senses," and tried to find in things a stable foundation for truth. But he also accepted the doctrine of innate ideas, though only in the sense that they exist in the mind from the time of our earliest experiences and remain there permanently. For instance, any external experience is knowledge of a mode of extension, and any mode of extension implies the idea of extension with all its properties; and the same is true of the idea of thought enveloped in any mode of thought. Régis' opinions contrast sharply with those of Malebranche who, as we shall see, had to answer the objections of his critics concerning the ideas which he saw directly "in God."

Régis assumed the role of defending Descartes against the attacks of Pierre Daniel Huet, who published his *Censura philosophiae Cartesianae* in 1689. Huet appears on the basis of his *Philosophical Treatise on the Weakness of the Human Mind,* written before 1690 but not published until 1723, to be a sensationalist and, consequently, a skeptic. The "species" of objects, because they pass through diverse media and then through our senses which alter them still more, are distorted by the time they reach us. But his skepticism is not, like that of the ancient Skeptics, a continuous search for truth. It is a definitive avowal of powerlessness, intended to "prepare the mind to receive faith." We must look with doubt upon everything that reason teaches us or at least believe that in divine things and even in human things reason can attain to certainty only through and in the light of faith. His attitude toward Descartes' rationalism is easily discerned; he criticizes Descartes for marshaling an arsenal of causes, all of them suspect since they can explain imaginary effects as readily as real ones. For example (p. 172), Huyghens was the first to discover Saturn's ring, which at the time of Descartes was assumed to be two satellites; Descartes "thought that he had adduced perfectly valid reasons to explain why the imaginary planets move quite slowly around Saturn." As for his criterion of clear and distinct ideas, its worth is refuted by the famous vicious circle for which he was criticized from the outset. In his *Reply to Criticism* (1691), Régis defended Cartesian physics in an odd manner. He maintained that "speculative physics can be dealt with only problematically, that whatever is demonstrative does not pertain to it," and that its role was limited to devising a mechanical arrangement for deducing effects from experience. As for the vicious circle, it was merely apparent; for it was on the human plane that the certainty of a true idea led to the existence of a perfect being, but it was on the plane of the absolute that the truth of an idea depended on the existence of this idea.

Toward the end of the century, in the opinion of many men less biased than Huet, Cartesian rationalism was dangerous simply because it was a form of rationalism. The "cause of God" was hard to defend through recondite arguments. "I have learned," said Jaquelot, for example, in his *Dissertations on the Existence of God* (1690), "that several metaphysical proofs do not have enough body to strike the heart perceptibly. The mind resists arguments that seem too subtle, even though it might find nothing to refute them." And to clinch his argument, Jaquelot substituted for proof of the existence of God his idea of the old proof *a contingentia mundi*. Furthermore, this was the age that witnessed the appearance of a number of refutations of the Cartesian proof, refutations that struck at the very heart of his philosophy. For instance, in his *Judicium de argumento Cartesii petito ab ejus idea* (Basel, 1699), Werenfels wrote that the idea of God is no more an immutable nature than is the idea of "horse," since we can arbitrarily eliminate one or more of its perfections. He added that we cannot know whether its existence is possible, since even if we grant that it is compatible with truths known to us, it can still be incompatible with unknown truths. Even Fénelon, though entirely sympathetic to Descartes, thought that he should begin his *Treatise on the Existence of God* by setting down the most obvious and popular proof, that of final causes written for "intelligent men" who did not have "a thorough knowledge of physics." In the period that lay ahead, more stress was to be placed on persuasion than on the invention of sound reasons.

BIBLIOGRAPHY

I to X

Texts

Descartes, René. *Œuvres*. Edited by C. Adam and P. Tannery. 13 vols. Paris, 1897–1913.
———. *Correspondance*. Edited by C. Adam and G. Milhaud. 8 vols. Paris, 1936–63.
———. *Œuvres et lettres*. Edited by A. Bridoux. New ed. Paris, 1953.
———. *The Philosophical Works*. Translated by E. S. Haldane and G. T. R. Ross. Repr. 2 vols. New York, 1955.
———. *Descartes' Philosophical Writings*. Translated by N. Kemp Smith. London, 1952.
———. *Philosophical Writings*. Edited and translated by E. Anscombe and P. T. Geach. Edinburgh, 1954.
———. *Philosophical Essays*. Translated by L. F. Lafleur. Indianapolis, Ind., 1964.
———. *Discours de la méthode*. Edited by E. Gilson. 2d ed. Paris, 1930.
———. *Les Méditations métaphysiques*. Edited by E. Thouverez. Paris, 1932.
———. *Correspondence of Descartes and Constantin Huyghens, 1635–1647*. Edited by L. Roth. Oxford, 1926.

Studies

Alquié, F. *Descartes: l'homme et l'Œuvre*. Paris, 1956.
Balz, A. G. A. *Descartes and the Modern Mind*. New Haven, Conn., 1952.
Beck, L. J. *The Method of Descartes*. Oxford, 1952.
———. *The Metaphysics of Descartes*. Oxford, 1965.
Brunschvicg, L. *René Descartes*. Paris, 1937.
———. *Le progrès de la conscience dans la philosophie occidentale*. Paris, 1927.
———. *Spinoza et ses contemporains*. 3d ed. Paris, 1923.
Delbos, V. *La philosophie française*. Paris, 1921.
Fischer, K. *Descartes and his School*. Translated by J. P. Gordy. New York, 1887.
Fouillée, A. *Descartes*. Paris, 1893.
Gibson, A. Boyce. *The Philosophy of Descartes*. London, 1932.

Gilson, E. *Index scholastico-cartésien.* Paris, 1913.
――――. *Études sur le rôle de la pensée mediévale dans la formation du système cartésien.* Paris, 1930.
Gouhier, H. *Essais sur Descartes.* Paris, 1937.
――――. *La pensée métaphysique de Descartes.* Paris. 1962.
Haldane, E. S. *Descartes: His Life and Times.* New York, 1905.
Hamelin, O. *Le système de Descartes.* Paris, 1911.
Jaspers, Karl. *Descartes und die Philosophie.* 3d ed. Berlin, 1956.
Keeling, S. V. *Descartes.* London, 1934.
Laberthonnière, LeP. *Études sur Descartes.* 2 vols. Paris, 1935.
Laporte, J. M. F. *Le rationalisme de Descartes.* Paris, 1945.
Lewis, G. *René Descartes, français, philosophe.* Tours, 1953.
Liard, L. *Descartes.* Paris, 1882.
Roth, L. *Descartes' Discourse on Method.* Oxford, 1937.
――――. *Spinoza, Descartes, and Maimonides.* New York, 1963.
Scott, J. F. *The Scientific Work of René Descartes.* London, 1952.
Sebba, G. *Bibliographia Cartesiana: A Critical Guide to the Descartes Literature, 1800–1960.* The Hague, 1964.
Serrurier, C. *Descartes, l'homme et le penseur.* Paris, 1951.
Smith, N. Kemp. *Studies in the Cartesian Philosophy.* London, 1902.
――――. *New Studies in the Philosophy of Descartes.* London, 1952.
Sortais, G. *La philosophie moderne depuis Bacon jusqu'à Leibniz.* 3 vols. Paris, 1920–29. Vol. III, *Descartes.*
Vartanian, A. *Diderot and Descartes.* Princeton, N.J., 1953.
Versfeld, M. *An Essay on the Metaphysics of Descartes.* London, 1940.
Meta-Meditations. Edited by A. Sesonske and B. N. Fleming. Belmont, Calif., 1965.

I

Studies

Adam, C. *Vie et œuvres de Descartes.* (*Œuvres,* Vol. XII.) Paris, 1910.
――――. *Descartes; ses amitiés féminines.* Paris, 1937.
――――. "René Descartes, Manuscrit de Göttingen," *Revue bourguignonne de l'enseignement supérieur,* 1896.
Baillet, Adrien. *La vie de Monsieur Descartes.* 2 vols. Paris, 1691.
Cantecor, G. "La vocation de Descartes," *Revue philosophique,* November, 1923.
――――. "A quelle date Descartes a-t-il écrit la Recherche de la Vérité?" *Revue d'histoire de la philosophie,* II (1928).
Cassirer, E. *Descartes: Lehre, Persönlichkeit, Wirkung.* Stockholm, 1939.
Cohen, G. *Écrivains français en Hollande dans la première moitié du XVIIe siècle.* Paris, 1920.

Gouhier, H. "Sur la date de la Recherche de la Verité," *Revue d'histoire de la philosophie*, III (1929).
——. *Les premières pensées de Descartes*. Paris, 1958.
Leroy, M. *Descartes, le philosophe au masque*. Paris, 1929.
Milhaud, G. "L'œuvre de Descartes pendant l'hiver 1619–1620," *Scientia*, January, 1918.
——. "Une crise mystique chez Descartes en 1619," *Revue de métaphysique*, July, 1916.
——. "La sincérité de Descartes," *Revue de métaphysique*, May, 1919.
Sirven, J. *Les années d'apprentissage de Descartes, 1596–1628*. Paris, 1928.

II

Studies

Alquié, F. *La découverte métaphysique de l'homme chez Descartes*. Paris, 1950.
Alquié, F., *et al*. Articles on Descartes commemorating the third centenary of his death, *Revue philosophique*, 1951.
Alquié, F., H. Gouhier, and M. Guéroult. *Descartes*. (Colloque de Royaumont.) Paris, 1957.
Berthet, J. "La méthode de Descartes," *Revue de métaphysique*, 1896.
Boutroux, P. *L'imagination et les mathématiques selon Descartes*. Paris, 1900.
——. "La signification historique de la Géometrie de Descartes," *Revue de métaphysique*, 1915.
Brunschvicg, L. *Écrits philosophiques*. Paris, 1951. I, 11–108.
Gibson, B. "The Regulae of Descartes," *Mind*, 1898.
——. "La géometrie de Descartes au point de vue de la méthode," *Revue de métaphysique*, 1896.
Guéroult, M. *Descartes, selon l'ordre des raisons*. 2 vols. Paris, 1958. Vol. I, *L'âme et Dieu*; Vol. II, *L'âme et le corps*.
Hannequin, A. "La méthode de Descartes," *Revue de métaphysique*, 1906. Reprinted in *Essais sur l'histoire des sciences et de la philosophie*. Paris, 1908.
Milhaud, G. *Num Cartesii methodus tantum valeat in sui opere illustrando quantum senserit*. Montpellier, 1894.
——. "La Géometrie de Descartes," *Revue generale des sciences*, 1916.
——. "Descartes et l'analyse infinitésimale," *Ibid*., 1917.
——. "La querelle de Descartes et de Fermat au sujet des tangentes," *Ibid*., 1917.
Vuillemin, J. *Mathématiques et métaphysique chez Descartes*. Paris, 1960.

III

Studies

Gilson, E. "L'innéisme cartésien et la théologie," *Revue de métaphysique,* 1914. Reprinted in *Études de philosophie médiévale,* Strasbourg, 1921, pp. 146 ff.

Natorp, P. *Descartes Erkenntnisstheorie: Eine Studie zur Vorgeschichte des Kriticismus.* Marburg, 1882.

Virgier, J. "Les idées de temps, de durée et d'éternité dans Descartes," *Revue philosophique,* 1920.

Wahl, J. *Du rôle de l'idée de l'instant dans la philosophie de Descartes.* Paris, 1920.

IV

Study

Boutroux, E. *De veritatibus aeternis apud Cartesium.* Paris, 1875. *Des vérités éternelles chez Descartes.* Translated by Canguilhem. Paris, 1927.

V

Studies

Blanchet, L. *Les antécédents historiques du "Je pense, donc je suis."* Paris, 1920.

Guéroult, M. *Nouvelles réflexions sur la preuve ontologique de Descartes.* Paris, 1955.

VI

Studies

Blondel, M. "Le Christianisme de Descartes," *Revue de métaphysique,* 1896.

Glison, E. *La doctrine cartésienne de la liberté et la théologie.* Paris, 1913.

Gouhier, H. *La pensée religieuse de Descartes.* Paris, 1924.

Hannequin, A. "La preuve ontologique de Descartes défendue contre Leibniz," *Revue de métaphysique,* 1896.

Laberthonnière, L. "La religion de Descartes," *Annales de philosophie chrétienne,* August, 1911.

———. "La théorie de la foi chez Descartes," *Ibid.,* July, 1911.

——. "Le prétendu rationalisme de Descartes au point de vue religieux," *Ibid.*, September, 1911.

Laporte, J. "La finalité chez Descartes," *Revue d'histoire de la philosophie,* II (1928).

Russier, J. *Sagesse cartésienne et religion: Essai sur la connaissance de l'immortalité de l'âme selon Descartes.* Paris, 1958.

VII

Study

Schwarz, H. "Les recherches de Descartes sur la connaissance du monde extérieur," *Revue de métaphysique,* 1896.

VIII

Studies

Belaval, Y. *Leibniz critique de Descartes.* Paris, 1960.

Carteron, H. "L'idée de la force mécanique dans le système de Descartes," *Revue philosophique,* 1922.

Gilson, E. "Météores cartésiens et météores scolastiques," in *Études de philosophie médiévale,* Strasbourg, 1921, pp. 247 ff.

Hoffman, A. "Die Lehre von der Bildung des Universums bei Descartes," *Archiv für die Geschichte der Philosophie,* XVII (1904).

Korteweg. "Descartes et Snellius, d'après quelques documents nouveaux," *Revue de métaphysique,* 1896.

Milhaud, T. "Descartes expérimentateur," *Revue philosophique,* 1918. Reprinted in *Descartes savant,* Paris, 1920.

——. "Descartes et Bacon," *Scientia,* 1917. Reprinted in *Descartes savant,* Paris, 1917.

——. "Le double aspect de l'œuvre scientifique de Descartes," *Scientia,* 1916. Reprinted in *Descartes savant,* Paris, 1917.

——. "Notes sur Descartes," *Revue philosophique,* 1918. Reprinted in *Descartes savant,* Paris, 1917.

Tannery, P. "Descartes physicien," *Revue de métaphysique,* 1896.

IX

Studies

Berthier, "Le mécanisme cartésien et la physiologie au XVIIe siécle," *Isis,* 1914.

Canguilhem, G. *La formation du concept de réflexe aux XVIIe et XVIIIe siècles.* Paris, 1955.

———. "Organisme et modèles mécaniques, Reflexions sur la biologie cartésienne (1)," *Revue philosophique,* 1955, pp. 281–299.

Gilson, E. "Descartes et Harvey," *Revue philosophique,* 1921 and 1922. Reprinted in *Études de philosophie mediévale,* Strasbourg, 1921, pp. 191 ff.

Sommer, E. *Die Entstehung der mechanischem Schule in der Heilknude am Ausgang des 17. Jahrhunderts.* Leipzig, 1899.

X

Studies

Boutroux, E. "Du rapport de la morale à la science dans la philosophie cartésienne," *Revue de métaphysique,* 1896.

Brochard, V. "Le traité des Passions de Descartes et l'Ethique de Spinoza," *Revue de métaphysique,* 1896. Reprinted in *Études de philosophie ancienne et de philosophie moderne.* Paris, 1912. Pp. 327 ff.

———. "Descartes stoïcien," in *Études de philosophie ancienne et de philosophie moderne.* Paris, 1912. Pp. 320 ff.

Espinas, A. *Descartes et la morale.* 2 vols. Paris, 1925.

Lanson, G. "Le héros cornélien et le généreux selon Descartes," *Revue d'histoire littéraire,* 1894.

Lewis, G. *L'individualité selon Descartes.* Paris, 1950.

———. *Le problème de l'inconscient et le cartésianisme.* Paris, 1950.

———. *La morale de Descartes.* Paris, 1957.

Mesnard, P. *Essai sur la morale de Descartes.* Paris, 1936.

Seailles, G. *Quid de ethica Cartesius senserit.* Paris, 1883.

XI

Studies

Balz, A. G. *Cartesian Studies.* New York, 1951.

Bouillier, F. *Histoire de la philosophie cartésienne.* 3d ed. 2 vols. Paris, 1868.

Mouy, P. *Le développement de la physique cartésienne, 1646–1712.* Paris, 1934.

Prost, J. *Essai sur l'atomisme et l'occasionalisme dans la philosophie cartésienne.* Paris, 1907.

XII

Text

Geulincx, Arnold. *Opera philosophica.* Edited by J. P. N. Land. 3 vols. The Hague, 1891–93.

Studies

Van der Haeghen, V. *Geulincx: Études sur sa vie, sa philosophie et ses ouvrages*. Ghent, 1886.
Land, J. P. N. *Arnold Geulincx und seine Philosophie*. The Hague, 1895.

XIII

Text

Clauberg, Johannes. *Opera*. Amsterdam, 1691.

Study

Müller, Hermann. *Johannes Clauberg und seine Stellung im Cartesianismus*. (Dissertation) Jena, 1891.

XV

Study

Seyfarth, H. *Louis de la Forge und seine Stellung im Occasionalismus*. (Dissertation) Gotha, 1887.

XVII

Texts

Régis, Sylvain. *Système de philosophie contenant la logique, la métaphysique, la physique et la morale*. Paris, 1690.
Huet, D. *Censura philosophiae cartesianae*. Paris, 1689.
———. *Traité philosophique de la faiblesse de l'esprit humain*. Amsterdam, 1723.

Studies

Bartholmes, C. *Huet, évêque d'Avranches, ou le scepticisme théologique*. Paris, 1850.
Sortais, G. "Le cartésianisme chez les Jésuites français au XVIIe et au XVIIe siècle," *Archives de philosophie*, VI (1929).

PASCAL

I *The Methods of Pascal*

BLAISE PASCAL (1623–1662) was not a philosopher. He was a scientist and an apologist for the Catholic religion. As a scientist he had a place in the tradition of mathematical and experimental physics that led from Galileo to Newton. As an apologist he did not start by attempting to demonstrate by reason all the truths of faith that are demonstrable. To answer the freethinkers he turned to history for evidence, to the whole spectrum of human behavior, just as he turned to experience and not to reason for proof of a physical truth. Descartes was also a scientist and, to a certain degree, an apologist, but his genius prevented him from being both without being a philosopher at the same time—without introducing science and apologetics into the "chain of reasons" from which he had excluded the truths of faith. Pascal's genius, on the contrary, allowed him neither to make science and apologetics an integral part of a philosophy nor to fail to take into consideration the truths of faith. The contrast between the two men, almost contemporaries, is so profound and so striking that in all probability nothing else in history can provide us with a better understanding of the nature of the human mind.

The *Essay on Conics,* written when Pascal was hardly out of his childhood (1639), reveals one of his characteristic intellectual traits. When dealing with a specific problem (to find the principle from which all the properties of conic sections can be deduced), he devised a specific method capable of resolving this problem and only this problem. Pascal discovered that every property of a conic section depended upon the invention of a certain hexagon, which he calls the mystic hexagram. Thus each problem requires a new inventive effort on the part of the mathematician, who must have the ability to discover the precise notions and principles needed for its solution. This explains why Pascal subsequently showed that in order to find the center of gravity of a cycloid and of the surfaces or volumes that depend upon this curve, we must take into consideration the properties of so-called triangular numbers. As he points out in his *Thoughts,* those who are not geometers will be repelled by definitions and principles that seem sterile to them and by propositions incomprehensible to them; they cannot see, immediately and intuitively, the slightest relation between the mystic hexagram and the properties of conical sections, between triangular numbers and the question of centers of gravity. The discovery of such relations depends not upon a method communicable to everyone but upon a certain mentality—the geometric mind—which is possessed by few men. "I was bothered by the fact that there were few men with whom I could discuss them," Pascal later remarked in speaking of the abstract sciences. He used the word "method" in the plural, for he maintained that there were as many methods— procedures to be devised—as there were problems to be solved. The geometer separates objects from one another, and the geometric mind in turn separates the geometer from other men.

The geometric mind is only part of the scientific mind. The Pascal who studied hydrostatics did not use the same intellectual endowments as the Pascal who invented the mystic hexagram. "Some people," he said, "have a clear understanding of the effects of water, which involves few principles; but their consequences are so subtle that only the most penetrating minds can reach them. Such men would not necessarily be great geometers, for geometry includes many principles, and a certain kind of mind may be able to gain a thorough grasp of a few principles and yet be unable even to begin to understand things that involve many principles." A "discriminating mind" with "power to penetrate" can be narrow and still serve to investigate the effects of water (since the principle of hydrostatics is unique); the geometric mind, on the other hand, must be able to grasp a great number of principles without confusion and is therefore broad even though it may be weak.[1]

As a scientist, Pascal also applied himself to other studies in which knowledge of principles is useless, or rather, in which the search for principles is futile. Cartesians may claim to establish the plenum through principles: "They say that because you believed as a child that boxes were empty when you saw nothing in them, you believed that a vacuum was possible. This is an illusion of your senses, strengthened by custom, and science must correct it. Or they say that because you were told in school that there is no vacuum, your common sense—which understood it quite clearly before this wrong impression—was corrupted and must be corrected by going back to your first nature" (No. 82). Consequently, no recourse to principles is possible in the question of the void. But experience establishes with certainty that the tube above the quicksilver in a barometer is empty, and with equal certainty that the weight of a column of quicksilver must be equiliberated by a pressure acting on the free surface. Furthermore, the celebrated experiment at Puy-de-Dôme, which showed that the height of the column decreases as the altitude of the apparatus increases, proved that the pressure is caused by the atmosphere. The existence of the vacuum or the weight of air can neither be affirmed nor denied on the basis of principles.

Geometric mind, discriminating mind, and experimental method —all these are modes of investigation that require different intellectual endowments. Pascal did not describe them or speculate on them from the standpoint of an outsider but entered into each mode with enthusiasm and passion. He was able to make a sharp distinction between these modes of investigation because of his

---

[1] *Pensées* (references are to numbers in Brunschvicg's edition).

experience with each of them. His success was prodigious in each instance, and in a few years he had managed to break new ground everywhere. In mathematics he created the calculus of probabilities, and one of his remarks about curves on a characteristic triangle suggested to Leibniz the procedure for the infinitesimal calculus. In physics his work with hydrostatics and barometry provided the stimulus for the study of the mechanics of fluids.

Adjusting the mind to the domain of the objects studied is the key to Pascal's approach. A mind that is "right" in its own domain will be "wrong and insufferable" if it changes its domain. The geometer Pascal learned this through his association with the Chevalier de la Méré and other men of the world. Many of them had sound judgment about manners and personalities. Had they reasoned like a geometer in reaching their convictions? Reasoned, yes; like a geometer, no. The geometer uses a large but finite number of principles; each principle has its own distinct formulation, is grasped perfectly by any attentive mind, and is linked to every other principle and to the conclusion. But the man of the world is not interested in these principles since they are of no use to him. His principles are "in common usage and there for everyone to see." How would he engage in geometric reasoning, using principles "which are sensed rather than known" and which can be communicated to others only "with infinite pains," with principles so numerous that demonstrating them in an orderly fashion would be "an infinite thing," with principles that cannot be formulated distinctly since "no man is capable of expressing them"? The man of the world does reason, but "he does it tacitly, naturally, artlessly." This is because he is endowed with a mind quite different from the geometric mind, the "discriminating mind" that consists primarily in "seeing the thing at a glance and not through progressive reasoning."

The discovery of the discriminating mind is of capital importance. Here we have an authentic type of reasoning which bears almost the same relation to geometric reasoning as Cavalieri's principle of indivisibles bears to the calculus of finite sums in mathematics; the relation is that between the infinite and the finite, the inexpressible and the expressible, intuition and discourse.

Pascal isolated and separated, whereas Descartes searched for a unity of method grounded on the unity of the intellect. But from another point of view he associated and compared. The worth of a "mind" depends on its appropriateness to the solution of problems in its own domain; but to estimate its worth in this way only is to judge it as a specialist, and we must also determine its worth for man as a man. On this point Descartes did not hesitate: all sciences fortify judgment because they represent a single intelligence employing a single method. Pascal acted as a specialist and concluded that to be productive in its domain, a mind must be exclusive: "Geometers rarely have discriminating minds and men with discriminating minds are rarely geometers." Is it good for men to devote themselves to studies that take them away from more important tasks? "When I began to study man, I saw that he is not fitted for abstract sciences and that I deviated farther from my condition by immersing myself in them than did others by ignoring them" (144).

Pascal devoted himself to the "science of man" only after he had undertaken his apology for the Catholic religion. This science and the apology are interconnected in his thinking. Human nature poses problems which can be solved only by revealed Christianity; without it, man cannot understand himself. In the new problem which he undertook to solve Pascal remained wholly faithful to his genius. He searched for a solution that would conform to every circumstance and omit none. The revelation of Christ has the same relation to the problem of man as the mystic hexagram to conics or triangular numbers to the center of gravity of cycloids; the solution to the problem will never come through analysis of its data no matter how penetrating. Original notions, whose relation to the question can be understood only by exceptional minds, must be found or forged. Such notions do not have the Cartesian intelligibility that pertains to notions considered independently; through them other things are intelligible. The same thing applies in the science of man. Here too, here especially, the solution must come from without—from the Christian religion which, unintelligible according to our human criteria, is alone capable of making man comprehensible to himself.

II *Criticism of Principles*

He we arrive at the element common to all of Pascal's speculations. He abhorred principles which could be applied indiscriminately and from which everything could be deduced. His antipathy toward the Jesuits' casuistry stemmed neither from partisanship nor even from contempt for lax morals. He detested the fact that men of their capabilities were adept at finding the subterfuge through which they could relate any action to an established principle and in this way justify abominable offenses. And his criticism of them in the *Provincial Letters* does not differ, from certain points of view, from the criticism of Descartes' physics which he expressed in his *Thoughts:* "We must say summarily that this is made by figure and motion, for it is true; but to say what these are and to compose the machine is ridiculous, for it is useless, uncertain, and painful" (79). Principles which are sufficiently universal to apply to everything, such as Descartes' mechanics, explain nothing with certainty.

But Descartes was wrong in thinking that he could start from principles intelligible in themselves and relate to them his whole chain of deductions. His mistake was the same as that of the atomists who believed they could first identify the elements that make up the whole and then reconstruct the whole by juxtaposing the parts, for "the parts of the world are all so related and linked to one another that I deem it impossible to know one without the other and without the whole" (72). The intelligibility of Gassendi's atom is illusory. But the intelligibility of Descartes' simple nature is no less illusory, for "man cannot understand what a body is, and still less what a mind is, and less than anything else how a body can be joined to a mind" (72). The impossibility of arriving at first principles in anything reflects a radical defect in human nature. Man, in the order of nature, is "a Nothing in comparison with the Infinite, an All in comparison with Nothing, a mean between nothing and everything." Furthermore, "his intellect holds the same position in the world of thought as his body occupies in the expanse of nature. All he can do, then, is to gain some idea of how things look from the center, in eternal despair of knowing either their beginning or their end."

What are the "principles" which are supposed to serve as a point of departure for human knowledge and which Pascal himself often mentioned in connection with the geometric or discriminating mind? The axioms and definitions of Euclid cannot be classed as principles in a strict sense, for the perfection of the geometric method would require defining and demonstrating everything—an infinite undertaking. We have to stop when confronted with indefinable and indemonstrable principles. Which of these is not suspect? Can we appeal to nature? "But there is no principle, however natural it may seem to be and even if it dates from childhood, that may not be a false impression attributable either to instruction or to the senses" (82). Descartes thought that he had established a clear distinction between nature and custom through methodical doubt. Pascal allied himself with Montaigne and the Pyrrhonians: "What are our natural principles but principles based on custom? A different custom would result in different principles. Custom is a second nature that destroys the first. But what is nature? Why is custom not natural? I greatly fear that this nature is itself a first custom" (92, 39).

Here Pascal's criticism of principles did not disagree with the use to which he put them in geometry and in physics, for he said that they were not absolute beginnings and that they were not intelligible in themselves. But nothing (and this is true of physics and geometry) prevented their being perfectly fitted to their role, which was to account for a certain number of properties known through reason, such as the properties of conical sections, or through observation, such as the height of the column of quicksilver in a barometer. "We always find that the thing to be proven is obscure and the thing used to prove it clear."

Pascal could break away from Pyrrhonism only by virtue of the source of knowledge and certainty that he called *heart* or, less frequently, *intelligence*. Heart or intelligence contrasts with *reason* which, in the language of Pascal, means reasoning or discourse in general, the knowledge of consequences. Reason "can be bent in any direction" (274), for the conclusion it reaches is determined by premises received from other sources. The heart provides knowledge in the sphere of principles—knowledge of God who is "sensible to the heart" (278) and the axioms of geometry. "The heart senses that there are three dimensions in space and that numbers are infinite." But was he not in a sense contradicting himself when he accepted both the views of the Pyrrhonians and, under the name of heart, a particular faculty for arriving at principles with certainty? By heart he meant not a faculty for acquiring knowledge of principles, but a certain manner of accommodating knowledge that would otherwise remain "uncertain and unsettled." Pascal often contrasted the faith of simple people, strong and sure, with the discourses of philosophers who used reason to demonstrate the existence of God. He knew that discourses, no matter how logical, are of little use in winning over the impious: "metaphysical proofs are so remote from the reasoning of men and so involved that they are not very convincing; and if they may be of use to some, it can only be during the time they witness the demonstration, for an hour later they are afraid of being mistaken" (543). Thus it is one thing to know truth through reason and quite another to sense it through the heart. Because principles are sensed as the believer senses God, the geometer can surmount Pyrrhonism.

III Pascal the Apologist

Pascal's religious apologetic therefore is not a demonstration of the truth of the Christian religion, or rather his demonstration (the traditional one through the Old Testament and the miracles) is but one part of a demonstration, the part where he remained in the main stream of tradition. But when he had to prove, as he set out to do, that the Christian religion answered all of man's needs, uniquely and completely, expedience took precedence over truth. Why should its perfect expedience make its truth superior to that of many other religions that are the fruit of our prejudices? Pascal knew, along with all other Christians, that the only proof of the truths of the Christian religion is revelation and that its only means of access to the human heart is divine grace. In the preface to the *Treatise on the Vacuum,* composed before his *Thoughts,* he wrote the well known pages in which he revealed that the only method of investigation of truth in religious matters is based on authority which has its source in God himself. In his *Thoughts* he treated revealed truths concerning our supernatural destiny and meditation on Christ as a datum or point of departure.

If traditional proofs in the form of miracles or prophecies were the same in nature as geometric proofs, the rest of the apologetic would be useless. But these proofs are such that they cannot convince the unbeliever; through them God conceals as much as he reveals about himself; and that is why faith remains meritorious and depends on grace rather than on reason.

Accordingly, instead of using proofs when he addressed the unbeliever, he had to show that only the Christian religion can make man comprehensible to himself. He therefore had to make man desire truth, to "free him from passions and prepare him to follow truth wherever he may find it."

But for this, man must know his own nature. According to Descartes, man's nature is revealed to the philosopher gradually, according to the order of reasons. Pascal, on the other hand, tried to concentrate all of man's knowledge of himself into a unique experience which would reveal to him simultaneously every facet of his nature. "When we seek effectively to reprove someone and show him that he is wrong, we must take note of the standpoint from which he is observing a thing, for from that angle it is generally true, and we must admit that truth to him" (9). This is the principle on which Pascal based his criticism of those who tried before him to determine the nature of man. He maintained, with Epictetus, that man's greatness is in his "thought"—that is, his faculty to judge all things, even including his own weakness; but the Stoics were ignorant of man's wretchedness and, consequently, their doctrine is ineffective and their advice sterile; their words were directed to a fictitious man capable of absolute self-control. Montaigne was right, therefore, when he showed the weakness and frailty of man, duped constantly by his imagination, accepting as natural justice something that is merely a custom of his country, endowed with a mental volubility that makes him incapable of choosing an exact point from which he could see himself and nature in the right perspective, so enslaved to opinion that he attaches more importance to the judgments that others pass on him than to what he himself is, subject to afflictions and to death, the "last act . . . always tragic, no matter how beautiful the rest of the comedy may be. Finally some dirt is thrown over his head, and that is the end of it all." Pascal put all the substance of Montaigne into his own work. Yet Montaigne's vision was defective, for he was ignorant of man's grandeur. That is why, through self-complacency and all the "foolish things" he said as a result of it, he finally reached a state worse than despair, an "indifference toward salvation, without fear and without remorse; . . . he thinks only of dying in a cowardly and indolent manner" (63). The tranquillity of soul that the Stoics and Montaigne tried to attain through opposing paths is illusory because, by eliminating certain traits from the picture, they made it more coherent than it actually is.

Here, too, there must be a total, unified experience. No matter what is stated as true concerning man, the opposite can always be asserted with equal veracity. Man is the epitome of incoherence and contradiction: a tragic incoherence inasmuch as it is not revealed to us as in a painting which we could ignore or which at most would entail an intellectual dissatisfaction; it touches our innermost being; it eliminates the very basis of our moral life, every vestige of our assurance—the confidence of the Stoic as well as the nonchalance of the Skeptic—leaving us bewildered and disoriented. "What kind of myth is man? How new, how chaotic, how contradictory, how prodigious! Judge of all things, a senseless earthworm; a storehouse of truth, a cesspool of uncertainty and error; the crowning glory and the riff-raff of the universe."

Many philosophers (after the Orphics) had, of course, looked upon man as an intermediate being composed of a celestial part and a titanic part engaged in a struggle; but they had intended (especially the Neo-Platonists) merely to make the situation comprehensible in itself by attributing it to the order of nature and assigning man to his logical place in the descending hierarchy of living beings. The new vision of the universe that the Renaissance had engendered made this relation to the totality of nature impossible. In the terrifying silence of infinite space, lost in the realm of nature, man is nothing. He knows neither his origin nor his destiny. He can no longer find support in the chimerical image of a finite, ordered universe in which his place is clearly indicated. He has to fall back upon himself.

What does he find in himself? His own self, which Montaigne had the "foolish plan" of depicting—a self which seeks to become the center of everything and which is at the same time unjust and irritating so far as others are concerned. Reciprocal politeness may indeed remove irritation, but not injustice (455). But even this is false, for man seeks through "diversion" to escape as much as possible from the self to which he sacrifices everything (139). Whenever he is alone with himself, he lives in an intolerable state of boredom. Conversations, games, reading, and thousands of other diversions prevent us from thinking about the weakness of the self that we love so much. But these external supports are also fragile and deceptive. The truth is that the diversions that seem to us to be remedies actually are much worse than boredom, for they "take us farther than anything else from the search for the cure to our ills." The result is that man, constantly tossed from self to things and from things to self, searches in vain for happiness "without ever finding contentment because it is neither in us nor in creatures but only in God."

This portrait of human suffering owes nothing to Pascal's Christianity. It must be clearly separated from the interpretation he offers. His interpretation of the portrait is as follows: every aspect of human nature can be explained in terms of the supernatural destiny of man revealed through Christianity. The philosopher was deluded by the notion that there is a nature to which everything can be related. We must change our perspective and see man in the supernatural drama in which he is an actor: his grandeur which derives from his divine origin, his wretchedness which originated with the fall of Adam whose children can no longer resist concupiscence, and his hope of salvation through the redemption of Jesus Christ in whose absence knowledge of God would be of no use to man. In keeping with the spirit of his age and milieu, Pascal ascribed a purely internal and religious significance to the three-act drama of creation, fall, and redemption which we have so often seen and which we shall again see as the frame (we recall the monotonous rhythm of station–procession–conversion) for the comprehensive representation of the universe.

The close correlation between Christianity and human nature is the thing that Pascal sought to emphasize, the thing that could attract the freethinker to religion. This explains his celebrated wager (333). Man has a penchant for gambling, and the gambler naturally places his bet on the table where, if the odds are all equal in other respects, he has a chance to win the most. Suppose the odds are equal with respect to the truth or falsity of the Christian religion. Suppose I place my wager first on its falsity and then on its truth: I give myself over to all the pleasures of concupiscence and pay no heed to the demands of the Christian life, or I perform the duties that can procure for me eternal salvation. Now we compute my gain or my loss in each instance: my net gain, if I free myself from all the painful duties of the Christian and find that the religion is false, is nothing when compared with the eternal salvation that I can obtain by leading a Christian life and finding that it is true. Since the odds favoring its truth and the odds favoring its falsity are presumed to be equal, it is obviously to my advantage to place my wager on its truth. Man is a creature of custom and imagination. True religion must also become a custom. "Take holy water; it will make you believe and will stupefy you." Pascal was not concerned with transforming human nature, for this is the work of God alone and of his grace. He sought simply to bring to light the points through which Christian truth could gain access to this corrupt and decayed nature. For this purpose he used not the art of demonstration (as we noted earlier, the proofs of religion are for believers), but the art of persuasion, adjusted to the hearer's disposition and "based as much on acquiescence as on conviction, since men are governed more by caprice than by reason."

BIBLIOGRAPHY

Texts

Pascal, Blaise. *Œuvres complètes.* Edited by L. Brunschvicg, P. Boutroux, and F. Gazier. 14 vols. Paris, 1904–14.
————. *Œuvres complètes.* Edited by J. Chevalier. Paris, 1960.
————. *Œuvres complètes.* Edited by L. Lafuma. Paris, 1963.
————. *Thoughts, Letters, and Opuscules.* Translated by O. W. Wright. Boston, 1888.
————. *The Great Shorter Works of Pascal.* Translated by E. Cailliet and J. C. Blankenagel. Philadelphia, 1948.
————. *Pensées* and *The Provincial Letters.* Translated by W. F. Trotter and T. McCrie. New York, 1941.
————. *Pensées.* Translated by H. F. Stewart. 2d ed. New York, 1965.

Studies

Bishop, M. *Pascal: The Life of Genius.* New York, 1936.
Blanchet, L. "L'attitude religieuse des Jésuites et les sources du pari de Pascal," *Revue de métaphysique et de morale,* 1919.
Boutroux, E. *Pascal.* Translated by E. M. Clark. Manchester, 1902.
Brunschvicg, L. *Le génie de Pascal.* Paris, 1924.
————. *Pascal.* Rieder, 1932.
————. *Blaise Pascal.* Edited by G. Lewis. Paris, 1953.
Cailliet, E. *Pascal: The Emergence of Genius.* 2d ed. Gloucester, Mass., 1961.
Chevalier, J. *Pascal.* Paris, 1922.
————. "La méthode de connaître d'après Pascal," *Revue de métaphysique,* 1923.
Fletcher, F. T. H. *Pascal and the Mystical Tradition.* Oxford, 1954.
Giraud, V. *Pascal, l'homme, l'œuvre, l'influence.* Fribourg, 1898.
————. "La modernité des Pensées de Pascal," *Annales de philosophie chrétienne,* 1906.
————. *Blaise Pascal, études d'histoire morale.* Paris, 1910.
Goldmann, L. *Correspondance de Martin de Barcos, abbé de Saint-Cyran.* Paris, 1956.
————. *The Hidden God.* London, 1963.
Hatzfeld, A. *Pascal.* Paris, 1901.

139

Jolivet, A., B. Romeyer, and J. Souilhé. Studies on Pascal. *Archives de philosophie,* 1923.

Jovy, E. *Études pascaliennes.* 5 vols. Paris, 1927–28.

Lacombe, R. E. *L'apologétique de Pascal, étude critique.* Paris, 1958.

Lahorgue, P. M. *Le réalisme de Pascal.* Paris, 1924.

Laporte, J. "Pascal et la doctrine de Port-Royal," *Revue de métaphysique,* 1923.

———. *Le cœur et la raison selon Pascal.* Paris, 1950.

Lhermet, J. *Pascal et la Bible.* Paris (no date).

Maire, A. *Bibliographie générale des œuvres de Pascal.* 5 vols. Paris, 1928.

———. *L'œuvre scientifique de Blaise Pascal.* Paris, 1912.

Malvy, A. *Pascal et le problème de la croyance.* Paris, 1923.

Mesnard, J. *Pascal: His Life and Works.* New York, 1952.

Mortimer, Ernest. *Blaise Pascal: The Life and Work of a Realist.* New York 1959.

Rauh, F. "La philosophie de Pascal," *Revue de métaphysique,* 1923.

Ravaisson, F. "La philosophie de Pascal," *Revue des deux-mondes,* 1887.

Russier, J. *La foi selon Pascal.* 2 vols. Paris, 1949.

Souriau, P. *L'ombre de Dieu.* Paris, 1955.

Stewart, H. F. *The Secret of Pascal.* Cambridge, 1941.

Strowski, F. *Pascal et son temps.* 3 vols. Paris, 1907–9.

Vinet, A. *Études sur Pascal.* 2d ed. Paris, 1856.

Webb, C. *Pascal's Philosophy of Religion.* Oxford, 1929.

Blaise Pascal, l'homme et l'œuvre. (Cahiers de Royaumont, Philosophie, I.) Paris, 1956.

THOMAS HOBBES

BORN IN 1588 at Westport, Thomas Hobbes was the son of a clergyman. He left the University of Oxford in 1608 to become private tutor to the son of William Cavendish (Lord Devonshire). He accompanied his pupil to France and Italy in 1610 and remained near him until 1628, the year of his death. The only fruit of this period was his translation of Thucydides, of which he was to say later in his versified autobiography: "Is democratia ostendit mihi quam sit inepta."

A second visit to France lasted from 1629 until 1631. Not until then did he become acquainted with Euclid's *Elements*, which was to serve thereafter as his model. A third visit to the continent, from 1634 to 1637, brought him into contact with Mersenne and all his learned associates in Paris, and with Galileo near Florence. In 1640 he wrote *The Elements of Law, Natural and Politic,* the first formulation of his philosophical and political system. In 1650 the manuscript was published, without his approval, as two separate works (*Human Nature* and *De corpore politico*). The work as a whole was not published until 1889.

In 1640, believing that he was in danger because of his royalist convictions, he fled to France, where he resided until Charles II was crowned kind of the Scots in 1651. He published *De cive* in Paris in 1642 and *Leviathan* in 1651. During the remaining twenty-eight years of his life in England he spent his energies in polemics with theologians, scholars, and politicians: with John Bramhall, the Arminian bishop of Londonderry, against whom he upheld the doctrine of determinism; with the mathematician John Wallis, who in his *Elenchus geometriae hobbianae* (1655) ruthlessly examined the mathematical errors in *De corpore,* published the same year; with the physicist Robert Boyle, who was a member of the Royal Society, closed to Hobbes because of his aversion to experience; with Chancellor Edward Hyde and several bishops who accused him of atheism and heresy "for making the Church dependent on the Crown," as he said by way of justification. He died in 1679.

Hobbes gave the following account of the state of his philosophical investigations at the time he published *De cive* (1642): "I had already advanced far enough to divide my work into three sections. In the first of these I dealt with bodies and their general properties; in the second I studied man from a particular point of view, his faculties, and his affections; and in the last part, I used as a basis for meditation the social polity and the duties of those who compose it. The result was that the first part included what is called first philosophy and some elements of physics; here I tried to discover the reasons for time, place, causes, powers, relation, proportion, quantity, figure, and motion. In the second I considered imagination, memory, intellect, reason, appetite, will, good, evil, honesty, dishonesty, and other things of this sort." *De corpore, De homine,* and *De cive* are the titles of the three sections. But this plan fails to give any indication of the manner in which Hobbes's thought was actually shaped. He had no idea of presenting a systematic outline of his philosophy when he composed *The Elements of Law, Natural and Politic* in 1640. In this political treatise, which covers the same ground as *De cive,* he makes no reference at all to the first two parts of his philosophy. Finally, although he had begun to conceive and execute his general plan after 1640, political circumstances caused him to publish *De cive* in 1644, long before he published the first two parts: *De corpore* in 1655, and *De homine* (still fragmentary) in 1658. And he stated plainly in the preface to *De cive* that "there was no danger in this reversal of the order, for it was clear that this part, grounded on its own principles, which are sufficiently known through experience, had no need of the first two parts."

The common link between his physics and his politics is his constructive and deductive spirit. In each of the two areas Hobbes begins by defining precisely the terms or notions that he will use in order that all consequences subsequently may be explained through simple reasoning. Philosophy is "such knowledge of effects or appearances, as we acquire by true ratiocination (*per rectam ratiocinationem*) from the knowledge we have first of their causes or generation; and again, of such causes or generations as may be from knowing their effects." [1]

Of course, Hobbes was an empiricist: "Sense [is] the principle by which we know those principles [by which we know all other things] and . . . all the knowledge we have is derived from it." [2] Still, against empirical knowledge based on the association of ideas and on the expectation of a future conforming to the past and suggesting prudence, he set purely rational knowledge in the form of wisdom or science. Such rational knowledge begins with the use of signs, which are the words of our language. "A *name* or *appellation* . . . is the voice of a man arbitrarily imposed, for a mark to bring to his mind some conception concerning the thing on which it is imposed." [3] Thanks to speech and to speech alone, the words truth, error, reasoning acquire meaning.

A proposition is said to be true or false, depending upon whether the subject and the predicate designate the same thing. "A triangle has three sides" means "this thing which has three angles is identical to this thing which has three sides." A syllogism enables us finally to link two names by virtue of a third that designates the same thing as the first two. We use names in our reasoning, just as we use numbers in our calculations, without ever considering things themselves. That is why, in spite of the continual flux of

---

[1] *Opera philosophica,* ed. Molesworth, I, 2.
[2] *Ibid.,* p. 317.
[3] *Elements of Law,* chap. v, sec. 2.

experience, we reach definite, certain knowledge that is quite distinct from empirical knowledge.

The philosophy of nature outlined in *De corpore* might be called "motionalism," according to one of Hobbes' recent interpreters: "Hobbes is the philosopher of motion, just as Descartes is the philosopher of extension." [4]

His philosophy (if we disregard logic) includes three parts: first philosophy, which shows the elements that comprise the notion of bodies, the theory of motion (*de rationibus motuum et magnitudinum*), and physics. First we consider physics, which aims to explain mechanically the way in which external bodies affect the human body and produce perceptions and related phenomena. Affected by the motions of external objects, the senses are set in motion, and their motion is transmitted by the brain to the heart; here begins a reactive motion in the opposite direction; the onset (*conatus*) of the reactive motion in the heart is the basis of sensation. Sensible qualities, sounds, odors, tastes, etc. are merely modifications of the affected subject, not properties of things. Memory, association of ideas, pleasure and pain are connected with sensation. We have memory when the motion which produced sensation continues in the absence of an object, association when experience establishes a link between two sensitive motions, pleasure or pain depending upon whether the flow of the blood is facilitated or impaired by sensible impressions.

Hobbes's physics is not, strictly speaking, a study of the external laws of nature, as in Galileo and Descartes, but a mechanical theory of perception and of mind. This was true from the time Hobbes composed his first work, his *Short Tract on First Principles,* which was intended to show how species given off by bodies act locally on animal spirits whose motions in turn constitute sensations, concepts, and judgments.

Thus when we see that in the first two parts of *De corpore* Hobbes, under the influence of Galileo and Descartes, superimposed

[4] Frithiof Brandt, *Thomas Hobbes' Mechanical Conception of Nature* (Copenhagen, 1928), p. 378,

on his physics the study of general notions of bodies and motion, we must bear in mind that his aim was not to achieve a comprehensive view of the universe but rather to lay a foundation for his mechanical theory of mind. The notions of body ("that, which having no dependence on our thought, is coincident or co-extended with some part of space"), space ("the phantasm of a thing existing without the mind simply"), and time ("the phantasm of before and after in motion") are not very original. He stated clearly, after Descartes, the principle of inertia: "Whatsoever is at rest will always be at rest, unless there be some other body besides it, by endeavoring to get into its place by motion, suffers it no longer to remain at rest. . . . In like manner, whatsoever is moved, will always be moved, except there be some other body besides it, which causeth it to rest" (p. 115). But he failed to realize the full significance of the second part of the principle and went so far as to assume (like Galileo) that it applied to circular motion as well as to rectilinear and uniform motion (p. 215). By the same token, his most important concept is that of *conatus* or endeavor, which bears directly on his preoccupations. In *De corpore* he defined endeavor as "motion made through the length of a point, and in an instant or a point of time." (Similarly, *impetus* is speed at a given instant.) Later, of course, mathematicians exploited his infinitesimal of motion, and Leibniz and Spinoza made use of this notion. We can be certain that Hobbes first used the notion of conatus to describe the motions of a living being. "This motion, in which consisteth pleasure or pain," he wrote in *The Elements of Law* (p. 22), is also a solicitation or provocation either to draw near to the thing that pleaseth, or to retire from the thing that displeaseth. And this solicitation is the *endeavor* [conatus] or internal beginning of animal motion." He also applied the notion of conatus to the effort made on the eye by the medium that transmits light. This is one of the main points of his discussion with Descartes on the subject of optics. Descartes spoke of an "action or inclination to motion" which he wished to separate from motion; to this Hobbes replied that "vision occurs through an action derived from an object, for any action is a motion, and a motion is propagated from light to the eye."[5] Generalizing this notion, he concludes that "weight is the aggregate of all the endeavors through which all the points of a body supported by the scale of a balance tend downward" (*De corpore*, p. 351). The notion of conatus then introduces motion everywhere, even where there appears to be absolute rest.

His politics is suffused with the emotions and concerns of his era. *De cive* was published prematurely because of the use to which it might be put in view of the conditions that existed in England at that time (1642). "In England," he explains in his preface, "people were beginning to engage in heated discussions concerning the right of the sovereign and the duty of subjects. These discussions, which began several years before the civil wars broke out, were a presage of the misfortunes that threatened and assailed my country. Thus, since I foresaw the conflagration, I hastened to complete this last part and the two parts that precede it even though I had communicated it a few years ago to only a small number of discreet persons." His fears were fully justified by the revolution that abolished the throne (1648).

The political thesis that Hobbes sought to establish on a rational construction of society was that of the absolute power of the monarch. From this thesis it can be deduced that any revolution is illegitimate. The thesis had gained ascendancy in England under Elizabeth and under James I; during the reign of Elizabeth the jurist Hooker denied that a political body could recapture, in whole or in part, sovereignty that it had once relinquished, and he held that the principle extended even to spiritual power. James I took the same stand when he made this statement concerning the divine source of his authority: "Whatever relates to the mystery of regal power ought not to be the subject of a debate; this would divest princes of the mystical veneration that pertains to those who are seated at the throne of God." The divine-right theory of sovereignty obviously clashes at all points with the theory of the social contract, which was prevalent during the Middle Ages and which placed

[5] "Tractatus Opticus," in *The Elements of Law*, ed. Tönnies, p. 171.

everyone on an equal footing by attributing the birth of society to an agreement between the people and the monarch. In 1606 the assembly of the Anglican clergy condemned those who held that "men roamed through woods and fields until experience taught them the necessity of government; that they then chose some from among them to govern the others, and that all power therefore is derived from the people."

The novelty and originality of Hobbes's system derives from the fact that he supported absolutism and at the same time subscribed to the theory of the social contract. For he did not believe he could construct society without the notion of a social contract, any more than he could explain the nature of intelligence without speech. Nor did he think that the social contract impaired absolutism in any way. On the contrary, he believed that the social contract, when rightly interpreted, of necessity led to absolutism. He was an absolutist without being a theologian, and this sets his doctrine apart from that of the other absolutists of the century, from James I to Bossuet.[6]

First we must examine the necessity of the social contract. Most political writers believe that we are born with a certain natural disposition to form human societies. This is false, according to Hobbes. The truth is that each man seeks in a civil society only that which seems good to him, and people are by nature as savage as the most ferocious animals: "Man is a wolf to man." The only instinct that Hobbes recognized in man was the simplest and most elementary, the instinct of self-preservation. If we call *right* the freedom each of us has to use his natural faculties in conformity to right reason, it follows that man has by nature the right to do whatever he deems good for his own preservation, that is, to do or possess whatever he likes. But at the same time reason shows man that the right to all things is of no use to him since it also belongs to all other men, who are his equals; if each man wishes to exercise his right, the result will be a war between all men, which is contrary to the preservation of all as well as of each. The experience of

---

[6] Fifth warning to Protestants, ed. Lachat, XV, 436–41.

civil wars shows that this *bellum omnium contra omnes* is not something imaginary but an ever present danger. Nature—that is, the instinct of self-preservation—guided by reason, therefore teaches us that for our own preservation we must seek peace if it is attainable; in our search for peace we must cease trying to exercise our own right in all things. Thus men are constrained by the law of nature and of reason to draw up contracts in which each of the parties divests himself of some of his rights and grants the other full freedom to exercise the natural right that both formerly held in common. Their pact or promise to observe the terms of the contract is motivated solely by the instinct of self-preservation. It follows that in the state of nature the pact is in no way binding if one party has reason to believe that the other is not observing it —that is, if he has reason to fear for his own preservation. Still, since compliance with the terms of such contracts is the guarantee of peace, natural law obliges us to observe them and to repay kindness with kindness rather than ingratitude; it commands us to show clemency; it prohibits vengeance, cruelty, insult, pride; it commands moderation and equity; it counsels us to submit our differences to impartial judges. All these laws are deduced not from some moral instinct or universal consent but from right reason which searches for means of self-preservation. They are immutable because they are conclusions drawn from a process of reasoning.

Reason shows that the state of nature and the accomplishment of natural laws are incompatible. In the state of nature men have no motive for respecting contracts, which are nevertheless the guarantee of peace. The only motive for respecting contracts is the fear of the consequences that might result from their violation. Fear must therefore be instilled in men—fear keen enough to offset the presumed advantage of exercising their natural right over all things. That is precisely the problem which the social state must resolve, and the conditions of the problem will determine the character of this state. Here reason alone speaks, for no instinct draws men together in a civil society. Men are not like bees or ants, and that is why animal societies are in no way comparable, according to

Hobbes, to civil societies made up of rational beings. Mutual agreement and the voluntary consent of all are too artificial and precarious in nature to insure peace. For "there will always be some persons who believe they know more than others, whose knowledge is superfluous, and who, through their innovations, stir up civil wars." It follows that there must be a single will to control all things necessary for peace: "This can be done only if each individual submits his will to that of another individual or an assembly whose counsel in matters concerning the general peace is followed absolutely and adopted as that of all those who compose the body of the republic." Natural law, as we have seen, dictated that we should relinquish a part of our natural right to all things; the social state generalizes and pushes to the limit this *dictamen* of natural law, for all men convey to the sovereign the right to exercise his authority; and the sovereign acquires such strength that he can cause all those to tremble who would break the bonds of concord.

The sovereign, whether it be a single man, a king, or a council in which the majority decides, is confronted by no multitude in possession of rights. The multitude is not a single subject capable of unified will or action: if people do not join together to form a social body, everything belongs to everyone; if they form a social body, they transfer their natural rights to the sovereign. Consequently the sovereign has the power to coerce, to punish, to wage war, to make laws. He outlaws doctrines such as popery or even Presbyterianism because of "the authority which many give to the pope in kingdoms that do not belong to him and which some bishops seek to usurp in their diocese," with the result that many wars break out. He is not himself subject to laws (and we recall that Chancellor Bacon had no scruples about setting the right of the state above all law). Putting it another way, his supreme law is the welfare of the people—protecting them against external enemies, promoting internal peace, and facilitating commerce.

But the objection might be raised that if the sovereign power issues from a contract, it can be dissolved by those who are parties to it. This objection seems natural to those who seek to ground regal authority on nothing less than divine right, but in practice it has no merit. Unanimous consent would be required for its dissolution. This can never be obtained, of course, and all revolutions that are accomplished through the deliberation of a small number of men are illegitimate. Even an assembly that deliberated publicly and in conformity to the laws was always suspect in the eyes of Hobbes. He feared the ignorance of the members of the assembly with respect to internal affairs and still more their ignorance of external affairs, which ought to remain secret. He also feared eloquence, which can give good the appearance of evil, and factionalism, which can give rise to sedition. That is why he preferred a king and a privy council selected by the king, even though a democracy with its public assemblies can be a legitimate government if individuals surrender their natural rights to the body politic. "The folly of the people and eloquence contribute to the subversion of States" (*De cive,* ii, 12, 13).

One serious difficulty inherent in his doctrine still remains: the relation between the sovereign and religion. Does not religion designate a power distinct from civil sovereignty—a power that exercises complete control over everything relating to eternal salvation? In Hobbes's time such a distinction was not only a subject for discussion but also the cause of serious conflicts all over Europe. "There is almost no dogma relating to the worship of God or to human sciences that does not give rise to dissensions, then to quarrels, to insults, and finally to wars. This happens, not because dogmas are false but because man by nature prides himself on possessing a certain wisdom and wants all others to hold him in equally high esteem." Clearly, then, religion is the concern of the sovereign inasmuch as it threatens civil peace. But even Hobbes, bold and indefatigable arguer that he was, was reluctant to advocate one radical solution—to permit the sovereign to impose his own beliefs and his own form of worship on everyone. "I do not see why he would allow anyone to teach and do things which in his judgment would entail eternal damnation," says Hobbes; "but I do not wish to get entangled in resolving this difficulty." The difficulty was indeed great in a country like England, where Catholic kings governed Protestant subjects. Though he disregarded the individual opinion of the sovereign, he nevertheless asserted that the state must institute a unique, obligatory form of worship, "for otherwise all the most absurd opinions relating to the Divinity and all the most impertinent and ridiculous ceremonies that have ever been seen would be found in a single city." The only restriction he imposed was that a subject must not obey a sovereign who commands him to revile God and to worship instead a man on whom he has conferred divine attributes.

But (since his only concern was the Christian religion) do we not have, either in the Decalogue or in the evangelical precepts, obligatory laws which have a different source from that of civil laws? Here a distinction must be made: the commandments of the Decalogue are civil laws, for Moses possessed temporal sovereignty over the Jews. Furthermore, a commandment such as "Thou shall not steal" makes no sense until laws have defined property, and the same condition applies to all the others. Thus it is only through civil laws that sin, justice, and injustice come into existence. As for the precepts of the Gospel, they are not laws at all, but an appeal to faith. We find in the Gospel no rule that allows us to discern what is yours and what is mine, no standard that serves as a basis for regulating exchange. Therefore the sovereign alone must establish what is just and what is unjust.

In short, the basis of religious harmony, which is necessary for social harmony, is not tolerance, as many of Hobbes's contemporaries thought, but conformity. Though the doctrine of *Leviathan* (1651) is the same, the title refers to the gigantic power represented by the state and reveals even more clearly than *De cive* Hobbes's critical attitude toward the Church. He was so critical, in fact, that even though he could pass for the stanchest supporter of the royalist cause, he had to break with the English royalist party, which counted on the Anglican church to insure its success.

Hobbes's "naturalism" in political matters is essentially the same as his "materialism." Both are expressed in his rationalism, which consists in reducing "nature" to elements simple and tractable enough for us to use them in a process of deduction capable of restoring concrete realities: body and motion on the one hand, instinct and self-preservation on the other. Hobbes required nothing else for the construction of his system of physics and of politics. "The seventeenth century," said Nietzsche, "is the century of reason and therefore of will." No one provides better justification for this idea than Hobbes: he was the logician of politics, the man who tried with unequaled determination to untangle incoherencies; but he was also—and this accounts for the severe beauty of *De cive* —a passionate man who could dominate his passions, an opinionated man who could examine even his most cherished opinions in the light of clear reason.

BIBLIOGRAPHY

Texts

Hobbes, Thomas. *Works*. Edited by W. Molesworth. 16 vols. London, 1839–45.
——. *Selections*. Edited by F. J. E. Woodbridge. Reprinted: New York, 1959.
——. *Body, Man, and Citizen*. Edited by R. S. Peters. New York, 1962.
——. *The Elements of Law*, Edited by F. Tönnies. 2d ed. Cambridge, 1928.
——. *The Metaphysical System of Hobbes*. Edited by M. W. Calkins. 2d ed. La Salle, Ill., 1948.
——. *The Citizen*. Edited by S. P. Lamprecht. New ed. New York, 1962.
——. *Leviathan*. Edited by Michael Oakeshott. Oxford, 1946.

Studies

Bowle, J. *Hobbes and His Critics: A Study of Seventeenth-century Constitutionalism*. London, 1951.
Brandt, F. *Thomas Hobbes' Mechanical Conception of Nature*. London, 1928.
Brandt, G. *Grundlinien der Philosophie von Thomas Hobbes*. Kiel, 1895.
Dewey, John. *The Political Philosophy of Hobbes*. (Studies in the History of Ideas, Vol. I.) New York, 1918.
Gough, J. W. *The Social Contract: A Critical Study of Its Development*. Rev. ed. Oxford, 1956.
Hönigswald, R. "Über Thomas Hobbes' systematische Stellung," *Kantstudien*, XIX (1914).
——. *Hobbes und die Staatsphilosophie*. Munich, 1934.
Hood, F. C. *The Divine Politics of Thomas Hobbes*. New York, 1964.
Laird, J. *Hobbes*. London, 1934.
Landry, B. *Hobbes*. Paris, 1930.
Levi, A. *La filosofia di Tommaso Hobbes*. Milan, 1929.
Lyon, G. *La philosophie de Hobbes*. Paris, 1893.
Macdonald, H., and M. Hargreaves. *Thomas Hobbes: A Bibliography*. London, 1952.
Macpherson, C. B. *The Political Theory of Possessive Individualism: Hobbes to Locke*. New York, 1962.
Mintz, S. I. *The Hunting of Leviathan*. London, 1962.

153

Peters, R. S. *Hobbes*. London, 1956.

Polin, R. *Politique et philosophie chez Thomas Hobbes*. Paris, 1952.

Robertson, G. C. *Hobbes*. London, 1886.

Sortais, G. *La philosophie moderne depuis Bacon jusqu'à Leibniz*. 3 vols. Paris, 1920–29. Vol II, *Hobbes*.

Stephen, Leslie. *Hobbes*. London, 1904.

Strauss, Leo. *The Political Philosophy of Hobbes*. Translated by E. Sinclair. New ed. Chicago, 1963.

Taylor, A. E. *Thomas Hobbes*. London, 1908.

Tönnies, F. *Thomas Hobbes: Leben und Lehre*. 3d ed. Stuttgart, 1925.

Warrender, Howard. *The Political Philosophy of Hobbes*. Oxford, 1957.

Watkins, J. W. N. *Hobbes's System of Ideas*. London, 1965.

Zagorin, P. *A History of Political Thought in the English Revolution*. London, 1954.

Hobbes Studies. Edited by K. Brown. Oxford, 1965.

SPINOZA

1 *Life, Background, and Works*

THE CIRCUMSTANCES relating to the life and background of Spinoza are complex. Born into the Jewish community in Amsterdam, he was influenced by his religious heritage, certain details of which are particularly interesting. He descended from Portuguese Jews who, along with their Spanish brothers, settled in Amsterdam toward the end of the sixteenth century. They brought with them a spirit quite different from that of the Jews in the Netherlands. Most of them descended from Marranos—men who were compelled to embrace Catholicism by Ferdinand's edict of 1492 but who remained Jews at heart. Under these circumstances the traditional teaching of their religion was denied them and they knew nothing about Hebrew or the Talmudic commentaries on the Bible. In Amsterdam they found a community in which the mysticism of the Cabala was studied almost exclusively and the profane sciences were neglected. This explains the dissension that existed among the Jews in Amsterdam throughout the first half of the seventeenth century; those who knew logic, metaphysics, and medicine resisted rabbinical instruction. One such man, Uriel da Costa, who was born in Oporto in 1585 and emigrated to Holland around 1615, denied the immortality of the soul and went so far as to write that "the law of Moses is a human invention" because of the contradictions that he found between it and "natural law."

Baruch Spinoza (1632–1677) was the son of a Jewish merchant of Amsterdam; he received the intensive but purely Hebraic training provided for all the children of the community: seven successive classes devoted to the learning of Hebrew, the reading of the Books of Moses, Kings, and the Prophets, and finally the study of the Talmud. He prepared himself for the office of rabbi and continued his studies after leaving school. Thus he learned about the Cabala and certain Jewish philosophers of the Middle Ages. Hasdai Crescas, whom he cited once in his Letters (*Ep.* XII), taught in the fourteenth century that the perfection of God consists not in knowledge but in love and that the perfection of a creature depends on his participation in this love; this doctrine, which corresponds closely to the beliefs of the Franciscans, is the one found at the end of Spinoza's *Ethics*. Spinoza may have been alluding to Maimonides or to a commentator on the Zohar when he spoke of ancient Hebrews who saw that God, his understanding, and the object of this understanding were identical (*Ethics,* ii, 7, scholium). Thus he came into possession of the Plotinian thesis of the identity of thought, the thinking subject, and the object conceived.

The son and grandson of wealthy merchants, he directed the family business from 1654 to 1656. Excluded from the Jewish community by the civil authorities (and not, as it is often alleged, by the Jewish theologians), he left Amsterdam and went to Leiden. A short time later he went to The Hague, where he lived on his earnings as a lens grinder and perhaps on the income from his commercial enterprise if it is true, as is now believed, that he continued after his departure to operate it through an intermediary. Even before his excommunication he had begun to frequent Christian circles where he found teachers who introduced him to the profane sciences, as well as friends and disciples. The physician Van den Enden taught him physics, geometry, and Cartesian philosophy. Van den Enden was an adept in the theosophy prevalent in Italy and Germany during the Renaissance and the seventeenth century which held that nothing existed apart from God. Through him Spinoza became acquainted with Bruno who, a century earlier, had asserted the unity of substance and the identity of God and nature, and who made a statement that would hardly seem out of place in Spinoza's *Ethics*: "The first principle is infinite in all its attributes, and one of these attributes is extension."

The Christians with whom he associated exhibited the two interdependent traits noted earlier: Christianity almost divested of dogma and a spirit of complete tolerance. Briefly, their Christianity was more practical than speculative and put more stress on living according to the precepts of the Gospel than on speculating about the nature of God. The Mennonites, for example, who had already been in existence for a century, abstained from any form of violence and refused to participate in war, to assume a public office, or to take an oath; furthermore, they rejected the priesthood and sacraments—even baptism—and denied all dogmas except the Trinity, the divine sonship of Christ, and salvation through Christ. The sect known as the Collegiants, among whom Spinoza found friends like Simon de Vries and Jan Bredenburg, a weaver of Rotterdam, was founded by Jan, Adrian, and Gilbert van der Kodde, after the Synod of Dort (1618-19), on the belief that the Holy Ghost was revealed to every pious man and that there was no need of theologians to interpret the Bible. They were also tolerant enough to accept into their fellowship members from groups as divergent as the Catholics and the Socinians.

Such a practical form of Christianity left the field open to religious speculations independent of dogmatic theology. In his *De veritate religionis christianae* (1687) Philip van Limborch used eternal salvation as a basis for classifying the diverse opinions of his era and he divided these opinions into three groups: those of the Christians, those of the Jews, and those of people he called *atheists* or *deists*. "I put these two together," he wrote, "not because the words 'atheist' and 'deist' have the same meaning but because most of the time deism hardly differs from atheism, and those who call themselves deists are generally atheists inwardly; both refuse to acknowledge God, or at the very least they change him into a natural, necessary agent and in this way completely subvert religion; furthermore, since they reject any revelation, they have no certain rule of life or, if they have one, it is no more perfect than the rule deduced from the principles of nature." With obvious malice Philip van Limborch included in this naturalism all speculations concerning salvation which were independent of dogmatic theology and which consequently evidenced an affinity with Spinozism. The Collegiants, who met twice a year in Rijnsburg, had no scruples about discussing the supernatural character of the mission of Jesus, the authority of Scripture, or the reality of miracles.

Indeed, it is the possibility of such free speculation, accompanied by the practice of Christian virtues independently of any formal confession of faith, that Spinoza himself, in his *Political Treatise,* asks the public authorities to secure for all men. Whereas Descartes left to the theologians the task of dealing with eternal salvation and to the princes the management of public affairs, allotting to each a distinct sphere, Spinoza follows the practice of all members of his milieu in affirming the radical unity of philosophical, religious, and political problems. His philosophy, as expressed in the *Ethics,* contains a theory of society and concludes with a theory of salvation through philosophical knowledge. His *Theologicopolitical Treatise* indicates the paths of salvation reserved for men who do not go beyond obedience to the prescriptions of positive religions. Finally, his *Political Treatise* describes an organization of the state that leaves freedom of thought to each man; and we know that Spinoza, though he did not participate actively in public affairs, was an ardent supporter of Jan de Witt, whose government guaranteed such tolerance until 1672, the year of the Orangist triumph.

Spinoza carefully avoided everything that might alienate his independence. Admired by the great Condé, who invited him to visit him in Utrecht during the campaign of 1673, he refused the offer of a pension and residence in France. The same year the Palatinate elector, Princess Elizabeth's brother, offered him a chair at Heidelberg University, where he could freely teach his philosophy; again he refused. It should be noted that his delicate health must have placed severe limitations on his activity; tuberculosis, with which he seems to have been afflicted, necessitates much rest and calm. His life, which was so orderly, so moderate, and so simple, was not that of an ascetic; it was that of an invalid for whom health is a priceless possession. In 1677, at the age of forty-four, he died.

Spinoza wrote two general expositions of his philosophy: the *Short Treatise on God, Man, and His Well-Being,* which he wrote in Latin for his friends (1660) and which has survived through two Dutch translations; and his *Ethics Demonstrated according to the Geometrical Order (Ethica ordine geometrico demonstrata),* which he attempted to complete on several occasions. The order suggested in letters written in 1661 to Oldenburg and De Vries differs from the order followed in the first part of the published version, and in 1665 he had almost completed the work, which then contained only three parts. But between 1670 and 1675 he revised the third part and made it the last three parts of the published version—the Passions, Slavery, and Freedom. Besides these two expositions, Spinoza wrote a treatise (unfinished) on method, *De emendatione intellectus,* before 1662. The *Theologicopolitical Treatise* was written between 1665 and 1670, and the *Political Treatise* (unfinished) between 1675 and 1677. Many years earlier, between 1656 and 1663, he had written *Renati Descartes principia philosophiae,* an exposition of Cartesian philosophy for the use of a pupil. *Cogitata metaphysica,* which explains the terms used in philosophy, dates from the same period. During his lifetime Spinoza published only *Principles of Cartesian Philosophy,* with the *Cogita* as an appendix (1663), and the *Theologicopolitical Treatise* (1670). But his *Opera postuma* which appeared as early as 1677, included *Ethics,* the treatise *On the Improvement of the Understanding,* the *Political Treatise,* and an important body of correspondence which unfortunately was revised and softened by his friends.

11 *The Improvement of the Understanding*

No other doctrine has aroused as much enthusiasm and indignation as Spinoza's. Few others have been interpreted in more different ways and judged more diversely. In the eyes of his contemporaries Spinoza was the denier of Providence, of final causes, and of free will, the critic of the authority of the Holy Word, the author of a pantheism in which the individual founders. As is frequently the case, his contemporaries were struck by the negations of his system rather than by its affirmations, which are nevertheless their counterparts.

Taken as a whole, the Spinozist doctrine is a doctrine of salvation through knowledge of God. The end of philosophy is to "search for a good which can be imparted and of which the discovery will insure throughout eternity possession of lasting and supreme joy." Thus it does not at first appear to be in line with the philosophies of Descartes and Bacon, who relegated to the sphere of faith the question of the ultimate end of man. Spinozism bears an external resemblance to the Neo-Platonic theosophies that have flourished throughout history.

Spinoza's first step is the same as that of many who theorized on the love of God during the Middle Ages: "All these passions (sadness, envy, fear, hate) are our lot when we love perishable things. But love that goes out to something eternal and infinite nourishes the soul with pure joy—a joy untainted by sadness." These words are the same as those found in the *Imitation of Christ* (ii, 7.1): "Qui adhaeret creaturae, cadet, cum labili; qui amplectitur Jesum firmabitur in aevum." In the sixteenth century Leone Hebreo used these words to explain the nature of this higher kind of love: "Although love is also found in corporeal and material things, it does not belong to them alone; but just as being, life, understanding, and every other perfection, goodness, or beauty depend upon spiritual beings and descend from immaterial things to material things, so love is found first and essentially in the purely conceptual world and descends from there to the world of bodies." [1] The practical problem posed at the beginning of *On the Improvement of the Understanding* is the same one which is resolved in the last propositions of the *Ethics*. All the rest of Spinoza's philosophy leads to the same propositions.

And yet Spinoza is far removed from the atmosphere of vague experiences, devotion, asceticism, and enthusiasm traditionally associated with divine love. "Love rests on knowledge. Before all else, then, one must think of a way of healing the understanding and of purifying it in such a way that it will know things successfully, without error and as perfectly as possible." Its power must be augmented. Here Spinoza's point of departure is meditation on the Cartesian method: there is a methodical chain of truths that begins with clear and distinct ideas and manifests the unrestricted fecundity of the understanding through the creation of mathematics and physics. Opposing this chain are the disconnected fragments of knowledge that come from the senses and the imagination, without any spiritual initiative. Spinoza is also a Cartesian when he assumes, in direct contrast to the Neo-Platonists, that the human mind cannot ascend by degrees from knowledge of sensible things to intellectual knowledge, as from an image to its model, but must achieve immediate intellectual knowledge. This theme is found in the passage in the *Improvement* in which he divides knowledge into various classes and retains only those that will serve his purpose. At the lowest level is *knowledge by hearsay,* knowledge that I have from the day of my birth and, in a general way, knowledge of everything that comes to me from tradition; next comes *knowledge based upon undisciplined experience,* knowledge coming from accidental comparison of similar occurrences—this is how I know men are mortal for example; then comes *knowledge that I have of cause through effect*—from the fact of sensation, for instance, I deduce the union of soul and body. These three kinds of knowledge— juxtaposed to one another, inert, and an end to themselves—are

---

[1] Quoted by H. Pflaum, *Die Idee der Liebe bei Leone Hebreo* (Tübingen, 1926), p. 105.

rejected because they will not serve to increase the power of the understanding. Quite different is *knowledge through which an effect is deduced from a cause*: from its definition I deduce the properties of a figure, for example. Quite different too is the certain, *intuitive knowledge* that I have of certain propositions. Such knowledge is truly productive. The merchant who applies the rule that he has been taught (hearsay) in order to find the fourth proportional when three terms are given, or who, having successfully carried out the operation in simple cases, applies the process that he has discovered to more complicated cases (undisciplined experience), arrives at the quantity to be discovered or at a result as surely as the mathematician who demonstrates a rule (knowledge of effect through cause) or the man who intuitively apprehends that the number sought is 6 when the terms given are 1, 2, and 3. But the merchant goes no further, whereas a Descartes, by meditating on proportionals, discovers the means of resolving equations of a higher degree.

From Descartes Spinoza also learned that the acquisition of certain knowledge precedes the discovery of a method. Through its natural force—through intuition and deduction "which cannot harm each other," according to Descartes—the understanding spontaneously discovers new knowledge; the basis of the method is reflection on the order that has made possible the attainment of new knowledge. The essentials of these developments are incorporated in the theses advanced in the *Improvement*. Just as the artisan first beats iron with natural instruments before fabricating a hammer with which he can forge it more perfectly, so the understanding expends its native strength in forging instruments with which it can advance its search. Method does not precede investigation and effective intellectual procedures; it follows them. It is knowledge of knowledge, for we know things through ideas before we know that we know them. The idea of the circle is knowledge of a thing that has a center and a periphery, but the idea itself has neither center nor periphery and is something quite distinct from the circle itself; consequently we can know a circle without knowing the idea of a circle. The method, in turn, is but the idea of the idea, that is, reflection on the true idea to the degree that the idea is an instrument or a standard for acquiring further knowledge. Here we have everything that separates the new spirit, which goes directly to things themselves, from ancient philosophy, which rests with analyses of concepts and a perpetual dialectic based on opinions.

The method of the *Rules* is complemented by the doubt of the *Meditations*. The method begins with natural certainties immanent in the mind and shows through the rule of order how these certainties can engender new knowledge. Doubt searches for a sure means of excluding everything uncertain, and it employs, besides the apparatus of methodical doubt, the *Cogito* and the guarantee of certainty through God. The whole of the second part of his work, according to Descartes, is indispensable in preparing the will to assent to that which the understanding perceives clearly and distinctly. Spinoza abandons Descartes at this point: true ideas, according to him, contain their own certainty; certainty is only "the objective essence of a thing," that is, the thing as it is represented in the understanding; it follows that the mind in possession of true ideas cannot fail to know that they are true; no truly sincere doubt can reach them, and they require no guarantee. We need only identify fictitious ideas (*idea ficta*), false ideas, or doubtful ideas in order to avoid confusing them with true ideas.

The distinction between true ideas and other ideas is the foundation of Spinozism, just as the doctrine of true and immutable natures is the foundation of Cartesianism. If there were the slightest suspicion that the mind can forge ideas such as those of God, substance, or extension, the whole structure of *Ethics* would collapse. Spinoza foresaw the difficulty when he wrote these lines: "It may be assumed that after we have forged the idea of a thing and stated freely and voluntarily that it actually exists in nature, then we are unable to conceive of it as existing otherwise." Spinoza was not disconcerted by the "absurdity" of a mind being deluded by itself and "compromising its own freedom." On what was his confidence grounded? A fictitious idea is identified primarily by its indetermination. We can arbitrarily imagine its object as existing or not existing; we can arbitrarily attribute such and such a predicate to a being whose nature is known to us imperfectly—for example, we can imagine that the mind is square; the fictive idea is the idea that permits an alternative. But if we possess the true idea of a being, indetermination disappears. To anyone who knew the entire course of nature the existence of a being would be either a necessity or an impossibility, and anyone who knew the nature of the mind could not suppose it to be square.

A false idea is in the same class. It attributes to a subject a predicate that is not deduced from its nature because the mind conceives its nature only in a confused, indistinct manner. Doubt springs from error. Descartes' celebrated hypothetical doubt, for example, is possible only because of a belief in the possible existence of a deceitful God. A true idea, on the contrary, is a completely determinate idea that contains the cause of everything that can be stated or denied concerning its object. For instance, in the mind of a worker the idea of a well regulated mechanism is a true idea when the relation between its parts is conceived distinctly even though the mechanism may not be realized. What constitutes a true idea is not its correspondence with an external reality but its "intrinsic character."

Here Spinoza is thinking of the power of the understanding to form, of itself, true ideas in mathematics. It begins with simple ideas which could only be true since, being simple, they have to be wholly determinate—extension, quantity, motion, for example. It forms complex ideas by linking simple ideas—the idea of the sphere, for example, which has its origin in the rotation of a semicircle around its diameter. Each such idea is a wholly determinate essence, and the mind never has to pass through universal, abstract axioms.

But is not the power of the understanding limited to the production of mathematics? Is it not here and here alone that the mind is a "spiritual automaton" acting in accordance with the laws of the understanding, whereas in knowledge of nature it "has the condition of a patient" subject to the senses and to "the operations that give rise to images produced in accordance with laws quite different from the laws of the understanding"? In short, is any knowledge of nature reached through the understanding? Methodical analysis of the conditions of the problem is the key to its solution. Knowledge of nature can pertain to the understanding only if it is capable of representing a true essence which is the universal cause of all the effects of nature, just as the essence of a circle is the cause of its properties. From the idea of the true essence the understanding deduces, objectively, the idea of all other things, so that our minds reproduce nature as perfectly as possible. The thesis of the intelligibility of nature through deduction of its principle is not, as we might at first assume, a new incursion of Neo-Platonism into philosophy, for the Neo-Platonic explanation moves through a descending hierarchy from the One or First Cause to the sensible world, to the world of duration, generation, and corruption: a spurious intelligibility, ignorant of the conditions of mathematical intelligibility in which only eternal verities can be deduced from eternal verities. Nature, which the understanding deduces from the objective essence of the principle, cannot be "the succession of singular things subject to change, but only the succession of fixed, eternal things (*seriem rerum fixarum oeternarumque*)." What are these fixed, eternal things? To understand what they are, we need to recall Cartesian physics, which posits in nature fixed essences and eternal verities, such as extension, the conservation of motion, and the laws of impact. Spinoza's "fixed, eternal things" are also the whole set of laws which constitute the permanent structure of nature, laws "according to which all singular things happen and are regulated." These *res fixae* then are also particular essences, well defined and determinate verities (just as the essence of a right angle or a circle is a determinate essence in mathematics), although they are present throughout nature and play the role of universals.

The rule of method prohibits Spinoza from deducing the sensible world as in emanative metaphysics. Moreover, he does not pretend to deduce the whole gamut of *res fixae* (in the manner of Plotinus, who caused an intelligible world to derive from the One), for "to conceive everything at once surpasses by far the powers of the human understanding." Just as we deduce one mathematical truth from another without ever reaching the end of the chain or using it to form a whole, Spinoza sees each of the *res fixae* as nothing more than a link in a chain or a moment in a progression and not as a part of a whole. And just as in mathematics, Spinozist deduction does not proceed haphazardly but is oriented; it is oriented toward the solution of the problem that was its point of departure—that of human nature, its power, and its union with God.

III *God*

Thus the design of the philosophy of *Ethics* owes its origin to the methodical exigencies developed in *De intellectus emendatione:* first, a theory of the first principle, God, on which all else depends; then the determination of the place of human nature and, in particular, the singular essence that is man, in the *res fixae et aeternae* deduced from divine nature. Spinoza indicated precisely the inner plan of *Ethics:* "The first part shows *in a general way* the dependence of all things on God; the fifth part shows *the same thing* but through consideration of the essence of the mind" (v, prop. 35, scholium). As in Descartes, who provided the model in his *Replies to the Objections,* the mathematical frame adopted by Spinoza, or more precisely, the Euclidean frame with its definitions, its axioms, and its propositions, is merely a procedure for explaining a truth once it has been discovered, not a method of invention. We find proof of this when we compare a letter written to Oldenburg in 1661 with the definitive revision of the *Ethics.* An axiom is restated as a proposition, the order of definitions is modified and new definitions are introduced. Such a synthetic exposition may be illusory and may suggest that what he has written is a traditional treatise on metaphysics that follows "the order of matter" and not "the order of reasons." Our illusion is dissipated as soon as we turn to *De emendatione,* for it reveals to us in the discovery of the notion of God the result of an exigency of method, and it should warn us that Spinoza's thought is thoroughly analytical, probing ever more deeply for the conditions under which nature and man can be apprehended through the understanding.

One of the main properties of the understanding is that "it forms positive ideas before negative ones." The idea of the finite is a negative one, for we call "finite in its class anything that can be terminated by something else of the same nature. For example, a body is called finite because we can always conceive a larger one" (*Ethics* i, def. 1), and in general "any determination is a negation." The paradigm of all positive ideas is the idea of God, "the absolutely infinite being, that is, the substance endowed with an infinite number of attributes, each of which expresses an eternal, infinite essence"; positive because it is a substance, that is, "that which is in itself and that which is conceived by itself, the concept of which has no need of the concept of something else from which to be formed." This is no Aristotelian substance, the hidden essence of things beyond the reach of the mind, which is limited to apprehending properties and accidents. Descartes taught that the essence of a substance was known clearly and distinctly through its principal attribute—for example, the essence of a body through extension. Spinoza follows Descartes in defining the attribute as "that which the understanding perceives of the substance as constituting its essence."

On the other hand, Descartes twice denied the positive character of the idea of substance. First, he believed that the real distinction between two attributes, such as extension and thought, each of which is conceived independently, forced us to posit two distinct substances, soul and body: to limit a substance to one attribute is to limit its reality. God, the absolutely infinite being, has an infinite number of attributes, each of which expresses his infinity; extension and thought, both infinite, are two such attributes of God. Descartes also believed that thinking substance and extended substance did not exist independently but had to be produced by the divine substance: "it pertains to the nature of the divine substance to exist," for to be conceived independently is to have need of nothing else in order to exist.

"Extension is an attribute of God." This is one of the theses that seemed most shocking to Spinoza's contemporaries. Did it not make God corporeal and attribute to him divisibility and passivity? Spinoza's assertion is comprehensible only in terms of Cartesian physics and the distinction it makes between extension as an object of the understanding and extension as an object of the imagination. Extension as it is imagined is infinite and indivisible; bodies are not its constituent parts but its limitations; the distinction between bodies is not a real distinction but a modal distinction. Modes are "the affections of substance—that which is in another thing and is conceived by this thing." From the standpoint of the physicist, bodies are modes of extension (they are conceived through extension), not parts of extension as it might be conceived by them. The Spinozist thesis is possible only because extension is the principle of intelligibility.

This clarifies the Spinozist notion that unique substance and universal intelligibility are one, provided that the relation of a substance to its attributes is not a simple relation of subject to predicate; an indivisible substance must be the reason that explains the existence of the modes in each attribute. All attributes, in spite of their essential difference, have one common trait—their capacity to explain the modes that are in them. Intelligibility does not depend on the nature of an attribute, for intelligibility is order, and the order according to which modes derive from each other in each attribute can be identical in spite of the distinction between attributes. Cartesian geometry enables us to understand how an order among ideas can be identical with an order among the affections of extension: the idea of the properties of a curve is linked to the equation of the curve just as its properties actually depend on its nature, with the result that the curve and its equation can be treated as one and the same being since their being is constituted by one and the same order. Unity of substance, therefore, signifies universal intelligibility provided that substance is not a subject but, more than anything else, the root of the unique order displayed in each attribute. "The order and relation of ideas is the same as the order and relation of things" (ii, prop. 7).

Everything in Christian dogmatism relating to a Creator who resolves of his own free will to produce the things conceived through his understanding and who subjects his will to the final cause of good is a fable in which anthropomorphism figures as prominently as it does in the accounts of the pagan gods. It is true that God is a cause, but a cause is a reason (*causa sive ratio*) that makes us understand an effect; in this sense God is an efficient cause, a cause of essences as well as of existences, an independent or absolutely first cause, a cause that acts according to the laws of nature or, putting it another way, a free cause—a cause that is efficacious only independently; he is also an immanent cause—one whose action does not pass to a being outside himself; consequently he is no different from what philosophers call nature (*Deus sive natura*).

IV *Human Nature*

The third exigency of method is to order things in such a way that the mind will not be exhausted by useless efforts; that is, to direct deduction only toward those things that yield knowledge useful to us—knowledge of human nature. Beginning with the second part, Spinoza devotes his *Ethics* entirely to the study of human nature to the extent that it can be deduced from the nature and attributes of God. But he must introduce first the notion of infinite mode, then the notion of finite mode.

Only two of God's infinite attributes—extension and thought—are known; each of them is simple, infinite, eternal. Alternately, the nature of man—body and soul—connotes duration, change, multiplicity, birth, corruption. How was it possible for the changing to spring from the eternal? This problem, which was the cross of every philosophy derived from Platonism, was transformed by Spinoza. Descartes' notion of extension could give birth to a physics only by virtue of motion which alone distinguishes one body from another, inasmuch as bodies are not distinct simply because they are extended; moreover, the quantity of this motion is constant, and the laws of its communication or distribution (which alone accounts for distinctions between bodies) are eternal verities. The constant quantity of motion, according to Spinoza, is a mode or affection of the attribute of extension, but it is an eternal mode like the attribute itself, and an "infinite mode" since it indicates the elements of immutability in "the aspect of the universe taken as a whole" (*facies totius universi*). But there is necessarily in the attribute of thought a mode that contains "objectively" the whole, immutable order of nature constituted by *facies totius universi*. This infinite mode is the "infinite intellect," or intellect of God, that contains "objectively," along with the idea of God, an infinitude of attributes and corresponding modes. Since these "infinite modes" are the expression of one immutable order that assumes a different aspect in each attribute, they have God as their "absolutely proximate cause." They make us pass from "naturing" nature (*natura naturans*) to "natured" nature (*natura naturata*) which consists in modes, but they do not take us away from the eternal and the infinite.

If we now consider a finite mode of extension, a body, which is nothing but an extended mass whose parts are animated by motions which are interrelated and transmitted from one part to another in such a manner that the whole persists for a certain term, we find in it nothing that links it to the eternal essence of the attribute of extension. The existence of the body has its reason in other finite modes, in other bodies that have imparted motion to it and, through their causality, actually make it what it is. The other finite modes, in turn, have their reason in other finite modes, and so on indefinitely. What is true of modes of extension is also true of modes of thought or ideas, for the order of objects in our thought reproduces the order of realities in extension in accordance with the correspondence of attributes. From this it follows that a finite mode has a manner of existing quite different from that of an infinite mode or an attribute. The infinite mode and the attribute possess eternity or infinite usufruct of being (*infinita essendi fruitio*), in which essence is merged with existence; but the finite mode, considered from the standpoint of its essence, is merely possible, since it begins to exist only when another finite mode produces it and ceases to exist as soon as another finite mode excludes it. Existence in duration is existence to the extent that it is distinct from essence, and it belongs solely to the finite being that has the causality of its being outside itself. Thus the finite world, with external causality and duration, is characterized uniquely by a deficiency and, as such, cannot be deduced immediately from the nature of the attribute of God, whose consequences are just as eternal as God himself. God is indeed its cause since the finite mode which is its cause is God himself modified in a certain manner, but he is its remote cause (*causa remota*).

Such was Spinoza's conception of human nature and its properties. Man consists of a body and a mind—that is, of an actual mode of extension and of an actual mode of thought constituted by the idea of this body. Spinoza tried to imagine what the individuality of a body could be within the universal mechanism. He saw it as the individuality of a machine whose different parts are arranged by external causes in such a manner that they impart motion in accordance with a permanent order; an individual being is itself formed of other individual beings, and the human body is therefore a very complex machine composed of other machines. In the attribute of thought is an idea which corresponds to a corporeal individual and which has no object other than the actual individual. It is the soul which begins and ends with the body and which has an external cause in other finite modes of thought corresponding to the modes of extension that are the causes of the body.

All the properties of soul are deduced from this definition: *the soul is the idea of the body*. But Spinoza's *idea* is not something outside the soul—"a mute image painted on a board"—waiting for judgment to give its assent. The idea, mode of a divine attribute, by itself affirms the existence of its object, and its affirmation persists as long as this existence is not excluded by the existence of another idea. What must be explained is not the position but the negation, and it is explained by the positive elements in whatever excludes the thing negated. Thus the idea of a body is not its reflection but rather the position and affirmation of its existence in thought. Besides, the idea is just as composite as the body itself, and the individuality of the mind, with the variety of perceptions that it includes, does not differ in nature from the individuality of the body.

But because the soul is a finite mode, the idea that it has of itself, the idea that it has of its body, and the idea that it has of external bodies are inadequate ideas. An idea is adequate whenever its cause or reason is known at the same time as its object; it is inadequate whenever the opposite is true. Alternately, any idea of a finite mode, limited to this mode, will of necessity be inadequate since the finite mode is essentially the mode that has its cause outside itself; the idea that the mind has of itself is therefore inadequate since, as a finite mode of thought, it has its cause in another finite mode; its knowledge of its body is inadequate since the existence and constitution of this body depend on an elusive influence exerted by external bodies; finally, its knowledge of external bodies depends on the impression they make on its own body. Thus external perception depends on the nature of our bodies more than on the nature of external bodies. Furthermore, if for any reason our bodies, in the absence of an external impression, happen to be disposed again as they were at the time of this impression, we perceive the external body as if it were present: hence memory or imagination. In fact, just like perception, the memory image implies the actual existence of its object; and the latter can be denied only if excluded by other ideas.

Man depends on a course of nature completely unknown to him. He is unintelligible to himself by his very nature. To be finite, according to Spinoza, is simultaneously to exist in time and to be unintelligible. To search for the finite modes that explain our existence would be a futile, impossible undertaking, for they are themselves unintelligible. Such is the first notion that we have of human nature.

Spinoza demonstrates that in the human soul, limited and incomprehensible to itself, in this detached, isolated fragment incapable of reattaching itself to the whole, reason must originate. To understand clearly his demonstration we must bear in mind the two notions of intelligibility which Spinoza categorically excludes: first, the Neo-Platonic notion of an intelligible world—a kind of ideal transposition of the sensible world; second, the notion of universals —blurred images of the intelligible world which the understanding, starting from the sensible world, attains through a complicated process of abstraction. The two types of intelligibility are both conceived, in effect, in terms of their relation to the sensible world, one as its model and the other as its extract. Spinoza thinks he has demonstrated that in the course of nature the mind can possess only mutilated and indistinct ideas. Descartes identified a completely different type of intelligibility in the absolute ideas which are detached from all other ideas and have inherent intelligibility: the idea of extension or of thought, for example. From human nature Spinoza deduces the presence in the mind of these absolute ideas. In Descartes they are characterized by the fact that they can be wholly present in a being no matter how limited it is; according to the *Meditations,* thought, whether considered in passion or suffering or in intellectual conception, is wholly in each of its manifestations, just as the total nature of extension is in each of its parts. Spinoza demonstrates that we necessarily have an adequate idea of that which is found in both the whole and the part; that we must have adequate ideas of the attribute of extension and of the attribute of thought for the very reason that we have an idea, no matter how mutilated and indistinct, of a mode of extension or of a mode of thought; and that we have an adequate idea of God whose nature is wholly present in each of the modes. These adequate ideas are *common notions* since they are equally present in each individual, and collectively they constitute reason. Thus we arrive at the notion of man as a rational being.

Man, then, acquires knowledge in several ways. The first kind of knowledge consists of the inadequate ideas that he has through the ordinary course of nature: sense perception and images linked together by a simple succession. The second kind of knowledge, or reason, consists of common notions and of everything deduced from them: knowledge whose object is abstracted from duration and entails the apprehension of things "under a certain aspect of eternity." Finally, all the rest of the *Ethics* shows how human nature gives rise to a third kind of knowledge in which the mind becomes intelligible to itself.

This conception of human nature is distinct from Descartes'. Spinoza shows how man, by his very nature, sometimes succumbs to error, sometimes attains to truth. Descartes imputed to man a free will capable of avoiding error and of giving its assent only to the clear and distinct ideas of the understanding. The root of Descartes' theory of error is his false notion of ideas: having interpreted ideas as simple pictures or images, he had to posit along with them the empty power to affirm and to deny what he called will. This "will" is but one of the universal terms which Descartes discredited. The power to affirm and to deny, and with it belief and volition, belong to each of our ideas. Error does not consist of assent based on an inadequate idea; it is the inadequate idea itself, at least in a certain sense, in so far as it is not excluded and denied by an adequate idea. For example, it is perception that makes us estimate that the sun is two hundred yards away, until the geometer has demonstrated its true distance. Error, then, is not perception but the absence of true ideas that correct perception, and the absence of doubt that accompanies error is not the same thing as assent to true ideas: the first is the mark of our weakness, the second of our strength.

Thus Spinoza introduces a whole new intellectual equilibrium into the theory of man: the object is no longer to justify but to demonstrate. Everywhere Descartes posited free wills—human or divine—engaged in the pursuit of an end posited as a good. He justified his method by relating it to the good of man, God's immunity from error by ascribing error to the will of man, and the passions by depicting them as something instituted by nature for the benefit of man. Spinoza demonstrates that man, whether succumbing to error or searching for truth, is a *spiritual being,* and he deduces the passions from human nature. The notion of a free will engaged in the pursuit of an end, the notion of good and evil —these are illusory, mutilated, indistinct notions.

v *The Passions: Bondage*

Error is a necessary product of human nature, and passion (contrary to the widely accepted opinion of the Stoics, who held that it contradicted nature and that the will had absolute control over it) is natural and necessary. Passion means that a living being experiences an affection of which the being itself is not the cause or of which it is but the partial cause; action, on the contrary, means that the being is the complete (adequate) cause of the affections which are in it. In the ordinary course of nature, man is of necessity subject to passion, since any affection experienced by his body, which is finite, has its source in a proximate body and so on by degrees throughout the whole order of nature; and the mind in like manner has inadequate ideas of which it is not the integral cause. But man also acts in so far as he has adequate ideas and deduces from them still other ideas of which he then is the total cause. Thus the natural course of the passive affections contrasts with the rational concatenation of ideas in the understanding just as the first kind of knowledge contrasts with the second kind of knowledge.

How, then, do inadequate ideas produce the passive affections that we call joy, sadness, and the like? "Every being tends to persevere in its own being," for every being is an expression, near or remote, of divine power; no being can be destroyed except by another being. The endeavor (*conatus*) to persevere, inherent in every being, is the first of the passive affections. In the body the immediate attachment to self is termed *appetite* (*appetitus*) and is the very essence of man; in the soul it is termed *desire* (*cupiditas*) and is simply the tendency to self-affirmation inherent in any idea. An idea is not only an image but also an affirmation of itself. It is obvious that desire, far from being dependent on any idea of a pursued good, is the principle of all the other affections. For instance, external causes act on our bodies and either promote or impede our endeavor to persevere in our own being, with the result that two affections arise: *joy,* which is the (adequate) idea of an increase in a body's perfection, and *sadness,* which is the idea of a decrease in its perfection. Furthermore, *love* arises when the idea of joy is combined with the (inadequate) idea of the cause believed to have produced it; *hatred* arises under the same conditions, when sadness is combined with the idea of its cause. The diversity of the passions is explained by the endeavor of the soul to imagine things that increase its power to act and to exclude images of things that prevent it from acting. It follows that all passions are modifications of love and hatred. Thus these two passions are spread by virtue of the laws of the imagination, from their primary object to objects which are themselves neutral but which were perceived along with it and bear some resemblance to it. For example, hatred for one individual may be transferred to every individual belonging to the same class or to the same nation. By virtue of associations linking it to objects which produce sadness, an object that arouses love or joy can arouse sadness and hatred at the same time, resulting in a state of *fluctuation,* which makes us love and hate the same thing. By virtue of the same laws, images of things produce the same affections as things themselves: *hope* and *fear* when we represent to ourselves something that will probably produce joy or sadness; hope and fear that become security and despair when we no longer entertain doubt concerning impending joy and sadness. The same laws also explain contentment and regret—images of joy and sadness produced by things we have hoped for or dreaded.

Another effect of the imagination: it is impossible for us to think of a human being similar to us, who is experiencing a certain affection, without experiencing the same affection ourselves. This explains *commiseration,* which is the sadness caused by our awareness of another person's sadness, and *emulation,* which is the desire caused by the image of the same desire in another person. It is for this reason that we try to promote joy in others; we desire to do whatever will please others, and when we imagine that they are acting in the same way toward us, we praise them.

Another consequence, however, is that we try to make others become similar to ourselves—to hate whatever we hate and to love whatever we love. Our ambition, identical in each of us, is thwarted by that of all the others who, in their turn, are trying to transform us according to their wishes, with the result that much hatred is generated. This law of the imagination which makes us love an object loved by another person also produces the modification of hatred called envy if the object in question can be possessed by only one individual, and man is thus torn between pity for the unfortunate individual and envy or jealousy with respect to those who are fortunate.

Now we see how resemblance engenders hatred which, having once sprung up, multiplies more or less independently. It is impossible for us to imagine that another person hates us without hating him in turn, and our hatred is necessarily accompanied by a desire for destruction which is manifested through anger or cruelty. But "hatred can be overcome by love, and hatred that has been overcome by love becomes love, which is greater than if it had not been preceded by hatred." For if I imagine a man whom I hate, feeling love for me, he is a cause of joy for me; I then begin to love him; and the joy I feel through this love promotes the endeavor made by the mind to banish sadness, which was enveloped in hatred.

Still to be explained are certain modifications of love and hatred that originate in the freedom that we imagine present in the object loved or hated. It is clear that love and hatred are stronger toward a being believed to be free than toward one bound by necessity, for I conceive the free being as the sole cause of my joy or sadness, but find it impossible, if I see that the cause of this joy or sadness has itself been produced of necessity by other beings, not to transfer my love or hatred to all these beings. For the same reason, modifications of our affections are different when they relate to a singular object which we imagine to have nothing in common with objects known to us. What is then produced is *admiration,* which becomes *consternation* if we dread the object, *veneration* if the man involved is superior to us, *honor* if he has vices that exceed the norm, *scorn* when we believe that he does not actually possess the qualities that caused us to admire him. Finally, if we ourselves are the cause of our joy or sadness, inasmuch as we imagine our power or lack of power to act, our joy becomes *self-satisfaction* and our sadness *humility.*

We see that all the passive affections relate to the endeavor of the soul to persevere in its own being. But each soul (and each body) has an individuality which distinguishes it and separates it from all others, and which itself changes with time. Consequently, different persons, and even the same person at different times, are not in agreement about the objects to be loved or to be hated. Passive affections express our own nature rather than the nature of external things, and believing that we are apprehending reality itself, we vainly call what we love *good,* what we hate *evil.*

Such is the mechanism of the passive affections that reveal to us man's bondage. The soul is a finite being that shifts its course with every wind, hating what it has loved and loving what it has hated under the influence of external causes. Our passive affections are determined by the whole course of nature, which has complete control over human nature inasmuch as it bears the same relation to human nature as does the infinite to the finite.

VI *Freedom and Eternal Life*

But not everything in man is determined by the course of nature: in proportion to the adequacy of his ideas, he acts. Moreover, not every affection is of necessity passive and linked to an inadequate idea. Joy, for instance, is the idea of that which increases our perfection. It is a passive affection if the cause of the increase is outside us, but it is an affection without being a passion if we ourselves are its adequate cause. In the same way, desire is passive affection only to the extent that we are able to continue in existence only through the concurrence of external causes, for if there is a part of ourselves of which we are the adequate cause, the affection of desire remains, without passion. Sadness alone (together with all the affections that depend on it) can be only passive, since by itself a being cannot seek self-destruction and since it is absolutely necessary for a being to have an external cause.

Given the fundamental tendency of a being to persevere in its own being, man must consider whatever promotes this tendency good and whatever hinders it evil. Good, then, is identical to self-interest, and virtue consists in loving one's self. It is clear that virtuous actions (those which increase our power as much as possible) are those determined by adequate ideas or grounded on reason, for we are their adequate cause, and an action of which we are the cause is the most perfect of all actions. On the other hand, we know that we shall find fewer obstacles to our good among other men in so far as they resemble us. We also know that all men are similar because of reason, which consists of common notions, and dissimilar and in conflict with each other because of their passive affections. To do everything possible in order to prevent such conflict is to act in conformity to reason: this is the purpose of the institution of society. It should be noted that in Spinoza's view the social power is not an educative power but only a coercive power. It is intended to prevent conflicts between us, not by making men rational but, in keeping with the principle that an affection cannot be destroyed except by a stronger affection, by using a stronger affection—fear of punishment—to oppose the passive affections that endanger the mutual security of men: hatred, jealousy, cruelty. In the state of nature each man has the right to decide what is good and what is evil according to his own constitution, which is of necessity determined by universal nature; consequently he has the right to avenge wrongs—something which now belongs to society. Sin and goodness, justice and injustice can now be defined only by society. We are therefore following the rules of reason when we decide that the passive affections declared illegitimate by society are bad and that all the affections which tend to unite men are good.

In a general way, all the affections that are conducive to self-preservation—even passive affections—must be judged good. Joy and gaiety can only be good: "a wise man will restore his body through moderate and agreeable nourishment, delight his senses with the scent and bright colors of plants, enjoy music, games, and spectacles" (iv, 45, scholium). In contrast, the passions that depend on sadness—particularly hatred, but also melancholy, fear, pity, humility, and remorse—are bad, debilitating, and always contrary to reason. But not all of the passions that depend on joy are good; those capable of excess, such as love, and those excessive in themselves, such as pride, are not good. Pride indicates an ignorance of oneself and a weakness matched only by contempt for oneself.

The principle common to all these judgments concerning the passions is obvious: just as truth destroys the error of sensible perception without destroying its positive elements, so reason welcomes the positive elements of the passions. "Appetite that produces the passions is *the same* as appetite derived from reason" (iv, 18, scholium). The endeavor to understand, characteristic of reason, is fundamentally identical to the endeavor to persevere in being, since the being of the mind is an idea; consequently, ideas of the passive affections that increase our being contain only that which is good and rational. Wisdom, which impels us toward whatever can preserve and increase our power, "is meditation, not on death but on life" (iv, 67). The wise man does not despise prudence which obviates perils, and in this way he attains the inner peace, the joy that results from the contemplation of our power to act. His is not the inner peace of a hermit: if the wise man strives to avoid the benefits of the ignorant, he still practices gratitude and good faith; and far from considering the laws of the city as obstacles to his freedom, "he is freer in the city where he lives according to common law than in solitude" (iv, 73).

The freedom of the wise man in no way depends, as Descartes

thought, on a hypothetical free will that would make man an "empire within an empire." According to Descartes there is interaction between body and soul. Whatever is passion in the soul is the result of an action of the body; inversely, however, the soul has the power to modify the pineal gland, with the result that it acts upon the motion of the animal spirits and acquires absolute control over its passions. Such a result is impossible if it is true that a perfect correspondence exists between the body and the soul; whatever is passion in the soul is equally passion in the body, for the word "passion" designates only the elements whose adequate cause is not contained in a being. We must not offer vain precepts for acting directly on the body but must try, always utilizing the same method, to determine whether we can deduce the conditions that will allow man to become the adequate cause of the affections of which he, in passion, is the inadequate cause. Such affections will no longer be passions but will become virtuous acts. For example, we know the passive affection called *ambition*—the desire of each man to make all other men similar to himself—and the serious conflicts that it engenders. But this is true only when the course of nature drives us to this affection. If we wish to make other men similar to ourselves with respect to our rationality, the same affection of which we are the adequate cause then becomes the virtue of *piety,* which promotes peace among men.

It is obvious why such a transformation is necessary. In passion no object is loved or hated for reasons drawn from its nature; consequently no object loved or hated is the true cause of our joy or sadness, but is merely an imagined cause. This joy or sadness not only *can* be separated from its apparent cause; it *must* be. As soon as we learn through reason that joy and sadness result from a universal course of nature, we cease to love or to hate the things that our imagination presented to us as their causes; similarly, sadness brought about by the loss of a good is assuaged in a singular manner as soon as we learn that the loss was inevitable. To overcome a passion is to know the passion, that is, to have an adequate idea of the affection it envelops. Alternatively, affections that originate in adequate ideas have a singular claim to survival and to constancy. If an affection varies in strength according to the number of causes that arouse it, no affection will be stronger than the one linked to adequate ideas; for whereas the objects of inadequate ideas are finite, changeable, and transitory, the objects of adequate ideas are constant and eternal; and whereas the objects of our passions are variable and diverse, when we consider the affections embraced by our passions we always find the eternal laws of nature. Adequate knowledge of our affection, in so far as it is adequate, expresses the perfection and power of our being; consequently it is accompanied by joy, whose true cause is traceable to God, the principle of the eternal laws of nature. This joy, accompanied by the idea of God, is love of God, and man is its adequate cause. Spinoza stressed how this love of God, grounded on adequate ideas, differed from the love of God discussed by theologians: it is constant and cannot change to hatred, as in the myth of the fallen angel; it cannot have as its counterpart any love of God for men, since God is exempt from any affection; finally, far from resembling the mystic's solitary love, it draws men closer to one another because it is grounded on reason.

Thus man achieves a certain degree of mastery over his passions by utilizing common notions of the second kind of knowledge. The idea that we have of our finite individuality as such is an inadequate idea. The idea that we have of God and of the principles of nature is an adequate idea, and we know that it is from this that all things, including ourselves and our passions, are of necessity deduced. This idea transforms the idea that we have of ourselves; we identify ourselves as beings determined by the laws of the universe and thus lose none of the positive elements of our individuality. Instead of eliminating the conatus through which we tend to persevere in our own being, we somehow draw support for it from the conatus of the universe (v, props. 1–20).

But such knowledge is universal. It is not our individual being as such that we relate to the universe but our individual being as a part of the universe, as having something in common with all the other parts. That is why the second kind of knowledge does not exempt us entirely from conflicts engendered by the passive affections or from life under conditions of duration, two things which are necessarily related. Superimposed upon the second kind of knowledge is the third kind, knowledge by which we apprehend intuitively—with the same clarity that characterizes our apprehension of the fact that 6 is the fourth proportional to the three simple numbers 1, 2, and 3—the necessary dependence that relates our individuality as such to the nature of God and his attributes. By the first kind of knowledge we were able to imagine ourselves as finite individuals, inexplicable in our isolation, besieged by insurmountable and unexplained forces; by the second kind of knowledge we know the universal laws of which we are the expression; but by the third kind of knowledge we are able to consider our individual being and to see that its uniqueness derives from the nature of God.

To know oneself in this way is to achieve eternal life, independent of any duration. Eternal life has nothing to do with survival of the soul following destruction of the body, or immortality, for the soul is the idea of the body and therefore can continue to exist only so long as the body itself continues in existence. But just what is eternal life? We must once again imagine the three moments in the idea man fashions of his own nature: at the outset he sees himself as a finite, singular being (first moment); next he imagines his reabsorbtion in universal necessity (second moment); finally he reappears to himself as a singular being, except that now he is eternal (third moment). Thus the *Ethic* reveals a kind of transfiguration of being as it passes from time to eternity, from finitude to infinity. That we are confronted here with something wholly alien to the spirit of Descrates, who relegated such questions to theologians, seems incontestable. All the difficulties that Spinoza found in Descartes' thought sprang from their divergent views on this basic point. The attribute of God which Descartes put in the foreground when he dealt with the relations between God and finite beings is his creative and providential will: God himself is the creator of eternal truths, the guarantee of the criterion of evidence through his veracity; he insures the constancy of motion, creates the world at each instant through a new act, institutes the union of soul and body for the good of man. These were all notions advanced by Descartes to establish the impossibility of deducing the nature of finite, singular beings from God and, consequently, the necessity of relegating to faith supernatural destiny and everything having to do with the union of the soul with God; these were also the notions vehemently criticized by Spinoza. Nevertheless, it would be wrong for us to draw a hasty conclusion, for instead of pondering Descartes' theology and metaphysics, we ought to consider his method and the way he applied his method to geometry and physics. The essence of his method was to leave universals aside and to proceed solely through intuition and deduction from one singular thing to another. In physics, for instance, we should note that (theoretically at any rate) his explanation of the singular bodies of nature, the heavens, or man left no unintelligible residue, and that his corporeal individual—manipulated and dealt with in this way by a physics which did not originate in sensation—was woven in its entirety from intelligible relations.

Such considerations should guide our thinking. How was Spinoza able to pass from time to eternity? it has been asked. But such passage, if passage there is, is an accomplished fact from the moment he begins to use the second kind of knowledge and common notions, for to use reason is to apprehend things under a certain aspect of eternity (*sub quadam aeterni specie*). But there is really no "passage" from time to eternity. Spinoza states this explicitly: "The desire to know things by the third kind of knowledge cannot arise from the first kind of knowledge." The whole treatise *On the Improvement of the Understanding* shows in fact that rational knowledge is a point of departure with which the soul must have direct contact if it is ever to reach its goal, though Spinoza adds that "it can arise from the second type of knowledge" (v, 28). This indicates that he assumes, on the contrary, a perfect continuity between knowledge *sub quadam aeterni specie* derived from common, universal notions and eternal life our knowledge of ourselves *sub specie aeternitatis*. The explanation—this bears repeating—is that the spiritual life was not conceived by Spinoza as a return toward an original state from which man has fallen but as a methodical progression; not one that makes us move from imperfect knowledge to perfect knowledge but one that makes us pass from perfect knowledge to knowledge deduced from it. The common notions of reason are sources of deduction: from the idea of God is deduced an infinitude of infinite attributes; from each attribute are deduced infinite modes, such as the infinite intellect in the attribute of thought and constancy of motion in extension. It is in this progression, which moves step by step toward singular things, and not in inert common notions that reason consists. And it seems at first glance that deduction ends here, for Spinoza does not deduce finite modes existing in time from the absolute nature of attributes even though the singular being that we are, soul and body, resides in these modes. But the fifth part of the *Ethics* shows precisely that such is not the case and that deduction, as it continues, brings us to the same singular beings, endowed now, however, with a different type of existence known not in time but *sub specie aeternitatis.* The individual is not an obscure quiddity; the corporeal individual was defined by a fixed, intelligible relation between motions (*Definition,* following ii, 13); therefore, if we consider the relation itself, without thinking of its existence in time, we apprehend it in its eternal essence as a necessary consequence of the infinite mode of extension represented by the laws of motion. And if the mind is the idea of the body, it follows that even if the actually existing body perishes, "some part of it, something eternal, must remain" (v, 23), namely its essence which proceeds eternally from the infinite or divine intellect, from an infinite mode of thought, just as its body proceeds from the laws of motion in extension. "We feel and know through experience that we are eternal" (v, 23, scholium), but demonstrations involve "the eyes of the soul."

The eternal life of the soul is like the internal development of the essence that proceeds from the divine intellect. By knowing this essence we acquire a better understanding of the principle from which it emanates, just as we know more about a geometric being as we deduce more of the consequences of its definition: "The more we know about particular things, the more we understand about God" (v, 24). Thus the third kind of knowledge is the most perfect knowledge that the mind can attain. It yields the eternal joy that culminates in beatitude, and an intellectual love of God arises in the mind when it identifies God as the source of this joy. The love which the soul feels for God and which is linked to his essence must itself have God as its cause; since God is absolutely infinite, he must love himself with an infinite intellectual love; the soul's love for God does not differ from God's love for himself but is rather a part of it. This joy and this love are affections which no longer include passive elements since by its nature the soul is their adequate cause. Yet, these affections do not differ essentially from the conatus which produced the passive affections, since the conatus, which constituted the essence of beings, is pure affirmation which posits beings without any temporal limits; they have lost only their limitations. *Omnis determinatio negatio* (statement from Part One) contrasts with *essentia particularis affirmativa* (statement from Part Five). A determination which is a negation is the limit of a being that does not contain its own reason; a singular thing which is affirmative comprehends itself because it no longer falls back upon itself egotistically but sees its dependence on the universe in its very singularity.

VII *Positive Religion and Politics*

In his *Theologicopolitical Treatise* Spinoza shows the contrast between an eternal life based on clear, distinct knowledge and the ways of salvation taught by religions. He seems to regard the latter the way revealed to him by philosophy: like the philosopher, the believer will be saved. How, then, are we to explain the outcries occasioned by the appearance of the celebrated *Treatise?* The reason is that Spinoza carefully isolates and separates two things united by religions—the teaching of truth and the rules of conduct to be followed. For religions consider their sacred books not merely as a set of commandments but as a revelation that has its source in God himself. In this way there arises, alongside a religion that prescribes piety and love among men, a theology which is based on the presumed authority of the divine revelation of Scripture and which shows us a God subject to every passion, to repentance, to jealousy, to anger, and to pity. Thanks to the allegorical method for which Philo the Jew had provided the model, the theologians in all probability had long been accustomed not to interpret literally expressions that were too offensive; but such half-measures assumed a passing from image to idea (from the first kind of knowledge to the second) and a similarity between them, in direct contrast to the Cartesian and Spinozist spirit; and in Spinoza's exegesis of Scripture, the powerful images that he throws into relief (the breath of life, the mythology of the angels, divine apparitions) show that in his opinion Moses and the prophets owe their hold on the common people to the strength of their imagination; they do not go beyond the domain of the senses and have no clear and distinct knowledge of things divine. It goes directly against the nature of God to enunciate particular laws which have a beginning in time and which are addressed to only one man or only one nation; only eternal consequences can be deduced from the nature of God. The edict that prohibited Adam from eating of the fruit "was a law only with respect to the one man Adam and necessitated by the defectiveness of his knowledge." That is also why God revealed himself to Moses as a princely legislator. If God had spoken to him immediately, he "would have perceived the Decalogue not as a law but as an eternal truth." Spinoza's was the first attempt, much more radical than Richard Simon's, to perform a purely literal exegesis of the Bible; thus he reached not the content of the precepts themselves but the reasons adduced to support them.[2]

The dissociation between the worth of biblical or evangelical narratives and the worth of the precepts they contained was accepted as a matter of course in the religious circles that attracted Spinoza's

[2] Louis Meyer, a close friend who published Spinoza's posthumous works, had written a *Philosophia scripturae interpres* (1666) in which he surmised that the standard for interpreting Scripture was the agreement between the truths it taught and reason.

sympathy. In short, all of them were animated by the Socinian spirit that consisted in expurgating religion of any theological teaching and in accepting only precepts conforming to the light of nature; moreover, they found in Scripture itself many passages that strengthened their conviction. Here, therefore, Spinoza constructed nothing; he had before him a religion of salvation in which saving faith consists not in the idea of God and the consequences deduced from it, but in the belief that obedience to the orders of God, considered as our king, can save us. He was fully aware of the value of faith. At the end of the *Ethics* he shows that "religion" is not dependent on knowledge of eternal life as outlined in his philosophy: "Even if we did not know that our soul is eternal, we would not cease to give first place among the objects of human existence to piety and religion—in short, to everything that relates to the intrepidity and generosity of the soul" (v, 41). The *Theologicopolitical Treatise* goes much further, for it declares that salvation is possible, even without the second kind of knowledge, through the simple, practical attitude of obedience.

The theory of salvation through faith is consonant with everything Spinoza observed around him. Is it equally consonant with his whole system of philosophy? F. Rauh noted that the human understanding, because of the infinite distance that separates it from the divine understanding, must admit that there are ways of salvation incomprehensible to it; and he noted that salvation, even in the *Ethics,* consists not in knowledge but rather in the affection of joy and blessedness which are associated with it and which can conceivably be associated with other conditions. We should add that Spinoza had direct experience with a religious life independent of philosophy, and that even though he criticized experience as a source of intelligibility, he never denied its worth as a source of certainty. Furthermore, the entire *Treatise* is devoted to separating the positive elements of this experience from the elements added by human error—a separation accomplished by virtue of adequate ideas of God provided by philosophy. Spinozism is perfectly compatible with the value of the religious experience.

Be that as it may, his outlook was linked to the spirit of tolerance that prevailed throughout the United Provinces, for it made religion independent of theoretical beliefs or rites that separated communities. The state itself must not support a particular belief but must stand as the defender of freedom of thought: that was the fundamental tenet of Spinoza's politics. We saw earlier that Spinoza's description of the origin of society was the same as Hobbes'; but whereas Hobbes concluded with the annihilation of the rights of the individual and the sovereignty of the state, Spinoza ended with a liberal state that did not abolish the natural rights of the individual even while it instituted civil rights based on a conventional conception of justice and injustice. This is true because his point of departure, notwithstanding appearances, was not wholly identical to Hobbes's: in Spinoza's view, the endeavor of a being to persevere in its own being when implicated in passion is the same as its endeavor when it has become rational; or, to use the language of Hobbes, agreement among men led by reason is effected through the same forces that unleash universal war. The state, therefore, is not to use violence to suppress these forces; its role is limited to using fear of punishment to prevent conflicting passions from being destructive; but for this very reason, it stimulates the rational affections that unite men, though it is incapable of producing them directly. From this it follows that individuals have the right to judge the state or to rebel if the state uses violence or excites hate among its subjects: a conclusion diametrically opposed to that of Hobbes, who wrote with the intention of preventing revolution in his country, whereas Spinoza continued to support the liberal government of Jan de Witt following the Orangist party's usurpation of authority.

VIII *Spinozists and Anti-Spinozists*

Spinozism remained an essentially religious and sectarian movement in Holland. Van Leenhof (1647–1712) and Van Hattem (1641–1706), both clergymen, popularized Spinoza's ideas on beatitude and eternal life through works written in the vernacular. "When we consider the necessity of hardships in the eternal order of God," says Van Leenhof, "and when we can fashion for ourselves an adequate idea of his sufferings, hardships are no longer hardships but contemplations of the order of nature that always contain elements of satisfaction." [3] The Spinozist sect was severely persecuted by theologians.

The doctrine was not favorably received by other philosophers. The Cartesians were particularly conscientious about replying to accusations such as those of Leibniz, who saw in Descartes "the seeds of Spinozism." The same accusations are found again in a work of Aubert de Versé entitled *The Sincere Unbeliever or Dissertation against Spinoza, in Which Are Refuted the Foundations of His Atheism* (1684). The work contained not only a refutation of Spinoza's impious maxims but also a refutation of the principal hypotheses of Cartesianism which were said to be the origin of Spinozism. These were the hypotheses of extended substance and continuous creation. Thus the refutations of the Cartesians continued without intermission. Among them were Wittich (*Antispinoza*, 1690), Poiret (*Fundamenta atheismi eversa*, in the second edition of *Cogitationes rationales*, 1685), Régis (*Refutation of Spinoza's Opinion of the Existence and Nature of God*, following *The Use of Reason and Faith*), and the Benedictine François Lamy (*New Atheism Destroyed, or Refutation of the System of Spinoza, Drawn for the Most Part from the Knowledge of Truth and of Man*, 1706).

But the anti-Spinozism of Bayle, the exponent of the critical spirit and of tolerance, equaled that of Leibniz, Malebranche, or Fénelon. We need only recall the many notes in his *Dictionary* against "the systematic atheist," "the first to reduce atheism to a system," the man who admitted that God was subject to extension and consequently divisible, who denied the principle of contradiction and

---

[3] *Le ciel sur la terre, ou description brève et claire de la véritable et solide joie, aussi conforme à la raison qu'à la sainte écriture, présentée à toute espèce d'hommes et sous toutes les formes* (1703). Quoted by Bouillier, *Histoire de la philosophie cartésienne*, I, 419.

said that God was subject to contrasting modes, who denied moral responsibility (for one must not say, "The Germans killed ten thousand Turks," but "God in the form of Germans killed God in the form of ten thousand Turks"). Bayle's indignation was passed on to Voltaire and even found its way into the *Encyclopedia*. Not until the German Romantic movement was there a rivival of interest in Spinozism.

It is true that in his *De ficto Baylii adversus Spinozam certamine*, Poiret charged that this indignation was spurious. In his article (Note O) Bayle did in fact attribute the origin of Spinoza's system to the objections of the Manicheans to the unity of the principle, on the grounds of the existence of evil. They note that these objections are invalid if (as in Spinoza) the principle is a necessary cause acting in accordance with the infinitude of its power but that they are all valid if this principle is a providential nature. Thus Spinozism gave Bayle an opportunity to call attention to the persuasiveness of the Manichean objections. Other pretended refutations of Spinoza—those of the Collegiant Jan Bredenburg (*Enervatio tractatus theologicopolitici*, Rotterdam, 1675) and of the Count of Boulainvilliers (*Refutation of the Errors of Benedict Spinoza*) also can be classed as disguised apologies intended to promulgate the doctrine.

Bibliography

I to VIII

Texts

Spinoza, Benedict de. *Opera quotquot reperta sunt*. Edited by J. van Vloten and J. P. N. Land. 3d ed. 4 vols. The Hague, 1914.
———. *Werke*. Edited by C. Gebhardt. 4 vols. Heidelberg, 1925.
———. *The Chief Works*. Translated by R. H. M. Elwes. New ed. 2 vols. New York, 1955.
———. *Earlier Philosophical Writings*. Translated by F. A. Hayes. Indianapolis, Ind., 1963.
———. *Ethics*. Translated by W. H. White. Edited by James Gutmann. New York, 1949.
———. *Short Treatise on God, Man and His Well-Being*. Translated by A. Wolf. Reprinted: New York, 1963.
———. *The Political Works*. Translated by A. G. Wernham. Oxford, 1958.
———. *The Correspondence of Spinoza*. Translated by A. Wolf. London, 1928.

Studies

Appuhn, C. *Spinoza*. Paris, 1927.
Bidney, D. *The Psychology and Ethics of Spinoza*. 2d. ed. New York, 1962.
Brunschvicg, L. *Spinoza et ses contemporains*. 3d ed. Paris, 1923.
———. *Écrits philosophiques*. Paris, 1951. I, 109–78.
———. "Le platonisme de Spinoza," *Chronicon spinozanum*, III (1923).
Carré, J. R. *Spinoza*. Paris, 1936.
Couchoud, P. *B. de Spinoza*. Paris, 1902.
Delbos, V. *Le problème moral dans la philosophie de Spinoza*. Paris, 1893.
———. *Le spinozisme*. Paris, 1916.
Duff, R. *Spinoza's Ethical and Political Philosophy*. Glasgow, 1903.
Feuer, L. S. *Spinoza and the Rise of Liberalism*. Boston, 1958.
Fischer, K. *Spinoza, Leben, Werke, und Lehre*. 5th ed. Heidelberg, 1909.
Frances, M. *Spinoza dans les pays néerlandais de la seconde moitié du XVIIᵉ siècle*. Paris, 1937.
Gebhardt, C. *Spinoza: Vier Reden*. Heidelberg, 1927.

Gilson, E. "Spinoza interprète de Descartes," *Chronicon spinozanum,* III (1923).

Gunn, J. A. *Benedict Spinoza.* Melbourne, 1925.

Hallett, H. F. *Aeternitas.* Oxford, 1930.

——. *Benedict de Spinoza.* Oxford, 1957.

——. *Creation, Emanation and Salvation.* The Hague, 1962.

Hampshire, Stuart. *Spinoza.* New ed. New York, 1961.

Joachim, H. H. *A Study of the Ethics of Spinoza.* New ed. New York, 1964.

——. *Spinoza's Tractatus De Intellectus Emendatione: Commentary.* Oxford, 1940.

Lagneau. "Notes sur Spinozisme," *Revue de métaphysique,* 1893.

McKeon, R. *The Philosophy of Spinoza.* New York, 1928.

Oko, A. S. *The Spinoza Bibliography.* Boston, 1964.

Parkinson, G. H. R. *Spinoza's Theory of Knowledge.* Oxford, 1954.

Pollock, F. *Spinoza: His Life and Philosophy.* 2d ed. London, 1899.

Rivaud, A. "Documents inédits sur la vie de Spinoza," *Revue de métaphysique,* 1934. Pp. 253–62.

Roth, L. *Spinoza.* London, 1929.

——. *Spinoza, Descartes, and Maimonides.* New ed. New York, 1963.

Saw, R. L. *The Vindication of Metaphysics: A Study in the Philosophy of Spinoza.* London, 1951.

Sérouya, H. *Spinoza, sa vie, sa philosophie.* 2d ed. Paris, 1947.

Sullivan, C. J. *Critical and Historical Reflections on Spinoza's "Ethics."* Berkeley, Calif., 1958.

Wolfson, H. A. *The Philosophy of Spinoza.* New ed. New York, 1950.

I

Studies

Colerus. *Korte dog waarachtige Levens-Beschrybing van Benedictus de Spinoza.* Amsterdam, 1705.

Von Dunin-Borkowski, S. *Spinoza.* Band I, *Der junge de Spinoza.* New ed. Munich, 1933. Band II, *Aus den Tagen Spinozas.* 4 vols. Münster, 1933–36.

Freudenthal, J. *Die Lebensgeschichte Spinozas in Quellenschriften Urkunden.* Heidelberg, 1899.

——. *Spinoza, sein Leben und seine Lehre.* 2 vols. Stuttgart, 1904.

Gebhardt, C. *Die Schriften des Uriel da Costa.* (*Bibliotheca spinozana,* Vol. II.) Amsterdam, 1922.

Meijer, W. "Wie sich Spinoza zu den Collegianten verhielt," *Archiv für die Geschichte der Philosophie,* XV (1901–2).

Meinsma, K. O. *Spinoza en zijn Kring.* The Hague, 1896.

Menzel. "Spinoza und die Collegianten," *Archiv für die Geschichte der Philosophie,* XV (1901–2).

Révah, J. S. "Spinoza et les hérétiques de la communauté judéo-portugaise d'Amsterdam," *Revue de l'histoire des religions,* 1958, pp. 173–218.

———. *Spinoza et le Docteur Juan de Prado.* Paris, 1959.

The Oldest Biography of Spinoza. Edited and translated by A. Wolf. London, 1927.

II

Studies

Gebhardt, C. *Spinoza Abhandlung über die Verbesserung des Verstandes. Eine entwicklungsgeschichtliche Untersuchung.* Heidelberg, 1905.

Léon, A. *Les éléments cartésiens de la doctrine spinoziste sur les rapports de la pensée à son objet.* Paris, 1909.

III

Studies

Bréhier, E. "Néoplatonisme et spinozisme," *Études de philosophie antique.* 1955. Pp. 289 ff.

Brochard, V. "Le Dieu de Spinoza," in *Études de philosophie ancienne et de philosophie modern.* Paris, 1912. Pp. 332 ff.

Huan, G. *Le Dieu de Spinoza.* Arras, 1913.

Lachièze-Rey, P. *Les origines cartésiennes du Dieu de Spinoza.* Paris, 1932.

Lasbax, E. *La hiérarchie dans l'univers chez Spinoza.* Paris, 1919.

Rivaud, A. *Les notions d'essence et d'existence dans la philosophie de Spinoza.* Paris, 1906.

IV

Studies

Baensch, O. "Die Entwicklung des Seelensbegriffs bei Spinoza als Grundlage für das Verständnis seiner Lehre vom Parallelismus der Attribute," *Archiv für die gesamte Psychologie,* XX (1918).

Freudenthal, J. "Über die Entwicklung der Lehre von psychophysichen Parallelismus bei Spinoza," *Archiv für die gesamte Psychologie,* IX (1907).

V

Studies

Godfernaux, A. *De Spinoza psychologiae physiologiae antecessore.* Paris, 1894.
Mielisch, G. *Quae de affectuum natura et viribus Spinoza docuit.* (Dissertation) Erlangen, 1900.

VI

Studies

Brochard, V. "L'éternité des âmes dans la philosophie de Spinoza," in *Études de philosophie ancienne et de philosophie moderne.* Paris, 1912. Pp. 271 ff.
Dyroff, A. "Zur Entstehungsgeschichte der Lehre Spinozas vom Amor Dei intellectualis," *Archiv für die Geschichte der Philosophie,* 1917.
Zac, S. *La morale de Spinoza.* Paris, 1959.

VII

Studies

Bonifas. *Les idées bibliques de Spinoza.* (Thesis) Montauban, 1904.
Borrell, P. "Spinoza interprète du judaïsme et du christianisme," *Annales de philosophie chrétienne,* 1912.
Francès, M. "La liberté politique selon Spinoza," *Revue philosophique,* July–September, 1958, pp. 317–37.
Gebhardt, C. *Spinoza als Politiker,* in Proceedings of the Third International Congress of Philosophy.
Karppe, S. "Richard Simon et Spinoza," in *Essais de critique et d'histoire de la philosophie.* Paris, 1902.
Rauh, F. *Quatenus doctrina quam Spinoza de fide exposuit cum tota ejusdem philosophia cohaereat.* Toulouse, 1890.
Zac, S. "Société et communion chez Spinoza," *Revue de métaphysique et de morale,* April–September, 1958.

VIII

Studies

Van der Linden, *Spinoza, seine Lehre und deren erste Nachwirkungen in Holland.* 1862.

Vernière, P. *Spinoza et la pensée française avant la révolution.* Paris, 1954.

MALEBRANCHE

I Life and Works

BORN IN Paris in 1638, Nicolas Malebranche completed—with little enthusiasm—his first courses in philosophy and
theology at the College of La Marche and the Sorbonne (1654–
1659), became a novice in the Oratory (1600), was ordained a priest
(1664), and except for occasional sojourns in the provinces, resided
in the Oratory of the Rue Saint-Honoré until his death. He is said
to have discovered the philosophy and method of Descartes in 1664,
upon reading the treatise *On Man* which La Forge had just published, and to have been so deeply moved by his discovery that he
quivered. Even if this account is not true, we can be sure that
meditation on the works of Descartes awakened in him an avid
interest in philosophy. In 1674 he published the first volume of his
Search for Truth, followed in 1675 by the second volume, then by
a third volume of *Clarifications.* During his lifetime the work went
through several editions. *Christian Conversations* (1676), a summary of the Christian doctrine, was published at the request of the
Duc de Chevreuse. His *Short Meditations on Humility and Pen-
itence* (1677) initiated a polemic with Arnauld on grace. Malebranche developed his theory of grace in his *Treatise on Nature and
Grace* (1680), which was censured by both Bossuet and the Jansenist. *"Pulchra, nova, falsa,"* wrote Bossuet on his copy; and
Fénelon, in agreement with him, published his *Refutation of*

197

Malebranche's System concerning Nature and Grace, while Bossuet reproved him publicly in the funeral oration of Marie Thérèse. Arnauld, in turn, began by attacking Malebranche's philosophical theses in his book *On True and False Ideas,* which was followed by many rejoinders and counter-joinders; furthermore, he brought charges against Malebranche in Rome and succeeded in having his book placed on the Index in 1690. Malebranche nevertheless defended his ideas by publishing the *Treatise on Morals* (1683), *Christian Meditations* (1683), and *Conversations on Metaphysics and Religion* (1688). In 1697 he wrote his short *Treatise on the Love of God,* which allied him with Bossuet in the famous quarrel over quietism. His relations with M. de Lionne, a bishop who served as a missionary in China, prompted the tract *Conversation between a Christian Philosopher and a Chinese Philosopher on the Existence of God* (1707). Finally, in 1714, Boursier's book, *The Action of God on the Creature,* elicited a reply from Malebranche in his last work, *Reflections on Physical Promotion.* He died in October, 1715.

II *Philosophy and Theology*

"He maintained his personal integrity in tumult as well as in tranquillity," wrote Lelong after the death of Malebranche.[1] His style, too, is uniformly pure and lively. Without irony or bitterness, but always with the appropriate tone, he depicted the intellectual inconsistencies of men, especially those of scholars, and also the danger of men with "powerful imaginations" who dominate weak minds solely through the vividness of their images and who are responsible for all kinds of superstitions. Erudition which appealed to authority and imagination which forcibly imposed itself were Malebranche's two great enemies. Inflexible in his beliefs, he yielded neither to Bossuet nor to Arnauld; moreover, each of his works is a new commentary on the same themes.

There is nothing, according to Malebranche, that will not lead

---

[1] Quoted by Blampignon, *Étude sur Malebranche,* p. 40.

us to God when properly used as a basis for meditation. This is the summation of his philosophy, which is essentially religious or rather which assumes that living according to reason is only a part of religious life. To take his most celebrated theses: the theory of occasional causes assumes that only the actions of God are efficacious and that we are duped by our imagination if we attribute efficacy in any form whatsoever to his creatures; the theory of the divine origin of ideas assumes that, because God is our sole light, any knowledge—even knowledge of material bodies—leads us to him; and meditation teaches us that self-love, far from separating man from God, leads him, when he has been enlightened, to the love of God. Malebranche's system is a vast act of conversion in which all things appear clearly to the mind and allow us to see that we depend upon God alone. "God is wholly everywhere," said St. Augustine, "and that is why we are able to remember him. Man remembers enough to turn toward God as toward the light which reaches him in some way even when he departs from it." Such thoughts were the object of constant meditations in the Oratory. Father André Martin (Ambrosius Victor), in his *Sanctus Augustinus: de existentia et veritate Dei* (1653), had brought together all of the saint's texts on this eternal truth, identical with God, uncreated, immense, infinite, superior to any created intelligence, yet accessible to man's understanding through the rules of geometry or moral precepts; and he had contrasted the intellectualist theory with the sensationalist theory which sought truth in sensible images and which denied that man could attain through ethics anything other than unstable precepts, or go beyond knowledge of bodies and whatever resembles bodies.

In minds so disposed, we find no exact line of demarcation between the limit of philosophical thought and the starting point of religious life; this is a resurgence of St. Bonaventure's spirit of Augustinianism. To appreciate thoroughly the integration of religious life and philosophy, we must recall the affinity of Augustinianism and Cartesianism which already existed long before the appearance of *Search for Truth*. Descartes, even more forcefully than St. Augustine, separated the intellect from the senses, saw truth only in the intellect, and grounded his philosophy on ascetic practices designed to isolate the mind from the sensible world and leave it face to face with God and itself. Contrary to what has often been alleged, we can be sure that Malebranche did not find universal sympathy for Descartes in the Oratory. When he entered the Congregation, his superiors took every precaution to make certain that the only doctrine taught was that of Aristotle, "the only one generally accepted and necessary for students." [2] But their precautions prove that there existed a current favorable to the idealistic views of Plato and Descartes. One thing is certain—Malebranche's profound admiration for Descartes. In 1673 he retracted the signature which he, along with all the others in the Oratory, had affixed to an anti-Cartesian statement.

He nevertheless abandoned a certain number of Cartesian doctrines. He denied that God is the creator of eternal truths, that man has an idea of God, that man has a clear and distinct idea of his soul, that soul and body are united through mutual interaction. That his negations and the general spirit of Augustinianism are in accord is easily discernible: truth is uncreated and infinite; the relation between soul and God is immediate; God cannot be represented by an idea; we find only obscurity when we retire within ourselves. His negations are equally consonant, however, with one general trait observable in the evolution of Cartesianism. The only type of clear and distinct idea is the notion of extension, which serves as the basis of mechanics in physics: anything that is not extension or number is not within the province of human understanding. Malebranche expressed his point of view clearly when, toward the end of his career, he commented on the whole of his work and took issue with Spinoza. "To demonstrate," he said, "is to develop a clear idea and to deduce with certainty whatever the idea necessarily includes; *and it seems to me that the only ideas clear enough to be used in accomplishing demonstrations are those of extension and numbers.* Not even the soul has any knowledge of itself;

[2] Quoted by G. Gouhier, *La vocation de Malebranche,* p. 53.

it has only an inward awareness of itself and its modifications. Being finite, it is even less capable of knowing the attributes of infinity. . . . As for me, I build only on the dogmas of faith in things regarding faith, because I am certain for a thousand reasons that they are solidly grounded; and if I have discovered a theological verity, I owe it mainly to these dogmas." [3] Here we are duly warned: apart from mathematics and physics, nothing is demonstrable because we have no clear idea of the basis of our demonstrations; this is the antithesis of the view of Leibniz, who was convinced that metaphysical truths are demonstrable.

It would seem to follow that Malebranche's philosophy embraces two points of view: that of the theologian who draws his inspiration from dogmas and tries to understand the divine scheme of nature and grace, and that of the scientist who works with physics and mathematics. But the question is by no means so simple, for contemporary theologians—Arnauld, Bossuet, and Fénelon—censured Malebranche mainly because he placed too much stress on the role of reason. As early as 1671 Rohault advised him not to shock people by appearing to *miscere sacra profanis*. But if we assume Malebranche's own point of view, the warning makes little sense. All of Malebranche's philosophical and religious speculation is governed by the following thesis: reason or the inward word that illuminates the meditations of the mathematician and the physicist is identical with the Word, the Son of God who became flesh in order to save men and who bestows on them divine grace. This identity is translated, despite mysteries incomprehensible to the human mind, through an analogous relationship that somehow exists between religious life and thought and philosophical life and thought. For example, prayers elicit grace, and the attention of the scientist is like a prayer which the Word answers by illuminating his mind with truth. The steps followed by God in creating the world are essentially no different from the methodical process through which man understands nature. "To consider the properties of extension

[3] "Correspondance avec Mairan," in Cousin, *Fragments de philosophie cartésienne,* p. 345.

in order," writes Malebranche, "we must begin, like Descartes, with their simplest relations and pass from the simplest to the most complex, not only because this way of examining our ideas and their relations helps the mind and is simplest, but also because it will give us a better understanding of the works of God, inasmuch as he always chooses the shortest course and acts in an orderly manner." [4] And, in a review of his whole system, he called attention to the identity of the "new philosophy" and religion: "The so-called new philosophy overturns all the reasons of the freethinkers through the establishment of the greatest of its principles, which is in complete harmony with the first principle of the Christian religion. For if religion teaches us that there is but one true religion, the new philosophy shows us that there is but one true cause." [5]

The influence of the new spirit is seen in his theology, which has two principles that are basically identical: God acts only through general manifestations of his will, and he acts through the simplest ways. We are stating the same thing when we say that God is concerned only with himself when he acts, that "his glory" determines all his acts, and that he wishes only to manifest his attributes. The consequences of this principle are obvious: Christian theology seems in effect to posit "particular" manifestations of the divine will in the sense intended by Malebranche. For instance, God willed the Incarnation as a consequence of Adam's sin and for the purpose of ransoming man; miracles, which are contrary to the ordinary course of nature, also seem to be particular manifestations of the divine will; the same thing applies to the election of those saved by grace. Malebranche, on the other hand, in his interpretation of these dogmas, tries to explain them without attributing to God any particular manifestation of his will. Creation, for example, is to God a problem of maximum and minimum: the problem was to obtain the greatest effect by the simplest means, and this excluded any particular end. The incarnation of the Son of God is independent

---

[4] *Recherche de la Vérité,* Book VI, Part Two, chap. iv, ed. Bouillier, II, 72.
[5] *Ibid.,* Book VI, Part Two, chap. iii, 68.

of the redemption of man; the redemption is its result and not its
end; the incarnation would have taken place even if Adam had not
sinned because the world would otherwise have been a production
unworthy of God. Miracles themselves fit into the scheme of things
inasmuch as they are objects of a particular will with respect to the
laws of nature and therefore are included in the more general laws
of the Kingdom of Grace. For Grace too (this is the part that stirred
most deeply the theologians of his time) has its laws. It would be
scandalous to assume that the Kingdom of Grace was subordinate
to Adam's sin and that God had willed a world, one of whose consequences would be sin, in order to establish the Kingdom of Grace.
He willed instead the Kingdom of Grace—the kingship of Christ—
through an absolutely general act of will to which even the act of will
through which he produced nature is subordinate.

Malebranche's aim is obvious: to eliminate from Christianity
everything that makes the vision of the universe a veritable drama
characterized by unforeseeable initiatives, everything that makes it
an actual history characterized by accidents. He is not trying to
submerge Christianity (following a pattern now familiar to us) in
a metaphysics in which the events of the sacred drama become the
necessary moments in the evolution of a divine reality and in which
physics is indistinguishable from theology; but he seeks to infuse it
with the Cartesian spirit which sees at the heart of reality only a
reason acting methodically and by its own initiative, and which can
isolate the clear and distinct ideas that will provide man with a
physics independent of theology.

One difficulty remains: is not original sin, which according to the
Christian faith transformed the conditions of human life, one of the
unforeseeable initiatives that do not fit into the scheme of things?

Malebranche's study of the soul is dominated wholly and from
the outset by the dogma of original sin, and it would be easy for us
to misconstrue his conclusions if we failed to realize that he always
made a distinction between two psychologies: Adam's psychology
before his sin, and Adam's psychology after his sin, which is our
own. Our psychology is characterized by the dependence of the

soul, which has become a plaything of the imagination and of the passions, upon the body. It is this dependence which we experience continuously and which the *Search for Truth* describes in detail. Reason, however, tells us that this dependence contradicts order inasmuch as the soul is superior in perfection to the body: normally the body ought to obey the soul. Thus "experience offers adequate proof that things are not as our reason tells us they ought to be, and it is ridiculous to philosophize against experience." Only Adam's sin and the dogma of its transmission to all men can explain the abnormal, confused psychology that is ours. The predominance of the body is the effect of sin. But sin did not change the scheme of things and Malebranche will show that confusion is the consequence of universal laws themselves, not of a modification in the conduct of God toward man following Adam's sin.

III *Human Nature*

Malebranche attributes to the soul faculties that belong to it independently of any connection with the body: *understanding,* which is the faculty to receive ideas, and *inclination,* which is the natural motion of the soul. Since we have no clear and distinct idea of the soul, the two faculties can be understood only by analogy with the modalities of extension, the only object of which we have a clear and unmistakable idea; understanding is to the soul what shape is to the body, and inclination is to the soul what motion is to the body. Both before and after Adam's sin, these faculties were operative only in connection with certain modifications of the soul caused by its union with the body. Intellection is always accompanied by images that originate in the senses, just as inclinations are always accompanied by passions, which are to inclinations what the senses are to pure understanding. Inclinations are the same in everyone, and so is understanding; by contrast, depending on the individual, there are many varieties of passions and sensations. Prior to sin, imagination was subservient to understanding, just as passions were subservient to right inclinations. We know that the image has a double role in Cartesian psychology: at times it is a cause of error, as when the senses deceive us with respect to the distance of the sun; at times it is an aid to the intellect, as when the intellect uses straight lines to represent abstract quantities. Malebranche referred to a state in which, before the Fall, the image was always an aid, and in which man, capable of directing his attention at will, knew how to eliminate useless or harmful sensations.

The same applies to passions: a passion implies a prior determination of inclination or will toward an object which the will represents as good or toward an object contrary to the one which the will represents as evil, and this determination is accompanied by feelings of love, desire, or aversion. Only then do passions arise; by virtue of the union of soul and body, the animal spirits move about in such a way as to put the body in the proper position to unite with good or to shun evil; and this motion generates in the soul an emotion accompanied by feelings of love or hatred much more intense than those that accompanied simple inclination. Thus passions belong to the order of nature, and before the Fall they had no role other than that of reinforcing right inclinations; but in the same way and in accordance with the same laws, they reinforce inclinations that have become bad and depraved.

It follows that sin did not create the union of soul and body, whose laws remained identical before and after the Fall, but it did change the union into a dependence. It also follows that understanding, even though it did not participate in sin, which was a result of the free initiative of the will, was nevertheless affected by it to the degree that its exercise depended on attention, a faculty of the will; though it lost none of its clear and distinct ideas, it was continuously submerged in the flow of images. This is the state depicted by Malebranche in the *Search for Truth,* in which five of the six books are devoted to an investigation of the causes of errors in the senses, imagination, understanding, inclinations, and passions.

Man subjects his judgments of material things to the senses, wrongly assuming that the senses give him the real qualities of things instead of expressing the relations of things to our own bodies. Imagination depends first on the constitution of the brain; fibers that are too delicate, like those found in women, rule out any mental application, for they cannot resist the invasion of images; fibers that are too hard, like those found in old people, do not allow new images to settle, with the result that an old man is dominated by his past. Imagination also depends on properties acquired by the brain: animal spirits follow most easily routes that they have already traveled. This accounts for the kind of spiritual inertia that gives us the illusion of finding again in new things the things that we already know. It also accounts for our absurd respect for authority, based on our first, irradicable impressions acquired through education. Finally, a man with a weak imagination is dependent on men with powerful imagination; he is seduced by poets, orators, writers, and simple storytellers who impose upon him images and beliefs. The understanding is also susceptible to errors when it fails to dominate images: such errors consist mainly in taking abstractions to be real, in introducing into things all the powers of occult forces which Scholastics accept as explanations.

As for inclination, its depravation through original sin is the basis of all our errors. Inclination, will, love—all are one to Malebranche. The motion of the soul is not apprehended through a clear and distinct idea—no more so than any other mental faculty—but since God has his end in himself, he could not have given to the soul any impulsion other than toward universal order, toward good in general. "The desire for formal beatitude or for pleasure in general is the gist or essence of the will to the degree that it is capable of loving the good." This impulsion includes love of self: "God wills that we should will the perfection of our being through the invincible love that he has for immutable order." In the theological controversies over quietism, Malebranche takes a decisive stand against the advocates of disinterested love who pretended that true love of God excluded love of self. "Through this [natural love for myself that God puts in me], when I put it to good use instead of pleasing myself like the Stoic sage, I seek only him, I tend only toward him." Sin is precisely the misuse of such love. Since God has endowed man with a motion that carries him toward the universal good, he always has enough power to go beyond particular goods presented to him by his understanding. But suppose he arrests his will in the presence of a particular good: then he sins. Thus sin is a kind of failure of the will—a failure of the will to exercise its full power. Then true love of self gives way to vanity and concupiscence; man turns toward a particular good the force that has been given to him for the universal good. Man is free to follow the divine impulsion; he is also free to still it and cause it to deviate. In either case, his freedom is not the creation of a force, for we know that according to Cartesian physics the deviation of a motion requires no supplementary force.

Foremost among these deviate inclinations which give rise to errors are the desire for knowledge, which spurs us on beyond the limits of our minds, the desire to appear wise, which produces the love of paradox, and the individual friendships that cause us to approve the thoughts of others uncritically.

In the absence of a clear and distinct idea of the mind, the dogma of original sin then allowed Malebranche to obtain in psychology a result analogous to the result reached by Descartes in physics: with his clear and distinct idea of extension, Descartes substituted for the confusion of sensible qualities a mechanistic physics in which the mind proceeds in an orderly fashion; with the dogma of original sin, Malebranche, in order to understand the disordered complications of our inner life, made use of a normative psychology which defines the relations of soul, God, and body according to the order of nature; the soul is then in subservience to God and in control of the body. This dogma, like all the others, enabled him to introduce order and reason into his interpretation of the universe.

Malebranche's moral philosophy is wholly dependent upon his conception of human nature. "Ethics demonstrated and explained through principles is to knowledge of man what knowledge of curved lines is to knowledge of straight lines"; it is what Apollonius and Archimedes are to Euclid. Mathematics has its source in the relations of magnitude which the mind contemplates in the divine Word; ethics derives from the contemplation of relations of perfection which are no less immutable and certain than the relations of magnitude. I can see with equal clearness that two and two are four, that mind is superior to matter, and that a beast is more estimable than a stone and less estimable than a man. Moral virtue begins with sustained attentiveness, made difficult by sin and perhaps impossible by the absence of grace, which allows us to see the immutable order of perfection and to cause our conduct, like God's, to conform to it; the difficulty is in "always suspending assent until the light appears." An act will be meritorious and will justify us in the sight of God only when accomplished through love of order based on our vision of relations of perfection. Love of order is common to all men and subsists even in the greatest sinners; thus it is our vision of order that is rendered impossible by the depravity of our inclinations, and only inner meditation, together with the suspension of action associated with it, can combat this depravity.

The cardinal virtues then are mental power and freedom. Power consists in "putting the mind to work in order to gain the life of the mind," that is, in not letting oneself be misled by sentiment but in arriving at clear ideas. Freedom consists in hearing the judgments of the world from all sides and in "retiring within oneself at every moment to listen and determine whether inner truth uses the same language." These virtues are quite different from the false virtues of the pagans: "One who endures the injuries inflicted upon him often is neither moderate nor patient. It is his laziness that makes him immobile and his Stoic pride that consoles him." Malebranche's own belief is that an effort of the will is impossible without meditation upon order, just as, in the sciences, all the work of the understanding is unproductive without method.

IV *Occasional Causes*

Even before Malebranche, of course, many Cartesians arrived at the theory of occasional causes. To consider a physical body as being identical with simple extension was to say that motive force did not belong to the body since it was not contained in the notion of extension. Indeed, Descartes identified the first cause of motion with God and, adopting the thesis of continuous creation, assumed that at each moment in time the divine act must be repeated. On the other hand, modes (idea or feeling in thought, motion in extension) always imply substance in the Cartesian sense, but substance never implies the effective existence of this or of that mode; consequently the existence of a mode is due to an efficient cause alien to substance which (unlike the substance of Aristotle or of Leibniz) receives its modes without producing them. Finally, as it is presented by Descartes, the distinction between soul and body makes any kind of interaction between the two substances unintelligible, and the correspondence that exists between them—in sensations, passions, or voluntary acts—necessitates recourse to a cause superior to both. Furthermore, the paradigm of mathematical intelligibility consists in constant relations which do not contain the idea of any efficient power.

Malebranche uses all of these arguments to refute the common belief that creatures have efficient powers. We can judge a thing only through its idea, and it is obvious that extension does not embrace a motive force or a force capable of producing modifications in the mind. But Malebranche goes further in his analysis. Considering independently the idea of efficient cause or of power to act, he shows that this notion includes something divine, for "a true cause is such that the mind perceives a necessary link between it and its effect." Only the will of an omnipotent being satisfies this condition. Any true causality is essentially creative: to say that the body can be modified through its own power is to say that it is capable of creating itself with modifications different from those willed by God.

Belief in the efficacy of natural causes was at the root of paganism, and Aristotle's doctrine was but one of its forms. We should note that this analysis alone enables Malebranche to deny any efficient causality in the soul even though he has no clear idea of this substance. He goes even further than his predecessors and denies it not only any power over the body but also any power over itself.

(Freedom, as we saw earlier, is not a true power of the soul.) Thus he puts on the same plane the philosophical exigency of intelligibility and the religious notion of the powerlessness of created beings.

The affirmation that God alone is an efficient cause is not the complete theory of occasional causes, but it is a first step toward such a theory. A similar affirmation on the part of the Muslim theologians of the ninth century introduced discontinuity and arbitrariness into the universe. But the God of Malebranche is a God who loves order and proceeds in the simplest ways and who therefore acts through immutable decrees and in accordance with universal laws. Furthermore, these laws produce the most varied results, just as a mathematical function, while yet preserving its identity, assumes different values when different values are assigned to the variable. Here the variable is this or that particular event— for example, the meeting of two bodies that collide under such and such conditions—and the constant is the laws by which motions are imparted, causing the bodies at this moment to assume determinate speeds in a determinate direction. The collision is then said to be the *occasional* or *natural cause* of the motion. A *natural cause* then is not a real, true cause but only an occasional cause, and it makes the author of nature act in this or that manner on this or that occasion; God continuously adjusts the efficacy of his action to the state of his creation. That is enough to satisfy experience, which requires only a constant relation between the modalities of nature and not an inherent power to act.

It is clear that experience is indispensable to the discovery of this constant relation. To state that God has a constant will is not to state the nature of his will in addition. Descartes deduced its laws from the rule of the conservation of motion, a rule which is itself based on the principle "that the action of the creator must bear the stamp of his immutability." "Nevertheless," says Malebranche, "experience has convinced us that Descartes is wrong, not because the metaphysical principle of his opinion is false but because the conclusion that he draws from it is not true, even though at first glance it seems highly probable" (*Search,* II, 397). Thus in 1698, in response to Leibniz' criticism, Malebranche changed the laws of impact which he had based on the principle of the conservation of motion in the first edition of his *Search.*

The notion of occasional cause, therefore, is linked closely to the notion of law. When Malebranche, speaking of the union of soul and body, says that in sensation or passion God has established certain modifications of the body which are the occasional causes of certain modifications of the soul, or that God has established in the will certain thoughts which are the occasional causes of certain motions, by the same token he is teaching the existence of laws governing the union of soul and body, and these are the laws he tries to determine through his psychophysiological investigations which play such an important part in his work. Moreover, a thought is the occasional cause of another thought in the soul; consequently the soul also has constant laws. Malebranche calls attention to one of these laws—the one which holds that attentiveness is accompanied by the perception of clear ideas. Finally, no man achieves justification independently but only through merit conferred on him by grace; yet it is his actions (prayers or good works) that have provided God with the occasions for bestowing grace on him in accordance with certain laws unknown to us.

Occasionalism, far from assuming a "perpetual miracle" (Leibniz' criticism), is therefore inseparable from a deterministic doctrine whose laws rigidly determine the whole series of events.[6]

v *The Nature of Knowledge and Seeing All Things in God*

All the philosophers inspired by Descartes dealt with the different "kinds of knowledge"; like Spinoza, however, they accepted the clear and distinct idea as the paradigm of perfect knowledge and viewed any other knowledge as an obscure and indistinct idea. Here Malebranche was a great innovator. In his work we find neither

---

[6] Principal texts: *Recherche,* Book VI, Part Two, chap. iii; *Méditations chrétiennes,* v and vi; *Entretiens,* vii.

the notion of an obscure and indistinct idea nor the thesis that whatever is not known through a clear and distinct idea is known through an obscure and indistinct idea. Whatever is not known through a clear and distinct idea is not known through any kind of idea. Here we find an implicit criticism of Cartesianism, for Malebranche implied that his concept of ideas was quite different from Descartes'. To Descartes, ideas were "images" of things which contained "objectively" whatever things contained "formally," objective existence being an inferior degree of formal existence. Malebranche rejected such a distinction, which seemed obscure to him, and attributed to the word "idea" only the Platonic sense of archetype or model. It is only in this sense that ideas represent things, with the result that things must be judged according to their ideas. Thus Malebranche had to assume three different ways of acquiring knowledge: from things themselves—for example, our knowledge of God, for it is obvious that he has no archetype and that the Infinite can see itself only in itself; from awareness or inner feeling—the knowledge we have of "all things that are indistinguishable independently" and the only knowledge we have of our souls; and from our ideas of things—knowledge that pertains exclusively to things different from ourselves and unknowable in themselves, such as our knowledge of natural bodies. It is important for us to note that the knowledge of bodies to which Malebranche here refers is not the analytical knowledge of the physicist but ordinary perception of external bodies.

If ideas are the archetypes of things they represent, Malebranche was bound to arrive at the celebrated thesis of *seeing all things in God*. Ideas cannot be the hovering species which Democritus made an intermediary between body and mind. Ideas are not creatures of the mind, for an idea, when one is no longer a prisoner of the senses, appears as a much truer reality than the material thing it represents. It has properties which the mind discovers in it and which somehow resist the mind. The idea of a square and the idea of a cube are two things that exhibit real differences, and to make both realities depend upon one creative act of the mind would be to attribute to it the omnipotence of God. Nor can it be said that these ideas are innate in the soul, for they appear to the soul one after the other in the succession of our perceptions; and if they were all assumed to be present in the soul, they would have to be accorded also the power to choose within this chaotic state. The process of elimination leaves only one possible hypothesis: they are seen directly in God. God must have within himself the ideas of all the beings he has created; in addition, the human soul is united immediately with God and always sees a particular, determinate being only as a limitation in infinite Being. Finally, God acts in the simplest ways by revealing to us in himself the idea of an external body at the moment when this body produces its impression, externally, on our own bodies.

Seeing all things in God was the subject of an ardent polemic with the Cartesians Arnauld and Régis, for criticism of Malebranche on this point was always made in the name of Descartes. Arnauld, though not very receptive to Malebranche's theses on grace, did not reply to his *Treatise on Nature and Grace* (1680), which Malebranche had brought to his attention a year earlier. He initiated his polemic against seeing all things in God with the book *On True and False Ideas* (1683); not until 1685 did he attack the theses on grace. Régis, who had supported Arnauld's opinion in his *System of Philosophy,* engaged in a discussion with Malebranche in 1694. In the long series of rejoinders and counter-rejoinders, the same arguments often reappear. One common postulate attributable to Descartes separates Malebranche from his adversaries. It was stated by Arnauld as follows: "It is quite true that our ideas [and not bodies] are the things which we see immediately and which are the immediate object of our thought." No one thinks of denying that knowledge of bodies is acquired through ideas. The sole aim is to determine the nature and origin of these ideas. According to Arnauld, the idea of an object is no different from the soul's perception of it; the known object is identical with the act by which it is known. This unique thing, this perception-idea, has only two relations: one to the soul that it modifies (perception), the other to the thing perceived in so far as it exists objectively in the understanding (idea). Here objective existence designates the manner in which "objects are wont to exist in the mind," a "much more imperfect manner of being than that through which an object is really an existent." Perception, Malebranche agrees, is a modification of the soul; consequently an idea is also a modification of the soul. It follows that the origin of ideas is adequately explained by the faculty of seeing bodies, with which God has endowed our minds. The thesis that all things are seen in God involves one very great difficulty, since it entails the admission that there are in God as many particular ideas as there are bodies, each with its contingent modalities.

Malebranche answers both questions: the first by making a distinction between perception and idea, the second by advancing the theory of intelligible extension.

The difference between ideas and perception, Malebranche wrote to Régis, seems as clear "as the difference between ourselves as knowing subjects and the knowledge we acquire." The contrast is indeed striking. As knowing subjects, we have no clear and distinct idea of ourselves. Our modalities, such as pleasure and sorrow or even the perception we have of our ideas, are obscure in so far as we ourselves are concerned. Man's substance, far from enlightening him, is unintelligible to him. In contrast, what we know—an idea— is clear and distinct, and I know it as something distinct from my soul. For example, I know the idea of a square together with its properties as something distinct from myself, and this would be impossible if it were a mode of my soul, for a mode cannot be apprehended apart from substance. Arnauld's thesis could be demonstrated only if ideas could be seen in the soul as distinctly as roundness can be seen in extension, and this is not possible.

Furthermore, Malebranche's reply to the first question is closely related to his reply to the second. For if it can be demonstrated that the mind really perceives not finite, limited, and contingent bodies (as Arnauld supposed) but rather an infinite intelligible extension, then it will follow that the idea is to the soul what the infinite is

to the finite; the mind, which is finite, lacks the capacity to produce a mode such as intelligible extension, which is infinite. "The
finite does not have enough reality to imagine the infinite."

His argument is valid only if the true object of the perception of
bodies is constituted not by as many particular ideas as there are
bodies but by a unique idea, the idea of *intelligible extension*. To
understand Malebranche's thinking on this point, it is necessary
for us to recall that extension, according to Descartes, is prior to
singular bodies, which are merely its limitations. In physics as well
as in geometry a body is determined by a limit in a pre-existing
extension. Our knowledge of the physical world, therefore, does not
go from parts to the whole; it does not consist in placing in juxtaposition with one another the finite bodies of which the world is
the sum. It goes from the whole to the parts; it can have its beginning only in infinity. Furthermore, according to Malebranche, this
is a kind of universal law of knowledge: any particular knowledge
is extracted in some way from an infinite source which the particular knowledge determines. Thus a general idea is not the result of
a summation of particular ideas, for it applies to an infinite number
of such ideas; consequently it implies—beyond the particular ideas
which exemplify it—the idea of universal or infinite being diffused
in some way over particular ideas. This generality cannot be drawn
from ourselves, for we are particular beings. The perception of external bodies obeys a general rule, drawing its support from the
apprehension of intelligible extension, which, according to Cartesian physics, constitutes the archetype of the world of bodies—the
unique idea to which we must turn in order to find out what they
are. Here as in any knowledge, the thought of infinity is always
prior to the immediate union of the soul with God and can exist
only by virtue of this union. Not that the soul understands infinity,
of course, for it can be perceived without being understood; that is,
a particular body is limited for us in an extension which we perceive
—an extension without limits but with a positive infinitude that we
can nevertheless apprehend.

The epistemological thesis, however, was matched, perforce, by a theological thesis that gave rise to new attacks. Intelligible extension is not a creature since it is infinite; it is therefore in God. But if everything which is in God forms part of his essence, to see intelligible extension is to see the very essence of God—an unacceptable but necessary consequence which Malebranche's adversaries used against him. He replied by introducing a concept of infinity wholly inspired by mathematics. In the seventeenth century the concept of infinity had become relative; infinities of different orders were assumed to be infinite only in relation to each other. A finite line, for example, can be viewed as an infinite sum of infinitesimal lines; the word "infinity" does not necessarily designate the whole of reality. Only God is not infinite in a relative sense, for he contains all being; when considered independently, he is infinitely infinite. But intelligible extension is simply the archetype of bodies and, consequently, God is not here considered independently but only in his relation to possible material creatures. When we see intelligible extension we do not see the essence of God: "Essence means the absolute being [infinitely infinite] that represents nothing finite"; we only see the substance of God "considered in relation to all creatures or in so far as they participate in it."

In the thesis of the intelligible world seen in God there remains one singularity that attracted the attention of Malebranche's contemporaries. Descartes had managed to posit extension as the principle of his physics only by using methodical doubt to eliminate sensible perceptions; through the concept of extension, then, common perception was excluded from this wholly intellectual knowledge. But common perception is precisely what Malebranche sought to explain. If intelligible extension—which is single and continuous, which lacks any variation or modification, and which is deprived of any sensible properties—is the principle of intellectual knowledge in physics, it is hard for us to see how it could produce the variety of perceptions that reveal to us a multitude of separate bodies endowed with sensible qualities which make them distinct. Malebranche explains common perception by reversing the operation accomplished by Descartes, who through analysis had isolated extension from the rest of sensible perception. Malebranche considers the two things separately: first extension, then sensations—of color, smell, and so forth—which, when considered by themselves, as qualities, are not related to extension. He stresses the contrast between the two: extension is the object of an idea, whereas sensations are purely and simply modalities of the soul, feelings which yield no knowledge. It would be futile, for example, for us to turn to the sensation of sound to find out what sound really is; acoustics rejects any sensation of sound and substitutes instead the study of intelligible mathematical relations. If sensations and feelings fail to give us any knowledge of things, they are connected according to precise laws (laws of the union of soul and body) to states of our bodies and their relations with external bodies, with the result that the external bodies are their (occasional) causes. These laws, established in the interest of the preservation of the body, warn the soul against the dangers it can incur.

Having accomplished a dissociation even more rigid than that of Descartes (inasmuch as sensation is not confused knowledge but no knowledge at all), Malebranche still has to determine how the two elements join together to produce external perception. A body is first perceived as an intelligible figure in unintelligible extension, for God applies intelligible extension to our minds diversely, depending on the diverse relations that exist between our bodies and external bodies. Modalities of the soul or sensations, produced at the same moment, extend through bodies; moreover, each limited extension may contain several sensible qualities which somehow interpenetrate, for the property of being extended belongs essentially to none of them.

"Man is often ignorant of things he thinks he knows, and he knows well certain things about which he thought he had no ideas." The perception of bodies is proof of this: we imagine that it provides us with knowledge of the external world, but it only establishes in us a relationship with the archetype of this world in God, and with the modalities of our soul. It follows that the existence of the external world is in no sense given; nor can it be demonstrated, as can the existence of a cause of our sensations, since we apprehend no efficacy other than that of God; it is established only by the revelation of sacred writings.

This final doubt gave rise to the last polemic of Malebranche in his correspondence (1713–1714) with Mairan, who tried to reduce his thesis to Spinoza's. "It seems to me that the main cause of this writer's errors," wrote Malebranche, "go back to the fact that he mistakes the ideas of creatures for creatures themselves and of bodies for bodies themselves and assumes that they can be seen in themselves." But if anyone is in error it is Malebranche, according to Mairan, because he is incapable of seeing any distinction between intelligible extension which is in God and extended material bodies, other than the distinction made by Spinoza between the attribute of God and modes. "We must not let ourselves be fascinated by the word intelligible," he wrote. "The essences of things are purely intelligible," and there is really no distinction between the extension contained in the concept of body and the extension called intelligible. "Once they are rightly interpreted the terms 'representative essence,' 'participable by bodies,' and 'archetype of bodies,' which seem to save and mitigate the consequence, are reduced to 'substance of bodies.'"

Nothing penetrates more deeply into the system of Malebranche than Mairan's criticism. Arnauld and Régis held that an idea was essentially representative; its being was limited to objective being, to the being of an image of things. Malebranche held that the idea is intelligible in itself since it is a divine archetype but that it is not essentially representative; it becomes representative only if God happens through his will to wish to create beings according to this model; his will can be made known to us, however, only by revelation. The knowledge that we have of bodies—physical knowledge —since it is knowledge of the unique idea of extension, is therefore completely independent of the knowledge of their existence and is complete without this knowledge.

This theory breaks the last link that seemed to bind the mind to something other than God. The mind no longer has to yield to the contingency of an existence independent of it. The resistance it encounters is only in itself. It is in the mind that knowing contrasts with sensing, ideas with feelings, inner truth which is immutable with personal inspiration which is forever changing, the clarity of the natural light with the vivacity of instinct. In each instance the first term designates the mental faculty that leads us to truth, the second the one given to us for the preservation of our bodies. Man errs by confusing them; the philosopher's task is to keep them clearly separated at all times.

VI *The Malebranchists*

In spite of powerful adversaries, the philosophy of Malebranche was widely acclaimed toward the end of the seventeenth century. It was popular among the elite and in the universities as well as in the Congregation of the Oratory and even among the Benedictines and Jesuits. Such eminent ladies as Mme Grignan were assiduous readers of the works of Malebranche, whose niece, Mlle Vailly, assembled the Malebranchists of Paris in her salon each week. He was himself a member of the Academy of Sciences and had among his colleagues dedicated supporters: among them, the Marquis de l'Hôpital, on of the advocates of the infinitesimal calculus; Carré, the mathematician to whom, according to Fontenelle, "the whole of geometry was but one step in the direction of his beloved metaphysics"; the engineer Renaud d'Elissagaray; and several geometricians who continued to favor Cartesian physics.

In the congregations it was difficult to support publicly the ideas of Malebranche, several of whose works were again placed on the Index in 1709 and in 1714. The Oratorian Thomassin (1619–1695) wrote *Dogmata theologica,* of which the second volume is entitled *De Deo Deique proprietatibus.* An avid reader of Plato, Plotinus, Proclus, and Dionysius the Areopagite, he followed the tradition of the Renaissance scholars and attributed to these philosophers "the same eternal wisdom that dictated the evangelical law." Though he never named Malebranche, he was probably influenced by him, especially when he attributed to Plato the doctrine that the first principles subsist eternally in the divine word and are continually present to every intellectual nature that seeks to attain them.

Malebranche's life came to an end at a time when the empiricism of Locke and the physics of Newton were on the verge of triumph. Nonetheless, throughout the eighteenth century there existed in England and France a current of antisensationalist thought. It appears in Montesquieu's *Persian Letters:* "Justice is an expedient relation between two things. The relation is always the same, no matter whether the being who considers it is God, an angel, or a man" (Letter 81). Jean-Jacques Rousseau related that he was introduced to philosophy in 1736 in books "which mixed devotion with the sciences; this is especially true of the ones from the Oratory and from Port Royal." More particularly, he "read and reread a hundred times" *Conversations about the Sciences,* by the Oratorian Bernard Lamy (1640–1715) who, in the third edition of his *Discourse on Philosophy* (1709), exalted the Malebranchist doctrine of external perception. This doctrine shows more clearly than any other man's exclusive dependence upon God.

The literature to which Rousseau alluded was copious and must have been widely read. A good example is Father Roche's *Treatise on the Nature of the Soul and the Origin of Its Knowledge against the System of Locke and his Supporters* (1715). It was also to refute the empirical tendencies of the Cartesian Régis that Lelevel, a resolute supporter of Malebranche, wrote *The True and the False Metaphysics* (1694). Moreover, many polemics involved the thesis of divine efficacy and the action of creatures. A Malebranchist like Fédé (*Metaphysical Meditations on the Origin of the Soul,* 1683) seemed to incline toward Spinozism by attributing to creatures an "infinite duration" by virtue of their connection with divine immensity. There was in any case criticism of Leibniz' pre-established harmony which, according to Lefort de Morinière (*On the Knowledge That Is in God,* 1718) and the Benedictine François Lamy (*On the Knowledge of One's Self,* 1701), attributed too much to human action. All the while Malebranche was being defended—as if against a calumny—against the charge of denying free will. This is one of the principal themes of the *Letters* which the counselor at the Châtelet Miron wrote in *Europe savante* (1718–1719). Father André of the Society of Jesus (1675–1764), in spite of the persecutions that he endured, was a faithful disciple of Malebranche, and wrote his biography. His *Essay on the Beautiful* and his *Discourses* propagated the spirit of the doctrine. He held that the philosophy of Aristotle, which was currently being taught by the Jesuits and "of which the great principle is that there is nothing in the mind that has not passed through the senses, obviously overthrows all the sciences, especially ethics."

The same polemic was also being conducted in England. In 1695 Locke was writing *An Examination of Malebranche's Opinion of Seeing All Things in God.* Two English translations of the *Search for Truth* had appeared in 1694. John Norris (1667–1711), a Malebranchist, criticized Locke's empiricism in the second part of *An Essay towards the Theory of the Ideal or Intelligible World* (1701–1704), censuring Locke mainly for posing the problem of the origin of ideas before determining their nature. His own thinking was suffused with the doctrine of St. Augustine.

During the eighteenth century, antisensationalist and Malebranchist theses were supported in Italy by Mattia Doria (*Difesa della matafisica contro il signor G. Locke*, 1732), by Ange Fardella (*Animae humanae natura ab Augustino detecta*), by Cardinal Gerdil (*Immateriality of the Soul Demonstrated against Locke*, 1747, and subsequently *Defense of P. Malebranche's View of the Origin and Nature of Ideas against Locke's Examination*); in France by Cardinal Melchior de Polignac (*Anti-Lucretius*, 1747); Abbé Terrasson, to whom Bouillier attributed, perhaps wrongly, the *Treatise on Created Infinity,* published under the name of Malebranche in 1769: a treatise which holds that matter is infinite, that mind is infinite, that there is an infinite number of worlds inhabited by beings similar to man, that there are as many incarnations of God as there are worlds, and that the duration of the worlds is infinite); and by Abbé Lignac (*Elements of Metaphysics,* 1753, and *Testimony of the Inner Sense,* 1760), who remained a stanch supporter of occasional causes.

BIBLIOGRAPHY

I to VI

Texts

Malebranche, Nicolas. *Œuvres*. Edited by Jules Simon. 4 vols. Paris, 1871.
———. *Œuvres complètes*. Edited by A. Robinet. 20 vols. Paris, 1959——
———. *Dialogues on Metaphysics and Religion*. Translated by M. Ginsburg. London, 1923.
———. *Correspondance avec J. J. Dortous de Mairan*. Edited by V. Cousin. New ed., edited by J. Moreau. Paris, 1947.
———. *Recueil de toutes les réponses du P. Malebranche à M. Arnauld*. Paris, 1709.

Studies

Church, R. W. *A Study in the Philosophy of Malebranche*. London, 1931.
Cousin, Victor. *Fragments de philosophie cartésienne*. Paris, 1852.
Guéroult, M. *Malebranche*. 3 vols. Paris, 1955–59.
Luce, A. A. *Berkeley and Malebranche*. New York, 1934.
Rodis-Lewis, G. *Nicolas Malebranche*. Paris, 1963.
Rome. B. K. *The Philosophy of Malebranche*. Chicago, 1963.

I

Studies

Père André Martin (Ambrosius Victor). *Philosophia christiana*. 6 vols. Paris, 1671.
———. *De la vie du Rev. Père Malebranche, prêtre de l'Oratoire, avec l'histoire de ses ouvrages*. Edited by Ingold. Paris, 1886.
Gouhier, H. *Malebranche: textes et commentaires*. (*Les Moralistes chrétiens*.) Paris, 1929.
Robinet, A. *Malebranche et Leibniz, relations personnelles*. Paris, 1955.
Roustan, D. "Pour une édition de Malebranche," *Revue de métaphysique*, 1916.

II

Studies

Blampignon, E. A. *Étude sur Malebranche*. Paris, 1862.
Blondel, M. "L'anticartésianisme de Malebranche," *Revue de métaphysique,* 1916.
Bouillier, F. *Histoire de la philosophie cartésienne*. 3d ed. 2 vols. Paris, 1868. II, 15–207.
Boutroux, E. "L'intellectualisme de Malebranche," *Revue de métaphysique,* 1916.
Delbos, V. *Étude sur la philosophie de Malebranche*. Paris, 1924.
———. *La philosophie française*. Paris, 1921. Pp. 91–132.
———. *Figures et doctrines des philosophes*. Paris, 1919.
Gouhier, H. *La philosophie de Malebranche et son expérience religieuse*. Paris, 1926.
———. *La vocation de Malebranche*. Paris, 1926.
Guéroult, M. "Étendue et psychologie chez Malebranche," *Les Belles-Lettres,* 1939.
Hubert, René. "Revue de quelques ouvrages récents sur la philosophie de Malebranche," *Revue d'histoire de la philosophie,* 1927.
Ollé-Laprune, L. *La philosophie de Malebranche*. Paris, 1870–72.
Pillon, F. "L'évolution de l'idéalisme au XVIIIe siècle: Malebranche et ses critiques," *Année philosophique,* 1893, 1894, 1896.
Rolland E., and L. Esquirol. "La philosophie chrétienne de Malebranche," *Archives de philosophie,* XIV (1938).

III

Studies

Van Biéma. "Comment Malebranche conçoit la psychologie," *Revue de métaphysique,* 1916.
Dreyfus, G. *La volonté selon Malebranche*. Paris, 1958.
Thamin, R. "Le traité de morale de Malebranche," *Revue de metaphysique,* 1916.

IV

Studies

Duhem, P. "L'optique de Malebranche," *Revue de métaphysique,* 1916.
Mouy, P. *Les lois du choc des corps d'après Malebranche*. Paris, 1927.

Novaro, M. "La teoria della causalita Malebranche," Reale Academia dei Lincei, 1890.

Prost, J. *Essai sur l'atomisme et l'occasionalisme dans la philosophie de Malebranche.* Rennes, 1909.

V

Studies

Delbos, V. "La controverse d'Arnauld et de Malebranche sur l'origine des idées," *Annales de philosophie chrétienne,* 1913.

Gaonach, J. M. *La théorie des idées dans la philosophie de Malebranche.* Rennes, 1909.

Gouhier, H. "La première polémique de Malebranche [with Foucher]," *Revue d'histoire de la philosophie,* 1927.

Pillon, F. "La correspondance de Mairan et de Malebranche," *Année philosophique,* 1894.

———. "Spinozisme et Malebranchisme," *Ibid.*

———. "L'idéalisme de Lanion et le scepticisme de Bayle," *Ibid.,* 1895.

VI

Studies

Père André Martin. *Œuvres philosophiques de Père André, avec une introduction sur sa vie et ses ouvrages, tirée de sa correspondance inédite.* Edited by Victor Cousin. Paris, 1843.

Bouillier, F. *Histoire de la philosophie cartésienne.* 3d ed. 2 vols. Paris, 1868. II. Ch. 17–19, 27–28, 30–31.

LEIBNIZ

I *German Philosophy before Leibniz*

IN A TRACT entitled *Aurora se initia scientiae generalis, Leibniz* contrasted the primitive, barbaric practice of drawing fire from friction generated by sticks with the scientific practice of borrowing fire from the rays of the sun: "On the one hand, heavy, terrestrial matter at first, then heat, then light; on the other hand, light first, then heat, and finally, through heat, fusion of the hardest substances." The title of the tract, like the symbolism of fire and light, was borrowed from Jakob Böhme. Here we enter a universe of thought quite different from that of Descartes and of Malebranche. We cannot ignore this fact if we are to understand Leibniz.

Germany, which produced Eckhart and Nicholas of Cusa, was the center of speculative mysticism, in contrast to the religious or contemplative mysticism of the Latin countries. Speculative mysticism, expressed in the vernacular, is represented at the end of the sixteenth century by Valentin Weigel (1533–1588), whose works were not published until 1618, and at the begining of the seventeenth century by Jakob Böhme (1575–1624). What Böhme's most recent biographer said of him can probably be said of all the other German mystics: "Böhme sought not gnosis but salvation; knowledge would have been given him only as a bonus and would even have come as a great surprise to him." [1] But if they wished first of

[1] A. Koyré, *La Philosophie de Jacob Boehme* (Paris, 1929), p. 30.

all to save themselves, the conditions under which they posed the problem of salvation led them to the vast metaphysical constructions which later provided the Romanticists with their models. For Weigel and Böhme were both hostile to the Lutheran thesis of salvation through faith, that is, to the belief that salvation is based on the merits of Christ and comes to us from without. They held that man achieves salvation through a positive, intimate transformation, through a veritable rebirth; such a rebirth implies a representation of God and human nature that constitutes a veritable theosophy.

Weigel's theosophy is based on the idea that God is primitively devoid of action, will, or personality, and that as he creates, he somehow reveals himself to himself and makes manifest all of his attributes. His creature contains elements of nothingness and for this very reason has the possibility of straying from him, of exerting its own will, and thus brings about the Fall—the fall of Lucifer and Adam, the true Hell that is within each fallen man. Weigel's originality seems to relate to his description of two modes of knowledge, one corresponding to the state of the fallen creature (natural knowledge) and the other to the state of the creature who has been saved and brought back to his source (supernatural knowledge). In the first state, the object (*Gegenwurf*) is passive from the standpoint of the knowing subject: "Knowledge and judgment are not in the object but in the man who judges what is before him." The external object is merely the occasion of his judgment; but "no object can judge itself," no truth, no wisdom can come from without. The opposite is true of supernatural knowledge. Here the object (God) is wholly active and man has nothing to do except to wait in silence; yet such knowledge is also internal, or is merely knowledge which God, who is in us, acquires of himself by using man as an organ. The salvation of man is therefore the last phase of the act by which God acquires knowledge of himself; supernatural knowledge is a transformation of being.

The famous Jakob Böhme was neither a popular preacher encroaching on the territory of pastors nor a sectarian leader competing for followers. "I do not keep company with the common people," he said. Böhme, who descended from prosperous peasants of Upper Lusatia and became a master shoemaker in Görlitz, did in fact have among his friends doctors who were disciples of Paracelsus and whose knowledge he assimilated, and enlightened members of the nobility. He was impelled to write "in order to give an account of his gift, his knowledge, and his experience," but not in a critical or proselytizing spirit.

Böhme began with the experience of evil, the feeling of melancholy and sadness that engulfed him when he saw that the impious man was as happy as the pious man; and his culmination was the "triumphant joy of the spirit," the veritable rebirth which followed the illumination that allowed him to understand the will of God and thereby to free himself from his sadness.

His liberating illumination suggested rather than formulated a doctrine which he expressed—following his custom—through images rather than ideas. An assiduous reader of the Scriptures, he was impressed by the striking images developed fully in Lutheranism—the wrathful God of the Old Testament with his avenging, destructive fire, and the God of love of the Gospels—but he was also acquainted with the hidden, ineffable God of the mystics. A friend of the alchemists, he saw in the attempt to transmute metals into gold through calcination an image of the purification through which the fallen soul achieves salvation.

His mind impregnated with such images, he finally settled on one theme, after considering many others: What is the relation between the bottomless abyss (*Ungrund*)—the eternal Nothing, the absolute being without essence which is absolute freedom—and the concrete, personal God who knows himself and is the creator of the world? It is necessary for him to posit with the *Ungrund* a will toward self-manifestation or self-revelation. As for the conditions of this manifestation, Böhme finds them through meditation on the identity of the God of wrath and the God of love: unifying love can exist only through victory over hate, light only through the heat that destroys and absorbs matter, pure gold only through the calcination of impure elements. All these images express the same graphic scheme, which may be formulated in the abstract as "*Yes* implies *no*." Böhme never tired of using the same scheme to express the inner life of God as well as his act of creation and the life of his creatures.

This scheme suggests a solution to the problem of evil. Since the created world expresses divine nature, there must be within it an obscure corner, conflicting forces, an egotistical desire; but above it and victorious there must be an ordering, harmonizing will to which it is subjugated. Though evil exists for the purpose of being over-come, it exists of necessity. But this solution runs counter to an-other: a man who has dark desire and disorder deep in his heart possesses complete freedom; he can imitate God and subordinate the fire of desire to the light of the spirit, or he can relinquish the victory to the forces of disorder, and through his fall bring about a new manifestation of God, as Savior. We find here the fundamental ambiguity between evil as a necessary condition of good—an image of the wrath of God in nature—and the introduction of a fugitive, contingent evil by man who, created in the image of God, has freely eradicated from his person the traces of his divine origin. This am-biguity persisted in the thinking of Leibniz and in German meta-physics of the nineteenth century.

II *Life and Works of Leibniz*

Gottfried Wilhelm Leibniz (1646–1716) studied ancient philos-ophy with Thomasius at Leipzig, mathematics with Weigel at Jena, and jurisprudence at Altdorf. At Nuremberg he became af-filiated with the Rosicrucians. In 1670, thanks to Johann Christian von Boyneburg, formerly first minister to the Elector of Mainz, he became councilor at the supreme court of the electorate. In 1672 he was sent on a diplomatic mission to Paris; in the same year he wrote a memorandum urging Louis XIV to put an end to the influence of the Turks by conquering Egypt. In France he associated with Arnauld and studied the mathematical works of Pascal; he resided there until 1676 (except for a trip to England in 1673 when he met Boyle and the mathematician Oldenburg). In 1676 he invented the differential calculus (as early as 1665 Newton had used the method of fluxions). In 1676 he returned to Germany by way of England and Holland (where he met Spinoza) and became librarian and private councilor to John Frederick, Duke of Brunswick-Lüneburg. He devoted part of his time to assembling the sources of the history of the house of Brunswick and, in 1701, began publication of the *Scriptures rerum brunswicensium illustrationi inservientes*. In Leipzig he founded the *Acta Eruditorum* (1682) and became the first president (1700) of the scientific society that Frederick I was to transform into the Berlin Academy. He did not abandon his idea of a union of the Christian nations against the Orient; having failed to persuade Louis XIV, he turned first to Charles XII, then, in 1711, after his defeat at Poltava, to Peter the Great. He next resided in Vienna, where he tried to effect an alliance between the Czar and the Emperor. He died in 1716.

Leibniz formulated the essentials of his philosophy in 1685. Prior to this date, his writings (*De arte combinatoria,* 1666, and *Theoria motus concreti et abstracti,* 1671) bear no trace of his fundamental doctrine of individual substances. A systematic account of the doctrine is given in his *Discourse on Metaphysics* (1686).

His work is a lush tangle, with countless short philosophical treatises in each of which he attempted to give a systematic account of his whole system; with all his plans for a universal science, for an encyclopedia of information; with all his practical projects (set down in the form of memoranda) for promoting the religious and political reconciliation of Christian nations and the religious organization of the earth; finally, with his voluminous correspondence with the scientists, philosophers, theologians, and jurists of his time. Both of his long philosophical works were completed as he was approaching old age: *New Essays concerning Human Understanding* (written between 1701 and 1709 and not published until 1765) in which he examined Locke's *Essay* paragraph by paragraph; and the *Theodicy* (1710), in which he explained his optimism by referring mainly to the objections raised in the article "Rorarius" in Bayle's *Dictionary*.

These works, in which he defended the thesis of innate ideas against Locke's empiricism on the one hand and supported the theologians who defended the thesis of Providence on the other, are not expositions of his system. The latter must be sought in his shorter writings, such as the *Discourse on Metaphysics* (1686), complemented by his correspondence with Arnauld, the *New System of Nature and of the Communication of Substances* (1695), and the *Monadology* (1714), written for Prince Eugene of Savoy (1714).

III *Initial Position of Leibniz: General Science*

If we compare Leibniz with Descartes, Spinoza, and Malebranche, their common traits are quickly noticed; like them, he is a mathematician; like them, he is a mechanist. But we also see contrasts: Leibniz the mathematician finds in Aristotle's logic the principles from which he will evolve his metaphysics; Leibniz the mechanist restores the substantial forms of Scholasticism and the use of final causes in physics. But the main difference lies in the rhythm of their thought. Descartes had reversed the order of philosophy by grounding the certainty of physics on reflective knowledge of God and of oneself; Leibniz goes back beyond Descartes to the traditional order. We will find nothing in his work that corresponds to Cartesian metaphysics, which is in fact a theory of knowledge; rather it is by beginning with matter and mechanics that he is able to rise to metaphysics and to God. Thus questions are reversed: what was preliminary to Descartes becomes final to Leibniz. "The question of the origin of our ideas," he said, "is not preliminary in philosophy, and it can be satisfactorily resolved only after much progress has been made."

Furthermore, and even more important perhaps (for this is his point of departure and his persistent idea), Leibniz views as a whole and as existing simultaneously parts of philosophy which Descartes subordinated to one another: those which, no matter what is being studied, admit of demonstration. Leibniz finds demonstrations to be in order not only in geometry but also in logic, metaphysics (especially in Plato and the theologians), and moral philosophy (particularly jurisprudence). He was attentive to the efforts of Erhard Weigel (1625–1699), who showed that Aristotle used the method of Euclid in his *Analytics,* and who wrote an *Ethica euclidea,* which Leibniz cites in a letter to Thomasius (1663). In one of his first dissertations (*Dissertatio de arte combinatoria,* 1666), he himself tries, after demonstrating different theorems concerning combinations, to show their applicability to the whole universe of the sciences, particularly logic, and also to jurisprudence.

Mathematics then is but one application of the art of demonstration, which can be extended to many other subjects. One of his dreams was to create a *general science* which had at its disposal a system of symbols or a *universal language* (*characteristica universalis*) which would have in all subjects the role that symbolism had in mathematics, and which would allow us to say "Let us calculate" instead of "Let us discuss," no matter what the question. "If we had [a language] such as the one I conceive, we could reason in mathematics and in moral philosophy; for symbols would stabilize our thoughts, too vague and too variable in these subjects in which imagination is of no help to us" (1677). The ideal of his science contrasts with the Cartesian ideal, whether we consider it from its starting point or as it progresses. To demonstrate, in his science, is to reduce given propositions to identical propositions in which the subject is the same as the attribute; but such a reduction is possible only if the notions that enter into the propositions can be analyzed into the simple elements of which they are composed and their identity is revealed, and only if the symbols chosen for the elements are such that the complex notion is of necessity deduced from the notions of the simple elements. "Reasoning in any form is merely the connecting or substituting of characteristic symbols; any substitution arises from a certain equipollence; [reasoning] is therefore a combination of symbols." Thus in a strict sense we can demonstrate that $1 + 2 = 3$ because we are dealing with numerical symbols completely and perfectly defined on the basis of the simple notions of 1 and $+$. Because Descartes prescribed self-evident propositions as the starting point, he failed to attain the goal; evidence is a subjective characteristic which varies according to the individual and which can engender only chimeras. Descartes generally failed to pursue notions that should be subject to further analysis, such as the notion of extension. Leibniz was not rigid enough to adopt the Cartesian method. He doubted that he was adequately acquainted with it, for it had proved sterile even "in its stronghold," the *Geometry* in which Descartes considered as insoluble to the human mind problems that Leibniz easily resolved through his infinitesimal calculus. Leibniz thought that his reductive analysis and his system of combination employed symbols that "ought to be useful in discovery and in judgment" if here, as in mathematical analysis, the new notions were simply combinations of previously acquired notions. Finally, according to Leibniz, one of the greatest advantages of method was the weighing of advantages and disadvantages through a process of deliberation and the calculation of probabilities.

Leibniz' initial position is therefore closer to Aristotle than to Descartes. His aim is not to describe the free, mental processes through which the human mind arrives at truth—doubt, reflection on evidence, and so forth—but to determine the necessary relations that compel the mind to pass from one proposition to another. Nothing is more abhorrent to him than Cartesian doubt, which would suffice to nullify any philosophical undertaking, for "if it is posited, the existence of God cannot remove it," especially if the fallibility of man is due to sin. The resolution of propositions into identities involves no doubt. "We acknowledge postulates and axioms not only because they are proved by an infinity of experiences but also because they immediately satisfy the mind; nevertheless, the perfection of science requires that they be demonstrated." Leibniz was on the path which led to the symbolic logic and the non-Euclidean geometries that came into being in the nineteenth century as a result of attempts to demonstrate postulates.

Leibniz' system of combination, therefore, consists essentially of fashioning all possible connections—that is, noncontradictory connections—between terms given initially, and thus proving a priori the reality of a concept as such. But such a method is generally inaccessible to the human mind, for there is no notion other than the notion of number that will enable us to determine by analysis the last "requisites." Clarity and distinctness of ideas are insufficient. Not only must an idea be clear (that is, not susceptible of being confused with other ideas, such as the idea of color) and distinct (that is, we must have a clear knowledge of the marks that set it apart from other ideas—for instance, extension in relation to thought); it must also be adequate—that is, the marks themselves must be analyzed into their last elements.

The possibility of a concept is proved, not a priori by method, but a posteriori by experience; and even in the clearest of the sciences—the science of numbers—we are sometimes obliged to leave it at that. For example, Leibniz cites one of Fermat's theorems involving prime numbers which could be verified in every concrete proof attempted but which had not been demonstrated (it finally was demonstrated by Euler, in 1736). What is needed, then, is "an art of instituting experiments that will supply what is lacking in our data."

IV *The Doctrine of Infinity*

The logic of concepts is traditionally linked to the doctrine of finitude: a fixed number of species constituted by a definite number of genera and differences; a finite world in space constituted in such a manner that species remain fixed as individuals change. Everything which in reality resists inclusion in this frame—individuality, continuity, infinity—is viewed as being excluded from the order and dependent on an unintelligible principle of disorder. In the sixteenth and seventeenth centuries the doctrine of infinity impregnated every sphere of mathematics and physics; at the same time the logic of universals collapsed. Leibniz, no less than Spinoza, is an impassioned advocate of the doctrine of infinity: any definite notion whatsover, any notion that does not envelop infinity, is according to him an abstract, incomplete notion. He holds that only the inexhaustible is real. Under these conditions, how would he and could he remain faithful to the spirit of Aristotelian logic and, to a certain degree, Aristotelian physics, since both are essentially finite? The expression he uses so often, "infinite analysis," shows the union, essential in his view, between the two aspects of philosophy, which must be infinite in so far as it relates to the actual universe and analytic in order to penetrate the sphere of intelligibility. Leibniz is concerned exclusively with creating a logic of infinity, and all of his doctrines and studies in mathematics, physics, metaphysics, theology, and moral philosophy are but its several aspects.

In geometry, infinite analysis seems impossible because the very definition of geometric continuity makes it impossible for us to find the elements which would, in sum, reproduce the *continuum*. Nevertheless, and for the same reason, we can imagine a quantity smaller than any given quantity, no matter how small. Leibniz' concept of *infinitely small* quantities contrasts sharply with Cavalieri's principle of *indivisibles,* which are the same in nature as finite magnitudes. For example, Cavalieri regarded the line as an infinite aggregation of points, a surface as an infinite aggregation of lines, and so forth. To Leibniz, however, the infinitely small quantity in the case of a line is an infinitesimal line. Leibniz then is able to turn to account one of Pascal's incidental observations concerning curves. The observation is based on the homogeneity of space, a property that enables us to imagine a similar figure corresponding to a given figure, no matter how small. It follows that the relation between two straight lines is independent of their absolute dimensions and can remain the same when the two lines become infinitely small. Leibniz shows that the direction of a curve at one of its points depends solely on the determination of the relation when the lines are infinitely small, so that we can have recourse to infinite analysis when we need to find the direction of the curve (that is its tangent) at any given point. The difference between his logic of infinity and Aristotelian logic is crystal clear:

his does not begin with given concepts whose relations are studied later, for these concepts would have to be composed of a finite number of elements; instead, it begins with a relation that engenders an infinite number of terms (the points of the curve).

Leibniz' philosophy is based essentially on the discovery in each instance of a kind of algorithm which plays *mutatis mutandis* the role of an infinitesimal algorithm in the infinitesimal calculus.

In mechanics, the law of the conservation of force, which should account for the indefinite series of mechanical changes in the world of bodies; in metaphysics, the notion of individual substance, which is simply the law of their consecutive changes or the pre-established harmony which is the law of the interrelationship of individual substances; in theology, the divine attributes—understanding, which is the law of essences, the will or choice of the better, which is the law of existences, and potentiality, which is the law of the passage from essence to existence; all these notions, no matter how different in appearance and origin, have no function except that of introducing universally the intelligibility of infinity which the infinitesimal calculus contributed to geometry. In each instance we must endeavor to apprehend a notion with an inexhaustible fecundity. We may distribute points on a surface as arbitrarily as we please; if we relate them on the basis of a continuous trait, an equation will give the law of distribution of these points. Our example brings into clear focus the thought that permeates Leibniz' whole system: there is always a law to explain infinite variation.

The most celebrated of Leibniz' doctrines—his dynamism, his theory of life, his theory of freedom and contingency—are corollaries of this unique idea, and considered apart from it they sometimes tend to present a rather disconcerting aspect. Furthermore, if his doctrines are the fruit of the same thought, we must not assume that they are contained in a coherent system in which we could easily relate them to one another or deduce them from one another. There have been attempts, for example, to relate his dynamism to his theory of substance on the ground that his notion of the monad derives from his notion of force; the truth is that each of the two notions had its origin in independent considerations, though they both fit into the same pattern of thought. We shall examine them one by one, but without exaggerating their systematic elaboration.

A common characteristic of these notions (of these sorts of algorithm) is that, unlike Descartes' clear and distinct ideas, they are not the object of intuition but are present as conclusions drawn by analysis from two universal principles applicable to all things— principles whose fertility was erroneously denied by the Cartesians. The two great principles are the *principle of identity*—A is A, when A is any given term—and the *principle of sufficient reason*—everything has a reason for being as it is and not otherwise; or: a cause is equivalent to its effect; or: any true proposition which is not self-evident is provable *a priori*. To these must be added the *principle of continuity* which states a property common to any diversity whatsoever: nature never acts by leaps—that is, a thing can pass from one state to another only through an infinite number of intermediaries. It follows that "whatever is discernible must be composed of parts that are indiscernible; nothing can originate suddenly—consciousness no more than motion." Reality then is always revealed to us as a continuum whose parts we cannot exhaust.

v *Mechanics and Dynamism*

Leibniz was first and always a mechanist and an advocate of the plenum. As early as 1669 he looked upon the modern explanation of all phenomena by size, figure, and motion as being the most acceptable one and even "the one closest to Aristotle." In 1670 he gave a systematic explanation of a system of mechanics in his *Theoria motus abstracti,* in which the notion of *conatus* (that is, an infinitely small quantity of motion), borrowed from Hobbes, is of first importance. Later, to explain how motion was transmitted in the plenum by impulsion, he had to imagine that solid bodies were swimming in a fluid that offered no resistance but was fluid only in relation to the solid bodies, that the fluid itself was composed of solid bodies swimming in a fluid still more subtle, and so forth *ad infinitum,* the subtlety of the fluids having no limit. In both Leibniz and Descartes, and for the same reasons, such a theory of mechanics ruled out any system of mathematical physics as conceived by Galileo, Pascal, or Newton; and whereas the calculation of fluxions provided Newton with the language needed for his physics, Leibniz never used his infinitesimal calculus to express the laws of nature.

Leibniz nevertheless heaped criticism on Cartesian physics. His criticism may be summed up in one statement: the principles posited by Descartes—extended substance, conservation of motion, and laws of nature derived from such principles—are not principles of unity capable of explaining the infinite diversity of things. First, extension cannot be a substance, for it is a "being through aggregation, and every being of this kind implies simple beings from which it derives its reality, with the result that it will have no reality at all if each being of which it is composed is still a being through aggregation"; extension, which is infinitely divisible, is an aggregate, not a substance. So there must be "something extended or continuous, and this is precisely what constitutes the essence of a body; the repetition of this (whatever it may be) is extension." Since extension is no different from the void, it contains nothing which would be the sufficient cause of resistance or mobility, nor does it explain the variety which characterizes the things that fill it. Motion, like time, "never exists, strictly speaking, because an aggregate never exists when it does not have its coexisting parts." The law of conservation of motion violates the principle of reason—*causa adaequat effectum* —since it wrongly assumes that motion is proportionate to force. A one-pound weight that has fallen four feet has obviously acquired the same force as a four-pound weight that has fallen one foot. That the motion of the first weight is to the motion of the second as 2 is to 4 easily determined by Galileo's laws. That what is identical in both instances is force—the product of the mass and the square of the velocity of the two weights (mv^2)—which is therefore the true constant sought by Descartes, is also easily determined. Descartes' laws of impact are, in turn, contrary to the principle of continuity, primarily because he often supposed that there was an instantaneous change in either the quantity or the direction of motion of the colliding bodies at the moment of impact. The principle of continuity should have warned him that in nature there can be only elastic bodies which, if they rebound on contact with another body, first lose their motion gradually (without a corresponding loss of any part of their force), then acquire it anew by virtue of their elasticity, which in turn results from the inner agitation of their parts. Elasticity therefore expresses an inner force, intrinsic to each body, which is not produced by the external bodies that determine its mode of action. Leibniz therefore cannot accept the perfectly homogeneous bodies represented by Descartes' elements, any more than he can accept atoms. The existence of elasticity and of inner forces supposes the infinite divisibility of actual bodies which accordingly cannot have exact, determinate shapes. So there is in nature no part of matter, no matter how small, which is not composed of still smaller parts, each of which is constantly in a state of agitation, and one body differs from another not by size or shape but by the inner force that it manifests.

In the elaboration of his rules Descartes also fails to appreciate the principle of continuity, which holds that when the difference between data becomes very slight, the difference between the results also becomes very slight. According to him, if two colliding bodies, B and C, have the same mass and velocity, they will both rebound with the same velocity; but if B is larger than C by even the slightest amount, its direction should remain the same.

It follows that if everything in nature is explained mechanically, the very principles of mechanics, namely forces and actions, are metaphysical. The Cartesians must have understood this when they introduced as the cause of motion and its conservation the arbitrary will of a *deus ex machina,* for the only alternative is to suppose that there is within bodies themselves something superior to them. And in fact force, as conceived by Leibniz, is indeed the permanent cause of all the actions a body can accomplish and of all the passions it can endure. It is "the first entelechy" which "corresponds to mind or substantial form." In discovering the constancy of force (mv^2)

to which he attaches as a corollary the law of conservation of *quantity of progression* (that is, constancy of the algebraic sum of the projection of velocities on an axis), Leibniz thinks that he has found a veritable reality.

What is the significance of Leibniz' dynamism or theory of the reality of force, which would constrain us to pass from physics to metaphysics? Particularly worthy of our attention is the contrast between his dynamism and the dynamism of central forces that was being evolved at the same time by Roberval, Huyghens, and Newton. Newton did not accept the plenum and saw as the paradigm of force the force of gravitational attraction which, following his investigations, became a particular instance of universal gravitation. We recall that, according to his famous pronouncement, physics must steer clear of metaphysics, with the result that the formula for gravitation was important (following the logic characteristic of the scientific current that linked Galileo and Newton) because it allowed him to calculate and foresee a great number of phenomena, and not because it revealed some hidden essence, such as a real force of attraction. In contrast, Leibniz, who thought that his formula (mv^2) disclosed a profound reality, could deduce from it nothing which could be used in the exact calculation of phenomena. Here we have, perhaps for the first time, the confrontation of two different minds. Paradoxically, it would seem at first glance that Leibniz' criticism of Newton in his letters to Clarke is identical with his criticism of Descartes: the inability to dispense with a *Deus ex machina* in physics. For it is easy to demonstrate that by virtue of the prolonged action of gravitation, a system such as the solar system will gradually deteriorate unless God repairs the machinery just as a mechanic repairs his contrivances. Their encounter sheds light on the degree to which Leibniz deemed the metaphysical superstructure of his physics to be indispensable. He shunned the arbitrary metaphysics which Descartes and Newton added, of necessity or by choice, to their physics. In force he had something real to account for all mechanical changes.

VI *The Notion of Individual Substance and Theology*

Everything in the system of Leibniz hinges upon the infinitude of the world and the impossibility of carving out any reality which is not in its own way infinite, any element which does not participate in its own way in this infinitude. Even in the world of bodies, as we have seen, extension is not divided into finite and limited bodies; instead, each body is infinitely subdivided; furthermore, each real substance contains in its own way the infinitude of the universe, and there is no state of a substance which does not contain traces of its whole past and the germs of its whole future.

But at the same time the exigency of infinity, inherent in each thing, is never satisfied. The infinity that we find in the universe is a "syncategorematic"[2] infinity which is typified by a mathematical series and which consists essentially in the impossibility of our ever arriving at the last term of a progression. A syncategorematic infinity has as its necessary complement a "categorematic infinity" which is the law of the series and which is of necessity outside the series. Similarly, as we shall see, Leibniz' concept of infinity in the sensible universe has as its necessary complement the laws of the series of changes which Leibniz identifies with individual substances. But substances or subjects, in turn, constitute not a real being but an indefinite multiplicity. Above this infinitude of substances we must therefore conceive an infinite being, a kind of law or "hypercategorematic infinite being," and this brings us to the consideration of infinitude in God—that is, to theology. Divine infinitude or perfection is to the eternally incomplete infinitude of the universe what the law of a series is to the infinitude of its terms in mathematics. Metaphysics and theology then are inseparable; the truth of a metaphysical notion, such as the notion of substance, can of course he proved "without mentioning God except when neces-

---

[2] A notion probably derived from William of Ockham, who had borrowed it from Peter of Spain. On the origin of the idea, cf. the notice on *Ennead* VI in my edition of Plotinus.

sary to indicate my dependence; but this truth is expressed more forcefully when the notion in question has divine knowledge as the source from which it is drawn." The same applies to all of the notions in Leibniz' philosophy, whether they are taken at their lower level (in the creature of God) or at their higher level (in their source in God) where analysis comes to an end.

Here we find a doctrinal scheme long familiar to us—the Neo-Platonic scheme according to which the same total reality finds expression at different levels, being more concentrated and closer to the One at the higher level and more divided and diluted at the lower level. We recall the Neo-Platonic design that became prevalent during the Renaissance and the intelligible world of Plotinus in which "each thing was all things" when we read that "in the soul of Alexander there reside eternally remnants of all that has happened to him and signs of all that will happen to him," and that "any substance is like a whole world and like a mirror of God or of the whole universe."

The crux of Leibniz' metaphysics is the notion of substance. "So long as we do not discern what is truly a complete being or a substance, we shall have nothing to halt us." But we must reach a halt, as Aristotle said, at least in the order of reasons. Descartes defined created substance as that which is conceived independently and has need only of the concurrence of God in order to exist. This meant on the one hand that the essence of a substance was reduced to a sole attribute (extension or consciousness), with the result that there could be no change in it, and on the other that it involved no relation to other created substances, with the result that doubt was cast on the very existence of a world, that is, the aggregate of interrelated substances. Cartesianism (and that is why it contains the germ of Spinozism) placed little value upon the individuality of substances, for mind as well as bodies had ceased to be substances and become modes of thought or extension.

As the language of Leibniz suggests, his notion of substance has its source in completely different traditions. For example, when he referred to "individual substance" in his *Discourse on Metaphysics* he was using the language of Aristotle and trying like him to make individual substances (which are merely subjects) the only true realities. Later he used the word "monad," a Neo-Platonic term which he probably borrowed from Bruno and which Proclus used to designate the "units" which are subordinate to the Supreme One and reflect from diverse points of view the whole multiplicity of the universe. But the dynamism of his physics is another source of his notion of substance and probably of his vitalism as well.

We need first to examine the notion of individual substance as it is revealed in his *Discourse on Metaphysics*. Here Leibniz, whose main concern is the solution of the theological problem (the problem of God's relation to his creatures), follows a method, showing how notions of individual substance, and then of divine attributes, issue from investigation of the conditions of what is called a *contingent truth*.

In contrast to *truths of reason,* which can be reduced to identities and of which the opposites imply contradiction, *contingent truths* or truths of fact are those of which the opposites do not imply contradiction; the "metaphysical necessity" of eternal truths contrasts with the absence of metaphysical necessity. But is the absence of necessity complete indetermination? It is not, for that would be contrary to the principle of sufficient reason. But does not determination entail necessity, that is, the impossibility of a different outcome? If so, contingency would not differ from necessity. Determination implies necessity but not metaphysical or logical necessity; there is also an *ex hypothesi* necessity, consequential or conditional, according to which a thing exists on condition that something else exists first. The metaphysical or logical necessity of an identical proposition issues immediately or mediately from the examination of its terms; but the necessity of a proposition of fact (Caesar has crossed the Rubicon) is due to prior events (Caesar's decision to secure his power). Since the prior events themselves are necessary only by virtue of their conditions, and so on indefinitely, it can be said that for Caesar not to have crossed the Rubicon remains metaphysically possible.

This accounts for the positive definition of contingent truths or truths of fact: truths whose integral reason could be identified only by an infinite analysis beyond the scope of the human mind. Truths of reason, on the other hand, may be demonstrated by a finite analysis.

The notion of individual substance is obtained by an application of the principle of reason to true propositions that have an individual being as their subject. "It is an established fact that any true predication has some foundation in the nature of things, and when a proposition is not identical—that is, when the predicate is not expressly included in the subject—it must be included potentially, and that is what philosophers call *in esse*. Thus the subject term always includes the predicate term, with the result that whoever understood perfectly the notion of the subject would also think that the predicate belonged to it. Therefore we can say that the nature of an individual substance or a complete being is to have a notion so complete that it is sufficient to embrace and to allow us to deduce from it all the predicates of the subject to which it is attributed." This is the application of the great principle which states that any true proposition is demonstrable a priori. But is not the *ex hypothesi* necessity of contingent truths transformed thereby into a metaphysical necessity if, here too, their truth issues from an examination of notions?

The objections raised by Leibniz' correspondents are worth considering. First, Arnauld, speaking as a theologian: To say that all changes in an individual being are deduced from its notion, as the properties of sphere are deduced from its definition, is to eliminate, along with contingency and freedom, any kind of true individuality. Then Volder, speaking as a geometer: "Everything deduced from the nature of a thing is invariably in the thing as long as its nature persists; thus from the notion of individual substance it would follow that nothing is active by nature, for action is always variation on the part of the creature." Leibniz here comes to grips with objections analogous to those which Aristotle was unable to resolve: he was called upon to choose between intelligibility that pertains only to necessary propositions and individuality that escapes intelligibility.

To answer the objections of the geometers Leibniz compares the nature of individual substance to the law of a series that embraces the indefinite progression of its terms or to the equation of a curve that allows us to determine at will an infinite number of points. But he quickly adds: "I believe this is the clearest statement I can make to geometric minds, although these kinds of lines [lines that constitute the infinite evolution of predicates] infinitely surpass those that a human mind can understand."

They infinitely surpass human minds for this reason: we know that the notion of a substance produces all its predicates, but we ourselves are never in possession of such a notion. This is true because "although we can account for a subsequent state in terms of its antecedent state, and then of the antecedent state in its turn, we can never come to a final cause within the series." But since there is always a connection that leads us indefinitely from one term to the next, no matter how far we go in the infinite series of terms which is never complete and will never be complete (Leibniz calls it syncategorematic infinity), we must assume that outside the series is a cause which makes all the terms and their dependence immediately intelligible (categorematic infinity). Thus we have infallible and a priori knowledge of each of the predicates that belong to substance, and such immediate recognition of an individual substance can belong only to God, the author of all things.

It follows that we must seek the root of contingent truths in God, and it is on this level that Leibniz takes his stand to answer Arnauld's objection. There is an a priori proof for any truth, whether contingent or necessary, drawn from the notion of its terms; if the truth is necessary, this proof is accessible to the finite mind; if contingent, proof exists only in God. But how can this proof, the total, unique "infallible vision" that God has of all things, not exclude all contingencies? In Cartesian theology, which makes eternal truths or essences as well as existences depend on the divine will, the real is not separated from the possible. Whatever is belongs of necessity to the same order, and Descartes' true successor is Spinoza. Descartes' error stemmed from the belief that the two great principles, identity and sufficient reason, were no longer applicable in theology. For when we apply them to theology, we see that necessary truths and contingent truths refer to distinct attributes of God. Through his understanding God conceives everything that is possible, that is, everything that does not imply a contradiction. Through his will he decides to create one of the possible worlds presented to him by his understanding. Consequently his infallible vision of real substances with their predicates cannot be of the same nature as his knowledge of the possibility of these substances; and his knowledge of the possibility of these substances, that is, of their essences, is distinct from our knowledge of the truths of reason. Knowledge of substances (and consequently of contingent truths) belongs in fact to the divine intellect in so far as the latter relates to will; knowledge of possible substances to a will which is itself possible; knowledge of real substances to the same will in so far as it is effective. Knowledge of the truths of reason, however, belongs solely to the intellect. Thus God's infallible vision is explained by the fact that he knows which of the substances conceived by his intellect he has decided to create through his will.

The distinction between the contingent and the necessary, therefore, is identical to the distinction between the real and the possible, between existence and essence. It has its source in the distinction between two divine attributes, intellect which relates to essences and will which relates to existences.

But God's vision of individual substances is infallible only if, by virtue of the principle of sufficient reason, his will is not arbitrary but determinate with respect to the choice of possible substances. The only choice worthy of the perfect being is the choice of "the best of all possible worlds," the wholly a priori principle of the famous Leibnizian *optimism* which cannot be proved or disproved by experience and which cannot be impaired by the mockery of Voltaire's *Candide*. The word "best," which Leibniz often exploded in the ears of theologians to assert more forcefully his anti-Spinozism, is sometimes replaced by the expression "maximum of essence." In fact, the existence of one possible can be incompatible with the existence of another; two or more possibles whose existence is compatible (that is, not contradictory) are said to be compossibles; among all combinations of possibles, there is obviously one which contains the maximum of reality or essence, and this is the one God chooses.

VII *Theology and Monadology*

The analytic exposition of Leibniz' system in the *Discourse on Metaphysics* was followed by a systematic exposition in which his debt to Plato is revealed in his concept of the monad.

At the summit, God: "At a deeper level in philosophy I manage to derive the supreme laws of natural things from some knowledge of divine perfections." The existence of the infinite and perfect being is established a priori on the basis of so-called ontological proof. But this proof, as it is conceived by Descartes, is incomplete. The existence of God is deduced from the idea of God, of course, but on condition that the idea is possible, that is, does not imply contradiction. The proof becomes: "God is necessary by virtue of his essence; therefore if he is possible, he exists." To show the possibility of the existence of God, Leibniz has recourse sometimes to his simplicity, since contradiction exists only in a concept whose elements are mutually incompatible, sometimes to proof *a contingentia mundi,* which thus becomes the preliminary step of the ontological proof. For we know of the existence of beings that exist through other, finite beings. Such beings are possible *a fortiori,* but if necessary being or independent being (*ens a se*) were impossible, beings that exist through others would also be impossible.

God has three attributes: power, intellect, and will. His power is creative, and his intellect is the foundation of essences or possibles. We might say that he corresponds to the intelligible world of the Platonists if there were not two important differences. In the first place, the field of possibles or of essences is infinitely greater than the field of existences, so that it is necessary for us to separate the possibles which will never come into existence from those which will come into being through an edict of will. In the second place, a possible which will become actual is not an ideal model but contains down to the smallest detail everything that will belong to the actual being. "My supposition," he said, "is not that God willed the creation of an Adam of whom he had a vague, incomplete notion, but that he willed the creation of an Adam whom he conceived as a definite individual." Thus in God, as Plotinus said, there are ideas of individuals. Finally, the will of God is the foundation of existences; through it God chooses the best combination of possibles and causes it to come into being.

Further elaboration of the divine attributes yields a clearer understanding of determination and its mechanistic character. If we grant that any possible tends toward existence (*exigit existere*) or that essence is merely the exigency of existence, creation becomes a problem of equilibrium and of maximum, for each possible achieves existence in so far as it is not blocked by other possibles—that is, in accordance with its degree of perfection—and the total combination is the one that possesses the maximum of reality.

From his metaphysical mechanism, linked to the optimal will just as his physical mechanism is linked to force, Leibniz deduces a priori the general characteristics of the universe.

We cannot speak of reality without speaking at the same time of infinitude. Only imaginary, abstract beings can be cut up into finite parts, and that is one more proof of their imaginary character. Leibniz, therefore, had to find a universe in which there could be nothing real which was not at the same time infinite. That is the origin of his notion of the *monad*. Leibniz began by substituting for what is commonly called the real universe a representation of the universe as it exists in the mind. The universe assumed to be real is merely an insubstantial phenomenon; reality is the mind with its representations. Furthermore, he generalized the idea of representation, which became equivalent to the idea of expression: "One thing becomes the expression of another (in my language) when there is a constant, regular relation between what can be said of one and what can be said of the other. Expression is . . . a genus, and natural perception, animal feeling, and intellectual knowledge are its species." From his reversal of the popular point of view and his generalization of the idea of representation, it follows that the representative beings whose aggregate constitutes the universe are not the minds that are endowed with intellectual knowledge and consciously perceived by us. Representation does not imply consciousness; indeed, we observe that within ourselves there are representations each of which involves an indefinite division into parts, without our having the slightest awareness of such perceptions. The sound of the surf, for example, is the sum of the sound of collisions between many tiny particles—elementary sounds of which we are totally unaware. Or again, a perceptible quality, color, or smell is deceptively simple, for it results from the aggregation of a huge number of elementary perceptions of unnoticed motions. And there are states, such as that of being in a faint, in which perceptions are no longer accompanied by any feeling. The same thing can therefore be expressed in countless ways since there are countless gradations in a distinct representation. Thus we not only can but must (since the universe has to contain the maximum of reality) conceive the universe as an aggregate of beings representative of the infinitude of the universe. There must be an infinity of such beings since there is an infinity of degrees in the clearness and distinctiveness of the representation of the universe.

Thus through generalization the notion of mind becomes the notion of monad. The universe of Leibniz is in a sense analogous to Plotinus' intelligible world in which the total reality of the world appears through each idea, and it is important for us to recall that the notion of a descending hierarchy in which each universe repeats all of the others at different degrees of concentration or of dilution is one of the most common notions in Platonic philosophy. This is indeed what monads are: each of them is a spiritual universe—a "windowless," isolated, and perfectly self-sufficient world; each is also a different expression of the same universe, and all such expressions constitute a hierarchy descending from the most perfect to the least perfect. But this is no longer Neo-Platonism: the gradational universes of the Neo-Platonists, taken in their descending order, exhibit less and less unity until finally, at the lowest degree, they reach the state of juxtaposition in space which characterizes the sensible world. Here nothing of the sort happens; each of the monads keeps the same indivisible unity from one hierarchy to the next. The reason is that Leibniz rejects the concept of the distinction between unity and dispersion, required by the realism of the spatial world he no longer accepts, and puts in its place the Cartesian concept of distinctiveness and clarity in contrast to confusion and obscurity, which remains wholly spiritual in nature. Monads then differ among themselves only in so far as they express the same universe with varying degrees of clarity. It is the spiritual nature of Leibniz' thought that introduces into the monad a dynamism that did not exist in the gradational worlds of the Neo-Platonists, for each monad not only expresses the whole universe at every instant with a certain degree of clarity but also tends spontaneously to express it in the best possible way. Each monad then has two attributes: *perception* or variety in the unity by which the infinite detail of things is represented in it at every moment, and *appetition* or the spontaneous tendency to pass from obscure perceptions to clearer perceptions. And there is a hierarchy of monads extending from the "naked monad" that has only perceptions without any apperception or feeling to the rational monad or mind that possesses, along with consciousness and reflective acts, knowledge of necessary truths. On an intermediate level are the animal monads which, thanks to memory, can predict the future by anticipating, when an event that has already taken place recurs, the event that followed it on the previous occasion (empirical successions).

Furthermore, any monad always contains traces of its whole past and is pregnant with its whole future. Everything about it, therefore, is determined by internal reasons. This we know a priori, and we must not rely on our experience. "I am uncertain as to whether I shall take a trip but I am not uncertain as to whether I shall always be myself, regardless of the trip. Such things seem indeterminate to us only because the signs or indications of them in our substance are not recognizable to us." The events that we call contingent are not indeterminate.

Monads are mirrors or expressions of the same universe. The only difference between them relates to the degree of clarity in their expression. But an infinitude of monads must be postulated, for the law of plenitude and continuity applies equally to forms and to extension. Furthermore, just as there is an infinity of other points between two points of a straight line, so there is an infinity of intermediate expressions between two expressions that differ in clarity. This is characteristic of divine infinitude: "Because God reveals from every aspect and in every way the general system of phenomena that he sees fit to produce in order to manifest his glory, and views every aspect of the world in every possible manner, letting no relation escape his omniscience, the result of each view of the universe from a certain spot is a substance that expresses the universe from this angle."

The infinity of monads (the aggregate) in no way constitutes a whole or a substantial reality that we might call the world. Taken by itself, it is one of the syncategorematic infinities whose unifying principle must be sought outside the series. The Leibnizian view is therefore diametrically opposed to the idea of a world soul or a universal mind.

VIII *Pre-established Harmony*

The serial law which relates monads to one another is called *pre-established harmony*. It is grounded on the belief that God, by his will and his wisdom, has acted on the being of monads in such a way as to make each monad's perceptions correspond to one another at every instant, each perception differing from the others because of the point of view from which the universe is seen or, without using a metaphor, because of its degree of clarity. Pre-established harmony means that God, in creating one monad, had all other monads in mind. The will to create a particular monad with all the events that issues from it is never a primitive or an absolute decree, for there is no fragmented will in God. But having willed the best of all possible worlds, he gave to each substance every possible perfection, with the result that his decree with respect to a particular substance or to an event involving this substance is always an *ex-hypothesi* decree resulting from the universal order.

Pre-established harmony explains the action or passion (always ideal) of a monad. The whole being of a monad is representative; action in a monad designates passage from a higher degree of clarity, passion to a lower degree. Further, by virtue of pre-established harmony an increase of clarity in one monad has as a necessary correlative a diminution of clarity in one or more other monads; the first is therefore said to act (ideally) upon the others. A particular case of such interaction is brought to light in connection with the problem of the union of soul and body. Between the two there is neither real influence, as Descartes maintained, nor occasional causality, as Malebranche maintained, but pre-established harmony like that between two clocks so well regulated by their maker that they will continue indefinitely to keep the same time. Such independence and spontaneity does not prevent us from speaking (ideally) of an interaction in the sense that whatever is action in one will be matched by passion in the other, and vice versa.

IX *Freedom and Theodicy: Optimism*

The problem of freedom also finds its solution in monadology. There is no modification of the monad which is not spontaneous and which does not come about independently, but there are monads of all types, ranging from those whose perceptions are more indistinct even than the perceptions that we have during a total loss of consciousness to the rational monads whose actions are determined by clear and distinct ideas. Such acts are called free, freedom being nothing except "spontaneity of intelligent being." Freedom then is in no sense indetermination, nor does it involve indetermination.

Free acts, derived like everything else from the internal law of the monad, manifest a kind of rational determinism. Arnauld countered Leibniz, however, by saying that such freedom implied no responsibility on the part of the author of the act. For example, if the notion of the creation of Adam and his sin is the object of a divine decree, then we must say that God is the author of sin. Every theologian since Plato had taken pains to set aside this very objection.

Leibniz dealt at length with the problem in one of his longer works, the *Theodicy,* which defends God against the charge that he is the author of sin and, in general, of evil. The book is inspired for the most part by the traditional teachings of the Stoics and St. Augustine, which Descartes also used in his fourth *Meditation.* Here Leibniz makes a distinction between *metaphysical evil* or imperfection, *physical evil* or pain, and *moral evil* or sin. Imperfection derives from the limits inherent in every creature; but if we realize that God created no being without awareness of its place in the whole and that he created the best of all possible worlds, we infer that within the total scheme of things every creature possesses at each instant its just proportion of perfection; since we can apprehend things only in isolation and abstractly, however, each creature seems to us to be less perfect than it might be. Physical evil or pain is explained as being a consequence, established by divine justice, of either imperfection (pain being associated with passivity) or sin. Last comes moral evil: Adam's sin is not a simple imperfection but a positive evil which sprang from his own initiative and which transformed the destiny of mankind; it introduced into things the kind of discontinuity that Leibniz sought everywhere to eliminate from his vision of the universe. How, then, could moral sin be reconciled with dogma? We should note that the difficulty was not peculiar to Leibniz, but was traditional in a theology which posited an omnipotent and omniscient God and which was therefore unable to account for God's not having known infallibly in advance that Adam, though free, would sin. We should also note that the solution, equally traditional, was provided by St. Augustine, who stated that God can foresee events but that events are not thereby predetermined. Leibniz' position is less tenable. The only way in which he can satisfy the theologians is to show how it is possible, in his system, to escape from Calvin's absolute decree. According to Calvin, it is by a decree dependent on the sovereign and arbitrary will of God that each man is destined either to salvation or to damnation. If this is true, then one can say that God willed Adam's sin and is responsible for it. Though the implication is that God created each man through one particular, original decree, we know this is not true, for the particular decree depends on the total decree by which God created the best of all possible worlds; consequently he allowed Adam to sin because Adam was entering the best of all possible worlds. God cannot be said to have willed Adam's sin since his will did not have Adam as its object; if he had created only Adam, he would not have made him a sinner, nor would he have created the best of all possible worlds. Leibniz believes, then, that he can avoid the absolute decree by imputing sin to Adam. It was certain that Adam would sin, but his sin was not necessary since it was metaphysically possible (that is, noncontradictory) for him not to sin, and the reason with which he was endowed enabled him to understand the sin that he was committing.

The nature of Leibniz' optimism made it possible for him to assume that the best of all possible worlds accommodated dogmas such as those relating to the small number of the elect. No pages bring out more clearly the significance of his doctrine of infinity than those in the *Theodicy* dealing with eternal damnation, the endless suffering which seems to provide a contrast intended to enhance the beauty of the universe. Here the tragic sense is completely absent, and divine justice is no more rigorous than a geometrical theorem. For the tragic sense can exist only for those who consider the destiny of man to be a kind of entity, isolated to some degree from the universe through an initiative of the will. But in a system in which only individual substances exist and everything issues from their spontaneity, even the slightest element has its function in the universe as a whole. This is because these individual substances are universes and contain, at least potentially, everything possible. Each substance, which seems to be complete by itself, is actually defined only by its relations with all other beings and by its definite place in a hierarchy that includes the damned as well as angels and the elect.

x *Living Beings*

Monadology also helps Leibniz resolve the problem of the nature of life. In a sense the problem of living beings, which never ceased to concern him, was at the outset one of the sources of his theory of monads. In 1671, when he was associating with alchemists and Rosicrucians, he expressed with them his conviction that there is a kind of invisible nucleus of the body which will subsist until the Resurrection. His attention was drawn quite naturally to the works of microscopists—Leuwenhoek, Swammerdam, and Malpighi—who made important discoveries between 1670 and 1690 concerning animals or animate elements invisible to the naked eye. The microscope enabled them to see in the living being not (in keeping with the ancient tradition of Aristotle) organs formed of homogenous tissues but organs whose parts were themselves organized. This offered a kind of experimental confirmation of the alchemists' subsistent nucleus, and it allowed Leibniz to introduce his infinitary ideas indirectly into biology. It also allowed him to universalize the concept of life, as Plotinus had already done, to the extent of assuming that there is nothing in nature which is not animate. It was sufficient to assume that matter is organized to infinity—that is, that every part, no matter how small, is itself organized. From this it follows immediately that we cannot assert that an animal is born or dies; we can only say that it grows until it becomes visible and then decreases until it becomes imperceptible; the germ of the animate being is indestructible. Infinite organization also allowed him to assume the "patterning of germs" to explain the pre-existence in Adam of the whole human race: germs are organisms and can decrease until they become infinitely small. Each organism, no matter how small, is composed of an infinite number of parts; there must be a law of their relation in the "central monad" whose representations correspond ideally to the relations between this organism and the rest of the material universe and which is to the organism as the soul is to the body. Corresponding to the growth of the body, to what we call its birth and its adult state, is an increase in the clarity of perceptions in the central monad. Thus Leibniz, who in his correspondence with Arnauld (1686) had seemed to concede that human souls were created at the moment of birth, later believed that they were pre-existent but raised to a higher degree of clarity with the birth of the body. Moreover, in his view rational souls not only subsist after death (like the souls of brutes, which fall back into their primitive state of confusion) but are also truly immortal—that is, a special decree of God enables them to preserve their reason and personality independently of their bodies.

Leibniz' biological and organic theory, therefore, allowed him to speak of unity in bodies. Such unity, as we have seen repeatedly, cannot be due to extension, which spontaneously crumbles. But do we not run into difficulty if we attribute it to an aggregate of monads? We have seen that the universe was formed of an aggregate of monads which did not constitute a whole or a unit; similarly, the aggregate of monads that corresponds to a body will not constitute a unit. That is why in his correspondence with Des Bosses (1706) he postulated a substantial bond (*vinculum substantiale*) between monads, thereby making constant application of the same principle: to realize, outside the infinite series of terms (here the infinity of monads in relation to a single body), the law of the series.

XI *Innate Ideas: Leibniz and Locke*

Monadology provided Leibniz with the solution to the problem of innate ideas. "The question is somewhat equivocal," he said, apparently referring to the way in which Locke had handled the difficulty which he examined in his turn in the preface and first book of the *New Essays concerning Human Understanding*. The first equivocation consists in thinking that we can refute the doctrine of innate ideas by showing that we do not always have actual knowledge of them—for their being known to us when we concentrate upon them is enough to make them innate. Furthermore, the word "innate" is equivocal: to the degree that everything comes from my own resources and I am subjected to no external action, there is nothing that is not innate in the monad that I am. But "in the common system" that postulates the influence of bodies on minds, that which does not come from sensible knowledge is called "innate," and this is the meaning implied by the famous adage which denies innatism: "Nihil est in intellectu guod non prius fuerit in sensu." This is also the meaning generally accepted by Leibniz, but the word embraces so many nuances that precision is not always easy. The mark of innatism is necessity, which pertains either to the primitive truths of reason—the axiom of identity and the principle of sufficient reason—or to the derived truths that can be reduced to the principle of necessity; to truths that may be proven a priori (the word a "priori" is used by Leibniz only with reference to such a proof). As for innate ideas, they are ideas without which a truth is inconceivable—the ideas of being, possible, same, identity, which enter into an innate truth. For example, it is impossible for a thing to be and not to be at the same time. All of our innate ideas taken as a whole constitute the intellect by which we think. Leibniz can therefore accept the Scholastic adage, but with one restriction: "There is nothing in the intellect which has not been in sensation, except the intellect itself (*nisi intellectus ipse*)." But necessity and apriority are merely marks of innatism. The word "innate" properly refers to that which is within us independently of any external experience—that is, to that which is the object of pure internal experience: "Inasmuch as sensations and inductions can never teach completely universal truths or that which is absolutely necessary, but only that which is, it follows that we have drawn such truths partially from that which is within us." So all ideas are reduced to "intelligible being"—to the "object of pure understanding" which is the self, constituted by inner experience. "The notion that I have of myself and of my thoughts, and consequently of being, substance, action, and identity, comes from an inner experience" or from "reflective acts," as he says elsewhere (*Monadology,* 30). And in a letter to Sophia Charlotte, he adds the following restriction to the Scholastic adage: "With the exception of the understanding itself or *whoever understands."*

But inner experience now designates something greater than the natural light of reason: it signifies everything which is naturally in us and which we see there when our vision is not obscured by the needs and inclinations that come from the body. Alongside reason is instinct, constituted by confused but innate knowledge: "One must pursue joy and avoid sadness," for instance—natural sentiments whose reasons are unknown and which are "difficult to untangle . . . along with customs, though it is generally possible for us to do so." Here, as in the thinking of Descartes, the innateness of an idea does not exclude its being indistinct.

XII *The Existence of Bodies*

Monads are the only substantial realities that exist in the universe. We saw how Leibniz removed substantial existence from the exterior world, such as it was conceived by the Cartesians. But did he deprive it of every mode of existence? We ought first to note that the mind, though "windowless," is quite certain, even in the absence of the complicated machinery of the Cartesian proof, that something exists in the outer world. Descartes knew only the first of two obvious truths: "I think, and there is great variety in my thoughts." For the second truth "proves that there is something other than ourselves which is the cause of the variety of the things that appear to us," since one and the same thing cannot be the cause of the changes within it. The representation of the external world then is to me a "well-founded phenomenon," founded on the existence of the substantial diversity of monads outside ourselves. But it is also by inner characteristics that "real phenomena" are distinguishable from the 'imaginary phenomena" of dreams: first, if we consider the phenom-enon in itself, by its animation, its multiplicity (the real phenome-non is endowed not with one but with several sensible qualities), and its permanence or integrity in time; then, if we consider other phenomena, by its agreement with prior phenomena, by the mutual agreement of minds, and by success in the prediction of phenomena. These we should note, are the criteria mentioned by Descartes: they are derived from the Academic and Skeptic schools of antiquity, and Leibniz brings out their true worth when he says that they provide moral certainty rather than metaphysical certainty.

If we examine, looking beyond things themselves, the order in which they coexist and succeed one another, we obtain space and time. Far from being realities antecedent to things or receptacles in which they are contained, as the Newtonians thought, they are ideal things possible and relative only to the beings of which they are the order. "I hold that space is something purely relative, like time, to an order of coexistences, just as time is an order of successions," Leibniz wrote to Clarke. "For space indicates in terms of possibility an order of things that exist at the same time in so far as they exist together, without entering into their ways of existing. And when we see several things together, we notice the order among the things themselves."

XIII   *Ethics*

From his theology and monadism Leibniz deduces a moral phi-losophy. "I submit," he wrote to Conring as early as 1670, "that ethics may require no more than a demonstration that the existence of God and the immortality of the soul are probable or at least pos-sible." Why? On one hand he assumes with Carneades that justice without an appropriate utility, whether present or future, is utter folly; on the other hand he sees clearly that justice seeks the gen-eral good or the good of the society to which we belong. Only a providential theology can resolve the problem of the just corre-spondence of virtue and utility—the problem attacked by Cicero in the *De officiis*—and "we cannot demonstrate with precision that man must do what is just unless we first demonstrate that there is a perpetual [avenger] of the public interest, that is, God and that inasmuch as he is clearly not always the avenger in this life, there must be another life."

Later, after he had discovered his system of monads and shown that minds are monads of a higher degree—"substances that think and are capable of discovering necessary truths"—he followed the ancient tradition of the Stoics and transmuted his universe into a "universal republic of Minds" ruled over by a monarch (God) whose subjects (ranging from angels to men) are Minds of every type. The law of his city is justice, which consists "in procuring for the world the greatest good that we can; this is certain [to contribute to our happiness] if there is a Providence that governs all things." These are formulas which we should not forget to translate into the language of monadology if we are to understand their full significance. Indeed, it is through a natural law derived from the will of God that each mind in the universe acquires at each instant the maximum of perfection compatible with the whole, but the mind acts consciously while the bare monad is divested of sensation; and the will that thrusts us toward the common utility is illuminated by knowledge of our own nature, with the result that virtue is actually "the inner power that keeps man from being diverted from the right path to happiness by the passions of his soul." Such is the *fatum christianum;* in a "good sense" *fatum* means the decree of Providence. "And those who submit to the decree through knowledge of divine perfections, of which the love of God is a consequence, do not (like the pagan philosophers) simply resign themselves to patient endurance but are even happy in the knowledge that whatever God ordains is for the best." But Leibniz thought that he could escape the *fatum mahometanum,* which denied that the decrees of God were interrelated, as well as quietism and "idle argument" since, in his opinion, knowledge engendered action.

It would seem that the idea of a universal republic should have persuaded Leibniz to accept a universal religion of some kind—a humanism superior to positive religions—but it did not. Theoretically, he tried to show that the positive elements of Christian dogmas were in no way contrary to reason; practically, as we have seen, he conceived a religious organization of the world in which Christians, politically reconciled and united in the same Church, would spread Christian civilization throughout the world. In keeping with his genius, his universalism is not the abstract universalism of the Stoic thinkers; instead, it assumes the most concrete forms and infiltrates the infinite realm of singular political realities.

One of his first works had been an anti-Socinian *Defensio Trinitatis* (about 1665), in which he boasted of having already found "a more profound philosophy" to supply him with precepts which were more applicable to meditation on sacred things and civic affairs as well as to physics, and which would allow him "to lead a tranquil life." Consequently he never separated these three objects: religion, physics, and civic life. He did everything possible to eliminate seemingly wide divergences between the discontinuity of the Christian vision of the universe and his own conception of continuity—for instance, as it was revealed to us in his theory of sin. Other elements of the Christian faith (miracles, transubstantiation) also seemed to interrupt the continuity of nature: the Port-royalist Arnauld objected that Leibniz' monadology excluded miracles, and the Jesuit Des Bosses believed it to be irreconcilable with transubstantiation. Drawing support from his doctrine of infinity, Leibniz defended his view of miracles as follows: we know that when points are indicated on a surface in any manner whatsoever, we can find the equation of the curve that contains them and accounts for their arrangement. Suppose, then, that we have an indefinite series of events and that some of the events obey natural laws as we understand them while others do not—in other words, they are miraculous; we must conceive, in divine infinitude, a law of the series that will embrace both kinds of events. The miraculous events, which interrupt what we call the natural order, have a place in the order of the universe, and their failure to have a place in it would contravene the divine attributes. As for transubstantiation, we saw how Leibniz in his reply to Des Bosses conceived the *substantial bond* to account for the unity of bodies; in transubstantiation the monads correspond to the subsistent bread, which is a "well-founded" phenomenon; but through a miracle the substantial bond of the body of Christ replaces the substantial bond of the bread.

In practice, almost all of Leibniz' activities were directed toward the triumph of Christianity. But he felt that its triumph could not be assured without a return to unity, which should have its beginning in the union of Lutherans and Calvinists,[3] followed by the reuniting of the Protestants in Germany with the Catholic Church. As early as 1673 he discussed the matter with Pellisson, through whom he tried to reach Bossuet, and in 1686 he wrote the *Systema theologicum* in which he proposed a formulary for conciliation. Pellisson died in 1693, but as late as 1701 Leibniz had not lost all hope: "You are right in judging me to be a Catholic at heart . . . ," he wrote to Mme de Brinon. "The essence of Catholicism is not to be in communion with Rome; otherwise those who are excommunicated unjustly would cease to be Catholics in spite of their wishes and without being inculpated in any way. The true, essential communion, which makes us a part of the body of Christ, is charity." In this spirit he tried, for the benefit of Bossuet, to attenuate the importance of doctrinal differences that separated the confessions, pointing out that they originated in the Council of Trent, whose ecumenical character was not even recognized in France, and that they were no more significant than the unending controversies about grace and divine love which did not destroy the unity of the Church within the Roman community. "What prevents reunion is not so much the dogmas as the practices" of the Roman Church. And with a (perhaps unwise) facility he called Bossuet's attention to the Gallican spirit that animated France, to the "limits placed there on the authority of the popes and other pastors." Bossuet also sought unity but on condition that the Protestants simply return to the Roman Church and recognize all of its decisions; unity did not include the variations and differences that Leibniz wished to safeguard.

[3] Cf. "Correspondance inédite," *Revue philosophique*, July, 1934.

Bibliography

I

Texts

Jakob Böhme. *Sämtliche Schriften.* Edited by W. Peuckert. 2 vols. Stuttgart, 1955–61.
———. *Sämtliche Werke.* Edited by K. W. Schiebler. 3d ed. 7 vols. Leipzig, 1923.

Studies

Boutroux, E. "Le philosophe allemand Jacob Boehme," in *Études d'histoire de la philosophie,* Paris, 1897.
Koyré, A. *La philosophie de Jacob Boehme.* Paris, 1929.
———. "Maître Valentin Weigel," *Revue d'histoire et de philosophie religieuse,* 1928.

II to XIII

Texts

Leibniz, Gottfried Wilhelm von. *Sämtliche Schriften und Briefe.* Edited by the Preussische Akademie der Wissenschaften. 40 vols. Berlin, 1923——
———. *Opera philosophica.* Edited by J. E. Erdmann. 2 vols. Berlin, 1839–40.
———. *Die philosophischen Schriften.* Edited by C. Gerhardt. 7 vols. Berlin, 1875–90.
———. *Die mathematischen Schriften.* Edited by C. Gerhardt. 7 vols. Berlin, 1849–63.
———. *Opuscules et fragments inédits.* Edited by L. Couturat. Paris, 1903.
———. *Textes inédits d'après les manuscrits de la bibliothèque de Hanovre.* Edited by G. Grua. 2 vols. Paris, 1948.
———. *Opuscula philosophica selecta.* Edited by P. Schrecker. Paris, 1939.
———. *Philosophical Papers and Letters.* Translated by L. E. Loemker. 2 vols. Chicago, 1956.

————. *Selections*. Edited by Philip P. Wiener. Reprinted: New York, 1959.

————. *Discourse on Metaphysics*. Translated by P. G. Lucas and L. Grint. Manchester, 1953.

————. *Monadology and Other Philosophical Writings*. Translated by Robert Latta. Reprinted: Oxford, 1948.

————. *New Essays Concerning Human Understanding*. Translated by A. G. Langley. 3d ed. La Salle, Ill., 1949.

————. *The Leibniz-Clarke Correspondence*. Translated by H. G. Alexander. Manchester, 1956.

————. *Theodicy*. Translated by E. M. Huggard. London, 1952.

Studies

Barber, W. H. *Leibniz in France from Arnauld to Voltaire*. Oxford, 1955.

Brindly, H. W. *Lectures on the Philosophy of Leibniz*. Oxford, 1949.

Carr, H. W. *Leibniz*. New ed. New York, 1960.

Joseph, H. W. B. *Lectures on the Philosophy of Leibniz*. Oxford, 1949.

Lovejoy, A. O. *The Great Chain of Being*. Reprinted: Cambridge, Mass., 1948.

Martin, Gottfried. *Leibniz: Logic and Metaphysics*. Translated by K. J. Northcott and P. G. Lucas. New York, 1964.

Meyer, R. W. *Leibniz and the Seventeenth-century Revolution*. Translated by J. P. Stern. Cambridge, 1952.

Saw, R. L. *Leibniz*. London, 1954.

Yost, R. M. *Leibniz and Philosophical Analysis*. Berkeley, Calif., 1954.

II

Studies

Baruzi, J. *Leibniz et l'organisation religieuse de la terre*. Paris, 1907.

Belaval, Y. *Leibniz critique de Descartes*. Paris, 1960.

Burgelin, P. *Catalogue critique des manuscrits de Leibniz*. Poitiers, 1914–24.

————. *Commentaire du Discours de Métaphysique de Leibniz*. Paris, 1959.

Daville, L. *Leibniz historien*. Paris, 1909.

————. "Le séjour de Leibniz à Paris," *Archiv für Geschichte de Philosophie*, 1922.

Friedmann, G. *Leibniz et Spinoza*. 4th ed. Paris, 1946.

Harnack, A. *Geschichte der preussischen Akademie der Wissenschaften*. Berlin, 1900. Vol I.

Ravier, E. *Bibliographie des œuvres de Leibniz*. Alcan, 1937.

Robinet, A. *Malebranche et Leibniz, relations personnelles*. Paris, 1955.

Stein, L. *Leibniz und Spinoza*. Berlin, 1890.

III

Studies

Balaval, Y. *Pour connaître la pensée de Leibniz.* Paris, 1959.
Boutroux, E. "Notice sur la vie et les œuvres de Leibniz, suivie d'une note de H. Poincaré sur les Principes de la mécanique dans Descartes et dans Leibniz," in Leibniz, *Monadologie,* Paris, Delagrave.
————. "Introduction a l'étude des nouveaux essais," in Leibniz, *Nouveaux Essais,* Book I, Paris, Delagrave.
————. *La philosophie allemande au XVIIe siècle.* Paris, 1929.
Cassirer, E. *Leibniz's System in seinen wissenschaftlichen Grundlagen.* Marburg, 1902.
Couturat, L. *La logique de Leibniz.* Paris, 1901.
Fischer, K. *Gottfried Wilhelm Leibniz.* 5th ed. Heidelberg, 1920.
Halbwachs, M. *Leibniz.* 2d ed. Paris, 1929.
Hannequin, A. *Quae fuerit prior Leibnitii philosophia ante 1672.* Paris, 1895.
Mahnke, D. "Leibniz als Begründer de symbolischen Mathematik," *Isis,* 1927.
Moreau, J. *L'univers leibnizien.* Paris, 1956.
Olgiati, F. *Il significato storico di Leibniz.* Milan, 1930.
Russell, Bertrand. *A Critical Exposition of the Philosophy of Leibniz.* 2d ed. London, 1937.

IV

Studies

Dunan, C. "Leibniz et le mécanisme," *Annales de philosophie chrétienne,* 1910.
Guéroult, M. *Dynamique et métaphysique leibniziennes.* Paris, 1934.
Hannequin, A. "La philosophie de Leibniz et les lois du mouvement," *Revue de métaphysique,* 1906.
Helmholtz, H. "Zur Geschichte des Princips der kleinsten Action," *Sitzungsberichte der berliner Akademie der Wissenschaften,* 1887, pp. 225 ff.

V

Studies

Couturat, L. "Sur la métaphysique de Leibniz, avec un opuscule inédit," *Revue de métaphysique,* 1902.

Jalabert, J. *La théorie leibnizienne de la substance.* Paris, 1947.
Werckmeister, W. *Der leibnizsche Substanzbegriff.* Halle, 1899.

VI

Studies

Albrich, C. "Leibniz's Lehre des Gefühls," *Archiv für die gesamte Psychologie,* XVI.
Dillmann, E. *Eine neue Darstellung der leibnizschen Monadenlehre.* Leipzig, 1891.
Penjon, A. *De infinitato apud Leibnitium.* Paris, 1878.
Rulf, J. *Die Apperzeption im philosophischen System des Leibniz.* (Dissertation) Bonn, 1900.
Vallier, C. A. *De possibilibus apud Leibnitium.* Bordeaux, 1882.

VII

Studies

Iwanacki, J. *Leibniz et les démonstrations mathématiques de l'existence de Dieu.* Paris, 1934.
Rodier, G. "Sur une des origines de la philosophie de Leibniz [Plotinus]," *Revue de métaphysique,* 1902. Reprinted in *Études de philosophie grècque.*
Zymalkowski, N. *Die Bedeutung der prästabilierten Harmonie im Leibnizschen System.* (Dissertation) Erlangen, 1905.

VIII

Studies

Cresson, A. *De libertate apud Leibnitium.* Paris, 1903.
Winhold, W. *Über den Freiheitsbegriff und seine Grundlagen bei Leibniz.* (Dissertation) Halle, 1912.

IX

Studies

Blondel, M. *De Vinculo substantiali et de substantia composita apud Leibnitium.* Paris, 1893.

Bois-Reymond, E. du. "Über leibnizsche Gedanken in der neueren Natur-wissenschaft," *Monatsberichte der berliner Akademie der Wissenschaften,* 1870, pp. 835 ff.
Peters, H. "Leibniz als Chemiker," *Archiv für die Geschichte der Natur-wissenschaft und der Technik,* 1916, pp. 85 ff.

X

Study

Hartenstein, G. "Lockes Lehre der menschlichen Erkenntnis im Vergleich mit der leibnizschen Kritik derselben," *Abhandlungen der sächsischen Gesellschaft der Wissenschaften, X* (1865), 411 ff.

XI

Studies

Van Biéma, E. *L'espace et le temps chez Leibniz et chez Kant.* Paris, 1903.
Volp, W. *Die Phenomenalität der Materie bei Leibniz.* (Dissertation) Erlangen, 1903.

XII

Study

Nathan, B. *Über das Verhaltnis der leibnizschen Ethik zu Metaphysik und Theologie.* (Dissertation) Jena, 1918.

XIII

Studies

Grua, G. *Jurisprudence universelle et théodicée selon Leibniz.* Paris, 1953.
———. *La justice humaine selon Leibniz.* Paris, 1956.

JOHN LOCKE AND
ENGLISH PHILOSOPHY

1 *Life and Work of Locke*

JOHN LOCKE (1632–1704), the son of a small land-
owner and attorney from Wrington, near Bristol, was sixteen when
the civil war began and his father enlisted in the army supporting
the parliamentary side. From 1652 to 1658 he was a student at
Oxford, where he took courses normally associated with prepara-
tion for service as a clergyman; in 1658, however, his interest
shifted to medicine and he completed courses in this field, but
without ever receiving the degree of doctor. In 1666 he formed close
ties with Lord Ashley, afterward Earl of Shaftesbury, whose tormented political life had its repercussions on Locke. He resided in
France on two different occasions, first in 1672 and later between
1675 and 1679, when he spent a year at Montpellier for the sake
of his delicate health; but his second period of residence in France
was prolonged by the disgrace of the Earl of Shaftesbury. In 1684
he had to leave England once again. Shaftesbury failed in his attempt to provoke a revolution and had to seek refuge in Holland
(where he soon died), and Locke, suspected by those in power,
decided that he in turn should make his way to Holland, where he
remained until the Revolution of 1688. Following his return to
England in 1689, he declined, primarily on account of his health,

267

the post offered him by the new king—the embassy to the Elector of Brandenburg—and accepted the office of Commissioner of Appeals. Concerned especially with religious and political as well as economic questions (it was then that he wrote *Some Considerations on the Consequences of the Lowering of Interest, and Raising the Value of Money*),[1] he also had to reply to numerous polemics. He retired to Oates, not far from his friends Lord and Lady Masham (daughter of the philosopher Cudworth), and remained there until his death.

In 1670 Locke, then thirty-eight, had been Shaftesbury's personal physician since 1667, and there was nothing as yet to suggest his philosophical vocation. A friend of the physician Sydenham, with whom he collaborated, and a member of the Royal Society since 1668, he had written two short medical treatises—*Anatomica* (1668) and *De arte medica* (1669), in which he stated "there is no knowledge worthy of the name except knowledge that leads to some new, useful invention. Any other speculation is an idle pursuit." General theories are injurious because they check and stabilize knowledge; only special hypotheses are useful—in apprehending immediate causes. In addition, he had reflected on the political and religious questions that were disturbing his country and had written *Sacerdos* and *Reflections on the Roman Republic,* in which he protested the encroachment of the clergy upon the civil authority; *Infallibilis scripturae interpres non necessarius,* in which he advanced the principle that the Bible is sufficient for our salvation; and *An Essay concerning Toleration* (1667), in which he reflected on the tolerance that should be manifested toward nonconformists (Puritans) who had not accepted the Act of Uniformity of Charles II.

In the winter of 1670–1671, following discussions with his friends (among them James Tyrell—the lawyer who was later to contribute to the revolution that overthrew James II and brought William of Orange to the throne—and the physician David Thomas) his

---

[1] The campaigns which he conducted at that time against factitiously raising the value of money culminated in a monetary reform and in the creation of the Bank of England in 1698. Cf. Rodocanachi's communication to the Academy of Moral Sciences, session of July 24, 1933.

thoughts took an unexpected turn. According to Tyrell's testimony, he noticed that it would be impossible for us to establish firmly the "principles of morality and revealed religion" without first examining "our own abilities to see what objects our understandings were, or were not, fitted to deal with." This was the origin of *An Essay concerning Human Understanding,* which does in fact end with a discussion of the certainty of moral truths (IV, 4.7) and of the relation between faith and reason (IV, 18). Although the *Essay* did not appear until 1690, as early as 1671 Locke had written *De intellectu humano* in which the reduction of all of our ideas to simple ideas was presented in the same was as in his *Essay,* which was the fruit of the rare moments of leisure afforded him by his turbulent career during the nineteen-year interval. After 1688 his ideas were accessible through an abridgement of the *Essay* published in Jean Le Clerc's *Bibliothèque universelle et historique.* The second edition (1694) contains many additions (II, xxvii; II, ix, 8; II, xxxiii; IV, xix) and changes (II, xxi; II, xxiii); Coste's French translation (1700), revised by Locke, also includes a number of additions and corrections.

II Political Ideas

The *Essay* was not devoted to speculation for its own sake. For this reason a brief analysis of Locke's political ideas will bring to light the conditions under which he wrote.

Locke struggled all his life against the Anglican theocracy, that is, against two interdependent theses: first, that by divine right the king wields absolute power; second, that the king's power is spiritual no less than temporal, giving him the right to impose on the nation a creed and a form of worship. In this doctrine the royal power appears to be something of a mystery, something pre-established and not susceptible to analysis. To criticize it Locke proceeded as he was to proceed in the study of the understanding. In the *Essay,* as we shall see, he reduces complex ideas to simple factors; here he tries to identify by analysis the simple factors into which the royal power can be divided. In neither case does their historical genesis come under consideration.

His analysis was favored or even made possible by the idea (then current) that since the social state is not natural to mankind but originates in a pact, we must first study, in the abstract, man in his state of nature prior to the pact. Is the state of nature the absence of a standard, as Hobbes maintained, which reduces any idea of justice and injustice to a convention, or is there a *lex insita rationi*—a natural moral law which was imposed prior to the pact? The second view, advocated by those who (following the Stoics) subscribed to the law of nations, is the one adopted by Locke. He accepts as natural law the right of property based on work and consequently limited to the expanse of land a man can cultivate, and paternal authority based on the premise that the family is a natural institution, not a political one. The school that inspired Locke is linked, however, to the doctrine of innatism which he rejects. He maintains that it is possible to demonstrate the rules of justice without recourse to the doctrine of innatism and predicates his demonstration on the commandment of God who established these rules and attached sanctions to them; consequently his demonstration depends on religious views.

The social pact creates no new right. It is an agreement between individuals who join together for the purpose of using their collective force to bring about the execution of natural laws, and who renounce the use of individual force in bringing about their execution. This conception is purely nominalistic and utilitarian; it reduces society to a stabilizing force effective in repressing infractions of the law. It follows that the royal power is subject to precise limitations. Citizens owe obedience to their king only with respect to permanent laws, not with respect to laws improvised from day to day. There are legislatures but they cannot act capriciously; more particularly, they cannot arbitrarily dispose of citizens' property by levying a tax without their consent. In a word, the pact between subject and sovereign is bilateral, and the subject has the right to revolt against any violation of the law. Such is the origin and the nature of royal authority; it has a legal basis and cannot be exercised illegally. The result is the total reversal of the doctrine of Hobbes, and Locke was one of those who gave their intellectual assent to the Revolution of 1688.

From such considerations the doctrine of toleration was derived. In England the object was not to prevent a spiritual power distinct from the temporal power, as in Roman Catholicism, from encroaching upon the temporal power in the name of eternal salvation for all men; on the contrary, in a country where, since the time of Elizabeth I, "the religion of the subject was determined by a law regularly debated in a parliament composed for the most part of laymen, statesmen, and businessmen," [2] the object was to determine whether the civil authority created by the pact could regulate the spiritual life of the people. Under these conditions Locke refused to grant absolute toleration. The sovereign is indifferent to the beliefs of his subjects except when they are expressed by acts contrary to the purpose of the political society; the king will therefore prohibit "papism," which allows the intervention of a foreign government, and will repress atheism since belief in God is the principle of the certainty of natural laws.

III The Doctrine of the "Essay": Criticism of Innate Ideas

The *Essay* contains the doctrine which was to establish religious and philosophical toleration by revealing the nature and limits of human understanding. But before taking up this doctrine we ought to consider one incident that will give us a better insight into its author's intentions. In 1678, while Locke was meditating on his work, Cudworth published *The True Intellectual System of the Universe*. Cudworth, one of the moving spirits of the Cambridge Platonists during this period, maintained that demonstration of the truth of the existence of God is inseparable from the thesis of innate ideas, and that the famous empirical adage, "Nihil est in intellectu quod non prius fuerit in sensu," led directly to atheism. If all science

[2] C. Bastide, *John Locke*, p. 131.

or knowledge is merely the informing of our minds by things situated outside us, he said (following the line of argument used in the tenth book of Plato's *Laws*), the world has to exist before there can exist a notion and knowledge of the world; nor can knowledge and intelligence precede the world as its cause; but this thesis is so fallacious, he wrote, that if carried to its logical conclusion it would exclude from existence not only reason and intelligence but even the faculty of feeling, for this faculty cannot be apprehended by the senses. Cudworth's thesis, if it were true, would upset Locke's whole system, for it was on the hypothesis of sensationalism that Locke sought to show the existence of the understanding and its nature, and to prove the existence of God. Why was the empirical hypothesis the only possible one? Because in order to have the right idea of things we must introduce the mind to their inflexible nature and to their inalterable relations, and not strive to introduce things to our prejudices. Innatism, however, begins with what is assumed to be immediate, inward knowledge and obviously accommodates all of our individual prejudices; thus the main theses that ought to bring us peace of mind—the theory of the understanding and the existence of God—are assumed to be inseparable from our prejudices.

The internal structure of the *Essay* is largely explained by Locke's concern to reply to the Cambridge Platonists, although he never names his adversaries. In Book I, which is a criticism of the doctrine of innate ideas, the long chapter on the existence of God and the chapter on enthusiasm complement and support each other.

In Book I, Locke clearly indicates his intention: to show that innatism is the doctrine of the prejudiced. If he were writing for unprejudiced readers, he would not criticize the doctrine itself and "it would be sufficient" for him to show "how men, barely by the use of their natural faculties, may attain to all the knowledge they have, without the help of any innate impressions, and may arrive at certainty without any such original notions or principles." But this is one of the most dangerous of all doctrines in that it leads to the proclamation of infallibility (I, ii. 20; I, iii. 24), that is, to an irreducible certainty based on nothing except the affirmation of an individual. He therefore sees in innatism a kind of individually inspired dogmatism characterized by groundless affirmations. For if there were truly innate principles, they would have to exist in all men, universally and eternally. But if we examine individually first the speculative principles (the principles of identity and contradiction) and then the practical principles ("Do unto others as you would have them do unto you," etc.), we see that they are known to few people, even in enlightened circles. Nor are they of any use. To decide that sweet is not bitter we need only perceive the ideas of sweet and bitter; we see immediately their dissimilarity, without having to resort to the principle that it is impossible for a thing to be different from itself.

This criticism of innatism is supplemented by the tenth chapter of Book IV in which the existence of God is proved by the simple use of natural faculties, without resort to innate ideas. This is a variety of proof *a contingentia mundi,* which, unlike ontological proofs, does not imply a preconceived notion of God; this notion is constructed with the proof itself. According to Locke, the existence of the contingent being that I am implies an eternal, omnipotent being who is also intelligent since he created in me the faculty of knowing, and who is the creator of matter, since he created my mind and it was much easier for him to have created matter. This proof alone can lead us to an exact, constant notion of the Divinity. Conversely, the notion that men have of the Divinity in the absence of such proof is confused and incoherent. There are even savage tribes who have no idea of God; among the common people the idea of God is suffused with anthropomorphism.

Finally, the chapter on enthusiasm (IV, xix, introduced in the second edition of the *Essay*) is a criticism of all of the individual illusions which in religious circles are ascribed to divine inspiration. This chapter corresponds to Malebranche's chapter on vivid imaginations and to Spinoza's *Theologicopolitical Treatise.* We should also note that in England the disease was endemic; it caused countless sects to spring up, and Locke recognized its danger more clearly than anyone else. He called attention to the contrast between such an imaginative, personal religion and the rational character of Christianity (in *The Reasonableness of Christianity as delivered in the Scriptures,* 1695), and he reduced all of the essential dogmas of Christianity to that which can be demonstrated by reason. It is clear that his condemnation of enthusiasm in religion corresponds to his condemnation of innatism in philosophy.

IV *Simple Ideas and Complex Ideas*

How can he introduce the mind to the inflexible nature of things and to their inalterable relations? Locke's system would be incomprehensible if we did not assume that reflection on the Cartesian doctrine was its source; it is, as his critics pointed out to him, "an idealism." What role do ideas play in his system?

All knowledge consists in the perception of similarity between ideas—yellow is not red, two triangles which have three equal sides are equal, and so forth; this perception is either immediate as in the first case or reducible by demonstration to an immediate perception as in the second. The idea, then, is to knowledge approximately what the term is to the proposition in logic. Ideas themselves are either complex (that is, formed of simple ideas into which they can be analyzed) or simple and irreducible. Locke's exposition is actually the reverse of the order just indicated; he first tries to determine the nature of simple ideas, then how they combine to form complex ideas (Book II), and finally how we perceive the similarity or dissimilarity between ideas (Book IV). We shall now follow the order of his exposition.

Actually his somewhat atomistic approach, which resolves the contents of sense and reflections into ideas, is more complicated than we might at first suppose, whether we consider elements (simple ideas) or their mode of combination. To begin with, the simplicity of an idea does not refer to its intrinsic character: ideas that cannot be communicated to us if we do not have them from experience (bitter, cold) are simple, and the absolute impossibility of our originating within us a single new simple idea (whereas we do form complex ideas) marks the limits of our knowledge. Our simple ideas are divided into three classes: simple ideas of sensation —warm, solid, smooth, hard, bitter, extension, figure, motion; simple ideas of reflection—that is, ideas of the faculties that we find within us, such as memory, attention, will (the word "reflection" designates only our inward perception of these faculties); and simple ideas of both sensation and reflection, such as the ideas of existence, duration, and number.

This is where complications begin: the Cartesian idea is representative; it is an image of things. Is Locke's idea also representative? Undoubtedly, for as we shall see, he raised the question of the value of representations and asked, at least with respect to simple ideas of sensation, which ideas actually represented the external world. But then such ideas would play two roles: on one hand they would be the points of departure or ultimate elements which constitute our knowledge and, by the same token, they would all be equal; on the other hand they would represent material things and, like intermediaries between us and things, would be quite unequal in value. As a physicist, Locke in fact adopted the conclusions of Boyle's mechanics: only extension, figure, solidity, and motion, together with the ideas of existence, time, and number, are "primary qualities" which represent to us things as they are. Colors, sounds, and tastes are "secondary qualities" produced in us by the impression made on our senses by the several motions of bodies so small that we are unable to perceive them. We should note that even with respect to primary qualities Locke failed by far to achieve the certainty of Descartes. To represent the external world the physicist uses these ideas because he cannot use others; for example, if we make impulsion the cause of motion, this is only because it is "impossible to conceive that body should operate on *what it does not touch* . . . or, when it does touch, operate any other way than by motion" (II, viii, 11; first edition); but that "impossibility" is not an irreducible objection to the physics of central forces which posits attraction as the cause of motion. Furthermore, the idea of extension is far from clear to Locke: the cohesion of bodies cannot be explained by it, and infinite divisibility is contradictory; and he is hardly faithful to Descartes when he states (II, xxiii, 16) that "by the complex idea of extended, figured, colored, and all other sensible qualities which is all that we know of it, we are as far from the idea of the substance of body as if we knew nothing at all." Thus simple ideas, even those of the primary qualities, ought not to be taken for the real elements of things.

The double interpretation of ideas of sensation—as the ultimate elements of knowledge and as representatives of the real world—did not persist among the "idealists" who followed Locke. Berkeley, among others, was decidedly opposed to it; he considered ideas only from the first point of view and abandoned the notion that they were representative.

By positing, along with simple ideas of sensation, simple ideas of reflection, and by conceding that our knowledge of the faculties of the mind cannot be reduced to our knowledge of sensible things, Locke eliminates the traditional link (as found in Hobbes) between empiricism and sensationalism. By means of the kind of inner experience which he called *reflection,* as original as external experience, he answers the strongest objections of the Cambridge Platonists against the atheism of the empiricists; and we saw how he used inner experience to demonstrate the existence of God without recourse to innate ideas.

Locke's speculation concerning complex ideas was to entail the elimination of vain philosophical discussions, for he showed the true origin of the ideas that were at issue. It is obvious that his "simple ideas" do not fit into the categories which traditional philosophy used to classify the objects of knowledge; they are neither substances nor modes of substance. One of Locke's most important innovations is that he considers such categories not as primary ideas but, as we shall see, as combinations of simple ideas.

Complex ideas are separated into two groups: those in which simple ideas are combined in the idea of one thing (the idea of gold or the idea of man), and those in which combined ideas continue to represent distinct but united things (the idea of "filiation" which unites the idea of son and father, and in general all ideas of relation). The first group is itself divided into two classes: ideas of modes which are the ideas of things that cannot subsist by themselves (a triangle or a number); and ideas of substances which are the ideas of things that subsist by themselves (a man). Modes themselves are divided into simple modes in which the same simple idea is combined with itself (for example, number which is a combination of units, and space or duration, each of which is a combination of homogeneous parts); and complex or mixed modes composed of different kinds of simple ideas, such as beauty or the idea of a murder.

Locke's composition (or deduction) of categories allowed him to resolve many controversial problems, among them the three problems of infinity, power, and substance which only theories of innate ideas were thought to be capable of resolving.

According to Locke, infinity is a simple mode since it consists of repetition of units of the same kind (number, time, or space); it differs from finitude only in that no limit is assigned to this repetition. Therefore it is not true that the infinite is prior to the finite, that the finite is a limitation of the infinite, that we conceive an infinity of perfection different from the infinity of quantity that we have just examined; the infinitude of God, in particular is conceived by us only as a number or an unlimited extension of his acts relative to the world. Of course, divine infinitude is different; actual infinity, which is realized, is in no way our idea of infinity, which is endless progression; similarly, eternity is not the endless duration which we conceive, for "what lies beyond our positive idea *towards* infinity lies in obscurity, and has the indeterminate confusion of a negative idea, wherein I know I neither do nor can comprehend all I would, it being too large for a finite and narrow capacity" (II, xvii, 15).

Analysis of the idea of power and of the idea of freedom which depends on it should, in Locke's way of thinking, put an end to the endless controversies over this question. The idea of power is a simple mode formed by the repeated experiencing of certain changes that we have noted in sensible things and in ourselves. When we perceive that our ideas change under the influence of sensory impressions or of voluntary choices, and when in addition we conceive the possibility of a similar change in the future, we have the idea of active power in that which produces change and of passive power in that which undergoes change. But in general the idea of active power is a reflective idea; it derives from the change that our will produces in bodies. The will, then, is an active power. Freedom is also an active power, but of another kind. It is the power to act or not to act according to the choice made by the will: a paralytic, for instance, who wishes to move his legs is not free to do so. To ask if the will is free is therefore to ask an absurd question; it is to ask if one power is invested with another power—a senseless question since a power can belong only to an agent. But we can ask if the agent who has the power to act on the basis of his knowledge and who is free—that is, has the power to perform or not to perform an action depending on whether he wishes to do so—is in addition free to will or not to will whatever is in his power: that question can be resolved through analysis of the motives of will. We are induced to will by uneasiness or dissatisfaction caused by privation of a good, but our uneasiness is not proportionate to the excellence of the good. Further, we have the power to compare one good with another and, on the basis of our examination, to suspend actions that would produce uneasiness. Freedom, then, is not a freedom of indifference but consists in making voluntary decisions on the basis of judgment rather than desire (II, xxi).

The question of the nature of substance (II, xxiii) is one of the most controversial. Substance was in any case considered by all to be the paradigm of primary realities, yet, no philosopher had been able to state clearly what he understood by this substratum of all attributes. Locke tried to resolve the question by showing that substance is a false simple idea—a complex idea mistaken for a simple idea. Here Locke's thought is not easy to penetrate, and its simplicity is illusory. The substance of gold seems at first glance to consist of simple ideas which are shown by experience always to be grouped together (yellowness, fusibility, ductility, great weight) and which, collectively, are always referred to by the same name. But in this case a substance would not differ from a mixed mode, which is also a constant group of simple ideas designated by a single name. Besides, Locke objects to being criticized for mistaking simple ideas for the real elements of things since it is in fact impossible for the mind to imagine these simple ideas as existing by themselves, apart from a substance in which they are inherent. If we use a single name to designate their group, it is because we believe they belong to a single thing and are actually linked to it in a union that constitutes a whole. For example, gold must have an intimate constitution—a real essence which, if known, would explain the relation of its properties. Locke states emphatically his belief in the existence of substance: "We cannot conceive how [simple ideas of sensible qualities] should subsist alone." But he states no less emphatically that we have no idea of this substance: to explain the cause underlying the relation of simple ideas—Aristotle's quiddity—is beyond our understanding, which can add nothing to these ideas beyond what we discover through sensation and reflection. Substance then is to Locke something like actual infinity: it exists, but we do not know what it is, and the only kind of investigation open to us is the experimental investigation of coexisting qualities. This is all we need to separate body (a mass of simple ideas of sensation) and mind (a mass of simple ideas of reflection); but it is not all we need to resolve the question of determining whether matter can or cannot think, for since we know absolutely nothing about what it is, we cannot be sure that the power of thinking is incompatible with its nature. That is why both Descartes, who assumed that man had knowledge of the intimate mechanism of things, and the Scholastics, with their substantial forms, attributed to man knowledge that belonged only to God or to angels.

Every idea, according to Locke, is representative. This is equally true of complex ideas and of simple ideas. To what extent do they correspond to the reality of things? Some ideas—ideas of substances —are always incomplete, for we can never know which of their unknown powers will be revealed to us by experience. Others, on the contrary, are always complete; these are the mixed or complex ideas that we have formed by uniting arbitrarily certain simple ideas—gratitude, justice, and all moral ideas can be nothing other than what we conceive them to be since they exist only by our conception. Furthermore, if we attribute to words that designate ideas the sense ascribed to them by unanimous convention, the idea of a substance can be complete when we think of everything designated by the word used to express it, and the idea of a complex mode incomplete if we omit an element of its conventional meaning. In the same way an idea is said to be true both when it represents something real and when we think of the sum of the characteristics that constitute the conventional sense attributed to it. In the first instance, the idea of a complex mode is always true since it has no reality other than the notion that we fashion of it, and the idea of substance in general is always false in the sense that it never expresses real essences; and it is sometimes false when it unites simple ideas shown by experience to be separated or separates ideas which are in reality united. In the second instance, when words are not given their exact meaning, ideas of individual substances are almost always true, the idea of mixed modes often false.

Finally, the analysis of ideas affords a definite solution to the famous question of universals. When and how can we legitimately say "This is lead" or "This is a horse"? If the universal term designates a real essence the answer is simple: Never. For if we are dealing with real essences we can never know precisely when a thing ceases to be of the species of horse or of lead. If, however, it designates a nominal essence fashioned from a collection of simple ideas associated with a name, we can know with certainty when such a proposition is legitimate and with even greater certainty as the convention becomes more firmly established.

But is this nominal essence in turn constructed arbitrarily by the mind? No, for according to Locke, general ideas, like all other ideas, are representative. In a chapter on the association of ideas (II, xxxiii), which corresponds to Malebranche's book on the imagination, Locke manages from his own point of view to separate general ideas that result from individual imaginings from those that are truly valid. Here experience and usage are our masters. Mixed modes, such as our moral or legal ideas (the idea of murder), are formed quite freely but not haphazardly; given social conditions (the existence of certain laws or customs) force us to choose certain combinations. Similarly, in the formation of general ideas of substances we not only conform with usage but must also follow nature and link together only simple ideas which are constantly linked together in experience; the last condition is possible and our general ideas can be valid only if there is a certain permanence in nature. The general idea of substance, then, is of human workmanship but founded on the nature of things. This correspondence between our ideas and nature raised many questions in the minds of Berkeley and Hume.

v *Knowledge*

Knowledge is the perception of agreement or disagreement among our ideas, expressed in a judgment. The bonds between our ideas can be of three sorts: *identity* or *diversity, relation* (there is a host of relations, such as father and son, greater and smaller, equal and unequal, similar and dissimilar), and *coexistence*. But identity and coexistence are merely singular instances of relation. Knowledge is therefore the perception of a relation. By definition knowledge is always certain, and what is commonly referred to as faith, belief, or probability always falls short of knowledge, which can nevertheless be either immediate—as when we have intuitive perception of agreement or disagreement—or mediate, as when we apprehend the relation of agreement or disagreement only through a demonstration that gradually brings us nearer to an intuitive perception.

But Locke identifies still a fourth sort of knowledge, "that of actual real existence agreeing to any idea." It is clear that the perception of existence cannot be reduced to the perception of a relation between two ideas, for existence is not an idea like that of sweetness or bitterness. Moreover, Locke identifies (IV, ix, x, xi) degrees of the certainty we have concerning the existence of real things: by reflection we have intuitive knowledge of our own existence; linked to this is demonstrative knowledge of the existence of God; but "the knowledge of the existence of any other thing, we can have only by sensation." Certainly it is absurd for us to doubt the reality of objects which are capable of producing in us pleasure and pain and which produce the impressions responsible for all of our ideas of sensation, and to doubt impressions that we cannot prevent, and pieces of sensory evidence that confirm one another. But Locke recognizes that such certainty is relative to practical situations in daily life, which do not require a higher degree of certainty.

The duality of these two judgments—of relation and of existence—is clearly illustrated in Locke's handling of the problem of truth. There are two categories of false judgments: in one the relation expressed by language in the proposition does not correspond to the intuitively perceived relation between ideas, and it is easy for us to correct it by returning to intuition; in the other the mistake consists not in perceiving a relation incorrectly but in perceiving it between ideas that do not conform to the real existence of material things. We can perceive with equal certainty relations between fanciful ideas (a hippogriff is not a centaur, for example) and true ideas, but only in the second case do we have real knowledge. It follows that real knowledge implies the union of the two elements that we have separated: the perception of the existence of a relation between ideas and the real existence of an archtype of which an idea is the representation.

From this it follows that there are two different ways of posing the problem of the reality of knowledge, depending upon whether we are considering mixed modes whose ideas, fashioned by the mind under the conditions we have examined, have no archetype other than themselves, or substances whose archetypes are outside us. In the first instance we have absolutely certain knowledge since everything is traceable to relations between notions posited by the mind: these are the mathematical and moral sciences (particularly the juridical sciences) which have the same certainty as mathematics since they are based on equally constant and secure notions. For example, we can use these notions to demonstrate that murder must be punished, and the soundness or our demonstration will equal that of a mathematical theorem. In the second instance experience alone will determine whether the coexistence of ideas in our judgments corresponds to reality.

Thus the dualism that we have noted in Locke from the very beginning—the dualism between the idea as an element of knowledge and the idea as a representation of reality—was finally translated into a radical distinction between ideal sciences and experimental sciences.

The English sage originated the ideological analysis that was to dominate philosophy for a long time: a compromise between a combinatory art which derives all possible knowledge from simple and distinct elements, and an empiricism which determines by experience and custom which elements and which combinations of elements are valid. This analysis reveals the limits of the understanding from two angles: it first eliminates all knowledge not obtainable through combination (such as knowledge of actual infinity, substance, real essence, free will), then all knowledge not justifiable by experience. To confine knowledge within these limits is to assure tolerance and social peace.

VI English Philosophy at the End of the Seventeenth Century

In England the transition from the seventeenth to the eighteenth century was marked by a resurgence of religious philosophy. Locke was the first witness to the intellectual ferment which characterized the eighteenth century. Three currents can be identified: (1) the Platonism of Cambridge; (2) natural religion, represented by Clarke; and (3) criticism of positive religions, as in Toland and Collins.

The oldest of these currents is Cambridge Platonism, which dates from the middle of the seventeenth century. Heirs to the erudite Platonism of the Renaissance, the Cambridge clergy preserved the traditions of Greek culture and evidenced their contempt for Scholasticism throughout the century. Their work is similar to that accomplished by French Oratorians like Father Thomassin. Like him they viewed Platonism not as a theory of mystical knowledge but as a theory of rational knowledge, and in 1670 one of them wrote a refutation of Böhme, whose ideas were being introduced into England. But the Cambridge Platonists, more liberal than Thomassin could be, viewed reason as a natural light which was not dimmed by the Fall and which is the necessary foundation of religion, whose essential dogmas (according to them) are few in number and intelligible to all. Their rationalism, though not mystical, lacks the aridity of Locke's. John Smith (1616–1652) followed Plotinus in ranking the enthusiast above the man who reasons with common notions and in ranking still higher the contemplative or intuitive man—one who, incapable of demonstrating the immortality of his soul logically, sees it in a superior light. Locke, who had been imbued with the liberal spirit of Cambridge (which, according to him, makes reason the judge of divine revelation), nevertheless condemned the innatism and enthusiasm of Cudworth. Still following Plotinus in their criticism of mechanism, Cudworth (1617–1688) and Henry More considered all bodies as having life in different degrees. Leibniz, who also attributed life to all things, was persuaded to take a position against the "plastic natures" posited by Cudworth—true forces which, since they act physically and construct organisms, differ markedly from Leibniz' monads.

The second current—natural religion—is well represented by Samuel Clarke (1675–1729), a London clergyman and a fervent Newtonian who delivered the Boyle lectures against atheism (instituted in his will by the physicist) which resulted in *A Discourse concerning the Being and Attributes of God*. According to its subtitle, the work was written "in answer to Mr. Hobbes, Spinoza . . . and other deniers of natural and revealed religion," and in order to establish the notion of liberty and prove its certainty, in contrast to reason and fate. Clarke attempted to convince unbelievers through reason and sought, setting aside revelation and even the diversity of proofs of the existence of God, to use an unbroken chain of closely connected propositions from which he could deduce successively the existence and attributes of God. Like Locke, he started from the principle that something has existed throughout eternity; from this eternity he then deduced all the attributes of God. He was a Newtonian, and he always found the best answers to materialism in Newton's *The Mathematical Principles of Natural Philosophy*. "The materialists," he wrote to Leibniz, with whom he corresponded frequently in 1715, "suppose that the structure of things is such that everything can arise from the mechanical principles of matter and motion, from necessity and fate; the mathematical principles of philosophy show on the contrary that the state of the universe (the constitution of the sun and the planets) is such that it can arise only from a free, intelligent cause." His identifying Newton with natural religion and his opposition to mechanism are important in the history of philosophy. Leibniz was trying vainly to demonstrate that his own mechanism could accommodate both theism and freedom.

The third current—free thought—which appeared almost surreptitiously at first, at the beginning of the century, among sects of materialists and "moralists," developed vigorously after the Revolution of 1688. We find in Toland (1670–1722) all of the themes that sustained the anti-Christian polemic during the eighteenth century: the diatribe against priests who allied themselves with the civil magistrate in order to delude the people and who invented dogmas such as those of the immortality of the soul in order to consolidate their power. He contrasted their religion with primitive Christianity —that of the Nazarenes and Ebionites, grounded solely on reason, with neither tradition nor priests. Moreover, in his *Pantheisticon* he advocated a pure mechanism—an eternal world endowed with spontaneous motion which leaves no room for chance, a theory of materialism which makes thought a motion of the brain. Anthony Collins (1676–1729) in *A Discourse of Free-Thinking, Occasioned by the Rise and Growth of a Sect Called Free-Thinkers* (1713) protested especially against the extravagances of the Bible and its miracles which were merely frauds, against the absurdity and incoherence of its official interpreters who, under the pretext of setting aside dangerous opinions and protecting him from error, prevented man from using his own judgment. Collins' *Remarks on a—Pretended—Demonstration of the Immateriality and Natural Immortality of the Soul* [3] is a reply to the letter which Clarke wrote against the theologian Dodwell, who maintained in 1706 that "the soul is a principle which is naturally mortal but which is rendered immortal by the will of God to punish or reward man." In his letter Collins showed the union of materialism and the sensationalist doctrine of knowledge: "Since thought is a consequence of the action of matter on our senses, we have every reason to conclude that it is a property or affection of matter occasioned by the action of matter."

Such were the three forms of rationalism prevalent at the beginning of the eighteenth century: the rationalism inspired by the Cambridge Platonists, the rationalism of Clarke, and critical rationalism. Shaftesbury (1671–1713), grandson of Locke's protector, set out on an independent course which drew its inspiration from the Cambridge Platonists and stressed the affective, sentimental, and aesthetic elements in their teachings. He maintained, contrary to Locke, that there is in man an innate moral sense which is love of order and beauty—an order which is expressed in the universe and society, and which has its perfection in God; natural affections whose development is responsible for all of the unhappiness of men. This view of universal order, in which apparent disorders disappear, provided a solution to the problem of evil—one which Leibniz recognized as being similar to his own optimism. But Shaftesbury was careful to call attention in his *Letter concerning Enthusiasm* (1708) to the difference between the false enthusiasm of the fanatic (observable in the English sects of his period) and true enthusiasm,

[3] Published in English as *A Letter to the Learned Mr. Henry Dodwell; Containing Some Remarks* . . . (2d ed., 1709) and in French under the title *Essai sur la nature et la destination de l'âme humaine* (London, 1769).

which is the awareness of a divine presence in the artist or the religious man. The letter affirms the preeminence of morality over religion. "This science," he added in *Soliloquy* (1710), "judges religion itself, examines inspiration, tests prophecies, distinguishes miracles; the sole standard is derived from moral rectitude." [4] On the whole, his thought resembles a commentary on Diotima's discourse in the *Symposium* and, after so much dry dialectic, is singularly refreshing.

[4] Quoted by A. Leroy, French translation of the *Letter*, p. 263, note.

Bibliography

I to V

Texts

Locke, John. *Works.* 3 vols. London, 1714. 10th ed. 10 vols. London, 1801.
———. *The Philosophical Works.* Edited by J. A. St. John. 2 vols. London, 1854.
———. *Selections.* Edited by S. P. Lamprecht. Reprinted: New York, 1928.
———. *Essays on the Law of Nature.* Edited and translated by W. von Leyden. Oxford, 1954.
———. *Essay Concerning Human Understanding.* Edited by A. C. Fraser. Oxford, 1894. Repr. 2 vols. New York.
———. *Essay Concerning Human Understanding.* Edited by John W. Yolton. 2 vols. New York, 1961.
———. *Locke on Politics, Religion, and Education.* Edited by Maurice Cranston. New York, 1965.
———. *Two Treatises of Government.* Edited by Thomas I. Cook. New York, 1947.
———. *Locke's Two Treatises of Government.* Edited by Peter Laslett. Cambridge, 1960.
———. *A Letter Concerning Toleration.* Edited by Patrick Romanell. 2d ed. Indianapolis, Ind., 1955.
———. *Original Letters of Locke, Sidney and Shaftesbury.* Edited by T. Forster. 2d ed. London, 1847.

Studies

Aaron, R. I. *John Locke.* 2d ed. Oxford, 1955.
Alexander, S. *Locke.* London, 1908.
Burtt, E. A. *The Metaphysical Foundations of Modern Physical Science.* 2d ed. Reprinted: New York, 1955.
Cox, R. H. *Locke on War and Peace.* Oxford, 1960.
Dewhurst, K. *John Locke (1632–1704), Physician and Philosopher.* London, 1963.
Fowler, Thomas. *Locke.* 2d ed. London, 1892.
Gough, J. W. *John Locke's Political Philosophy.* London, 1950.

Hefelbower, S. G. *The Relation of John Locke to English Deism.* Chicago, 1918.
Hofstadter, Albert. *Locke and Skepticism.* New York, 1936.
Lamprecht, S. P. *The Moral and Political Philosophy of John Locke.* New ed. New York, 1962.
Macpherson, C. B. *The Political Theory of Possessive Individualism.* New York, 1964.
O'Connor, D. J. *John Locke.* London, 1952.
Smith, Norman Kemp. *John Locke.* Manchester, 1933.

I

Studies

Bonno, G. *Relations intellectuelles de Locke avec la France.* Berkeley, Calif., 1955.
Fox, H. R. *The Life of John Locke.* 2 vols. London, 1876.
Cranston, M. *John Locke: A Biography.* London, 1957.
Lord King. *The Life of John Locke with Extracts from his Correspondence, Journals and Commonplace Books.* New ed. 2 vols. London, 1829–30.
Yolton, J. W. *John Locke and the Way of Ideas.* Oxford, 1956.

II

Studies

Bastide, C. *John Locke: Ses théories politiques et leur influence en Angleterre.* Paris, 1906.
Polin, R. *La politique morale de John Locke.* Paris, 1960.

III–V

Studies

Carlini, A. *La filosofia de Locke.* 2 vols. Florence, 1920.
Frazer, A. C. "Locke," in *Encyclopaedia Britannica,* 9th ed., 1882.
———. *Locke.* London, 1890.
———. "John Locke as a Factor in Modern Thought," *Proceedings of the British Academy,* I (1903), 221 ff.
Gibson, J. *Locke's Theory of Knowledge and Its Historical Relations.* New ed. New York, 1960.
Hertling, G. V. *Locke und die Schule von Cambridge.* Freiburg im Breisgau, 1892.

Jackson, R. "Locke's Distinction between Primary and Secondary Qualities," *Mind*, XXXVIII (1920), 56 ff.
Lamprecht, S. P. "Locke's Attack upon Innate Ideas," *Philosophical Review*, XXXVI (1927), 145 ff.
Marion, H. J. *Locke: Sa vie et son œuvre*. 2d ed. Paris, 1893.
Ollion, H. *La philosophie générale de Jean Locke*. Paris, 1908.
Tellkamp, A. *Das Verhältnis John Locke's zur Scholastik*. Münster, 1927.

VI

Texts

Clarke, Samuel. *Works*. Edited by B. Hoadley. 4 vols. London, 1738–42.
Cudworth, Ralph. *The True Intellectual System of the Universe*. 2 vols. London, 1743.
Lord Herbert of Cherbury. *Autobiography*. Edited by S. L. Lee. London, 1886.
———. *De veritate*. Translated by M. H. Carré. Bristol, 1937.
———. *De religione laici*. Translated by H. R. Hutcheson. New Haven, Conn., 1944.
More, Henry. *Opera omnia*. 3 vols. London, 1679.
———. *Philosophical Writings*. Edited by F. I. MacKinnon. New York, 1925.
The Cambridge Platonists. Edited by E. T. Campagnac. London, 1901.

Studies

Albee, Ernest. "Clarke's Ethical Philosophy," *Philosophical Review*, XXXVII (1928), 304 ff. and 403 ff.
Cassirer, Ernst. *The Platonic Renaissance in England*. Translated by J. P. Pettegrove. London, 1953.
Hutin, S. *Les disciples anglais de Jacob Boehme*. Paris, 1960.
Lantoine, A. *Un précurseur de la franc-maçonnerie, John Toland, suivi de la traduction française du Pantheisticon*. Paris, 1927.
Leroux, E., and A. Leroy. *La philosophie anglaise classique*. Paris, 1952.
Lyon, G. *L'idéalisme anglais au XVIIIe siècle*. Paris, 1888.
Muirhead, J. H. *The Platonic Tradition in Anglo-Saxon Philosophy*. London, 1920.
Passmore, J. A. *Ralph Cudworth: An Interpretation*. Cambridge, 1951.
De Pauley, W. C. *The Candle of the Lord: Studies in the Cambridge Platonists*. New York, 1937.
Pawson, G. P. *The Cambridge Platonists and Their Place in Religious Thought*. London, 1930.
Powicke, F. J. *The Cambridge Platonists*. London, 1926.

Prior, A. N. *Logic and the Basis of Ethics.* Oxford, 1949.

Tulloch, J. *Rational Theology and Christian Philosophy in England in the Seventeenth Century.* 2d ed. 2 vols. Edinburgh, 1872.

Tuveson, E. L. *Imagination as a Means of Grace.* Berkeley, Calif., 1960.

Ward, R. *Life of Henry More.* New ed., edited by M. H. Howard. London, 1911.

BAYLE AND FONTENELLE

1 *Pierre Bayle*

THE PRINCIPAL works of Pierre Bayle (1647–1706), prior to his celebrated *Historical and Critical Dictionary* (1697), date from the grievous period when Protestants were expelled from France or forced to become converts. Bayle himself, who was from a Protestant family and who returned to the reformed religion after he had embraced Catholicism briefly (1669), left the Academy of Sedan where he had been teaching philosophy and, in 1680, fled with several coreligionists, including Pierre Jurieu, to Rotterdam, where he spent the rest of his life. All of his subsequent works—*Diverse Thoughts Written to a Doctor at the Sorbonne on the Occasion of the Comet which Appeared in December MDCLXX* (1681), the *General Criticism of Louis de Maimbourg's History of Calvinism* (1682), and *Philosophical Commentary on These Words of Jesus Christ: Compel Them to Come in* (1686)—are demands for tolerance, but their tone is wholly different. Bayle did not speak as a member of a humble, outlawed sect, nor did he protest, like Jurieu, in the name of a religious truth which was the exclusive property of Calvinism, for his intellectual awareness of the absurdity of intolerance was no less acute than the feeling of revulsion caused by the horror of the religious persecutions. He knew that Calvinism was just as intolerant as Catholicism; all theologians, even when they at first agree to discussion, end like the "converters of France; around 1680 these gentlemen began to offer to discuss their religion with their errant brothers; they promised to hear their doubts, to enlighten them, to instruct them cordially; but after answering two or three times, they would no longer endure contradiction and insisted that anyone who would not accept their explanations was opinionated. That is what they should have said from the beginning, for it is ridiculous to enter into discussion unwilling to listen to an oppenent's reply" (*Dictionary,* article on Rufin, Note C). No matter which side he was on, no theologian observed the law of discussion. Bayle himself found a most implacable enemy in the person of the Protestant minister Jurieu.

How, then, did this spirit evolve? The great metaphysical systems which dominate the seventeenth century conceal the profound interest in history that characterized this period, yet nothing was then more widespread. "For one investigator of physical experiences," writes Bayle, "or for one mathematician, you find a hundred serious students of history and its dependencies." Bayle strongly condemns the "disdainful maxims" of those who scorn historical investigations. Mathematicians may contrast the clarity of their logic with the darkness in which the investigation of human facts leaves us, but Bayle reasons that historical facts can be known with a degree of certainty perfect in its own right; in addition, the historian, in contrast to the mathematician, deals not with beings that are merely "ideas of our soul" and cannot "exist outside our imaginations" but with true realities. Mathematicians, Bayle adds (and here we are bound to recall Leibniz), stress the great ideas of the infinitude of God yielded by the "abstract depths of mathematics"; against this the historians set the priceless knowledge yielded by investigations of the failings and limitations of human reason.

The tendency is obvious: thanks to Bayle, scholars broke out of their narrow fields of investigation and became interested in philosophy. They sought to provide more profound and more important data on the nature of man than had ever been provided by philosophers versed in geometry. As a matter of fact, as he noted in the first draft of his *Dictionary,* Bayle's intention was not to refute factual errors found in the dictionaries and works of historians who had preceded him, by checking their sources, but rather to challenge the validity of the opinions held by theologians and philosophers. He criticized all the great metaphysical systems of his time. He was implacable toward Spinoza, he used blunted weapons against Leibniz who answered him in his *Theodicy,* and he disapproved of the dogmatism of philosophers no less than that of theologians.

What was the nature of Bayle's criticism? It is obvious that he was intrigued by the spectacle of the medley and variety of human opinions, but his interest was not the same, either fundamentally or formally, as that of a skeptic like Montaigne. Bayle belonged to an age of impassioned (and excessive) controversy: never had there been so much dry debate over "grace" or "the way of examination and the way of authority." Bayle himself was a controversialist when he locked horns with Jurieu in defense of tolerance. Moreover, the opinions which were upheld in a controversy were presented in the manner most appropriate to their defense—that is, as established doctrines marked by inner coherence and based on universally accepted principles. It was this form, appropriate to controversy, that Bayle tried to give to the theses which he examined; that is how he tested them, and he rejected them because they did not withstand the test. Leibniz' monadology failed the test because of "all the impossibilities that strike in the imagination"—for example, a substance which is simple and which is nevertheless capable of causing its perceptions to vary spontaneously and of passing from one perception to its opposite in the absence of any external reason. The first step toward putting an end to controversy was to show that neither of the two adversaries understood himself or said anything intelligible.

He was quick to sense not only the slightest incoherence but also relationships between ideas even when these relationships were veiled or dissimulated by the partisan spirit of the controversialists. For example, a considerable part of his *Thoughts on the Comets* is based on the rather explicit assumption of an affinity between miracles officially accepted by the Church and the prediction of future events accepted by the common people on the basis of the appearance of comets; that his method of criticism was effective is obvious. On the thorny question of grace he suggests to adversaries that they cannot fail to understand each other once they agree to examine their doctrines instead of championing their causes: "On the matter of liberty there are only two stands to take. One is to say that all of the distinct causes that converge in the soul confer upon it the power to act or not to act; the other is to say that they make it resolve to act in a certain way that it cannot resist. The first stand is that taken by Molinists, the other that taken by Thomists, Jansenists, and Protestants of the confession of Geneva—three groups who oppose Molinism and *who therefore must have essentially the same dogma*. But the Thomists vehemently insisted that they were not Jansenists, and the Jansenists insisted with equal vehemence that they were not Calvinists on the matter of liberty . . . and all of this for the purpose of avoiding the dire consequences envisioned in case of agreement on some point with either the Jansenists or the Calvinists. On the other hand, there has been no sophism which the Molinists have not used to show that St. Augustine did not teach Jansenism" (*Dictionary,* article on Jansenius, Note C). Bayle likes, however, to separate things which we, because of our prejudices, deem to be indissolubly united. For example, he notes (a then novel idea which was to be of great significance in ethnological investigations) that belief in magic and demonic powers does not imply belief in God; and he was able to cite as evidence the religions of the Far East which were then becoming known in Europe.

This relentless criticism, based on unreserved intellectual sincerity, foils biased opinions by taking individual theses and revealing their inner contradictions or unintelligibility, by showing the affinity that sometimes exists between opposing theses and, by contrast, the arbitrariness of the bond that unites certain affirmations. This relentless manipulation of ideas, this collation of theses is pursued indefatigably (to the unending delight of the reader) throughout the pages of the *Dictionary*.

But was this criticism as widely disseminated as we might at first assume? It was precisely because of its dissemination that Bayle tried to attenuate the significance of his reflections, which are "rather free and hardly conform to ordinary judgments: . . . If a rank, undistinguished layman like me called attention to an error in vast historical collections involving religion or morality, there would be no reason for anyone to be concerned. . . . No one chooses as a guide in such matters an author who speaks only in passing and incidentally, and who, for the very reason that he scatters his sentiments like needles in a haystack, clearly indicates that he does not wish to be followed." Montaigne's ideas, he continues, did not begin to disturb theologians until they were reduced to a system by Pierre Charron.

In reality we find in all of Bayle's criticisms a dialectical movement which always retains its identity and which is singularly effective. It consists in depriving metaphysical and religious theses of any support in human nature or human reason, with the result that Bayle, while pretending always to subscribe to orthodoxy, managed to relegate them solely to the divine authority to which they laid claim. Almost all of the great metaphysical systems since Descartes had implied that certain theological theses were linked to the very nature of human reason: existence and unity of God, Providence, immortality of the soul. At the same time even the most liberal advocates of tolerance were nevertheless reluctant to leave in peace the atheists or materialists whose opinions were thought to be contrary to any moral life. It was this presumed connection between the main religious dogmas and the fundamental needs of reason and morality that Bayle's criticism gradually undid.

In dealing with the existence of God, Bayle said: "On this point there is ample liberty." "Provided that a doctor acknowledges that this existence can be proved by some other means, he is allowed the liberty of criticizing this or that particular proof" (Article on

Zabarella, Note G). In plain language he is saying that there is no universally accepted proof. In fact, the Aristotelian proof by means of the first mover implies the eternity of the world—an unacceptable notion. Furthermore, it can be used to prove a multiplicity of prime movers just as surely as it can be used to prove that there is one God. The Cartesian proof was criticized from all quarters. A doctor from the Sorbonne, L'Herminier, was able freely to reject every Thomist proof and accept only the proof grounded on the order of the universe. On this question, therefore, there was no absolute evidence. Luther's teacher, Biel, had stated moreover that "proofs of the existence of God provided by reason are only probable."

Providence is Bayle's favorite question, the question to which he returns time after time. The problem of theodicy had in effect been stimulating vain discussions for centuries but had never been resolved. The existence of evil could not be reconciled with the existence of an infinitely good and omnipotent principle; either its goodness must be limited if it permitted the existence of evil which it could have prohibited, or its power must be limited if it wished to prohibit evil but could not. Everything said to justify God makes him an absurd despot. To say, for example, that he permits sin in order to manifest his wisdom is to see in him "a monarch who would allow sedition to spread in order to acquire the glory of having brought a remedy." Only Manicheism, with its theory of the two principles, one good and the other bad, could resolve the issue. Thus human reason found itself in a most singular situation: "Who will not marvel at and who will not deplore the destiny of our reason? Take the Manicheans: with a totally absurd and contradictory hypothesis they explain experiences a hundred times better than orthodox thinkers with their righteous, necessary, and uniquely true hypothesis of an infinitely good and omnipotent First Principle" (Art. *Pauliciens,* Note E). Bayle's irony, though veiled, is unmistakable.

Can the immortality of the soul, in its turn, be proven rationally? Pomponazzi's treatise clearly showed that Peripateticism could not prove its immortality: "Here only the system of Descartes has laid down firm principles." But, the Cartesian principle itself (the spirituality of the soul) is not evident to all, and Gassendi's reply to Descartes satisfied many people (Art. *Pomponazzi,* Note F).

It might be alleged in defense of these dogmas that they are indispensable to public morality, but experience reveals that atheists sometimes have good morals and that believers may be criminals. Bayle gave his approval to Pomponazzi's observation "that a great number of rogues and rascals believe in the immortality of the soul while several saints and righteous men do not."

Thoughts on the Comet, in which Bayle repeatedly stressed the existence of ethical principles among atheists, had caused many adversaries to raise their voices against him. "This is because they do not wish to admit that religious motives are by no means our only motives for action," he says; "there are others. The Sadducees who denied the immortality of the soul were more virtuous than the Pharisees who were meticulous in the observation of the law of God" (Art. *Sadducées,* Note E). We would know little about men if we believed that "our morals are corrupted because we doubt or fail to learn that there is another life after this one" (Art. *Sanchez,* Note C). The illusion springs from the assumption that men always act according to their principles, so that it can be demonstrated *a priori* that belief in a future life will serve as a moral restraint. But nothing is so uncommon as consistency in our opinions and practices. Jurieu, for instance, who conceded that our religious beliefs depend on our mental dispositions and tried logically to deduce tolerance since tastes are not open to dispute, proved to be the most intolerant of men. Furthermore, it is wrongly assumed that religious motives are our only motives for action; there are in fact many others—love of praise, fear of infamy, and many more—which are often stronger than religious motives and capable of leading to virtuous actions" (*Dictionary,* ed. of 1715, III, 988).

These few indications reveal the infinite patience with which Bayle pursued his work of removing one by one every prop supporting the metaphysical and religious truths inherent in human nature, every argument adduced to make them a human necessity;

in short, every reason for believing derived from the essence of man. He nevertheless pretended that he was not removing a single true and solid support for religion: what is fallible human reason in comparison with infallible divine authority? Every doubt raised by the problem of theodicy was eliminated by authority: "This is surely the right choice and the true way to remove doubts: God said it, God did it, God permitted it; it is therefore true and just, wisely done, wisely permitted" (Art. *Rufin,* Note C). Recourse to authority and to authority alone is obligatory. Bayle cites, not without approval, this letter from Perrot d'Ablancourt to Patru: "You believe in the immortality of the soul because your reason dictates this course, and I against my judgment. I believe our souls are immortal because our religion commands me to believe in this way. Consider both views and you will probably admit that mine is much better" (Art. *Perrot,* Note I).

Thus he puts metaphysical truths on such a high plane that they no longer have any human interest. Reduced to its own domain, separated from rationality and ethics, isolated in its majesty, religion remained helplessly suspended. Will authority provide a basis for agreement? No, not so long as human judgment intervenes to assess its worth. "Scripture is used to support both sides of a question" (Art. *Semblançay,* Note C). There is no agreement on the interpretation of Scripture. Nicole and the Catholics supported the method of authority which made the Roman Church an infallible interpreter; but who, in the absence of lengthy investigations not accessible to the faithful, can assure us of the unity of this tradition? The method of critical examination, supported by Protestant ministers, itself engendered disputes. Thus there is no human method for evaluating authority. What recourse is there except to believe that men are led to religion by purely irrational means, "some through education and others through grace?" This time any tie between religion and reason has been broken, duly and decisively; religion is wholly divine but it is in no way human. Or perhaps, as we might infer from the first means of access to it—education—religion is after all a mere custom, traceable like other customs to

the accident of birth. Bayle's thought may be expressed in these reflections which he attributes to Nihusius: "When one belongs to a
certain communion by education or birth, the resulting disadvantages are not a legitimate reason for leaving it unless something is
to be gained by the change—a better position, for instance; for what
would we gain by abandoning the communion that has produced us
and shaped us if by leaving it we only exchanged one sickness for
another?" (Art. *Nihusius,* Note H).

Thus Bayle's negative dialectic resulted in tolerance which removed religious conviction from the domain of human disputes,
but it had as its positive counterpart (and this, especially, accounts
for its significance) a concrete, historical, and human conception of
human nature which had no transcendent term as a referent.

II *Fontenelle*

Bernard Fontenelle (1657–1757), who first devoted himself to the
writing of minor poems, pastorals, and an unsuccessful tragedy,
must have reflected more than any of his contemporaries on revolutions in public taste, on "changes that are forever occurring in the
minds of men, tastes that are imperceptibly replaced by new tastes
in what might be described as a relentless, mutually destructive battle or an eternal revolution of opinions and customs." [1]

Do these changes in taste follow no rule? "It is not by chance that
one taste supplants another; there is ordinarily a necessary but hidden link" (II, 434). Here he was obviously being attentive to public
taste. He was aware of his contemporaries' distaste for the preciosity
of the age of Voiture and the Hôtel de Rambouillet, and in his *Conversations on the Plurality of Worlds* he demonstrated that he knew
how to interest the ladies in astronomy.

But after he became secretary of the Academy of Sciences, he began to meditate on the scientific movement of his time, particularly
in mathematics and physics; thus he became the historian or rather

---

[1] *Sur l'histoire,* II, 434 (this and subsequent references are to Fontenelle's *Œuvres,*
Paris, 1818).

the historiographer of the sciences through eulogies written for deceased members of the Academy, and he discerned, beneath ephemeral changes in taste, the emergence of a new spirit among the intellectual elite and, beneath the new spirit, the fundamental traits of the human mind of which it was but one form. Fontenelle's sole interest in his essays (sometimes uninspired), in the prefaces to *The Analysis of Infinitely Small Objects, The Geometry of Infinity,* and *The Utility of Mathematics and Physics,* in his short *History* and *The Origin of Fables,* and in his somewhat longer *History of Oracles* (whose subject matter he borrowed from Van Dale), was to arrive at a description of the human mind which would take into account the prodigious advances that had occurred in the mathematical and physical sciences during the seventeenth century.

Fontenelle saw these advances as the point of departure for an ascending movement whose future could not be foreseen: "We may assume that the sciences are just approaching birth," he wrote to his colleagues. "The task of the Academy is to provide an ample supply of authenticated facts, for the structures of physics cannot be raised until experimental physics is able to provide the necessary materials" (I, 37). What direction would this progress take? The example of progress in infinitesimal geometry in the seventeenth century is topical; all of the great geometers—Descartes, Fermat, Pascal, Barrow, Mercator—"each one following his own particular route was led either to infinity or to the brink of infinity. It permeated all things, followed the geometers everywhere, and would not allow them freedom to escape" (I, 21). Newton and Leibniz came along and discovered the means to employ in calculus "this infinity which could no longer be rejected." Thus knowledge does not begin with unity but tends toward unity. It is not the analytical development of common principles accepted by everyone; it is the unanimity of efforts, at first dispersed, which are harmonized thanks to the inspired discovery of a general principle: "When a science like geometry is just coming to birth, we can apprehend almost nothing but scattered truths which do not cling together, and we prove each of them separately, as best we can and almost always with considerable difficulty. But after a certain number of these unitary truths have been found, we see how they fit together and their general principles begin to emerge" (I, 27).

It is clear that the expression "general principle" here signifies nothing comparable to the principle of identity or its analogues; it is rather a principle that accords science a deductive form, such as the infinitesimal calculus in all problems of quadrature or the law of attraction in every particular law in astronomy. The deductive form is an ideal remote from science, but it is nevertheless the idea of any science, even history. Fontenelle sees an affinity between the system of motive powers by which Tacitus explained the history of the Roman emperors and the system of vortexes by which Descartes explained natural phenomena, and he entertains the notion of going even further and constructing a priori a history in which a sequence of historical events will issue from the principles of human nature, once these are thoroughly understood (II, 429).

Progress in the direction of principles, though it implies the spontaneity of separate thoughts, is nevertheless subject to a regulative order: "Each item of knowledge comes to light only after a certain number of prior items have been clarified and when its turn arrives" (I, 21). But this regularity implies that the same force is always at work in human development. The mind does not, in fact, have two ways of proceeding; it always explains the unknown by comparing it with the known. This is the same procedure that gave birth to fables, which are only the sciences of primitive man, and which later caused the advance of the sciences. Fables are generally explained (and here Fontenelle is probably thinking of Bacon) by the uncertain faculty of the imagination. In reality many people, from antiquity on, assumed that myths were etiological—that is, intended to explain phenomena. Fontenelle was a vigorous exponent of the etiological theory; Homer and Hesiod were the first Greek philosophers, but even "in those crude times men of extraordinary intelligence were naturally inclined to seek out the cause of whatever they saw"; if water always flowed in a stream, they reasoned that there must be a nymph holding an urn from which water flowed without ceasing (II, 389). Fontenelle offers a singular proof of the rational character of fables, namely, the identity that he finds (thus anticipating comparative mythology) between the fables of the Greeks and those of the American Indians (II, 395). Gods and goddesses, therefore, issued from the same principle which regulated modern sciences: the relating of the unknown to the known. Fontenelle concludes: "All men resemble one another so closely that the stupidities of any tribe whatsoever should make us shudder" (II, 431). The superiority of modern man is attributable to the development of his knowledge and not to his intelligence, which Fontenelle equates with that of primitive man.

Fontenelle went still further in his thinking, but he had to take every precaution before expressing himself. One of the foundations of Christianity is the action of God in history—an action translated by the miracles and the Incarnation. Fontenelle envisions a positive history which teaches man only about himself; the spirit of Voltaire's *Essay on Morals* contrasts sharply with that of *The City of God*. Fontenelle points out that "there are two parts of history to be studied": the fabulous history of primitive times, which is wholly the invention of men, and the true history of times closer to us. The two histories will reveal "a detailed portrait of man, after the general portrait has been provided by morals"; their usefulness is in the discovery of "the soul of facts," which in the first instance consists of errors and in the second of passions (II, 431). One could hardly be more explicit, though Fontenelle made an attempt to be so in his *History of Oracles*. One of the historical proofs of the power of Christ was said to be that the pagan oracles, which were necessitated by demons, had ceased to speak at the time of his coming. Following the account of Van Dale, Fontenelle first shows that explaining oracles through demons is unsound because of their very commodiousness, which made it possible for the Christians easily to explain the miracles of paganism; then he shows that the fact of the cessation of oracles is itself spurious.

If in all of his essays Fontenelle, like Bayle, implies the negation of the action of God in history, he suggests, by way of counterpart, that God must be sought in nature: "Physics follows and untangles the signs of the infinite intelligence and wisdom which produced all things, whereas history has as its subject the effect of the passions and whims of men" (I, 35). Fontenelle's God is no longer the God of history—the God manifested in the intolerant sects of religions—but the God of nature who acts through fixed laws. Physics itself "is elevated to the status of theology."

BIBLIOGRAPHY

I

Texts

Bayle, Pierre. *Dictionnaire historique et critique.* 3 vols. Rotterdam, 1697. 3d
ed. 4 vols. Rotterdam, 1715. New ed., edited by A. J. Q. Beuchot. 16 vols.
Paris, 1820–24.
———. *Œuvres diverses.* 4 vols. The Hague, 1727–31.
———. *Selections from Bayle's Dictionary.* Edited and translated by E. A.
Beller and M. du P. Lee, Jr. Princeton, N.J., 1952.
———. *Historical and Critical Dictionary, Selections.* Translated by Richard
H. Popkin. Indianapolis, Ind., 1965.

Studies

Barber, W. H. "Pierre Bayle: Faith and Reason," in *The French Mind.* Ox-
ford, 1952. Pp. 109–25.
Constantinescu-Bagdat, E. *Pierre Bayle.* Paris, 1928.
Delbos, V. "Fontenelle et Bayle," in *La philosophie française.* Paris, 1919.
Pp. 133 ff.
Delvolvé, J. *Essai sur Pierre Bayle, religion, critique, et philosophie positive.*
Paris, 1906.
Labrousse, Elisabeth. *Inventaire critique de la correspondance de Pierre Bayle.*
Paris, 1961.
———. *Pierre Bayle.* 2 vols. The Hague, 1963–64.
Lévy-Bruhl, L. "Les tendances générales de Bayle et de Fontenelle," *Revue
d'histoire de la philosophie,* I (1927), 50 ff.
Mason, H. T. *Pierre Bayle and Voltaire.* London, 1963.
Puaux, F. *Les précurseurs français de la tolérance au XVIIIe siècle.* Paris,
1881.
Robinson, H. *Bayle the Sceptic.* New York, 1931.
Smith, H. E. *The Literary Criticism of Pierre Bayle.* New Haven, Conn.,
1912.
Pierre Bayle: Le philosophe de Rotterdam. Edited by Paul Dibon. Amsterdam,
1959.

305

II

Texts

Fontenelle, Bernard de. *Œuvres*. 5 vols. Paris, 1825.
──────. *Histoire de l'Académie royale des sciences*. Paris, 1702–33.
──────. *De l'origine des fables*. Edited by J. R. Carré. Paris, 1932.
──────. *Dialogues on the Plurality of Worlds*. Translated by J. Glanvill. New York, 1929.

Studies

Carré, J. R. *La philosophie de Fontenelle, ou le sourire de la raison*. Paris, 1932.
Cosentini, J. W. *Fontenelle's Art of Dialogue*. New York, 1952.
Delbos, V. "Fontennelle et Bayle," in *La philosophie française*. Paris, 1919. Pp. 133 ff.
Delorme, S. "Études sur Fontenelle," *Revue d'histoire des sciences*, 1957, pp. 288–309.
Grégoire, F. "Le dernier défenseur des Tourbillons, Fontenelle," *Revue d'histoire des sciences*, 1954, pp 220–46.
──────. *Fontenelle: une philosophie désabusée*. Nancy, 1947.
Lévy-Bruhl, L. "Les tendances générales de Bayle et de Fontenelle," *Revue d'histoire de la philosophie*, I (1927), 50 ff.
Marsak, L. M. *Bernard de Fontenelle*. Philadelphia, 1959.

INDEX

Loamhedge

For my good friend Martha Buckley, who inspired my Martha.
For Heather Boyd, who cheered me from her hospital bed to mine.
and
To the memory of two brave warriors:
Nolan Wallace, who became Lonna Bowstripe,
and Eric Masato Takashige Boehm, who fought the good fight.

Text copyright © 2003 by The Redwall La Dita Co., Ltd.
Illustrations copyright © 2003 by David Elliot.
All rights reserved. This book, or parts thereof, may not be reproduced in
any form without permission in writing from the publisher,
PHILOMEL BOOKS,
a division of Penguin Young Readers Group,
345 Hudson Street, New York, NY 10014.
Philomel Books, Reg. U.S. Pat. & Tm. Off. The scanning, uploading and dis-
tribution of this book via the Internet or via any other means without the
permission of the publisher is illegal and punishable by law. Please
purchase only authorized electronic editions, and do not participate
in or encourage electronic piracy of copyrighted materials. Your
support of the author's rights is appreciated.
Published simultaneously in Canada.
Printed in the United States of America
Text set in 11-point Palatino
Library of Congress Cataloging-in-Publication Data
Jacques, Brian.
Loamhedge : a tale from Redwall / Brian Jacques ;
illustrated by David Elliot. p. cm.
Summary: While a group of adventurers from Redwall seeks out the an-
cient abbey of Loamhedge in hopes of curing a young haremaid's paralysis,
Redwall is besieged by vermin.
[1. Animals—Fiction. 2. Fantasy.] I. Elliot, David, ill. II. Title.
PZ7.J15317 Lm 2003
[Fic]—dc21
2003000716
ISBN 0-399-23724-0
1 3 5 7 9 10 8 6 4 2
First Impression

BRIAN JACQUES

Loamhedge

Illustrated by DAVID ELLIOT

PHILOMEL BOOKS NEW YORK

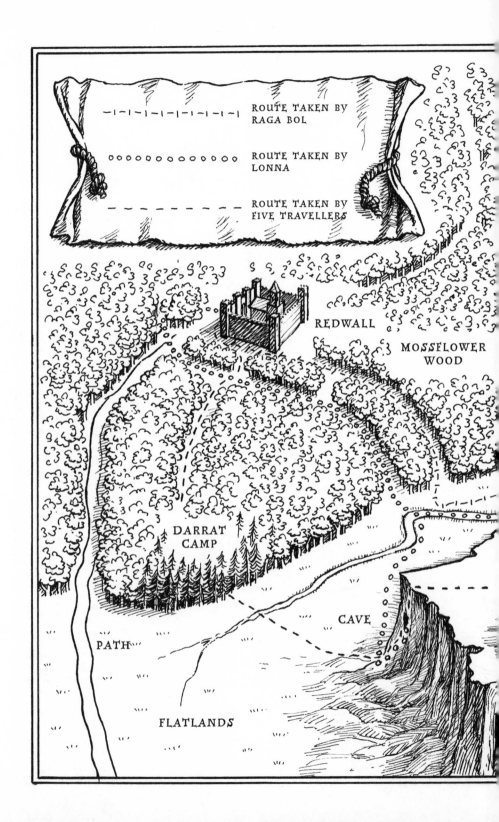

ROUTE TAKEN BY
RAGA BOL

ROUTE TAKEN BY
LONNA

ROUTE TAKEN BY
FIVE TRAVELLERS

REDWALL

MOSSFLOWER
WOOD

DARRAT
CAMP

CAVE

PATH

FLATLANDS

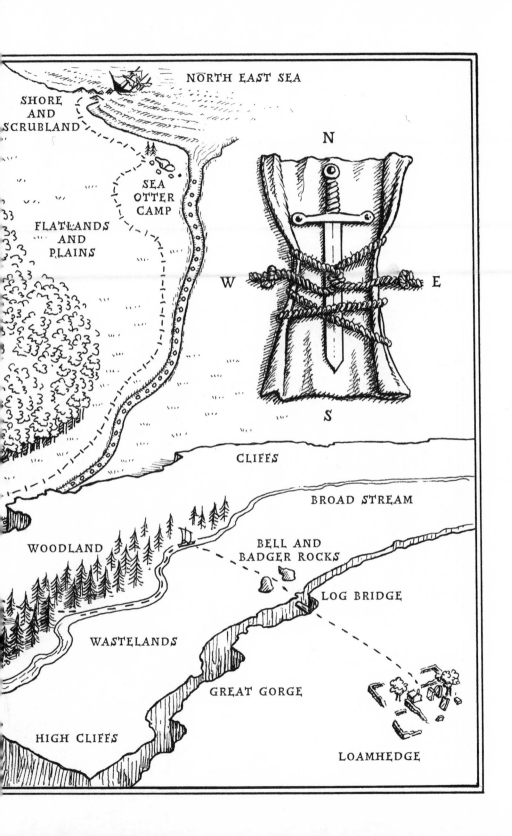

NORTH EAST SEA

SHORE
AND
SCRUBLAND

SEA
OTTER
CAMP

FLATLANDS
AND
PLAINS

N

W   E

S

CLIFFS

BROAD STREAM

WOODLAND

BELL AND
BADGER ROCKS

LOG BRIDGE

WASTELANDS

GREAT GORGE

HIGH CLIFFS

LOAMHEDGE

Prologue

Have you been travelling, my young friend? Come in out of
the darkness and rain. Sit by the fire, eat, drink and rest
yourself. Life is one long journey from beginning to end,
you know. We all walk different roads, both with our bodies and our minds. Some of us lose heart and fall by the
wayside, whilst others go on to realise their dreams and desires.

Let me tell you a story of travellers, and the paths they
followed. Of young ones, like yourself, sometimes uncertain of their direction, and often reluctant to listen to the
voices of sense and wisdom. Of a mighty warrior, set on a
course of destiny and vengeance, unstoppable in his resolve. Of an evil one and his crew, cruel and ruthless, bound
on a march of destruction and conquest. Of a simple maid
and her friends, homebodies whose only aims were peace
and well-being for all. Of wicked, foolish wanderers, chasing fantasies and fables, consumed by their own greed. Of
small babes who dreamed small dreams, not knowing what
the future held in store for them. And, finally, of two friends,

1

faithful and true, who had roamed many highways and together chose their own way.

The lives I will tell you of are intertwined by fate—good and evil bringing their just rewards to each, as they merited them. Listen whilst I relate this story. For am I not the Teller of Tales, the Weaver of Dreams!

BOOK ONE

"They're not as big as I thought they'd be"

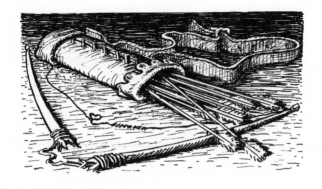

1

Lashing rain, driven by harsh biting winds from the sea, scoured the land from the bleak salt marshes to the stunted scrub forest. Abruc the sea otter bent against the strain of a loaded rush basket. It was tied to his shoulders and belted across his brow to stop it from spilling backward.

Holding on to his father's paw, young Stugg trotted alongside, plying his parent with interminable questions, which Abruc did his best to answer.

"H'are you veddy veddy strong?"

Scrunching his eyes against the wind, Abruc could not help smiling at his inquisitive little son. "I have t'be strong. I've got to feed you, your mamma an' the whole family. That's my job, I'm a father."

Stugg sucked his free paw, digesting this information whilst he thought up another question. "Den why can't Stugg sit atop of your basket no more?"

Abruc adjusted the belt to ease the strain on his neck. "Because you've growed since last season. Yore gettin' to be a big feller now, a fine lump of an otter. Soon you'll be carryin' yore ole dad an' the basket. Let's put a move on, Stugg, so we can make it into the woods by dark. It'll be good to take a rest out o' this weather."

With the sound of the grey northeast sea pounding in

their ears, both the sea otters squelched through the desolate salt marshes toward the weather-bent scrub forest.

Daylight ebbed into early evening as they entered the shelter of the trees. With a grunt of relief, Abruc swung his basket to the ground. It was brimfull of edible seaweed, scallops, mussels and shrimp—a full two days' work, gleaned from the coast of the barren northeast waters. Abruc sat on a fallen pine. Sensing his father's weariness, Stugg climbed up behind him and began gently rubbing his brow.

Abruc relaxed, sighing gratefully. "Hmmmm, that's nice. I was beginnin' to think that strap'd cut the top off me skull. Huh, where'd I be then?"

Stugg giggled. "Wiv a half offa head, silly ole farder!"

The sea otter cautioned his son. "Hush now, not so loud. There might be Coast Raiders about. Huh, they'd cut the tops off'n our skulls, just to watch us die."

Wide-eyed, Stugg crouched down against his father, speaking in a hushed whisper. "Mamma says Coaster Raiders be's naughty vermints!"

His father pushed dry pine needles into a small heap, shaking his head grimly. "Naughty ain't the word for that scum. They're evil, cold-blooded murderers. Cruelty is just fun to the likes o' them. Right, young 'un, I suppose yore hungry now?"

Nodding eagerly, Stugg whispered, "I'm starfished!"

Abruc chuckled. *Starfished* was a word all the young ones used, a cross twixt *starving* and *famished*.

He patted Stugg's head fondly. "Nothin' worse'n a starfished otter. You stay here, keep yore eyes'n'ears open, an' lay low. I'll go an' find us a snug berth for the night."

He pulled a sack from under his cloak, tossing it to his son. "Sort through the rest of those rations an' see wot you want for supper. I'll be back soon."

Abruc knew the woods well, he recalled a spot not too far off. It was a good dry place, sheltered by a rock ledge. Silent

6

as a night breeze, he weaved his way through the dark, twisted trees, straight to the exact location. He had camped there before. Halting slightly short of his destination, he paused. Something did not feel quite right about the area. Abruc sniffed the air and listened carefully, his animal instinct aroused. He caught the faint sound of ragged breathing. Drawing his long dagger, he crept forward, peering keenly into the shadows, his neck hairs bristling.

For supper Stugg had selected two flat loaves, some of his mamma's apple and blackberry preserve and their last flask of plum cordial. If his father lit a fire, they could make toasted preserve sandwiches and warm cordial. The young otter was a pretty fair cook, often having helped his mamma to prepare meals. There was not much else to do but wait in silence for his father's return. Stugg set out the food and sat next to the basket of supplies.

Abruc came speeding out of the darkness to his son's side. Crouching beside Stugg, he gripped his paws tightly. The sea otter's voice was urgent and breathless from running.

"Listen carefully, little mate. Could you find yore way back home to our holt on yore own?"

Stugg was taken aback by the unusual request. "Er, I fink so, what's a matter, farder?"

Abruc gripped his son's paws tighter. His voice sounded harsh. "Answer me—yes or no! Could you find yore way back home?"

Stugg had never seen his father like this. He nodded, his own voice sounding small and scared. "Yes, Stugg know d'way!"

Abruc released the young otter's paws. "Good, now here's wot y'must do, son. Find Shoredog. Tell him to bring the crew to the spot by the rock ledge, he'll know where I mean. Say that they best bring rope, canvas an' poles. Enough t'make a stretcher to carry a wounded, giant stripedog. That's if'n he's still alive when they reach here."

Words poured from Stugg's mouth like running water. "A giant, a stripedog, a wounded one? I never see'd a giant stripedog afore! What happened? Will he get deaded . . ."

Abruc grabbed Stugg and shook him, something he had never done before. He hissed at him through clenched teeth. "Shut yore mouth, son! Don't stand here askin' questions! Go now, run, don't stop for anythin'. The life of another creature depends on you. Go!"

Young Stugg took off like a madbeast, pine needles scattering from under his paws as he tore homeward through the nighttime forest. Abruc watched until his son was out of sight, then gathered up their belongings and dashed back to the camp beneath the ledge.

Swiftly he heaped dry pine needles and cones with a few twigs. Using the steel of his knife blade against a chunk of flint, he soon had a small fire burning. It was sheltered by the overhanging rock and could not be seen from a reasonable distance. Abruc viewed the scene around him. Two badgers, one very old, the other about two seasons into his adult growth, lay stretched out, side by side. Small and grizzled, the oldest of the pair was obviously dead, slain by various weapon thrusts. As he turned to the younger badger, a brief glance at the churned-up ground and the blood-flecked rock confirmed the sea otter's suspicions. His jaw clenched angrily. "Dirty murderin' Raiders!"

The younger badger was still alive. Abruc had seen one or two badgers in his lifetime, but not as big as this fellow. He was truly a giant—tall, deep of chest and broadbacked with massive paws and powerfully muscled limbs.

The sea otter winced as he inspected the fearsome wound to the badger's head. A long jagged slash, from eartip to neck, had ripped across the badger's face. Narrowly missing the eye, it had ploughed across the brow, through the wide-striped muzzle, across the jaw line to the side of the creature's throat.

Abruc, with only a limited knowledge of healing, staunched the blood with his cloak. Lifting the badger's

8

head, he cradled it in his lap, dabbing away at the dreadful rift and murmuring to the unconscious beast.

"Seasons o' salt, matey, 'tis a miracle yore still alive! Y'-must have a skull made o' rock. I know you can't hear me, but don't worry, big feller, our crew will do the best we can for ye. There's one or two good healers at our holt."

Abruc sat rambling away to the senseless badger, knowing he could do little else until help arrived.

It was close to midnight. Rainladen wind hissed through the scrub forest, carrying with it salt spray from the thundering seas. Beside the guttering embers of his little fire, Abruc had dozed off, still holding the badger's head.

At the front of the otter crew, Shoredog pointed with his lantern, hurrying forward. "There they are, mates!"

Little Stugg reached his father first. "I bringed them, farder!"

Abruc patted the youngster's paw. "Yore a good ole scout. Unnh, somebeast get me out from under this giant's head. Me limbs have gone asleep on me from holdin' his weight."

Willing paws assisted him upright. Shoredog shook his head as he viewed the injured badger. "Great seasons, lookit the mess the pore creature's in. I fears there ain't much hope for 'im. I never set eyes on a wound bad as that 'un!"

Stugg caught sight of his mother and tugged at her paw. "Issa giant stripedog goin' to die, mamma?"

Abruc's wife Marinu nodded at Shoredog's grandma, Sork. "Not if'n we can help it, Stugg. Come on, crew, get some warm blankets around that badger an' strap him to a stretcher. Easy now, don't jolt the pore beast too much."

Everybeast knew that Marinu and Sork were the best healers in all the southeast.

Stugg grinned broadly. Now that he had succeeded in his mission, he proceeded to take charge of the situation, striding about and issuing orders. "You all hear my mamma, pick dat stripedog up careful!"

9

Marinu was about to pull her son to one side when Abruc murmured to her, "Let the young 'un be, he did well tonight."

As the otter crew manoeuvred the huge badger onto the huge stretcher, Shoredog gave a surprised bark. "Blood'-n'thunder, lookit that!"

Beneath the injured creature a mighty bow and a quiver of long arrows lay half covered in the loose sand and pine needles. The badger had fallen backward upon the bow, his hefty bulk breaking the weapon in two pieces. One jagged half was stuck into his hip. Marinu halted the bearers until she and Sork had extracted the splintered yew wood. The big fellow grunted faintly as they padded and dressed the wound.

Stugg jumped up and down triumphantly. "He be's alive, d'stripedog maked noise!"

Old Sork looped the birchbark quiver over Stugg's head. It scraped the ground, the arrows were taller than he. Sork shooed the young one aside. "Aye, mayhap he is. Now you carry those an' stay out the way."

A score of otters bore the badger off on a litter of pine poles, sailcloth and rope, padded with dead grass and soft moss. Stugg stayed behind with his father and Shoredog to bury the dead badger. It was only a shallow grave, but they found slabs of rock to top it off with. Abruc wedged the two pieces of broken bow, with the string still joining them, into the foot of the grave. They would serve as a marker. All three sea otters gazed down at the sad resting place.

Abruc shook his head. "Pore old beast, we don't even know wot name he went by. He looked weak, an' small. A badger that age should've spent out his seasons restin' in the sun. I wonder wot kin he was t'the big 'un. Mebbe his father?"

Stugg pressed his face against Abruc and wept. He could not imagine anybeast losing a father. He sobbed brokenly. "Who would kill someone's farder like that?"

Shoredog looked up from smoothing the earth around

the stones. "Only beast I knows who kills like that is Raga Bol."

The name struck fear into Abruc. "Raga Bol! Has he been here?"

Shoredog stood upright, dusting off his paws. "While you an' Stugg were gone, Rurff the grey seal visited our holt. He saw the Searats' ship wrecked on the rocks, further north up the coast. Raga Bol an' about fifty vermin crew came ashore. They headed down this way, but pickin's are scarce on this northeast coast, so they've probably marched inland. They ain't got a ship anymore. I was just rousin' our crew to search for you an' Stugg, when the young 'un comes runnin' to tell me you need help."

Shoredog took one of the straps on Abruc's basket. "Let me help ye with this, mate, 'tis a good haul."

They set off back to their holt, with Stugg stumbling over the quiver of long arrows.

Abruc shrugged philosophically. "It's a bad spring, cold an' stormy. Let's hope summer's a bit better when it comes. At least we won't have Raga Bol an' his villains to worry about. I suppose we should count ourselves lucky, really."

Young Stugg hitched the arrows higher on his back. They still dragged along the ground as he muttered aloud. "More luckier than d'poor stripedogs, I appose."

A brief smile crossed Shoredog's weathered face. "That young 'un of yores is growin' up quick, mate!"

Dawn glimmered chill and blustery over the heathlands some two leagues west of the northeast sea. Wet, hungry and dispirited, Raga Bol's crew of Searats huddled round a smoking fire down a ravine. They stared miserably at a deep, rain-swollen stream running nearby. From further up the bank the vermin could hear their captain's shrieks and curses rending the air.

Rinj, a sly-faced female, gnawed at a filthy clawnail, glancing from one to the other. "Ye t'ink Bol's lost the paw? I t'ought Wirga cudda sewed it back on, she's a good 'ealer."

A lanky, gaunt rat named Ferron picked something from his teeth and spat it into the stream. "Sewed it back on! Have ye gone soft in the skull? Last I saw, Cap'n Bol's paw was 'angin' on by a string o' skin. We should've stayed well clear o' those two stripedogs!"

Rinj wiped firesmoke from her blearing eyes. "The little ole one wuz no trouble, he didn't know wot 'it 'im, gone afore ye could wink."

Ferron winced as Raga Bol's screeches and curses redoubled. "Aye, but wot about the big 'un, eh? I thought Cap'n Bol killed him wid the first blow of his big sword!"

Glimbo, the captain's first mate, pushed Rinj away from the fire and installed his fat, greasy bulk close to the flames. One of his eyes was a milky sightless orb; the other roved around the crew as he warmed his paws.

"Never in me days seen Bol 'ave to strike a beast twice wid that blade. But that big stripedog came back after the first whack an' got his teeth in good. Just as well that Bol struck again, or he would've lost more'n one paw. Mark my words, stripedogs are powerful dangerous beasts!"

The heathland was a barren region, made drearier by the day's unabated rain. Down in the ravine a huge bonfire blazed to dispel the harsh weather. Every Searat of the crew sat watching their captain. Tall and sinewy, with a restless energy that could be glimpsed in his fiery green eyes, Raga Bol was an impressive rat by any measure. He sat wrapped in a fur cloak, his left pawstump hidden from view. The Searat's right paw rested on the carved bone hilt of a heavy, wide-bladed scimitar, protruding from his waistband. The crewbeasts could feel Raga Bol's eyes on them. Rain sizzling on the fire and wind fanning the flames were the only sounds to be heard as they waited on their captain's word.

Finally, Raga Bol rose and snarled bad-temperedly at them, firelight reflecting from his hooped brass earrings and gold-plated fangs. "We march west at dawn. Anybeast who don' want to go, let 'im speak now, an' I'll bury 'im right 'ere!"

Not one of the Searat crew said a word. Raga Bol nodded. "West it is then. Blowfly, get me two runners."

An enormously fat rat, with a whip curled about his shoulders, motioned two lean crew members forward.

Raga Bol sat looking at them in silence, until they squirmed under his unwinking gaze. His jaw clenched as he moved the stump where his left paw had been. "You two, go back to where I slew the stripedog. Find the carcasse, an' bring me back his head."

Each of the runners touched a paw to his ears. "Aye aye, Cap'n!"

Raga Bol stood watching them climbing the sides of the ravine, then turned his attention to an old female Searat crouching nearby. "Wirga, is that hook ready yet?"

"It'll be ready by dawn, Cap'n." The old one gave him a toothless grin. "So thee wants the big stripedog's head, eh?"

Raga Bol drew his cloak tight and sat, staring into the fire. "Nobeast ever took a paw o'mine an' stayed in one piece, dead or alive. Now get that hook ready if'n ye want to keep yore head, ye withered old torturer!"

2

Far over to the west, a brighter spring day had dawned. Ascending meadowlarks heralded the sun beneath a soft, pastel blue sky. Drawn by the sudden warmth, mist rose from the greenswards, transforming dewdrops to small opalescent pearls amid the dainty blossoms of saxifrage, buttercup, capsella and anemones. Mossflower woodland trees were blessed with a crown of fresh green leaves. Life was renewed to the sounds of little birds, calling to their parents with ceaseless demands for food.

Toran Widegirth loosed his apron strings, satisfied that he had completed his duties as Redwall Abbey's Head Cook. Leaving his kitchens, the fat otter sought the beautiful spring morn outdoors. Heaving a sigh of relief, Toran sat down on an upturned wheelbarrow at the orchard entrance. He was joined by his friend Carrul, the Father Abbot of Redwall. The mouse sat down beside the otter, both relaxing in silence, blinking in the sunlight and savouring the first good weather that spring.

Carrul glanced sideways at his companion. "Not going with Skipper and otter crew this season?"

Toran watched an ant negotiating its way over his footpaw. "Much too early, it ain't summer yet. But you know

14

Skipper an' the crew, first sign o' sun an' a skylark an' they're off like march hares to the west seashores for the season."

Abbot Carrul chuckled. "Fully provisioned I trust?"

Toran nodded wearily. "Aye, I saw them off myself at dawn. Pushin' a cartload o' victuals I'd made special for 'em. Singin' their rudders off, dancin' like madbeasts!"

Carrul's smile widened. "I know, they woke me up, I saw them from my window. Good luck and fair weather to them. So why didn't you go? I gave you permission to take as long as you wanted to go on leave."

Toran shrugged. "Oh, I'm gettin' too old for that sort o' thing. Leave it to the younger ones."

Carrul snorted. "Too old? Too big in the tummy, you mean! If you're too old, then what about me, eh? I was your teacher when you were only a tiny Dibbun at Abbey School!"

The ottercook tweaked his friend's bony paw. "Aye, an' ye haven't gained a hair's weight since then. How d'ye do it, you skinny, ancient mouse?"

The Abbot looked over his small square spectacles good-humouredly. "I don't spend my whole life down in those kitchens like you do, my friend. Oh, Toran, isn't it just a glorious day? I hope the summer is a really golden one."

Toran snuggled more comfortably into the wheelbarrow. "Makes ye feel good t'be alive, don't it, Carrul?"

They both lapsed into silence again, gazing around and taking in the beauties of their Abbey.

Behind them, Redwall reared—a legend in pink, dusty sandstone with its high walls and turrets, stained-glass windows and buttressed arches, belltower, attics and steeple, all complemented by a background of verdant woodland and cloudless blue sky. Toran took in the stout battlements and picturesque gatehouse of the outer wall, whilst the Abbot contented himself by viewing the lawns and orchards, peacefully shimmering in the sunlight.

Carrul's gaze took in the Abbey pond, down near the south ramparts. "What creature could not count himself lucky to be dwelling in such a paradise. Ah, look Toran, there's our young friend Martha, taking a little nap in her chair, just by the rhododendron bushes on the far side of the pond."

Toran saw the young haremaid, her head nodding down to a heavy volume, which lay open on her lap.

The ottercook eased himself from the barrow. "I'll just take a stroll over there and check she's alright."

The Abbot stretched luxuriously into the position Toran had vacated. "Dearie me, you're like an old mother hen with that young 'un. Why don't you tell her that lunch will be served late, out in the orchard? In fact, tell everybeast, 'twill cheer them up after being kept indoors by the rain for so long. We'll all lend a paw to help."

Toran smiled happily. "What a good idea!"

The ottercook approached Martha carefully, not wanting to disturb her. She was very special to him. Toran could recall the winter's day, twelve seasons ago, when Martha Braebuck had arrived at Redwall. She had been nought but a tiny babe, strapped to the back of her ancient grandmother. Her brother Hortwill, two seasons older, had stumbled along, clutching the old hare's cloak. Toran's heart had immediately gone out to the pitiful trio. They had walked from the far Northlands, the only survivors of a vermin attack which had wiped out an entire colony of mountain hares. No sooner were they through the Abbey gates than the poor grandmother had collapsed and died from exhaustion. A sad occurrence, made sadder by the fact that Martha had never learned to walk from that day forth. Her brother grew up as sprightly as any young hare, but despite the most tender care, the babe Martha was immobile from her knee joints to her footpaws. There were no signs of any apparent wound or injury, no scarring or broken bones. No reason, in fact, why the little one should not learn to walk. Some of the

16

wiser heads, like old Phredd the Gatekeeper, Great Father Abbot Carrul and Sister Setiva, the healer shrew who took care of the Abbey infirmary, said it was due to shock. That perhaps Martha's long trek from the Northlands, strapped to her grandmother's back, coupled with witnessing the murder of her family and kin, had caused the problem. Still, the Redwallers were completely puzzled.

Toran did everything possible to help her. He believed firmly that one day she would stand and walk. Meanwhile, the kind ottercook provided Martha with the means to get about. Taking a light comfortable chair, he fixed it to the base of a kitchen trolley, adding two large wheels to the back. The young haremaid learned to propel herself about quite easily. Toran also fashioned a crutch for her, but Martha used it only to get at things which were beyond her reach.

Martha Braebuck grew up an extremely bright young creature with a thirst for knowledge. She was a formidable reader and scholar, the equal even of the venerated mouse, Sister Portula, Redwall's Abbey Recorder. Martha could solve riddles and equations, write poems, ballads and even sing. According to popular opinion, she had the sweetest singing voice ever heard within the Abbey walls. She never complained about being chairbound, and was invariably cheerful and willing to help others. The maid was a welcome and useful member of the Redwall Abbey community.

Toran watched silently as her head drooped lower. The volume slid from her lap rug onto the grass. Toran grunted as he bent to retrieve it.

Martha came awake, stifling a yawn and rubbing her eyes. "Dearie me, I must have nodded off!"

Returning the hefty volume to Martha's lap, the ottercook winked at her. "Who'd blame ye, with all this sun about. I could lie down right here an' take a nap myself!"

Martha saw a group of Dibbuns approaching from

around the orchard hedge. "You wouldn't sleep for long, my friend. Look, here comes trouble!"

The Abbeybabes descended upon the haremaid's chair. Muggum, a tiny mole who was their ringleader, climbed up onto Martha's lap, rumbling away in his quaint mole-speech. "Yur, Miz Marth', do ee singen us'n's ee song?"

The haremaid eyed him good-naturedly. "Which one would you like me to sing?"

Toran interrupted with his suggestion. "A pretty day deserves a pretty song, miss. Sing a spring song!"

The squirrelbabe Shilly added her request. "Da one where uz clappa paws!"

Buffle the shrewbabe, who was the smallest of all, nodded solemnly. "Gurbbadurrguddun!"

Shilly translated. "Him says that be a good 'un."

Martha sat up straight, exchanging a smile with Toran. "Well, Buffle's word is good enough for me. Here goes."

The Dibbuns raised their paws, ready to clap, as Martha's melodious voice soared out.

"The rain has gone away . . . Clap Clap!
and larks do sing on high.
Sweet flowers open wide . . . Clap Clap!
their petals to the sky!
'Tis spring . . . Clap clap! 'Tis spring,
let us rejoice and sing,
the moon is queen the sun is king,
so clap your paws and sing . . . Clap Clap!

There's not a cloud in sight . . . Clap Clap!
the leaves are bright and new.
This day was made for all . . . Clap Clap!
for me my friend and you!
So sing . . . Clap Clap! . . . So sing,
let summer follow spring,
from golden morn to evening,

18

we clap our paws and sing . . . Clap Clap!
    . . . Clap Clap!"

Although the clapping missed its beat once or twice, it was
with joyous vigour. The little ones danced around, whooping and squeaking wildly, "Sing us'n's a more!"

Martha was coaxed into singing the lively air again. She
finished quite out of breath, amid yells for a third performance.

Toran took charge, slapping his rudder loudly on the
bankside. "Hold up there, ye rogues, pore Miz Martha's
tuckered out. Now lissen t'me. If ye promise t'be good, we'll
have lunch out in the orchard today, seein' as 'tis sunny!"

His suggestion was greeted with roars of approval.
"Lunch inna h'orchard, 'ooppee!"

Martha smiled happily. "Oh, what a splendid idea!"

Little Shilly sped off toward the Abbey, calling to the
other Dibbuns. "Come on, we 'elp Granmum Gurvel wiv
lunch!"

Toran watched them go. 'I don't think old Gurvel will
thank me for lettin' that lot invade the kitchens."

Martha settled the big volume more comfortably on her
lap. "Bless their little hearts, they mean well."

Toran cast a glance at the haremaid's book. "That's a
heavy ole thing t'be readin', miss. Wot's it all about?"

Martha opened the book at a page marked by a silken
ribbon. "I borrowed it from Sister Portula's library. It's a
rare and ancient account of Loamhedge mice."

The ottercook looked thoughtful. "Loamhedge mice, eh?
I've heard of them. Weren't they the ones who helped
t'build our Abbey? Aye, they were led by old Abbess, er,
wotsername?"

"Germaine." The haremaid corrected him. "It was she
and Martin the Warrior who helped to build and design
Redwall. Germaine and her followers once lived at the place
they called Loamhedge. It was a peaceful and prosperous

19

community, almost as large as our Abbey, some say. But they were forced to abandon it and flee for their lives. Loamhedge was left deserted to the four winds."

Toran's interest was roused. Although he was no great reader himself, he liked to hear his friend tell of what she had read. "Why did they have to leave? Does the book explain?"

Martha riffled back to a previously read page. "It says here that a great sickness fell upon Loamhedge. A plague, brought by vermin, possibly Searats. First there was sickness, then a few deaths. Abbess Germaine was wise enough to realise that it would grow into an epidemic, which would wipe them all out. So she took her mice and fled. They went wandering for many seasons, far from home. One day their journey took them into this part of Mossflower territory. It was here they met Martin the Warrior and his friends. Germaine joined forces with the Woodlanders, helping to rid the lands of powerful enemies. When peace was achieved, Martin and Germaine were free to realise their dream. They built a mighty stone fortress, an Abbey, where goodbeasts could live in safety and happiness together. That's how, countless ages ago, Redwall came into being. . . ."

Martha was interrupted by her brother Hortwill. He came bounding and splashing through the shallows and threw himself upon her.

"Wot ho, wot ho, wot ho, me pretty young skin'n'blister!"

She ducked her head, laughing as he showered her face with kisses. "Stop that this instant, Horty! I'm not your skin'n'blister, I'm your sister. Oh, look now, you've splashed water all over Sister Portula's precious book!"

Hortwill Braebuck, or Horty, as everybeast knew him, was Martha's brother, older than her by two seasons. An overpowering character—ebullient, quaint of speech, always in trouble, he was roguishly gallant, sentimental to a fault, and possessed a gluttonous appetite. In short, a typical hare.

Throwing up both paws and ears in mock horror, Horty declaimed, "Well, flog me twice round the jolly old orchard an' chop off me ears with a rusty blinkin' axe, wot! Splashed a bally spot o'water on Sis Peculiar's blessed book? Lack a day, fifty seasons in the cellar for me. What say you, Toran old scout? Either that or instant death. Wot wot?"

Toran played along with Horty's dramatic mood. Squinting an eye, he growled fiercely, "Instant death's the only thing!"

The young hare threw him a smart military salute. "As y'say, sah, sentence t'be carried out on the blinkin' spot!"

Without further ado, Horty flung himself into the pond and vanished underwater, still saluting.

Martha sat bolt upright in her chair. "Oh the fool, save him Toran, quickly!"

Lumbering into the pond, the ottercook fished Horty out with one huge paw.

Grinning like a madbeast, and still saluting, Horty spouted a mouthful of water into the air. "Beloved blinkin' friend, you've saved me life. I'll never forget you, an' I'll always dine at your excellent kitchen!"

Keeping a straight face, Toran looked at Martha. "I'd better chuck him back in, miss, think of the food we'd save!"

Martha nearly fell out of her chair with laughter. "Hahahaha! Oh no, please sir, hahaha! I beg you, spare his gluttonous young life. Hahahahaha!"

Shooting a last jet of pondwater skyward, Horty said fondly, "A chap's confounded lucky to have such a merciful sister, wot!"

Toran growled as he frog-marched Horty ashore. "Ye certainly are, matey. But if'n I hears ye callin' Sister Portula, Sis Peculiar again, back in the pond ye'll go. Aye, an' those two ripscuttle pals o' yores, Springald an' Fenna. A lesson in manners wouldn't harm them, either!"

Martha dabbed the book pages dry with her lap rug. She could never be angry with her boisterous brother. Horty had always been close by, ready to cheer her up when she was sad or depressed. Her inability to run free like other young ones sometimes put Martha in low spirits.

She held up the volume for Toran to see. "No harm done really, it's perfectly dry now. Come on you two, let's go back to the Abbey!"

On the way up, they met Muggum and several other Dibbuns who had been banished from the kitchens by Granmum Gurvel, the old assistant molecook.

Muggum tugged his snout respectfully to the haremaid. "Yur, mizzy, oi'll push ee to ee h'orchard furr lunch."

Reaching down, Martha lifted the molebabe onto her lap. "That's very thoughtful of you, Muggum, but I'm sure Horty and Toran can manage the job quite well."

Patting the young haremaid's paw, the molebabe nodded sagely. "Oi thankee, Miz Marth'. Coom on, zurrs, you'm pushen us faster'n'that, us'n's bee gurtly 'ungered furr lunch!"

3

Redwall orchard was a riot of blossoming fruit trees and bushes. Pink and white flowers clustered thick on every branch, their petals carpeting the grass. Apple, pear, cherry, beech, hazelnut and almond trees flourished in rows, fronted by raspberry, strawberry, red currant and whortleberry. Summer promised an abundant yield.

Toran cast an eye over three trolleys laden with buffet lunch—spring vegetable soup, brown bread and cheese, dandelion and burdock cordial, followed by a dessert of damson preserve pie. "Who did all this?"

Abbot Carrul bowed apologetically, knowing how touchy the ottercook could be about trespassers in his kitchen domain. "I offered to help Granmum Gurvel. You looked so hot and weary when I met you in the orchard for a breath of fresh air. Gurvel and I decided to help you out. Is it to your liking, my friend?"

Toran bowed thankfully to them both. "My thanks to ye. I couldn't have done it better!"

Redwallers sat in the tree shade, laughing and chatting amiably as lunch was served. Sister Portula spread a rug, and Toran lifted Martha onto it. All four sat beneath a wide chestnut tree at the orchard's far end. Sunlight and shadow dappled them as they watched the inhabitants of Redwall enjoying lunch. Martha appreciated such moments because the elders always included her in their discussions. The young haremaid felt she had become an honorary member of the Elders Council.

Martha laughed at the antics of the Dibbuns, who were beginning to get a bit rowdy. "They do get excited after a rainy spring indoors. Look at baby Yooch, he's eating flower petals!"

Sister Portula shook her head. "There's Shilly and some others doing it. I'll wager 'twas Muggum who started it all. Muggum, Shilly and Yooch are more trouble than any ten Dibbuns. I call them the Terrible Trio!"

Toran's stomach shook as he chuckled. "Yore right, marm. Hi there, Springald, go an' tell those little 'uns to stop eatin' the petals, or Sister Setiva will have to dose 'em with physicks."

The mousemaid Springald shrugged carelessly. "Flowers won't do 'em any harm. I used to eat petals myself."

Abbot Carrul glanced sternly over his glasses at her. "Do as you are bidden, miss, and don't argue!"

Springald curtsied slightly, then flounced off to do as she was told.

Sister Portula pursed her lips and tutted. "Yonder goes more trouble. She's one of the other three. Horty, Springald and Fenna, the young rebels. They aren't babes anymore, they should know better."

Martha put aside her cordial beaker. "Oh, they'll grow out of it, Sister, they're all good creatures at heart, I'm sure."

Portula helped herself to bread and cheese. "Huh, let's hope they do, before there's really trouble. I'm sure we were never like that at their age, were we, Father?"

Abbot Carrul raised his eyebrows. "Weren't we, Sister? I can recall two young ones sailing a dining room table on the pond. Aye, with an embroidered linen tablecloth for a sail. Hmm, let me see now, what were their names?"

Sister Portula fidgeted uncomfortably with her sleeve

hem. "But that was only a bit of fun. You and I were well behaved as a rule."

Martha could scarcely believe her ears. "You two? Well, you rascals! Did you get caught, Father?"

Behind his small glasses, the Abbot's eyes twinkled. "Oh, we were caught sure enough, and both set to work in the kitchens as punishment. Remember that, Sister?"

Portula nodded ruefully. "How could I ever forget five days of scrubbing greasy pots and scouring pans? My little paws stayed wrinkled for half a season!"

Martha winked cheekily at the Recorder. "Horty and his two friends seem innocent compared to you and Abbot Carrul. What a pair of rogues you were!"

A light smile hovered on Portula's kind face. "Listen, missy, if you think we were naughty, you should have seen two Dibbuns who were younger than us at the time. Bragoon and Saro, an otter and a squirrel. Now those two really were a twin pestilence!"

Martha turned to Toran. "I've heard you telling the young ones tales about Bragoon and Saro, but I always thought they were make-believe creatures. Were they actually real?"

The ottercook nodded vigorously. "Oho, missy, that they were! Bragoon was my big brother, five seasons older'n me. Sarobando, or Saro, as everybeast knew her, was a Dibbun squirrel, his best little pal. Sister Portula's right, ye never saw two villains like 'em! Hah, 'twas just as well they ran off whilst they was still young 'uns. If'n Bragoon an' Saro had stayed, we mightn't have a roof over our heads. They would've demolished the Abbey between 'em!"

Whilst Toran had been talking, some of the Dibbuns and a few of the young 'uns had gathered around.

Muggum scrambled up onto Toran's lap. "Yurr zurr, you'm tell us'n's ee story 'bowt Zuro an' Burgoon!"

Toran chuckled. "I can't bring one to mind right now, but I can recite a poem I wrote about 'em for the Harvest Feast many seasons back."

Taking a swig of cordial, he tried to recall the words.

Shilly waggled her tail impatiently. "Well, 'urry up an gerron wiv it, Cooky!"

The ottercook twitched his nose at her. "Silence, ye liddle rip!"

Draining his beaker, Toran launched into the recitation.

"I'll tell ye a tale of two Dibbuns,
who lived here long ago,
an otter who was named Bragoon,
an' a squirrel known as Saro.
Aye, little Bragoon an' Saro,
what a pair o' scamps they were,
their names rang through the land oh,
there was nought they didn't dare!

Good Granmum Gurvel molecook,
made puddens, cakes an' pies,
they vanished off the kitchen shelf,
before her dear ole eyes.
'Bragoon an' Saro, I'll be bound,'
the poor ole beast would say,
'they'll eat me out of house an' home,
they'll turn my fur to grey!'
Bragoon an' Saro, gracious me,
I dread to hear those names,
come hearken whilst I tell ye,
of those two scoundrels' games.

Who filled the Abbot's bed with ants,
who nailed up all the doors,
who was it glued the bellrope,
and stuck the ringer's paws,
who filled the pond with beetroots,
and turned the waters red,
who baked poor Foremole's sandals,
inside a loaf of bread?

The dreaded Bragoon an' Saro,
I'm here to tell ye all,
there's never been two like 'em,
at the Abbey of Redwall!"

The Dibbuns jumped up and down in delight, roaring with laughter at the escapades of the infamous pair. Horty and his friends, Springald and Fenna, laughed, too.

Toran put on a stern face, wagging a cautionary paw at his listeners. "I tell ye, 'twasn't so funny for the poor creatures who were the butt o' those tricks!"

Horty scoffed. "Oh I say, sah, you don't actually believe all that dreadful twaddle about Bragoon an' Saro, wot?"

Abbot Carrul answered him. "Toran's right, 'tis all true. I was a young 'un here myself at the time, I saw it!"

Fenna fluttered her long eyelashes prettily. "Oh really, Father Abbot, you don't expect us to believe all that about Bragoon and Saro. We're not Dibbuns anymore. Toran makes up the stories to amuse the little ones—they'll believe anything, but we know better."

Martha spoke out sharply. "If the Abbot and Toran say it is true, then I'm certain it is. What reason would we have to doubt them?"

Her words, however, went unheeded by the three young 'uns, as they strolled off together, still unwilling to credit the existence of the fabled duo.

Horty scoffed again. "Bragoon an' Saro, wot? Load of jolly old codswallop, if y'ask me. Tchah!"

Springald giggled. "If I swallowed that lot, I'd be looking out for fishes nesting in trees and flying!"

Martha was so angry that she almost rose from the rug, but then she fell back again.

Abbot Carrul helped her to sit up. "Don't upset yourself, Martha. One day our young friends will wake up and find themselves somewhat older and a little wiser, just wait and see. I was a bit like them at that age, but one lives and learns."

The young haremaid sighed. "I hope it happens to my brother soon. I don't like to say this, Father, but Horty seems to behave more outrageously each day."

Toran helped Martha into her chair. "Don't ye worry. Horty's a hare, they're always a bit wild when they're young."

Martha retrieved her volume and straightened her rug. "Perhaps you haven't noticed, Toran, but I'm a hare, too!"

Sister Portula dusted a stray flower petal from Martha's head. "Ah, but you're a very rare and special kind of hare, my dear. Anybeast can see that!"

Hostile weather still reigned on the plains and heathlands of the far east. Raga Bol and his Searats had not made much headway in three days of trekking westward—the Searat captain's pawstump pained abominably. They camped on high ground, in the lee of a rocky projection. Apart from a few chosen cronies, the crew avoided the captain, making their own fire sufficiently far away to evade his sudden wrath.

Raga Bol sat by his own fire, with Glimbo and Blowfly in attendance. The two runners had been sent out to retrieve the badger's head but had returned empty-pawed. They crouched at the far side of the blaze, panting from their long journey. Raga Bol watched reflecting flames glinting from the polished silver hook where his paw had once been. His luminous eyes shifted to the runners.

"Are ye certain 'twas the spot where I slew the giant stripedog?"

Both heads nodded. "Certain shore, Cap'n!"

"I'd swear me oath on it, Cap'n Bol. The stripedog was gone, there was no sign of 'im anywhere's about!"

The Searat captain's terrifying stare never left either of the two quivering vermin. "But the old one, he was buried there?"

"Aye, Cap'n, right on the spot where ye slew the big 'un."

"He's right, Cap'n, the very spot. All the tracks were wiped out, too. Wasn't nothin' we could do but come back 'ere, fast as we could, to tell ye!"

Raga Bol dropped his gaze to the steaming ground at the fire's edge. "Speak to none about this, or yore both deadrats. Now get out o' my sight!"

Glimbo and Blowfly scuttled off, relieved to be still among the living, after having brought their murderous captain such bad news. Hunching against the bleak cold at his back, Raga Bol sat silent. His eyes roved between the silver hook and the roaring, wind-driven fire.

Blowfly whispered to Glimbo, "I reckon dat giant stripedog must still be alive, mate!"

The fat Searat's hushed whisper was barely audible, but Raga Bol heard it. He stood slowly and faced them both. With lightning swiftness his hook shot out, latching on to Blowfly's broad belt. The Searat was dragged forward to find himself facing Bol's upraised blade and threatening snarl.

"Did ye ever see a beast alive after I'd struck 'im wid me blade? Well, did ye?"

Blowfly watched the heavy scimitar poised, one stroke away from his quivering double chins. The rat's voice went squeaky with panic. "N . . . no, Cap'n!"

Raga Bol bared his gold-plated teeth in a wolfish grin. "Shall I prove it to ye, Blowfly?"

The rat sobbed brokenly. "Aw, don't do it, Cap'n Bol, please. Nobeast ever lived after yew 'it 'em wid yore sword!"

The captain's pale eyes lighted on Glimbo. "You should know, mate, tell 'im!"

Glimbo loved life too much to remain silent. Words poured from his mouth like running water. "Dat stripedog's kinbeasts must've carried 'im off, fer a fancy buryin'. I bet they buried the old 'un where he fell, 'cos they couldn't haul two carcasses. Mark me words, Blowfly, it don't matter 'ow big the stripedog was, he's deader'n any doornail now. Once Cap'n Bol's sword swipes 'em, they're well slayed. I'd take me affydavy on it!"

Blowfly fell to the ground as the hook pulled loose from his belt. Bol ground the scimitar and leaned on it.

"There's yore answer, mate, the stripedog's dead. I don't want to 'ear no more talk of such beasts from my crew. Now set four guards around me, so I can sleep."

The sentries crouched miserably in the darkness, waiting for the dawn. Wrapped in his cloak, Raga Bol lay alongside a roaring fire. But sleep did not come easily, and, when it did, his dreams were troubled by visions of the giant stripedog coming slowly but surely after him with the light of vengeance burning in his eyes.

Abruc the sea otter, his wife Marinu and their son Stugg sat on the streamside, beneath an overhanging bank canopy. They enjoyed their evening meal outside, away from the bustling noise of the holt. Stugg sucked noisily at the contents of his bowl.

Abruc patted his stomach and winked at the young creature. "Now that's wot I calls a sea otter chowder. Nobeast can make it like yore mamma does, ain't that right, me 'eart?"

Marinu refilled her husband's bowl. "I wager you used to say that about yore own mamma's chowder. All it takes is clams, mussels an' shrimps, with some beans, chestnut flour, seaweed, carrots an' a few pawfuls of sea salt an' hot-root pepper. 'Tis simple to cook up."

Young Stugg held out his bowl for a refill. "But you make it da best, 'cos yore our mamma!"

Marinu dipped her ladle into the pot they had brought out. "You'll soon be as big a flatterer as yore dad! Wipe that chin, you've got chowder all over it."

Abruc looked over the rim of his bowl at Marinu. "So, how are you an' old Sork gettin' along with our big badger? D'ye reckon he'll live?"

Marinu wiped Stugg's chin with her apron hem as she spoke. "It looks like he will, though whether or not he'll waken fully we don't know. He might just fade away, after one of those death sleeps that last a few seasons. I never thought anybeast could be so deeply wounded an' live. Sork used fish glue to mend his skull bone. When that was all clean and set, I used long hairs from his own back as thread to stitch the skin back over. We set lots of spider web over it all. Give it a few days, then we'll wash it gently with valerian and sanicle to deaden any pain. Shoredog says he'll have to be moved to the old cave where it'll be quieter. We'll make him a big bed of silver sand and moss."

Abruc nodded. "That should help. I'll keep a warm fire of pine an' sweet herbs burnin' there, night an' day."

Marinu rose. "I'm going back inside. Sork wants to borrow some of the broth off'n my chowder to feed him. A hard task with such a big beast who's still senseless."

When she had gone inside, Abruc and Stugg finished off the remaining food. The young otter sat watching his father attach a slim line, from the end of his rudder, to a thick root growing from the bankside. Abruc took a chunk of beeswax and began rubbing it into several more loose lines of tough flaxen fibre.

The sea otter eyed his young son. "Shouldn't you be off to yore bed, 'tis getting' late."

Stugg rubbed some of the beeswax on his paw curiously. "Wot are you doin' wiv dat stuff, farder?"

Abruc explained as he worked. "I'm makin' a bowstring, a good stout one that won't rot or break under strain."

Young Stugg pursued his enquiries. "Wotta you be wantin' a bowstring for, farder?"

Abruc answered patiently. "T'aint for me, it's for our big badger. I've got a feelin' he'll be well again some day. When the time comes, he'll be leavin' us to go westward."

Stugg persisted. "Is a bowstring good to go westward wiv?"

His father began deftly plying the waxed fibres together.

31

"Aye, son, that big feller's an archer. He'll have t'find 'imself the right wood t'make a new bow, but the least I can do is to plait him a proper bowstring. Then he'll be well armed to settle up with the vermin who tried to slay him an' murdered his ole friend."

Stugg nodded. "I bet they be sorry then!"

Abruc stopped working momentarily. "Sorry ain't the word, young 'un. When a badger goes after his enemies, there ain't noplace they can run or hide from him. I'll wager our big beast will come down on 'em with the Bloodwrath!"

Unfamiliar with this strange word, Stugg posed a new question. "Wot's a Bloodraff, farder?"

Abruc shook his head decisively. "Bloodwrath is terrible, somethin' you don't ever want t'see or know about. Go on now, off to bed with ye, me son!"

4

Old Father Phredd was the Redwall Abbey Gatekeeper. He had once been Abbot, but his seasons caught up with him. Passing the position over to Carrul, he retired to the gatehouse. Phredd was ancient, probably the oldest hedgehog in all Mossflower, and enjoyed being very old, and rather eccentric as well. Although the Old Gatekeeper sought the privacy of his beloved gatehouse and slept a lot, when he was up and about, he could be rather sprightly. His skinny form, with drooping silver spikes, often caused a smile around the Abbey and its grounds. Phredd spoke to stones, trees, plants and flowers, carrying on long conversations and debating with the most everyday objects.

He had arrived late for lunch, shunning the main crowd that was now gathered in the orchard. Preparing his own plate in the deserted kitchens, Phredd first chose a scone. He prattled on to it as he made his way around the tables.

"Hee hee, you're a fine fresh fellow. Now what'll I have to go with you, eh, eh? Speak up!"

Placing an ear close to the scone, he cackled. "Teeheehee! Of course, some honey, a piece o' cheese and a beaker of soup—not too hot, just right for swigging, eh?"

Granmum Gurvel, the old molecook, came in from the orchard to draw off more cordial. She spied Phredd and watched him chatting away to the food until he caught sight of her.

Phredd waved his scone at her. "Oh, er, young Gurvel, g'day!"

She chuckled. "Hurr hurr, goo day to ee, zurr. Wot bee's ee soup sayin' to ee, sumthin' noice oi 'opes?"

Phredd sipped at the beaker and smacked his lips. "Oh yes, indeed, miss. 'Tis saying that you cooked it very nicely. Oh, it also asked if there was any pie about, eh?"

Gurvel went to her larder and took out a large pie. It was preserved plum and apple, the golden crust liberally dusted with maple frosting.

She cut a generous slice and gave it to him. "Thurr naow, old 'edgepig, doant ee let nobeast see that. Oi baked it speshul furr supper."

Phredd nodded his thanks and skittered off out of the kitchens, conversing with the pie slice. "My my, you're a handsome fellow! What a splendid dessert you'll make. Come on, let's find a nice quiet corner, eh?"

Granmum Gurvel shook her head at Phredd's antics. She picked up the remainder of the pie. "Coom on, pie, back in ee larder again!"

The realisation of what she was doing caused the old molecook to smile. "Gurr, lack ee day, that Phredd got oi a talkin' to moi own pies naow, gurt seasons!"

Martha had finished her lunch. She, too, sought peace and quiet to continue her reading. Leaving her friends, she wheeled the chair indoors. Crossing Great Hall, she went straight to her favourite place. Harlequin hues of sunlight shafted down through the high, stained-glass windows onto the worn stone floor. Between two towering sandstone columns, a lantern glowed beneath a wondrous woven tapestry with a sword suspended to one side of it. The hare-maid halted her chair in full view of the scene, golden motes of sundust floating slowly on the serene air.

Martha paused before opening Sister Portula's heavy book. She gazed up at the central figure in the tapestry, Martin the Warrior. A heroic, armour-clad mouse, the hero and champion of Redwall Abbey. Martha loved looking at his face—so strong and protective yet kindly, with a secret smile forever hiding in his eyes. The sword he was leaning on was the very same one that hung on the wall—a legendary warrior's weapon, its only adornment, one red pommel stone set on the hilt. Martin's swordblade had been forged at Salamandastron, the badgers' mountain fortress on the west seashore. It had been made from a star fragment that had fallen from the skies.

No matter what position Martha took up when she visited the tapestry, Martin's eyes always seemed to be watching her. The haremaid could feel his presence so strongly that she often spoke to him. Keeping her voice low in the echoing hall, she nodded toward the warrior mouse.

"The rains stopped today. You can see by the sunlight in here that it's a beautiful spring day outside. I've come to do a bit of reading in peace. You should hear those Dibbuns singing in the orchard—they're so happy! Did you ever do much reading, Martin?"

"Hee hee, I don't suppose he did, a warrior like him, eh?" Phredd emerged from the shadows, where he had installed himself behind a column to enjoy his lunch.

Martha was slightly surprised at the old hedgehog's appearance. "Oh I'm sorry, sir, I didn't know you were here."

Phredd picked pie crumbs from his cheek spikes. "No need to be sorry, pretty miss, you carry on talking to your friend. I've had many a long chat with him, eh!"

The haremaid continued looking at the tapestry. "He looks so understanding, like a friend anybeast could talk to. Do you think he can hear us?"

Phredd patted her shoulder lightly. "Of course he can. I'm sorry for intruding. You carry on, miss. I'll just pop off to my gatehouse for an afternoon nap. Good day to you."

He shuffled off, though Martha heard him reprimanding a corner bench. "You mind your own business an' don't be eavesdropping now, eh, eh!"

Martha opened the book but was only able to concentrate on it for a short while before her eyelids began to flicker and then droop. The peacefulness of her surroundings, combined with the warm sunlight pouring down from the windows, had woven its own spell. There, in the silence of Great Hall, the small figure in the chair slept in a pool of tranquillity. Floating through the corridors of her mind came two mice—one, a maid of her own age clad in a gown of green; the other, Martin the Warrior.

His voice was as reassuring as soft breezes through a meadow. "I never did read much, Martha. It is good to read, all learning is knowledge. Read on, young one. Learn of Sister Amyl and the mice of Loamhedge."

The haremaid could hear her own voice replying, "Learn what? Who is Sister Amyl?"

The young mousemaid standing beside the warrior pointed to Martha and spoke, every word burning itself into Martha's mind.

"Where once I dwelt in Loamhedge,
my secret lies hid from view,
a tale of how I learned to walk,
when once I was as you.
Though you cannot go there,
look out for two who may,
travellers from out of the past,
returning home someday."

Both Martin and Sister Amyl raised a paw in farewell. The dream faded like wisping smoke as Martha slept on.

Around midnoon Martha was awakened rudely, her chair jolted as three pair of paws latched on to it. Horty, Springald and Fenna ran her speedily across Great Hall, whirling perilously around the huge stone columns.

Martha gripped the chair tightly. "Whoo! Slow down, please. Where are we going?"

Horty jumped up beside her, shouting, "Out to enjoy the jolly old fresh air, my beautiful skin'n'blister, you'll go mouldy sittin' indoors, wot! I say, you chaps, can't you make this thing go faster? Yaaaah!"

The chair struck a table edge and upturned. Springald and Fenna leapt aside, but Martha and Horty were shot out. Luckily, Martha landed on top of her brother, clutching Sister Portula's volume to her. The chair skidded on a short distance, then lay still, one of its wheels still turning slowly.

Horty looked up into his sister's face. "Dreadfully sorry about that, old gel, just a bit of fun, wot. I say, are you hurt?"

Martha glared down from where she was sitting on him. "Lucky for you I'm not. Is my chair damaged?"

Springald and Fenna set the chair upright and examined it. "No, not a mark on it, Martha!"

"Haha, old Toran knew what he was doing when he built this thing. Stay there, we'll lift you back in!"

In frosty silence, Martha allowed them to lift her back into the chair. The trio fussed about, folding the rug neatly about her lap and laying the volume on it.

Fenna smiled sweetly. "There, no real harm done, Martha. We were only trying to cheer you up, didn't mean to throw you like that."

Hastily Springald backed her up. "Yes, we were going to take you for a quick spin around the walltop. Lovely view from there on a day like this."

Horty waggled his ears in agreement. "Right you are, m'dear. There's still time for a toddle round the battlements, though we'll go slower this time. Word of honour, wot!"

Martha shook her head firmly. "Oh no, you three wildbeasts aren't taking me anywhere. Now go away! Please, leave me alone, I'm quite happy here!"

Horty scuffed his footpaw guiltily along the floorstones.

"I say, y'won't tell anybeast about what happened, will you?"

Martha tapped her chair arm pensively. "Any beast like who?"

Horty fidgeted with his belt tab. "Er, like Toran, or Abbot Carrul or blinkin' old Sis Peculiar."

Martha reminded him of the Infirmary Keeper. "Or Sister Setiva?"

Fenna's eyes went wide. "Oh please, don't tell her!"

The other two miscreants joined in with their pleas.

"She'll make us scrub the infirmary out and stitch sheets!"

"Aye, an' physick the blinkin' life out of us. Oh come on, charmin', beautiful Sis, say y'won't snitch to that monster!"

They looked so sorry for themselves that Martha relented. "Alright, I won't say anything—provided you go away immediately and leave me in peace."

Without a word the trio began to scramble away and were almost at the door when Martha suddenly recalled her dream.

"Wait, come back here, there's something I need you to do!"

Horty dashed back so hastily that he almost tripped and fell onto his sister's lap. "Anything, dear old skin'n'blister, we're yours to flippin' well command!"

Martha issued her modest requests, but she spoke firmly. "Fenna, I want you to go and seek out Abbot Carrul. Horty, you go and find Sister Portula, and mind how you address her. The message for both of them is this: Ask politely that if neither is too busy, would they please come to the gatehouse. There is an important matter I would like to discuss with them. Springald, push my chair to the gatehouse—at a reasonable pace, please."

Brother Phredd poked his head around the gatehouse doorway, blinking and yawning. "Ah yes, young wotsername, come in please, and your friend, too. Always nice to have afternoon visitors, eh!"

As Springald pushed Martha over the threshold, the haremaid heard the mousemaid muttering. "Huh, I'm not stopping in some dusty old gatehouse on an afternoon like this!"

Martha fixed her with an icy smile. "Oh, you don't have to stay, you run off to the kitchens now. Have a word with Gurvel or Toran—tell them I'd like afternoon tea for four."

Springald looked puzzled. "Afternoon tea for four?"

Martha wheeled round to face her. "Yes, afternoon tea, you know, scones and slices of cake, and a large pot of mint tea with honey. Hop along now, bring them straight back here, and don't spill the tea. Off you go, miss!"

To ensure Martha's silence, Springald had no option but to obey. With a sweep of her skirt she flounced off.

Old Phredd addressed the chair he was about to sit on. "Afternoon tea, how does that sound to you, quite nice, eh?"

In due course, Abbot Carrul and Sister Portula arrived. Both knew that Martha was a sensible creature and would not summon them on some foolish errand. Brother Phredd had just seated them both, when another knock came on the door. He scratched his drooping spikes and muttered. "More visitors, quite an eventful afternoon, eh?"

Springald pushed the laden trolley in. She curtsied impudently at the Abbot. "Afternoon tea for four, Father!"

Martha forestalled any further smartness by nodding graciously at the mousemaid. "Thank you, miss, you may go now!"

Sister Portula watched the back of Springald's head shaking with rage as she exited the gatehouse and slammed the door. "Gracious me, you certainly put that young mouse in her place!"

Martha smiled demurely. "Yes, Sister, but she does need it now and again, doesn't she?"

Abbot Carrul took the haremaid's paw. "What was it you wanted to see us about, Martha?"

Over afternoon tea, Martha explained to her friends how she had fallen asleep. She told them of Martin's visitation, and of the young mouse who had accompanied him, ending with the short poem, which she recalled precisely.

"Where once I dwelt in Loamhedge,
my secret lies hid from view,
the tale of how I learned to walk,
when once I was as you.
Though you cannot go there,
look out for two who may,
travellers from out of the past,
returning home someday."

Abbot Carrul sat forward in his armchair. "Strange. What do you think, Sister?"

Portula put aside her tea. "Not many Redwallers are honoured by a visit from Martin the Warrior. We must heed all he says. His spirit is not just the essence of valour and honour, he is also the voice of knowledge and wisdom. Now, what is your own opinion of this incident, Martha?"

The haremaid tapped the cover of the book. "This is the history of Loamhedge that you loaned me, Sister. I think the answer lies inside it. That's why I called you here. I am still young, but you three have the knowledge of seasons on your side. I was hoping that you could help me. I never dreamed that there might be an answer to why I can't walk. Do you think there is?"

Old Phredd picked up the big tome and laid it on the table. He spoke to it, as it if were a living thing. "Well now, you dusty old relic, are you going to assist us with this little one's problem, eh, eh?"

He turned and gave Martha a toothless grin. "Heeheehee, I think he will. Though one can never really tell what a book says until one reads it, eh?"

Abbot Carrul opened the book. "This may take some time, but we're on your side, Martha. If there is a way to make you walk, rest assured, we'll find it."

Martha could feel tears beginning to brim in her eyes. She blinked them away swiftly. "Thank you all, my good friends. But there is something that I don't think the book can tell us. Who are the ones we must look out for? The two travellers from out of the past, returning home someday?"

Sister Portula gazed out the window into the sunlit noon. "You're right, Martha. I wonder who they could be."

5

North of Redwall, spring eventide filtered soft light through the leafy canopy of Mossflower Wood. Amid aisles of oak, beech, elm, sycamore and other forest giants, slender rowan, birch and willow stood like young attendants, waiting on their stately lords. Blue smoke drifted lazily upward through the foliage which fringed a shallow stream. Somewhere nearby, a pair of nightingales warbled harmoniously.

The tremulous beauty was lost upon a small vermin band who had trekked down from the far Northlands. They had camped on the bank to fish. A fat, brutish weasel called Burrad was their leader. Beneath his ragged cloak he carried a cutlass, its bone handle notched with the lives he had taken. Burrad's sly eyes watched his band closely. They were spitting four shiny scaled roach on green willow withes to grill over the fire.

Drawing the cutlass, Burrad pointed it at the biggest fish. "Dat'n der is mine, yew cook it good fer me, Flinky!"

The stoat called Flinky let out a pitifully indignant whine. "Arr 'ey, Chief, I caught dis wun meself, 'tis me own fish!"

Despite his bulk, Burrad was quick. Bulling the stoat over, he whipped Flinky mercilessly with the flat of his blade.

Covering his head, the victim screeched for mercy. "Yaaaaaargh, stop 'im mates, afore he kills me pore ould body! Yeeegh, spare me, yer mightiness, spare me. Aaaaagh!"

Cruel by nature, Burrad thrashed Flinky even harder. Throwing himself upon the hapless stoat, he pressed the blade against Flinky's scrawny neck, snarling viciously.

"Wot d'yer want, the fist or yore 'ead? 'Urry up an' speak."

The cutlass blade pressed savagely down. Flinky wailed. "Yeeeeh, take de fish, I've only got one 'ead. Take de fish!"

Burrad rose, grinning wolfishly as he kicked Flinky's bottom. "Cook dat fish good, or yore a dead 'un!"

He turned on the other eleven vermin gang members. "Wot are youse lot gawpin' at, eh? Gimme some grog!"

A female stoat called Crinktail, whose tail was shaped almost like a letter Z, passed Burrad the jug of nettle grog. Snatching it roughly, the bully sat down, taking long gulps of the fiery liquid.

He watched Flinky like a hawk. "Crispy outside an' soft inside, dat's de way I likes fish."

The others averted their eyes; there was no doubt about who the leader of their gang was.

Crouched low in the reeds on the far bank, two creatures viewed the scene. One was an otter, the other a squirrel, both in their late middle seasons.

The otter squinched his eyes, letting them rove over the gang. "Hmm, about twelve o' them over there, I'd say."

The squirrel nibbled on a young reed. "There's thirteen."

Her companion shrugged. "I won't argue with ye, 'cos my eyes ain't as good as they used t'be. I tell ye though, mate, that's one sorry gang o' vermin. Looks as if they got rocks in their skulls instead o' brains."

The squirrel chuckled. "Aye, campin' there without a single sentry posted, an' a fire smokin' away like a beacon. 'Tis a wonder their mothers let 'em out alone."

The otter nodded. "See ole lardbelly yonder, the big weasel? Leave him t'me, I enjoy takin' bullies down a peg."

The squirrel commented drily, "Watch he don't fall on ye, he'd flatten ye like a pancake. Are those fish ready yet?"

Her companion sniffed the air. "I'd say so. Right then, are we ready t'go an' pay 'em a visit?"

The squirrel sighed. "Aye, layin' here won't get us any supper. You go in the front, an' I'll make me way around back."

The lean, aging otter grumbled. "It's always me wot has t'go in the front. Why can't I go in the back?"

The squirrel cut left along the streambank, replying, " 'Cos I'm the best tree climber. Give me time t'get ready, mate, don't walk in too early. Good luck!"

Tucking his rudder into the back of his belt, the otter draped his ragged cloak to conceal it. He bound a faded red bandanna low on his brow, disguising both ears and scrunching down over his eyes to make them look short-sighted.

Picking up a polished hardwood staff, he splashed into the stream shallows, muttering to himself. "Huh, I'm gettin' too old for this game!"

Little Redd was the youngest of the vermin gang. Small and runty, he was often the butt of their coarse jokes.

Seeking about for firewood, Redd glanced sideways. He saw the bedraggled creature wading across the stream, and called to Burrad. "Aye aye, Chief, looks like we got company!"

Burrad took his mouth from the grog jug. He cast a contemptuous glance at the hunched figure struggling toward the bankside. "Wot'n de name o'bludd is dat?"

The otter sloshed ashore, calling in a quavery voice. "A good evenin' to one an' all. Seems I'm just in time for supper. Mmm . . . roasted roach, me favourite vittles!"

Burrad's cutlass was drawn and wavering a whisker's breadth from the unwanted visitor's nose. "Who are ye? Huhuhuh, or should I say, wot are ye?"

The stranger avoided the blade neatly. Ducking under it, he stood at the vermin leader's side, wrinkling his nose comically. "Wot am I, young feller? I'm a ferroat, o' course!"

Flinky looked up from the cooking fire. "A ferroat? Ah' shure, an' wot sort o' beast is dat now?"

The intruder replied airily. "Oh, just a cross twixt a ferret an' a stoat. I was a small sickly babe, or so me ole mum'- n'dad told me. That's why I look like this."

Ignoring his fish-cooking task, Flinky continued. "An' who, pray, was yore muther an' father?"

The stranger replied, straight-faced. "A rat an' a fox, I s'pose, but they was terrible liars."

Flinky scratched his head. "Liars? Huh, I'll say they was!"

Burrad interrupted by thwacking Flinky between both ears with the flat of his blade. "Who asked yew, pud- dle'ead? Gerron wid cookin' dose fishes!"

He turned to the odd-looking creature. "Wot's yore name, ferroat, an' wot d'ye want 'ere?"

The newcomer pointed to himself. "Just told ye, haven't I? Me name's Ferroat, an' I'll sing an' dance fer me supper. That's if ye'll allow me, kind sir."

The vermin gang winked and sniggered among them- selves. Burrad, a kind sir? This old fool was begging to die.

Testing his cutlass blade by licking the edge, Burrad leaned close to his intended victim and grinned. "Allow ye, eh? If'n yore dancin' an' singin' ain't to me likin', I'll allow this blade to chop ye into ten pieces. Then I'll allow me gang to roast ye over that fire. If ye don't taste nice, we kin always use ye fer fishbait!"

Smiling affably, the odd beast bowed creakily. " 'Tis a fair offer, sir, I thankee kindly."

Shuffling about in a curious jig, the creature twirled his staff and began singing.

"I'll always recall wot Ma said to me,
ere I went a rovin' a minstrel to be,

beware of the vermin, they ain't got no class,
an' they ain't got the brains Mother Nature gave grass!
Rowledy dowlety toodle um day.

I soon found out me dear mother was right,
I met up with some vermin the followin' night,
they were strangers to bathin', an' that made me think,
why didn't Ma tell me that all vermin stink?
Rowledy pong and a toodledy pooh!"

The comic-looking old ragbag of a beast jigged and shuffled
around. Raucous laughter greeted his performance followed by tears of merriment that coursed down the vermin's cheeks. It was only at the start of the third verse, when
vermin's faces were compared to toads' bottoms, that Burrad realised the singer was insulting him and his gang.

Roaring with rage, the fat weasel rushed the disguised
otter. Whirling his cutlass, Burrad aimed a mighty swipe
that should have left the singer headless. However, far from
being slain, the odd creature ducked under the blow, came
up under Burrad and tweaked his snout.

Purple with spleen, the gang leader grappled with his
opponent, yelling to his second in command. "Skrodd, gut
this old fleabag wid yer spear, I've got 'im!"

The tall, evil-looking fox dashed forward, plunging with
his spear. But the otter was fast and more clever than both
vermin. He butted Burrad under the chin, wriggled from
his grasp and scuttled to one side in the blink of an eye.

Burrad stood gaping at the spear protruding from his
stomach. He raised his clouding eyes to the open-mouthed
fox, faltering. "Ye've killed me, yer blather-brained foo . . . !"

Burrad crashed over backward, slain by his own gang
member. Amid the drama, nobeast noticed the four fish
vanish up into the willow foliage, hauled on a thin twine by
the green withes they were spitted upon.

Skrodd's surprise was only momentary. His brain was already reacting to the fact that he was now the vermin gang's

new leader. Leaving the spear stuck in his former chief, the tall fox grabbed the cutlass from Burrad's limp grasp. He came at the otter with a blurring barrage of swift slashes.

Whizzzzzthonk! A slingstone from the trees suddenly rendered him senseless. Skrodd's fellow vermin looked on in horror as his body collapsed in a heap. Before the gang could move, the squirrel dropped from her perch. Danger glinted in her eyes as she twirled a loaded sling expertly.

"There's twoscore more of us layin' in the bushes, just waitin' on the word!"

Shedding his disguise, the otter knocked daggers and other weapons from the vermin's paws, with sharp raps of his polished staff. He looked nothing like the ragged, dancing fool he had been a moment ago. His voice was stern and commanding.

"Everybeast stand still, right where ye are! Believe Saro, we've got a full crew ready to pounce on ye!"

Halfchop, a rat who was minus a paw, gulped. "If'n that un's called Saro, yew must be Bragoon?"

Flinky look at the pair in astonishment. "I've heard of ye, Bragoon an' Saro. Two mighty warriors!"

Bragoon leaned on his staff and nodded. "That's us, an' there's forty more trained fighters like us, just waitin' to get a crack at you lot. So have the brains to stay alive an' listen to wot we say."

Flinky bowed politely. "Anythin', yer honour, sure we're in no position to be arguin' wid ye."

Saro pointed at a wobbly-nosed ferret called Plumnose. "You, where have ye come from? Speak!"

Gesturing back over his shoulder, Plumnose replied, "Durr, we cummed from der Nort'lands."

Saro nodded. "The Northlands, eh? Then listen carefully to my friend Bragoon."

The otter let his fierce eyes wander round the hapless vermin as he ground out an ultimatum. "Get yoreselves back to the Northlands, 'cos if yore anywhere south of here by nightfall, yore all deadbeasts! We're goin' now, but our mates'll stay hidden, watchin' ye. Sit still here until 'tis properly dark, then break camp an' get back to where ye came from—sharpish! We'll be passin' this way again tomorrow. Make sure yore not still here. Is that clear?"

Flinky's head bobbed up and down like a yo-yo. "Ah, sure, 'tis certain clear, yer mightiness. We've all got the message, an' a fine important one it is, sir!"

Bragoon and Saro backed out of the camp. A moment later they were lost in the surrounding trees. The vermin sat wordlessly staring at one another until Plumnose broke the silence.

"Wodd duh we do now?"

Flinky's mate, Crinktail, was in no doubt. "Like they said, we wait 'til it's dark, then we gets out of here. I don't know about youse, but I'm goin'."

Flinky agreed. "Aye, ye don't disobey two like Bragoon an' Saro. Best do the sensible thing, mates."

Recovering from the slingstone blow, Skrodd sat up groaning. "Unnnh, wot hit me?"

Slipback, a weasel with most of his back fur missing, toyed with the cutlass that had belonged to Burrad.

"Ye were knocked cold by a slingstone, mate."

Skrodd felt the lump on his skull and winced. "Who did it?"

Flinky chuckled. " 'Twas none other than a famous squirrel called Saro. Yore lucky she did, 'cos the one you was goin' after wid yore blade was 'er partner, Bragoon."

Skrodd stood slowly and walked across to Slipback. Suddenly he dealt the weasel a swift kick to the chin. As Slipback fell, the tall fox grabbed Burrad's cutlass.

"Keep yer paws off dat blade, 'tis mine now. I slew Burrad, an' I'm the new chief round 'ere!"

Slipback avoided a second kick. "Only by accident—dat don't make yew chief!"

Skrodd turned to face the rest of the gang, wielding his

new weapon. "Accident or not, Burrad's dead. Does anybeast want to challenge me? Come on!"

None came forward. They knew the tall fox's reputation as a fighter; even Burrad had never kicked him about.

Skrodd smiled grimly. "Right, up on yore hunkers, we're goin' to track those two down!"

Little Redd exclaimed, "Didn't ye hear Flinky? Those two are dangerous warriors, Bragoon an' Saro."

Skrodd turned on the little fox. "Ye mean that ole ragbag who was jiggin' about an' tryin' to sing for his supper? Wot did the other one look like, Flinky?"

The stoat shrugged. "Small an' oldish, why d'ye ask?"

Skrodd curled his lip scornfully. "A pair o' little ole tattered ragamuffins, an' ye lot believed they was Bragoon an' Saro. Real famous warriors are big an' tough. Any two beasts could say they was Bragoon an' Saro. Those two were nothin' but a pair of ole impostors. Now come on, let's get after 'em. Nobeast knocks me down wid a slingstone an' lives t'brag about it. I'll gut the two of 'em!"

A hefty-looking rat called Dargle remained seated. "They said we was to sit 'ere 'til it was dark, then head back t'the Northlands. The otter said there was twoscore fighters layin' nearby, an' that we'd be dead meat if'n we didn't do like we was told."

Skrodd shook his head in disbelief. "An' ye believed 'im? That's the oldest trick in the book. Watch, I'll show ye twoscore o' fighters!"

Furiously grabbing anything that came to paw—firewood, pebbles and soil—the tall fox flung them at the surrounding trees, yelling out defiantly. "Now then, ye mighty fighters, come out an' show yerselves. I'll fight ye all at once, or one by one if'n ye ain't frightened o' me! Get out 'ere, ye mangy frogbait!"

Silence greeted the challenge. Skrodd spat contemptuously into the fire, glaring at the vermin gang. "Wot a bunch of addlebrains! Up on yore paws an' get movin' ye bunch o' ditherin' oafs. After I've slain those two ole relics, we'll get the rest o' this job done. Move!"

As they moved southward into the woodlands, Little Redd discussed the situation with Flinky. "Skrodd ain't takin' us to that Abbey place that Burrad was always goin' on about, is he?"

Flinky nodded. "Ah sure, it looks like he wants t'be the big bold beast who gets the magic sword. Huh, magic sword! I wonder where ould Burrad heard that tale?"

Juppa, the weasel who was Slipback's mate, joined the conversation. "Burrad said his father told 'im about it, just afore he died. Said there was an Abbey, a big place called Redwall. Accordin' to 'im, there's only a few peaceful woodlanders lives there. They keep a magic sword at Redwall. 'Tis said that the warrior who holds that sword is the greatest in the land!"

Slipback confirmed his mate's story. "Aye, none can stand against the sword owner, I've heard the tale meself."

Skrodd, who was leading the gang through the darkened woodlands, overheard Slipback's remark. He stopped and questioned the weasel. "Wot have ye heard? Tell me."

The garrulous Flinky spoke up. "Ah sure, 'twas me that told him. I sat wid Burrad's ole dad many a night, yarnin' away. He was a fine ould feller, not like his son. Anyhow, he told me all about the magic sword, so he did."

Skrodd was fired with the idea of possessing such an enchanted blade. He stared hard at the gabby stoat. "Right, then, you tell me everythin' the ole beast said."

Flinky liked to talk, but he was also aware that the tall fox was not one to be taken lightly. "Ah, well let me see now. There's this place, see, a grand ould Abbey called Redwall that stands on a path somewhere in the centre of the land. Sure, an' a fine buildin' it is!"

Little Redd interrupted. "I've 'eard o' Redwall."

Skrodd froze him with a glare, gesturing Flinky to continue. "Aye, Redwall was built by a mighty warrior long ago.

He carried a great sword made from bits o' the moon 'n stars. A marvellous blade, magic enough t'make a champion fighter out o' anybeast. That warrior's long dead now, but the sword still hangs in the Abbey."

This time it was Skrodd's turn to interrupt. "Then why doesn't one of the creatures at Redwall Abbey wear it?"

Flinky shook his head. "Ah no, they're all only simple woodland beasts. They're farmers an' such, not fighters. Hah, what need d'they have o' swords, 'tis said that Redwall is a place of peace an' plenty."

Little Redd's eyes shone with longing. "I wish I had a magic sword!"

Skrodd shoved him roughly. "A runt like yew, huh, you'll have to fight me fer it. That sword is goin' t'be mine!"

The hefty rat Dargle muttered under his breath. "If ye think ye can take it, fox!"

Skrodd looked around at the vermin behind him. "Did somebeast say somethin'?"

Flinky rubbed his stomach. "Ah no, Chief, 'twas just me ould guts rumblin' away. I knew that fish wasn't fer me somehow."

Bragoon and Saro had made camp in a grove of conifers, some miles south of where they had encountered the vermin.

Burying the fishbones beneath the deep layer of pine needles, the otter wiped his mouth. "Bit o' fish like that makes a nice change, eh mate? Did ye manage to lay paws on any o' that stuff they was drinkin'?"

The aging squirrel wrinkled her nose disgustedly. "That poison? Vermin-brewed nettle grog. Small wonder they're stupid—it must've rotted what little brains they had. Best stick with clean streamwater until we get back to Redwall an' get some decent drink."

She lay back, viewing the star-dusted skies through the treetops. "Aah, t'be back home in the good ole Abbey. D'ye think they've forgiven us for the old Dibbun days?"

Her companion chuckled. "I certainly hope they have, we were a fearsome pair, mate. Hmmm, wonder if ole Granmum Gurvel's still the Abbeycook. Hoho, the pies'n'scones we swiped off'n her kitchen windowsill. No wonder she turned grey!"

Saro shrugged. "There's a lot o' seasons run under the bridge since we were Abbeybabes. I don't suppose pore old Gurvel will still be livin'. She was a great cook though."

Bragoon nodded. "Aye, she was that. I'll bet that little brother o' mine Toran is Abbeycook now. Gurvel taught him a lot, y'know. He was always a goodbeast around kitchens an' ovens."

Saro hopped up and spread herself along a bough, directly above Bragoon's resting spot. She reminisced hungrily.

"Scones, or fresh bread, with meadowcream an' damson preserve. That's what I could eat right now!"

Stretched on the ground, Bragoon yawned and sighed. "Don't even mention it, mate. Let's get a good night's shut-eye. We could make Redwall by afternoon tea tomorrow. You can fill yore face then. G'night, Saro."

The squirrel ignored her friend and continued yearning. "October Ale! What could be nicer than a foamin' beaker of good October Ale. Mmmm, with some brown farlbread an' some yellow cheese with roasted hazelnuts in it. Simple but satisfyin', eh Brag?"

The otter opened one eye. "Very acceptable. Now go t'sleep!"

Saro carried on as if she had not heard. "What would y'say to an apple'n'blackberry crumble, spread thick with meadowcream?"

Bragoon growled. "I'd say button yore lip an' sleep. So goodnight!"

But Saro could not forget the subject of food. "Howsabout ice cold mint tea an' a thick slice of heavy fruitcake with honey crystals in it. Ooooh!"

Bragoon sat up slowly. "I'd say ye was makin' my pore stomach gurgle with all this vittle talk. Good . . . night!"

Saro licked her lips. "Or some of yore favourite, a big carrot'n'mushroom pasty, with onion gravy drippin' an' oozin' out the sides, an' . . . Yaahoooow!"

She was catapulted into the air as Bragoon hauled down hard on the bough, letting it go suddenly. Rising from the ground, Saro dusted herself off indignantly.

"Gettin' touchy in yore old age, aren't ye? Goodnight to ye, ole grumpy rudder!"

Bragoon snorted. "I swear ye were born chatterin'. Now goodnight, old gabby whiskers!"

Silence fell over the glade. Both lifelong friends drifted into the realm of slumber. They dreamt golden-tinged memories of their Dibbun seasons at the place they called home—Redwall Abbey.

6

The big badger's eyes flickered, then opened slowly. He lay quite still, taking in his strange surroundings—a cave, peaceful and warm, with sweet aromatic wisps drifting languidly from a rockbound hearth. A fireglow cast flickering shadows across the rough-hewn walls. He felt secure and safe there with moss and soft, silver sand beneath him.

A movement near his head caught the badger's attention. A young sea otter emerged.

"De old stripedog who was slayed, was he yore farder, sir?"

Though it pained him, he strained his neck to get a closer look at the young one. The badger's voice, echoing in the cavern, sounded strange to his ears. "Nay, he was my friend, though a father could not have been kinder to me. He was called Grawn. I trust you put him to rest decently."

The youngster nodded several times. "Shoredog an' my farder made a bury hole. They putted rocks on him an' yore bow, 'cos it was broked in halves."

The badger's big dark eyes glistened wetly. "I must thank your father and Shoredog. What do they call you?"

The young beast held out his paw politely. "I bee's Stugg, son of Abruc an' Marinu, sir."

A massive paw took Stugg's smaller one, enveloping it.

54

" 'Tis a pleasure to meet ye, Stugg. I am called Lonna Bow-stripe. Is your father hereabout? I would speak with him."

Lonna listened to young Stugg scamper from the cave calling shrilly. "Farder, farder, come quick! De big stripedog bee's awake, his name be Lonna!"

In a short while, two male sea otters entered the cave, followed by two females, one very old, and Stugg following up the rear.

Lonna leaned forward slightly. "Thank you, my friends, for saving my life, caring for me and putting old Grawn to rest. Stugg told me you buried him well."

Abruc pressed Lonna back down gently. "We did what was right for your companion. Only vermin leave the dead unburied. As for ye bein' cared for, 'twas my wife Marinu an' ole Sork who saw to yore well-bein'. You lie still an' rest now, Lonna. By an' by ye'll get stronger. We'll see to that."

The big badger's paw touched the long scar ridge that crossed his face diagonally from eartip to jaw. "I must grow strong again to repay the vermin who did this and murdered poor Grawn. Did you see them?"

Sork placed Lonna's paw by his side. "Be still, bigbeast, an' thank the seasons ye are still alive. That face still needs a lot of healing, aye, an' yore back, too. We'll bring ye food an' drink." Sork and Marinu departed.

Shoredog stood over Lonna, looking down into his injured face. "We never saw the vermin, but we know 'em. Raga Bol the Searat an' his crew were the ones. His ship was wrecked beyond repair. They have gone westward, inland to where the weather's fair an' the pickin's easier. Do ye know Raga Bol?"

Lonna's scar twitched faintly. "I do not know the scum, but I know of him. They say he kills for fun."

Young Stugg scowled. "My farder says Raga Bol be's wicked!"

Abruc tugged his son's rudder. "Go an' help yore mamma now."

Lonna watched the young otter shuffle off. "He'll grow up to be a fine big creature someday."

Abruc smiled. "Aye, Stugg's a good liddle son."

Abruc sought Lonna's paw and pressed something into it. "Yore weapon was too badly broken to fix. I wove ye a new bowstring. Mayhap ye'll need it when y'leave here."

Lonna held the cord where he could see it better. "Thankee, friend. 'Tis a fine, tough one, well woven and waxed. This is a good and thoughtful gift."

Abruc flushed with pleasure. "Ye have only to ask if ye need ought else. We'll do our best to find it."

The giant badger closed his eyes, speaking softly. "I'd be obliged if you could get some ash shafts for arrows, and a few long stout yew saplings, so I can choose one to make a new bow from."

Shoredog replied. "We saved yore quiver an' the arrows, too. Me an' Abruc know some stream otters not too far from here. They coppice a yew grove. We can have ye a selection of good saplings by tomorrow night. Now sleep, Lonna, ye must rest if yore goin' to get better. Relax an' sleep."

A short time thereafter, Lonna allowed Marinu to feed him. Then he drifted off into slumber whilst Sork tended to his hurts. In his sleep he visioned Raga Bol, swinging down at his face with the broad-bladed scimitar. The big badger concentrated all his energy and thoughts on the Searat's savage features.

Mentally he began chanting, over and over, "Look and you will see me! Know that I am Lonna Bowstripe! The earth is not big enough for us both! I will come on your trail! I will find you, Raga Bol! I will seek you out no matter where! The day of your death is already written on the stones of Hellgates!"

Whilst the big badger was sleeping, young Stugg crept in to see him. The expression of hatred on Lonna's ruined features was so frightening that the young sea otter ran from the cave.

Raga Bol was still out on the heathlands, trekking west with his Searats. They were camped on the streambank in what had once been a vole settlement. Amid the smoke and carnage of burning dwellings and slain voles, the barbarous crew fought among themselves over the pitiful possessions and plundered food.

Wirga, the wizened old Searat who had healed Raga Bol's severed stump, stood watching her master chewing on a strip of dried fish.

With the silver hook tugging at the fish as he pulled to tear it apart, Bol grinned wickedly at Wirga. "See, I told ye, the further west we go, the better the pickin's get. This stump o' mine ain't painin' so much now. Aye, an' the weather's gettin' better, too."

Wirga gestured round at the slain vole bodies lying on the bank. "Fling 'em in the stream an' this'd make a good camp for the night, Cap'n."

Bol picked his teeth with the hooktip. "Aye, 'tis nice'-n'restful 'ereabouts now. Hahaha!"

Dutifully, Wirga laughed with him. Her cackling trailed off as she saw her captain go off into a vacant silence, his eyes opening wide as the fish fell unheeded from his mouth.

Wirga stared at him anxiously. "What is it, Cap'n, a bone stuck in thy gullet? Let me take a look!"

As she bent toward him, Raga Bol recovered and kicked her roughly away. "Break camp, we're movin' out!"

The healer was bewildered at this sudden change. "But Cap'n, thee said . . ."

Wirga narrowly dodged an angry slash from the silver hook.

Bol booted the fire left and right, scattering it. "I said we're movin' out, we ain't stayin' in this place. Now shift yoreself an' get the crew together!"

He strode off, to the top of a small rise, peering back at the route they had come along. Wirga passed the word on to Glimbo.

The one-eyed Searat rolled his milky orb in puzzlement. "Why does 'e wanna move? 'Tis nearly dark!"

Wirga picked up her stolen belongings. "Hah! Yew go an' ask 'im, if'n thee feels tired o' livin'."

The crew gathered in sullen silence, watching their leader. He was still gazing eastward from the top of the rise. None of them dared make a move until he did.

Raga Bol stared at the hostile heathland, muttering to himself. "Yore dead, stripedog, or ye should be. In the name o' blood an' thunder, where are ye?"

He drew his cloak about him and shivered. Somewhere in Raga Bol's evil mind he had felt Lonna Bowstripe's threat.

In the gatehouse at Redwall Abbey, Martha and her friends were studying the history of Loamhedge. It made harrowing reading.

Abbot Carrul shook his head sadly. "This is not the story of one creature, it is the history of many, all related to one writer, who set it down as a chronicle. I think that this poem, "The Loamhedge Lament," by Sister Linfa, sums up most of the tragedy. I'll read it out to you."

Martha's eyes misted over as the Abbot recited the poem.

"Where are the carefree sunlit days,
when once amid tranquil bowers,
Loamhedge mice would take their ease,
to dream away happy hours?
Where did the laughter go?
Who stole the joy away?
Heavy the heart that goes
far from its home to stray.
A sickness stole in to blight our lives
like a spectre of unwanted doom.
Midst grief and anguish it lingered,
creeping through hall and room.
Like wheat before the sickle,
it laid our loved ones low,

leaving us only one answer,
to flee our home and go!
Stalked by desolation now,
left open to wind and rain,
only in old memories dim
would Loamhedge live again."

The day's last gleaming shone through the open door. Toran stood framed there, wiping his eyes on his cook's apron. He had entered unnoticed and heard the whole thing.

"Leave this now, and come back to the Abbey for supper, friends. Tomorrow morning ye can sit out on the wallsteps in the sunlight and study some more. Martha, come on, 'tis far too sad, sittin' here at night readin' of sickness an' death."

The haremaid cast an imploring glance at Abbot Carrul. "But we must find out about Sister Amyl's secret, and we must find out a way to discover where Loamhedge lies!"

The Abbot shepherded her to the gatehouse door. "Toran's right, miss, the night hours can be long and oppressive for such heavy stuff. Let's go to supper in Cavern Hole and shed our sad mood for tonight. We'll be much brighter, and more alert, in the morning."

Old Phredd the Gatekeeper waved them off. "Hmm hmm, you run along now. I'll stay here awhile."

He watched them go, then wandered back into the little building, talking to a cushion he had picked up. "Hmm, the way to Loamhedge, now where've we seen that before? Chronicle of some bygone traveller I expect, eh, eh?"

Climbing upon a chair, he peered at a row of books on a high shelf. Selecting one, Phredd blew the dust from its covers and smiled benignly at it. "Ah, there you are, y'old rascal. Hiding up there, heehee. Didn't think I could see ye? Now what've you got to say for yourself, eh, eh?"

Settling down in an armchair, he brought a lantern close and opened the book's yellowed pages. "Heeheehee, we've met before, haven't we? The recordings of Tim Churchmouse, now I recall ye! The journey to seek out Mattimeo, son of the warrior Matthias. Aye, that covered the Loamhedge Abbey territory, I'm certain it did!"

Toran had been keeping his eye on Martha throughout supper. The ottercook did not like to see his young chum so downcast. He chivvied her, hoping to lighten Martha's mood.

"Cheer up, beauty. If'n ye keep lookin' like that, it'll teem down rain tomorrow. Wot's the matter, my mushroom 'n'barley soup too cold? Has the bread gone stale, the cheese too hard, not enough plums in the pudden? Speak up, droopy ears, does that strawberry fizz cordial taste musty?"

The haremaid managed a wan smile. "No, Toran, it's not that, the supper is delicious. It's just that . . . oh, I don't know."

Toran collared Horty, just as he was reaching for another helping of plum pudding. "Hear that, young starvation face? Yore sister doesn't know wot's wrong with her. Sing her a song an' liven her up, or y'don't get any more plum pud!"

Horty had done this once or twice before, when Martha was a bit down. That, and Toran's threat to cut off his plum pudding supply, galvanised the greedy young hare into action. He let rip with a special ditty he saved for such occasions.

"What a gloomy little mug, wot wot,
come on, let's see you smile.
With a scowl like that you'd frighten
every beast within a mile.
So chortle hahaheeheehoho!
and brighten up for me,
or I'll send you to that Sister
from the Infirmary.

She'll say 'Wot have we here, wot wot?
A face like a flattened frog?
This calls for a bucket o' physick, aye,
now that should do the job!
Will somebeast grab her nose,
so she can't hold her breath,
then I'll be able to grab a ladle,
an' physick the child to death!
I'll not have it said of me, I couldn't do my job,
an' send a young 'un to her grave,
with a grin upon her gob!'

So chortle hohohahahee,
an' smile an' giggle a lot,
you can't sit there all evenin'
with a face like a rusty pot. Wot wot!"

Martha was chuckling when she spied Sister Setiva, the
Infirmary Keeper, making a beeline for her brother.

Setiva had a stern manner, and a marked northern accent, coupled with a dislike for impudence. "Ach, ye flop-
eared wretch, ah'll physick ye tae death if'n ah lay paws on
ye!"

Horty hid behind Toran. "I say, sah, 'twas only a blinkin'
joke, y'know. Don't let that old poisoner get me!"

Martha wiped tears of merriment from her eyes as the
Abbot leaned across to her and asked, "Better now, miss?"

She nodded. "Yes, thank you, Father. Oh, that Horty!"

Sister Portula gave the Abbot a sidelong glance. "It's all
very well making plans to continue our studies out on the
steps tomorrow, but look at the ruckus today. They were
crowded around the gatehouse to see what we were doing
inside. I think we'd best get ready to have lots of company
tomorrow, Father—unless you can think of another way to
keep our creatures distracted."

Abbot Carrul touched a paw to the side of his nose. "I've

already thought of that, Sister. Do you not know what day it is tomorrow?"

Portula shrugged. "A day like any other. Sunny, I hope."

Abbot Carrul stood up and murmured to her as he banged a ladle upon the tabletop to gain order. "Tomorrow is the first day of summer."

He raised his voice. "Your attention please, my friends!"

A respectful silence fell upon the boisterous Redwallers. Everybeast was eager to hear what their Abbot had to say.

"It is my wish that, as tomorrow is the first day of Summer Season, a sports day and a feast shall be held within the grounds of our Abbey. My good friend Foremole Dwurl will be in charge of the proceedings. I trust you will cooperate with him. Foremole Dwurl!"

Redwall's mole leader, a kindly old fellow, bowed low to the Abbot. Amid the raucous cheering and shouting, he climbed upon the table and stamped his footpaws to gain order.

"Thankee, zurr h'Abbot. Naow, you'm all coom to ee h'orchard arter brekkist, an' oi'll give ee yurr tarsks. Hurr hurr, an' all you'm Dibbuns make shore you'm be proper scrubbed!"

Abbot Carrul looked over the top of his tiny glasses at Sister Portula. "Does that solve your problem, marm?"

The good Sister looked slightly nonplussed. "But Father, Summer Season doesn't start for two days yet."

Foremole Dwurl wrinkled his snout confidentially. "If'n you'm doant tell 'um, marm, us'n's woant. Hurrhurr!"

Silence reigned in Cavern Hole. Every Redwaller was tucked up in bed, anticipating the coming day's delights. Summer Season feast and sports was always a joyous event on the Abbey calendar.

Abbot Carrul pushed Martha's chair across Great Hall to her bedroom, which was next to his on ground level. His voice echoed whisperingly about the huge columns as they went.

"Did you notice that Old Phredd didn't come in for supper this evening?"

Martha voiced her concern. "Oh dear, I do hope he's not ill!"

The Father Abbot reassured her. "Not at all, that old fogy's fit as a flea. He was rather anxious for us to get out of the gatehouse, though. I'll wager a button to a barrel of mushrooms that rascal has information about Loamhedge hidden in his dusty archives, sly old hog!"

Martha sat up eagerly. "Do you really think so, Father?"

Carrul nodded. "I'm certain of it, miss. D'you know, I think our search is going to turn up some interesting and exciting stuff tomorrow."

The young haremaid wriggled with anticipation, since any prediction the Abbot made invariably came to pass. "Oh, I do hope so, Father. Maybe we'll discover Sister Amyl's secret. Wouldn't that be wonderful!"

Martha looked up as they passed the great tapestry. Was it just a trick of the flickering lanterns, or did she really see Martin the Warrior's eyes twinkle at her?

7

Some leagues north of Redwall Abbey, the ragtag vermin gang blundered their way through the nighttime thickness of Mossflower woodlands. Skrodd swiped at the undergrowth with his former leader's cutlass as he led the party.

The big rat, Dargle, kept muttering under his breath, continuously criticising Skrodd. "Fancy trackin' two beasts when yore lost, huh!"

Tired and sleepy, the other vermin managed a weary murmur of agreement. Skrodd did not want to challenge Dargle directly—it was the wrong time and place for such a move. So he asserted his authority by bullying all and sundry. He turned on them, brandishing the cutlass.

"Shut yer gobs an' keep movin'. Lost? Hah! Youse'd be the lost ones if'n I wasn't leadin' ye!"

Flinky enjoyed causing trouble. Disguising his voice, he called out behind the big fox's back. "That's no way t'be talkin' to pore pawsore beasts!"

Little Redd agreed with him. "Aye, we should be sleepin' now instead o' wanderin' round an' round all night long!"

Although Flinky was the instigator, Redd was the unlucky one whose voice Skrodd identified. With a savage kick, Skrodd sent the small fox sprawling.

Laying the cutlass blade against his neck, he snarled, "Ye

liddle runt, say the word an' ye can sleep 'ere fer good. I've took enough of yore moanin'!"

Realising that he had gone too far, Flinky tried to remedy the situation by pulling Redd upright as he appealed to Skrodd. "Ah, come on now, sure he's only a tired young whelp. No sense in slayin' one of yore own mates. Let's step out a bit, an' I'll sing a song to help us along, eh?"

Skrodd relented, pointing his blade at the stoat. "Right, you sing. The rest o' ye march, an' shuttup!"

Flinky's ditty put a little fresh life into the gang's paws.

"Ferrets are fine ould foragers,
though frequently furtive an' fey,
stoats can sing sweetly fer seasons,
so me sister used to say,
but foxes are fine an' ferocious,
when faced with a fight or a fray,
an' rats remain rambunctious but only for a day!
But wot about weasels, those wily ould weasels,
they're woefully wayward an' wild,
the ones they've whipped an' walloped,
will wail that weasels are vile,
they've bullied an' beaten an' battered,
they've tormented tortured an' tripped,
I'm sure any day their pore victims would say,
steer clear o' the weasel don't get in his way,
for of all the vermin ye'd care to recall,
the weasel's the wickedest wretch of all.
An' virtuous vermin will all agree,
any weasel is worse than me!"

There were four weasels in the gang: Slipback; his mate, Juppa; and two taciturn brothers, Rogg and Floggo. All of them protested volubly at Flinky's song.

"That ain't right, foxes are worse'n weasels!"

"Ye sing dat again, an' I'll wallop ye alright!"

Skrodd's bad-tempered shout quickly silenced them.

"Shut yore faces back there, or I'll show ye 'ow ferocious foxes can be. Sing somethin' else, Flinky, an' don't insult nobeast!"

Dargle called out, "Aye, an' be nice to foxes, they're easy hurt!"

Skrodd fixed the big rat with an icy glare. "Aye, an' they can hurt rats easily, too!"

Dargle stared fearlessly back at him. "Ye don't scare me, fox. Burrad was slayed by mistake. Us rats don't make mistakes when we fight!"

Skrodd never answered. Turning away, he continued to march, but the challenge was out in the open now. The rest of the gang exchanged nods and winks—a fight to the death was not far off. Skrodd pulled Little Redd up to the front with him and allowed him to walk by his side. The small fox felt honoured; normally he would be left trailing at the back of the gang.

Keeping his voice low, the bigger fox took on a friendly tone with the young one. "You stay by me, mate. Us foxes've got to stick together."

Little Redd had to glance around to make sure Skrodd was not talking to some other beast. He was more used to kicks and insults than to kind words.

The big fox winked at him. "I been keepin' an eye on ye, mate. Yore a smart little feller, not like this other lot!"

Redd hated being called "little," but he was quite pleased to know that Skrodd thought of him as smart. He returned the wink, speaking out of the side of his mouth.

"I ain't no fool, an' I ain't so little, either. I'm growin' fast. One day they'll call me Big Redd."

Skrodd got to the point. "Lissen, mate, I want ye t'do me a favour. Do ye think yore smart enough t'be useful to me?"

Little Redd walked on tippaw, swelling his chest out. "Just tell me wot ye want doin', mate!"

Skrodd leaned close. "Keep an eye on the gang, especially Dargle. That rat's gettin' too big fer his boots. I want ye to watch my back, sort o' be my second in command."

Redd hid his delight, replying gruffly, "I'll do that, just watch me. Soon they'll be callin' me Big Redd. I won't let ye down, mate!"

Skrodd patted the small fox's back. "Good! When I gets this gang sorted out, we'll give ye a proper vermin name. Big Redd don't mean nothin'. How does Badredd sound to ye, eh?"

The young fox was squirming inside with joy. However, he kept his voice tough, in keeping with his new position. "Sounds great t'me, mate. Badredd—I like that! 'Tis a real killer's name. Badredd!"

After a fruitless night rambling through woodland thickets, the gang watched a rose-tinged dawn break over the tree-tops. They were soaked through by heavy dew, which was dripping everywhere from boughs and leaves.

Dargle's temper was on a short fuse. Emerging into a clearing on the bank of a stream, he struck out at Little Redd with his spear haft.

"Keep outta my way, runt! Every time ye come near me, I get soaked wid the water ye knock off the bushes."

Redd looked appealingly at Skrodd. The big fox cast a glance of mock pity at Dargle and snarled scornfully. "Scared of a few drips o' dew, are ye? Look at us, we're all wet through, an' we ain't moanin'."

Dargle faced up to Skrodd right away. "Hah! Wet through an' weary, an' wot for, eh? We never found the otter an' the squirrel. No, we just tramped around all night followin' you, an' now we're good an' lost. Some leader you are, Skrodd!"

The big fox bristled. "Don't talk silly, we ain't lost!"

It was Dargle's turn to sound scornful. "Oh, ain't we now? See that rowan tree, I marked it wid me spearblade not long after we started marchin'. Look!"

Flinky inspected the fresh scar on the rowan bark. "Aye, 'tis a new spearmark sure enuff. Dargle's right!"

Leaning on his spearbutt, the hefty rat grinned teasingly.

"We've been goin' round in circles, mates, an' now our great leader's got us lost. Well, Skrodd?"

The fox held his blade at the ready and challenged Dargle. "If'n yore so clever, then you find the way. 'Tis easy to stand there talkin' smart all day, Dargle. Go on, show us how ye are, an' find the right way!"

The rat squatted down on his haunches, chuckling. "Sort out yore own mess, I'm stoppin' here an' restin'."

Halfchop ventured a suggestion. "Burrad would've sent Plumnose to find the way, 'cos he's a good tracker."

Relief flooded through Skrodd as he realised that Halfchop had provided the solution to a sticky problem. Taking advantage, he quickly re-established his position as leader of the gang.

"Right, Plumnose, get on yore way! Ferget the two beasts we were trackin', they'll keep for another day. Find us the way to this Redwall Abbey place an' report back here."

Always one to seize an opportunity, Flinky nodded his head admiringly. "Ah, that's a grand ould move, Chief. I see ye noticed the fine campsite we're at. We can lay up here fer a day or two an' rest, once we're sure of the way. Lookit, we got a stream wid fish an' freshwater an' lots o' trees full of fat birds sittin' on nests packed wid eggs. The place is filled wid roots an' fruit an' firewood!"

Skrodd looked sage. "That's wot I was thinkin', a day or two here'll freshen us up for the rest o' the journey. We'll make camp an' rest awhile, mates."

Only Plumnose was not happy with the new plans. His huge nose wobbled from side to side as he complained. "Duh, id's nod right. I'b tired, too, j'know!"

Rogg and Floggo, the weasel brothers, notched arrows to their bows and fired a pair of shafts near Plumnose's paws.

"Yore the tracker, Plum, now git goin'!"

"Aye, ye could track a butterfly underwater wid a hooter like that. Hohoho!"

Throwing twigs and grass clumps at the unfortunate creature, the gang drove Plumnose from the camp. Glad

they had not been selected to go tracking, they shouted after
him.

"Don't trip over yer nose, Plum!"

"Aye, an' don't sniff any big boulders up. Heeheehee!"

The tension was broken for the moment. Gathering wood
and foraging for victuals, the gang busied themselves.

Flinky dug a firepit on the streambank, singing a cheery
ditty.

"Ah 'tis luvverly bein' a vermin,
'cos ye lead a simple life,
leave the snufflin' babes behind,
run off from the naggin' wife.
There's nought to do but ramble,
an' plunder on the way,
just look bold, rob all ye can hold,
an' bid 'em all good day.
A vermin, a vermin, that's wot I'll always be,
I'm base an' vile, 'cos that's me style,
an' I'll bet ye envy me!"

By late morn they had a good fire burning. Flinky and his
mate, Crinktail, were in their element. They boiled woodpigeon eggs, grilled fish, and made a passable vegetable
stew from various roots and wild produce which grew
plentifully roundabout. Neither Dargle nor Skrodd made
any move to help. Sitting close to the fire, they helped themselves, glaring at each other across the flames.

Skrodd collared Little Redd and gave him whispered orders. "Scout round an' find me somewheres safe to rest.
Make sure 'tis soft an' comfortable. Pick a place far away
from that rat, an' someplace close for yourself, so ye can
guard me. Go on!"

Puffed up with his own importance, Redd went to seek a
suitable resting spot. He chose the base of a spreading oak,
not too close to the stream. It was a basin-shaped depression
between two thick roots.

When the gang finished eating, they settled down for a much-needed sleep. Most of them stayed by the fire, but Dargle chose a fernbed on the opposite side of the camp from Skrodd. From there the rat could see his enemy and lay plans.

Little Redd proudly showed Skrodd the spot at the base of the oak trunk. "That's it, mate, nice an' snug, see!"

The small fox lay down, gesturing. "There's plenty o' room for both of us. I can guard ye good from here, mate."

Skrodd shook his head disapprovingly. "Nah, ye go an' lay by the fire with the others. That'll put ye halfway twixt me'n Dargle. But don't go sleepin', keep yore eyes peeled on those ferns where he's layin' low. Soon as Dargle makes a move, come runnin' an' let me know."

Little Redd rose reluctantly. "I kin watch him just as well if'n I stop 'ere with you, mate."

Skrodd hauled him roughly upward, thrusting him toward the fire. "Ye'd do better to heed my orders. Now get goin'. I'm chief round 'ere, see!"

Stinging from the rebuke, Redd slouched over to the fire. Sullenly, he slunk down amid the snoring vermin.

With not a breeze to rustle the trees, warm noon sunlight shone down on the camp. Bees hummed gently, and butterflies fluttered silently around blossoming bushes. Near the ashy embers of the cooking fire, Little Redd drifted into a slumber. Only one of the gang was still awake—Dargle. Now was the time to put his plan into action. Draping his cloak over the ferns so it would look like he was still there, the rat inched his way backward out of the foliage. Flat on his stomach, he took a careful route, circling the campsite. When the rear of the spreading oak came in sight, Dargle rose into a half crouch. Gripping his spear firmly, he crept up on his sleeping enemy.

Skrodd woke momentarily, but only to die. A muffled grunt of agony escaped him as Dargle's spear thrust into his body.

Dargle leaned down on the spearhilt, grinning triumphantly. "*Now* who's the chief, eh?"

It was the rat's only mistake—it turned out to be his last. Skrodd had lain down to sleep with the cutlass held tight in his paw. Now, with one spasmodic jerk, he whipped the broad blade across his assassin's neck, almost severing Dargle's head. The ambitious rat fell slain on top of his victim's dead body.

Little Redd was wakened by Flinky kicking him in the back. The small fox sat up rubbing his eyes and muttering at the still-sleeping stoat. "Keep yore paws to yoreself, ye great lump!"

Flinky rolled over and emitted a huge snore. To avoid a second kick, Redd rose stiffly and looked around. Dargle's cloak was still draped over the ferns. He let out a sigh of relief and wandered over to check on Skrodd. Redd was dumbfounded by the sight that greeted him—Skrodd and Dargle, both dead!

Little Redd circled them slowly, poking both beasts with a stick and uttering their names softly. There was no doubt about it, they were still as stones. His first thought was to run and tell the others. He had already opened his mouth to shout when a thought struck him. Who would be the next to claim leadership of the gang? Little Redd sat down and did some serious thinking. It did not take him long to reach a decision. He would be the new chief. Getting the cutlass loose from Skrodd's paw was a difficult task, but he managed it somehow. Dargle was almost decapitated by Skrodd's death blow. Two good chops of the hefty blade finished the job.

Flinky was roused by a painful feeling he knew well, the slap of a flat cutlass blade. He sprang upright, rubbing his rump, expecting to see Skrodd standing over him. Instead, there stood the small fox, whacking away at the other gang vermin and yelling aloud.

71

"Up on yore hunkers, all of ye!"

The weasel Juppa grabbed a chunk of firewood and advanced on the small fox, snarling. "Ye snotty liddle runt, who do ye think y'are, smackin' me wid the chief's blade?"

Redd jarred the wood from Juppa's paws with a blow from the cutlass. His voice was shrill but commanding. "I'm the new chief round here, that's who I am. Come an' see this, all of ye!"

The gang stood around the two carcasses in awed silence as the small fox explained. "I saw Dargle run Skrodd through with his spear. So I rushed in, grabbed the cutlass an' slew the dirty murderin' sneak with one swipe!"

Crinktail looked at him disbelievingly. "You, Little Redd, took off Dargle's block in one go?"

Redd was getting the feel of the heavy sword now. He took a pace back, then leaped forward, swinging the cutlass in both paws, shouting fiercely. "Aye, one swipe! D'ye want me to show ye how? I'm the chief now, this sword's mine, I killed to get it!"

He was gratified to see fear shining from Crinktail's eyes as she backed away from him swiftly. "No, no," she pleaded, "if you say ye did it, I'm not one to argue with ye!"

Ever the one to seize an opportunity, however, Flinky confronted Redd and held out his paws placatingly. "Ah now, don't go upsettin' yoreself, Little Redd. We all think ye'll make a grand chief. Anyway, better'n the last two. Isn't that right, mates?"

He turned to the gang, winking broadly at them but making sure the small fox could not see his gesture.

"C'mon now, raise yer paws an' salute the great new chief!"

A newfound confidence flooded through Redd as he watched the remaining nine vermin acknowledging his leadership with raised paws. He suppressed a shudder of joy. For as long as he could recall he had been ignored, bullied or pushed about. Now, in the course of one day, he was in command of the gang.

Deciding to assert his authority, Little Redd glared haughtily at the ratbag vermin. "My name ain't Little Redd no more. From now on ye'll all call me Badredd. Is that clear?"

Flinky threw him an elaborate salute. "Badredd it is, yer honour, sure an' a fine ould name it is! Well now, Badredd sir, wot's yore pleasure—do we stop 'ere awhile in this grand camp? There's water an' vittles aplenty roundabout, an' 'tis a pleasant spot."

Badredd nodded imperiously. "Aye, we'll stop 'ere awhile!"

As they prepared the evening meal, Flinky's mate, Crinktail, whispered to him. "Badredd, huh! Wot'n the name o' blood made ye support that liddle fool?"

Flinky winked at her as he turned a roasting woodpigeon on a willow spit over the fire. "Trust me, mate, better a liddle fool than a big bully. I can 'andle this 'un. Badredd'll do like I suggest, ye'll see. We've 'ad enough o' weasels, big foxes an' bullyrats in this gang. This Mossflower territory's a good soft place to stay, plenty of everythin'. Better'n those ould Northlands. Leave the thinkin' t'me, we'll live the good life from now on. Badredd'll do like I tell 'im."

The newly elected Badredd sat on the streambank, picking a roasted woodpigeon leg and watching the westering sun die in a crimson haze. He listened to Flinky singing as he dished out supper to the gang, who lay about looking contented enough.

"Oh this is the place to be,
where the fruit falls from the tree,
where eggs an' birds jump out of the nest,
right in me pan they come to rest.
Oh this is the place for me,

73

far from that Northland sea.
Here the good ould fish leap out of the stream,
an shout, 'Please, sir, cook me,'
where the sun shines all the day,
an' the cold wind stops away,
an' the water's clean 'n' fresh 'n' clear,
I'll make ye a promise now, me dear,
I'll take a bath so don't ye fear,
in ten summers' time if I'm still here,
'cos this is the place for me!"

Badredd, however, had totally different plans. Not for him all this lying about on sunny streambanks. Ambition had entered his being. To be the owner of the magic sword and ruler of that place Skrodd had spoken of—Redwall Abbey.

8

Lonna Bowstripe sat outside the cave, savouring the approach of summer in the harsh northeast coastlands. Pale sunlight glimmered out of a watery, cloud-flecked sky. It was breezy, but the chill had died out of the wind. Green buds were shooting out of the scrublands, seabirds mewed across the marshes.

The huge badger shifted his position near the fire, wincing momentarily and arching his back. Young Stugg sat beside him like some constant shadow, always close to the big creature. Lonna fascinated the young sea otter.

"You back still be hurted, Lonn'?"

Lonna smiled down at his companion. "A bit, but it's getting better every day, mate. Pass me the bow, please."

Stugg ambled across and carried the yew sapling to him. Out of six lengths, this was the one Lonna had chosen to use for fashioning his bow. Stugg inspected it closely. The wood had seasoned out until it was strong as sprung metal. Lonna had shaved away the bark, leaving a broad band at its centre that he had bound and whipped with green cord to make a pawhold. At both ends, the wood was circled and notched deep to accommodate bowstrings. Stugg watched as the badger tested the yew's strength by bending it against his footpaws.

"Wot you think, Lonn', bee's it ready?"

The badger applied heavy pressure, bending the bow until it formed a deep arc. He straightened it slowly and then responded. "As ready as it will ever be, young 'un. This is a good bow!"

Stugg jumped up and down impatiently. "Putta string on it, Lonn'. Fire a h'arrow for Stugg!"

Abruc wandered out of the main holt cave toward them. "Ahoy there, young pestilence! Are ye still botherin' Lonna? Yore more trouble than a sack o' frogs!"

The giant badger tugged Stugg's little rudder fondly. "Oh, he's no trouble, Abruc. Stugg's my good old workmate."

Abruc sat down beside them. He could not keep the curiosity out of his voice. "Well, bigbeast, is yore bow finally ready?"

Lonna used the bowstaff to pull himself upright. "Let's string it and see, shall we?"

A short time thereafter, all the sea otters had gathered to watch the testing of the bow. Lonna limped slightly as he went back into the cave to fetch his quiver of arrows.

Stugg stood outside, holding the bow and declaiming proudly to everybeast, "All stan' back now, please. I help Lonn' to make dis bow. 'Tis a very dangerful weapon, so watch out!"

The big badger emerged with the birch bark quiver. It was packed heavily with two score of long ashwood shafts, which Abruc and Shoredog had helped to fashion. Each one was fletched with grey gull feathers, gleaned from the shoreline. The arrows were tipped with flint shards, sharpened and ground to lethal points.

Lonna took the bowstring which Abruc had woven and looped it over the notch in the yew staff.

After knotting it with a skilful hitch, he remarked, "If this bow fails, it won't be for want of a good string. This is the finest one I've ever seen, thanks to you, friend."

76

Abruc flushed with pleasure. "Thankee. 'Tis a special string, worthy of a mighty bow."

Lonna braced the yew sapling against his footpaw, with the string at the bottom end. Tying a loop into the free end, he leaned down heavily on the centre of the wood.

A gasp arose from the otters as the yew bent in a great arc. With the graceful ease of an expert bowbeast, Lonna slipped the loop deftly over the notched top end. It was a bow now, a mighty and formidable longbow that only a beast the size and strength of Lonna Bowstripe could draw. Taking three arrows, he set them point down in the earth and selected one, explaining as he did, "Height, distance and accuracy are what an archer needs."

Whipping the bow up, he laid the first arrow on it, heaved back powerfully and let fly, all in a split second. Swift as lightning the shaft sped upward and was immediately lost to sight.

Shoredog let out a growl of surprise. "Whoo! Where did it go?"

Stugg gestured airily. "Stuck inna moon I appose, eh Lonn?"

A rare smile creased the badger's scarred face. "Aye, I suppose so, mate. Let's try for distance next."

The second arrow he laid flat against his jaw, squinting one eye and holding the bow straight.

Zzzzip! Out across the stream over marsh and scrubland it flew, until it was lost on the seaward horizon.

Abruc clapped his paws in delight. "Speared a big fish I bet, eh Stugg?"

The young otter smirked. "Prolably two, anna big crab!"

Lonna scanned the countryside. "I need a target now." He bowed to Abruc's wife, Marinu. "Lady, would you like to choose one? Anything will do."

She looked around, then pointed. "There's a piece of driftwood just beyond the marsh, see? To the right of that rivulet which runs out onto the shore. I don't know if you can reach that far, Lonna. Shall I pick something a little closer? I'm afraid I don't know much about firing arr . . . !"

Her words were cut short as the chunk of driftwood went end over end, pierced through by the badger's arrow. A rousing cheer went up from the spectators.

Lonna unstrung his bow, passing it to Stugg. "Well, mate, it looks like we made a proper bow. Thank you for all your help."

The young otter nodded. "Searats better watch out now!"

Lonna took supper in the sea otters' main cave that night— a large seafood pie, followed by a preserved plum crumble, washed down with beakers of last summer's best cider. He sat by the fire with Abruc and Shoredog, with Stugg dozing on his lap.

Old Sork made Lonna hold still whilst she inspected his facial scar. "A luckybeast is what ye are. 'Tis healin' better'n I hoped. So what are ye lookin' so miserable about, eh?"

The big badger shrugged. "Every day that I sit here, Raga Bol and his crew get further away. Soon there'll be no trace of them to follow."

Abruc refilled his beaker with cider. "Never fear, Lonna. A Searat like Raga Bol always leaves a trail, a path of murder an' destruction that anybeast with half an eye could follow. I've been watchin' ye since you've been up an' about. I know yore impatient to begone from here. Well, summer's almost in, the time'll soon be ripe."

Lonna stared into the flames as he replied. "Raga Bol and his crew won't live to see the leaves turn gold this autumn. I leave tomorrow!"

Shoredog helped himself to more cider, peering curiously at the big badger. "Then we'll go with ye, Lonna, us an' a dozen of our best fighters. Even a warrior as big as yoreself will need help with Bol an' his crew!"

The badger shook his huge scarred head. "I'm grateful, friend, but this is a thing I must do alone. You stay here and care for your families. There will be a hard time ahead for me. Raga Bol knows I am coming."

78

Abruc replenished the fire with driftwood and sea coal. "He probably thinks yore dead, mate. How could he know yore comin' after him?"

Lonna never took his eyes from the flames as he explained. "I never knew my mother and father. Grawn, the wise old badger you buried, was the one who reared me. Not only did he teach me all the skills of a bowbeast but also many other things. When I was very small, Grawn told me that I was gifted with something few other badgers possess. He said that I was born with the power of a Seer. Old Grawn used to question me a lot. One day he said to me, 'You have the keenest eyes of any bowbeast I have known, but you also have another eye, inside your mind. You can see things the rest of us cannot, strange things that will shape your destiny.' It has always been so with me. Even when I was lying wounded in the cave, I could see Raga Bol. I can stare into this fire and see his face. Believe me, he knows I am coming. I want him to know, to fear me. He is evil and must die!"

Shoredog felt the fur on the nape of his neck begin to prickle. "But if yore a Seer, ye must have known Grawn was goin' t'die, didn't ye?"

Lonna's eyes left the flames momentarily. "Aye, I knew the old beast had not long to go, but I didn't know the manner of his death. Grawn was old and very ill. He wished to end his days at the badger mountain of Salamandastron. I was taking him there, and I knew my own fate was also linked to the mountain."

Abruc leaned forward. "Do ye know where this mountain is?"

Lonna turned back to contemplating the fire. "I have never been there, but I feel I am guided to it by my mind's eye. It is far to the west, on the shores of the great sea. When my business with the Searats is done, that is where I'll go. I will not return to this place again. That is why I must travel alone."

*

79

As they sat silently by the fire, Marinu came and lifted the sleeping Stugg from Lonna's lap. All the other otters had retired for the night. Only the three of them—Lonna, Abruc, and Shoredog—remained.

Shoredog broke the silence. "Garfo Trok, he's the answer!"

Abruc nodded vigorously. "Right, mate, good ole Garfo!"

Lonna stared from one to the other. "What are you talking about—who's Garfo Trok?"

Shoredog rose and picked up his warm cape. "Skipper o' the Nor'east Riverdogs, that's who Garfo is. He runs a riverboat. Garfo will take ye westward along the waterways. That should save time an' strain on that back o' yores, Lonna. Ye'll pick up Raga Bol's trail in half the time ye'd take limpin' along step by step."

Shoredog hurried from the holt, calling back to Abruc. "I'll be back with Garfo by midday. Tell the cooks to pack plenty o' vittles, especially nutbread!"

Abruc nudged Lonna cheerfully. "Ye'll like ole Garfo, that otter knows waterways like the back of 'is rudder."

Happy but puzzled, Lonna smiled at the sea otter. "I'm sure I will, but what's all this about vittles and nutbread? I eat only lightly when I'm travelling."

Abruc stood up and stretched. "Ye may do, Lonna, but Garfo Trok ain't a beast that's ever stinted 'isself when it comes to vittles, particularly nutbread. Why, that ole dog'd go to Hellgates for a loaf! Now get yoreself off an' rest, ye've a big day tomorrow!"

After Abruc had gone, Lonna stretched out by the fire, intending to sleep there for the remainder of the night. Before he closed his eyes, he spent several minutes intensely concentrating on the red embers, repeating mentally, "Rest not too deeply, Raga Bol! Know that I am coming for you! As surely as night follows day, I am coming!"

Raga Bol and his crew were sleeping. They had made it out of the hills and moorlands into the first fringes of heavy forest. A spark from the campfire touched Ferron's nose, startling him awake. The gaunt rat sat bolt upright, rubbing at the stinging spot. He saw Raga Bol sit up as well, waving his silver hook and mumbling as he tried to come fully awake.

"Go 'way, yore dead! Get away from me, d'ye hear?" The Searat captain caught Ferron looking strangely at him across the fire. "Who are ye gawpin' at, long face, eh?"

Ferron knew better than to answer back. Instead, he lay back down and closed his eyes. All the crew had been saying the same thing. Lately Cap'n Bol was acting very strange.

9

Dawn was only moments old, but Redwall Abbey was awake and buzzing. Today was the special day Abbot Carrul had promised. Breakfast was already being served from a large buffet table, set up in the passage outside the kitchens. With laden platters, the Redwallers sat down to eat at anyplace which took their fancy. Horty and his friends looked out from the dormitory window at the scene below. Dibbuns thronged together on the broad front step of the Abbey, spooning down bowls of oatmeal mixed with honey and fruit. Anybeast wanting to dine outside had to step carefully over them to reach the lawns or the orchard. It was a jumble of happy confusion.

Muggum waved his beaker at the passing elders, who tippawed around him. "Yurr, moind ee paws, you'm nearly trodded in this choild's brekkist. Whurr's ee manners? Hurr!"

Warm sunlight was rapidly dispersing the mist into a golden haze. Fenna the squirrelmaid leaned out over the dormitory sill and dropped a fragment of scone down into the hood of Sister Setiva's habit, giggling as she drew back inside.

"Did she notice it?"

Horty reassured her. "Not at all. She's toddled off down

to the pond with Brother Gelf. Hahaha! I expect old Setiva'll be set upon by the first blinkin' bird that spots it. Should liven her up, wot!"

Springald watched the Infirmary Sister balancing her tray gingerly as she crossed the lawn. "Huh, pity help the bird who tries to set upon her. She'll bath it in the pond and physick it silly. Look out, here comes Father Abbot!"

The mischievous trio ducked below the windowsill as Abbot Carrul, Toran, Sister Portula and Martha emerged from the Abbey. Toran lifted Martha's chair over the step and assisted Portula with a trolley full of food. They set out for the gatehouse together, with Abbot Carrul stretching his paws and breathing deeply.

"My my, it's a good-to-be-alive day. Let's hope we get a few hours of peace to tackle our studies."

Toran had to rap loudly on the gatehouse door to gain attention. Old Phredd could be heard inside, arguing with an armchair.

"Come out my way and let me see who 'tis. It's your fault, being so comfy and allowin' me to sleep like that!"

A moment later, his frowzy, prickled head poked around the door. "Oh, er hmm. Good morning, I suppose it's morning, isn't it? Of course, if 'twas noon, the sun would be much higher, eh, eh?" Dabbing his face in a bowl of water, the ancient hedgehog absentmindedly wiped his eyes on Martha's lap rug. "There, that's better. Oh good, I see you brought breakfast with you. Splendid, I'm starving!"

Martha ate very little, trying to hold back her impatience as Phredd slowly munched his way around the food. Toran, however, got to the point right away.

"Well then, sir, how did yore studyin' go? Did ye find out anythin' useful about Loamhedge?"

Phredd nodded toward a dusty book lying on his bed. "Oh, that. Take a look in the old volume there. I read it until I could keep my eyes open no longer. Hmm, quite interesting really, an exciting little story, eh?"

Martha opened the book, its pages yellow with age and

83

so brittle that they were cracking and beginning to flake. She read aloud from the neatly scribed lines of purple, faded ink. "Written by Tim Churchmouse. Recorder of Redwall Abbey in Mossflower country . . ."*

Phredd interrupted her as he dealt with a hazelnut roll. "It was written in the seasons of Abbot Mordalphus. The account of Mattimeo, son of Matthias the Abbey Champion. All about abduction and slavery, a search, a chase and so on. If you're looking for a route to the old Abbey of Loamhedge, the descriptions are very long and complicated, but there's a map included that should be a help. Actually I only got a third of the way through the account before I dropped off. . . ."

Abbot Carrul shook his head in wonder. "In the seasons of Mordalphus, . . . Dearie me! That book must be nearly as old as time itself!"

Sister Portula put aside her beaker of mint tea. "The land will have changed a lot since then, what with rains and floods altering water courses and storms blowing down trees. There'll be new areas of woodland grown over the ages, and I don't know what. Do you think it will be much help, Toran?"

As she had been speaking, the noise of stamping paws and singing voices had been swelling outside.

Toran went to the door. "Who knows, Sister? Great Seasons, what's all that rackety din about?"

Old Phredd chuckled. "They're singing the Summer Feast song. What a happy sound! Let's go out and watch, eh, eh?"

Martha was less than enthusiastic, since she wanted to continue studying the book. But the Abbot patted her paw encouragingly. "You know, we can study the problem at our leisure, but next summer's first day is a long time away. They sound so joyful and excited! Come on, young 'un, let's go and see."

*See *Mattimeo*

Smilingly, the haremaid relented.

Up and down the wallsteps and all over the lawns, Redwallers, led by Horty, were joining paws and skipping about, singing lustily to the jolly tune.

"The sun could not shine brighter
upon this summer's day,
my heart could not be lighter.
I've heard our Abbot say
there'll be a feast this evening,
so listen one and all:
This afternoon we'll run a race
around the Abbey wall!

Come form up in a line, pals,
and listen for your names,
it's ready steady set and go,
for Redwall Abbey games!

There's vittles in the kitchen,
good ale and cordials, too,
fine singers and musicians,
to play the evening through.
But first I'll gird my robe up,
so I don't trip or fall.
I'm going to be the first around
that high old Abbey wall!

Come form up in a line, pals,
and listen for your names,
it's ready steady set and go,
for Redwall Abbey games!"

Martha could not resist the merry cavalcade. Clapping her paws in time to the lively song, she laughed happily. Sister Portula, whooping like a wildbeast, grabbed Martha's chair and dashed off into the throng.

Abbot Carrul winked at Phredd. "My mistake for starting all this, but who could sit indoors studying on such a wonderful day?"

Toran, in complete agreement, shepherded both of his friends out of the way of the dancers. "You two stay here. I'll go an' bring two armchairs an' the rest o' the food out of the gatehouse. Ye can sit back an' watch the whole thing in comfort. We can always look through dusty ole books tomorrow."

Old Phredd spoke to a buttercup growing by the wall. "Heehee, now there's a sensible young creature. Beasts like that make a body enjoy his old age, eh, eh?"

Bragoon and Saro stood outside the main gate. Memories flooded back as they touched the stout oak timbers.

The aging squirrel looked misty-eyed. "Dear ole Redwall Abbey! Sounds like they're havin' a good time in there, mate. Well, do we knock for the Gatekeeper?"

Bragoon scuffed the gravel path with his rudder as he pondered the question. "Hmm, we've been a long time gone. Suppose nobeast knows us anymore. Or worse, supposin' they do recognise us an' recall wot a pair of scoundrels we were! They might not want us back. Wot d'ye think?"

Saro gnawed at her lip. "Aye, I think yore right, Brag. Tell ye what, let's just slip in unnoticed an' sort of mingle with the crowd. That way we can judge the lay o' the land."

The otter grinned furtively at his companion. "The way we used to come an' go, through the ole east wall gate. I'll bet ye can still open it."

Saro clapped his back with her bushy tail. "Great idea! Come on, let's give it a try. We'll disguise ourselves up a bit so as not to cause too much of a stir!"

Brother Weld, an old bankvole who was Abbey Beekeeper, perched on the arm of Abbot Carrul's chair to watch the fun. Some of the other games were in progress, and competition among the Dibbuns was fierce.

The Abbot watched them fondly as he reminisced. "I was pretty good at the nut and spoon race in my younger seasons."

Weld kept his eyes on the games as he observed drily, "Aye, Father, you beat me three seasons on the run. Then they caught you sticking your nut to the spoon with honey."

Abbot Carrul cautioned him. "Not so loud, Weld, keep your voice down. We can't have the young 'uns discovering that a Dibbun who cheated at nut and spoon is now their Abbot!"

Three of the Dibbuns—Muggum, Shilly and Yooch—were trying madly to win the greasy pole event. A big bag of candied chestnuts hung from the top of the pole. It resisted all their efforts. Each time, they ended up skimming dismally down to earth, caked with a mixture of soap and vegetable oil. After some earnest plotting, they hatched up a joint plan. Muggum stood tippaw, grasping the base of the pole. Yooch scrambled up the molebabe's back and stood on his head. Both clung tightly to the pole, then Shilly climbed up over them onto Yooch's head. Holding the pole with one paw, the squirrelbabe strove with her free paw to reach the bag. Unfortunately, the combined height of all three Dibbuns was still short of the prize. Muggum could not look up, his tiny face squinched by the weight of his two pals. But that did not stop him yelling out words of encouragement.

"Gurr, goo on Shilly, grab ee chesknutters naow!"

Shilly roared back at him. "I carn't not gerrem, me paw bee's too likkle'n'short!"

Yooch the molebabe grunted his contribution. "Moi pore bee's flattinged, 'urry up!"

Amid the spectators' shouts of support and hoots of laughter at the spectacle, Fenna came bounding out. The squirrelmaid hopped up the backs of all three Dibbuns.

87

Launching herself from the top of Shilly's head, she made a graceful leap. Fenna effortlessly unhooked the bag of candied chestnuts. Performing a spectacular somersault, she landed neatly on the ground, without a speck of grease anywhere on her.

She smiled smugly. "No trouble at all, the prize is mine!"

Martha's voice cut across her jubilant cries. "Not fair! it's the greasy pole you're supposed to climb, not the greasy Dibbuns. You should forefeit the nuts, Fenna!"

Fenna stuck her lip out and pouted. "But I won them!"

The Abbot left his armchair and took possession of the bag. "The object is to get the nuts. There's no hard-and-fast rule about climbing greasy poles. But be fair, Fenna. The little ones tried so hard, and they gave us all such fun. I suggest we split the nuts four ways betwixt you and them."

Whilst everybeast was applauding the decision, Toran caught Shilly and Yooch as they fell backwards from the pole. Horty was left with the task of unsticking Muggum, who was practically plastered to the pole with grease. He tugged his snout politely to the young hare.

"Thankee, zurr, oi thort oi wuz stucked thurr fer loife!"

Horty gazed down at his clean tunic, now coated with the mess. "Oh, think nothin' of it, old lad. My pleasure, wot!" He slipped and fell flat as he stumbled away from the pole.

By the pondside an old female squirrel, her face hooded against the sun by a cowl, was bathing her footpaws in the reeded shallows. An otter of medium size, his face also hooded, sat next to her. Sister Portula sought a seat in the reedshade alongside them, fanning her face with a dockleaf.

"Whew, this is certainly going to be a memorable summer!"

The otter glanced sideways at her. "Has afternoon tea been served yet, Sister?"

Portula swiped at a flying midge which was tormenting

her. "We never serve afternoon tea when there's going to be an evening feast. You knew that, didn't you, Brother?"

The female squirrel sighed. "Oh no, I was lookin' forward to some nice scones with strawberry preserve an' meadowcream."

Portula had to raise her voice to be heard over the sounds of sporting revellers. "The walltop race will be starting soon. I think first prize for that might be a cream tea with scones."

The squirrel jumped upright, surprisingly spry for one of her long seasons. "Right, I'll enter an' win first prize!"

The Sister shook her head doubtfully. "You'll have lots of competition from younger and fitter creatures, I'm afraid."

The otter smiled knowingly. "Oh, don't ye worry about that, Sister. If'n there's a prize of afternoon tea goin', my mate'll win it. Right, Saro?"

The squirrel threw off her cowl. "I'll give it a good try, Brag, an' maybe I'll share it with ye."

The good Sister stared open-mouthed at the aging squirrel. "Saro, is it really you?"

Saro took the old Recorder's paw and shook it warmly. "Aye, Portula, my ole friend, an' guess who this creakin' ruddered lump is?"

Portula was all aflutter. "Wait, don't tell me now. . . . Oh, seasons o' mercy, it's Bragoon!"

She raced off, waving her paws wildly and shouting, "They're back! It's Bragoon and Sarabando! They're back!"

The squirrel watched her go. "Hear that, I got me full title!"

The games were abandoned for the moment. Redwallers crowded to the pond to see the legendary duo. Both beasts were overwhelmed by pawshakes, kisses, backslaps and the embraces of old friends. Banter and welcomes went back and forth as they were reunited with the comrades of long-gone seasons.

"Saro, you bushy-tailed rogue, 'tis me, Phredd the Gatekeeper!"

89

"Old Phredd? I don't believe it. Are you still here?"

"Och, 'tis that dreadful Dibbun Bragoon! Where've ye been, ye bold wee scamp?"

"Sister Setiva, a pleasure t'see yore face, marm. Been? Oh me'n Saro've been as far as there an' back a few times!"

"Yurr, oi'd know ee thievin' likkle face anywhurrs, Miz Saro!"

"Granmum Gurvel, my ole beauty, give me a hug, quick!"

"Haharr, who's that—not young Carrul the nut'n'spoon cheat?"

"Bragoon, friend of my Dibbun days, oh 'tis so good to see you! Ahem, the name's changed now, I'm Father Abbot Carrul. But what a pleasure to see you, and Saro, too!"

"Look out, who's this big, rough-lookin' villain, eh?"

"Oi bee's Muggum, marm, bee's you'm really Sabburandum?"

Suddenly Bragoon found himself swept off his paws and hugged in a viselike grip. Tears flowed freely down Toran's face.

"Brother Brag, you've come home to Redwall!"

Planting a kiss between Toran's ears, Bragoon wheezed. "Brother Toran, I won't see sunset if'n ye crush me t'death. I missed ye, Toran, y'great lump of an otter!"

Greeting upon greeting followed, everybeast seemed at once to be embracing the pair. The air resounded to cries of "Well I never, my oh my, just look at ye, welcome home!"

Springald, Horty and Fenna stood to one side. Like most teen-season creatures, they were embarrassed by all the hugging and kissing among elders.

Springald muttered in resignation. "I suppose that means the end of the Games Day. Huh, I'd have won the wall race easily if they hadn't turned up."

Fenna passed each of them a piece of candied chestnut, musing aloud. "So, that's the famous Bragoon and Saro. Huh, they're not as big as I thought they'd be. They look pretty old, too—creaky, I'd say. What do you think, Horty?"

The young hare shrugged. "After all the tall stories we've

heard about 'em, wot? Actually, old bean, you could be right. Those two ain't exactly the huge giants we've been told about. A bit blinkin' old, an' jolly ordinary, too, though everybeast seems tip over tail to see 'em back, wot? Let's toddle over there now that the huggin'n'kissin' is all done with. Come on, chaps, I want to get a closer dekko at the bold blinkin' Bragoon an' the startlin' Sarobando."

Martha was being introduced to the pair by Sister Setiva.

Bragoon shook the haremaid's paw gently. "Martha, eh? A pretty name for a pretty maid. Well, Martha, you don't look anything like us two when we were young. I wager you've heard a lot o' stories about the villainy we got up to in the old days."

Martha thought Bragoon had a kind face; she liked him immediately. She tried changing the conversation from his past misdeeds. "How did you and Sarobando get into the Abbey, sir, with the gate locked and barred?"

Old Phredd scratched his scrubby beard. "Aye, how did you get in, eh, eh?"

Saro shrugged modestly. "Oh, 'twas nothin' really, just a little trick we used to do with the east wallgate. Don't worry, Phredd, we locked it behind us."

Fenna interrupted. "Mister Bragoon, I heard that you were once a Skipper of Otters. Is that true?"

The aging otter nodded. " 'Tis true enough, miss, but ole Saro didn't fancy bein' an otter. So I gave it up to go rovin' with her."

Springald enquired, rather pertly, "Are you as good a cook as your brother Toran?"

Bragoon chuckled at the idea. "Wot, me? No, pretty one, I'll wager that Toran's the best cook anywhere. Huh, I'd prob'ly end up burnin' a salad!"

Ignoring the Abbot's stern gaze, the mousemaid continued. "Miz Saro, are you as quick as they say you are? I bet I'm faster than you. I won the Abbey wallrace last summer."

Saro grinned from ear to ear and shook Springald's paw.

"My congratulations, missy! So then, I'll have a bit o' competition in this wall race. I'm plannin' on runnin' in it for a prize of an afternoon cream tea. Mmm! 'Tis many a long season since I tasted one."

Springald blurted out, "You're too old, I'll beat you easy!"

Abbot Carrul was shocked by her behaviour. "Springald, show some respect for your elders!"

However, it was Saro who interceded on her behalf. "Not at all, Father, I like to see a young 'un with a bit o' spirit. She's like me at her age. Don't ye fret now, 'twill be a fine race, I'm sure. Let's go to the wall an' get it started. No time like the present, eh, mate?"

Supremely confident, Springald winked at Horty and whispered to Fenna. "That old relic's in for a surprise."

Turning to Saro, she bowed mockingly. "After you, marm!"

10

The crowd gathered under the threshold of the gatehouse. None of the wall racers was interested in entering. Everybeast was talking about it, eager to see the race between Springald and Saro.

The Abbot held up his paws. "So be it, the wall race will start from the threshold above this gate. One circuit of the entire rampart's area, ending back on the same spot. Pushing or shoving means instant disqualification. Runners may use all of the walkway, including the battlements. Any questions?"

Shilly the squirrelbabe piped up. "Farver h'Abbot, worrabout uz likkle 'uns an' the very very h'old 'uns?"

She was referring to the ground race, which was run over the same distance but from the ground level. This was for Dibbuns and Elders, mainly to avoid the dangers of falling from the walltops, where only fit and experienced runners competed.

The Abbot watched as Foremole Dwurl scored a deep line along the ground with his formidable digging claws. "Of course, we mustn't forget the ground race. All competitors come up to the line, please. No crowding or jostling!" He checked the walltop, where Springald and Saro were standing level.

93

Brother Weld, acting as walltop official, waved down to the Abbot. "All ready up here!"

Bragoon and Toran sat on the lawn where they could see both races at the same time. Toran patted his ample stomach.

"Me racin' days are long gone. What about ye, Brother? Yore the same age as Saro, why ain't you runnin'?"

Bragoon folded his paws and settled back. "I'm far too old. Saro was born on the same day as me, but she's an hour younger."

Toran scoffed. "An hour, that's nothin' in a lifetime!"

His brother Bragoon maintained a straight face. "Oh it isn't, eh? Ye try holdin' yore breath for an hour, matey!"

Every Dibbun in Redwall was hopping and leaping on the line, waiting for the start.

Abbot Carrul held up a big spotted red 'kerchief, taking one last look around as he called, "Is that all now, last chance for any late entrants!"

Horty came bowling up, pushing Martha in her chair as she protested. "No, please Horty, I've never raced before!"

The garrulous hare pushed his sister onto the line. "Oh piffle'n'twodge, miss. We'll show these blighters what us Braebucks are jolly well made of, wot! Two stout runnin' paws an' a splendid set o' wheels. Hahah, we'll leave 'em all bally well standin', wot wot!"

Toran and Bragoon applauded from the sideline. "That's the stuff, give it a go, miss!"

Springald stood in a ready stance. Saro glanced sideways at her as she pawed the line.

"Good luck to ye, young 'un!"

The mousemaid kept her eyes set on the course ahead. "Aye, good luck to you, too, old 'un. You're going to need it!"

Several of the Dibbuns made overenthusiastic false starts, causing a slight delay as Toran and Bragoon got them back into line.

Abbot Carrul stood out on the lawn and shouted as the 'kerchief fluttered in the breeze.

"On your marks . . . Ready . . . Steady . . . Go!"

Away everybeast went, young and old, on walltop or ground, running at top speed.

Carrul sat on the grass with the two otters. "Dearie me, some of those Dibbuns have raced off in the opposite direction."

Toran laughed. "Oh, let 'em go. They'll still run the same distance at the finish. Flyin' fur'n'feathers! Lookit young Springald go, ye'd think she had wings on 'er footpaws. Looks like Saro is laggin' behind a bit. D'ye think she's in trouble already, Brag?"

The otter shook his head. "She's just pacin' herself, keepin' the mousemaid lookin' back over her shoulder, ye'll see."

Both walltop runners were almost at the north wall corner, with Springald a good two paces in front.

Below on the grass, chaos ensued. A molebabe and a tiny shrewlet had decided to stop and share some candied chestnuts between them. Another molebabe tripped over them. He forgot the race and joined the pair.

"Hurr, worrum ee got thurr, candee chesknutters, oi'm gurtly fond o' they'm, boi 'okey oi arr!"

The shrewlet passed him a few. "Den h'eat dese up, nuts make y'go faster, we still winna race, mate!"

Martha clung tight to the chair as the little cart bounced and bumped furiously forward, with Horty yelling out a warning to them. "I say there, you bounders, make way or we'll run ye down. Watch out for the corner, me old skin'n'blister. Steer quicker, or we'll knock a hole in that wall, wot!"

Abbot Carrul shook his head in admiration as he viewed the walltop runners. "My word, the speed of those two, they're nearly at the east corner already. Look at them go!"

As Toran saw them negotiate the corner and tear off along the parapet southward, he groaned softly, "Aaaah, pore ole Saro's flaggin' now. See, Springald's stretched her lead, I think she's bound to win."

95

A slight smile played about Bragoon's lips. "The race ain't over 'til the winner crosses the line. You watch, Saro'll soon take the spring out o' Miss Springald."

But by now the mousemaid had turned the south wall-corner, leading by three paces.

The Abbot commented. "I think that young 'un's got the field to herself now."

Bragoon did not answer; instead, he put both paws to his mouth and emitted a single sharp whistle.

Springald was panting heavily, but still she took time to glance back at Saro as she gasped, "Give up, old 'un, you're beat!"

Saro was breathing like a bellows, still hard on her opponent's heels. At the sound of Bragoon's whistle, Saro summoned up all her energy and put on a massive burst of speed. As the finishing line loomed up, Springald set her eyes dead ahead, racing wildly for it. Saro made a mighty leap. She sailed up and over, passing above the startled mousemaid's head, to land beyond the line, half a pace ahead, right beside Brother Weld, who roared out, "Saro wins!"

Completely shocked, Springald collapsed in a heap on the walkway. Fighting for breath, she gasped, "Wh . . . wh . . . what h . . . happened?"

Weld the Beekeeper was holding Saro's paw high, shouting, "The winner by a half pace—Miz Sarobando!"

On the ground, three quarters of the way around, more contestants were put out of the race as they met the reverse runners. They collided and fell in a jumble, roaring and arguing.

"Yurr, wot ways bee's you'm foogles a runnen?"

"Uz norra foogles, you knock uz over 'cos we winnin'!"

Martha steered the cart around them, yelling in panic, "Slow down, Horty, watch out for those Dibbuns!"

Her brother narrowly missed the melee, speeding up as he shouted, "Forward the buffs! Onward t'death or flippin' glory! Blood'n'vinegar, me jolly lads! Redwaaall!"

Howling and hooting, he rushed over the finishing line, grinding to a halt and losing a back wheel in the process. "Hoorah, me beautiful ole skin'n'blister, we won. Wot Wot Wot!"

"Nay, you'm diddent, zurr. Uz wunned—Shilly an' oi!"

Horty's mouth fell open. "But . . . but . . . how . . . wot . . . but?"

Martha almost fell from her chair laughing. "Hahahahaha! Muggum and Shilly were first over. Heeheehee, they won. Stop your but butting, Horty, we were second. A great effort on your part, sir. Thank you kindly!"

She did not tell him that, when they almost collided with the fallen Dibbuns, she had rescued Muggum from the heap as they whizzed by. Muggum had hold of Shilly's tail, so she, too, was swept aboard the chair. Both of the little ones hopped off the cart, over the line, just ahead of it. Luckily they landed either side of the vehicle.

The Abbot, who had his suspicions as to who the real winners were, eyed the Dibbuns sternly. "Who won? I want the truth!"

Muggum was the picture of infant innocence. "Troofully, we'm wunned, zurr. Us'n's farster'n woild bunglybees, moi paws nurrly tukk foire!"

The Father Abbot shook his head in disbelief until Martha reassured him. Toran and Bragoon backed her up stoutly.

"Aye, 'twas the Dibbuns who won, fair'n'square!"

"Right, mate, would we lie to a great Father Abbot?"

Folding both paws into his wide sleeves, the Abbot wandered off, muttering, "Why shouldn't I believe three good and honest creatures? Frogs can fly, fish make nests in trees. Who am I but a poor Abbot who knows nothing?"

It was still some time until nightfall and the commencement of the Summer Feast. Under the Abbot's instructions, the kitchen crew had already made a substantial afternoon tea.

Saro threw a friendly paw around Springald's shoulders.

"That was the closest race I've ever run. Come on, young 'un, you'n yore friends must take tea with me. Let the winnin' Dibbuns an' Martha sit with us, too."

The banks of the Abbey pond made a perfect setting as the Redwallers sat in the lengthening noon shadows, watching sungleams on the cool, dark water. Junty Cellarhog, the big hedgehog who took care of Redwall's famous cellars, personally served them with ice-cold rosehip and mint tea. Everybeast gossiped animatedly whilst enjoying the excellent food. Most Redwallers wanted to know more about the famous pair and their adventures. Bragoon had to do most of the answering, as Saro was lost in the ecstasy of scones, meadowcream and strawberry jam. Even Horty was amazed at the amount of food that Saro could put away.

He remarked in awed tones, "Good grief, marm, you can certainly deal pretty roughly with scones when you've a blinkin' mind to, wot!"

Bragoon shoved more meadowcream over to his companion. "Don't disturb Saro while she's eatin', she gets fierce."

Horty nodded politely. "Know wotcha mean, sah. I expect it was jolly tough, wot. All those seasons o' fightin' rascally vermin. Must've given the lady a confounded keen appetite!"

Bragoon nodded. "Many's the time I've had to count me paws after sittin' too close to Saro at vittlin' time!"

Toran beckoned to his friend Junty. "Now then, ole cellarspikes, wot about a bit o' music? Brought yore fiddle?"

Junty Cellarhog took a small, beautifully crafted fiddle out of the hood of his cloak. He tuned it deftly. "Rightyo, any pertickler tune ye'd like?"

Horty volunteered. "Play the Dawnsong. I'm sure Martha will sing for us. The jolly old skin'n'blister has a rather charmin' voice, y'know."

Everybeast began calling for Martha to sing. Junty struck

a chord or two. The haremaid bowed in deference to the two guests.

"Only if Bragoon and Sarobando would like to hear it."

The otter chortled. "Like to hear it? I'd *love* to hear ye sing, Martha. All I ever hear is my mate Saro, an' she's got a voice like a frog bein' strangled!"

The squirrel looked up indignantly from a half-eaten scone. "Hah, lissen who's talkin'. Let me tell ye, missy, to hear ole Bragoon singin', 'tis like listenin' to a nail trapped under a door!"

Fenna giggled. "Then you'd best be singing, Martha. Those two'll curdle the meadowcream if they start warbling."

Martha paused until Junty's fiddle had played the opening bars, then she began to sing.

"I have a friend as old as time,
yet new as every day.
She banishes the night's dark fears,
and sends bad dreams away.
She's always there to visit me,
so faithfully each morn,
so peaceful and so beautiful,
my friend whose name is Dawn.

She fills the air with small birds' song,
and opens all the flowers.
She bids the beaming sun to shine,
to warm the daylight hours.
She comes and goes so silently,
to leave the earth reborn,
serene and true, all clad in dew,
my friend whose name is Dawn."

There was silence as the last poignant notes hovered on the still air, then wild applause.

Bragoon's tough face softened as he sniffed. "I never heard anythin' so pretty in all me days!"

Horty puffed out his chest. "I told you she could sing!"

Saro, having forgotten her afternoon tea, sat transfixed. "Sing, did ye say? Listen, even the birds've gone quiet at the sound of the maid's voice. I'm retirin' from singin' as of now. Wot d'ye say, mate?"

Bragoon had borrowed Junty's fiddle. He plucked the strings as he gazed in admiration at the haremaid. "Our lips are sealed, Miss Martha, ye put us t'shame. Mind ye, I can still knock a tune out on the ole fiddle, an Saro ain't a bad dancer. Shall I play a jig for ye?"

Muggum had a swift word in Martha's ear, causing her to smile. "Do you know a Dibbun reel called Dungle Drips?"

The Abbeybabes leaped up and down, shouting eagerly. "Play ee Dungle Drips, zurr!"

Bragoon raised the fiddlebow, winking at Saro. "Haha, Dungle Drips. We danced to that 'un a few times when we was Dibbuns, eh mate?"

The aging squirrel leaped up. "Aye, I'll say we did! Right, c'mon, me liddle darlins, I'll show ye a step or two. I once was Redwall's Champion Dibbun Dancer!"

Even before the first notes rang out, the Dibbuns clasped paws and whooped. Saro was whirled off amid a crowd of molebabes, tiny mice, infant squirrels and small hoglets. All the Dibbuns roared the molespeech lyrics with gusto, hurtling themselves into the wild reel. Martha was convulsed with laughter at their antics and amazed at Saro's skill. The squirrel was a born dancer, twirling and somersaulting recklessly as she sang out in mole dialect along with the Dibbuns.

"Whooooaaah! Let's do ee jig o' Dungle Drips,
woe to ee furst likkle paw wot slips,
chop off ee tail, throw um in bed,
wiv a bandage rownd ee hedd!
Feed ee choild on strawbee pudd,

gurt fat h'infants uz darnce gudd,
Dungle Drips naow clap ee paws,
tug moi snout an' oi'll tug yores.
Bow to ee h'Abbot, gudd day zurr,
twurl ee rounden everywhurr,
Dungle Drips bee's gurt gudd fun,
oop t'bed naow likkle 'un. Whoooooaaah!"

The dance grew more frantic, the singing faster as Bragoon speeded up his fiddling. Muggum and his crew performed some very fancy pawwork—shuffling and high kicking, raising raucous cheers and calling for the fiddler to play even faster. The scene of wild abandon suddenly stretched out into a double line with Saro bringing up the rear as the Abbeybabes cavorted furiously across the lawns and vanished into the Abbey.

Bragoon stopped playing and blew upon his heated paws. "Whew! Wot happened there, Carrul?"

Bewildered, the Abbot shook his head. "I've no idea. Sister Setiva, do you know what those babes are up to?"

The shrewnurse shrugged. "Och, the wee beasties must have danced off tae their beds. 'Tis no great surprise, ah'm thinkin', after all that racin', eatin' and jiggin'. Ye ken, they must be rare wearied."

The Redwallers sat sipping tea for quite some time. There was no sound from within the Abbey. Then Saro emerged. Chuckling to herself, she sat down wearily, accepting a beaker of tea gratefully.

"Whew, I ain't as young as I used t'be! That was some dance, I tell ye. Those Dibbuns jigged through the Abbey, up the stairs they went, straight into their dormitory. Before you could say boo, they were flat out on their beds an' snorin'! I felt like joinin' 'em myself. Huh, looks like the liddle 'uns have called it a day."

Toran looked perplexed. "But wot about the Summer Feast?"

Abbot Carrul saw the look of disappointment on his friend's face. "Cheer up, Toran, we'll have it at midday tomorrow. 'Twill keep until then."

Horty's ears drooped mournfully. "I say, you chaps, all I've had to eat is a few measly scones an' a drop o' tea."

Martha slapped his paw playfully. "Shame on you, I wouldn't call three plates of scones measly. Don't pull such faces, you'll last until tomorrow."

The gluttonous young hare went into a sulk. "Jolly easy for you t'say, wot. Skin'n'blisters never scoff much anyway, not like us chaps. So be it then! If none of you lot see me round an' about tomorrow, you'd best take a blinkin' good search. You won't be smilin' then. Not when you find the skeleton of a gallant young hare in some lonely corner. Oh yes, indeed, that'll be me, perished t'death from flippin' hunger, wot! Woe is us, you'll cry, an' weep absolute buckets o' tears, thinkin' we should've let the poor brave lad have a small extra scoff last night."

Bragoon played along with Horty, shaking his head sadly. "An' wot'll yore skeleton reply to us, ole mate?"

Horty sniffed. "It'll say, too blinkin' late, but I told you so, an' yah boo sucks to you, cruel rotten lot! I leave you to your guilty consciences, you heartless bounders. My famished lips are sealed. Wot!" He stalked frostily into a corner whilst stealing the last scone from under Sister Portula's nose.

11

It was still warm as darkness fell. When the Redwallers stopped by the water, enjoying a faint breeze, talk turned to the life of Redwall Abbey and gradually to Martha's story. Bragoon and Saro, who had become very fond of the pretty young haremaid, listened intently. Abbot Carrul, Sister Setiva, Toran and Sister Portula all contributed to the narrative, with Martha filling in the details.

When the tale ended, Bragoon sat staring at the haremaid's unmoving footpaws, peeping from under her lap rug. The aging otter's voice was extremely sympathetic. "What a terrible thing t'happen to a young 'un! An' you've never been able to walk since ye can first remember?"

Martha shook her head. "No, sir, though 'tis not for the want of trying. I collapse every time I do, as if my footpaws were held there by two pieces of wet string."

Saro was impressed by the young one's frankness. "That's a hard thing for anybeast t'bear. If'n ye don't mind me askin', Martha, wot d'ye do with yourself all day?"

Martha shrugged. "Oh, I get around. There's always my kind friends to push me, though I can wheel myself around if I need to. I do a lot of reading and studying, too. Oh, that reminds me, Sister Portula, I left your book in the gate-

103

house. Old Phredd's still up, I can see the light at his window from here. Let's pay him a visit."

They all strolled across to the gatehouse with Bragoon and Saro pushing Martha's chair. Unusually for Phredd, he was wide awake and answered the door promptly.

"Young Martha, I was hoping you'd come. I see you brought all your friends, eh? Well come in, everybeast. You'll have to find somewhere to sit, there's not much room, y'know!"

Phredd spoke to the latch as he closed the door behind them. "Heehee, got something to show this haremaid, haven't we?"

Martha sat up eagerly. "Have you found anything, sir?"

The old hedgehog sat on the side of his bed, opening Sister Portula's book at a page he had marked. "Found something? Hah, the moment that race was over and I could rescue my armchairs back in here, I did some serious reading. There's more important things in life than running oneself silly around walltops, y'know. After all, Martin the Warrior sent you a message that mustn't be ignored, missy."

Bragoon suddenly became interested. "Martin the Warrior sent ye a message, Martha? What did he say?"

The haremaid explained. "I fell asleep near the tapestry. Martin and another young mouse named Sister Amyl appeared to me. Martin told me to read, because reading is knowledge, then Sister Amyl spoke this rhyme to me.

"Where once I dwelt in Loamhedge,
my secret lies hid from view,
the tale of how I learned to walk,
when once I was as you.
Though you cannot go there,
look out for two who may,
travellers from out of the past,
returning home someday."

104

Saro looked very serious. "I remember Martin the Warrior spoke to me an' Brag when we were young."

Abbot Carrul peered over his spectacles in astonishment. "Martin spoke to you two? Did he really?"

Saro kept her face straight. "Oh aye, I'll tell ye wot he said.

"Seek adventure, liddle mates,
go ye forth from Redwall's gates.
Both of ye, wild and unchecked,
begone afore my Abbey's wrecked!"

Bragoon chuckled. "She's only jokin', of course."

Old Phredd glared at them both. "This is no joking matter. As soon as I saw you down by the pond today, I knew you were the two travellers from out of the past. Eh, eh, the two that Sister Amyl's poem spoke of, right?"

Horty's eyes went wide as saucers. "Right indeed, wot!"

Phredd tapped the open book he held. "Stop jabbering and listen, please, this is most important. I have found the story of Sister Amyl. It was written by another, Recorder Scrittum. He was the Loamhedge brother who put most of this story together—and very well he did it, too. Listen to this!"

They sat entranced as Phredd's wavery tones brought the past back to life for them.

" 'The plague has come to Loamhedge, a great sickness is upon us. This morning we buried four, three sisters and one brother. Our infirmary is packed with the ill and suffering. I fear this Abbey has become a pest hole. Abbess Germaine and her Council have reached a bitter decision: if we are to survive, we must leave Loamhedge. It is almost unthinkable, is it not? Having to forsake our beautiful old home to wander in the wilderness. Germaine speaks of travelling to Mossflower country, where she has friends who will give us shelter. We are to take very little with us and live off the land as we go. These are hard and sad times, indeed.

" 'However, there is no other way for it. Poor Sister Amyl is a young mouse who has never walked. She makes her way about in a wheeled chair. Amyl has decided not to go with us. I pleaded with her, saying that I would care for her and push the chair to wherever we were bound, but she would not hear of it. Amyl said that the journey would be far too arduous and feared that she would hold us back. In a way she is right, since a wheeled chair cannot be hauled over hill and dale. There would be bad weather to contend with—rivers, swollen streams, rocks and swampland. Also, it will soon be wintertide. The Abbess does not know of Amyl's decision yet. It is my sad duty to tell her of the situation. Young Sister Amyl is such a good creature. It will break my heart to leave her at Loamhedge, amid the dying.' "

Toran interrupted the narration by sniffing loudly and grubbing a paw across his moist eyes. "Pore liddle thing, left t'die in a deserted Abbey. I'd never leave ye to a fate like that, Martha, no matter wot it took!"

Bragoon grasped the haremaid's paw. "Me either, miss!"

Martha forestalled Saro and the rest by holding up a paw. "I know you wouldn't, none of you. . . ."

She caught sight of Old Phredd, glaring about impatiently. "Oops, sorry sir, we'll be quiet, I promise!"

The Gatekeeper huffed, then leafed on to another marked page. "Thank you! Now let me read further into this narrative. Here is a section by Recorder Scrittum, concerning setting up camp on the first evening of the journey.

" 'Let me tell you of a miracle! Can I believe my eyes, you must take what I tell you as true, I have always been a faithful recorder, and never given to lying. Here was I, trudging along carrying my writing equipment and a sack of provisions. We were heading for a streambank with high sides, where there would be shelter for the brothers and sisters. I was travelling somewhere in the centre of the column, not having seen the Abbess, as she was leading up at the front. I came away from Loamhedge, filled with shame and remorse, being too overcome with grief to bid Sister Amyl farewell. I slunk off like a thief. Then, from the rear of the marchers, a mighty cheer rose up. I trekked back to see what was causing such jubilation. There across the heathland, limping slowly but walking without any shadow of a doubt, came young Sister Amyl!' "

Again, Phredd's recital was interrupted when a hearty cheer came from his listeners. The old hedgehog made as if to slam the book shut.

"Do you want to hear the rest of this, or shall I lay back on my bed and go to sleep, eh, eh?"

Somewhat embarrassed, Abbot Carrul replied, "Forgive us, friend, we'll stay silent. It was just that we felt so happy for Sister Amyl, we had to cheer."

Phredd went back to his book, muttering, "Aye, so did I when I first read it. Ahem, allow me to continue. 'Was it a miracle, or some sort of magic? I had told the Abbess of Amyl's plight. She was sorrowful, of course, but informed me she would have a word with Amyl. What came of their conversation, I did not know. But here was my young friend, as large as life and up on her footpaws. Later that evening we sat by the fire, exhausted after the day's long march. Sister Amyl lay wrapped in her cloak sleeping deeply. I sought out Abbess Germaine and spoke to her about the amazing happening. Here is what our great and wise Mother Abbess told me. She said that she had recalled a formula, given to her by an old healer, many seasons ago. Searching through her belongings, she had found the parchment. This she gave to Amyl, telling her that she must decide on her own whether to stay or whether to read the formula, learn from it and undertake the journey. Obviously, Sister Amyl must have read what was written on the parchment. Was it a magic spell, or some remedy of herbal medicine? The Abbess would not tell me.' "

Martha stifled a cry of disappointment, nevertheless listening dutifully as Phredd continued reading.

" 'Next morning I dropped to the rear of the column and

107

walked with Sister Amyl, whose pace was getting stronger and more sure as the day went on. I told her what I had gleaned from the Abbess and faced her with the question: What was written on the parchment?

" 'Amyl gave me one of her rare, secretive smiles and refused to speak of it. All that day I persisted, harassing her to divulge the information. It was only after a full day's march through sleeting rain and harsh country that she relented. We were camped beside a rocky tor, huddled in our cloaks around the fire, when she finally spoke. Her words are etched into my memory, and here they are, for what it's worth. "The message on the parchment would be of no use to you. It would only have a meaning for somebeast who is greatly troubled in mind or body. Once I had learned what the old healer's rhyme was, I left the parchment behind at Loamhedge. I carry its power within me now, but any creature in need of those words must seek it out for themselves.

" 'Beneath the flower that never grows,
Sylvaticus lies in repose.
My secret is entombed with her,
look and think what you see there.
A prison with four legs which moved,
yet it could walk nowhere,
whose arms lacked paws, but yet they held,
a wretched captive there.' "

Phredd closed the book decisively, addressing its cover. "My bed calls me. I bid you a weary goodnight."

Bragoon protested. "Is that all there is?"

Abbot Carrul reassured the otter. "If there was more, my old friend would have told you. Right, Phredd?"

The ancient Abbey Gatekeeper reached for his nightshirt. "Right indeed, young Carrul. I have given you all the information that is of interest to you, namely, Sister Amyl's story. We already have a map of the route to Loamhedge that was used by Matthias in his search for his son Mattimeo."

108

Saro yawned and stood up stretching. "We'll look at that tomorrow. After all that racin' an' jiggin', I'm ready for bed, too. That poem of Sister Amyl's, 'tis a real tail twister an' no mistake. Flowers that never grow, prisons with four legs an' no paws. An' who in the name o' fur'n'bush is Sylvaticus lyin' in repose?"

Old Phredd poked his head through the neck of the nightshirt. "Sylvaticus was the first Abbess of Loamhedge. Don't know where I learned that, must have been at Dibbun School. Hmmm, that was more seasons ago than I care to remember. Funny how old little facts stick in one's mind. Don't slam my door when you leave, it doesn't like being slammed. Goodnight!"

They strolled back to the Abbey through the balmy night air, discussing the whole thing.

Martha turned to Bragoon and Saro, who were pushing her chair. "Phredd said that you were the two travellers from the past. Do you believe him?"

Bragoon nodded. "Of course we do, beauty. Don't ye fret now, me'n my mate'll bring that parchment back from Loamhedge for ye. Ain't that right, Saro?"

The aging squirrel's reply left Martha in no doubt. "Aye, I'll wager a split acorn to a cream tea on it, missy. We'll have ye up'n'dancin' in no time!"

The haremaid's face was a picture of joy to behold. "I will dance someday just for you, my good friends. Tomorrow I'll make a copy of Sister Amyl's poem so you can take it with you in case you forget the words."

Horty did a small hopskip of eagerness. "Splendid idea, my wise an' pretty sis. I'll take charge of it, like a sort of jolly old mapfinder. Wot!"

Bragoon and Saro exchanged glances, and the otter murmured, "We'll have to see about that."

Further discussion was cut short. Sister Setiva met them at the Abbey doorway. She stood in a pool of golden light, holding up a lantern. The stern old Infirmary Keeper cast a jaundiced eye over the new arrivals.

"Ah'm tae shew ye to yore beds. There's two spare ones in the room next tae mine."

Bragoon bowed appreciatively to her. "It'll be a treat to sleep in a real bed again, Sister."

Saro agreed. "Aye, after some o' the places we've laid our heads down. But we'll be up at the crack o' dawn, ready to lend a paw with yore problem, Martha."

Bragoon thumped his rudder down firmly. "Ye can bet yore brekkist on that, missy. We won't let ye down!"

Martha clasped their paws fondly. "Pleasant dreams to both of you."

The pair found themselves being prodded, none too gently, with Setiva's blackthorn stick.

She commanded them in a no-nonsense voice. "Follow me tae mah sickbay, an' 'twill be woe betide either of ye if ah hear just one wee snore disturbin' mah rest, d'ye ken?"

Bragoon saluted her smartly. "Oh, we're kennin' away like a pair o' good 'uns, Sister. Lead on!" They grinned at each other, listening to the shrewnurse while she chunnered away to herself as she shuffled upstairs.

"Ach, I'll have tae dig oot fresh sheets an' coverlets! Ah'm thinkin' they're big enough tae make their ain beds, great roarin' villains! Ah'll nae sleep a whit taenight, knowin' they two are in the next room tae mine!"

Opening the infirmary door, she glared at her guests. "Wipe the mud off ye're paws an' the silly grins offn'n ye're faces. Ah'll be inspectin' yon sickbay on the morrow, an' ah'll skelpit the pair o' ye if'n there's one wee thing oot o' place, d'ye ken? Ah bid ye a silent guidnight!" She slammed the door and retreated into her own chamber.

Bragoon burst out sniggering as Saro called out in imitation of Setiva's far northern accent.

"Aye, we ken, Sister, an' a guidnight to ye, too, the noo!"

The Sister's strict tone rang out from the adjoining room. "Ah'll be in there wi' mah stick if there's anither sound, so get tae sleep an' no talkin'!"

Saro whispered in Bragoon's ear. "Goodnight, mate."

12

Early morn found the northeast skies showing more promise of decent weather. Outside the holt of Shoredog, pleasant sunlight was turning the mist into a warm yellow haze over the stream.

Lonna Bowstripe limped out with the rest of the sea otters to witness the arrival of the otter known as Garfo Trok. He had come in a peculiar-looking craft, a long, battered old boat with rounded stern and for'ard ends. It had a rickety cabin erected amidships and sported a square, heavily-patched sail, which was furled around a much repaired crosspiece.

Garfo was a stream otter, a jovial, fat beast. He wore an old iron helmet that resembled a cooking pot, and a permanent smile on his broad, friendly face. Shipping his paddling pole, Garfo waddled ashore and began singing in a dreadfully toneless voice.

" 'Tis a long ways down the stream, me lads,
when a beast ain't got no grub oh,
wid a belly like a wind-blowed sail,
aboard this leaky tub oh.
If I fell overboard like this,
all thin'n'pale'n'slack oh,

111

a pike'd take one look at me,
an' quickly chuck me back oh!

Me ribs are showin' through me fur,
I'm frightened o' the weather,
in case a sudden gust o' wind,
whips me off like a feather.
Me cheeks are sunken hollow,
an' me nose is wintry blue, lads,
me rudder's covered in green mold,
I'm sufferin' from the Doodads!

Take pity on this riverdog,
an' feed me good ole vittles,
some skilly'n'duff to stop me bones,
a-clackin' round like skittles.
A pot or two o' barley stew,
an' nutbread by the plateful,
an' a bathtub full o' custard, lads,
would find me ever grateful!"

The sea otters laughed and applauded Garfo heartily, then
gathered round as he shook paws, patted backs and kissed
babes, all the while hooting in booming tones, "Whoohoohoo,
slap me rudder an' curl me whiskers! Lookit ye lot. Wot
'ave youse been feedin' yoreselves on? Y'all look so
chub'n'sparky! Ma Sork, me ole tatercake, are ye still bakin'
the primest nutbread in the northeast?"

Old Sork whacked him playfully with her ladle as he
picked her up and hugged her. "Put me down, ye great fat-
barrel. I've been up all night bakin' nutloaves to feed yore
hungry gob!"

Garfo put her down and cast a jolly eye over Lonna.
"Whoohoo, shrivel me snout an' gravel me guts! So this is
the giant stripedog I'm carryin' as cargo. Hah, I thought I
was a big 'un, but ye could eat dinner of'n me head, mate!"

Lonna shook Garfo Trok's paw. "Pleased to meet you,

mate, but I'm not just cargo. My name is Lonna Bowstripe, and I can wield a paddle as good as most."

Garfo was big and well built for an otter, but Lonna's giant frame towered over him. He released the badger's huge paw.

"Wield a paddle, big feller? Whoohoo, ye look strong enough t'carry me an' my old boat *Beetlebutt* up a waterfall on yore back! Belay, Lonna, let's get some brekkist afore we sail."

Lonna had already eaten, so he sat nibbling a crust of ryebread and sipping some plum cordial whilst Garfo dealt with breakfast. The otter was a mighty eater and extremely odd in his choice of food. He spread nutbread with honey and dunked it into hotroot soup. Breaking up an apple pie, he crumbled it into a bowl of mushroom stew, daubing plum preserve on an onion-and-leek pastie.

Clearing the lot in a remarkably short time, Garfo stood up, patting his big stomach. "Ahoy, Lonna, pack that bow'n' arrers an' let's go sailin'. Can't waste a fine mornin' sittin' here vittlin', like some I've seen. Never could abide greediness in a beast!"

The otters had packed *Beetlebutt* with an amazing array of provisions. Lonna looked around at the faces of all these otters that he had come to like so much. It was going to be a sad experience saying good-bye to them. Garfo stood, waiting to push off, as the badger went in turn to each of his otter friends—Shoredog, Sork, Marinu and many others, saving his last farewell for Abruc and young Stugg. Lonna embraced Abruc warmly and clasped his paw. A tear coursed down the big badger's scarred face.

"Farewell to you and your family, my good friend. I will never forget you and your son. You saved my life, cared for me, fed and nursed me. All I can give you in return are my thanks and undying friendship!"

Abruc scuffed the ground with his rudder, then looked up at the big badger. "Friendship is the greatest gift one can give to another. You are a goodbeast, Lonna. I know ye would've done the same for me an' mine if'n ye found us lyin' hurt. Go on, mate, you go now, an' know our thoughts are always with ye!"

Stugg tugged at Lonna's paw until the badger lifted the young otter and held him level with his eyes. His face solemn, Stugg wiped a tear from Lonna's striped muzzle.

"Lonn', der is somet'ink you can do for me an' my farder. Get Rag' Bol an' dose Searats, so they don't hurt no more pore beasts!"

The badger put Stugg back down and stepped aboard the boat. Raising his bow, he called out as Garfo pushed off into the midstream.

"Stugg, my little mate. I swear by the fine string your father made for this bow. I will wipe Raga Bol and his Searats from the land forever. This is my oath, and my promise to you. Good-bye!"

Putting aside the bow, he joined Garfo Trok at the paddling poles.

Fighting away the tears, Lonna did not look back as they sped downstream. Behind him the tribe of Shoredog stood on the banks, singing an old sea otter song of farewell.

"When the sun sets like fire,
I will think of you,
when the moon casts its light,
I'll remember, too,
if a soft rain falls gently,
I'll stand in this place,
recalling the last time,
I saw your kind face.
Good fortune go with you,
to your journey's end,
let the waters run calmly,
for you, my dear friend."

Garfo Trok had spent his life amid the northeast streams and rivers. There was no waterway for leagues that the burly otter was not familiar with. Lonna obeyed his every order, backing and tacking down the broad stream. They made good progress. Midday found the *Beetlebutt* running smoothly with a fair breeze running astern.

Garfo shipped his long paddle, gazing up at the blue, cloud-flecked sky. "Let the ole lady drift for awhile, mate. Belay that paddle an' we'll haul sail an' take a bite o' lunch."

They released the sail and made its ends fast to the cleats. Lonna had been wondering when the otter's appetite was going to reappear. Together they sat on the roof of the little midships cabin, drinking cider and eating nutbread.

Garfo chuckled as he watched the big badger consume his lunch. "Whoohoo, ain't nothin' wrong with a beast who kin eat hearty, mate! That limp o' yourn will soon clear up with a good cruise. Ye won't be walkin' so much." Lonna liked the feel of a boat beneath his paws; he felt rested and well.

Gesturing ahead, he enquired, "How long can we go by water, Garfo?"

The otter refilled his beaker. "Almost into Mossflower. This ole stream takes a turn there an' runs back east. I kin see yore wonderin' 'ow far ahead those vermin are."

Lonna eyed him keenly. "Aye, can ye tell me, mate?"

Garfo scratched his rudder thoughtfully. "Raga Bol has t'go by land since they ain't got no boat an' there's too many of 'em for small rivercraft. Those Searats should be well into Mossflower Wood by now. I'd say ye was about ten days behind 'em, Lonna. But I kin cut that down to eight, wid some canny sailin'. Don't fret, mate."

The badger's eyes narrowed, the look on his ruined face caused the otter to shudder. Lonna laughed mirthlessly. "Oh, I'm not fretting at all. I'll catch up to them for sure!"

The country they were sailing through was open, with no tree cover. Gradually it ran into hills and gorges, the stream-banks growing higher on either side.

Garfo pointed to a steep bend up ahead. "When we

115

round the point of yon bend, we'll be meetin' up with Buteo. Now I know yore not a-feared of anybeast, but don't start anythin' wid him. I've knowed Buteo a long time."

Lonna was intrigued. "Just as you say, mate, but who is Buteo?"

Garfo crumbled some nutbread on the cabin roof. "Oh, ye'll find out soon enuff, matey, soon enuff!"

Beetlebutt took the bend smoothly, keeping to midstream. Halfway around it, Lonna was startled to feel a slight cuff on the back of his head. Buteo landed like a bolt of lightning, silent and menacing. He was a honey buzzard—a large, savage-looking bird of prey. From fawn-barred tail to mottled chest, and huge wingspan to lethal-hooked beak and a fierce eye, Buteo looked every inch a killer. Folding his wings, the buzzard stared disdainfully at the crumbled nutbread that Garfo had put out for him, then pointed a lethally sharp talon at them.

"Heek! This be Buteo territory, I rule here. Heeeeeekah!"

Garfo replied cheerily. "So ye do, me ole burdy, but we ain't trespassin', just passin' through."

Buteo cocked his head to one side, glaring at them. "Ya-heeek! I riddle you riddle, you spin me a spin. Only pass here if you win. Good?"

Garfo cautioned Lonna to silence with a warning glance. The badger watched as the otter appeared to consider this proposition.

"Good it is, Buteo. You go first."

The honey buzzard stared up at the sky, a thing that honey buzzards do when trying to appear mysterious. "Heeeeekoh! What be brown'n'yellow, fat'n'mad, an' if you slow, sting you bad?"

Garfo scratched his rudder, shaking his head, as if really perplexed. "Frazzle me whiskers, Buteo, that's a real poser!"

Buteo pecked up the crumbled nutbread, sniggering. "Keeheeheehee! Stupid riverdog not crossing through my country. Buteo much clever. Keehar!"

Garfo tipped a sly wink to Lonna, then jumped up shouting. "I got it, 'tis a bumbly bee!"

Both Garfo and Lonna had to avoid the buzzard's wings as he beat the air in frustration. "Yeekeeha! How you know?"

The otter twitched his nose modestly. "Oh, I just took a guess. But it was a great an' clever riddle."

Buteo stalked up and down, digging his talons angrily into the cabin roof. Then he turned and wheeled on Garfo. "Yeeee! You still not go 'til you spin me. This time I win!"

The crafty otter produced a flat pebble from his helmet, spat on one side of it and held it up for the bird to see. "Right, I'll spin ye—dry side I win, wet side you lose. Good?"

The honey buzzard nodded eagerly. "Keehee! I take wet!"

Garfo spun the pebble into the air, chanting, "Up she comes, down she goes, how she lands, nobeast knows!"

Buteo's keen eyes watched every spin of the stone until it clacked down flat on the deck.

Garfo grinned from ear to ear. "Wet side, you lose!"

The buzzard hovered over the otter, glaring murderously at him. Garfo sat munching a chuck of nutbread, looking the fierce bird straight in the eye. "Ye've got to let us pass now, mate, or you ain't a bird whose word can be trusted."

Fearing that the buzzard was going to attack Garfo, Lonna braced himself to spring upon it.

The bird's black and gold eyes dilated wildly as it screeched. "Allbeast know Buteo be a bird of honour, my word always good. I slay anybeast who say different. Yeeeeeekaaaah!"

Snatching the nutbread from the otter's paw, he soared off into the air—up and up, until he was a mere dot in the sky.

Lonna relaxed gratefully. "That was a close call, my friend. Buteo looked like a bird who would fight to the death. How did you manage to hoodwink him like that?"

Garfo Trok winked knowingly. "I been doin' it a long time, mate, whenever my journeys take me by this way. Pore ole Buteo's memory's scrambled from too many battles. Besides, he ain't the brightest o' birds. Funny how he loses every time. I'll let him win on the return trip, 'cos I'll be bound back nor'east anyway. That's fair enough."

Lonna could not help laughing at the sly otter. "You great fat fraud! Shame on you, Garfo Trok!"

Nibbling on a piece of cheese he had found, Garfo waved his rudder nonchalantly. "Better'n havin' to fight t'the death wid a mad buzzard. You said so yoreself, mate. Anythin' for an easy life, that's my motto."

13

The Searat Blowfly sat on a rotten log, cooling his footpaws by rubbing them in the rich, damp loam. Gazing up at the trunks of mighty woodland trees, with their canopy of sun-pierced green, he murmured to the Searat sitting alongside him.

"I likes this 'ere Mossflower place, better weather 'ere than on that nor'east coast. Plenny o' shelter an' prime vittles, too!"

His companion, a sad-faced Searat called Rojin, rubbed his blistered footpaws tenderly as he complained. "Huh, if only we wasn't marchin' so much. I ain' cut out fer all this trekkin'. I'm a Searat, norra landlubber!"

Hangclaw, another rat, limped over to join them. Rooting with his daggerpoint at a splinter in his footpaw, he spat in disgust.

"Right y'are, shipmate, just look at me pore trampers. Why are we walkin' all the time. Where's ole Bol got us bound to? We're traipsin' around all day an' 'arf the night!"

Glimbo, the one-eyed rat who had been first mate aboard ship, had been loitering nearby, eavesdropping on the three crewrats. Sneaking up behind them, he gave the rotten log a hard shove with his spearpoint, sending the trio sprawling into the loam.

"Gerrup on yer paws an' quit whinin', ye slab-sided sons o' worms. If the cap'n catches ye, he'll leave youse here to rest as food fer the ants. Now march!"

Raga Bol had been marching up in front of the others but had looked back over his shoulder so often that the crew could not fail to notice. The Searat captain dropped back until he was level with Glimbo. Catching his mate's sleeve with the deadly silver hook, Bol swiftly dragged him behind a broad sycamore trunk.

Glimbo's sightless eye rolled in its socket as he saluted. "They're all on the march, Cap'n!"

Raga Bol poked his head out from behind the tree and snarled at the backstragglers. "Keep movin', I'm watchin' ye!" Then he turned his attention to the trembling Glimbo. "They're talkin' about me, wot're they sayin'? The truth!"

The mate was trembling so hard that the back of his head made a noise on the tree trunk like a woodpecker. "N . . . nothin', Cap'n, they ain't sayin' nothin'.."

He heard the slither of cold steel as Bol drew his scimitar. As Raga Bol pulled him close, Glimbo could see the glint of his captain's gold teeth. He knew how dangerous the captain's moods were becoming.

With his scimitar upraised, Bol hissed, "They must be sayin' somethin', ye mud-brained idiot!"

Words poured out of Glimbo at breakneck pace. "On me oath, Cap'n, the whole crew's sayin' 'ow thankful they are to ye for bringin' 'em 'ere, where 'tis sunny an' there's easy pickins. It's just that they ain't used to all this marchin' . . . some of 'em gotten sore paws."

Thunk! The scimitar blade cut deep into the sycamore, taking off a tuft of Glimbo's whiskers. "Sore paws, is it? You tell any beast moanin' about sore paws that I'll chop 'em off an' make 'em march on the stumps! Aye, an' ye can tell all the crew to quit starin' at me all the time. An' ye can tell 'em another thing, too. Any rat I 'ears mentionin' that giant stripedog, I'll make 'im eat his own tongue. There ain't no big stripedog follerin' me, d'ye hear?"

120

Glimbo gulped hard, knowing how close to death he had come. Raga Bol wandered off without warning, leaving him to pull the scimitar loose and return it. The mate was surprised to see his captain sit down in the loam and speak in a voice that almost had a sob in it. "I ain't been sleepin' at nights. Post extra guards around me when it gets dark."

Glimbo dislodged the blade and returned it to his captain. Raga Bol grabbed the scimitar, staring suspiciously at him.

"Stop starin' at me like that, thick'ead. Gerrabout yer business an' make 'em march faster!"

Glimbo saluted and walked off bemused. This was not the Raga Bol he knew from the seafaring days. The captain was definitely acting strange. He glanced back at Bol, but the captain did not notice him looking, because he, too, was peering back over his shoulder.

Badredd felt the early sun on his muzzle as he lay on a soft patch of moss, with both eyes closed, feigning sleep. He listened to the voices of the gang, identifying each one as they spoke.

"Sure 'tis a luvly morn, an' a grand ould spot t'be enjoyin' it in!" Flinky had an unmistakable accent.

His mate, Crinktail, was next to speak. "Which way d'ye want these woodpigeon eggs boilin'?"

Flinky replied, "Keep 'em nice'n'soft, me ould darlin'. I've never been fussy on hardboiled eggs."

Crinktail sounded cheerful. "I'll cook night an' day for ye, if'n yew can fool that little fox into lettin' us stay by this water for a few more days."

Badredd heard Juppa's voice chime in. "Aye, this is a prime spot. See if'n ye can fool the liddle idjit to stop 'ere fer a score o' days!"

Flinky oozed confidence. "Leave it t'me, mates. I'm a silver-tongued ould charmer when I wants t'be!"

Badredd yawned convincingly, then, opening his eyes, sat up lazily and stretched. "Boiled woodpigeon eggs, eh? Bring 'em over here, Flinky, I 'ope they're done nice'n'soft."

The stoat gritted his teeth but obeyed the new chief's orders. "Top o' the mornin' to ye, sir, an' another grand day 'tis, t'be sure. Now ye enjoy those eggs, there's plenny more around. We was just sayin' wot a fine spot ye chose fer us. Yore a wise leader, so y'are!"

Badredd put the eggs to one side and stood up, sword in paw. Scowling darkly, he asserted his authority. "Don't get to like it too much, you lot, 'cos we're movin' on as soon as we've eaten. So pack up yore gear an' stand by, ready t'-march as soon as Plumnose gets back!"

Halfchop's face was the picture of dismay. "But didn't ye say we wuz stayin' 'ere for a coupla days?"

The little fox gripped his cutlass tighter. "Well, I just changed me mind. A chief can do that!"

Slipback stood paws on hips, facing up to Badredd. "Changed yore mind, eh, jus' like that! An' where d'ye think yore takin' us, eh?"

Raising the cutlass, Badredd took a pace forward and snarled nastily at the weasel. "We're goin' to this Abbey place, if 'tis any business of yores. So git yore tackle t'gether!"

Slipback turned to the others, scoffing insolently, "Hah, looks t'me like the liddle fox needs a magic sword t'make 'im look bigger!"

Badredd's temper snapped. He swung at the weasel's unprotected back, chopping off his tail with a single blow.

Slipback screeched in pain. "Yeeeaaaargh, me tail!"

His mate, Juppa, hastily slapped a pawful of bank mud on the severed stump. Slipback lay moaning, half fainting with the agony.

Juppa glared accusingly at Badredd. "Ye had no call t'do that to 'im!"

As the fox once again flourished his cutlass, the gang fell back. He saw the fear in their eyes and exulted in it. "Next time anybeast talks t'me like that, I'll slay 'im! Oh, I know wot ye've been sayin' be'ind me back. Think ye can fool me, do ye? Well, dig the dirt out yore lugs an' lissen. I'm rulin' this roost, an' wot I say goes! I'm goin' to own that magic sword, aye, an' take the Abbey, too. Anybeast who sez diff'rent, let 'em speak now!"

Flinky raised his paws placatingly. "Ah, sure now, who'd be wantin' t'get themselves slayed by battlin' wid a fine great warrior like yoreself? 'Tis just that we thought ye was goin' to stop 'ere a few days."

It was then that Badredd knew he was really the leader of the gang. A feeling of power surged through him. Now he could be as cruel and commanding as Burrad or Skrodd. Had he not just drawn blood? Curling his lip contemptuously, he growled, "I do the thinkin' from now on. We're goin' to the Abbey. Come on, Slipback, up on yer hunkers, ye ain't dead yet."

With a poultice of mud and dockleaf tied to his severed tail, the weasel rose slowly, fixing Badredd with a stare of hatred. "There's eight of us an' only one of you, fox. Don't get too big'n'fancy wid yore ideas, 'cos ye've still got to sleep at nights. I wouldn't turn me back on us too often if'n I was you—ye can't kill us all!"

Badredd realised the truth in Slipback's statement, but now that he had all this newfound power he was not backing down. With his cutlass blade, Badredd upset the small cauldron of water over the campfire. It went out with a hiss and a cloud of steam.

At that moment, Plumnose came lumbering back through the woodlands. The ferret's oversized nose wobbled from side to side as he took in the scene. "Huh, wod's bin goin' on, mates?"

Flinky began explaining. "Ah well, Plum, me ould messmate, wait'll I tell ye wot . . ."

Badredd shoved the stoat roughly aside. "I'm the chief now—make yore report t'me. Well, wot did ye find?"

Plumnose pointed in the direction he had been scouting. "Er, over der, I'b found a path dat runs south't'north. I t'ink dat's der way to the h'abbey. Id's aboud h'a day's march, Chief, to d'path I mean."

123

Badredd pointed with his blade. "Get movin', you lot. Plumnose, you go up front an' show 'em the way. Slipback, Juppa, Crinktail, Flinky an' Halfchop, up front wid 'im. I ain't walkin' wid youse behind me. Rogg an' Floggo, you bring up the rear wid me."

He shook the cutlass at Flinky. "An' remember this, old silver tongue, no gossipin' an' plottin', 'cos I'll be watchin' ye. There'll be no more coaxin' me inter things wot I don't wanna do. Now move yoreselves!"

It was pleasant walking through the woodlands. Patches of light and shade mottled the grass, and many forest blossoms were coming into bloom. The weasel brothers, Rogg and Floggo, were a taciturn pair. Since both of them carried bows and arrows, Badredd had kept them back with him. He explained their duties as he watched the backs of the gang, marching ahead. Badredd confided to the weasel brothers as though they were lifelong friends.

"Stay by my side, mates, I'll make ye both my seconds in command. Keep yore eyes on the rest of that gang an' watch me back. Aye, ye two look true'n'blue t'me. When we conquer that Abbey place, I'll reward ye well. Mark my words, ye'll live the lives o' kings!"

Rogg and Floggo were not at all impressed by the little fox's brags and promises. They had seen gang leaders come and go, each one as ruthlessly cruel as the next. Keeping a stolid silence, the brothers marched dutifully on. Badredd kept a half pace behind them, carrying the cutlass over one shoulder like a spear. He had tried wearing it thrust into his belt, but the blade was too long. It dragged along the ground and got caught twixt his footpaws, causing undignified stumbles. Leaders could not afford to look foolish to those serving them.

Morning wore on to midday. The gang's initial feelings of a brisk march through pleasant country began to pall as the going got more difficult. Those who were marching in front began complaining when they had to pass through a wide area of stinging nettles. Badredd roared at them to carry on in silence, which they did but only briefly. They had come upon marshy ground—not too deep but very uncomfortable—and soon were grumbling loudly. Swarms of midges attacked as the vermin struggled through the smelly, oozing mud. This time they ignored Badredd's shouts and threats, even hurling insults back at him. After what seemed like hours, the front marchers emerged onto firm ground. Badredd and his bodyguards Rogg and Floggo hurried to catch up with them.

The gang had found a dry, sunny clearing where they lay, looking sullen and rebellious. One glance at their mud-splashed, insect-bitten faces warned their leader of trouble to come should he start roaring out orders to continue marching. Badredd forestalled this by sitting down wearily and commenting, "Ye did well there, mates, let's rest 'ere awhile. Ahoy, Plum, are ye sure this is the right way? Are ye sure that hooter o' yores didn't wobble in the wrong direction, eh?"

Not even a snigger greeted his little joke. Picking dried mud from his nosetip, the ferret replied dully, "Dis is duh way h'I went awright."

The vermin gang had no supplies with them and were too tired to forage. Crinktail and Halfchop stretched out and began taking a nap in the warm sunlight. Plumnose, Juppa, Slipback and Flinky sat in a group, conversing in muted tones. Rogg and Floggo slouched nearby, their eyes half closed.

Badredd began feeling dozy in the midday heat, but he forced himself to sit up and look alert. He saw Slipback glance his way, then whisper something to Juppa. The little fox pointed the cutlass at them.

"Cut out the whisperin', I'm warnin' ye!"

Flinky grinned impudently and threw a lazy salute. "Ah sure, they wasn't sayin' ought bad about ye, sir. Wid yore permission, would it be alright if we was to sing?"

Badredd relaxed, shrugging indifferently. "Sing 'til yore

tongues drop off, if'n ye've a mind to. But none o' that gossipin' an' whisperin' to each other!"

The four exchanged sly winks. Flinky began singing a lullaby in a soft soothing voice.

"All the walkin' today that I've done, done, done,
trampin' through mud in the sun, sun, sun,
it reminds me of the days when me dear ould mother
    said,
come on now liddle feller, time for bed . . . bed . . . bed.
So hush a-bye, looh ah-lie, baby close yore eyes,
an' dream about the moon up in the starry skies."

He repeated the verse again, even softer, with the other three vermin humming gently in the background.

Badredd's head drooped forward slightly, the cutlass lying limp in his open paw. His thoughts drifted back to his own young seasons. Through a golden haze of memory, he was barely aware of Flinky's singing. It was the same tune but with different words.

"It looks like the fox has gone to sleep, sleep, sleep,
Slippy now be quiet as ye creep, creep, creep,
an' stick a good sharp spear straight through his head,
then the moment that he wakes up he'll be dead, dead,
    dead!
So hush a-bye, don't ye cry, foxy close yore eyes,
an' ye'll soon make lovely vittles for the ants an' flies!"

The murderous scheme might have worked out successfully had it not been for Plumnose. He thought that the altered words were so funny that he clapped his paws and broke out into hearty guffaws.

"Duh, haw haw haaaw! Dat's a gudd 'un, I like dat, Flink! Haw haw haw, wake up dead, berry gudd!"

Badredd snapped immediately back to reality. He caught

Slipback, brandishing a spear not three paces from him. Grabbing up his cutlass, the fox raised it threateningly.

"Wot are yew up to, weasel?"

Slipback veered and went past him. He started jabbing at the shrubbery at the edge of the glade.

"Thought I saw those bushes movin', Chief. It might've been that otter an' the squirrel, er, Sagroon an' Bando!"

Flinky interposed. "I know who ye mean, Bragoon an' Saro. I saw the bushes move, too, Chief. Slipback could be right!"

Thinking swiftly, Badredd turned the situation to his advantage. "No sense in takin' chances then. We'd best git movin' fast. Come on, up on yore paws!"

Badredd drove them hard for the remainder of the day by adopting a simple but effective scheme. He ordered Rogg and Floggo to fire off arrows from time to time. The deadly shafts fell just short of the marchers' rear, causing them to hasten forward. Oaths and curses accompanied the arrival of each arrow, but they kept going, knowing they were only getting tit for tat. The plot to rid themselves of the little fox had failed, but they realised that, had it been Burrad or Skrodd in Badredd's place, Flinky and Slipback would have been slain as retribution. They were getting off lightly.

Progress was good. By evening, Badredd was heartened to hear Plumnose calling out, "Dere's duh path at de end ob the trees!"

Sure enough, they had reached the border of the woodlands. In front of them lay the path, which ran down from the north to the south.

Flinky leaned on an elm trunk, smiling cheerfully as the fox came up to see. "Ah well, there ye are now, Chief. All we gotta do is follow that road t'the left an' keep goin' 'til we hit Redwall Abbey!"

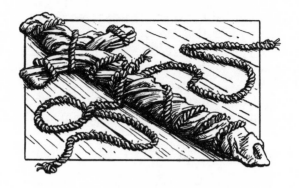

14

Larks soared joyfully on the flatlands outside of Redwall, singing their hymns to the newborn day. Chiming a melodious bass line, the Abbey's twin bells boomed out warmly. Indoors, all the young ones were already up and about, anticipating the arrival of Summer Feast.

Sister Setiva invariably rose to the tolling bells. Up and dressed, tidy and neat, she rapped on the sickbay door with her blackthorn stick, berating the sleepers within.

"Oot o' those beds, ye great dozy lumpkins. If your no' out here in a braces o' shakes, ah'll be in there an' haul ye both oot by your tails!"

Bragoon poked a sleepy head from beneath his coverlet. "Hear that, mate? I think we'd best get up. Huh, I'd sooner face a regiment o' vermin than that ole shrewnurse!"

Reaching out a paw, Saro grasped a bedside stool and rattled it noisily on the floor, calling out. "We're both up, Sister, just makin' the beds an' tidyin' round. We'll be out there in a tick!"

Setiva's shrill warning came back loud and clear. "Och, you're a braw fibber. Ah'll be doonstairs, keeping an eye out for ye. Laggardly sluggards!"

The pair sat up at the sound of her retreating stick taps. Saro yawned and thumped her head back on the pillows.

"Just leave me here for the rest o' the season, Brag. I'd forgotten how comfy a real bed feels. Mmmmmmmmm!"

Leaping out of bed, the otter swished water from a ewer on his face and towelled it vigourously. "Fair enough, me ole bushtail, you stop there. I haven't forgotten how good a Redwall brekkist tastes."

Without bothering to wash, Saro pursued him downstairs. "I'm right with ye, ole ten bellies. You ain't scoffin' all the vittles afore I gets a crack at 'em!"

Martha had just finished making up a tray for herself and Old Phredd when she saw the pair rush in and begin loading up two trays from the long buffet tables set up in the kitchen passage. She giggled at the sight of them, helping themselves to some of everything, chuckling with delight at the food.

"Almond wafers with raspberry sauce, my favourite!"

"Oatmeal with apple'n'honey, just the stuff! Granmum Gurvel, me ole beauty, pass me some o' that pastie. Wot's in it?"

"Burr, ee mushenrooms an' carrot, zurr, wi' h'onion sauce."

"Onion sauce! Gimme two portions, one for Starvation Saro!"

"Hah, lissen to ole bucket mouth! You get us two mint teas, Brag, an' I'll fill two beakers o' Junty Cellarhog's best damson cordial. Oh great, hot scones! Gimme, gimme!"

Leaving the buffet, they beamed at the haremaid over the tops of their laden trays. "Mornin', Miss Martha, we're just makin' up for the lost brekkists, ain't that right, Bragg?"

The otter winked roguishly. "Haharr, sleepin' in a real bed gives a beast a powerful appetite."

Martha looked up at their heaped trays. "I'm sure it does. Perhaps you'd like to take breakfast in the gatehouse with Phredd and me, away from all this bustle."

Balancing the tray skilfully on his head, Bragoon began wheeling Martha's chair. "An honour an' a pleasure, miss. Besides, 'twill get us out of Sister Setiva's way. Come on, afore she finds we ain't made our beds or tidied the sick-bay."

Halfway across the lawn, Abbot Carrul caught up with them. "Oh dear, Martha, I've brought breakfast for Phredd, too."

The haremaid indicated her two companions. "Don't worry, Father, it won't go to waste!"

The old hedgehog Gatekeeper welcomed them in. He reached for his nightshirt, then shook his head absent-mindedly. "Hmm, must've gone to bed in my daytime habit. Look at me, putting my nightshirt on to start the day. What's it all coming to, eh, eh?"

Phredd gestured at the volume lying on the table. "The account by Tim Churchmouse about the route to Loamhedge, when Matthias was searching for his son. If you two read it, you'll learn of how to get there."

Saro leafed briefly through the ancient pages. "Me'n Brag ain't champion readers like you, sir. We'd rather see the map—that'll tell us more."

No sooner had Martha showed them the copy she had made of the map, than the squirrel and the otter glanced at one another and nodded.

Bragoon tapped his paw upon the map. "We've travelled this country afore. I can recall most of it—those high cliffs, the pine forest, river, desert an' the great gorge. Dangerous country, eh Saro?"

The aging squirrel held the map this way and that as she studied it. "Aye, bad territory, though we came to it a different way. I remember those rocks, the ones shaped like a bell an' a badger's head, but I can't bring that tall tree to mind."

Bragoon tapped his rudder thoughtfully against the floor. "It prob'ly collapsed with age. This map was made seasons afore we were born. But 'tis the same area alright, riddled with vermin an' all manner o' perils. I was glad to get away from it!"

Martha looked disappointed. "Does that mean it's too dangerous to make the journey?"

The otter laughed. "Haharr, wot ever gave ye that idea, me beauty? Danger's wot me an' Saro live on. We'd both end up dead afore our seasons was out livin' at Redwall."

The squirrel nodded mournfully. "All the good vittles an' soft beds, that'd finish us off. Huh, if Sister Setiva didn't."

Abbot Carrul poured mint tea for Old Phredd. "Then when will you be going?"

Saro selected a hot scone and bit into it. "Straight after the Summer Feast, if'n we can still walk. Late noon prob'ly. We'll travel southeast."

After breakfasting they set off for the orchard to help with the festive preparations. Horty, with his two friends, Springald and Fenna, came out of the Abbey, carrying a trestle board. The young hare hailed Bragoon and Saro.

"Hello there, you chaps. Well, have you sorted out a jolly old way to Loamhedge for us, wot?"

Bragoon answered him rather abruptly. "Aye!"

Springald bounced up and down eagerly. "Oh good, when are we leaving?"

Fenna's eyes shone happily. "A journey to Loamhedge. Great seasons, I've been looking forward to this!"

Horty looked from Bragoon to Saro excitedly. "Come on then, you bounders, who's got my copy of the bally map? Remember, I'm the flippin' pathfinder, y'know."

Bragoon turned to face the trio, his voice stern. "This ain't no daisy dance! Me'n my mate Saro'll be makin' the journey to Loamhedge . . . alone!"

Horty's ears drooped. "But you said . . ."

Saro interrupted him. "We never said nothin', young 'un. Yore the one whose been doin' all the sayin'. Bragoon an' me knows the country we got to go through. We can make it alone, but it'd be far too dangerous with three young 'uns in tow."

Fenna was outraged. "You mean you aren't taking us?"

Bragoon nodded. "That's right, missy. 'Tis too much responsibility. We couldn't show our faces back in this Abbey if'n ye were slain by vermin or killed in an accident. We're goin' alone, an' that's that!"

Springald tried to make an appeal to the Abbot. "What's he talking about? We've as much right to go as they have! Martha's our friend, too. Father, you're the Abbot of Redwall. You make all the decisions here, tell them!"

Abbot Carrul beckoned the three young ones to him. Putting his paws about their shoulders, he spoke kindly. "Now, now, what Bragoon and Saro say makes sense. None of you has ever been further than the main gate. You're far too inexperienced to make such a trip, trust me. Our two friends are thinking of your own good."

Horty pulled away from the Abbot, his ears standing stiffly with indignation. "Tosh'n'piffle, sah! We're young and strong. We can put up with anythin' those two old fogies can! Bragoon and Saro are old chums of yours. That's why you're blinkin' well siding with 'em. And anyhow, what flippin' right have you to stop us goin', wot?"

Springald and Fenna supported him volubly. "Horty's right, it's not fair. You let us think we were going all along, then changed your mind at the last moment!"

"Aye, it's just because we're young, and those two old wrecks want to grab all the glory for themselves. What do you think, Martha? Come on, tell them we're right."

Martha shook her head. "If the message from Sister Amyl, when she appeared in my dream with Martin the Warrior, had mentioned that you should go, I'd be the first to say yes. But only the two travellers, Bragoon and Saro, were included in the rhyme. So I'm afraid I must say no—not that my decision matters. Our Father Abbot has forbidden you to journey to Loamhedge, so you must abide by his word. Also, I trust Bragoon and Saro. They know of the dangers and are far more experienced at things like this than the three of you."

Horty exploded. "It's nothin' but a confounded plot against us. Shame on all of you, shame I say!"

Abbot Carrul put his footpaw down sternly. "Enough of this talk! Arguing and casting insults is not the way in which any decent Redwaller should behave. Any more of this from you, Horty, or your two friends, and there'll be three empty seats at the Summer Feast this afternoon!"

Horty glared back at the Abbot, his temper completely out of control. "Keep your rotten feast, blinkin' bounders!"

The Abbot's paw shot out. "Go to your rooms and stay there until you are ready to apologise, all three of you!"

The trio ran off, shouting, "Don't worry, we wouldn't be seen dead at your Feast!"

"Come on, leave those old greywhiskers to themselves!"

"You'll be jolly well sorry, we'll stay in the blinkin' dormitory until we die of flippin' starvation. So there!"

Abbot Carrul comforted Martha, who had become so upset that she had begun weeping. "There, there, Martha, don't you waste tears on those three. Could you imagine Horty starving himself to death? 'Tis as unlikely as me trying to leap over the belltower. Give them a day and they'll have changed their minds, trust me." Carrul bowed slightly to Bragoon and Saro. "Please forgive the bad manners of those three young ones."

Saro smiled wryly. "No need to apologise to us, friend. I can recall two, younger'n'Horty an' his pals, two more bad-mannered liddle scuts ye never did see!"

Martha blinked through her tears. "Were you really that bad?"

Bragoon shuffled his rudder awkwardly. "Oh, much worse, missy. Take me word fer it!"

Abbot Carrul chuckled heartily. "Aye, now that you've come to mention it, 'tis a wonder you turned out so well!"

Bragoon clapped him on the back. "An' ye, too, Carrul. Ye wasn't exactly a model Dibbun as I remember!"

Whipping out a clean kerchief, the Abbot busily wiped away at Martha's eyes. "Yes, well, that was a long time ago. Now then, missy, are you going to keep weeping and bring on the rain, or are you going to smile for our Summer Feast?"

133

She smiled happily. "Are you still going to carry on with the feast, Father, I mean after what just took place?"

Abbot Carrul reassured her. "Of course I am, no need to halt it because of three surly young 'uns. If they want to join in, all they have to do is apologise for their bad manners. Come on, friends, I wouldn't miss my Summer Feast for anything!"

Set in the orchard against a background of ripening fruit and summer flowers, complete with sumptuously decked tables, the feast turned out to be a huge success. Freshly washed and dressed, the Redwallers took their places, waiting on the Abbot to start the proceedings. Martha sat between Bragoon and Saro. The three of them stared in awe at the magnificent spread. Salads, pasties and savouries were still being brought on trolleys by the servers. These were placed among the pies, tarts and flans. Jugs of various cordials and fizzes stood between trifles, crumbles, puddings and candied fruits. Loaves of many shapes and types, still fresh from the ovens, were set amid cheeses of different hues—from pale cream to golden yellow.

Everybeast, even the Dibbuns, ceased their chatter as Abbot Carrul stood up and recited a verse, specially written for the event.

"We celebrate this happy day,
with fair and right good reason,
in friendship, let us share the fruits,
of this fine summer season.

We seed and plant the fertile earth,
to use what she may give,
and thank the kindly summer sun,
which gives us joy to live."

Granmum Gurvel, resplendent in a new floral-embroidered apron, called out. "You'm never spoked truer wurds, zurr!"

With that, the Summer Feast began in earnest. Junty Cellarhog tapped a barrel of strawberry fizz, which he had made the previous summer. Dibbuns squealed with delight as the bubbles tickled their mouths. Carving a wedge from a soft hazelnut cheese, Bragoon added it to his salad. Toran noticed him brushing away a teardrop.

"Wot's the matter with ye, brother?"

The otter looked mournfully at the festive board. "Nothin' really, I was just thinkin' of all the Redwall feasts I've missed since me'n Saro left the Abbey."

Toran scoffed. "Don't fret, it looks like yore makin' up for it with a will!"

Saro adopted a wheedling tone toward the ottercook. "Anybeast who can cook vittles like these should be famous. Toran, ole pal, why don't ye come adventurin' with me'n yore brother? You could cook for us an' everybeast we meet."

Toran lowered his eyes modestly. "No thankee, marm. I'm a mite too round in the waist for travellin'."

Sister Portula put aside her plate in mock indignation. "Take our ottercook, indeed! Mayhaps you'd like to take Junty Cellarhog, too, in case you feel the need of a drink?"

Bragoon chortled. "Haharr, a capital idea, Sister!"

Abbot Carrul's eyes twinkled as he joined the conversation. "I'm with you, Bragoon, a marvellous scheme! Take Toran and Junty, they'd make life much easier for you and Saro. However, I must insist that you take Sister Setiva along. If ever you are wounded, or fall ill, you'll surely need a dedicated creature to care for you both. Agreed?"

Bragoon suddenly became interested in a bowl of plum pudding and meadowcream. He mumbled hastily, "Me'n' Saro will make the journey alone, thankee Carrul."

Good-humoured banter and cheerful gossiping carried on into the warm summer noontide, a perfect accompaniment to the delicious feast. Having eaten their fill, the Dibbuns ran off to play within the Abbey grounds.

After awhile, Saro glanced at the sun's position and announced, "We'll have t'get goin' soon. Best be on the road afore we lose the daylight."

Her otter friend patted his stomach. "Aye, though I reckon we won't need much feedin' for a day or two. That was the nicest food an' the best company I can ever recall. Thankee, friends, for everythin'."

The Abbot smiled. "It was our pleasure. I knew you'd be going today, so I've had two packs of provisions made up by Granmum Gurvel. They should last you quite a time. Inside them you'll find all you need—the map, the poem telling of the location of Sister Amyl's secret and extra garments to wear. Now, is there anything else you two would like to take, anything?"

Bragoon replied without hesitation. "I'd like to take with me the memory of a sweet song. Martha, would ye sing us a song to send us on our way?"

Saro added. "Aye, go on, missy, put the birds t'shame!"

The haremaid's clear voice rang out into the still noon air. She sang for her two friends as she had never sung before. They sat entranced by Martha's beautiful voice.

"I planted her gently last summer,
all in quiet evening shade,
within an orchard bower,
her little bed I made.
Alone I sat by my window,
as autumn leaves did fall,
they formed a russet cover for
My Rose of Old Redwall.

Through winter's dreary days she slept
beneath the cold dark ground,
when all the earth was silent,
white snows lay deep around.
Bright stars came out above her,
as to the moon I'd call,

136

take pity on my dearest one,
My Rose of Old Redwall.

How the grass grew green and misty,
soft fell the rain that spring,
her dainty budded head arose,
and made my poor heart sing.
Then summer brought her just one bloom,
so white, so sweet and tall,
with ne'er a thorn to sully her,
My Rose of Old Redwall."

Both the hardy old adventurers were sobbing like babes. Saro scrubbed roughly at her eyes. "Come on, mate, time to go. We'll push ye as far as the gate, missy, so ye can wave us good-bye."

They were met at the gatehouse by Foremole Dwurl and Granmum Gurvel, each carrying a pack of provisions. Old Phredd emerged from the gatehouse with a long, slender bundle, which he presented to Bragoon.

The otter stared at the strange object. "Thankee kindly, Phredd. What is it?"

Abbot Carrul answered. "It is the sword of Martin the Warrior. I want you to take it on your quest for Loamhedge. Should you need a weapon to defend yourselves, you could not have a finer one. I trust you both with the sword, and I know when the journey is done, you will bring it back safe to Redwall. May the spirit of Martin go with you, my friends, and the good wishes of all in this Abbey!"

Bragoon bound the still-wrapped sword across his shoulders. "Ye do us great honour. How could we fail with Martin's sword to keep us company? Go back to yore Summer Feast now, an' don't fret. Me an' Saro'll bring back Sister Amyl's secret—that is, providin' it makes ye walk, Martha."

The young haremaid's eyes shone with resolution. "Walk? I'll do better than that! One day I'll dance for both of you. I'll dance on top of that wall, right over the threshold, for my heroes Bragoon and Sarobando. I swear it upon my solemn oath in front of you both!"

Bragoon laughed. "Haharr, that's the stuff, me darlin'!"

Saro swung her pack up on one shoulder. "So ye will, beauty, so ye will. Good-bye!"

They had only taken a dozen paces down the path to the south when Toran came running up and threw himself upon Bragoon. "Take care of yoreself, brother, an' look out for Saro, too!"

Bragoon gasped for breath as he tried to pull free of Toran's embrace. "We've taken care o' each other since we was Dibbuns. If'n ye don't let go of me, I'll get me ribs crushed afore the journey's started!"

Toran released his brother and stood weeping on the path. Bragoon looked away as Saro kissed the ottercook fondly.

"Go on now, ye great lump, back to yore feast. We'll be just fine. But keep this in mind, Toran Widegirth, when we come back to Redwall ye've got to make us a feast, as good as the one we had today. Promise?"

Toran ran back to the Abbey, shouting, "That 'un today'll look like afternoon tea to the feast I'll make ye when ye return, I promise!"

They watched him go inside, then walked to the south wall gable and struck off southeast into Mossflower.

15

Horty stood at the dormitory window, watching as Toran returned and assisted Old Phredd in closing the main gate. Both beasts then headed for the orchard and what remained of the Summer Feast. The young hare turned to his two companions, who were sprawling about on their beds.

"Well, chaps, Toran's back an' the gate's closed, wot! That means those two aging relics have finally gone off on the quest. Is everything ready, you blighters?"

Springald leaned over and pulled three bulging sacks from under her bed. "These are going to take some carrying!"

Horty scoffed. "Pish an' tush, m'gel, one can't have enough tuck. It's vital, mark m'words, bally vital!"

Fenna gathered their walking staffs and three travelling cloaks from the wall closet. "But how do we get out of the Abbey without being spotted? It won't be dark for hours yet. Huh, you'd think Bragoon and Saro would've waited until dawn tomorrow."

Horty sat down on his bed, ruminating. "Hmm, you've got a jolly good point there. I'll have to think up a cunning plan. Spring, pass me one of those sacks. A chap can't think on a blinkin' empty tummy, wot!"

Springald kept a tight grip on the foodsacks. "Forget your

confounded stomach, Horty! Get thinking, and be quick about it. We can't sit around here until it's dark and we've lost their trail."

Horty rose and strode back to the window, muttering, "Forget one's tum, wot? Easy for you t'say, Miss Mouse. I'm a flippin' hare, y'know. Forgetfulness of the old stomach is bally impossible to types like me . . . Ahah, Dibbuns, the very chaps!"

Flinging the window open, Horty called down to Muggum and a crew of Abbeybabes who were cavorting on the lawn below. "What ho there, my pestilential friends!"

Shilly the squirrelbabe looked up and pointed an accusing paw. "Naughty 'orty, you been sended up t'stay inna dormitee."

Horty stared down his nose at the little squirrel. "Let me inform you, my broom-tailed friend, I am here merely out of choice. I can come down when I flippin' well please. Now listen closely, you little bounders. Would you like to hear a secret, wot?"

Muggum wrinkled his button nose. "Ee seekurt? Us'n's gurtly fond o' seekurts. Ho urr aye!"

Fenna called out in a hoarse whisper. "Horty, what are you up to? Who are you talking to?"

Waggling his ears at her, the young hare looked secretive. "I've just thought up a super wheeze, a plan t'get us out unnoticed, wot. Create a diversion, that's the idea. Leave this to Hortwill Braebuck, marm!"

A hogbabe named Twiglut, having grown impatient, squeaked up at the window. "Are ya goin' a tell uz dis seekrut? Well 'urry h'up, or we go an' play wiv sticks!"

Horty waved his paws earnestly to gain the Dibbuns' attention. "No no, don't go an' play with sticks, my tiny pincushion. I'll tell you the secret. This mornin' we went down to the pond, an' guess what? We saw lots of big fishes . . ."

Muggum butted in. "Wurr they'm gurt hooj fishies, zurr?"

Horty stretched his paws wide, indicating their size.

"Huge? They were blinkin' colossal! Anyhow, they gave us rides on their backs all round the jolly old pond. Oh, it was loads o' fun, I can tell you, absoballylutley top hole an' all that, wot!"

The Dibbuns began dancing with excitement.

"Will ee fishies still be thurr?"

"Uz wanna ride on der fishies!"

Horty scratched his ears. "Hmm, they said they'd be there late afternoon, just before evenin'. I say, you chaps, it's round about that time now, isn't it?"

Roaring delightedly, the Dibbuns thundered off in the direction of the Abbey pond.

Horty called after them. "Have fun, you little savages. Tell the fishies Horty sent you!"

The realisation of what was taking place suddenly hit Springald. Leaping up, she hurled Horty away from the window. Cupping both paws to her mouth she yelled. "No, don't go! Come back this instant, all of you, come back!"

But the Dibbuns could not hear because of the din they were setting up. Like a small stampede, they ran out of sight around the Abbey corner.

Springald turned on Horty. "You blathering fool, what have you done? Idiot!"

Horty flapped his ears airily. "Creatin' a small diversion. No need to get your fur in an uproar, old thing, wot?"

Fenna's tail went stiff as Horty's foolish act dawned on her. "You puddenbrain! Can't you see that those babes will be drowned if there isn't anybeast responsible to watch over them?"

The young hare slapped a paw to his brow. "Oh corks, you're right! I never gave that a flippin' thought." Leaning wide out of the window, he bellowed, "I say, little chaps, come back this very instant. D'ye hear?"

"Dearie me, what's all the shouting about?"

Horty found himself staring down into the questioning face of Brother Gelf, who was returning some bowls to the kitchen when he heard the commotion.

Fenna pushed past Horty, her voice shrill with anxiety. "Hurry, Brother, the Dibbuns are down at the pond alone. There's nobeast with them. Oh hurry, please!"

The mouse sped off as fast as his paws would carry him.

In a trice, the bells of Redwall were tolling out an alarm. Creatures could be seen hurrying toward the pond. Toran was out in front, shedding his apron as he ran and plunging straight into the water. Luckily, none of the Dibbuns was harmed. Most of them were garnered from the shallows by willing paws, though Toran had to swim for Muggum. The molebabe was well out of his depth, floating about like a ball of downy fur. Foremole Dwurl's resounding bass tone could be heard, calling to the Abbot, as he panted up, pushing Martha's chair.

"They'm awright, zurr h'Abbot, oanly ee bit wetted!"

Horty was shaking all over as he turned to his friends and laughed with relief. "No harm done, chaps. At least my diversion worked, wot?"

Springald and Fenna leapt upon him, boxing his ears and kicking his bottom. They were furious.

"No thanks to you and your bright ideas!"

"You great waffling flannel-brained nincompoop!"

Horty broke loose and seized the travelling gear. "What's done is done. Sorry, chaps, an' all that. We'd better make ourselves scarce. Let's go while the goin's good!"

Sister Setiva was towelling the babes dry with Toran's apron and her shawl; others were helping, using anything that came to paw. The shrewnurse railed on at the Dibbuns, alternately drying and hugging each one.

"Och, why wid ye want tae do sich a silly thing, mah babbies? Have ye no been told aboot playin' alone by the water, eh?"

Under the stern eyes of Abbot Carrul, Martha and a dripping wet Toran, the whole story emerged. Martha could scarcely believe her ears when she heard that it was her brother who had encouraged the little Dibbuns. Seething with righteous wrath, she turned to Toran.

"Mr. Widegirth, would you kindly push me up to the Abbey? I wish to have some severe words with that brother of mine!"

The ottercook bowed politely. "Certainly, Miz Braebuck. I'm shore there's one or two wants words with Master Horty, one of 'em bein' me!"

A procession of Redwallers followed Martha into the Abbey. The Dibbuns were enjoying the affair hugely, seeing some other beast getting blamed for their escapade. They tagged along, muttering darkly of tail chopping and bottom-skelping punishments. Some were even speculating that Horty would be boiled in a soup pan.

Their delight, however, was short-lived. Sister Setiva and some molewives whisked them off, down to Cavern Hole.

"Intae the bath, ye filthy wee beasts. Och, there's nae tellin' whit muck'n'mire ye picked up in yon pond!"

The Abbeybabes wailed piteously but to no avail.

Boom! Boom! Toran's hefty paw reverberated on the dormitory door. After a moment's silence, his voice rang out harshly.

"Master Horty, yore sister an' Father Abbot want a word with ye downstairs. Miz Fenna an Miz Springald, ye'd best show yoreselves, too!"

Martha sat down in Great Hall and waited. Soon she heard the dormitory door slam, followed by the sound of Toran's footpaws pounding down the stairs. Abbot Carrul looked over his glasses as the grim-faced ottercook entered the hall.

"Don't tell me they're gone?"

Toran sat down on a table edge. "No trace of 'em, Father. I searched that dormitory from top't'bottom, but I'll wager they're hidin' someplace. You leave it t'me, I'll find those villains."

The Abbot began pushing Martha's chair toward the

kitchens. "I don't think you will somehow. Follow me, please."

Granmum Gurvel met them as they entered the kitchen. Clearly in a proper tizzy, the poor old molecook began chattering angrily. "Foive gurt h'apple puddens, ee gurt meadowcreamy troifle, strawbee scones, celery an h'onion flans, pasties full o' carrut'n'gravy. They'm all be gonned? Burrrrooooh! Wait'll oi get'n moi paws on ee Dibbun rarscalls. H'all moi luvverly arternoon bakin' furr tomorrers lunchen an' supper. Varnished!"

Martha kept her eyes downcast as she informed Gurvel, "It wasn't Dibbuns, Granmum. It was my brother Horty and his friends, Fenna and Springald. They're the thieves who raided your kitchen. Now they've run off to join Bragoon and Saro on the quest."

Toran's rudder rapped loudly on the floor. "Of course, that's it, Martha! But why'd they have to cause so much upset to everybeast—us, an' the Dibbuns, an' Gurvel? Why?"

Abbot Carrul raised his eyes and sighed. "Sadly, that's the way most young 'uns behave at that age. Forbidding them to do something is like encouraging them. Unfortunately, they do things without thinking."

Old Phredd shuffled in, bowing creakily to the Abbot. "I just found my main gate open, but me and young Toran barred it shut this afternoon. How did that happen, eh, eh?"

Carrul patted the Gatekeeper's bony paw. "No doubt you've closed it again, Phredd. It was Horty, Fenna and Springald—they've gone off adventuring."

Phredd chuckled drily. "Just like Bragoon and Saro when they were younger, eh, eh?"

Junty Cellarhog, who had just come into the room and heard Phredd, thrust his big paws into his apron belt. "No, ole feller, not like Saro an' Bragoon at all. Them two was born tough, rovin' was in their blood. But young Horty doesn't remember anytime afore comin' to Redwall, an' both maids was borned 'ere. They don't know wot 'tis like out there in the big world. I think they'll 'ave to learn t'grow up fast."

Martha felt a pang of alarm at Junty's words. "What does he mean, Toran?"

The ottercook explained. "Well, miss, look at their vittles. Apple puddens, strawberry scones an' a meadowcream trifle? No proper travelbeast'd take such stuff along. Huh, it'd be smashed t'bits afore they got a day's march in, eh Gurvel?"

The old molecook nodded wisely. "Aye, et surpinkly wudd, zurr. Oi maked speshul marchin' vikkles furr ee uther two. Lots o' cheese, ee h'oatbreads, summ candied fruits an' canteens o' moi gudd dannelion'n'burdock corjul furr drinken."

Martha grasped Toran's paw. "You don't think they'll come to any harm, do you?"

The ottercook's eyes softened. "Don't ye fret yoreself, Martha. If'n they picks up my brother an' Saro's trail, they'll be safe enough. Mind, though, they won't get no special treatment. Horty an' his pals will learn the hard way. Now, if'n they lose the trail, Redwall's stickin' up in plain view for a good distance. Once yore brother gets hungry, he'll dash back to this Abbey like a scalded toad. The others are sure to follow. If'n ye pardon me sayin', Martha, Horty's a natural glutton. He won't stray too far without vittles—starvation's a hard taskmaster!"

The haremaid fiddled with the fringe of her lap rug. "I'd feel happier if somebeast could overtake them and bring them back, so they don't get lost or hurt."

The Abbot looked at Toran and Junty Cellarhog, both big, stout beasts and very competent. "Perhaps our Martha is right. Do you think you two could catch up with them before it gets too dark?"

Junty took off his canvas apron and nodded to the ottercook. "We'll give it a try, Father. Are ye ready, mate? Come on!"

They left the Abbey by the main gate. No sooner had Carrul and Old Phredd closed and barred it then Junty and Toran were pounding on the timbers to get back in.

Toran's voice was loud and urgent.

"Open up quick! There's vermin comin' down the path from the north! They're headin' this way. Hurry and let us in!"

BOOK TWO

"If only they were back here at Redwall"

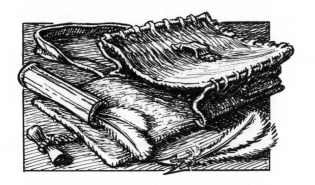

16

Late that same afternoon, the vermin gang had been keeping to the woodlands. On Badredd's orders they followed the path. Stopping for a breather, the little fox sighted Redwall Abbey in the distance, showing above the trees. He scurried out onto the path, pointing and yelling.

"Aharr, there 'tis, mates, the Abbey place! I told ye I'd find it, 'twas me who saw it first!"

As he ran forward, the cutlass, which he had pushed into his belt, tangled in his footpaws, causing him to trip. He lay sprawled on the path, still shouting. "Wait'll I gets me paws on that magic sword!"

Halfchop sneered. "Look at 'im, willyer, the flamin' fool. I swear, Flinky, dat stoopid oaf'll get us all killed!"

The crafty stoat chuckled. "Ah, sure enough, he's a grand, brave beast. I'd sooner serve under Badredd than Burrad or Skrodd. Those two would have made us march in front, an' led from the rear. Let the fearless chief run an' meet the foe. Us pore ould pawsloggers will just keep our heads down an' follow from a safe distance."

Crinktail was in agreement with her mate. "Aye, whoever's inside o' that place will prob'ly see us comin' from their walltops. Wot was it that Burrad said, that those Abbey creatures was all peaceable Woodlanders? So we may as well put on a show o' force. The sight of a vermin gang might make 'em open up those gates to us—providin' they knows wot's good for 'em!"

The crew strolled out onto the path, deliberately setting a slow pace, keeping Badredd well ahead of them. Flinky sang a quiet ditty as a warning to his mates. The little fox could not quite hear the words, but he assumed it was some sort of song for marching into battle. He swaggered along, a good half-spearthrow in front, waving the unwieldy cutlass with regained dignity, feeling every inch the great Badredd, commander of a vermin crew. The others followed at a safe distance, sniggering at the words of Flinky's song.

"When the clouds of arrows fly,
keep yore heads down.
Let the brave ones charge on by,
keep yore heads down.
When the heroes' blood runs red,
an' yore scared to raise yore head,
just be glad that you ain't dead,
keep yore heads down!

Ye won't win no medals here,
keep yore heads down.
Don't be fools who know no fear,
keep yore heads down.
We can all lay low an' sing,
duckin' spears an' stones from sling.
Let 'em chuck most anything,
but keep yore heads down!"

Amid smothered giggles and hoots, Slipback and Juppa made disparaging remarks behind their leader's back.

"Haw haw, lookit the way 'is bottom waggles when 'e puts on a swagger. Looks like two sour apples in a sack!"

"Aye, an' if'n 'e don't stop wavin' that blade around, 'e'll chop 'is own tail off. Wot d'ye reckon, mate, does that liddle smidge look like a vermin warrior who'd terrify those Abbeybeasts?"

"Maybe they'll laugh theirselves to death at the sight of 'im. Heeheeheee!"

Flinky gazed up in awe as the impressive red sandstone Abbey loomed closer. He muttered to Rogg and Floggo. "Huh, if Badredd gives the order to charge that place, well, I'll be chargin', shore enough. I'll be runnin' the other way, like a duck wid its tail on fire!"

The weasel brothers were not much given to merriment, but Flinky's remark tickled them so much that they guffawed loudly.

Badredd came running back brandishing his cutlass. "Wot's so funny, eh, can I share the joke?"

Flinky shrugged disarmingly. "Ah now, we wasn't laughin' at ye at all. 'Twas just that we're 'appy for ye. Yore a good chief, an' soon the magic sword'll be yores. Ye deserve it fer bein' a grand ould leader, so ye do. Ain't that right, mates? Badredd's the best boss we've ever 'ad!"

Half believing Flinky's flattery, Badredd eyed the gang and nodded approvingly. "Lissen, mates, we could be a good crew if'n we tried. Now wipe the grins offa yore gobs an' form up in twos. We'll march straight up to that Abbey an' put the fear o' Hellgates into those peaceable bumpkins. Try t'look more like a gang o' killers. Wave yore weapons about an' snarl loud, as if yore ready t'do murder!"

Flinky glanced up at the high battlements. Already he saw heads poking up over them in the gathering gloom. Thinking quickly, the stoat slid down into the ditch on the path's opposite side. He beckoned Badredd. "A nighttime charge might go wrong, Chief. D'ye not think we oughta figger out some kind of ould plan, afore we go rushin' at a buildin' that size?"

The little fox turned his attention to the walltops. Lots of heads were beginning to appear there. He climbed down into the ditch, alongside Flinky, knowing that what the stoat said made sense. "Aye, let's, er, make up a scheme. . . . Everybeast down 'ere!"

The remaining gang members obeyed promptly. Flinky patted Badredd's back. "Sure, that's wot I likes about ye, Chief, yore a true fox, a born slayer, but a grand an' crafty ould planner. Hoho, those creatures in there'll get the shock o' their lives when we turns up outside their doorstep tomorrer!"

Badredd was puzzled. "Tomorrer?"

Crinktail caught on, knowing her mate was trying to put off invading Redwall for as long as possible. She backed Flinky up. "Haharr, clever move, Chief. Tomorrer's the best time t'do it!"

Beyond a straight charge, Badredd had no real plan. He decided to hear Flinky out, knowing the stoat was no fool.

Flinky explained eagerly. " 'Tis dark now, y'see, an' we're in strange territory. The gang can get a good night's rest down 'ere. When you've thought up yore scheme, we'll be ready fer a fresh start, an' catch 'em nappin' at dawn! Now that's wot I calls a smart move, thought up by a smart fox!"

Unaccustomed to compliments, Badredd enjoyed the feeling of having everybeast waiting on their leader's word. Flicking his tail round slowly, he stroked it as foxes do when they are pleased. "Right, we rest 'ere, gang, that's my orders!"

He missed the nudge exchanged between Crinktail and Flinky as they lay down and closed their eyes. Flinky murmured but loud enough to be heard by all. "Ain't we the lucky ones, havin' a gangleader like Badredd."

Starlit darkness had fallen as Abbot Carrul made his way up the north wallsteps onto the ramparts. A frown creased his brow when he saw the throng of Redwallers crowding the parapet.

"Friends, listen to me, please. There's no need for all of you up here. With vermin about, it's not safe to stand looking over the battlements. Anybeast who is not required up here, please go down now. Sister Setiva, Sister Portula, will you see those Dibbuns down the stairs, it's time they were in their beds anyhow."

Toran and Junty, who had already joined Foremole Dwurl and Brother Weld, were at the northwest wall corner. Carrul hastened to join them. "Is there really a vermin band out there? Where are they now?"

Toran answered reassuringly. "There's no great army o' them, Father, I only counted about eight. Might be more to come, but I ain't spotted 'em yet."

Junty made way for the Abbot to look between the battlements as Toran pointed. "Look, they've lit a small fire, in the ditch, just further up the path there. Wonder wot they're up to?" A red-gold glow showed from the ditch, where Toran was pointing.

Foremole blinked. "Oi aspeck they'm cooken ee supper."

The Abbot looked to Toran. "What do you think?"

Thumping his rudder thoughtfully against the wallside, the ottercook speculated. "Well, there's no way a crew that size could attack Redwall. I think we'd best do nothin' for the present, Father. But let's watch every move they make. We'll post sentries on the walls, just a few who can watch 'em, while keepin' low. Who can tell—maybe they're only passin' by this way. Per'aps they're bound someplace else. I wish Bragoon an' Saro would've stayed a day or two longer—we could really do with 'em right now!"

Foremole smote the wall with a heavy digging claw. "Boi 'okey we'm cudd, they'm udd know wot to do abowt ee varmints. But thurr bee's h'only us'n's, yurr!"

Toran could sense that the Abbot was waiting for him to take charge. He waved down to Martha, waiting in her chair on the lawn, then spoke. "Father, maybe ye an' Martha could get a few helpers an' search around for anythin' that would be useful as a weapon. I've got a feelin' they won't make a move 'til tomorrow. We should be ready for 'em by then, though it prob'ly won't come to that. I'll stay up here with Junty, Weld an' Foremole on watch."

The Abbot went down to the lawn and pushed Martha back to the Abbey, explaining what was happening and what he had seen. The young haremaid could tell by Abbot Carrul's face that he was very worried.

Wirga was long past her best seasons, a wrinkled, toothless old Searat, yet Raga Bol kept her with his crew. She was useless as a fighter or a forager, but she possessed other skills. There was little that Wirga did not know about wounds and the treatment of injuries. Her powers as a healer and her knowledge of herbs, nostrums and remedies made the old vermin invaluable to the ignorant crewrats. But there was yet another art Wirga practiced—that of a Seer. Raga Bol, as captain, was the only one she allowed to consult her, and then only in times of crisis.

Wirga crouched by the fire, watching Bol. They were camped among some wooded hills where the red sandstone rocks of Mossflower jutted out in shelflike formation. It was twilight. The Searat crew had slain a small colony of wood-mice, and were leisurely plundering their shattered dwellings. Raga Bol and Wirga sat on a hilltop, isolated from the noisy rabble below.

The old Searat knew that her captain wished to consult her. He had given her half a roasted dove and a goblet of his personal grog—this was always a sign that she was needed. Wirga took out her pouch of charms and selected half a large musselshell. It was edged with yellow on the inside, glistening grey at the centre, with three partially grown purple mussel's pearls protruding from its broad end.

Filling the shell with water, she gazed into it. "Thy appetite is not good of late?"

Raga Bol licked the sharp tip of his silver pawhook in silence as Wirga continued.

"Sleep eludes thee, thou are weary. None can rest easy in thy presence. Even I fear to speak of certain things—aye, things that trouble thee."

With a curt nod, the Searat captain dismissed the four guards who attended him from twilight to dawn. When they had gone off to join the others, he took a furtive glance over his shoulder.

Drawing close to the Seer, Raga Bol dropped his voice to a hoarse whisper. "Fear not, speak openly to me, ye won't be harmed."

Keeping her eyes on the water-filled shell, the old Seer proceeded, her voice now a sibilant hiss. "If thine enemy lives, he must die. Only then can Raga Bol find peace of mind. Thy foe's death will release thee."

The Searat captain's eyes shone feverishly. "Does the stripedog still live? Tell me!"

Wirga turned away from the shell, confronting him. "When did thou last see this stripedog?"

Bol's red-rimmed eyes stared back at her. "This very noon, aye, in full sunlight. 'Twas when we stopped to rest. I was so tired that I dozed off awhile. The sun beat through my closed lids, makin' everythin' go red. That's when I saw the stripedog. Gettin' off a strange craft he was, where that broadstream from the nor'east bends away from the trees an' woodlands. Ye recall the spot, 'twas where we slayed those two shrews. The stripedog pointed to the bodies an' looked straight at me. 'They will be avenged, I am coming for ye, Raga Bol!' Those were his very words."

Wirga went back to contemplating the water in the shell, then continued. "Thee told him to go away and join the deadbeasts at Hellgates, because he was already slain by thee. But the giant stripedog kept coming. He was frightening to look upon, with his face cleaved wide, but scarred an' stitched together by somebeast. Do I not speak truly?"

Raga Bol gasped, in awe of the Seer and her powers. "Aye, true, but how did ye know? Did ye see the beast, too?"

She smiled. "Wirga sees many things unknown to others."

What she did not say was that she had been observing her captain for days—listening, watching, taking all in. Every nightmare, every time Raga Bol called out, in the brief times he did sleep, were memorised by Wirga. She had a complete picture of it all—from the moment Raga Bol had struck the badger to every event since.

The Searat captain brought his face even closer to the Seer. His breath was hot on her jaw, his voice half threat and half plea. "I can't fight a dream, so I'm waitin' on yore word. Tell me wot t'do, I must be rid of the stripedog!"

Wirga replied. "Knowest thou my three sons?"

Bol knew the ones she spoke of, though not too well. They were a furtive trio, a bit undersized for Searats, always last to fight but first to grab the plunder. He was not impressed with them, and saw the three as background vermin who never put themselves forward or appeared bold, like proper Searats often do.

The captain shrugged. "Aye, I know 'em, they ain't no great shakes as fighters. That big stripedog could eat the three of 'em!"

Wirga rocked back and forth on her haunches, chuckling. "Heehee, well said. But give 'em a skilled tracker, one who could lead 'em to the place of thy dream, an' my sons will make an end of thy stripedog, believe me!"

Raga Bol drew his scimitar, allowing the firelight to gleam across its lethal blade. "If'n' I never finished the bigbeast with a blow o' this, how could three runts like that do the job?"

Wirga drew from her pouch a section of bamboo, cut off near the joint and sealed at one end with beeswax. Carefully, she broke away the wax and upended the cylinder. Six long thorns spilled out, each one tipped with crimson dye and plumed with the short feathers of some exotic bird. She stayed Raga Bol's paw as he reached to pick one up.

"Keep away from such things. They can kill ten times more swiftly than the most venomous snake!"

The Searat captain pulled back his paw. "Poison?"

Using her long pawnails, the Seer divided the thorns into three groups of two. "Once one of these little beauties pricks the skin, even the greatest warrior cannot stand. Poison, from far isles across the southern seas. My three sons know how to use these darts. Warriors they may not be, but assassins they surely are. Give 'em a tracker to lead 'em to the streambend. They will seek out thy stripedog an' slay 'im."

Raga Bol stood abruptly, peering over the hilltop rocks at his crew below until he saw the one he required. "Ahoy, Jibsnout!"

A big, competent-looking Searat saluted. "Cap'n?"

Raga Bol called back to him. "Bring Wirga's three sons up 'ere. I've got a task for the four of ye."

Night had fallen as the sons of Wirga left the hilltop, following Jibsnout. The tracker had a blanket with some food rolled into it thrown over his shoulder, and a well-honed dagger dangling from a cord around his neck.

Once they were off the hill and bound back along the trail, Jibsnout halted and glared contemptuously at the three smaller rats. It was obvious he did not enjoy their company. He pointed the dagger at each of them in turn.

"Lissen t'me, slimesnouts. I don't like yew three one liddle bit. But I gotta do the job wot Cap'n Bol gave me—to take ye back to where the broadstream bends at the edge o' this forest. Wot ye do then is carry out the cap'n's orders. 'Tis up to ye how y'do that, an' nought t'do wid me. But get this straight: Ye do yore job an' I'll do mine. So stay outta my way an' mind yore manners around me. Step on my paws or look the wrong way at me an' I'll gut all three o' ye wid this blade o' mine! Unnerstood?"

The sons of Wirga never answered; they merely looked at one another and exchanged sly leers. This did not improve Jibsnout's opinion of them. Turning on his paw, he set off at a rapid pace into the dark woodlands, growling back to the odd trio.

"Move yoreselves! We'll be marchin' night'n'day, an' only stoppin' for a bite or a nap when I says so. If'n ye don't keep up, I'll leave ye behind. Hah, try explainin' yoreselves to Raga Bol when ye get back then, I dare ye!"

17

Three days earlier, Lonna had bid farewell to Garfo Trok at the broadstream bend. The last he saw of the otter was Garfo singing loud ballads about food, or the lack of it, paddling back upstream to the northeast country. Lonna had enjoyed his time with the garrulous otter aboard his boat *Beetlebutt*. The big badger felt lonely as he trudged off into Mossflower, but soon his loneliness was replaced by rage, as he remembered the pitiful bodies of the two dead shrews. Before they parted, he and Garfo had buried them on the bankside.

All that day the scar across Lonna's face felt sore and tight. His head ached whenever he thought of Raga Bol and his murderous crew, and his back wound began bothering him, causing him to limp as he pressed doggedly onward. The woodlands were quiet and peaceful, with sundappled green light cascading through the overhead foliage. Distant birdsong sounded muted, bees droned lazily in the midday calm. Lonna ignored the beauties of nature, his eyes constantly darting from side to side, paws ever ready to seek bow and shafts.

At midnoon the big stripedog halted by a rippling brook in a mossy sward. Resting awhile, he ate sparingly from the sea otter's food pack—a crust of nutbread, some fine ripe cheese and a few scallions he found growing nearby—and drank deeply from the brook. Still sitting with his footpaws in the water, Lonna washed his head and face, then, leaning forward, immersed his face and head for several long intervals. The cold, clear brookwater refreshed him greatly. He stood up to leave, rubbing the small of his back and swaying from side to side, testing the limp in his footpaw, to judge how it was feeling.

A sense that he was being watched came over Lonna. Continuing his exercises, he spoke out in a voice loud enough for any eavesdropper to hear.

" 'Tis not good manners to spy on a beast. Come out and show yourself. Don't be afraid, you can see I'm no Searat!"

An elderly female squirrel, clad in a russet and yellow tunic, dropped out of the trees, landing right in front of him. She was a perky, cheerful-looking creature, but he could see by the way she toted a small javelin she was ready for anything.

Looking him up and down, she chattered boldly away. "Chahah! Me could tell ya wasn't Searatta. Warramarrer bigbeast, ya back be hurted?"

Completely disarmed, Lonna smiled ruefully. "Just a bit, marm, but 'tis getting better by the day, thank ye. My name is Lonna Bowstripe."

The squirrel bobbed him a neat curtsy. "Me's Figalok Twigbenda, pleasin' t'meetcha. I fix ya back, Lonna, folla me!"

Lonna took an immediate liking to Figalok, following her without question. She was so very swift that he had to hurry to keep up. Figalok halted alongside a big, ancient hornbeam tree and began giving rapid orders.

"See da branch stickin' out up above? Me wancha t'jump up an' grab it tight. Chakahoo! Berra take offa dat bigbow an' arrers. Cheeh! Howcha make dat—cut a yewtree down an' purra string on it? Dat a big bow, sure 'nuff!"

Lonna smiled at her observation. When he took off his bow, it stood near three times the height of Figalok. Placing his quiver of arrows to one side, he leaped up, grabbed the hornbeam limb and hung there, dangling. The branch was quite stout enough to hold his weight.

"Is this alright, marm? What do I do now?"

Figalok walked around him. "Ya jus' hang there like a h'apple. Are ya plenny strong, Lonna?"

He stared down at her. "Aye, strong enough."

Figalok jumped up and sat on Lonna's footpaws, facing him. She grabbed his legs to steady herself. "Keep ya paws still now, bigbeast, don't ya kick me off!"

Figalok began jerking Lonna back and forth, using him like a swing. "Chahah, dis do ya good, keep tight hold!"

For what seemed like an eternity she continued the swinging motion, back and forth, forward and back. Lonna's own bodyweight, with the added burden of the squirrel, began to tell after awhile. She stared up at his clenched jaws.

"Ya wanna leggo now? Dat was a good ride."

Lonna gasped. "Aye, I'd best come down before I drop!"

Figalok leapt to the ground, skipping to one side. "Right-ee, ya can leggo, Lonna!"

He dropped gingerly, expecting the fall to jolt his back. Surprisingly, it did not.

The squirrel gave his back a thump. "Wassamarra witcha? Walk round, jump 'bout! Chahah, ya back be good as new now. Me fixed lotsa backs!"

Lonna's back felt easy and relaxed, he was not getting a single twinge from the footpaw, which had been bothering him. He walked, then trotted, jumping up and down force-fully, putting all his weight on back and footpaw. Revelling in the newfound freedom of movement, Lonna dashed at Figalok, meaning to embrace her.

"I'm better, there's no more pain! Figalok, you marvellous creature, how can I thank you?"

She shot up the trunk of the hornbeam, protesting, "Keep ya big paws offa me, or I be crushed flat! Betcha hungry, eh? Bigbeasts must get plenty hungry. Folla me!"

Figalok scuttled through the woodlands, with Lonna hard on her tail. She halted at the base of a three-topped oak, which grew in close proximity to a beech, an elm and a sycamore. The upper limbs of all three trees intertwined with the oak, forming a wide platform.

The squirrel twitched her tail at Lonna. "Ya wait der, me send ya rope down!" She shot lightly up the oak trunk, vanishing into the foliage.

A moment later Figalok reappeared, surrounded by a crowd of tiny squirrelbabes. They squeaked and squealed at the size of Lonna, pointing and giggling.

"Cheehow, nanny, wherecha find dat 'un?"

"Weehoo, must be da biggest beast in alla lands!"

"Choowhee, never see'd not'ink like 'im in me life!"

Shoving them out of her way, Figalok pushed a thick rope down. It was knotted at close intervals to make climbing easy. Shouldering his bow and quiver, Lonna began scaling the rope. Figalok was hard put to keep back the press of little squirrels.

"Chahah, gerra ya back an' make way for me friend. Take no notice a dese likka pesters, Lonna, up ya come!"

Lonna found the climb quite easy. The squirrelbabes shrieked and scurried off as he joined Figalok on the bough. She nodded approvingly.

"Not'ink wrong wirra dat back now. Me make a squirrel outta ya, bigbeast. Berra get vikkles quick, afore they alla gone!"

The squirrels' dray was an amazing sight. Branches were cunningly woven twixt the network of bows and limbs between the four trees. Lonna found it safe to walk upon, though he trod carefully. At the oak's centre was a wide platform with a charcoal oven set on slabs of slate. Upward of a dozen older squirrels were preparing a meal there. Literally scores of babes and young ones festooned the place, hanging by their tails or balancing nimbly on the slenderest of twigs.

Figalok proudly introduced her newfound friend to the assemblage. "Ya see this 'un, he be Lonna bigbeast. Figalok finded 'im. Lonna be hungry, berra give 'im lotsa vikkles!"

Four older squirrels hurried to serve the big badger, plying him with huge portions of a thick, sweet porridge. It was a mixture of wild oats, fruit and nuts boiled in honey and rhubarb juice. Lonna was given a full flagon of elderflower and pennycress cordial. Both the food and drink tasted delicious. Figalok sat beside him, watching in awe as he satisfied his considerable appetite.

"Cheehoo! Betcha mamma was glad when ya leaved home!"

Lonna chuckled. "Who knows, maybe she might have been, but I don't ever remember having a mother."

Gradually the squirrelbabes had been inching closer to the big badger. When he mentioned that he had never known a mother, their sympathy was instantly aroused. They surrounded Lonna, sitting on his lap and shoulders, climbing on his back and paws. He was totally engulfed by the babes, one of them even perched upon his head.

Their tiny paws patted him as they squeaked sorrowfully. "Aaaaah, never haved no mamma, pore bigbeast!"

"Must bee'd tebbirle, not 'avin' no mamma!"

"Didya cried an' weeped alla time for ya mamma?"

Figalok waved her paws at them. "Chachafah! Shooshoo! Gerroffa 'im, leave Lonna alone!"

But the badger defended them. "Let them be, marm. I like the little 'uns, they're so small and friendly. Besides, they're not at all afraid of my face, the scars and stitching."

Figalok shrugged. "Chaaaah, why be they 'fraid? Likkle 'uns never see'd a bigbeast afore. They know ya be a goodbeast, me see dat, too. Not matter what ya lookin' like."

Before he could express his gratitude for the kind words,

163

a tubby squirrel mother, with a fine bush of tail, took the empty bowl from Lonna and called to the little ones. "Hachowa! Sing for a bigbeast, sing 'im Twing Twing."

The elders stood by, smiling fondly as the squirrelbabes sang their simple song for Lonna. What they lacked in melody, they made up in raucous enthusiasm, some of them performing dancing leaps and hops in time to the tune.

"Twing twing up inna trees,
twirlin' me tail around,
lighter'n fevvers onna breeze,
never not fall to a ground!"

These were the only words they seemed to know, but they carried on singing the verse again and again, with the renewed gusto of babes enjoying themselves. Lonna held both paws wide, his face wreathed in a happy grin. The little ones swung on him, squeaking away lustily.

They were well into the seventh repetition of their song when one of the elders gave forth a piercing whistle. Like lightning, both infants and elders vanished into the foliage. A massive black shadow flew low overhead.

Lonna looked around, but not a squirrel could be seen anywhere. He called out into the densely leafed treetops. "Figalok, where are you, what's going on?"

The elderly squirrel popped her head out from behind a branch, her eyes wide with fright as she chattered. "Bad, bad! Rakkaw Ravin badbird! Look ya uppina sky!"

Glancing upward, Lonna beheld a raven of startling wingspread, circling high in the bright afternoon sky. Reaching for his bow, he picked an arrow from the quiver and laid it on the string, keeping his eyes on the raven.

"Don't worry, marm, that bird won't harm you while I'm here."

Figalok stayed under cover, shaking her head sadly. "Rakkaw Ravin after babes, ya watch 'im, he soon be down.

Steal likkle 'un, take what he want. Badbird, bigga strong an' fast. Nobeast stoppa Ravin!"

As Figalok spoke, a tiny squirrel panicked. Squealing shrilly, she hopped out on a long branch. There she stood, covering her face, rigid with terror, and in clear sight of the foe. Sensing a quick kill, the raven folded its wings and dropped down like a thunderbolt.

Instinctively, Lonna stretched the bowstring tight against his clenched jaw. Closing one eye, he aimed at the bird and loosed his shaft. With a sound like an angry wasp, the arrow zipped upward, taking the raven through its glossy, plumed body. Instantly slain, its huge wings spread wide open, the raven cartwheeled through the air like a dark, tattered cloak, landing with a thud on the woodland floor beneath the oak, transfixed by the badger's well-aimed arrow.

Chattering madly, the squirrels started pounding the body. The older ones used small slings, from which they hurled small pebbles. Emerging from cover, the babes tossed down pawfuls of leaves and pieces of twig, all the while screeching insults at their slain enemy.

"Yaa yaa, not eat us no more, Rakkaw!"

"Yeeheeee, eata dis twig if ya be hungry, bigbird!"

"Hahaaay, Rakkaw, we burn ya, burn ya, burn ya!"

Some of the older squirrels threw down glowing charcoal from their oven. The smell of charring feathers reached Lonna's nostrils. Shocked by the frenzy of hatred the squirrels were working themselves into, he called out in a stern voice.

"Here now, stop that, you'll cause a woodland fire!"

Sensing the danger, Figalok joined Lonna. "Chahah, ye heara bigbeast, stoppa throwin' fires!"

They obeyed reluctantly. Figalok sent some older squirrels down to fetch water and quench the smoking embers. She touched the big badger's taut bowstring.

"Dat a good bigbow, me thank ya, Lonna. Rakkaw Ravin gone'd forever now, thank ya!"

Hanging up his bow and quiver on a nearby branch, Lonna sighed. "I wish that had been a Searat!"

Figalok pointed west and slightly south. "Searatters over data way."

The badger became immediately alert. "Where, over that way, have you seen them?"

Smiling slyly, the elderly squirrel nodded. "Ho, me see 'em, awright! Lotsa Searatters marchin' through. Chahah, they no see us, though. Squirrel know how ta hide." She tapped her paw four times against the oak tree. "Me see dat many Searatters a-comin' back thisaway though."

Lonna grabbed up his bow and quiver. "Where, when?"

Figalok explained. "Yistaday. Me was far from this place, lookin' for a h'almind nuts. See dem, one bigbeast."

She tapped her paw on the oak three times. "Dis a many smalla Searatters comin' disaway. No worry, Lonna, dey not see ya, we hide up here plenny good, eh? Asides, dey still more'n a day 'way, not travel fast like squirrel."

Lonna seized the thick, knotted rope and began clambering down to the woodland floor. "Searats at last! I've got a score to settle with those murdering scum. Figalok, will you show me where they are?"

The squirrel made it down to the ground before him. "A course me will—least I can do for ya, bigbeast. We go now, catch 'em around at dawn, travel alla night, eh?"

Lonna shook her small paw gratefully. "Thank you, my friend!"

The squirrels appeared much upset at Lonna leaving, particularly the little ones. "Don't go bigbeast, ya stay here wid us for longa time!"

One bold little maid thought she knew the reason for the badger's departure. She shook her head at the others. "Gorra let Lonna go, he gotta find 'is mamma."

Lonna ruffled her downy little brush. "That's right, miss. Now take care of your mammas, and watch out for ravens."

Figalok kicked the dead bird's carcass scornfully. "No

more Rakkaw Ravin come here. We hangin' dis one up inna tree, dat scare 'em off. Chahaah, you betcha!"

Following the agile Figalok, Lonna trotted off south and west into the thickness of Mossflower. As they went, he envisioned the evil face of Raga Bol—concentrating hard on it, as only a creature of fate and destiny like a badger can.

"I'm coming, Raga Bol! I am Lonna Bowstripe, and I'm coming!"

18

After marching all night on what he had fondly imagined was a southeast course, Horty was totally fatigued. In dawn's pale light, he slumped down in a fern grove, grumbling.

"It's no blinkin' use, you chaps, I've got to take a jolly old snooze. Ahah! But first we must deal with the inner hare. Brekkers beckons the poor lad's slim stomach, wot?"

Furious, Springald grabbed the provision sack from his paw, ranting on at him. "Food, food, food, don't you ever think of anything else? Here we are, in the middle of nowhere, and you're yowling about brekkers after eating all night as we marched! We're lost, you lop-eared oaf, lost!"

Horty tried unsuccessfully to tug the sack back from her. "Lost? Don't talk piffle'n'woffle, m'dear gel, we're merely restin'. Now don't be so flippin' moody, an' pass the scoff!"

Springald dealt him a wallop with the soggy ration sack. "You've no idea where we're going. You've completely lost Bragoon's and Saro's tracks, and we could have been walking in circles for all you know! You're an idiot, d'you hear me?"

Horty twiddled his ears and smiled at Fenna. "Rather pretty when she's angry, ain't she? Spring, me old beauty, why don't y'give your face a rest. We'll find the right track sooner or later. Or would you prefer to toodle back to the Abbey an' face the blinkin' music, wot wot?"

Fenna sat down wearily beside Horty, then closed her eyes. "Good grief, I'm bone worn-out. He's right y'know, Spring, arguing isn't going to get us anywhere. Let's have a bite to eat and a rest. Give him the bag."

Springald threw herself moodily down amid the ferns. "Here, take your confounded food. I wish I'd never left Redwall in the first place."

The gluttonous young hare seized the sack eagerly. "I wish you hadn't, either—there'd be more scoff for me an' Fenn, wot. Hawhawhaw!"

Fenna looked into the sack to select her breakfast. She drew back with a look of disgust. "Yukk, I'm not eating any of that mess. Look at it, pie and trifle squashed up with onion gravy pastie. Just the sight of it makes me sick. Nobeast could stomach that!"

Horty dipped his paw in and came up with an unappetising lump of sludge. "Well tut tut, little miss fussy apron. What's wrong with the flippin' scoff, it's good food ain't it? Please yourself, marm, but I'm jolly well starved."

He began eating with evident relish. "Mmmmm, you bods don't know what you're missin'. Nothin' like a spot o' tucker to settle the old tum for a good sound snooze, wot!"

This time it was Fenna who lost her temper. She tugged Horty's ears sharply. "Listen to me, you great ten-bellied buffoon, you were supposed to be supplies officer, remember? You appointed yourself in charge of provisions. There'll be no naps or snoozes for you while us two are still hungry, so shift yourself and get us some breakfast, right away!"

Horty made a languid gesture. "There's two other sacks there, or ain't you blinkin' well noticed? You can open 'em yourself!"

Where Fenna upended one of the sacks, a great splodge of squashed pastie and meadowcream trifle splattered among the ferns.

Springald inspected the contents of the other sack. "Ahah, scones and cheesebread. But guess what, pals? Our genius packed 'em along with a flask of mint tea and one of strawberry cordial. Of course he never made sure the stoppers of the flasks were on tight, so we've got another sackful of sludge. Oh, Horty, how could you?"

The gluttonous hare was munching pawfuls of the mixture from the second sack. He smacked his lips loudly. "Sorry about the blinkin' flask stoppers, chaps, but I didn't want to make too much noise, y'see. Mmmm, rather good this stuff. Hawhaw, I've just invented apple'n'rhubarb'n'-gooseberry surprise. Hmm, there's some soft white celery cheese in here, too . . . excellent mixture. I must give old Gurvel the recipe when we return t'the jolly old Abbey, wot!"

Springald peered into the third sack, wrinkling her nose in distaste. "How could anybeast even think about eating that?"

Horty took the sack and sampled a pawful. "An' what, pray, is the matter with it? 'Tis perfectly top-hole scoff! Trouble with you two is y'don't know how to blinkin' rough it. You've become spoiled by Abbey life, too picky by far!"

Springald took hold of a sack. "Go and get a bath, Horty."

The young hare grinned at her. "Not right now, thanks, I don't need a bath."

She upended the sack over his head. "You do now!"

Horty rose slowly, making two eyeholes in the mess of flan and pudding, then sucked his paws. "Gettin' a bit touchy, aren't we?" He saw Fenna take hold of another sack and fled. "Hello out there, any frogs or tadpoles know a good stream where a chap can get a wash an' brush up, wot?"

Fenna sat down and rested her head between both paws. "We should've known better than letting him go for supplies. 'Tis our own fault, I suppose. The fool never even thought of bringing a flint along to make fire."

Springald produced a chunk of crystal from her belt

pouch. "That's no trouble. I got this off Old Phredd. He told me how to use it . . . watch this."

She held the crystal close to some unlit twigs and moss, focussing until it caught the sunrays and concentrated them in a small bright point. Instantly, the moss began smouldering. After a short while, a single puff of the mousemaid's breath caused a slim column of flame to rise.

Fenna was both delighted and astonished. "That's marvellous! At least we can boil some water and pick mint leaves to make tea. There's plenty of wild mint growing round here. What's the matter, Springald?"

The mousemaid kicked the sack she had upended. "Guess what? Horty forgot to bring anything along to boil it in."

Fenna sat down beside her friend. "Right, that's the last time I listen to the mad plans and stupid ideas of a hare. We'd best go back to Redwall!"

Springald did not relish the suggestion. "Redwall? Imagine having to face the Father Abbot, and Sister Setiva, and Granmum Gurvel and all the rest! I'd sooner sit out here for a season or two and starve, until they've forgotten about us drowning those Dibbuns, plundering the kitchens and disobeying the Abbot. Lack a day, we'd be scrubbing floors and washing pots until we were old and grey!"

Springald's despairing thoughts were interrupted by Horty's voice. "Yowch ouch, I say, leggo me blinkin' ears, you bounders!"

Horty appeared, dripping wet, with six big, mottled rats dragging him along. Their garb was a curious mixture of leaves, shrubbery and purple tattoos. All of them were armed with cudgels and long knives.

Springald let out a cry of alarm, Fenna seized an old kitchen knife and leapt up. Soon they were surrounded, as more rats stepped out from the trees.

Their leader—a tall, brownish-white mottled vermin carrying a long spear—growled warningly. "T'row down der knife, or you're deadbeasts!"

Something about his bleak stare told Fenna it would be wise to obey the order. She let the knife fall.

Horty indignantly took up his case with the tall rat. "I say, d'you mind tellin' these chaps to stop swingin' on me blinkin' ears? They'll pull 'em out by the flippin' roots, tuggin' at 'em like that, wot!"

A sudden jab of the tall rat's spearbutt jolted into the young hare's stomach, leaving him doubled up and gasping for breath. The rat turned the point swiftly, covering Fenna and Springald as they leapt forward to intervene.

"Be still or die! I am Birug, High Kappin of de Darrat. You be prisoners for invadin' our lands!"

Springald protested. "We're not invading anybeasts' land, only passing through. We are innocent travellers!"

Birug sneered. "Shut you mouth, shemouse, you not talk to High Kappin like dat. Bring dem along!"

Fenna was shocked to see that they were surrounded by at least a hundred rats. Horty regained his breath, but before he could speak he and his two friends were gagged with thick pieces of rope. Darrat rats swarmed over the trio, binding their forepaws tightly and linking their footpaws together on a long rope. They were helpless. The squirrelmaid barely had time to cast a frightened glance at her companions before sacks were pulled roughly over their heads. Cudgels prodded them, none too gently.

Birug's voice rang out. "March now!"

Stumbling and bumping into one another, they were hauled swiftly along, dragged upright and cuffed soundly whenever they fell by the wayside. The unhappy trio bumbled along in the midst of their captors, terrified witless and ruing the day they had set paw outside of Redwall Abbey.

Sarabando and Bragoon lay in the treeshade, out of the shimmering midday heat. They sipped dandelion and burdock cordial and nibbled at oatcakes, supplemented by some watercress they had found near a stream. Saro tootled a small reed flute and played a melody. Bragoon sang the tune quietly.

"I know not young 'uns or a wife,
no scolding tongue I fear,
I live a carefree traveller's life,
from yon to hither and here.
O'er mountain hill and lea,
I'm bound to wend my way,
cross river lake or sea,
with never a beast to say,
Sit down! Stand up! Stay here!
O ring a lairy lay.
Stand back! Be still! Just wait!
Farewell my dear, good day!"

Saro began piping the tune to a second verse, when Bragoon ceased singing and held up a paw. "Ssshhh! Did ye hear somethin', mate?"

Ears cocked, the squirrel looked around. Silently she nodded, pointing over to the dense growth of trees on her left. Putting aside the flute, Saro pointed to her friend, indicating that he should stay put. In a flash she was gone, nimbly scaling a beech trunk and vaulting away through the foliaged upper terraces of Mossflower.

Bragoon sat perfectly still, his eyes roving from side to side as he searched the woodlands. Several minutes elapsed before Saro somersaulted back to earth from the high treetops. She picked up a twig, then snapped it and flung it away, muttering darkly to herself.

Bragoon raised his eyebrows. "Wot's upset ye, matey?"

The squirrel began gathering up her possessions. "Upset? I ain't upset, buckoe, I'm steamin' fit t'burst! Those three young fools from Redwall, Horty an' the two maids—they've got themselves captured by a hundred or so big spotty rats!"

173

Bragoon sighed heavily. Buckling the sword across his back, he dusted himself off and made ready. "You shore 'twas them?"

Saro checked her sling and pouch of stones. "Aye, I'm sure enough. They was bound t'gether an' had sacks over their heads, but it's got t'be them. Wot other young hare, squirrel'n'mouse would be wanderin' willy-nilly through these woodlands, eh? They've sneaked out o' Redwall an' come searchin' for us, to share the adventure. Huh!"

Bragoon shook his rudder in disapproval. "Fivescore o' big spotty rats, ye say? Well, they'll get their share of the fun—that's if'n the three idiots live long enough. Ye recall those spotty rats we battled with last time we was up this way?"

The squirrel nodded grimly. "Aye, they were flesh eaters!"

19

Evening was crimsoning the sky over the western reaches as Birug led his Darrat vermin into camp. The Darrat tribe gathered around to see what he had captured. A huge old rat—almost white, with a few brown flecks—pulled himself out of a hammock which was slung under a rocky ledge. Bulling his way through the crowd, he indiscriminately kicked babes, young ones, females and males out of his way. Studying the bound and hooded creatures lying exhausted on the ground, he addressed Birug in a shrill voice totally unsuited to his bulk.

"Lemme see dem!"

Horty felt the sack being pulled from his head and a knife slitting the rope gag in his mouth. He spat out the gag and found himself looking at the huge, fat one. Immediately the young hare began complaining.

"Y'don't mind me sayin', sah, but this is all a bit bally much! Is this the way y'treat jolly peaceable wayfarers, wot?"

A slap from the huge rat silenced him. "Shutcha face, rabbert, d'great Hemper Figlugg don' like talky rabberts!"

He glared at Springald and Fenna, who had been unhooded and had their gags removed. "Don' like talky mouses or squirrels either!"

A shrunken and incredibly ugly female pushed her way through to Hemper Figlugg's side. Ignoring him, she began pinching the three captives, nodding approvingly as she did so. Hemper Figlugg whispered something in her ear.

She nodded, replying aloud. "Burcha Glugg!" The Darrat tribe nodded in agreement and laughed.

Always ready to take advantage of a situation, Horty winked at his two companions. "At least they seem happy, must be a good joke, wot! Burcha Glugg, wasn't it? Watch this."

He grinned at the assembly and repeated the words, "Burcha Glugg!"

The Darrat tribe howled with laughter at Horty's remark. A tiny ratbabe wrinkled his nose at the young hare and squeaked, "Burcha Glugg!"

Horty favoured him with a kindly smile. "Aye old lad, Burcha Glugg, indeed, wot! Yowhoooo, y'little savage. Gerroff!" The ratbabe, who had bitten Horty's footpaw, clung on grimly. High Kappin Birug pulled the ratbabe off and cuffed it.

Hemper Figlugg nodded at his prisoners. "Glugg cayjizz!"

They were picked up bodily and borne to two large cages, formed of thick branches lashed together, one of which was open. Into this the three companions were thrown. The Darrat tribe dispersed and went about their business. Seeing they were being ignored, Springald began loosing herself from the ropes binding her forepaws and the running rope about her right footpaw. The other two did likewise.

Fenna watched the fat Hemper Figlugg settling himself back into the hammock. "What now, I wonder?"

Springald answered hopefully. "Well, we're still alive, aren't we? Where there's life there's hope, they say."

Horty rubbed his stomach—as usual, his mind was on food. "I won't be alive much longer if somebody doesn't feed us. Chap gets hungry, bein' captured an' all that, wot?"

He called out to a passing rat. "Hi there, I say, me old vermin, how about somethin' to jolly well eat?"

He pantomimed eating and pointed inside his mouth. "Eat! Y'know, just like starvin' chaps do. Grub, food or whatever you savages call it."

The rat grinned and pointed to his own mouth. "Glugg!"

Horty clapped his paws together. "Hoho, that's the stuff. Glugg!"

Something suddenly dawned on Fenna. "Glugg, that must be their word for food. Oh, great seasons!"

Horty winked. "Leave it to me eh, wot! I can translate any bally thing when it comes to food!"

Springald understood all too well. She clapped a paw to her brow. "Glugg, that's what we are. Food!"

Horty patted her reassuringly. "No no, old gel, you've got it all wrong. They said Burcha Glugg—that prob'ly means feed them, or give these bally prisoners some food, they look hungry."

Just then, four Darrat males bore a big cauldron to the cage. They placed it outside the bars, within the captives' reach. It was filled with a form of porridge, full of berries and sliced fruit.

One of the rats indicated they should eat. "Burcha Glugg, you eat all up."

Horty smiled. "Told you so!"

Fenna asked the rat, "What does Burcha Glugg mean?"

The rat shrugged. "Old Darrat way of saying good food."

Springald's worst fears were confirmed. She whispered in a shaky voice. "They're fattening us up before they eat us!"

Horty dipped a paw into the cauldron and scooped some up. "Oh, don't be silly! Nobeast'd dare to eat us, shockin' idea. I say, this tastes rather good, wot. Come on, you two!"

They shrank to the back of the cage, shaking their heads. "I couldn't bear to touch it!"

"Oh Horty, how could you eat at a time like this?"

One of the rats unwound a whip from about his waist, gave it a sharp crack and shouted at the pair. "Eat or whip!" They were forced to dip their paws in and eat. However, with the prospect of what they were being fed for, the food, as good as Horty said it was, turned to ashes in their mouths.

Fenna and Springald could only manage a small mouthful apiece, but Horty bolted the porridge down until his snout and whiskers were crusted with it.

"Mmmch, no sense in a chap bein' eaten, grmmfff munch, on an empty stomach. Capital stuff, wot!"

Night fell, bringing a cloudless vault of carnelian blue, dusted with stars. Bragoon lay alongside Sarobando, among some rocky hillocks that skirted the Darrat camp. The otter watched as campfires glimmered low.

"Let the vermin settle down, they prob'ly outnumber us by a couple o' hundred to two."

Saro chewed on a dandelion stalk. "What then?"

Bragoon raised his head, risking a glimpse of the camp area. "They're in a cage, over by that long rocky ledge. We'll have to work out a plan to break 'em out an' escape without bein' seen."

The squirrel lay back and closed her eyes. "Yore good at schemin', mate. What's the plan?"

The otter lay down and closed his eyes also. "First a short sleep, wait'll the camp's quiet."

Saro opened one eye. "An' then?"

Bragoon stuck Martin's sword into the ground, close to paw. "I don't know just yet, but ye'll be the firstbeast I tell when a good idea comes along. I'm goin' to sleep, wake me in an hour. Otters get good ideas when they take naps."

Saro rolled over onto her side. "No, you wake me, 'tis your turn."

Her companion watched the starlight playing along the swordblade. "How can I wake ye when I'm makin' the plan? You wake me!"

The squirrel grumbled. "Huh, 'tis always me. Alright, you take a nap an' do all the plannin', I'll wake ye in an hour." The only answer she received was a pretend snore from the otter.

The midnight hour had just passed. Silence reigned over the Darrat camp, broken only by protracted snores mingled with nighttime woodland sounds.

In the cage, Horty sat clasping his stomach and grimacing. Fenna came over to sit by him. "Tummyache, eh?"

The young hare answered dolefully. "Absolute agony, doncha know. No use upsettin' you an' Springald, so a chap's got to be brave an' silent, even though he's dyin'. It must've been somethin' I ate."

Springald overheard him and snorted. "Something? You great glutton, 'tis not something, but how much of that something you ate. That big cauldron's almost empty!"

Horty winced. "Ah me! Maids can be beautiful but cruel. I only scoffed that porridge because you two wouldn't touch it after the first mouthful. Ha, 'twas me that saved you a jolly good whippin'. Sacrificed meself for your rotten sakes, that's all the gratitude a chap gets, wot?"

One of the three guards in front of the cage snuffled and grunted at the sound of Horty's raised voice. The captives sat in frozen silence until he settled back down with the other two rats. The three guards snorted in soft unison.

Springald whispered, "Look at them—not a care in the world. We'd be that way, too, snoring in the dormitory. Huh, that's if we'd had the sense to listen to the Abbot and your sister Martha. Wish we were back at Redwall now."

Fenna murmured, "Wishing isn't much use. What we should be doing now is escaping while the guards are asleep."

Horty forgot his pains for a moment. "By jingo, you're right, old gel. Escape, that's the bally idea! Right, chaps, anybeast got a scheme or a plan of some type, wot?"

They sat racking their brains for a while, until Fenna ad-

179

mitted limply, "We've got no chance, locked in a cage and surrounded by armed guards. They'd cut us down before we managed to get two paces!"

Numbly they stared at one another. A tear trickled down Springald's cheek; Fenna's lower lip started quivering. Horty blinked and sniffed.

"We've really gone an' done it now, haven't we, chaps, wot!"

Then a rope fell from above, close to the cage. Attached to it was a sharp knife and a piece of bark that had charcoal writing scrawled on it: "Hush, take knife, escape. Tie rope to pot. Wait."

Horty peered up through the bars at the overhead rock ledge. Bragoon's tough-lined face was staring back at him. The otter held a paw to his mouth, signalling silence. Working feverishly, Springald took the knife and tied the rope to the cauldron handle. At a wave from Fenna, the cauldron rose upward, halting just above the cage.

Gripping the rope firmly, Bragoon began swinging the iron cauldron from side to side until it moved back and forth in mighty sweeps like a giant pendulum. Horty watched it as it swung, lower and lower, whizzing close to the cage front, until it reached the level of the three snoring Ratguards. Then the cauldron jerked outward. *Kurblunggggggg!* It struck two of the rats, laying them out senseless. The remaining one sat up, rubbing his eyes.

"Wot was th . . ." *Podongggg!* The cauldron caught the third rat on the return swing, knocking him head over paws.

Springald was sitting on Fenna's shoulders, slashing at the ropes which kept the wooden roof bars in place. The sharp knife made short work of them.

Hemper Figlugg awoke. He heard the cauldron toll like a muted bell as it hit the last rat. Waddling out of his hammock, he went to investigate the noise. Seeing Fenna's head poking out of the cagetop, he hastened forward, shouting wheezily, "Burcha Glugg 'scapin'! Wakey wakey, Darrats!"

Borlongggggggg! The swinging cauldron biffed him on the back of his great fat head. Hemper Figlugg performed a somersault, raising a big puff of dust as his back hit the ground. His shout, however, had roused the Darrat horde, who came staggering from under the ledges and thick bushes, grabbing for weapons.

Bragoon roared down to the escapers, "Cut that pot loose an' grab on to the rope!"

Springald slashed the cauldron free, and they took hold of the rope.

Saro's head appeared above the high ledgetop. "One at a time, we can't pull ye all up t'gether!"

Horty grabbed the spear from a fallen Ratguard. Taking charge, he rapped out orders like a veteran sergeant. "Steady the buffs, chaps! Spring, you go first, Fenna next! I'll hold these bounders off, wot!"

The Darrat had just realised what was taking place. Around half a dozen of the boldest came at the young hare.

Spear at the ready, Horty challenged them bravely. "Step up there, laddie bucks, meet a flippin' Redwall warrior, wot! Two or ten at a time, doesn't blinkin' matter to Bonebreaker Braebuck. Have at ye, scurvy nosewipes! Come on, don't be shy, ye wiltin' wallflowers. Wot!"

A big broad mottled rat charged at him, waving a hatchet. A slingstone flew from above, and the rat stood still, tottered, then collapsed in a heap.

Horty threw himself at the other five rats, who had been advancing on him slowly. He was in his element.

"I'm the son o' the roarin' buck! D'ye want to visit your ugly ancestors, eh? Well, I'm the one who'll send ye to Hellgates. Yaaaaaaah!"

At the top of the ledge, Fenna and Springald stood with their rescuers. Bragoon shook his head. "Is he mad? Look at 'im!"

Horty was like a whirling demon, lashing out with his long hind legs as he thwacked wildly about with the spear. Rats went down like ninepins before his onslaught.

181

Sarobando nodded in admiration. "That young 'un's got the makins of a powerful warrior, but he's still a hotheaded learner. Soon as he tires they'll overpower 'im an' bring 'im down."

Springald yelled down to her friend. "Horty, get to the rope, hurry!"

The young hare looked at the pack of rats charging toward him. "Right away, marm, cover me jolly old back, chaps!"

Saro used her sling, while the others pelted the rats with rocks from the ledge as Horty ran for it. He reached the rope and looped it about his waist.

"Haul away!"

Kappin Birug flung a wooden club that caught Horty square between both ears, before bouncing off his head.

Horty grinned. "Yah missed me!" Then he fell unconscious.

Ducking slingstones and a few arrows, the rescuers—along with Fenna and Springald—hauled Horty's limp figure up onto the ledgetop.

Bragoon peered anxiously down as more archers began appearing. "Better get goin' an' move out o' range. They mean business!"

They struck off into some thick pinewoods, carrying the senseless figure of the hare between them.

20

It was a long and wearying night, but the Redwallers kept going. Pines grew thick about them, obscuring even the stars in the sky. Stumbling on through the dense carpet of rotting pine needles, Springald bumped into a tree trunk.

"Oof! There won't be a part of me that's undamaged if we go on at this rate. A torch would help us to see where we're going."

Bragoon urged her on. "Just keep goin', missy, there'll be no torches. One spark can start a fire among pine trees, an' the whole woodland'd be ablaze bafore ye could blink. Besides, a torch would be like a beacon for those vermin to follow."

Springald felt foolish. "I'm sorry, I didn't realise."

The otter said nothing, but he was exhausted and bad-tempered after having to run all night, burdened with Horty. He snapped at the mousemaid. "'Tis not much good bein' sorry now, Miss Mouse. If'n you three would've stayed put at the Abbey, we wouldn't be in this fix!"

Fenna came to her friend's defence. "We only came after you because we thought we could help. Besides, now that we're free, we can get on searching for Loamhedge."

But Bragoon was not to be appeased. "Free, eh, don't make me laugh! You think those rats won't come after us?

Lissen, I know rats, they won't rest 'til they've got us all in the cookin' pot. Ask Saro, we've fought flesh eaters like them afore. The only way to make 'em give up is to kill 'em, an' there's too many of the scum for that!"

A quavery voice echoed out of nowhere. "Oh, far too many! They've eaten most of us, you know."

Bragoon stood stock still, his eyes scouring the night woods. "Who said that?"

From a small hillock of pine needles built up round the base of a trunk, the voice answered, "If you remove your great heavy rudder from my neck, I'll tell you!"

The otter leaped to one side as an old rabbit shoved his head through the mound.

"Sorry to startle you like that, I'm sure. If the Darrat are hunting you, I'd be pleased to hide you. Only for awhile, though—they eat anybeast who harbours fugitives." The ancient rabbit shrugged. "But Darrat will eat a creature for no reason at all. So, d'you want me to hide you?"

Saro indicated the unconscious Horty. "Just until this 'un's fit for travel agin, thankee."

The rabbit's name was Cosbro. He took them to the hollow log in which he lived. It was a cunningly contrived dwelling, a great elm trunk overgrown with all manner of moss and nettles. One end of it backed against a standing rock, the other was artfully concealed by thistles and wild lupins. Cosbro carefully parted these, creating a little gap which allowed them to squeeze through one at a time. Once they were all inside, the old rabbit rearranged the outer thistles and lupins, rendering the entrance invisible to the casual observer.

Springald looked about: it was a very neat little home. Lit by four lanterns containing fireflies, its illumination dim but adequate. They sat down on a carpet of dried grass and springy moss.

Fenna made Horty comfortable, remarking, "I've never heard of a rabbit living inside of a tree before."

Cosbro preened his meagre whiskers. "Neither have the Darrat, young 'un. That's what makes it such a perfect place. I've often sat in here, listening to them digging holes as they searched for rabbits—they dig out anything that looks like a burrow. Clods, they have no imagination at all."

Bragoon smiled at the old one. "But where do the other rabbits around here live?"

Cosbro shook his head sadly. "There are no other rabbits left. Only me, sitting inside this log, poor fool that I am."

Saro patted his paw gently. "You ain't no fool, me friend. It takes a clever beast to survive in this country. How many rabbits were there, an' how'd ye come to be livin' here?"

Cosbro shrugged. "We were too many to count one time, long ago. Our families had no written history. All I have to remember my ancestors by are ancient poems and ballads passed down by word of mouth. Woe is me, sometimes I think I must be the last rabbit left in all the land."

Saro felt sorry for the pitiful old creature. She passed him a flask of dandelion and burdock cordial.

"Wet yore whistle with this, ole mate. Maybe ye'd like to tell us one of yore poems from the ole days, eh?"

Cosbro sipped the cordial, closing his eyes blissfully. "Ahhh, dandelion and burdock, tastes like nectar to me. Aye, 'tis many long seasons since I tasted ought as good as this. Have you ever heard of a poem called 'The Shadowslayers'?"

He looked from one to the other, but they shook their heads. Helping himself to a longer sip, Cosbro licked his lips. "When I was younger, I could skip through such verses. But, alas, the weight of seasons has descended upon me. My mind forgets a lot of things these days. So, my friends, here is the poem, as best as I can recall it.

"Lo the golden days are gone,
the happy laughter long fled,
now silence falls o'er Loamhedge walls,

lone winds lament the dead.
The Shadowslayers sent us forth,
some south and east, some west and north.

The wise ones said 'twas vermin foul,
their blood, their teeth, their fur,
which brought the plague that laid us low,
with more than we could bear.
When families die before our eyes,
we learned, 'tis folly to be wise.

Leave everything ye own now, flee,
run if ye can, go far and wide,
linger not here, to grieve and weep,
those tears have all been cried.
The mouse Germaine said, 'Woe, 'tis true,
The Shadowslayers will come for you.'

The mice went first, escaped their fate,
they traversed north and west;
what was left of us remained,
to lay our dead to rest.
We travelled then, us piteous few,
who'd seen what Shadowslayers could do.

My father's father spake these words,
as had his kin, from time untold,
wand'ring exiled o'er the land,
growing up, and growing old.
Recalling to their dying breath,
how once the Shadowslayers brought death."

Cosbro took another drink and sighed wearily. "I myself
wrote that final verse, though there were many more. They
told of our family names and histories. But I've forgotten
the words, shame on me!"

Fenna thought it was the saddest thing she had ever
heard.

Springald spoke comfortingly to the ancient hare. "I hope

186

that if ever I live to your age, I would remember the half of it, sir."

Horty chose that moment to waken from his stupor. "Remember what, wot? I say, did we escape those blighters? Jolly good show, chaps, where are we now? Someplace far a-blinkin' way, I hope. Owch, my flippin' head's given me jip!"

He tried to stagger upright and banged his head on the log. "Yowhooyooch! Who left that up there, confounded oaf!"

Saro threw herself across his face, stifling further cries. She whispered fiercely. "Shuttup, addlebrain, I can hear somethin' goin' on outside!"

Kappin Birug and a crowd of Darrat rats halted alongside the log. Those inside held their breath in frozen silence. Sounds of the vermin poking about with spearbutts and slashing at shrubbery could be heard by those in the log. Outside, Birug climbed up and sat upon the log. Dawning sunlight slanted through the trees as he glanced down at the Darrat rats resting upon the grass.

"Any of you be High Kappins, eh?" They stared owlishly at one another, then shook their heads. Birug jumped up, performing a dance of rage upon the log. Pointing his spear at them, he screeched.

"Den why you not searchin', mudbrains? Search! Search! Find dem, y'want me to do everythink, eh? Search!"

They dispersed hastily, trying to look busy and diligent as they probed amid the woodland trees. Birug laid about with his spear shaft, spittle going everywhere as he took out his bad temper on anybeast standing close.

"Hemper Figlugg got bad sore skull, big lump onna 'ead! Dose beasts die slow when I catch 'em. Only make Burcha Glugg out of wot be left of dem!"

Birug hurried over to a rat who had returned to investigate the fallen log. Dealing the unfortunate several hard kicks to the rump, the Kappin screeched hoarsely at him. "Wotcha be doin', dumbum—y'think they be beetles, hidin'

187

inna falled treelog? You never be High Kappin, that be sure!"

As Birug chased the rat back to search with the others, Cosbro crept to the log opening and called out in excellent imitation of the gruff Darrat dialect. "Der dey goes! Ober dat way, quick!"

There followed a stampede of pounding Darrat paws, with Birug bellowing as he hastened in pursuit. "Not kill 'em, catch 'em priz'ner, that a h'order!"

As the sounds retreated, the fugitives breathed easier. Springald was visibly shaken. "Good grief, that was a bit close for comfort!"

Saro removed herself from Horty's face. He was the picture of sputtering indignity.

"Pshaw, phoo! I'll be spittin' wodges of your bally tailfur for days t'come, marm. No blinkin' thanks to you, I was near smothercated, wot! But who am I to complain, chaps? Me flippin' head's poundin', achin' to blue blazes. There's a lump like a duck egg on me young skull. The poor old stomach is painin' an' swollen from savin' the ungrateful comrades. An' to top it all jolly well off, a great lump of a squirrel has been layin' on my tender young mouth for absolute ages. Phwaaaw, phutt! Never feed your young on squirrelhair, tastes vile!"

Bragoon's paw shot out, pinching Horty's nose in a viselike grip. "Are ye finished moanin', after ye nearly got us all captured, young sir?"

Horty tried to nod. "Yith, juth leggo ob be dose pleathe!"

The otter released his grip, growling threateningly. "One more whimper an' I'll pull it right off, so keep quiet!" He turned to question Cosbro. "Ye mentioned Loamhedge in yore poem, mate, an' Abbess Germaine, too. She ruled there, from wot I've 'eard. Loamhedge is where we're bound for. Any idea which way it lies?"

The ancient rabbit pointed in a general southeast direction. "I can't be sure, but I've always imagined it being somewhere over that way. I've heard 'tis savage country—deserts, chasms, wide rivers, and numerous foebeasts."

Saro nodded. "Aye, me'n Bragoon have seen a bit of it, though that was quite a few seasons back. Over that way, eh?"

Cosbro began moving the vegetation from his log entrance. "When you see a great line of very high cliffs, you'll know you're on the right track. Er, by the way, have you any of that excellent cordial to spare? I'm too old to travel now."

Bragoon passed him a fresh flask. "Take this, friend, an' thankee kindly for yore help!"

They emerged into calm morning sunlight and fresh, green woodlands.

Saro waved to Cosbro. "Good fortune be with ye, matey. We'll travel now, while the coast's clear. You take it easy!"

Cosbro brought something out of his dwelling and gave it to Bragoon. It was a large coil of rope—thin but incredibly strong, with big knots every three pawlengths.

The otter inspected it closely. "Haharr, 'tis a climbin' rope, an' a fine one, too. If'n I ain't mistaken, this'll come in useful at the high cliffs. Where'd ye get it?"

Cosbro explained. "I made it myself, when I was a lot younger. Never got round to using it, though. I've forgotten my dreams of high cliffs long since. You take it."

Bragoon drew Martin's sword and held it up in a warrior's salute. "A gift from a friend is somethin' to be valued. Thankee, sir, an' may the seasons be kind to ye!"

To avoid bumping into the Darrat, they set off at a southerly tangent through the woodlands. Cosbro stood watching until they were out of sight. Wiping a paw across his rheumy eyes, the ancient rabbit murmured wistfully to himself, "And may the seasons be kind to you, friends. May the breeze be at your backs, and the sun never in your eyes. Ah me, I wish that I were young enough to go with you."

The lonely rabbit shuffled back to his home, thinking of the high mysterious cliffs and the lost opportunities of his earlier seasons, now that old age leaned heavily upon him. Cosbro took one last look at the far horizon as he bent to enter the log dwelling.

"Ah well, at least my rope won't be wasted—if they live long enough to use it."

21

Martha did not sleep a wink on the night that the vermin were sighted. It was as if some unreasoning panic was welling up in her. Vermin, at the very gates of her beloved Abbey! Restlessly she roamed Great Hall, propelling the little cart which held her chair, by pulling it along with the crutch that Toran had made for her.

Moonlight sent pale shafts of light in varied hues as it shone through the stained-glass windows onto the worn stone floor. Travelling through the patches of dark and light, the young haremaid arrived at the tapestry of Martin the Warrior. She gazed up at the figure of the heroic mouse. It was illuminated by a small lantern on either side.

Martha voiced her fears and worries to her friend. "Oh Martin, what shall we do? Sarobando and Bragoon have left the Abbey, and all on my silly little behalf. Abbot Carrul gave Bragoon your great sword to take with him. I'd stay in my chair forever, if only they were back here at Redwall. The safety of this Abbey and all my friends here is far more important than foolish dreams of being able to walk. With my brother and the other young ones gone, who will help us against the vermin? The very thought of those cruel, murderous vermin getting inside our gates is horrible!"

"Here now, young Martha, what's all this?"

She gave a start as the Abbot loomed up out of the shadows. "Father Abbot, I thought you'd gone to your bed."

Carrul sat down on the edge of the cart and looked over the top of his glasses at her. "And I thought you had, too, miss."

The sound of the main abbey door opening caused them both to pause. The Abbot's loud whisper echoed around the hall columns.

"Who's there?"

Toran's voice replied. " 'Tis only me an' Foremole Dwurl, Father. We just been relieved o' wallguard by Junty Cellarhog an' Weld." The pair joined Martha and Abbot Carrul.

Dwurl tugged his snout politely. "Wot bee's you'm a-doin' settin' daown yurr? Shudd be snorin' abed, 'tis orful late."

The Abbot put on his wise face. "Oh, we were just discussing a few things, weren't we, Martha?"

The haremaid managed an important little cough. "Ahem, yes, just small bits of business. What's it like out there, Toran? Any more news of the, er, vermin?"

The ottercook sat back on his rudder. "No, miss, they ain't up to much. Their fires are burnt low, I think they're sleepin'. We've been watchin' the ditch outside the front gate, t'other side o' the path, makin' sure they don't try t'sneak along it."

Martha asked the question she had been anxious to have answered. "Aren't you afraid?"

Toran rubbed his wide midriff thoughtfully. "Bless yore 'eart, pretty one, o' course we are. Only a fool'd say he wasn't. We're afraid as any sensible beast should be, but we ain't scared. Wot I mean is, we're only afraid for the safety of others—Dibbuns, an' young 'uns like yoreself. But if'n we got to do somethin' about it, we ain't scared o' vermin."

Foremole licked his lips. "Oi'm afeared."

Toran raised his eyebrows at this remark. "You, afeared?"

A huge grin creased the mole leader's homely face. "Aye,

192

zurr, afeared oi'll fall asleep an' miss ee brekkist. Oi'm a-thinken oi'll go to ee kitchens an' get a h'early wun!"

Martha laughed at the mole's comical logic. "What a great idea, sir, I think we'll join you!"

The kitchen was crowded with Redwallers of a like mind, even Dibbuns. Nobeast could sleep with the excitement of the night. Granmum Gurvel and three young moles were busy filling baked apples with honey and chopped hazelnuts.

Gurvel curtsied to the Abbot as she bustled by. "Coom in an' sit ee daown, zurr, an' you'm h'others, too. Et bee's a gudd job moi ole bones can't be a sleepen, so oi'm a keepen moiself bizzied."

They found seats around the kitchen table and began pouring a sauce of meadowcream and rosehip over their baked apples. Everybeast was watching the Abbot as he paused before eating to address them.

"What we need are some good contingency plans, my friends. Seeing as most of us are here, I'll take any suggestions."

Muggum was sitting up on a shelf, among the spice jars, with his cohort of Dibbuns. The molebabe raised his spoon. "Oi says chop ee vermints tails offen wi' a gurt rusty knoife, an' barth 'em in 'ot soapy watter. Hurr, they'm soon bee's glad to run away arter that. Ho urr aye!"

This met with hearty applause and much sneezing from the Dibbuns, two of whom had opened a hotroot pepper jar. Amused by this, Abbot Carrul tried to keep a straight face as he spoke to Sister Portula, who was recording the meeting. "Not a bad idea! Write it down, Sister, and don't forget the bit about hot soapy water. We'll keep it in mind."

Sister Setiva, after wiping several noses and glaring the Dibbuns into silence, held up a paw. "As soon as ah've finished eating, ah hope some o' ye will join me tae search around for more things tae use as weapons."

Martha was among those who volunteered. But Toran

193

had other plans for her. "You'd never be able to search the attics upstairs, me beauty. I think ye should be in charge of the Dibbuns' safety. Seasons forbid that anythin' should happen to the liddle 'uns with vermin camped next to our gates. Will ye do it, Martha?"

Immediately the haremaid agreed. "I'd be glad to. Right, come on you villains, off that shelf and up to bed. Last one up washes all the pots and dishes, eh, Granmum Gurvel?"

Gurvel picked up her big ladle. "You'm said the vurry thing oi wuz abowt t'say, Miz Marth!"

An almighty scramble followed as Dibbuns climbed down from the shelves and fled upstairs squealing.

Abbot Carrul waited until the noise subsided. "Next suggestion please!"

Badredd lay awake down in the ditch, trying to ignore the stentorian snores of those around him. He longed for the dawn, when he could take possession of his magic sword. What did it look like? He imagined it as a solid gold blade with a crosshilt and grip crusted with rubies, pearls and emeralds. Of course, he would not mind too much if it were made from silver with jetstones and sapphires for adornment.

Mentally he went through a speech he had prepared for the woodland bumpkins who lived behind the wall. Badredd silently practised it, making sweeping paw movements to emphasise its drama. "Throw wide your gates! Tremble at my name, for I am Badredd, commander of a vermin horde."

He paused here, wondering if his scruffy little band could constitute a horde. No matter, those woodland oafs had probably never seen a horde, much less taken a head count of one. He continued his oratory. "You are looking at death, all of ye! Unless you deliver unto Badredd the magic sword that is rightfully his."

He questioned the last phrase—it needed something, a word or two to prove that the sword's ownership was never in doubt. Hah, that was it! He embellished his flowery recitation thus: "For did not my father, Reddblade, Warlord of the Northern Mountains, proclaim it so? 'Give unto my son Badredd his sword. It lies within Wallred, I mean, Redwall. To the mighty warrior goes the magic sword!'" He flung out his paw and caught Halfchop a smack on the chin.

The rat awoke, holding his chin in his good paw. "Mmmph, wot did ye do that for, Chief?"

But Badredd was too fired up to waste time with arguments. "Get further along that ditch an' see if'n ye can make it so that yore level with the big gate!"

Halfchop peered at him in the predawn darkness. "Wot for?"

Badredd shoved him forward. "If'n ye make it safely, give me a signal. I'll follow up with the rest o' the crew. That way we'll be in place when it gets light. They'll get the shock o' their lives when they see me climb out o' the ditch an' demand the magic sword. Go on, don't hang about!"

Blundering forward, Halfchop stepped on a thistle and banged into the ditch's sidewall. "'Tis no good, I can't see a thing. Why don't ye wait 'til dawn?"

Badredd drew his cutlass. "Because I want it done now. There'll be one less in the crew if'n ye stand there rubbin' yore chin an' makin' excuses. Now get goin'!"

Halfchop picked up a red-ended branch from the embers of a fire. He went off, blowing it back to burning light and muttering, "Alright, then, but I ain't goin' without a light!"

Up on the northwest rampart corner, Brother Weld nudged Junty Cellarhog. "Is that somebeast coming along the ditch carrying a light?"

The burly hedgehog watched as a small burning beacon grew closer. "Aye, so 'tis, Brother. I wager that's a vermin, up to no good, I'll be bound. Better stop the rascal afore he sets fire to our front gate."

There was always a variety of things in Junty's big apron pocket. He dug a paw in and rummaged about. A slow smile lit up his heavy features as he produced a big barrel bung made from a knot he had gouged out of an oak log. "This should do!"

Though ponderous and not given to quick flings, Junty was accurate and very powerful.

Halfchop was never very sure of what fractured his muzzle and wrecked his nose. But he never forgot the sound as it hit him. *Kachunk!*

Badredd saw the rat's light snuffed out with a gentle hiss as it fell into some stagnant water. He went and shook the weasel brothers, Floggo and Rogg, awake. "Rouse yore bones there. Go an' fetch ole Halfchop back 'ere. He went wanderin' off up the ditch. It looks like the idiot's fallen over. Go on, move! It'll soon be dawn."

When they returned, hauling the senseless rat, Badredd blew on the embers and stirred the fire. He winced as he saw the damage to Halfchop's face. Awakened by the commotion, Flinky dug some dried herbs out of his pouch and lit them so that they smouldered. The weasels held the rat's head steady as Flinky pushed the smoking herbs under his nose. Halfchop's eyes opened immediately when the pungent fumes got to him.

Badredd squatted beside him. "What happened?" Halfchop looked at the fox quizzically as he repeated the question. "Who did that to ye, what happened?"

Halfchop spoke . . . just one word—"Kachunk!"

Flinky put aside the smouldering herbs. "Wot did ye say, mate?"

Halfchop looked at Flinky as if seeing him for the first time. He looked at Badredd the same way and spoke the word again. "Kachunk!"

Losing his patience, Badredd pawed the cutlass edge menacingly. "Talk sense! I asked ye wot happened. Keep sayin' that stupid word an' I'll kachunk ye, good an' proper!"

Halfchop leaned close and whispered in the fox's ear. "Kachunk!"

As Flinky saw the cutlass beginning to rise, he stepped in and stayed his crew leader's paw. "Ah now, leave him alone, Chief. The pore ould rat's not in his right mind at all. How d'ye feel, matey, better now?"

Halfchop smiled foolishly over his swollen muzzle. "Kachunk!"

Dawn crept in from the east, pale pink and lilac in a creamy haze. Dewdrops bedecked the flatlands beyond the ditch. Redwall Abbey's twin bells tolled out the opening of a new summer day. Martha watched Toran, Abbot Carrul and several others mounting the gatehouse steps. Frustration tinged the haremaid's plea to them.

"Let me come up on the ramparts, I want to see what's happening. Oh please, I feel so helpless down here!"

Toran shook his head. "It might get a bit dangerous up here, me pretty. Best ye stop down there an' look after the Dibbuns."

Little Shilly the squirrelbabe made a scramble for the steps. "Cummon, we all go up onna wall. Then Miz Marth' gotta be up dere wiv us'n's!"

Sister Setiva ran down and blocked the Dibbuns' way. "Och no ye don't, mah wee babes. Ah'll come o'er tae the orchard wi' ye an' Martha. We'll see if any blackberries are ripe enough tae be picked yet. A guid idea, eh?"

Squeaking with delight, the Abbeybabes pushed Martha's chair across the lawns so fast that the haremaid was forced to hold on tight to the arms.

Sister Setiva chased after them, shouting in her thin, reedy voice, "Slow down, ye naughty creatures, go easy wi' Miss Martha!"

Junty and Brother Weld kept an eye on the ditch as they made their way along to the threshold over the main gate.

Throwing a brief salute, the Cellarhog made his report to the Abbot. "Looks like they're makin' a move, Father. Comin' this way!"

The wall party was armed with a variety of window poles, kitchen utensils and tools. Apart from one or two slings and bags of pebbles, there were no real weapons to be found within the bounds of the peaceable Abbey. Toran gave Junty a sling and some stones. He tossed a long ash stave to Brother Weld.

"These ain't much, but they're better'n nothin', friends."

Now the vermin crew had reached the spot directly below where the Redwallers stood. They halted, only the tops of their heads visible. Silence fell as they waited, standing in a muddy pool of ditchwater.

Toran whispered to Abbot Carrul. "Let them state their business first."

The silence from below became rather protracted, then a voice spoke out. "Kachunk!"

This was followed by Badredd hissing, "Somebeast, shut that fool up!"

Curiosity overcame Old Phredd the Gatekeeper, who called out, "What do ye want? Speak up!"

Badredd had envisioned himself leaping boldly from the ditch to state his demands. However, he was far too short for such a thing, so several of the crew had to lift him up and boost him onto the path. It was a totally undignified procedure. The little fox landed, sprawling on the dust and gravel. He sprang up quickly, took a swaggering step forward and tripped over his cutlass.

Having heard a few stifled giggles from the walltop, Badredd glared up frostily at the assembled Redwallers, putting on his toughest snarl. "Ye'll laugh the other side of yore faces afore this day's done!" Puffing himself up to his full height, he continued. "I'm Badredd, Warlord of the Vermin Horde. Nobeast can stand against me. I come from the Northlands where we drink our enemies' blood!"

The Abbot bowed his head politely. "I bid you a good morning, Sir Badredd. I am Father Abbot Carrul of Redwall. Is there any way I can be of service to you? Mayhaps you might need food or supplies to continue your journey?"

At the mention of food, the rest of the vermin crew climbed out of the ditch eagerly, but the little fox forestalled them by answering the Abbot scornfully. "We don't want yore food, mouse. Our journey's end is here, at this Wallred place. You've got a magic sword here. I want it—bring it t'me now!"

The Abbot stared coolly down at him. "There is no such thing as a magic sword at Redwall Abbey."

Badredd drew his cutlass with a swish, pointing it at Carrul. "You lie! Bring that sword out to me, old fool, or it will go badly with ye!"

Toran stepped up to the Abbot's side, roaring down at the fox, "Don't ye dare call the Abbot of Redwall a fool or a liar! If he says there's no magic sword here, then you'd best get the mud out o' yore ears an' listen. Now shift yoreself, vermin. Get up the road with that raggedy-bottomed bunch. Quick, or I'll come down there and kick yore tail back t'the Northlands!"

Shaking with rage, Badredd turned and nodded to his two archers, the weasel brothers. "Fire!"

Two arrows zipped from their bows. Toran flung himself upon the Abbot, knocking him down below the battlements. One arrow flew harmlessly overhead, the other grazed the ottercook's shoulder.

Toran winced as he yelled, "Down, everybeast!"

The Redwallers immediately dropped below the parapet. Junty Cellarhog fitted a stone into his sling and whirled it. He popped up and let fly. Though it was a speedy shot, and not too accurate, it did hit Badredd on the footpaw. He screeched out in pain as Crinktail and the rest of the crew jumped back into the ditch, taking him with them.

There was an uneasy silence. Then Flinky called out in a

wheedling voice. "Ah, look now, friends, why don't ye just throw the ould magic sword to us an' we'll be on our way, I promise!"

This was followed by a tirade from Badredd. "Sword or no sword, I vow I'll slay ye all an' take yore Abbey from ye. This is war, d'ye hear me?"

Two broken halves of the arrow which had struck Toran were flung into the ditch. The ottercook sat watching Sister Portula bind his wound with her apron. He laughed and shouted back contemptuously to the fox, "War, eh? Go on then, let's see ye take Redwall from us. A dirty liddle band o' vermin scum, ye'd have no chance!"

Down in the ditch, Flinky gazed levelly at Badredd and nodded. "Sure an' I believe the big riverdog's right. How could a crew as small as ours take that fine big place? 'Tis all made o' stone an' locked up tight."

Badredd nursed his footpaw, shooting a hateful glance at the stoat. "Whose side are ye on, theirs o' ours?"

Flinky spread his paws expressively. "Ah now, Chief, I'm with you. But ye got to admit, things ain't exac'ly goin' our way, are they now?"

Badredd narrowed his eyes, well aware that Flinky could be a sly one at times. "So, what d'ye suggest?"

The stoat winked secretively. "Make 'em think we've gone away. I'll wager we could catch 'em off guard after a day or two."

Granmum Gurvel came panting up the wallsteps, carrying a big wooden pail of kitchen rubbish with the arrow that had missed the Abbot sticking out of it. The old mole blinked indignantly. "Yurr, see wot appinged? Oi wurr just crossin' ee lawn to put ee rubbish on moi compost 'eap. That thurr h'arrer comed roight out'n ee sky an' stucked in moi pail!"

Junty Cellarhog took it from her. "Don't fret, marm, it missed ye!"

*

200

Back in the ditch, Badredd was mulling over Flinky's idea. "How many days do we wait?"

Junty's voice interrupted further conversation. The Cellarhog was whining piteously. "Sir, we've got somethin' here for ye."

Badredd leaped up. "Lend a paw 'ere, get me outta this ditch. We won't be waitin' any longer. Hah! They've seen sense at last, that'll be my magic sword!"

They boosted him up out of the ditch. He was back a moment later—dripping with leftover oatmeal, potato peelings, onion skins and old cooking oil. Laughter and hoots of derision rang out from the walltops. Badredd was speechless with rage. The crew backed off from him, holding their noses at the odour from yesterday's kitchen rubbish.

He clawed at the mess. "I don't care how long I got to wait, they're deadbeasts, all of 'em. They can't treat Badredd like that!"

Halfchop smiled at him. "Kachunk!"

Toran sat in the orchard, surrounded by the Dibbuns, telling the tale to them whilst Sister Setiva and Martha tended his wound. The incident, while being humorous, worried Martha.

"I wish Sarobando and Bragoon were here now."

The ottercook patted his newly bandaged shoulder. "Don't upset yourself, young 'un. Those vermin'll leave when they find there's nought here for 'em except the ole pail o' rubbish. Ain't that right, Sister?"

Setiva knotted off the bandage neatly. "Aye, like as not. Ye say there's but ten o' the rogues altogether. Hmm, they shouldnae be much trouble. Aye, but 'twould be fine if we had some otters or shrews aboot the place."

Toran stood up and flexed his paw. "Huh, ye'll not find otters around here, save for me. They've gone off to camp on the seashores all summer. As for shrews—well, they go wherever the streams an' rivers take 'em. I know we ain't got many at Redwall of fightin' age, but we'll do at a pinch."

Martha folded the rug across her lap. "I hope you're right. I'd hate to see vermin get into Redwall. What would happen to these little ones?"

Muggum picked up a stick. "Uz foight 'em, miz, we'm gurt fierce Dibbuns. B'ain't that roight, Shilly?"

The squirrelbabe, and all the other Dibbuns, set up a fearful clamour. Brandishing sticks, wooden spoons and stones, they paraded up and down, scowling, growling and shouting dire threats.

Though Martha could not help smiling inwardly, she covered her ears and looked shocked. "Dearie me, I wouldn't like to be a vermin with all these great rough warriors around. Would you, Toran?"

Her friend nodded. "Aye, miss, thank the seasons we can sleep safe in our beds. These liddle 'uns are reg'lar terrors!"

The smallest of the Dibbuns, the tiny shrew called Buffle, picked up a stone which was far too big for him. He fell over backward and sat there muttering unintelligible sounds.

"Gurrumvurbilbultumcuchachukchuk!"

Toran removed the stone from Buffle's stomach. He picked the babe up with one paw and set him on Martha's lap. "Well, I wonder what that's all about?"

Yooch, who seemed to be the only one who could understand Buffle, translated. "Buffle sez he eat vermins all up!"

Sister Setiva cleaned a few dandelion seeds from the shrewbabe's whiskers. He tried to bite her paw. Setiva raised her eyebrows. "Och, ye wee terror, don't ye dare tae eat me all up!"

Buffle clenched his tiny paws and came out with a long torrent of garbled baby talk.

Martha turned to Yooch. "What's he saying now?"

Yooch giggled. "Buffle sayin' lotsa naughty fings!"

Sister Setiva looked shocked. "Time for your nap, young shrew!" She swept him off protesting loudly. Setiva was a no-nonsense shrewnurse and ignored Buffle's tirade. "Och, ye can stop all that gobbledygook—ah'm no' impressed!"

22

Badredd and his crew had left the ditch and crossed back into Mossflower Wood. With all manner of fruit, berries and wild vegetables to be had there during this summer season, the vermin had no difficulty finding food. Crinktail and Juppa gossiped as they prepared food for the others. Neither was very optimistic.

Juppa plucked away at a moorhen, which Rogg had brought down with his bow. "I tell ye, 'twill be a long time afore we see the Northlands again. Badredd's more determined than ever now."

Crinktail chopped away at dandelion roots and wild celery with a thin-bladed dagger. "Aye, that's true enough. Where is our fearless chief? I ain't seen him round lately."

Slipback strolled in and threw down a sizeable bunch of watercress. "Who, Badredd? That 'un's takin' a bath in the stream, tryin' to get the smell o' that rubbish off 'im. He ain't too pleased, I can tell ye, two baths in two seasons is hard on a beast. He only took a bath last spring."

Flinky emerged from the undergrowth, his tunic full of pears. "Ah sure, any vermin knows that bathin' weakens ye. How's the vittles comin' along, me ould darlin'?"

Crinktail winked fondly at her mate. "They'll be ready soon enough, ye great starvin' stoat. Sit by the fire here an' stir the pot awhile. Ye can give us a song while yore at it."

Flinky knew more vermin songs than all the crew put together. He sang aloud, hoping the strains might reach Badredd whilst he was taking his bath in the stream not far away. The rest of the crew drifted in to listen, sniggering and nudging a bit at the words.

"Oh hear my song, young vermin,
and take heed to wot I say,
I had a fine young son like you,
who bathed most every day.
Whenever he saw water, straight off he'd dive right in,
a-scrubbin' an' a-washin' of himself, then he'd begin:

Ooooooooohhhhhhh! I smell just like a rose,
from me tail up to me nose,
why, even all the blossoms envy me.
An' all I'll ever lack,
is a mate to scrub me back,
I'm the cleanest vermin that you'll ever
see . . . eeeeeeeeeeeeeee!

I'm clean as a weasel's whistle,
shiny as a stoat's best coat.
Just pass the scented essence,
in camomile I'll float.
All lathery suds an' lilac buds an' pine tree fragrance,
    too,
with me teeth so white an' me fur so bright an' eyes of
    baby blue."

The last verse was sung sadly and with great feeling.

"But then one summer dawn,
I had to weep an' mourn,
I went down to the bathing pool that day.
There was not one poor young hair,

just a sweet aroma there.
Alas, he'd gone an' washed himself away.
Awayeeeeeeeeeee!"

Badredd strode to the fire, dripping wet. Jiggling a claw in one ear, he gave Flinky a frozen stare. "Get them vittles cooked an' shut yore stupid gob. When we've eaten, we're movin' on, fast!"

Flinky returned his stare blankly. "Ah sure, an' wot's the hurry, yore 'onour?"

The little fox buckled his cutlass on. "I want to take a look round the back o' that Abbey, there's got to be a way in!"

Flinky passed a secret wink to Crinktail, who tried to fob Badredd off with an excuse. "But, Chief, by the time we've finished the meal and got round there, it'll be dark."

Badredd picked up a bowl and held it forth to be filled. "Good, that'll be the ideal time to get the job done!"

Abbot Carrul felt much relieved as he surveyed the path and the ditch from the west walltop. "Thank goodness there's no sign of the vermin. What do you think, Toran, have they gone for good?"

The ottercook had lashed sharp kitchen knives to the tops of two window poles. He and Junty each had one. Toran peered up the path into the gathering darkness.

"Looks like they have, Father, but I'm takin' no chances. Me an' Junty'll stay guard up here an' keep a weather eye out. If the things are still all clear tomorrow, we'll do a patrol around the outer wall just to make certain."

Carrul patted his friend's stout back. "As you wish, I'll have food sent up to you."

It was a fine warm night. Cavern Hole was packed with Redwallers, all happy and relaxed since hearing the news their Abbot brought, that the vermin fear had passed. Granmum Gurvel and her molemaids served a celebratory supper of mushroom and barley soup, harvest-baked loaves and a dessert of apple and blackberry crumble made from fresh ingredients, which the Dibbuns had gathered from the orchard.

Foremole sat down next to Sister Portula, digging into his bowl of crumble and smiling happily. "Gudd arpatoit to ee, marm, ee trubble bee's gonned naow!"

Portula raised a beaker of October Ale. "Good appetite to you, sir. Hmm, look at young Martha, she doesn't seem to be enjoying herself. I wonder what's the matter with her."

Foremole pondered the situation for a moment, then pronounced his judgement. "Oi 'spec Miz Marth's missin' urr bruther."

Sister Portula called across to the haremaid. "Don't fret about Horty, he'll be back soon, eating us out of house and home, no doubt. You'll see!"

Martha smiled wanly. "I'm sure he will, Sister, but I can't help feeling concerned about him."

Abbot Carrul put aside his supper and stood up. "What you need is a jolly song. Shall I sing you a little ditty I once learned from a sea otter?"

This surprised Martha. "You singing, Father Abbot?"

Carrul raised his eyebrows. "What's so odd in that, may I ask, miss? Gurvel once said I had a voice like a bird!"

Brother Gelf chuckled. "Aye, a dying duck. Come on then, Carrul, let's hear ye."

The Abbot took a deep breath. "Right, here goes. But you must sing this line at the end of each verse. *Heave haul away, twice around the bay. Yaah!*"

All the Redwallers wanted to see their Abbot singing, so they agreed readily. Carrul tapped the tabletop until he had the rhythm, then launched into the song. For an old mouse, he had quite a strong, ringing baritone.

"On the good ship *Leakylea*,
the captain was a frog,
the mate was a bumblebee,

and the cook was an old hedgehog.
  Heave haul away, twice around the bay. Yaah!

I was born at an early age,
and sent straight off to sea,
with a flea in an iron cage,
on the good ship *Leakylea.*
  Heave haul away, twice around the bay. Yaah!

We sailed the seas so rough,
and never washed the dishes,
ate pans o' skilly'n'duff,
and laughed at all the fishes.
  Heave haul away, twice around the bay. Yaah!

We ate all we could chew,
my flea grew bigger'n me,
'cos he'd ate more'n all the crew,
aboard the *Leakylea.*
  Heave haul away, twice around the bay. Yaah!

The the ship sank in a gale,
I was rescued by my flea,
we're all that's left to tell the tale,
of the poor old *Leakylea.*
  Heave haul away, twice around the bay. Yaaaah!"

Martha applauded, laughing along with the other Red-wallers.

Abbot Carrul bowed modestly and winked at Brother Gelf. "Not bad for a dying duck, eh?"

Remembering her responsibility to the Dibbuns, Martha called to them. "Bedtime, little 'uns, come on now!"

Strangely, the three who were most likely to protest—Muggum, Shilly and Yooch—went quietly. The other Abbeybabes made their usual loud protest, but to no avail.

Sister Setiva wagged a severe paw at them. "Up tae your beds, this verra instant, or ye'll have me tae reckon with!"

Martha watched the last one—Buffle the shrewbabe—scamper through the doorway, where he turned and glared at everybeast. "Kumfuggleworragarrumbubbub . . . Kurch!"

Setiva picked up a ladle and made as if to chase him. "Ah cannae tell what you're sayin', ye wee rogue. But, like as no', 'tis somethin' verra naughty! Ye'd best get toddlin' afore I catch up wi' ye!"

Buffle stood his ground long enough to twiddle a paw to his nose at the shrewnurse, then he bolted off, giggling.

Martha tried hard not to laugh. "Perhaps we'd better go up and tuck them in, Sister?"

Setiva waved a dismissive paw. "Och no, we can do that later. Ah've got tae go an' take supper tae Toran an' Junty first."

The haremaid pushed her chair away from the table. "I'll come and help you. Poor old Toran, I'd forgotten about him. Never mind, there's plenty of crumble left."

Badredd halted his crew at the east wickergate. There was a small door set in the centre of the Abbey's rear wall. He held up a paw for silence. Gently pressing his weight against the timbers, the small fox tried the circular iron ring handle. It was firmly locked shut.

Plumnose held up a little lantern close to the door. "Huh, id's shudd, Chief!"

Badredd had difficulty controlling his voice. "Is it now! Thanks for lettin' me know, bouldernose!"

Plumnose grinned. "T'ink nodding ob it." He turned to Halfchop. "Duh likkel door's locked, I t'ink."

The rat wiped a ribbon of drool from his chin. "Kachunk!"

Badredd rounded on the pair, hissing viciously. "Shut-tup, you two, an' get back into the trees—go on! Flinky, are ye any good at openin' locks?"

The stoat scratched his grimy cheek. "Ah, well, there's locks an' locks, if ye get my meanin', yer 'onour!"

Badredd whipped out his cutlass and thrust it under Flinky's nose. "I never asked ye for a lecture about locks! I said, are you any good at openin' 'em—well, are ye?"

Flinky heaved a sigh and took the cutlass from his chief's paw. "Sure an' I don't know until I try. Shall I give it an ould go?"

Badredd waved him to the door impatiently. "Well, put a move on, we haven't got all night!"

Flinky wedged the swordblade between the door jamb and the wall. He slid the blade down until it clinked dully against something.

"Hah, there's yore problem, Chief, 'tis a bolt. D'ye want me to try an' chop through it?"

The fox exhaled irately. "Anythin', just get on with it!"

Flinky requested the aid of Floggo and Rogg. "Come over t'this door, buckoes. Now put yore shoulders to it. Push now. That'll widen the gap so I can get a grand swing at the bolt. Push, put those ould bows down an' push!"

The door moved slightly under the pressure, creating a thin space. Flinky took the cutlass in both paws, raising it within the gap. Then he struck, whipping the blade down with all his might.

Piiing! As it struck the iron bolt, the blade snapped in half.

Badredd stared in silent horror at the stoat, who—still holding the handle and half a blade—was hopskipping in agony, both paws numbed by the reverberation of metal upon metal.

The vermin leader's voice rose to a disbelieving squeak. "Me sword! Me luvly cutlass! Ye've ruined it! Idiot!"

Tears squeezed from the corners of Flinky's eyes as he flung the half cutlass on the ground. "Aarh, it broke its stupid self. Yore s'posed t'be the chief, why didn't you have a go?"

Badredd seized the broken weapon. "Have a go? I'll have a go at you if ye ain't careful, idiot! An' you lot, a fine crew

I've got, sittin' round scratchin' yerselves among the trees. Up on yer paws, doltheads, we'll have to find someplace else where we can get in. Jump to it!"

As Badredd strode off in foul mood, Plumnose called to him. "Chief, me an' Halfchob hab got de door oben!"

Badredd dashed back to where Plumnose and Halfchop stood in the small doorway. Finding the door still closed, he fumed at them. "Ye blither-brained, wobble-nosed, broken-snouted loafheads! Get goin', afore I carve cobs off'n ye with what's left o' me sword!"

But then, as Plumnose pushed the wicker door gently, it swung inward. "Duh, hawhawhaw, oben!"

Halfchop walked through the open door and grinned. "Kachunk!"

Flinky inspected the wall alongside the door. "Well now, ain't I the clever beast! I must've hit the bolt so hard that it broke through the ould soft sandstone it bolts into. See, there's a chunk of it missin'. Oh, here's the rest of yer grand cutlass, Chief."

He presented the fox with the other half of the blade. Flinging it from him, Badredd turned on the crew and hissed, "You lot, keep yore mouths shut, not a sound out of ye. Foller me, don't go cloghoppin' all over the place. We're goin' to take a look around. Next move is t'get inside the big buildin'. Quietly now . . ."

After taking food out to the west walltop for Toran and Junty, Martha and Sister Setiva returned to the Abbey. Martha stayed in her chair below stairs whilst Setiva went up to the dormitory to check up on the Dibbuns. The shrewnurse was away only for a brief space of time when a dismayed cry reached Martha. Setiva came hurrying back downstairs carrying little Buffle, who was imprisoned in a pillowcase with only his head sticking out.

The Sister's voice shook with barely controlled anger. "Och, jist let me get mah paws on those rascals. Ah'll give 'em somethin' tae remember me by!"

Buffle strained against the pillowcase knotted at his neck. "Goourr, 'ascals!"

A look of fear crossed the haremaid's face. "What's happened, Sister?"

Setiva began trying to release Buffle. "Ooh! Those Dibbuns, Muggum, Shilly an' Yooch. They've gone missing. All the rest o' the wee ones were fast asleep, except Buffle. D'ye see what they did? Trapped 'im in this auld pillowslip so he couldnae follow 'em. Where in the name of all fur have they got to?"

Buffle pulled a paw free and pointed out the Abbey door.

Junty Cellarhog ran his paw around the inside of his bowl and licked it. "Ah, apple'n'blackberry crumble, mate, nothin' like it!"

Toran gazed longingly back toward the Abbey. "Aye, pity we're on wallguard all night. If the Abbot sends out a relief, there might be some left when we get off duty." Toran's keen eye suddenly noticed three small, white-clad figures trundling across the lawn in his direction. Two were waving sticks and one swinging a ladle. He peered hard.

"Look there, mate, that ain't no relief!"

It was at that moment when things began happening fast.

Framed in a shaft of golden light from the Abbey door, Martha and Sister Setiva were pointing to the Dibbuns and calling aloud to them. "Come back here this instant, or you're in real trouble!"

The trio split, Muggum running south and the other two hurrying off to the north.

Toran saw them and chuckled. "Escapin' Dibbuns, eh? They won't get far . . ."

Junty interrupted him roughly. "Look, vermin!"

Badredd and his crew were sneaking quickly out across the lawn, trying to grab Muggum, who was heading for the pond where he planned on hiding in the reeds. The little mole was completely unaware of the enemy. Sister Setiva had come out onto the Abbey steps. As soon as she saw the vermin crew, she began dashing to save Muggum.

Junty was already hurtling down the gatehouse wall-steps, calling back to Toran, "Get the other two little 'uns inside!" He shouted at the shrewnurse. "Stay where ye are, Sister. I'll bring that Dibbun in!"

With his paws, Toran swept up the giggling Shilly and Yooch—this was all one big game to them—then the ottercook turned and pounded toward the Abbey door.

Slipback came within a paw's length of grabbing Muggum, when Junty fetched him a massive whack to the chest, laying the weasel out flat. Then the big Cellarhog seized the molebabe and ran as fast as his footpaws would carry him, with Badredd and the crew hard on his heels. Without stopping, Junty snatched up Sister Setiva from where she had been standing in his path, rigid with fright.

Thud! Thud!

Two arrows from the bows of the ferrets buried themselves in the Cellarhog's broad back. He staggered slightly but kept running. Muggum was screeching, the hedgehog's sharp spines were sticking in his paws as the molebabe tried to struggle free.

Toran sped into the Abbey, dropped both of the other Dibbuns into Martha's lap. "Get ready to slam the door shut!" He panted as he turned and ran back outside to help Junty.

One arrow grazed Toran's cheek, another hit Junty in his right shoulder. Toran shot past the Cellarhog, whirled hard, and caught Crinktail across the face with a huge smack of his rudder. He turned and pushed Junty, with both his burdens, up the steps and into the Abbey, roaring, "Bar the door!"

Redwallers, who had come pouring out of Cavern Hole to see what all the commotion was about, assisted the haremaid in slamming and barring the door in the face of the charging vermin crew. Two more arrows made a hollow sound as they flew into the strong oak timbering. A crash and a tinkle sent Foremole and Brother Weld hurrying to the lower windows.

Toran urged others along with him. "Get tables an' benches! Barricade the lower frames before they get in!"

Badredd waved his broken cutlass. "Keep at it there, crew, we've got 'em on the run!"

Flinky watched a dining table blocking a broken window. He muttered out the side of his mouth to Juppa. "Keep slingin' rocks, but let 'em barricade those windows. They'd eat our liddle gang if'n we got inside. We'd be well outnumbered, mate."

Juppa looked puzzled. "Well, if'n we ain't goin' in, wot's the next move?"

Flinky had served under lots of different vermin chiefs, all a lot smarter than Badredd. He winked confidently at the weasel.

"Lissen t'me. If'n we ain't goin' in, well they ain't gettin' out. Did ye see that great orchard we passed as we came through?"

Badredd came marching around, prodding Flinky with his broken blade. "Wot's that sling doin' empty? Keep chuckin' rocks at those windows until I tell ye to stop. Both of ye!"

Flinky loaded a large pebble into his sling. "Ah, we'll be doin' that, yer 'onour, right away. I was just tellin' ould Juppa here what a clever move ye made."

Badredd was eager to know just what the clever move was. "Aye, well that's alright. You explain it to 'er, she was never too bright. Go on, tell the long-tailed oaf." The small fox stood listening to Flinky's explanation.

"Hoho, we've got the sillybeasts locked up tight now. Prisoners in their own Abbey, 'tis called a siege. There's only a limited supply o' food an' drink in there. Take us now, the chief knows we got the orchard an' the pond. They'll either starve t'death in the Abbey or surrender after awhile. Ain't that right, Chief?"

Only a moment before, Badredd thought he had lost the encounter, but the realisation of what Flinky had just said made him shudder with delight. So that was what a siege was all about.

Keeping a straight face, the fox nodded wisely. "Aye, 'tis a siege, sure enough. Now you two keep slingin'." He swaggered off, shouting orders to the other vermin. Juppa watched him go. "A siege, eh? What a clever idea!"

Flinky launched another stone but missed. He jumped neatly aside as it bounced back at him. "Ah sure, the ould chief is full o' clever ideas, especially when some otherbeast thinks 'em up for 'im. Little fool, he couldn't find his bottom wid both paws!" The weasel and the stoat loaded their slings again, laughing hilariously.

Martha had pulled herself from her chair. She sat on the floor, both eyes shut tight, clutching Junty's paw to her cheek as she rocked back and forth. The Cellarhog was lying where he had fallen, face up. Muggum was wailing as Sister Portula pulled spikes from his side and paws.

Sister Setiva was similarly engaged. "Och, ye've got some fine sharp quills on ye, mah guid Cellarhog. Ah'll be with ye soon as I've got them out o' me. Hauld him still, Martha, how is he?"

With her eyes still shut, Martha kissed his limp paw. "He's dead, Sister. Junty is dead!"

23

A squabbling flock of starlings, disputing rights to an ants' nest, woke Jibsnout in the hour following daybreak. With a cavernous yawn, the big Searat heaved himself upright. He cast a jaundiced eye over the three sons of Wirga who were curled up together, sleeping beneath a wych hazel.

Jibsnout cuffed the trio roughly, stirring them into wakefulness. "Up on yer hunkers, whelps, we're on the move again!"

The three smaller rats rose reluctantly, one of them glaring balefully at the Tracker and hissing. "We only lay down an hour afore dawn."

Jibsnout smirked. "Aye, 'tis a shame, ain't it? Move yerself, snotty snout, an' don't argue wid me. If'n I say ye march, then ye march, so button yer lip!"

Quivering with anger, the smaller rat picked up his little spear—each of his brothers carried one, too. Jibsnout had seen them use the deadly weapons, but not as spears. Although they were actually hollow rods, the spearpoints could be removed, transforming them into blowpipes through which poisoned darts could be shot with lethal accuracy. The big Searat stroked his long dagger fondly and moved closer to the sons of Wirga. He fixed the angry one with a cold stare.

"Go on, mamma's liddle rat, use it, I dare ye. Think yore brave enough t'slay me, eh?"

Lashing out swiftly, Jibsnout knocked the spear from the smaller rat's paws. Whipping out his blade, he menaced the other two. "Just try raisin' one o' those things against me, an' poison or not, I'll rip yer throats out! Well, come on, ye gutless wonders, who's ready fer a fight t'the death?"

The sons of Wirga stood silent, their eyes cast down. Jibsnout curled his lip scornfully, turning his back on them. "Hah, I thought so! There's more backbone in an egg than in youse three put t'gether. Scringin' cowards!"

Each of the three blowpipes was already charged with a poison dart. Silently slipping the head from his spear, the rat whom Jibsnout had insulted placed the hollow rod to his mouth. His cheeks bulged as he prepared to propel the dart.

Zzzzzzip!

A long arrow struck the little rat, driving him back a full four paces. He was dead before he hit the ground.

Diving to either side, the remaining two sons of Wirga sought cover. Lonna emerged from out of the trees, fitting another shaft to his bowstring. The badger's eyes were red with the light of vengeance, the snarl on his scarred, stitched face transforming him into a terrifying apparition. Frightened though he was, Jibsnout, a seasoned fighter, acted swiftly. Wielding his dagger, he dashed forward, hoping to get so close to his adversary that the bow and arrow would be rendered useless.

Lonna was in a dilemma: he could see one of the Searats glancing around a treetrunk, ready to fire a blowpipe, and Jibsnout thundering toward him. With lightning speed the badger acted. Falling into a crouch, he fired his arrow, but only narrowly missed being shot himself as a poison dart whipped by overhead. Jibsnout roared in pain as the arrow transfixed his paw to the ground. As Lonna rose, taking another shaft from his quiver, the Searat who had fired the dart fled off into the woodlands.

The remaining son of Wirga came from behind a fir tree,

certain that he could not fail to hit a target as big as the badger. As he placed the blowpipe to his mouth, Figalok the squirrel appeared directly in front of him, hanging by her tail from an overhead branch. She grabbed the opposite end of the vermin's blowpipe and blew hard. Clutching his throat, the horrified rat fell writhing to the ground, choked on his own poison dart.

Figalok dropped out of the tree, nodding to Lonna. "Cha-haah, gotta be plenny quick wirra Searatta!"

The big badger put up his bow, striving to master the Bloodwrath that was coursing through him. "You saved my life, friend, but I'll have to thank you some other time. One of the Searats got away. I must hunt him down now while his trail is still fresh."

The squirrel gestured at the wounded Jibsnout. "Warra 'bout dissa one, ya goin' to slay 'im?"

Jibsnout crouched over, his face creased in agony. The arrow that had pierced his footpaw was buried half its length into the ground. He glanced up at Lonna, expecting no mercy from him.

"If'n yore gonna finish me off, make it quick, stripedog!"

The badger strode over and grasped the arrow. With a sharp tug he pulled the arrow out, growling at Jibsnout. "I'm no Searat, I don't kill defenceless beasts!" Ripping the sleeve from the rat's frayed tunic, Lonna grabbed a pawful of damp moss and dockleaves.

The puzzled rat watched his enemy binding the wound up tight. "Ye mean yore lettin' me live?"

The badger hauled him upright, slamming him against a tree. "My name is Lonna Bowstripe. Take this message to Raga Bol. Tell him that he and all his crew of murderers are walking deadbeasts. I will find them and slay them, one by one. Even you. Now begone from my sight and deliver my message to your captain. Tell him I am coming, nothing will stop me!"

Lonna and Figalok watched Jibsnout limping painfully off until he was obscured by the trees, then together, the two friends took a brief meal. The squirrel wielded a blow-pipe spear and poison darts taken from the slain Searats.

"Chahaah! Me betcha dis keep Ravin away from squirrel. Lonna Bigbeast, ya goin' after dat Searatta who runned away? Me go witcha, we find 'im afore tomorra."

But the badger would not hear of it. "No, my friend, you have your own home and kinbeasts to protect. This is something I must do by myself. I am sworn by my own oath to rid the earth of Raga Bol and all his vermin. But I thank you for saving my life, Figalok!"

The elderly squirrel took his paw. "Chahaaw, so be't, Lonna, ya are d'true warrior. Ya saved us fromma Ravin, glad Figalok could save ya, too. Me no ferget ya alla me life, always think of ya!"

Averting his eyes, Lonna inspected the long dagger he had taken from Jibsnout, pleased that it was a good blade. When he looked up again, Figalok had gone, vanished into the treetops.

The Searat's trail had gone off to the southeast. Lonna picked it up and followed the tracks. As he walked, the badger fashioned a holder for his dagger, fitting it to his upper left arm close to the shoulder. By late afternoon, the dense woodlands thinned out into pine groves and sand-hills. In the distance, Lonna could make out a dark shape to his left on the horizon. The trail of Wirga's remaining son was running parallel to the mysterious mass. Just before sunset, the badger crested a rise which afforded a clear view of the country he was travelling through. On the one side, the hills bordered a vast, dusty plain, almost like a desert wasteland. On the other side, the odd dark mass reared up into a towering line of forbidding cliffs. After awhile it grew too dark for tracking. Reaching the cliff face, Lonna sighted what he knew was a cave. He climbed up and made camp there for the night.

There was no need for a fire. The night was still and

warm, with heat waves drifting in from the plain. Knowing he could pick up the Searat's tracks at dawn, Lonna sat in the cave entrance, eating an apple and some dried fruit. He gazed up at the night sky, where a sliver of moon, resembling a slice of russet apple, was surrounded by myriads of stars twinkling in the firmament. The words of an old song rose unbidden to his mind.

"When weary day does shed its light,
I rest my head and dream,
I ride the great dark bird of night,
so tranquil and serene.
Then I can touch the moon afar,
which smiles up in the sky,
and steal a twinkle from each star,
as we go winging by.

We'll fly the night to dawning light,
and wait 'til dark has ceased,
to marvel at the wondrous sight,
of sunrise in the east.
So slumber on, my little one,
float soft as thistledown,
and wake to see when night is done,
fair morning's golden gown."

Since Lonna had no recollection of his parents, he surmised that the lullaby had been taught to him by Grawn, the old badger who had reared him.

Lonna stayed that night in the cave on the cliffside. As day dawned he spotted a tiny puff of dust, on a hilltop off to his right. The big badger knew instantly that it was his quarry. The Searat must have spent the night amid the hills, not far from the cave. Pausing only to grab his bow and quiver, Lonna set off in pursuit.

He had travelled no further than the base of the first foothill when he was faced by a small patrol of ten Darrat rats. Their leader eyed him insolently up and down.

"Dis be Darrat land. You give me bow'n'arrers, stripedog. We take ye to Hemper Figlugg!" He grinned at the other rats, murmuring to them, "Much Burcha Glugg, eh?"

Had it been ten rats or twenty, Lonna did not like either their manner or their disposition, so he charged them without warning. They went down like ninepins under the giant badger's onslaught. Seizing the leader of the patrol, Lonna hurled him bodily into the other rats. Then the big badger was among them like a whirlwind—punching, kicking, butting, thrashing them with their own spears. So surprised were the Darrat that they fled in panic, kicking up sand widespread as they scuttled off amid the hills.

Lonna picked up his bow and quiver. Then, throwing back his great striped head, he gave vent to the fearsome warcry of hares and badgers. "Eulaliiiiiaaaaaa!"

However, with much more urgent business to attend to, he let the Darrat be, and didn't give chase. Instead, Lonna set off swiftly on the trail of the Searat.

When the Darrat saw they were not being pursued, they halted on the plain beside the foothills. The patrol leader limped up, carrying half a broken spear. He watched the big badger crossing a hilltop, some distance off.

Turning to his subordinates, who were sitting licking their wounds, he snarled, "We was sent to catcher rabbert, mouse an' squirri', not stripedog! Huh, let High Kappin catcher that 'un—'e be over dat way wid many Darrat!"

The Searat saw Lonna coming after him. Deserting the hills, he dashed out onto the dusty plain. It was a mistake, the last mistake he was ever to make. The badger's arrow found him. Once Lonna had the range, nobeast could outrun a shaft from his big bow. Though Wirga did not know, she had lost all three of her sons.

Lonna sat down in a hollow amid the hills and made breakfast from the food in his pack.

*

Out on the flatlands the five travellers pushed forward, keeping the distant cliffs in view. They marched shoulder to shoulder because, as Saro had pointed out, that way they would not be eating one another's dust. Since their rescue, Springald and Fenna were paying more attention to Bragoon and Saro. Seasoned campaigners both, the squirrel and the otter were ever ready to share their knowledge with the younger, less experienced trio.

Horty was feeling rather chipper now that any immediate danger was past. He struck up a jolly marching song, to which he himself had written the lyrics. As was usual with hare songs, it dealt mainly with food.

"Oh wallop me left an' stagger me right,
an' buffet me north an' south,
if I could teach a stew to walk,
it'd march right into me mouth!

To pasties an' pies of convenient size,
I'd beat a tattoo on me drum,
so jolly forceful, each tasty morsel,
tramp over me gums to me tum!

As each of 'em trips in through me lips,
all skippin' along to the beat,
why all of a sudden I'd grab a fat pudden,
an' leave it no way to retreat!

Form up in line, you vittles so fine,
watch y'dressin' that salad back there,
a quick salute to trifle'n'fruit,
then charge down the throat of the hare!

Quick march! One two! Scoff 'em all! You an' you!
Left right! Left right! Here comes supper for tonight!"

A grey, black-flecked Darrat scout came loping into the camp in the foothills of the high cliffs. He threw himself flat in front of High Kappin Birug, the Darrat leader. Pointing back to the scrubland, the rat scout shouted, "Burcha Glugg!"

Birug dashed past him to the top of a hill. He crouched, peering at the small dust cloud with the travellers marching in front of it, not half a mile away. Smirking with satisfaction, Birug turned to the others who had followed him.

"Hemper Figlugg, trus' me, ho yar, I know dey only go one way. Run for bigrocks. We wait, they be come to us. Burcha Glugg!"

Darrat vermin shook their heads in admiration of Kappin Birug's cunning. One of them piped up. "Hemper be 'appy to see Burcha Glugg come back." The more excited of the Darrat leaped up and down, waving spears.

Birug growled a warning at them. "Keepa 'eads down, idjits!"

Horty glanced up at the sky. "Cloudin' over up there, chaps. We might have a spot of jolly old rain before nightfall, wot?"

Bragoon sniffed the light breeze. "Bit more'n a spot, matey. Looks like we're in for a downpour afore dark. Keep movin', step the pace up. Mebbe we'll find shelter in the lee of those big cliffs."

Fenna let out a gasp and sat down. "Ouch, my footpaw!"

They gathered around her, crouching down to take a look. The squirrelmaid spoke through lips that hardly moved. "Stay down, all of you, don't look toward those foothills!"

Bragoon kept his eyes on Fenna. "Why, what's goin' on?"

She quickly responded. "Rats ahead, they look like those flesh-eating ones!"

Springald automatically began to look up, but Sarobando pressed her head back down. "Listen to Fenna an' keep yore eyes down, miss. How many d'ye reckon there are?"

Bragoon interrupted. "Plenty, I'll wager. Too many for us to fight off. I told ye, those vermin don't give up easily.

They've been waitin' in the foothills for us to show up. Well, mates, wot's t'be done, eh?"

Fenna shrugged. "I suppose we'll have to run for it."

Bragoon shook his head. "Bad idea! They'd outcircle us."

Horty began shrugging off his backpack. "Does any chap mind me makin' a suggestion, wot?"

Saro saw that the young hare looked serious. "As long as 'tis sensible. Go on then, wot's yore idea?"

Horty shed his backpack. "Give me some old, dead brush, an' I'll decoy the rotters. A hare can jolly well outrun 'em if anybeast can. I'll take the villains off one way, while you lot go runnin' off the bally opposite way. See that black hole up there, about halfway along the cliffs? I'll meet y'back there after dark. Well, what d'you think?"

Springald objected. "It's far too dangerous. You'll be caught."

Saro stared at Horty. "I say give it a try, it might work. Otherwise, we'll just stick together and get nabbed."

Bragoon winked at the hare. "Right, go to it, young 'un. Good luck!"

Two Darrat spies peeped over the hilltop, to where the dust cloud had stopped. One whispered. "Warra dey do now, jus' lay dere?"

The other one leaped up as the dust plume started again, moving swiftly north. "Musta see'd us, dey runnin' now, fast!"

He waved his spear, calling to Birug, who had the rats standing ready, "Kappin, dey go lef' plenty fasta!"

Horty pelted along with a bunch of dead bracken tied to his tail, raising a dust cloud that stood out light brown against the lowering clouds. Glancing sideways, he saw the Darrat rats pouring over the hill, veering in his direction. He muttered between clenched teeth.

"Ahah! That's the way, you vile vermin. Come on, you shower, follow Hortwill Braebuck, skimmer of the scrublands!"

Fenna raised her head. In the distance she could see the dust cloud off to her left. "Good old Horty, he's whipping along like a whirlwind!"

Still crouching low, they watched their friend's progress, comparing it to the crowd of Darrat vermin chasing him. Horty was indeed a Redwaller, brave and courageous. Springald felt elation and pride surging through her. She clenched her paws.

"Go on, mate, there's none faster than you! Flesh eaters, hah! All those scum will eat is the dust in his wake! Run them, Horty, show those rats what a hare from our Abbey can do!"

As soon as Bragoon saw the two dust plumes, he realised that the Darrat had come out of the hills and hit the scrubland. Their intended quarry was far and away out in front. The otter's eyes shone with admiration.

"I said that young 'un has the makins of a real warrior. He'll lead 'em a merry dance alright. Oh, drat, here comes the rain!"

24

Large drops began falling, slow at first, sending up small puffs of dust as they struck the dry plain. A distant thunder rumble echoed from the high cliffs, followed by a faroff flash of lightning that illuminated the southeast horizon. Then the deluge fell in earnest. Saro stood upright, blowing water from her nosetip as she blinked at the sheeting curtains of heavy rain.

"Nobeast can see us now. Let's head straight for the cliffs!"

Joining paws, they jogtrotted toward the foothills, battered by the relentless downpour. Lightning ripped over the dark skies in blinding sheets, while thunder boomed and banged overhead. Dust turned quickly to mud, their paws squelched into it. Springald tightly gripped the paws of Fenna and Saro. The intensity of the storm was frightening, she had never been out in open country at such a time before. At Redwall, it had been relatively easy to run inside and shelter from the elements, but out here it was different.

They gained the foothills, slipping and sliding up the wet grass. Bragoon shielded his eyes as he glanced upward.

"Keep goin', it ain't too far now. Yonder black hole that Horty spotted looks like it could be a cave of some sort. Let's make it up that far an' shelter."

Horty's wet paws slapped down in the sludge and mud. Wiping water from his eyes, he chanced a backward glimpse at his pursuers. Although the main body were still a respectable distance off, three fast runners had broken away and were coming doggedly onward, closing the distance considerably. The young hare bit his lip. The trio were armed with spears; if they got within throwing range, he would be finished. It was time for a change of plan. Still with stamina in reserve, Horty shot off to the right, back among the foothills, where he stood a chance of losing the Darrat mob.

Birug panted, squinching his eyes against the rain as he saw the hare change course and dart into the dunes. The High Kappin urged his rats on. "Catchim, or Hemper Figlugg make Burcha Glugg outta you!"

Topping a rise, Horty spotted the barely discernible hole in the cliffside, far along to his right. He tripped and went rolling downhill. Spitting grit and coated with sand, he swiftly picked himself up and pounded on to the next dune, muttering to himself, "Ears up, old lad, keep pickin' 'em up an' puttin' 'em down, wot. Huh, if only the young skin'n'blister could see her handsome brother now—a blinkin', gallopin' sandbeast!"

A spear buried itself in the sand, not far behind him.

Birug appeared at the top of the hill that Horty had just come over. Two others trailed behind him. He seized the spear from one of them and flung it. The Darrat leader's aim was bad—he watched the spear strike the hillside flat and slide back down. Birug rested a moment on all fours, fatigued.

Horty gained the next hilltop and turned. Holding a paw to his nose, he wiggled it and called out cheekily, "Bloomin' old flesh scoffer, go an' boil your own head an' eat it, wot wot!"

Stung by the hare's jibe, Birug hauled himself upright

and came after the hare with renewed energy. Horty scuttled off, chiding himself for his momentary foolishness.

"Have to keep the old lip buttoned, wot! Seems a jolly determined type o' cove for a rat, full of the old vermin vinegar. Curse his caddish hide!"

Afternoon passed, without the rain slackening its intensity. It was humid, without a trace of breeze. Rivulets gathered into swollen streams, racing down the cliffside in floods of umber-hued water.

Bragoon was first to reach the black hole. His prediction had been correct: it was a cave—large, dark and deep. He helped Springald and Fenna enter first, while Sarobando brought up the rear. Once inside, all four flopped down, exhausted. The otter shook himself like a dog and shrugged off the packs he had been burdened with.

"Whoo! Wretched weather, wonder when this rain's due to stop?" He sat up against the right wall, peering out. "Come on Horty, mate, where've ye got to?"

Fenna joined him. "I hope he's alright!"

Springald rose and began to wander off to explore the big cave, but Bragoon pulled her back.

"You stay close up here, miz. We don't know wot might be back there. Can't risk a fire, either—too dangerous. Break out some vittles, if'n they're still dry enough, and a drink, too. Funny how ye can be out in the rain all day an' still be thirsty."

The mousemaid found dry oatcakes and some crystallised fruit, which they washed down with some home-brewed cider. Fenna stared out into the persistent downpour, then jumped slightly as thunder boomed out overhead.

Saro patted her shoulder. "Nought t'do but sit an' wait, matey. Don't fret now, that young rogue'll make it."

The squirrelmaid forced a smile. "If he's not here soon, I'll light a fire and make a pot of soup. Horty can smell vittles a league away. He'll show up then, I wager."

She sat miserably, pondering the foolishness of her statement. Horty could be lying slain out there in the rain.

Horty staggered gamely on, the three rats not more than six paces behind him. They had picked up their spears again and thrown them at him several times. With the courage of desperation, the young hare, having managed to avoid the throws, remained unscathed. Birug and his two rats had left the spears where they fell, and carried on, stubbornly pursuing the fugitive. It was only a matter of time now, and they would have him. As the High Kappin blundered forward, Horty moved out of his reach.

With his tongue lolling, the rat gasped out, "We . . . catcha!"

Horty stumbled, tripped and wriggled out of his reach. Gaining his footpaws, he stood panting. "Couldn't . . . catch your old . . . grannie . . . Slobberchops!" He blundered on another pace or two, then collapsed.

Birug nodded to the other two rats. "Gerrim . . . now!"

All three crawled forward on their bellies, reaching out to lay paws on the fallen hare when, without warning, the hillside gave way, sliding down a tremendous avalanche of wet sand. It enveloped the three rats completely, burying them under a huge mound.

Horty lay at the edge of the mass, covered right up to his neck. He was trapped fast. A paw, almost the size of his own head, seized both of the hare's long ears and yanked him out with one mighty pull. Horty revived with the pain, his eyes flickering open. He stayed conscious just long enough to see a lightning flash illuminate the head of a giant badger with a scar running lengthwise down its striped muzzle.

The young hare blinked. "Nice weather, wot . . . Oh, corks!" Then he passed out.

Only the Dibbuns slept upstairs in their dormitories that night, while every other Redwaller guarded the barricades.

It was the longest, saddest night Martha had ever witnessed. The still form of Junty had been wrapped tenderly in blankets and borne down to the place he loved best, his cellars. Clearing the barrels and lifting some floorstones, Foremole Dwurl and his crew dug a grave for the good Cellarhog. Junty was laid to rest. Once the grave was filled in and the flooring stones replaced, Abbot Carrul took a charcoal and wrote words upon it. At some later day the moles would chisel the words into the stones as a permanent epitaph for a beast whom all Redwallers loved dearly. Tears often smudged the charcoal letters as Carrul wrote:

"Here lies a fallen warrior, slain by vermin whilst helping his fellow creatures. Hard working, good and faithful. A credit to his kind. Always a kind word or smile to all. Junty Cellarhog, Keeper of Redwall Abbey cellars. His October Ale was the best. Rest peacefully, old friend."

Above stairs, Martha rolled her cart around Great Hall, relieving those who were wearied. When she was not doing that, the tireless haremaid helped Granmum Gurvel to ferry food from the kitchens.

Toran watched Martha—she was never still, always finding something to do for the common good. He halted the little cart with his rudder. "Come on, beauty, time ye took a nap or ye'll be worn out."

Martha protested. "I'm fine, honestly I am!"

But, deaf to her pleas, the ottercook opened the lap rug and tucked it beneath the haremaid's chin. "No arguments now. I'll wake ye if'n yore needed, miss. You stay out the way here, in this quiet corner away from broken glass an' slingstones. I'll have t'go an' get more stuff to barricade those windows."

He hurried off to assist Brother Weld, who was struggling with a door he had taken from its hinges. "Here, Brother, you take one end an' I'll take the other."

Weld sighed thankfully. "We're getting a bit old for this sort of thing. D'you think we'll hold them off, Toran?"

Gritting his teeth, the big otter growled. "Filthy scum, if

they get in this Abbey, 'twill be over my dead body. Don't worry, Brother, we'll keep 'em out!"

Old Phredd helped them to shore the door up against the windows. "Huh, the way I see it, we're under siege. 'Tis those vermin who are keeping us in!"

Toran clenched his paws tightly. "That's right. Strange ain't it, bein' kept prisoner inside yore own home."

Old Phredd added miserably, "Aye, what do we do if the food runs out?"

Toran's clenched paw wagged under the ancient Gate-keeper's nose. "Quit that kind o' talk now, d'ye hear me? There's vittles aplenty for all, so don't go scarin' every-beast!"

Badredd watched the dawn wash the skies in rosy hues. The small fox was in his element. "Flinky, Crinktail, c'mere. I got a plan o' me own at last!"

Both stoats, stuffing themselves on orchard produce, continued eating as Badredd explained his scheme.

"Load up a couple o' sacks an' take a stroll through the woods south of here. Eat what y'like as ye go."

Flinky tossed away a half-eaten pear. "Sounds like a good ould job, Chief, but what're we supposed t'be doin'?"

The little fox grinned craftily. "Recruitin' more vermin. We need more beasts to take this place. Tell 'em that Red-wall is bein' conquered by Badredd an' a vermin crew. Aye, an' tell 'em there'll be plenty o' vittles an' booty for anybeast who'll serve under me. Have ye got that?"

Flinky saluted elaborately. "Leave it to us, Chief. We'll bring ye back a gang o' the best, so we will. No old or fee-ble ones, just grand fightin' vermin. But wot about all this ripe ould fruit?"

Badredd snorted impatiently. "Use yore head, give it away to any vermin ye come across. Show 'em we got plenty of vittles. Say there's lots more where that comes from, if they'll come an' serve under me. Do I have to tell ye everything?"

Crinktail touched the side of her nose knowingly. "We unnerstand, Chief, leave it to me'n Flinky." The pair hurried off to the orchard to load up sacks of fruit.

Badredd began issuing orders to his depleted crew. "Floggo, Rogg, watch that big door, an' the windows, too. Keep yore bows'n'arrows at the ready. Kill anybeast wot pokes his nose out!"

The little fox was glad he had the weasel brothers to serve him. They never argued and usually obeyed all orders.

"Juppa, Slipback, Plumnose, Halfchop, keep slingin' stones at those windows. Whatever ye do, don't stop!"

Juppa was pawsore and weary of slinging stones. "But we've smashed all the windows. Wot else is there t'keep slingin' stones at?"

Badredd could feel his temper fraying. His voice gained a squeak as he shouted in the weasel's face. "The idea of breakin' the windows is so that ye can hurl stones through an' hit anybeast inside the place. Or are ye too stupid to realise that?"

Juppa stood her ground, arguing back swiftly. "No, I ain't stupid, but I'm hungry an' tired! Us four've been chuckin' stones at that Abbey all night. Oh, an' there's one more thing we ain't too stupid to realise. We're runnin' outta stones to throw, while yore marchin' about givin' orders out an' doin' little else!"

Badredd waved his broken cutlass about threateningly. "Don't ye dare talk t'me like that, I'm the chief around here!"

Slipback muttered loudly. "Wot're ye goin' t'do, run 'er through wid a broken sword?"

The little fox threw his half cutlass aside and stamped his footpaw down so hard that it hurt. "I heard that, Slipback. Do? I'll tell ye wot I'm goin' to do. I'm goin' t'show ye three how to sling stones properly! Throw down wot stones ye got left an' give me yore slings. Plumnose, Halfchop, start slingin' alongside me. Come on, move yoreselves, take these slings an' load up!"

Halfchop picked up a sling and loaded it with an apple he had been munching on. He grinned at Badredd. "Kachunk!"

The little fox glared speechlessly at the hapless rat. He shouted to Plumnose, "Teach that idjit to throw stones!"

Furiously, Badredd began slinging at a mad rate. The slingstones went everywhere—a few through the window spaces, some backward across the lawns when he released them too early. Others bounced back off the solid sandstone walls.

Slipback dodged a ricochet, grinning slyly. "Hah, let's see 'ow long the mighty chief can keep that pace up!"

Juppa started moving out of range, ducking a pebble that had gone the wrong way. "Let's get out of 'ere afore we get slain!"

She raised her voice, calling to Badredd, "We're goin' to get somethin' to eat an' take a rest!"

The fox kept hurling stones like a madbeast, panting. "Get out o' my sight, ye useless lumps! When y'come back, bring more stones, a lot more!"

Plumnose, who was slinging at a much steadier rate, called happily to Badredd. "Huhuh, we'b godd lots ob stones, me'n my mate!"

The fox screeched back at him. "Sharrap an' get slingin'!"

Halfchop had found a black-and-red banded pebble among his stones. He polished it on his fur and spoke to it. "Kachunk!"

25

Abbot Carrul and Granmum Gurvel were going around Great Hall, distributing beakers of hot barley and leek soup to the defenders. Martha was wakened by a stone pinging off a nearby column. Gurvel ladled soup from a cauldron standing on a trolley. The Abbot served it to Martha. Then Carrul called Toran over and gave him some.

Toran accepted it gratefully. "Well, Father, the windows are barricaded tight now. There's only the odd stone comin' through. Let the vermin wear themselves out. Apart from broken panes, there ain't much damage—unless they try burnin' the window barricades."

Carrul tried to remain calm, though he could not help sounding anxious. "Have you a plan in mind, Toran?"

Scratching his rudder, the ottercook stifled a yawn. "I wish I had, but I'm far too tired an' upset about pore Junty."

Martha straightened the rug across her lap. "We'd do better if we went upstairs to the dormitories. Perhaps up there we could retaliate against the vermin."

Abbot Carrul nodded. "Sounds sensible to me, Martha. Carry on."

Warming to her own idea, the haremaid explained. "We could make slings and throw stones at them. I'll wager Foremole and his crew could provide us with rubble."

Gurvel sighted Foremole Dwurl coming up from the cellars. She beckoned him to join them. "Coom over yurr, zurr."

Dwurl waved a heavy digging claw. "Wutt can oi do furr ee?"

Martha made her request. "Would it be possible to get a load of rubble and pebbles up to the dormitory windows, please?"

The mole nodded his velvety head. "Surpintly, miz! Oi take ett ee bee's goin' t'give yon varmints a gudd peltin', hurr hurr!"

Immensely fond of Foremole Dwurl, Martha took his work-lined paw in hers. "Great minds think alike, my friend. We need lots of stones, and some rubble, to tip on the vermin if they start lighting fires. Water is too precious to waste in our present position."

Toran looked at his young friend with a new respect. "Hear that, Carrul? Our Martha certainly has a wise head on her shoulders, eh?"

Martha turned to the ottercook, her eyes shining fiercely. "Aye, and I don't intend to lose it to a band of murdering vermin. It was vermin who slew my family when I was a babe and too young to do anything about it. This time 'tis going to be different. No matter what happens, those evil scum are not going to take Redwall Abbey from us. We'll defeat them!"

They all clasped paws on the arm of the haremaid's chair. Her resolution ran like wildfire through them all.

Father Abbot Carrul's voice echoed around Great Hall. "Everybeast upstairs to the front dormitories. We're going to fight them. Redwaaaaaaalll!"

A great cheer went up as Martha had united them in a common cause: taking the attack to the foebeast. The Redwallers thundered upstairs, shouting and roaring.

"We'll teach 'em a lesson they won't forget!"

"Aye, they'll regret the day they came to our Abbey!"

"No vermin's goin' to bully us!"

234

"Blood'n'vinegar, that's what they'll get!"

Sister Setiva was minding the Dibbuns as the dormitory door was flung open wide. Redwallers crowded in, still shouting. The Abbeybabes did not quite know what was going on, but they joined in lustily, issuing dire threats against the enemy.

"Cutta tails off wiv rusty knifes!"

"Boil ee varmints in roasted baffwater!"

"Gurr, smack ee bottoms wi' gurt sticks!"

Little Buffle stuck out his stomach and bellowed, "Yukkumbumgur!"

Setiva was becoming able to translate Buffle's baby language. She raised her eyebrows in horror. "Och, ye wee scallywag, I'll wash your mouth out wi' soap if ye even think o' sayin' that again!"

Martha was carried up, chair and all, by Brother Weld, Toran and several stout moles. Immediately she related her plan to all the Abbeybeasts.

"Sisters Setiva and Portula, could you set about making lots of slings? Good, strong braided ones. Brothers Gelf and Weld, I want you to check the downstairs barricades as often as you can. Make sure they're still holding firm, and report back to me each time. Foremole, sir, can you bring up as much stone and rubble as you can lay your paws on?"

Dwurl saluted. "We'm got loads o' rubble an' rock frum our diggin's in ee basement, miz. Oi'll bring et roight aways."

The haremaid nodded to Toran. "Can you search about, friend, to find anything we can use as weapons? Anything!"

Muggum and the Dibbuns clung to the chairarms, pleading, "Uz 'elp ee, Miz Marth', give us'n's summ jobs!"

Sister Setiva turned in the dormitory doorway, shaking her blackthorn stick and berating the Abbeybabes. "Och! Ah'll give ye jobs. Get straight intae yon beds an' stay oot o' Miss Martha's way, this verra instant!"

Martha saw the sad little faces on the Dibbuns and interceded on their behalf to the strict Infirmary Keeper. "Please,

Sister, they only want to help. Let me find a job for them. Granmum Gurvel, have you any sieves or riddles? We'll need them to sift out slingstones from Foremole's rubble when it arrives up here. Could you find some?"

Muggum brightened up. "Oi'll tell ee a riggle, Miz Marth'."

Gurvel took the molebabe's paw. "Gurr, liddle pudden 'ead, that bee's ee wrong sort o' riggle. Cumm to ee kitchens, an' oi'll foind ee sum proper riggles."

Everybeast hurried to their tasks, while Martha tried to keep some organisation amid the ensuing chaos.

Molecrews trundled in and out of the dormitory, bearing stretcherloads of rubble. Sister Portula and some elders ripped old fabric into strips and began weaving slings. Redwallers on kitchen duty came scurrying up with drinks and meals. Martha wheeled her chair about, giving directions, calling encouragement and keeping the constant traffic moving back and forth.

"Don't block the doorway, please. Bring that stretcher right in and empty it there, by the window." She seemed to be everywhere at once. "Oh, that's a nice strong sling, put it over there with the others. Don't leave that cordial and soup by the rubble, it'll get dust all over it. Shut it inside that wardrobe for the present."

Badredd soon grew tired of slinging stones. His paws were aching: more than once, a stone had stayed in the sling, causing it to wrap around his paw and strike it sharply. That, plus the fact that he was an abominable shot, made him toss the sling away angrily.

"Blood'n'skulls, I've got better things t'do than stand here chuckin' stones all day. Where's the rest o' this lazy lot, eh? Stuffin' vittles or layin' about sleepin', I bet. Well, I'll soon liven their ideas up, the dirty layabouts!" He stalked off in high dudgeon.

Plumnose and Halfchop dropped their slings and trailed

after him. The little fox turned on them furiously. "Where are you two deadbrains goin'? Did I tell ye t'stop slingin'? Get back there afore I flay ye both!" The pair went back wearily and continued slinging.

Plumnose complained resentfully to his companion. "Huh, he'd inna bad mood, iddent he?"

Halfchop nodded in agreement. "Kachunk!"

Martha kept track of Badredd from her position at the front dormitory windows. "I wonder where he's off to now."

Toran stood behind her chair. "Who knows, miss. He's up t'no good, though, an' jumpin' mad by the look o' him."

Foremole gestured at the considerable mound of earth and stone piled up close to the windowsills. "Hurr, ee vurmint can jump all ee looikes, we'm ready for 'im!"

Granmum Gurvel staggered in, dragging a bulging sack. "Yurr, lookit oi finded, ee gurt sack uv 'otroot pepper. Ee 'hotters leaved it yurr afore they'm go'd off. Oi'm b'aint a keepen it in moi kitchens, no zurr, orful sneezy stuff!" Gurvel dumped it next to Martha's chair. The haremaid quickly pulled out her kerchief as dust rose from the sack. "Kerchoo! Aah . . . Aah . . . Achoo! Beg your pardon, dearie me!"

Baby Buffle stared down at the sack from the top of the rubble mound. "Sumakivalikkasaccasaccavurgimchoochoo!"

Martha dabbed at her nose with the kerchief. "What's he chunnering on about now, Sister?"

Setiva translated the shrewbabe's language. "Och, pay no heed tae the rascal. He says we should throw et at yon vermin. 'Tis a silly idea—we'd be sneezed tae death doin' a thing like that. The breeze'd carry et right back in 'ere."

Gurvel spoke up. "Nay, marm, not if us'n's makes ee likle sacks uv pepper, boi 'okey. We'm cudd frow slingers at ee varmints."

Martha clapped her paws delightedly. "What a great plan! Thank you, Buffle and Gurvel. Let's try it!"

The ancient molecook took charge of the operation. Soon, she and several Dibbuns donned bandannas of wet cloth to protect their noses and mouths against the fiery hotroot pepper. Carefully, they ladled measured portions of the pepper onto flimsy squares of thin, birch-bark parchment. Each of these was fashioned into a tiny bundle, tied at the top with thread. Toran weighed one in his paw. "Just right for throwin'. Hoho, these'll cause a few sneezes if they land on some scummy noses!"

Yooch the molebabe had scrambled up onto a windowsill. Jumping up and down, he waved his tiny paws and squealed, "Look out, look out, d'vermints bee's cummin'!"

Badredd kept a paw on the broken cutlass in his belt, not drawing the weapon lest they see it was only a half-bladed thing. Behind him stood the rest of the available vermin crew—Halfchop, Floggo, Rogg, Slipback, Plumnose and Juppa.

The little fox shouted boldly. "Where's yore chief? I wanna talk!"

Abbot Carrul showed himself at the dormitory window. "Say what you have got to say, fox!"

Badredd puffed out his narrow chest. "Lissen, we've got ye well boxed in up there. You ain't warriors, ye can't fight back or hurt us. So I'll tell ye what I'll do. Open yore doors, we won't attack. Just let me'n one o' my crew come in. When we've found yore magic sword, an' other bits o' loot that we fancy, we'll leave ye in peace an' go."

The Abbot shook his head firmly. "Never! You'll not set paw in Redwall Abbey, none of you!"

Badredd passed a paw signal to Rogg from behind his back. The weasel casually notched an arrow to his bowstring.

Keeping his temper in check, the fox replied, "Never? We'll see about that. Wot ye got to unnerstand is that yore under siege—we could starve ye out or keep attackin' until one by one yore all slain. Oh, I've got lots o' bright ideas, mouse, take yore pick. Either that or just do as I command. 'Twill save ye a lot o' grief."

Carrul stood his ground. "No matter what you say, you will not enter this Abbey. Now, let me make a suggestion. Take your vermin, plus all the fruit you have stolen from our orchard, and leave here. If you do this, you will save yourself a lot of grief. Take my word for it!"

Badredd shrugged. "Ain't no use of talkin' to ye, mouse."

As the vermin leader stepped aside, Rogg hurried forward and let fly. Inside the dormitory, some of the pepper dust had got to the Abbot, causing him to sneeze. "Yaachooo!"

As Carrul's head went down with the force of the sneeze, the arrow tipped his headfur, ending up quivering in the dormitory ceiling.

Cursing inwardly, Badredd forced himself to stay nonchalantly calm, even to smile. "Saved by a sneeze, eh? Yore a lucky mouse!"

Suddenly Toran appeared at the window, a pepper bomb in each paw. "You won't be so lucky. Sneeze on this, snottynose!"

In quick succession, two bags of pepper struck Badredd's face. Then the dormitory windows were packed with Redwallers, hurling their new weapons and shouting.

"Try a sniff of this, uglychops!"

"Yurr, stuff this'n oop ee nose, zurr vurmint!"

"Och, take a whiff o' this, ye wicked rabble!"

"Sorry we ain't got no salt, so here's a little more pepper for ye!"

Literally peppered by bags of the stuff, the vermin crew fled—spitting, sneezing and rubbing at their burning eyes as the fierce hotroot pepper did its work. Between sneezes, they bumped blindly into one another, wailing and screeching.

Martha held up a paw. "Stop now, no use wasting pepper. They've learned their lesson, a good hot one!"

A rousing cheer went forth from the Abbeybeasts. "Red-waaaaaallll!"

Martha hugged Toran's waist from her chair. "We did it, friend, we defeated the vermin!"

The ottercook stood watching the vermin as they hurled themselves into the Abbey pond. He stroked the haremaid's head absently. "Aye, beauty, we did it for now. But they'll be back, an' next time they do, those vermin will try to slay us all."

Sister Portula was in agreement with him. "Right, Toran, so what'll we do then?"

Martha surprised herself by shaking a clenched paw. "We'll just have to give back as good as we get. Don't forget, there's more of us than them. I'd risk my life willingly any day if it meant defeating those scum!"

Growls of agreement rang out, even from the Dibbuns. Abbot Carrul was taken aback by the warlike mood of the Redwallers, and even more so by Martha's fighting spirit. He held up his paws until order was restored.

"You are right, of course, my friends, but let us not do anything haphazard. There has to be a proper plan to rid our Abbey of these vermin!"

Flinky and Crinktail were in no special hurry to run about seeking recruits for Badredd's gang. The pair wandered deep into Mossflower, glad to be away from the bickering and squabbling of the small vermin gang. They rambled onward, consenting with each other to desert their fellow vermin and find a new life together, far away from it all.

Unfortunately, they walked right into trouble and ambled straight into the camp of Raga Bol. A huge, fat Searat with one milky, sightless eye grabbed the luckless pair by the scruffs of their necks. Both their stomachs churned in fear at the sight of the savage Searat crew. For the first time in his life, Flinky was rendered speechless as he beheld a real Searat captain.

Raga Bol was the complete picture of a barbarian chief-

tain—from his hooped brass earrings and tawdry s
ery, to his silver hook, gold teeth, curved scimitar ar
lethal stiletto he was using to pick at a roasted pike. He
a fishbone into the fire and picked at his teeth with
hook. Looking both stoats up and down, Raga Bol con
sulted the fat rat.

"Who are these two barnacles, Glimbo?"

Flinky began stammering out an answer. "If it please,
yore 'onour, we was just . . ."

Splat! Raga Bol leaned forward and struck Flinky a slap
across his mouth with the pike. "Did I speak to ye, stoat?"

The hook shot out, catching Flinky's jerkin. He was
yanked forward, under the cold glare of the wickedest eyes
he had ever looked into.

He felt the Searat's hot breath on his face as the rasping
voice growled out, "Guard yore tongue, mudbrain, or I'll
carve it out an' feed it to ye. Speak now, wot's in those
sacks?"

Flinky's throat bobbed as he gasped out, "F . . . f . . . fruit,
sir!"

Raga Bol stuck his stiletto in the sack Flinky was holding.
He booted the stoat backward, causing the blade to rip
through the sack. Flinky went sprawling amid the fruit
which spilled out onto the ground.

The Searat scowled. "Fruit? Is that all ye brought? No
booty, weapons, not even a brace o' birds or a decent fish.
Just fruit!"

Glimbo wrenched the sack from Crinktail. He emptied it
over Flinky, who lay cringing on the ground. "Sink me! This
'un's brought fruit as well, Cap'n. They must be both
stoopid in d'brain!"

Gripping hold of Crinktail, Glimbo shook her until her
teeth rattled, bellowing in the hapless stoat's face. "Yore
stoopid in d'brain, wot are ye?"

Crinktail gabbled out something that sounded like
"Stooballainnabrab!"

The Searats crowded round laughing. They tore the

jerkins from both stoats, and robbed them of their belts and knives.

Stripped to the fur, Flinky and Crinktail huddled together, eyes wide with terror as the Searats licked their knifeblades and winked wickedly at them.

Raga stroked under his chin, with the polished curve of his pawhook. "The woodlands round here are packed with fruit, an' ye bring me two sacks o' the stuff? Right then, me beauties, I'll tell ye what we'll do. What'd ye like, an apple or a pear?"

Crinktail spoke, her voice quivery with terror. "Apples, sir."

Raga smiled, showing several gold-capped fangs. "Haharr, apples it is then. Ferron, jam an apple apiece in their gobs, 'twill stop 'em singin' out while they're roastin'!"

Ferron, a tall, gaunt-faced rat, sorted through the fruit until he came up with two large, rosy apples. He strode over to the two victims, but before he could start, Flinky yelled, "Loot! Treasure! Booty an' magic swords!"

Raga's long blade rasped out of its scabbard. Resting the point against Flinky's nose, the captain spoke just one word—"Where?"

The stoat answered speedily, knowing his life depended on it. "Sure, 'tis at the Abbey o' Redwall, sir, only a good ould march from here. All the plunder yore 'eart could desire!"

The swordtip lifted as Raga looked around the ugly faces of his leering crew. "Give 'em back their stuff. Come 'ither, mates. Sit 'ere by me, where I can carve cobs off'n ye if yore tellin' me fibs. I can't abide fibbers, can you, messmate?"

Flinky shook his head vigourously. "Sure those fibbers are the worst ould kind of beasts ever born, ain't that right?"

Crinktail hastened to agree with him. "Fibbers are villains!"

Raga Bol narrowed his frightening eyes and glared at his prisoners, who sat as if hypnotised. Suddenly he threw back his head and roared with laughter. "Aharrharrharrharr!

That's wot I like to 'ear, me liddle fishes. Avast there, Blowfly, bring grog fer our messmates!"

Blowfly, a malodourous, greasy-looking rat, brought three gigantic pottery jars and a keg of grog, which he rolled along by kicking it. He filled the jars brimful, issuing one to each of them. Both stoats quailed at the sight of the fearsome-smelling brew. Bol drained half of his at one huge swig, smacked his lips and winked broadly at them. "Good 'ole seaweed'n'fish'ead grog, ain' nothin' like it! Aharr, Raga Bol can't abide prissy liddle creatures wot don't like grog. Drink 'earty now!"

Gagging and spluttering, Flinky and Crinktail tried to sup the fiery liquor. The Searat crew gathered round, grinning and guffawing as they watched the stoats trying to cope with the grog. Finishing his swiftly, Raga observed his victims closely. "Cummon, buckoes, no shilly-shallyin' there, bottoms up, an' don't ye leave none for the fishes!"

Grog was dribbling down Flinky's chest fur by the time he finished. Something odd was happening to his eyes. In front of him sat three Raga Bols. His head was whirling, and his tongue felt as though it belonged to someone else. He hiccupped. "Heeheehee, hic! Sure, that was a prime ould, hic, droppa grog, hic hic! Ain't that right, hic, eh, Crinky, hic!"

Crinktail gazed woozily at her empty jar and giggled. "Sh'marvelloush! Makesh y'feel like a battlin' badger, heehee, whoops!"

She was knocked flat on her back. Raga, who had kicked her over, stood glaring down at the stoat, his sabre drawn. "Badger, wot badger? Is there a badger 'ereabouts? Have ye sighted a great giant of a stripedog? Tell me!"

Crinktail attempted to rise, but fell flat. She looked up at the Searat captain with owlish solemnity. "Wot badgersh? Heehee, we ain't seen no shtripedogs around 'ere. Don' worry, Bragger Roll, we'll fight 'em all for ye, me'n Shlinky!"

She giggled again, then passed out, senseless. A fleeting

glimpse of relief crossed the Searat's face. He turned his attention to Flinky, who was swaying from side to side, and blinking drunkenly. "Ahoy, buckoe, let's talk, me'n you. I'll ask the questions, an' ye give me all the answers. The right ones if'n ye value yore skin! This Abbey o' Redwall, tell me everythin' about it. An' worrabout yore crew, 'ow many strong are they, who's yore leader, wot's 'e like? No lies, now, c'mon!"

Raga Bol's crew listened avidly as Flinky related the entire sorry tale to their captain. The stoat was drunk, but not so drunk that he didn't know what would please the murderous Raga Bol. A good portion of his story was outright lies. He told of witless Abbeybeasts, and a fabulous treasure, laying great emphasis on the magic sword. Flinky was good at what he did, having spent most of his life lying and pleasing others. The captain and his crew believed the yarn. There followed much winking, nudging, whispering and gleeful rubbing of paws, even from Raga Bol. This was going to be a picnic, an orgy of looting and slaughter. A real Searat's dream come true!

The Searat crew made ready to march. Raga Bol delayed moving, since there was one thing still bothering the captain's mind—the fate of the giant stripedog. Giving orders for the crew to stand ready, he marched back along their trail alone, looking for signs of his assassin's return.

After an hour or so, Raga Bol glanced up at the sky. Dark rolling clouds, coupled with the distant rumble of thunder, presaged the arrival of a sizeable storm. He turned his gaze to the path ahead, where the foliage was swaying in the hot wind. The Searat's keen eyes and ears missed nothing. He saw the shrubbery moving the wrong way at one point and heard the moans and laboured gasping of somebeast coming slowly up the trail toward him.

It was Jibsnout, leaning heavily on an impromptu crutch he had fashioned from a branch. Raga Bol hastened to intercept him, frowning with false concern. "Jibsnout, matey, are ye wounded? Have ye news of the stripedog? Where are those sons of Wirga, 'ave they deserted ye?"

The stolid Searat slumped wearily down, his tongue licking the first fat drops of rain that fell through the woodland canopy. He looked up at Raga Bol kneeling at his side.

"Cap'n, we stood no chance! That stripedog 'ad a squirrel wid 'im, they ambushed us! Two of Wirga's sons were slayed. The other one ran away, though 'e wouldn't'a got far, I wager. I was shot through the footpaw by the stripedog, then 'e took my blade. I thought 'e was gonna kill me, but 'e tended to the wound an' sent me back to ye wid a message, Cap'n. The stripedog sez to tell ye that 'is name is Lonna Bowstripe, an' that 'e's comin' after ye, Cap'n Bol. Aye, yoreself an' all the crew, me too. We're all deadbeasts, d'ye hear me, walkin' deadbeasts! That big Lonna beast is goin' to slay us one by one, every ratjack of us! Take me word fer it, Cap'n, 'e's a mighty warrior but a real madbeast! I saw it in 'is eyes, they was red as fire. The stripedog'll finish us, all of us, I believe wot 'e said!"

A jagged lightning flash lit up the gloomy woodlands; thunder rattled closer and the rain came in earnest. Raga Bol held Jibsnout close to him, murmuring softly. "Hush now, mate, no stripedog's goin' to harm ye. This storm'll wash out all our tracks, nobeast'll find us then. Besides, we'll be snug inside of a big stone fortress, wid vittles to spare an' more loot than ye've ever clapped eyes on. Hahaarr, 'ow'll that suit ye matey, eh?"

Jibsnout blinked rain from his eyes. "That'll suit me good, Cap'n."

Bol held him closer, whispering in his ear, "Ye won't breathe a word about no stripedog to the crew now, will ye, me ole mate?"

Jibsnout smiled at his captain. "You know me, Cap'n Bol. None of 'em will 'ear a word from my mouth!"

Raga Bol smiled back at Jibsnout. "So they won't, mate, yore right."

He slew Jibsnout with a single thrust of his stiletto. Shoving the body into the bushes, Raga Bol sloshed back through the battering downpour, muttering to himself. "They all talks sooner or later, but you was right, Jibsnout. Nobeast'll 'ear a word from yore mouth."

26

The storms which had been battering the high cliffsides slackened off to a steady downpour. Fenna popped her head outside the cave, shielding her eyes. "It's hard to see anything properly on a rainy night. No sign of Horty yet, I do hope he's alr . . ."

A monolithic shape loomed out of the darkness, silent as a moonshadow. The squirrelmaid staggered backward as a badger of massive proportions padded in. Over his shoulder lay Horty, draped like a limp rag. The badger carried on past them, to the back of the cave, his deep growl echoing.

"I found your friend, never fear, he'll come to his senses before too long. Be still now until I get a fire going."

Bragoon's paw stayed Springald from rising. "Be still, Spring, do as our friend says."

They heard steel strike flint, as the badger's soft breath coaxed flame from the sparks that fell onto the tinder. Soon a pale light flickered. It became a proper fire when the badger added dried grass and twigs to it. He banked it up with broken pine branches, waited a moment, then turned to face the travellers. Bragoon had encountered a badger or two before, but none like this one. Warrior was written all over this giant beast—from the great bow he carried, to the long quiver full of arrows, to the lethal dagger strapped below his shoulder. He wore a simple smock of rust-hued homespun, belted with a woven sash.

But it was his face that denoted his calling. A deep, jagged scar ran lengthwise across the broad-striped muzzle, with stitchmarks pocking either side. The dark eyes remained impassive, reflecting the firelight. The otter judged him to be one of those fated creatures cursed with that malady called Bloodwrath—the red tinge mixed with the creamy eye whites betrayed it. Bragoon had heard tales of such badgers that described them as terrible to behold and unstoppable in battle. The otter held out his paw, flat, with the palm upward, a sign of peace. The badger did likewise. Then he placed his paw on top, making Bragoon's look like the tiny paw of a Dibbun. He introduced himself.

"I am Lonna Bowstripe. This is not my cave, but you are welcome to stay here until the hare recovers. I saw you escape those rats today and knew you would shelter up here. I watched from the hills what a brave thing your friend did. I killed those three rats who tried to capture him—vermin are bullies and murderers, they are no great loss to anybeast. Who are you, why are you in this country?"

The otter bowed respectfully. "I am Bragoon. This is Saro, Fenna and Springald. The hare is named Horty. We are travellers." He gestured upward toward the plateau on top of the cliffs. "We are seeking a place called Loamhedge. It lies somewhere up there."

Lonna began stringing his bow. "A dangerous quest, friend. There are many Darrat rats out there still. Their captain was one of the three I slew. You need to reach the clifftops without interference from them. Your journey will be hard enough without rats following you. Perhaps they are camped in the area. I will warn them off. Pass me an arrow, Fenna."

The squirrelmaid took a shaft, nearly as long as she was, from the badger's quiver. They watched Lonna blunt the point by jamming an old pinecone over it. He held it to the fire until it was blazing and crackling. Testing the air outside the cave, the badger seemed satisfied.

"It's not raining too heavily now, the shaft should burn for a bit before it goes out." With a single graceful move, Lonna set the blazing arrow on his string, drawing the shaft back until the burning end almost touched the bow. *Whooooosh!* It shot off like a rocket, into the night sky above the dunes.

Throwing back his head, the big beast roared out in a thunderous voice that echoed around the cave and along the cliffsides. "I am Lonna Bowstripe! I eat rats! I will taste the blood of any who are here by dawn! Eulaliiiiiaaaaaaa!"

He returned to the fire as they took their paws from ringing ears and began tending to Horty. Lonna smiled and shook his head as Horty began to stir. "He looks hard to kill—I've heard it said that hares are perilous beasts. This one will be a warrior one day."

The giant badger looked so large and ferocious in the firelight that Springald could readily understand how the rats would fear him. She enquired politely, "Sir, you didn't really eat three rats, did you?"

The smile still lingered on Lonna's lips. "Nay, little maid, don't believe all you hear. The language of death and violence is all that vermin understand. I'd sooner devour a crushed toad that was four seasons dead than eat rat. I eat only the same food as you do."

"Eat? I say, did some chap mention eats? I'm famished!"

Bragoon assisted the incorrigible hare to sit upright. "Oh, this 'un's awake, sure enough. Well, how d'ye feel, young famine belly? Oh, ye'd better thank the beast who saved ye. This is Lonna Bowstripe."

Horty did an exaggerated double take at the huge badger. He winked cheekily. "Good grief, sah, bet you can pack the jolly old provisions away, wot wot?"

They pooled the resources of their packs and were soon toasting yellow cheese and oat scones over the fire. Saro poured dandelion and burdock cordial for the company.

Springald split some loaves of nutbread and spread them with honey.

Lonna glanced sideways at Horty, taken aback by the young hare's appetite. "Great seasons, talk about packing provisions away! Where do you put it all? You're a bottomless pit!"

They all burst into laughter at the sight of Horty's indignant face.

Over the next few hours, they exchanged their stories. The five friends told Lonna all about Redwall and its creatures. They also explained Martha's situation and the reason for their quest. When the giant badger related his own personal history, they were greatly saddened and angry, too. There was a hushed silence when he came to the end of his narrative. Lonna ran his paw down the fearsome scar, tracing it across his still face.

"They will pay with their lives, Raga Bol and all his vermin crew. As sure as the days break and the seasons turn!"

The five travellers did not doubt a word that he uttered.

Lonna rose and replenished the fire. "You must sleep now. Tomorrow will be a hard day's climbing. I think the plateau above the cliffs is no place for the fainthearted. Take a good rest tonight, I'll guard the cave entrance."

Bragoon uncovered his sword. "I'll keep ye company, Lonna. Two guards are better'n one, an' four eyes can see more than two."

They sat together at the cave entrance. Lonna could not take his gaze from the otter's sword, drawn to it like a magnet to metal. "That is indeed a wondrous weapon you carry, Bragoon."

The otter let the firelight play along the blade. "Aye, 'tis so, though it don't belong t'me. Abbot Carrul of Redwall loaned it t'me the day we left. I think he did it not just for our protection, but as a sort o' good-luck charm for the journey. This sword belongs at the Abbey. 'Twas owned in the far olden seasons by a mouse. His name was Martin the Warrior, one o' the founders of Redwall. I was told stories of Martin an' his sword when I was nought but a Dibbun. They say it was forged an' made by a great badger lord, a warrior himself, an' a very skilled swordsmith, as ye can see. He made it from a lump of ore that fell from the sky, a piece of a star, I was told. This badger, he was Lord of Salamandastron, a mountain fortress. Did ye ever hear of that place, Lonna?"

The dark eyes of the giant flashed. "Every badger knows the name of Salamandastron. I will go there myself someday. I feel my days will end there—but only when my score with Raga Bol is settled."

Bragoon sat up with a start, realising that he had dropped off to sleep during the night, something he would never have done in his younger seasons. Dawnlight was filtering into the cave, and Lonna Bowstripe was gone. As Saro was rekindling the fire from its embers, the three young ones were just waking.

She gave Bragoon a beaker of hot mint tea. "Mornin', matey. Well, our bigbeast left while it was still dark. I saw 'im go, y'know."

Fenna poured tea for herself. "Lonna's gone?"

Saro nodded. "Aye, you lot were all asleep. Horty's snorin' woke me, sounded like a tribe o' stuffed-up frogs."

The young hare huffed indignantly at her, but Saro carried on. "I was lyin' there wide awake, watchin' Lonna in the fireglow. He'd picked up the sword o' Martin to admire it. Well, next thing that badger went stiff as a frozen pike, sittin' there starin' at the blade as if it was speakin' to 'im. I watched for a while, then Horty started snorin' agin. So I gave 'im a good kick an' settled back to catch a nap."

Horty interrupted. "Blinkin' cadess, kickin' a chap in mid slumber? Rank bad manners, I'd say. Hmph!"

The elderly squirrel shrugged. "When I woke up agin, he'd gone."

Bragoon slapped his rudder against the rock floor. "I'll wager 'twas Martin the Warrior, speakin' to Lonna through

251

the sword. He told the badger where t'find Raga Bol, an' Lonna took off after the villain!"

Bragoon wrapped the sword up reverently as Horty chuckled. "I bet old Raggaballoon wotsisname wouldn't be too pleased with Martin, if he knew. Snitchin' about him to that bally great hulk. I'd hate to be in his way when he feels peevish. Frazzlin' frogs, imagine what old Lonna'll do to that vermin when he catches up with him, wot wot!"

Bragoon began packing his belongings. "I wouldn't like to imagine, mate. That's Lonna's business, an' I'm sure he can take care of it well. But we've got our own problems to tend. Up an' on to Loamhedge, mateys!"

Morning boded bright as they left the cave and began climbing the cliff to its top. It was hard going until the two squirrels, Saro and Fenna, went ahead. Soon they were on top of the cliff. Lowering down a rope, they heaved up all the packs, then secured the rope around a rock, allowing the other three to haul themselves up.

It was a breathtaking panorama from the plateau. Horty's keen eyes spotted a small dark smudge, moving across the scrublands in the distance. He pointed. "I say, you chaps, that could be thingummy, er, Lonna!"

Springald shaded her eyes. "So it could! He's headed northwest, that's the direction we came from. Saro, d'you suppose he's going to Redwall?"

Sarobando felt they were wasting time sightseeing. "I couldn't really say, missy, but one thing's shore, we ain't goin' to Redwall. 'Tis Loamhedge we want. So stop lookin' backwards an' let's go for'ard. Quick march!"

Shimmering flatlands, devoid of vegetation or shade, rolled out before them. Small swirls of dust eddied in spirals on the hot breeze. Sarobando squinted her eyes against the distance.

"Miss Fenna, yore in charge o' the drinks, we'll have t'be stingy with liquid. It might be some time afore we run across water by the look o' things."

Immediately after the squirrel mentioned drinks, Horty

began feeling thirsty. "I say, Fenna old gel, pass me that canteen, there's a good little treebounder. I'm parched!"

Fenna marched right on past him. "We'll drink at midday and not before, so forget about it and keep going."

The young hare appealed to his comrades. "Wot? Did you chaps hear this heartless curmudgeon?"

Bragoon grinned pitilessly at Horty. "Aye, loud an' clear, mate. Wot's the matter, are ye thirsty already?"

The incorrigible hare clapped a paw to his throat dramatically. "Me flippin' mouth's like a sandpit, an' the old tongue feels like a bally feather mattress. A drink, for pity's sake, marm!"

Saro levelled a paw at him. "Ye drink when Fenna tells ye. Now get a slingstone pebble an' suck it. That'll keep the thirst off as y'march, 'tis an old trick."

Horty pulled a pebble from his pouch, looked at it in disgust, then put it back. "Permission to sing, sah!"

The otter waved a paw in the air. "Sing y'self blue in the face for all I care, but forget about drinkin'."

Horty had to dig through his store of ballads and ditties, but he soon came up with an appropriate one.

"I knew a jolly old spider, and she always used t'say,
she could dive in a bath of cider, an' swim around all
    day.
Oh I would like to be that spider,
floatin' round in sparklin' cider,
she'd drink an drink, 'til she started to sink,
there'd be so much cider inside o' that spider!

I once knew a friendly flea, to whom I used to chat,
his favourite drink was ice-cold tea, what d'ye think of
    that?
Oh I would like to be that flea,
sippin' cups of ice-cold tea,
all in fine fettle from a rusty kettle,
'til I drank as much tea as that flea!

253

O cider spider, tea an' flea,
'tis all good manner o' drinks for me.
I'm an absolute whizz for strawberry fizz,
I'll sup old ale 'til I turn pale,
I'd never bilk at greensap milk.
Give this ripsnorter some rosehip water,
or cordial fine made from dandelion,
give me a barrel it's mine all mine,
just tip me the nod or give me a wink,
an' I'll drink an' drink an' drink . . .
an' dri . . . hi . . . hi . . . hiiiiiiiink!"

Saro covered her ears with both paws and roared, "Enough!
I can't stand no more o' that caterwaulin', give that hare a
drink. Give everybeast a drink!"

Fenna passed the canteen around, allowing each of the
group one good mouthful. Horty was onto his second swig
when the otter snatched the canteen from him and stop-
pered it. "Ye great guzzlin' gizzard, don't ye know when
t'stop?"

Horty gave him a hurt look and belched. "Beg pardon,
sah. Miserable blinkin' bangtail, I barely wet me lips, wot!"

Bragoon grabbed the young hare by his fluffy tailscut and
tugged hard. "One more word and ye'll be wearin' this as
a bobble twixt yore ears. Now belt up an' march!"

It was hard, hot and dusty out on the flatlands, but they
trekked doggedly onward. Even the breeze was like the
heat from an open oven door. With neither shade nor
shadow to shelter from the ruthless eye of the blazing sun,
it soon became an effort to walk.

Bragoon licked his dry lips. Dropping his pack, he
crouched down on his hunkers. "Phew! I tell ye, mates, I
never knew a day could get so hot. We'll rest here awhile."

The aged squirrel set about making things comfortable.
She laced their cloaks together and made a lean-to. Weighting one end of the cloaks with their supply packs, she
propped up the other end with two travelling staves.

"That'll give us a bit o' shade. Get under it, an' we'll take another drink. Mebbe we'll have a nap 'til it gets cooler. Then we can travel in the evenin'."

The otter dug a beaker out of his pack. "Good idea, mate. Fenna, pass me the canteen. I'll measure our drinks out, so nobeast gets any less." Here he glanced at Horty. "Or more than the others!"

They were each allowed one half-beaker, which they sipped gratefully.

Horty quaffed his off in a single gulp. "Bit measly, wot! Where's the food?" He was the only one who felt like eating; the others stretched out and tried to rest.

Fenna watched the hare stuff down candied fruits. "That will make you even thirstier. The sweetness will start you wanting to drink more."

Horty waggled his ears at her. "Oh pish tush an' fol de rol, miss, I like eatin', doncha know!"

Bragoon opened one eye, remarking ironically, "Ye like eatin', really? I'd never have known if'n ye hadn't told me so! Put that haversack back on the cloak ends, or the wind'll blow our shelter away."

Springald dreamt she was back at Redwall, paddling in the Abbey pond. Cool, wet banksand slopped between her footpaws as she splashed happily about. Sister Portula and the Abbot came strolling across the dewy lawn. Although the mousemaid could hear what they were saying, their voices sounded different.

"All gone! Every flippin' thing is confounded well gone, wot?" Springald wakened to see the reddish evening light through clouds of dust. Horty was stamping about outside the lean-to entrance, sobbing hoarsely. "Every blinkin' drop t'drink, an' every mouthful of scoff. Gone, gone, we've been robbed, flamin' well looted!"

Bragoon grabbed the hare and shook him. "Stop that bawlin', calm down an' tell us wot 'appened."

Springald gathered round with Fenna and Sarobando to hear Horty's woeful tale.

"Couldn't sleep, y'know, too bally hot, wot. I was jolly thirsty, too, so I got up an' went outside t'get the canteen out of the haversacks. Some blighter's filched the lot. They've left rocks in their place. Go an' see f'y'self!"

It was true: five rocks sat holding down the rear of the lean-to, where the five packs of food and drink had been stowed.

Saro held up her paws. "Be still, there may be tracks, pawprints or dragmarks!"

She went down on all fours, eyes close to the dusty earth, nose twitching as she sniffed. A moment later, she stood up with a look of disgust on her face. "Nothing! Not a single trace. Must've been an experienced thief who did it."

Bragoon commented wryly. "A beast would have t'be clever to survive in this wasteland. Well, that's it! No good weepin' o'er stolen supplies, we'll just have t'get on with it. While 'tis dark the weather's cooler, so we'll travel by night, at the double. Right, Saro?"

The old squirrel nodded and began issuing guidelines. "Aye, mate. March fast an' silent, no talkin'. We don't know wot's out there in the darkness. 'Tis strange territory, so stick together an' hold paws. There'll be no time for restin'."

She wagged a stern paw at the young hare. "Listen good, Horty, this ain't a game anymore, see. If you start yammerin' on about food'n'drink, or causin' any upset, ye'll be riskin' our lives. Just march, do as yore told an' shut that great mouth o' yours, d'ye hear?"

Horty placed a paw over his own mouth and drew the other paw across his throat in a slitting motion.

Springald nodded. "I think he's gotten the idea. Quick march!"

Off they went into the day's last crimson-tinged twilight—without food, drink or any hope of rest. The five small figures were dwarfed by the immensity of a dust-blown, trackless desert. Hidden eyes watched their departure, and sinister shapes rose from the earth to follow the questors.

27

The storm broke over Redwall at about the same time that Raga Bol killed Jibsnout. Foremole Dwurl gazed gloomily out of the dormitory window at the windswept deluge outside. He blinked as lightning illuminated the room and thunder barraged overhead.

"B'aint no use a throwen pepper at vurmints in ee gurt rainystorm. Bo urr, nay, zurr!"

Martha wheeled her chair to the window and peered out. "Hmm, I wonder how the vermin are coping with this downpour."

Abbot Carrul sighed. "Who knows? Martha, please keep an eye on them. Right, let's get on with this Council Meeting."

Outside, fat raindrops beat a deafening tattoo on the walls of the Abbey, its lawns nearly underwater. Badredd and his gang had commandeered the gatehouse. They lay about, wrapped in sheets, blankets and window curtains, using the material to dab at their sorely inflamed nostrils. Sneezing had become pure agony, with the membranes of their nostrils and throats red-raw from the bombardment of hotroot pepper.

Plumnose was having the worst of it. Each time he

sniffed, his pendulous nose wobbled and vibrated. Throwing off the bedspread he had been wearing, the suffering ferret made for the gatehouse door.

"Duh, I'b goin' oudd inna rain tuh lay dowd an' ledda rained water clear be node. Id mide wash idd out!"

Halfchop sneezed painfully as he volunteered to accompany him. "Kachuuub!"

The Abbey Council had decided on a desperate scheme. Twoscore of the most able-bodied Redwallers would storm the gatehouse and make an end of the vermin. They stood ready to go, each armed with some form of homemade weapon: kitchen knives tied to window poles formed spears, long-handled garden spades, forks and hoes, together with coopering mallets and stave hatchets from the cellars.

Toran, serving as commander of the group, leaned against the windowsill, going over the scheme for a second time. "Listen, friends, 'tis no use barricadin' 'em in the gatehouse. We've got to make an end to it, invade the place, break in an' slay every last one o' them. No half-measures if we want a peaceful life for us an' the little 'uns. I'll go through the door first, the rest o' you follow me. Show no quarter once yore inside! Sister Portula, Foremole Dwurl an' yore two moles there, Burney'n'Yooler, you stay outside an' get any who tries to break out an' run off. Any questions?"

Muggum saluted with a copper ladle he had brought from the kitchen. "No, zurr, oi'll do moi dooty, doan't you'm wurry!"

Martha lifted him onto her lap and took the ladle. "Your duty is to stay here with the rest of us and guard the Abbey door. This storm has set in for a good while yet. Once it goes dark, Toran and his friends will have the advantage of night cover and rain. The vermin won't be expecting them to attack. Meanwhile, we'll guard the door and make sure only Redwallers get back inside. It's a very important job, Muggum. Can you do it?"

The molebabe narrowed his eyes, glaring suspiciously at Toran's attack party. "Ho, oi can do et, Miz Marth', doan't ee fret. They'm b'aint a-getten back in yurr iffen they'm b'aint theyselves!"

Toran shook the molebabe's paw. "Well said, matey!"

Abbot Carrul stood up on one of the truckle beds and delivered a homily to his beloved Abbey creatures. Everybeast fell silent, respectfully bowing their heads as he spoke out.

"Fortune and fates be with you all,
you who fight for the right,
some will stand, others fall,
never to return this night.

But fear ye not, my loving friends,
be strong of limb and heart,
knowing that peace depends on you,
let courage play its part.

Tranquillity and calm spread wide,
through this our dear homeland,
justice and truth go by your side,
which evil cannot withstand."

Though Martha did not say it, she wished now more than ever that her two friends, Sarobando and Bragoon, had stayed.

Thunder exploded overhead; jagged forks of lightning tore through the fading light. Raga Bol and his Searats pounded on Redwall Abbey's main gate. Hearing the noise, Halfchop and Plumnose padded soggily to the gate.

Plumnose placed an ear against it, calling out, "Who'd dat?"

A sabre was at Flinky's neck as he answered. "Sure, 'tis

only me'n me mate Crinktail. We're gettin' drowned out here. Open up an' let us in, Plummy!"

The two crewbeasts lifted the wooden bar, allowing the door to swing inward. Flinky and Crinktail were flung in, landing face down in the mud as the Searats poured through. Raga Bol seized the ferret's nose and twisted it, bringing Plumnose up on his pawtips, squealing in agony.

"Yeeee! Ledd go!"

The captain let go and kicked Plumnose flat in the mud. "So yore the big bad warrior wot put this place to siege, eh?"

He roared with laughter as the ferret held a paw tenderly around his bruised nose and pointed to the gatehouse. "Nodd me. Badredd's in dere, he did idd!"

The little fox was half asleep as the gatehouse door crashed off its hinges. He was dumbstruck at the sight that greeted him. Raga Bol strode forcefully in, squinting one eye as he glared ferociously around.

"Which one of ye is Badredd?"

The crew, terrified out of their wits by half a hundred Searats leering through the doorway at them, pointed quickly at the fox. Raga's polished pawhook latched into Badredd's belt, jerking the fox face-to-face with him. The barbaric captain's murderous eyes bored into the fox's numbed gaze. "So then, liddle laddo, yore the mighty Badredd?"

Speech deserted him, Badredd could only stammer. "Y . . . Y . . . Yu . . . Ya . . . y-y-y-"

Raga Bol shook him like a rag doll, covering the little fox with spittle as he roared into his face. "Don't stan' there makin' noises like an idjit! Are ye or aren't ye Badredd, ye runty buffoon?"

The fox nodded furiously, as he heard his own voice squeak out, "Yis!"

The sea captain turned to his crew, gold fangs asparkle as he grinned at them. "Well now, ain't that nice. Say 'ello to our new cap'n, buckoes!"

There was loud guffawing and shouts of ridicule from the Searats.

"Pleased t'meet yer, I'm shore!"

"Mercy me, 'e do look fierce, don't 'e?"

"I'd watch 'ow ye talk to ole Badredd. Looks like an 'ard master t'me, a cold 'earted killer!"

"Hawhawhaw! Aye, lookit 'is sword. Hawhawhawhaw!"

The Searat captain wrenched the broken cutlass from his victim's belt. He held it under Badredd's nose. "Does your mamma know ye've been playin' wid this? Dearie me, yew could cut yerself. Naughty fox!"

Raga Bol's crew laughed until tears ran down their cheeks. When the fox's own crew began smiling and chuckling, the big Searat turned on them savagely.

"Wot are you lot laughin' about, eh? Stupid clods, lettin' yoreselves be ordered about by a liddle oaf with a busted sword. Gerrout of 'ere, all of ye, clear out!"

The vermin scurried to obey, cringing and ducking as they had to pass Raga Bol, who was partially blocking the doorway. Still dragging Badredd along by his belt, Raga strode out into the sheeting rain, issuing orders to his Searats.

"Glimbo, Ferron, Chakka, you stay in the liddle 'ouse wid me. Ringear, lock that big gate, nobeast gets in or out. Post a watch on it. The rest of ye, take shelter where ye can find it. Blowfly, take a rope's end an' keep an eye on this lot."

He indicated the fox's crew with a nod. Finally, Raga turned his attention to the hapless Badredd. Thrusting the broken cutlass into the fox's shaking paws, he snarled, "Now then, me laddo, yew'd better be a good cook, or ye'll find yoreself bein' served up as vittles. D'ye hear me?"

Badredd nodded miserably as Raga Bol continued barking out orders. "Git yoreself down t'that pond an' take yore crew along. I wants fish fer me brekkist, a good fat 'un, an' no excuses. Just 'ow yer catches an' cooks it is yore bizness. But if'n it ain't on the table, done perfectly, when I wakes up . . . then ye'd best cut yore own throat wid that toy sword, 'cos ye won't wanna face Raga Bol. Now get to it sharpish!"

He flung Badredd face first into the mud. Then, turning on his paw, the big Searat strode inside the gatehouse.

The little fox raised his head, weeping and spitting out wet soil, thankful he was still alive. But for how long? The barbarous rat had set him a near impossible task. How was he going to catch a big fish and cook it in the midst of a thunderstorm, with rain pounding furiously down?

Thud! A blow from a knotted rope's end made him arch his back. Blowfly landed another one, this time across Badredd's rump.

"Up on yore hunkers, foxy! Yew 'eard wot the cap'n said. Step lively now. Youse others, bring that blanket t'make a tent fer me. I ain't sittin' round in the rain watchin' ye makin' Cap'n Bol's brekkist. All down t'the pond now, at the double!"

He drove them forward with the rope's end.

A horrified silence had fallen over the Abbey dormitory. One word from Old Phredd cut the air like a knife. "Searats!"

Shilly followed this up with a question. "Wot bee's a Searat?"

Toran bent down to the small truckle bed and pulled up the covers to the squirrelbabe's chin. All around the dormitory, Dibbuns were sleeping peacefully. The ottercook wrinkled his nose at Shilly.

"A Searat, me dear? Just some naughty ole beast. Nothin' for ye to get upset about, go t'sleep now."

Abbot Carrul sat down on a hill of slingstones in the middle of the floor. "How many of them are in the grounds of our Abbey?"

Martha replied from her seat at the window. "Hard to count in the dark and rain, Father, but there's certainly more than twoscore of them, all rats, and armed to the fangs. Surely we can't overcome that many!"

An old mousewife called Mildun began sobbing in a panic. "We'll all be dragged out of our beds and murdered, I know we will, us and those poor little babes. Oooooooohhhhhh!"

The haremaid immediately issued a harsh scolding. "Stop that right now!"

Shocked into silence, Mildun shrank from the sharp reproof, listening intently as Martha continued in a stern voice. "There's no call for that behaviour, marm, all you'll do is cause worry to everybeast. Don't let me hear an outburst like that from you ever again. Now if you've anything to say, then make it helpful. Don't be a beast of ill omen, and keep your voice down. We don't want the little ones taking fright. Do you hear me?"

Mildun sniffed and mumbled into her kerchief. "Sorry, Martha."

Abbot Carrul turned grateful eyes to the haremaid. "Thank you, miss. Well, the whole situation has changed now—for the worse, I'm sad to say. An attack against such numbers of those savage rats is out of the question. So what do we do now? I'm open to helpful suggestions."

Foremole Dwurl raised a powerful digging claw. "Tunnels owt, zurr, me'n moi moles can make ee gurt tunnel. Uz'll all be safe frumm ee vurmints then, oi reckerns!"

As hope sprang anew in the Redwallers, they began chattering and clamouring aloud.

Toran silenced them with a sudden bark. "A fine idea, sir, but let's not be too hasty. Yore plan calls for a bit o' discussion. Now one at a time—you first, Father Abbot."

Carrul folded both paws into his wide sleeves. "Thank you, Toran. First, let me say this. Our Foremole's plan is a sensible one. The Dibbuns, and anybeast who chooses to go with them, will be safe from harm. As for myself, I must remain here where my duty lies. I could never desert my beautiful Abbey."

The ottercook seconded him. "Nor I, Carrul. It ain't right leavin' Redwall wide open to Searats an' vermin. I stay!"

Martha struck the arm of her chair resolutely. "Redwall Abbey is my home, the only home I've ever known. I'm not moving from here!"

Every voice in the room was raised. "We stay! We stay!"

Foremole Dwurl wrinkled his nose apologetically. "Oi bee's sorry oi menshunned et naow."

Abbot Carrul placed a paw about the faithful mole's shoulders. "You've no need to be sorry, friend, it was a good idea. The trouble is that nobeast wants to go now. So what do we do next?"

Muggum would not be denied his say. The molebabe waved the copper ladle, which had become his chosen weapon. "Us'n's foights, zurr, that bee's wot us do. Foight!"

Sister Setiva relieved Muggum of the ladle to stop him from giving anybeast a whack as he waved it about. "Och, ye wee terror, hush now an' pay heed tae yore elders!"

Toran picked up the molebabe and made an announcement to the assembly. "This liddle feller's right, we must fight. But it won't be no kill-or-be-killed sort o' last stand. Oh no, mates, we'll fight an' defend the Abbey, stave off any attacks. Even if that means we'll have t'fight all summer long, until the Skipper brings his ottercrew back 'ere from the Northshores. Then together we can deal with those savages outside."

Sister Portula brandished the hooked window pole she had armed herself with. Normally a quiet and reserved old mouse, she surprised everybeast by calling out, "Well spoken, Toran. That's the most sensible thing I've heard so far. We can be what we are, not warriors but defenders! We can stick it out and delay them all summer until help arrives from Skipper and his crew. But it will be no easy thing. Remember that we are under siege. Food will run short, drinks will have to be rationed, water cannot be used freely anymore. . . ."

Baby Buffle interrupted the good sister by piping up, "Nonomorragerrabaffinwirrawater!"

Martha gave Shilly a puzzled look. "What did he say?"

The little squirrel grinned from ear to ear and did a somersault. "Iffa water bee's short, Dibbuns can't not get baffed. Yeeheeheehee!"

Nobeast could resist laughing along with the overjoyed babes.

The storm finally subsided to a light drizzle. Scratching the back of his neck with his silver hook, Raga Bol rolled out of Old Phredd's bed and exited the gatehouse. Swigging from a flask of grog, he listened to the whimpers and wails from the pond. Blowfly was keeping Badredd and his little gang hard at it. The Searat captain gazed up at the majestic grandeur of Redwall Abbey. What a sight! Anybeast would be mad to bother with ships when he could own a place like this. Smiling wolfishly, he shouted toward the Abbey.

"Yore goin' to meet Cap'n Raga Bol tomorrer, mousies!"

28

Marching all night was a harrowing experience for the younger creatures. Saro and Bragoon, being used to such hardships, plodded doggedly on in silence. Fenna stumbled alongside them, her eyes constantly drooping shut. The squirrelmaid sorely regretted ever leaving Redwall and all its comforts. She did not know which she yearned for most—sleep, food or water. Springald was of a like mind, trudging onward in a straight line with her four companions, keeping quiet and trying not to inhale too much dust.

It was a cruel and forbidding outlook, the wasteland stretching all around, flat, silent and gloomy in the nighttime darkness. After what seemed like an eternity, daylight showed on the eastern horizon, a pale, misty mixture of dove-grey and orange.

Bragoon watched the faint apricot edge of morning sun slowly rising. He spoke softly. "That's a pretty sight, ain't it, mates?"

Horty hardly gave it a second glance. "Pretty, y'say? Pretty bloomin' awful if y'ask me, wot. I'd swap the blinkin' lot for a drop of water! Can't we stop now? You said march by night an' sleep durin' the day. Well, there's the jolly old day, an' I'm pawsore an' weary. So let's lay the old heads down, eh chaps?"

Saro pushed him onward. "Not just yet, we've got to keep goin' while 'tis cool. When the day gets hot, that's the time for sleep. The more ground we cover, the sooner we'll be out o' this wasteland. Keep marchin', don't stop now."

None of the travellers wanted to, but they carried on, knowing that it was the only sensible thing to do.

By midmorning, the sun was beating down remorselessly as small dust spirals danced on the hot breeze. There was still no sight of trees or streams amid the dun-hued wastes.

Bragoon finally halted. "We'll rest here until late afternoon!"

Saro began setting up a lean-to with cloaks and staves, weighting the cloak edges down with pieces of rock.

Horty raised a dust cloud as he slumped down. "If I could only lay paws on the rotters who swiped our grub'n'water. By the left! I'd kick their confounded tails into the middle o' next season, wot!"

Bragoon rested on his stomach in the small patch of shade. "Don't think about it, mate, yore only makin' things worse."

Springald looked back at the ground they had covered. "Funny how the land seems to wobble and shimmer out there."

Fenna curled up and closed her eyes. "That's just the heat on the horizon. It's a mirage, really."

Saro shielded her eyes, peering keenly at the spectacle. She nudged the otter, directing his attention to it. "Don't look like no mirage to me, wot d'ye think, Brag?"

Bragoon squinted his eyes and watched intently. His paw strayed to the sword which lay by his side. "It might be just the heat waves, but it seems t'be movin' closer toward us. Then again, it could be the earth dancin'. Remember the ground shakin' like that the last time we was in this territory, Saro?"

The squirrel never let her gaze waver from the shimmering. "Aye, it made a rumblin' sound, too."

Horty laughed wildly. "Hawhawhaw! Just listen to 'em,

chaps. We're in the middle of bally nowhere, bein' baked alive, not a flamin' drop t'drink or eat. Now what, the ground has to start bloomin' well dancin'! Am I goin' off me flippin' rocker, or is it those two ramblin' duffers, wot?"

Bragoon and Saro exchanged glances, then went back to their watching.

Horty, however, would not be ignored. Gesturing with his paws, he flopped his ears dramatically.

"They're tellin' me the ground's doin' a jig. An' here am I, without a pastie to shovel down me face or a bucket o' cordial to wet me parched lips! Ah, lackaday an' woe is the handsome young hare, languishin' out here an' losin' me mind! I'm goin' mad, mad I tell ye! Stark bonkers an' ravin' nuts! 'Tis the dreaded thirstation!"

Springald shook her head. "Thirstation? Shouldn't that be thirstiness, or just thirst?"

Bragoon whispered to Saro. "That couldn't be the earth dancin', or we'd have felt the rumbles."

Horty continued with his tirade. "Rumbles, rumbles? How could benighted buffoons such as you know about the rumblings of a sad tragic hare, whose life is bein' cut short by the contagious thirstation an' tummyrumbles?"

The otter's tail caught him a firm thwack across the rear. "Shuttup, young 'un, get to sleep an' quit yore shoutin'!"

Horty subsided meekly, but still muttered to have the last word. "Beaten by the bullyin' Bragoon into shallow slumber. Goodnight, fair comrades, or is it good day, wot?"

Within a short time, the three young ones were asleep. Sarobando was dozing, too, but Bragoon lay on his stomach, chin resting on both paws. Through slitted eyelids he scanned the wastelands to the rear of the lean-to. They drew closer. Now he could distinguish them, not as heat shimmers but as small, patchy bumps. Moving silently, betrayed only by odd puffs of dust, they edged nearer. Then they halted. One bump detached itself from the pack and advanced.

Saro came awake as Bragoon touched her ear. He nodded

toward the moving object, twitching his tail against the squirrel's footpaw. Saro prepared herself, knowing the signal well. One . . . Two . . . On the third twitch they both attacked. Springing in the air and leaping forward, both beasts threw themselves bodily on the thing. It squeaked aloud. Immediately the ground came alive. Squeaking and whistling, hundreds of small shapes raised an enormous dust cloud as they fled. The captured one wriggled and bit madly, but it could not escape its captors. It was disguised by a cloak woven from tough, coarse grass. Bragoon and Saro swiftly wrapped it into a bundle, trapping the beast within.

Saro drew a small blade. "Haharr, got ye, thief, be still or I'll slay ye!"

Bragoon crouched with his sword poised, defending his friend's back against attack. Saro dragged the bundle inside the lean-to, rapping out orders to the trio, who were now awake.

"Grab ahold o' that. Jump on it if it tries to escape!"

Springald and Fenna held the thing tight. Horty pulled off the covering. It was a small, goldish-brown mouselike beast with a long tail and a white-furred stomach. Temporarily stunned, it lay gazing up at them through huge, dark eyes.

The otter came bounding in; sword upraised he menaced it. "Our food'n'water, where is it? Speak or die, robber!"

The creature gave vent to a piercing cry. "Feeeeeeeeeeeee!"

This was followed by a sound from outside, like hundreds of tiny drums.

Saro stepped out of the shelter. "Curl me bush, come an' take a look o' this, mates!"

A billowing dust cloud was rising from footpaws drumming the earth. When it settled, a hundred or more of the mouselike beasts stood facing them. They all wore grass cloaks about their shoulders.

Fenna whispered to Saro. "Good grief, what do we do now?"

The older squirrel answered quietly out of the side of her mouth. "Say nothin'. Leave this to me, mate."

Bragoon emerged from the shelter, dragging his prisoner by the tail. Hoisting the creature up, he swung the sword of Martin. The otter's voice roared out. "Give us back our food'n'water, or this 'un's a deadbeast! D'ye understand me? I'll slay 'im if'n ye don't obey!"

For an answer, they once again set up a loud drumming with their footpaws: *Brrrrrrrrrrr!* Then they stood silent, watching Bragoon as the dust settled.

The captive one glared fearlessly up at the otter. "Chiiiii-iirk—kill me! We of the Jerbilrats give nobeast water. Chiiik, sooner give our blood than water!"

Springald was surprised. "Rats? They're handsome little things. They've got beautiful, big dark eyes. They look far too nice to be rats!"

Saro turned fiercely on the mousemaid. "Just shut yore mouth, miss, I don't care 'ow nice they look. They've told ye wot they are—a rat's a rat, an' that's that. Hold yore tongue, an' leave the talkin' to Brag!"

The otter yelled back at the massed Jerbilrats. "Hah, so ye can unnerstand me. D'ye think I'm foolin'?"

He struck with the sword, snipping a whisker from the Jerbilrat. As the drumming resumed, Bragoon raised his sword. "Next one takes this robber's head off. Give us our supplies!"

Fenna whispered urgently to Horty. "He's not really going to chop off a defenceless creature's head, is he?"

Horty shrugged. "Simple case o' survival out here. Either we get the rations back or we peg out an' perish, wot!"

The Jerbilrat actually smiled at Bragoon. "I die, one less mouth to feed—that saves water. Kill me, riverdog."

Saro sighed. "Don't give us much choice, does 'e?"

The otter let his sword drop. "I never slew a helpless beast."

Saro winked. "I know, mate, we ain't murderers. Let me try."

Hauling the Jerbilrat up by its ears, she dealt it a slap. "I know ye ain't givin' us our supplies back, but I'll slap ye round 'til sunset if'n y'don't tell me where water is."

Saro made a wavy motion, describing a stream or river. "Water, like this." She gave the beast a heavier slap. "Talk!"

The Jerbilrat shrugged. "Two days southeast maybe, don't know."

Saro struck again. "Then find out, 'cos yore comin' with us!"

The creature snarled. "I'm Jiboa the Jerchief. I'll kill you—I'm not afraid to kill, like that riverdog is!"

Saro took a length of rope, knotting it firmly around Jiboa's neck. She smiled grimly. "Ole Bragoon's the merciful one, I ain't so soft 'earted. I don't take no lip from cheeky-faced rats. Now take us to the water, or I'll make ye wish my mate had killed ye!"

A swift kick to the rear set Jiboa moving. "Your water might be gone now. Dancing earth can shift streams down great cracks in the ground."

Saro flicked the rope against the back of his neck. "Ah, go an' tell that t'the frogs. Ye just get us there."

Cancelling all plans to sleep by day, the travellers broke camp and set off into the dry, hot morn. They kept glancing back as the entire Jerbilrat pack continued to follow them. When Jiboa thrummed his footpaws, the rats drummed back in answer. He smirked at Saro.

"Feeeeeee! Old toughbeast, eh? Jerbilrats can go without water longer than you and the others. You'll weaken sooner or later. Then my rats will slay you all, you'll see."

Saro jerked the rope sharply, causing Jiboa to fall on his own tail. She winked craftily at him. "Funny 'ow ye can't do two things at once. Seems every time ye try, then ye fall over."

Jiboa scrambled upright. "Stupid treejumper, I can walk'-n'talk!"

Saro tugged the rope and pulled him over again. "Wrong! Every time you say somethin' nasty, bump, down ye go.

But if'n ye was to shout out that y'can see water, ye'd regain yore sense o' balance right away. Unnerstand?"

There was neither shade nor shadow when the sun was directly overhead. Horty began complaining once more. "Oh shed a tear for a thirsty young hare, an' if it's wet I'll drink it, wot. I say, you chaps, wouldn't you just love to wet the old whistle at a cool runnin' stream? If the odd fish swam by, then one could eat an' drink at the same jolly old time, wot. Phew, I'm so hot'n'dry that you could make a blanket of my tongue!"

Fenna gave him a sharp nudge. "You're showing us up in front of those Jerbilrats, moaning and whining like that. They'll think we're soft and weak. Now try to behave like a Redwaller, and stop all that nonsense!"

Horty stiffened his ears, saluted and stepped out smartly. "Right, old gel, leave it to Hortwill Braebuck, Esquire. I'll sing t'the clod-faced old savages, wot, here goes!"

Horty, with his talent for making up songs as he went, launched into an insulting ditty about Jerbilrats. Fenna and Springald giggled as they joined in the refrain at the end of each verse.

"Oh a Jerbilrat's a creature,
without one redeemin' feature,
beware of him, pay heed to what I say.
He'll sneak up on one quite sudden,
and devour one's pie or pudden,
an' he'll rob your bloomin' water anyday . . . Anyday!

If one ever meets a jerbil,
one must be extremely careful,
an' keep one's drinks tight under lock and key,
for 'tis a widely held belief,
that the scruffy little thief,
will sup every single drop quite happily . . . Happily!

For a jerbil's just a rat,
who has never had a bath,

so be careful that you stay upwind of him.
'Cos the smell would blow one's hat off,
or put any decent rat off,
an' kill all the flies around a rubbish bin . . . Rubbish
    bin!

Jerbil manners are disgraceful,
they're so spiteful an' ungrateful,
so arrogant an' sly an' so unjust.
Every ugly son an' daughter,
is a stranger to bathwater,
jerbils wallow round all day beneath the dust . . . 'Neath
    the dust!"

Horty waved to the Jerbilrats, who were squealing and
drumming their footpaws angrily. "What ho, chaps, sorry I
can't warble anymore for you. The old tongue's all swollen."

Saro halted Jiboa until the others caught up with her.
"This sun is gettin' too much, let's take a rest, mates."

Shading their heads beneath the cloaks, they squatted on
the hot earth. Dozing off was unavoidable in the intense
heat. Late afternoon shadows were lengthening as Saro was
jerked awake. Jiboa had gnawed through the rope. He sped
off in a wide arc, trying to get back to the other Jerbilrats.

The squirrel chased after him, shouting out, "Grab 'im,
Horty, he's loose!"

Quick off the mark, the young hare gave chase. He was
reaching out to grab Jiboa, when a piercing shriek came
from above. *"Kyeeeeeeeeee!"*

Jiboa threw himself flat, but Horty was knocked ears over
scut by a massive shape. A great buzzard—chocolate-and-
white plumed—snatched Jiboa up in its fierce, hooked
talons. It bore him off squeaking, high into the blue. Three
more of the deadly predators swooped down on the Jerbilrat pack, each one seizing a victim, as the rest tried vainly to
burrow into the dust. Then they were gone. The rest of them
fled westward, thrumming and wailing fearfully.

273

Then there was silence. Horty sat up, dusting himself off. "Stifle me whiskers! Did you see the size o' those birds? That's a pretty awful thing to happen to anybeast, even a Jerbilrat. Fancy bein' scoffed by a flippin', flyin' feather mattress, wot!"

Springald gazed around at the dusty, deserted plain. "Those poor creatures, no wonder life in this area makes them hostile to others. I hate this dreadful place!"

Fenna's voice sounded small and frightened. "How are we going to find water now that we're completely alone?"

Bragoon shouldered his sword wearily. "Just press on. Jiboa knew there was water over this way. We've got t'keep goin'!"

They staggered onwards, but as evening arrived Fenna collapsed. Saro rushed to her side, fanning her brow and rubbing her paws. The aging squirrel looked up at Bragoon. "Pore young thing, the heat an' thirst have got to 'er. We don't even have a damp cloth t'wet 'er lips. Fenna'll die if'n we don't get some water soon."

The otter covered the little squirrel with his cloak. "Right, mates, that's it. Horty, ye come with me! Spring, ye stay 'ere with Saro an' Fenna. Me'n Horty will find water, or die tryin'. If'n' we ain't back by tomorrer noon, ye'll know we never made it. But don't fret, we'll be long back by then with water!"

Sarobando and Springald shook their friends' paws.

"Good luck, an' fortune go with ye!"

"We'll be alright here, hurry back now!"

Horty bowed gallantly. "To hear is to jolly well obey, marm!"

The two comrades struck off into the gathering dark.

Saro and Springald settled down to their vigil. After awhile, Fenna began murmuring as she tossed and turned feebly. "A beakerful, is that all, Father Abbot? I'm thirsty . . . so very thirsty, Father."

The mousemaid cradled her friend. "Hush now, Fenn, lie still."

Softly, Springald began singing an old lullaby, from when they were Dibbuns together at the Abbey.

"Peace falls o'er vale and hill,
silence fades the light,
moon and stars watch over
little ones by night.
Dawn will send the day bright,
larks will sing for thee,
streams of slumber flow now,
round this babe and me."

Saro smiled. "That's a pretty song, I remember it from Redwall long ago. Ol' Sister Ormel used t' sing it in the dormitory. Happy days, Ormel was a good ol' mouse."

Springald sniffed. "I learned it from her, too. Sister Ormel passed on three winters back. She was well loved."

As they nursed Fenna, in hostile country, far from their beloved Abbey and its friendly creatures, Saro and Springald sat silent with their thoughts of Redwall.

Horty staggered gamely onward, though his paws were wobbling and his body bent with fatigue. Bragoon was in slightly better shape, but every step he took was an effort. Side by side they stumbled along through the night. Then the young hare tripped and fell, bringing the otter down with him.

Through cracked and swollen lips, Horty mumbled, "Beg your pardon, old lad, tripped over a confounded bush. Wonder what oaf left it there, wot."

He grunted as Bragoon scrambled over him and grabbed a pawful of leaves. Thrusting his nose into them, the otter whooped. "Wahoo! This ain't no bush, mate. 'Tis a big clump o' comfrey. There's water nearby, I'm sure of it. Water!"

Leaping up, they plunged forward with renewed hope and energy. The otter suddenly ground to a halt, pulling

Horty back. He pointed ahead, to where a soft glow emanated from behind the bulk of a widespread willow tree. Beyond that, the trickle of running water could be clearly heard.

Drawing his sword, Bragoon thrust the young hare behind him, uttering a quiet caution. "Stick close t'my back, an' don't do anythin' foolhardy. There's a fire burnin', t'other side o' yon tree. I 'ope there's friendly beasts sittin' round it."

Horty snorted. "Fat chance in this neck o' the woods, pal. All we've met is bounders'n'cads since we climbed those cliffs. Huh, friendly y'say, prob'ly so friendly they'll chop off our blinkin' heads on sight, wot?"

The otter's paw clamped over Horty's mouth. "Stow the gab an' stay behind me, we'll soon see!"

There were six reptiles in all—two large frilled lizards, three fat toads and a grass snake—lounging around the fire. They were grilling a mess of bleak and minnow on green twigs. Having made a bit of noise as they approached, both travellers were expected. One of the lizards stood barring their way to the water, which appeared to be a small streamlet flowing away into a dense pine forest. The rest of the reptile crew crouched, ready to back the lizard up.

Bragoon nodded civilly to them, noting that all eyes were on his sword. "Evenin' to ye, we've come for water."

One of the lizards sniggered nastily, trying to imitate the otter's voice. "H'evannin' to ye, we've a-come f'waterrrr!"

Horty noticed several large gourds of water nearby. "That's the jolly old stuff, water, you know, that pleasant liquid which is rather nice t'drink. I say, those tiny fish smell rather toothsome, wot. Don't suppose you'd like to donate a few to a worthy cause, a hungry but honest hare, eh?"

The reptiles edged around, circling the pair. The largest of the lizards picked up a crude, flint-tipped spear, pointing it at Bragoon.

"Watersss not a free, iz all oursss. You wanta fisssshes an' drrrrrink, give usss bright a blade!"

Ignoring him, the otter turned to Horty. "I don't know wot it is wid the beasts in this country, but they seem t'think we're dim-witted. Our stream, our water, our fish. While pore young Fenna's dyin' for a drop o' water. I've taken about enough of all this claptrap, mate. Ye take my sword, don't do anythin', just stay there, that's an order!"

Horty took the weapon and saluted. "As y'say, sah! An' pray, what d'you intend doin', if one may ask, wot?"

A slow, savage grin spread across the otter's tough face. "Nothin' much, I'm just goin' t'get us some water."

Roaring out a warcry, Bragoon launched himself at the reptiles. "Make way fer Bragoon o' Redwaaaaaallllll!"

Horty could not have moved if he had wanted to. He stood wide-eyed with shock, watching six reptiles take the most fearsome beating he had ever witnessed.

Bragoon broke the spear of one of the lizards over its head, then picked the reptile up and hurled it into the stream. He went at the others like a madbeast. Flinging himself through the air, he butted a toad heavily in its enormous stomach. As air shot out of the toad in a whoosh, he rudderwhipped it hard, thrice across the head, laying it senseless. He turned and grabbed the other lizard, running it forcefully, snout on, into the willow trunk. Seizing the grass snake, he used it like a flail, cracking the jaws of the other two toads with the snake's head. Bragoon leaped high. Still holding the grass snake, he landed on the two toads' stomachs, then booted all three toads into the stream. The other lizard sat facing the tree trunk, nursing its broken snout. Knotting the snake around its neck, the otter looped them both to a low branch.

Dusting off his paws and breathing heavily, Bragoon took the sword from the astounded young hare. Putting the swordpoint at the lizard, he growled, "In the future, mind yore manners an' be polite to visitors!"

The lizard clutched onto the coils of the senseless grass snake around its neck. The snake was looped to the branch above, keeping the lizard on tip-paw. Bragoon put his face close to the reptile and roared thunderously, "Yore all dead-beasts if'n I clap eyes on ye agin! D'ye hear me, slimeguts?"

Dipping a paw into one of the gourds, the otter tasted the water and spat it out in disgust, then called to his companion. "Git yore gob out o' that stream, young 'un. Wash these things out an' fill 'em wid fresh water. I'll get the fish." He stowed the sword over his shoulder. "Don't dillydally, mate. Fenna an' the others'll be waitin'. Put a move on!"

Horty hurried to do Bragoon's bidding, holding a conversation with himself as he rinsed and filled the containers. "Seasons o' soup'n'salad, 'pon my word! That crackpot must've been a right terror in his younger days, wot? Curl me crusts! A chap'd do well to stay the right side o' that otter, he's a bloomin' one-beast army!"

Bragoon's voice cut sharply into his meanderings. "Stop chunnerin' an' get 'em filled, ye great gabby windbag!"

Horty filled the last gourd with one paw, saluting furiously with the other. "Chunnerin', sah, who, sah, me, sah? No, sah, not never, nohow. Last one filled, sah, all correct, wot wot!"

Bragoon had chopped branches with his sword. He and Horty carried the gourds, strung on the wood and yoked across their shoulders, two to each of them. They had drunk sufficient water and chewed on the cooked fish as they trekked back to their friends.

Sighting the lean-to in dawn's pearly light, they dashed forward, slopping water, with Horty yelling, "Toodle pip there, you idle lot, here come two handsome water carriers. I say, we've got fish, too! Jolly good, eh?"

There was no reply from the shelter. Bragoon hurried forward, only to find it deserted.

BOOK THREE

"We lived one summer too long"

29

Morning sunlight filtered like molten gold through the gatehouse. Raga Bol picked his teeth with the silver pawhook, spitting a bone back onto the remains of a well-grilled fish, which he had breakfasted on.

The Searat captain was in a expansive mood, having slept dreamlessly without any giant stripedog nightmares. The whole incident surrounding Lonna had faded into the background since his arrival at the Abbey. He felt a sense of power, sheltered by the monumental red walls which he knew would be his new home. No more scouring the cold northeast seas. This was a place of fair weather, a fortress from where he could rule all Mossflower. Lord Raga Bol, he liked the sound of his new title.

Badredd quaked with pent-up tension as he awaited the Searat's verdict on his cooking. Blowfly stood behind him, twirling his knotted rope's end. Relief flooded through the small fox at the sound of the captain's coarse but satisfied chuckle.

"Haharr, I've eaten worse an' lived! Wot kinda fish was that 'un, matey? Wot 'erb did ye use on it, eh?"

Badredd answered promptly. " 'Twas a grayling, sir, grilled with button mushrooms an' dill. I did it special."

Bol patted his stomach. "Graylin', that's a nice-soundin'

name. Blowfly, wot are we goin' t'do wid this cook—flog 'im to a jelly wid yore rope's end or gut 'im wid this 'ook?"

Blowfly smiled, not a pretty sight. "Gut 'im, Cap'n, go on!"

The hook lunged out, capturing Badredd around his neck. He was dragged forward until Bol was breathing in his face.

"Make yoreself useful round 'ere, me liddle graylin'. Clean this place up, scrub it out an' make the bed. Blowfly, you stay 'ere, tickle 'im up wid yore rope's end if'n 'e slacks!"

Thrusting both scimitar and stiletto in his sash, the captain swaggered out onto the sunlit lawn. "Glimbo, rally the crew. 'Tis time we went for a parley wid our new friends!"

All night long, Foremole and his molecrew had been carrying rubble up to the dormitory to be used as extra defence material. Martha sat close to the window with Toran and Abbot Carrul.

Granmum Gurvel laid breakfast out on the windowsill for them. "You'm bee's h'eaten ee brekkist naow, 'tis gudd furr ee!"

The trio had already laid their plans. Toran poured honey and beechnut flakes over his oatmeal, pointing to the gatehouse. "Stand ready, everybeast, they're comin'!"

Raga Bol sauntered up with twoscore of Searats, as though he was out for a morning stroll. He waved up at them.

Toran grunted. "Don't look like they're goin' to attack right now."

"It wouldn't pay to!" Martha muttered grimly, reaching for one of Redwall's latest pepper bombs. Abbot Carrul stayed silent, polishing his glasses nervously on his habit sleeve.

A Searat brandishing a rusty axe snarled up arrogantly at the dormitory windows. "Get yerselves out 'ere, or we'll come in an' drag ye down!"

Drawing his scimitar, Raga Bol dealt the Searat a swinging blow to the jaw with its bone handle. He placed a sea-booted footpaw on the sprawled-out rat and spoke reprovingly. "Tut tut, I'm surprised at ye, mate. Is that anyways to be addressin' gennelbeasts?" Returning the blade to his sash, the Searat captain lectured the rest of his brutish crew. "Mind yore language when ye talks to the goodbeasts up there, that's an order!"

He winked broadly and turned away from them, performing a flourishingly elegant bow. His gold fangs glinted as he smiled up at the dormitory windows. "My 'pologies, an' a good day to ye all, messmates. Me name's Raga Bol, fer want of a better 'un. I'm 'ere to parley wid yore cap'n. 'Twould be a kindness if'n 'e'd speak t'me."

Abbot Carrul showed himself. "I am Father Abbot Carrul of Redwall. What exactly do you want, sir?"

Raga Bol put his head to one side, almost managing to look coy. "Ho, a bit o' this an' a bit o' that. Nothin' fer you to bother yore dear old grey 'ead about, Father Abbot. I'm nought but a simple beast who likes pretty trinkets."

Toran felt that Carrul had taken enough verbal fencing. Recalling the arrow which had been shot to slay his Abbot, he came forward, placing himself in front of Carrul. In one paw he held a long cook's knife; in the other, a pepper bomb.

"Wot would ye like, silvertongue—a bit o' this or a bit o' that?" He indicated both weapons as he spoke. "Make yore choice, 'cos that's all ye'll get from us. Redwallers aren't born fools. We know scum, even when they try to talk fancy!"

Realising that the otter could not be cajoled or wheedled, Raga hurled himself at the Abbey door, hacking at it with his sabre and knife and yelling to his Searat crew, "Attack! Break this door down!"

"Redwaaaaaallllll!" A warcry rang out as the defenders fired slingstones and pepper bombs down upon the foebeasts. A slingstone pinged off Raga's jaw, leaving it gashed.

283

He retreated from the door, bellowing, "Back! Out o' their range. Back!"

They stumbled back across the lawn to where they could see missiles coming and better dodge them.

Martha was shocked but elated. It had all happened so fast: one moment she was listening to the talk going back and forth, the next moment she was screeching like a wild-beast and madly launching off slingstones. She held her trembling paws up to her eyes, willing them to be still.

Toran winked at her. "Well done, beauty!"

His attention was distracted by Raga Bol, shouting, "Ahoy there! Is that the way ye treat creatures wot comes in peace? Aharr, ye wretches, I'll show ye the Searat way o' fightin' back. I'll burn ye out!"

The Searat captain marched off, back to the gatehouse. Some of his crew were nursing wounds, while others fled blindly, their eyes streaming as they sneezed uncontrollably and headed for the pond.

Martha could feel panic welling inside her. She clasped Toran's paw. "Will they really try to burn us out?"

Seating himself on the windowsill, the ottercook stared down at the Abbey's main door, directly below. "Aye, I thought they'd get around to that, sooner or later. But the Searats' plan won't work. How much of that soil an' rubble is there, Dwurl?"

Spreading his hefty digging claws, Foremole shrugged. "Much as ee loikes, zurr. We'm gotten gurt 'eaps o' durt'n'rubble, hooj marsess uv ee stuff!"

The Abbot looked over his glasses at Toran. "What are you thinking of, friend?"

The ottercook turned from the window. "Our Abbey is built o' stone, Father. Ain't many ways they can burn an entrance in. The big Abbey door is the one way. If that went afire, we'd be lost, sittin' on the other side of it, waitin' for the door to burn down. So I plan on blockin' it completely. We'll do it right now. Ain't no sense in losin' time, so we'd best work hard'n'fast. Pay attention, everybeast, this is the plan. . . ."

Raga Bol's mood had turned sour. He had supposed that his show of force would have gained him an easy victory rather than a shameful retreat. But it had become apparent that the Abbeybeasts were not afraid to fight, no matter how great the odds. He retired to the Abbey pond where he sat sullenly watching those of his crew who had been struck by pepper bombs dousing their heads in the shallows. Flinky and the rest of Badredd's gang were there, ineptly trying to catch another grayling. The captain took his spleen out on them, booting Flinky headfirst into the water.

The stoat rose spluttering, as he tried to placate the irate Searat. "Sure we was only tryin' to catch a fat ould fish for yer 'onour's supper. Ain't that right, mate?"

Halfchop nodded enthusiastically. "Kachunk!"

Raga Bol drew his scimitar menacingly. "Gerrout o' me sight, ye witless idiots, make yoreselves scarce. Now!"

Avoiding the keen blade, Flinky and the rest fled the scene.

Ferron, the gaunt rat, slung a flat pebble, bouncing it over the pond surface. "I wouldn't give 'em 'til sunset, Cap'n. I'd burn those beasts out now!"

Bol was loath to destroy any part of his new home. He looked to Wirga, his Seer. "Wot say ye, old one?"

Wirga was drawing patterns in the banksand with a stick. She shrugged. "If the sons of Wirga were here, they could use their darts on anybeast who showed at the windows."

Raga Bol glared at her. "But they ain't 'ere, are they? So do we burn 'em out, or have ye got a better way?"

The Seer sensed the danger in his tone. She made her reply diplomatically. "Set a fire in full view of the windows. Then send a messenger to give them one last warning. The sight of flames should alter their minds."

This was the answer the captain desired. He gave orders.

"Ferron, Glimbo, gather wood an' get lamp oil. Then set up a blaze on the lawn, where they kin see it. Wirga, take Chakka wid ye. Go an' warn those fools wot'll 'appen if'n they don't surrender t'me!"

Badredd had just finished mopping the gatehouse floor clean and was about to unbend when Blowfly slapped his rump smartly with the rope end.

"Yew missed a corner be'ind the door!" The fat Searat caught Flinky peering in through the open window at him. "Now then, slysnout, wot do yew want?"

The stoat smiled apologetically. "Beggin' yore pardon, sir, but 'tis the cap'n, 'e wants ye down by the pond."

Blowfly gave Badredd another sharp rap. "This place better be shipshape when I comes back, or I'll flay the back offa ye. Ahoy there, stoat, lend 'im a paw. I kin find me own way t'the pond." Blowfly waddled off, twirling his rope end skilfully.

The small fox tossed Flinky a damp rag. "You start on the windows, I'll see t'the floor."

The stoat pulled him upright, whispering urgently. "We're gettin' out o' this place. Come on now, while they're all at the pond we can make a run fer it!"

Badredd gazed dumbly at Flinky, as if not understanding what he had said. The stoat grabbed the cleaning rag from him and flung it away. "Don't stand there wid yore jaw flappin'! Are ye comin' wid us, or d'ye like bein' a slave? The rest o' the gang are hidin' by the gate, waitin'. All the Searats are down by the pond, there's not a sentry on guard at all!"

Badredd's limbs began trembling. "But wot if they catch us?"

Flinky could not keep the contempt out of his voice. "Huh, some grand ould leader ye turned out t'be. Yore better off stayin' here if'n yore too scared. We're goin'!"

He ran from the gatehouse to where the others were waiting. "Get that gate open, quick now!"

Soon Badredd came running from the gatehouse to join the escapers, shouting out, "Wait for me, mates. I'm comin', too!"

A moment later they were off, dashing south down the path and cutting off east into Mossflower Wood, leaving the main gate swinging lazily in the summer breeze.

Raga Bol was putting an edge to his blade on a stone he had found on the pond's edge. He glanced up sourly at Blowfly's approach. "Wot do y'want, eh?"

The fat Searat saluted with his rope's end. "Dat liddle stoat, the gabby one, 'e said yew wanted ter see me, Cap'n."

Blowfly dodged a swipe from the silver hook as Bol roared, "I never said no such thing. Get back to that gate'ouse an' see wot they're up to. Go on, move yer fat bum!"

He glanced up despairingly at the sight of Wirga and Chakka arriving back from the Abbey building. Both were caked from eartips to tails in a mixture of soil, rubble and sloppy debris, which clung to their bodies. The Searat captain shook his head in disbelief. "Well, make yore report. Wot 'appened to youse two?"

Wirga spat out grit. Pawing soil from her ears, she hawked and coughed to clear her mouth. "They didn't give us a chance to speak. We went round there like thee told us, but they wouldn't listen, would they Chakka?"

She waded into the pond and began washing the mess off as Chakka continued. "They was pourin' muck outta the winders, Cap'n. We tried to give 'em yore warnin', but a crew o' those moles lobbed a big 'eap o' rubble down on us. Not only that, but they kept tippin' stuff down until we was knocked flat. We 'ad to dig our way out afore we was buried. It looks like they're coverin' the Abbey door, so we can't put a light to it, Cap'n. Those beasts are killers, we was near suffocated!"

Raga Bol put aside sharpening his scimitar. "Have the others lit the fire on the lawn yet?"

Wirga emerged dripping from the pond. "Aye, the wood is burning."

Raga Bol hurried up from the pond, past the orchard and out onto the lawn at the front of the building where he could take in the full scene. He could see the top few timbers of the Abbey's main door. The rest had disappeared under a heap of debris, which was still pouring out of the window, forming a great hill of rubble, which completely blocked the doorway.

Quivering with rage, Bol strode up to the fire, which his crew was fuelling with logs, branches and planks. He smote at the blazing wood with his scimitar, scattering it onto the lawn. "Glimbo, git yoreself over 'ere! Stop burnin' the wood, we'll need it to pile up agin that load o' rubble!"

The one-eyed Searat, who had been enjoying the blaze, saluted his leader quizzically. "Ye don't want a fire then, Cap'n?" He recoiled, his face now splattered with spittle from the captain's furious rant.

"Can't ye see they've blocked the doorway, fool? Rubble won't burn, we need that wood to pile up agin that 'eap. We can climb up on it through the winders!"

Raga Bol sat down on the lawn, chopping at the grass with his blade and shouting out, "Can't ye use yore brains? 'Ave I got to do all the thinkin' round 'ere?"

Blowfly came plodding up from the gatehouse. "Cap'n, the vermin gang are gone. The gate's open, they must've escaped!"

Bol gritted each word out slowly, as if he was speaking to a dim-witted infant. "Well, go an' bring 'em back! Glimbo, you go wid 'im, an' don't show yer ugly faces back 'ere widout every last one of 'em. Go!"

Martha had heard every word. She smiled at the Abbot. "Well, that's a few less to bother us."

Sister Setiva ducked her head aside as a stretcher load of debris hurtled out of the window space. "Och, but did ye hear yon Searat? They're goin' tae make a ladder tae scale the heap o' muck. Whit are we to do now?"

Just then, Foremole Dwurl clumped into the dormitory, his face wreathed in a happy smile as he announced, "We'm no need to wurry o'er water nomores, zurr. Moi molers h'uncovered a gurt well, daown in ee cellars!"

Sister Setiva pursed her lips. "Och grand, but ah don't see how that's goin' tae help us fight Searats off!"

Toran shook Dwurl by his muddy digging claw. "That's a spot o' luck, me ole mate! Keep throwin' rubble out o' the windows, an' tell yore crew to start bringin' up pails o' water, as much as they can!"

The ottercook winked roguishly at Martha. "We'll see 'ow far the rats get, tryin' to scale a mudhill."

The haremaid clapped her paws gleefully. "Very good, Toran, what a splendid idea! Gurvel, keep making those pepper bombs. In a day or two those Searats will wish they'd never heard of Redwall Abbey!"

Little Muggum flung a pawful of debris moodily out the window. "Hurr, they'm founded watter. Oi 'speck uz Dibbuns bee's a getten barthed agin."

Sister Setiva patted the molebabe fondly. "Och aye, but ye can throw the soapy bathwater oot o'er the rats!"

Within the hour, Old Phredd had penned a poem about what he envisaged. Martha laughed along with the rest as the ancient Gatekeeper read it aloud to the defenders.

"They won't leave this Abbey, all filthy and scabby,
    when this war is done.
Our foes will retreat, looking clean nice and neat,
    every Searat's son.
Oh won't it be splendid, when this siege is ended,
    like roses they'll smell,
washed by bathwater sweet, looking fresh in defeat,
    as away they run.

Come one and come all, dirty vermin we'll call,
    should you need a scrub,

don't worry or fear, we've got bathwater here,
    you may take a tub.
Wash the mud out your ears, so you'll hear us my dears,
    for 'tis truth to tell,
you will know how it feels, with a clean pair of heels,
    from a Redwall Farewell!"

Raga Bol watched as Ferron and Rojin barred and shut the big wallgates. Wirga followed him inside the gatehouse, waiting silently on his command. The Searat slumped down on Old Phredd's bed, speaking his thoughts as he gazed up at the ceiling.

"Tonight, once 'tis dark, we attack. You stay 'ere wid a few o' the crew. Light a fire, make lots o' noise, they'll think we're all round by this gate'ouse. I'll take the rest an' storm the Abbey by surprise. Tell Ferron to gather all the wood that ain't burned. We'll need it to get up the rubble. I'll be inside afore that ole Abbotmouse knows it. I'll teach those bumpkins to defy Raga Bol. The floors in there'll be awash wid blood by the time I'm done!"

Wirga ventured some questions. "Do I leave the gates locked, Cap'n? What if Blowfly an' Glimbo return with the prisoners? Or my three sons, what if they return with Jibsnout?"

Raga Bol looked sideways at his Seer. "They got paws'n'voices, ain't they? Let 'em bang on the gates or call for ye to open up."

Wirga humbled her tone, knowing she was touching on a delicate subject. "Jibsnout and my sons are gone overlong now, they should have returned. Thou wouldst know then if the big stripedog still lives."

Bol snapped up off the bed. "Wot do I care about yore whelps, or Jibsnout, eh? I gave 'em a job to do, they should be doin' it. As fer the stripedog, mention 'im agin an' I'll let daylight through yore skinny carcass. Now get out an' give my orders to Ferron an' the crew. We attack tonight!"

30

Horty looked around blankly, spreading his paws. "Gone? Where in the name o' seasons have they gone to? They were supposed t'wait here, wot!"

Bragoon held up a paw. "Quiet, mate, don't move, stay still!" He cast around, starting in a small circle and going wider. "If ye go shufflin' about with those big paws o' yores, this dusty ground'll get disturbed. Ahah! Here's their tracks, aye, an' one other, too. Quick, mate, grab all the gear an' foller me!"

Horty gathered up the cloaks and staves which had formed the lean-to. Burdened by this, plus the two gourds of water on his yoke, he staggered after the otter. Bragoon, having shed his share of the water, was forging ahead swiftly.

Horty protested. "I say, old bean, that's a bit wasteful, ain't it, leavin' behind good water that you had to carry half the blinkin' night?"

Bragoon kept his eyes on the trail as he answered. "Can't stop now, got t'get to our mates fast—'tis a matter o' life an' death. Keep up as best ye can!" Hurrying forward, the otter began emitting an odd, piercing whistle.

Horty plodded on, twitching his ears in disapproval. "Huh, matter of life'n'death, an' the bounder's whistlin' if y'please? Wouldn't mind, but it's not even a flippin' catchy tune. The bally beast's brains have gone to his rudder if y'ask me, wot!"

Eventually Bragoon spotted the three figures, out on the arid plain. Springald and Saro were shuffling along facing backwards, supporting Fenna. Closely following the otter and his three companions, an adder was slithering, its forked tongue flickering out, sensing prey, the fatigued trio ahead of it. Hearing the sound of Bragoon's high-pitched whistle, the snake turned, bunching its coils and hissing viciously. Not as big as some serpents the otter had encountered, it was a male, just beginning to get its growth. But angry and deadly enough to deal a fatal bite with one speedy strike of its venomous fangs. Continuing to whistle, Bragoon drew his sword and moved closer, making ready to fight if necessary. The otter smiled grimly. His ploy had worked: the hunting adder had now become the hunted, its fate sealed.

Before the old warrior could strike, the young hare bawled out a warning. "Look out, pal, here come those blinkin' buzzards again!"

Like thunderbolts out of the blue vaults of morning, two large adult birds whizzed down. With total disregard for the snake's venomous fangs, they struck their quarry with lightning speed. The murderous beaks and talons of both buzzards snuffed out the adder's life with savage skill and ferocity. The dead snake was still writhing in the dust whilst they continued their frenzied attack. Then it went still, and the hawks screeched out their victory cry.

Shielding her eyes against the sun, Saro watched the predators bearing their limp prey off into the cloudless sky as Bragoon and the hare approached her.

She shook her head ruefully. "I wish I'd learned t'do that whistle. Never could get the hang of it, though. Burn me brush! Is that water you've got there, Horty?"

Shedding all his trappings, the young hare sank wearily

down. "Indeed it is, marm, but I'm afraid you'll jolly well have to com'n'get it for yourselves. I'm whacked out!"

Bragoon took the yoke from him and sat it across his shoulders, then lifted the two gourds. "Ye did well, mate, take a rest now."

The elderly squirrel and the two Abbeybeasts sat amid the wasteland dust, gulping down the life-giving liquid. The otter soaked a cloth, allowing it to dribble into Fenna's mouth. He wiped her face with the damp material, cautioning them, "Drink slower, or ye'll be sick. This young un'll be right as rain soon. So, wot 'appened, mate?"

Saro looked up from the gourd. "Just afore dawn, I scented the adder. Huh, I can sniff those things a mile off!"

She continued drinking as Springald took up the tale. "We knew it was somewhere close, stalking us. It was too dangerous to stay inside the lean-to, the snake would've found us. So we sneaked quietly off, but the adder saw us and came right on our track. I've never seen an adder before—horrible beast! I was scared clean out of my wits. Good job you found us in time, we couldn't have carried Fenna much further. And, Bragoon, will you teach me that whistle? It saved our lives!"

The otter lifted Fenna onto his back. "Some other time, miss. Let's get this 'un into the pineforest shade. We found a stream over that way. I'll take ye to it."

Saro closed her eyes dreamily. "A pine forest an' a whole streamful o' beautiful babblin' water. Lead on, mate!"

They entered the pines when it was midday. Horty raced ahead until he found the stream. He ran toward it, turning his head to shout, "This is the place, chaps! Hawhaw, wait'll I tell you what old Brag did to a gang of bullyin' reptiles last night. He gave 'em the towsing of their lousy lives, he . . . nunhhhhh!"

Without paying attention, Horty had run full head-on into a thick, low pine branch. He was laid flat out, unconscious.

Saro ran to him and lifted his head. "Stone-cold senseless!

That makes two we got to nurse now. Why didn't the lop-eared gallumper look where he was goin'?"

The remainder of the afternoon was spent beside the stream. Springald looked after her two friends whilst the older pair went foraging for food. It was so pleasant in the shade of the tall pines. Besides tending the invalids, the mousemaid had time to paddle and wash in the stream. It was a cool and peaceful spot with sunlight and shadow dappling everywhere. Fenna was recovering nicely when Bragoon and Saro returned. The two old campaigners brought with them wonderful chestnut-coloured mushrooms, wild onions, dandelion buds and a variety of edible roots and berries.

Bragoon was heartened by the sight of the squirrelmaid. "Feelin' better, eh, beauty? Well, we can't light no cookin' fires in a pine forest like this, 'tis too risky. Do ye fancy a nice salad, miss?"

Fenna watched the otter chopping everything finely with his swordblade. "Salad would be perfect, thank you!"

The moment the aroma of freshly cut food assailed his senses, Horty revived. "Oh goody! I say, you chaps, please pass the salad. Owchowchoooh! Me flippin' bonce is splittin'. Can y'see any of me brilliant young brains leakin' out, wot?"

Fenna could not stifle a giggle. "Oh, poor Horty, you've got a lump like a boulder, right twixt your ears. I'm sorry for laughing, it must be very painful."

The young hare winced when he touched the large swelling. "Painful ain't the word, Fenn old gel, it's absobally agonisticful. Don't think I'll last the day out, actually. Don't shed too many bitter tears when I turn me paws up an' peg out. 'Twas all done bravely in the line of duty. Wot!"

Saro inspected the injury. "Hah, it looks like a duck egg growin' out o' yore skull. Don't worry, though, you'll live. I've got just the thing for that. Sit still an' eat yore salad while I go an' make a poultice."

She spent some time at the stream, gathering certain things and soaking them in the water. On her return, the aging squirrel tore strips off a cloak for binding.

Horty pulled back apprehensively. "Don't hurt a dyin' young beast in his final moments. Be merciful, marm!"

Bragoon held the hare's paws as Saro worked. She tweaked Horty's whiskers whenever he moved. "Be still, ye great ninny! This is a compress of duckweed, dock, watercress, sainfoil an' streambed mud. Twill do ye a world o' good!"

When she had finished, the others had to turn away their faces to keep from bursting out into laughter. Horty sat dolefully munching salad. Atop his head sat a high turban of cloak strips, herbs and mud, secured with a tie beneath his chin. Both of Horty's ears flopped out at the sides. He glared at Bragoon, who was biting down on his lip to contain a guffaw.

"What's the flippin' matter with your face, chucklechops? D'you find somethin' funny about a wounded warrior, wot wot?"

The otter brought himself under control. "Who, me? No, mate, but I wouldn't go near any bumblebees if'n I was ye. They might be lookin' fer a new hive! Hohohohoho!"

Seeing there was no salad left, Horty rose regally and stared down his nose at the mirth-struck quartet. "Tut tut, I shall be carryin' on alone, without any aid from those I once called friends. Huh, bunch of whinnyin', witless woebetides. Fie upon you all, say I!" He stalked off in high dudgeon, his turban dressing awobble as he stooped to avoid branches.

Fenna grasped her sides, tears of laughter rolling down both cheeks as she gasped out, "Heeheehee, come on, I'm, haha, well enough to travel now. Ohahahahhh! We'd better go along with him just in case he, heeheehee, backs into a sharp branch, and we, hahahahaaaa, have to tie a turban to his tail. Whoohoohoohoo!"

295

The pine forest was a vast area. As evening fell, it became dark, swathed in a gloomy, green light. Horty was still not talking to anybeast, but the urge to utter some noise was so great that he struck up a mournful dirge.

" 'Tis a sad lonely life, I have oft heard it said,
to go wanderin' about with this wodge on one's head,
for I travel alone o'er desert an' lea.
Why, even the midges and ants avoid me,
while the ones I called pals an' the comrades I know,
all laugh 'til their rotten, cruel faces turn blue.
There's a grin on the gob of each pitiless cad,
as they scoff at the plight of a poor wretched lad,
but I'll carry on bravely, I won't weep or cry,
an' I'll have my revenge on 'em all when I die.
My ghost will sneak up while they're laid snug in bed,
an' I'll hoot spooky whoops through this thing on my
   head.
Then they'll cry out 'Oh Horty, forgive us, please do'
as my spirit howls loudly . . . 'Yah boo sucks to you!' "

When night fell, Horty broke down and wept inconsolably. Springald crept through the gloom and found him sitting on a log, feeling sorry for himself. She put a paw around him.

"Horty, don't cry. What's the matter? This isn't like you."

He shoved her paw away. "Yaaah, gerroff me, you don't care, no flippin' one bally well bloomin' cares about me!"

Bragoon took a firmer approach. "Come on now, mate, wot's all this blubberin' about, eh?"

Horty snapped a small twig and flung it at the otter, but it missed. "You ain't no mate o' mine, none of you lot is! I'm starvin' t'death, I've got a molehill growin' out me head, my poor skull aches like flamin' thunder, an' now I'm goin' blind. I can hardly see a paw in front o' me!"

Fenna took over, grasping the weeping hare's shoulders.

"Don't be silly, Horty Braebuck, and listen to me. What's all this carrying on for, eh? You're hungry, right? Tell me when you *aren't* hungry! What then, your head's aching? Stands to reason, you've suffered a nasty bang on it. But as for going blind, that's nonsense! It's so dark in this forest at nighttime that none of us can see much. Here, take hold of this stick and follow me. Don't keep fiddling with that dressing on your head or it'll never get better. Saro, have you any food left?"

The squirrel produced a few mushrooms. "I saved these."

Fenna gave the mushrooms to Horty. "Eat them slowly, take small bites and chew each mouthful twenty times. Come on, up you come, we've still got a lot of ground to cover yet."

They marched all night, with Bragoon scouting ahead and Saro keeping them on course. The otter returned in dawn's first glimmer, bringing with him a heap of ripe bilberries in his cloak.

"Lookit wot I found! I think there must be a river ahead, I could hear the sound of running water in the distance. Sit down an' get yore gums round a few o' these, Horty mate, they're nice'n'ripe. We'll rest 'ere awhile."

Horty was considerably less sorrowful when there was food in the offing. "Mmmm, better'n those measly mushrooms. I say, you chaps, I can see better. Flippin' bandage must've fell down over me eyes last night, wot. Oh corks, now everything's gone flippin' green! Why's it all green?"

Springald explained. "Because it isn't properly light yet, it's the day breaking over the treetops. Pines grow so thick in here that it makes the light look green."

But Horty would not be convinced. "Fiddlesticks, you're only sayin' that t'make a chap feel better. Ah well, I don't mind spendin' the rest o' me life in a green fug. Hawhaw, lookit old Brag, sour apple face, an' you, too, Spring, little lettuce features, an' you Fenn, young grassgob!"

Saro stared at him pointedly. "Ye missed me out?"

Having devoured all the available berries, Horty lay back and closed his eyes. "Hush now, let a chap get some rest, cabbage head!"

The squirrel chuckled. "That's more like the ole Horty we all know an' dread."

Midmorning found them back trekking once more, eager to be out of the oppressive pine forest. The further on they went, the more pronounced came the sound of flowing water.

Saro stopped to listen. "Sounds like a fairly wide river. Have ye got that ole map from the Abbey, mate?"

Bragoon produced the map, which had been made during the journey of Matthias of Redwall in search of his son Mattimeo. He scanned it closely. "Aye, we're on the right course, though I think we took a different route t'get to it. This is the high cliffs, here's the wastelands an' this is the pines we're in now. There should be some sort of open area ahead, then a big river. We'll soon see, mates. Press on, eh!"

They emerged onto the edge of a deep valley, the hill below them thickly dotted with smaller pines and lots of shrubbery. Below it was the narrowest strip of bank. Beyond that, a wide, fast-flowing river glimmered in the sunlight. Halfway down, the travellers halted on a shale ledge. They still had some way to go, and the descent looked fairly steep. Horty sat down, yawning in the heat. He rested his face in both paws.

Saro prodded him. "Are ye alright, head achin' is it?"

The young hare nodded. "A bit, but I'm more tired than anything."

Saro indicated an overhang that was screened by bushes. "Tuck yoreself in there young 'un an' take a snooze. I'll call ye when we're ready to move."

The four travellers slithered and bumped down the steep hillside, grasping trees and bushes to slow their descent. They were about halfway down when Bragoon sighted the reptiles. He halted, pointing.

"Down yonder on the riverside below us. Those reptiles I dealt with last night are waitin' for us. Trouble is, they've brought a pile o' their gang with 'em!"

Saro counted the assorted lizards, newts, toads, smooth snakes and grass snakes awaiting them on the shore. There were about thirty in all, with another twoscore camped on the opposite bank of the river.

A thin reed lance zipped upward, narrowly missing Fenna's cheek. She stumbled, almost overbalancing, but Bragoon managed to grab her. "Take cover quick, they're throwin' lances!"

To one side of the slope, a fallen pine had lodged flat between two standing trees. Crouching behind it, Saro fitted a stone to her sling and launched it off at the reptiles. Cautiously, she peered over the log, noting that a toad had hopped out of the way of her stone. "They ain't movin', just waitin' for us down there. Let's give 'em another couple o' slingstones, mate!"

Both she and Bragoon slung more stones as Springald and Fenna threw lumps of shale. They were forced to duck fast as a half dozen of the sharp, thin lances came back at them.

The otter thumped his rudder down irritably. "Well, this ain't goin' t'get us to Loamhedge. Those cold-blooded scum 'ave got us pinned down 'ere!"

Springald picked up one of the lances and threw it back. "It's a stand-off, what are we going to do?"

Sarobando passed her sling to the mousemaid. "Ye can use this, 'tis a good sling. But I'll want it back later. This is wot we'll do. While you three keep slingin' stones, I'll slide off through the trees an' take a scout round downriver. I'll find a good quiet spot where the river narrows for an easy crossin'. Then I'll slip back 'ere an' let ye know. Once 'tis dark, we can all sneak away an' escape. Right?"

Fenna nodded. "Sounds like a good idea!"

Bragoon raised his eyebrows. "Sounds like? Let me tell ye, missy, when my ole mate gets an idea, 'tis always a good 'un!"

Saro gave him a quick grin. "Thankee, Brag. Now let's give 'em a good rattlin' volley to keep their 'eads down while I pop off unnoticed. One . . . Two . . . Three!"

Slingstones and lumps of shale peppered down at the foebeasts below. When Springald looked up, Saro had gone. Bragoon shoved the mousemaid's head back down as more lances came.

"Always duck fast once ye've throwed, Spring. There's more pore beasts been injured or slain in fights by lookin' up to see where their stones went. Ready agin, come on, let's give 'em a spot o' blood'n'vinegar. Yahaaar! Try some o' this, ye scum-backed, bottle-nosed crawlers!"

Horty slept on beneath the overhang, blissfully unaware of what was taking place.

31

Saro put some distance between herself and the skirmish. Ahead lay a sweeping bend in the river. Making her way down to the bank, she skirted the bend and began jogging steadily along the shore. It was peaceful and quiet, with only the crunch of pebbles beneath her footpaws mingling with the murmur of riverwater, echoing off the high, wooded slopes on either side. As she got round the bend, Saro caught the sound of deep, gruff voices singing a river shanty. She pressed on toward the singing. It was a song she knew, and she was fairly certain who the singers would be. The aging squirrel joined in with the melodious music.

"Wally wally dampum dearie,
I'll sail back home next spring.
Kiss all the babies for me,
an' teach the lot to sing.

Toodle aye toodle oo, me daddy's a shrew,
whose face I can't recall,
but I'll stay home all season long,
until I hears him call.
Logalog Logalog Logalog Oooohhhh!

Ringa linga ling me darlin',
there's ribbons for yore hair,
I'll bring to ye a bonnet,
an' a fine red rockin' chair.

Toodle oo toodle ay, just wait'll the day,
Daddy comes paddlin' in.
I'll grow up big'n'strong then,
an' sail away with him.
Logalog Logalog Logalog Oooooooooohhhhhh!"

Cupping both paws to her mouth, Saro bellowed for all she
was worth. "Logalogalogaloga loooooooog!"

Six shrew logboats hove into view, sailing upriver. The
lead craft was by far the largest, carved from a mighty oak
trunk and fitted with a single square sail of scarlet with an
ornate letter *B* emblazoned on it. All the logboats were
packed with shrews, about a hundred of the small, fierce
beasts. Each spiky-furred shrew wore a multicoloured
headband and a kilt held up by a broad, copper-buckled
belt into which was thrust a short rapier. Their leader, a
solid old patriarch, with a thick, silver beard, stood in the
prow of the front craft. He signalled for the rowers to pull
into the shore.

No sooner had the vessel nosed in to land than the shrew
chieftain leaped ashore and seized Saro in a viselike bear
hug. He roared cheerily, "Sarobando, me ole squirrelcake,
where've ye been a-hidin' yoreself? Oh, it does me eyes a
power o' good to see ye agin! Belay, where's that rip-
ruddered rascal Bragoon? Is the ole villain still alive? Ha-
harrharrr!"

Saro tugged the shrew's big beard and kissed both of his
cheeks. "Log a Log Briggy, ye barrel-bellied ole riverroarer,
I knew 'twas you as soon as I 'eard yore song. Let go o' me,
mate, while me ribs are still in one piece. Lissen careful to
wot I got to tell ye!"

After loosening Saro, Log a Log Briggy listened as she told him the facts. "There's trouble upriver. Bragoon an' some young mates of ours are pinned down on the 'illside by reptiles. There's about thirty o' the scum on this side o' the water, an' more on the other side. We need yore 'elp, Briggy!"

The shrew chieftain's brows lowered menacingly as he gritted out the words. "Reptiles, eh? I can't abide the creepy, cold-eyed scum. They think they rule the roost up that end o' the river. Don't fret, matey, I'll put my oar in an' show 'em who the real bigbeast is in these waters. No reptile's goin' to mess wid good mates o' mine!"

He began issuing orders to the captains of the other five logboats. "Moor those vessels on the other bank, we'll come back for 'em later. Jigger, take twenty goodbeasts an' go wid Saro. Bring extra clubs along wid ye. Raffu, Fregg, Scordo, Fludge, you an' the rest foller me along the far bank. Keep 'idden among the trees, an' don't make no noise. Bring me Aggie Frogslapper, look lively now!"

One of the shrews passed Log a Log Briggy a hefty carved sycamore war club, which he wielded lovingly. "Ole Aggie's slapped a few frogs in 'er day. Hah, there'll be a lot o' reptiles won't be comin' back for a second kiss from ye, Aggie me old gel!"

Briggy introduced Saro to a young shrew who was the model of himself in bygone seasons. "This is me eldest, Jigger. 'Tis only his sixth season out as a Guoraf warrior, but he's shapin' up well. Jigg, me darlin' son, go wid Saro. When ye get yore fighters set up, wait for yore dear ole dad's call afore ye charge the scurvy foe."

Jigger shook Saro's paw. "Let's make tracks. I hate bein' late fer a fight, marm!"

Armed with clubs, rapiers and slings, the shrews set off with Saro and Jigger at a swift trot around the riverbend. Log a Log Briggy took his logboat with the other five craft across the river to the opposite bank. He was first ashore, stroking his club, Aggie Frogslapper, and murmuring fondly, "Aharr, 'tis a long time since ye had a good outin', me dearie!"

Night had descended over Redwall Abbey. Brother Gelf and Brother Weld sat by the dormitory window with Toran and Martha. The vermin had extinguished the fire on the Abbey lawn. Only the glow from a fire by the gatehouse could be seen. Abbot Carrul came up from the kitchens, threading his way through the Redwallers, who were resting on the dormitory floor. He pushed a trolley along to Martha and the watchers.

"I thought you might like some leek and chestnut soup. There's freshly baked cheesebread here, too."

Toran nodded admiringly. "Ole Granmum Gurvel's a treasure. All the strife we're goin' through, but she still finds time to cook good vittles for us. Thankee, Father!"

Abbot Carrul stared out the window. "Pretty calm out there. I imagine the vermin are taking their supper by that fire near the gatehouse. You can hear their voices when the wind drifts this way. Do you think they'll bother us tonight?"

Brother Weld exchanged glances with his friend Brother Gelf. "Well, you heard them say they'd attack us when it got dark. Don't let that little decoy by the gatehouse fool you, Abbot, they'll be coming shortly."

Carrul poised his ladle over the soup cauldron. "You'll excuse me saying, but we don't look exactly ready to stand off an attack, with everybeast sitting about on the beds and the floor. How will you know if the Searats are stealing up on us under cover of darkness?"

Brother Gelf chuckled. "Oh, we'll know sure enough, Father."

From out on the lawn, shrieks and curses rent the air, together with the clatter of falling wood. Martha said calmly, "That'll be them now. Right, friends, all to the windows and take up your positions."

The Abbot ducked to avoid a hooked window pole that Foremole Dwurl was carrying. "Will somebeast pray tell me what is going on out there?"

Martha patted the paws of the two brothers beside her. "It was their idea. We knew Raga Bol and his Searats would come once night fell. So Brother Weld and Brother Gelf had the bright idea of throwing broken glass, from the windows of Great Hall, out onto the lawn. Then, if the Searats tried to sneak up in the dark, they'd naturally let us know. It worked rather well, Father. Just listen to them!"

Raga Bol lurched about on the darkened lawn. He grabbed one of his crewrats, cuffing him about his ears. "Silence, ye fool, wot's all the yowlin' about?"

The Searat limped this way and that, trying to dodge the blows. "Somethin' sharp is stickin' right into me footpaw. I couldn't 'elp it, Cap'n, I swear!"

Bol shoved him away scornfully. "Somethin' sharp, eh? I'll give ye somethin' sharp if'n ye don't shuttup. Any chance we 'ad of a surprise ambush is long gone now. Never mind yore footpaws, get some fire in yore bellies an' try t'be like real Searats. Avast there crew . . . Charge!"

Keeping his voice low as he heard the captain bellowing, Toran the ottercook gave his own orders. "Up t'the winders, mates, let go the water!"

Sturdy moles trundled forward to the windows. They hurled out the contents of bowls, pails, pots, pans, cauldrons and buckets. Water cascaded over the rubble heap, which piled outward, protecting the Abbey door.

The first ranks of Searats flung tree limbs, planks and long branches against the heap. Raga Bol dashed about, shouting encouragement. "The fools won't stop us wid a drop o' water! Up ye go, buckoes. Board the place like it was a ship an' slay 'em all!"

Crewrats began scaling up the timbers. Unfortunately for them, the wood started sinking into the rubble, which had turned into a big mudheap, owing to the water drenching it. However, three of the longest planks spanned the mess, their ends resting on the sandstone lintel above the door.

When Raga Bol saw this, he waved his scimitar about wildly. "Ferron, Hangclaw, Rinj, gerrup those long bits. Come on, all paws t'the planks. Get through those winders, look sharp!"

Clenching blades in their fangs, the Searats clambered skilfully up the wooden lengths. The planks bellied under their combined weight but held.

Raga Bol laughed like a madbeast. "Haharr, keep goin'. We'll make it, mates!"

But they never quite made it. Hotroot pepper bombs burst on the heads of the lead climbers. Vermin wobbled on the planktops, trying to hold on whilst fending off the searing packages that pelted them.

Toran and the Redwall defenders appeared at the window spaces bringing their long, hooked window poles into play. The ottercook and four others latched on to a centre plank and heaved it out from the wall.

"Push, friends! Put yore backs into it an' shove!"

Under the concerted effort of the Abbeybeasts, the plank was forced outward. Searats clung shrieking to it, as the pole moved it away. With nothing to support it, the plank teetered for a moment, then toppled over backwards with vermin clinging to its underside.

Willing paws plied more window poles. Sister Setiva, Sister Portula and a crowd of elders pushed the left plank. Brothers Weld and Gelf, assisted by Gurvel, Foremole and three of his crew, pushed the one to the right. They strained and grunted, leaning their weight against the bending window poles.

Martha gripped the arms of her chair, lifting her body forward. She could hear herself roaring. "Push hard as you can. Push!"

The planks fell, one to either side of the windows. Wood scraped against stone as they plunged sideways. Wailing

Searats threw themselves clear—some going headlong into the mudheap, others thudding on the paving stones below.

The defenders fell in a heap on the dormitory floor, yelling out a great victorious cry. "Redwaaaaalllllll!"

Martha was about to drop back into her chair when an awful sight froze the breath in her throat. The Searat Ferron was crouching before her, framed in the window. He had leaped from the first plank before it had begun its backward journey. Latching on to the sill, Ferron had hauled himself up onto the windowledge. Now he perched there, snarling, a long dagger in one paw, ready to kill. In front of him, the Abbot had risen from the jumble on the floor and was standing with both paws raised wide, joining in the joyous shout of Redwall, with his back to the window.

Time stood still, Martha's voice had deserted her. She was holding herself up, with her paws still gripping the chair arms. In front of her, Abbot Carrul stood, smiling at the haremaid and cheering lustily. Behind him, the Searat raised his dagger, preparing to stab at the Abbot's unprotected back. Alarm bells were clanging furiously in Martha's brain, coupled with the voice of Martin the Warrior, thundering at her, "Save your Abbot!"

It was over in a flash! Martha stood upright. Charging past Carrul and pushing him to one side, she hit the Searat, knocking him right out of the dormitory window.

Toran came bulling forward. He grasped the haremaid's waist, pulling her back into the room. "You walked, Martha! You walked! You walked! You walked!"

32

Down on the lawn, Raga Bol turned and strode away from the scene of his defeat. The Searat Rojin limped up to him. "Cap'n, there's no way we kin get at 'em. Those beasts ain't as simple as they look."

Bol carried on walking without even looking back at Rojin. "Have ye only just realised that? Call the crew off. There's got t'be a way into that Abbey, an' I'll find it. Ye can take my oath on it, 'cos I ain't movin' from Redwall. 'Tis mine, d'ye hear me? Mine!"

Somewhere southeast, deep along a woodland trail in Mossflower Wood, Flinky stopped running. Breathless and shaking, he collapsed to the ground. The little gang of escaped vermin flopped down beside him. Badredd slunk at the back of the group, with nobeast paying him the slightest attention. Gone were his days as gangleader. Now all the vermin looked to the stoat, Flinky, as their saviour. He had taken them out of the Searats' clutches.

Panting hard, Crinktail clutched her mate's paw gratefully. "We did it, we got away!"

Halfchop grinned fondly at Flinky, his new hero. "Kachunk!"

Understanding what his pal meant, Plumnose nodded in agreement. "Wodd duh we doo's now, Flink?"

The triumphant stoat was never stuck for words, despite trying to regain his breath. "Ah well, Plum, we can't run anymore tonight. Let's just stow ourselves under those bushes an' take a good ould rest while we lay low there an' 'ide. Tomorrer we'll 'ead south, where nobeast will ever find us agin. Sure, we'll find a comfy spot where there's plenny o' vittles growin', clean water an' grand weather. That'll do fer us, a good plan, eh?"

Juppa's voice was full of admiration. "Aye, that it is. We're with ye all the way, Chief!"

Rolling beneath the bushes, Slipback settled down amid the leaf mold. The rest joined him, with Flinky still chattering on.

"Ah, sure, we musta bin mad, lettin' greedy ould fools an' oafs lead us. Ferget all the magic swords, sieges an' great abbeys. Wot more could a body want than layin' round in the sun all day, fillin' yore stummick wid vittles an' never an argument twixt the lot of us anymore. After wot we bin through, I reckon we deserves a taste o' the good life, mates!"

Owing to the size of his nose, Plumnose was gifted with a keen sense of smell. His voice carried a note of disgust as he called out in the darkness beneath the bushes. "Duh, sumthink smells h'awful round 'ere!"

Juppa gave vent to a horrified gurgle. "Yurgh, wot's this?" She shot out of the bushes on to the other side of the trail. Wringing her paws, the weasel performed an anguished little dance.

"There's a deadbeast in there! Yukk, I put me paw on its face. Creepy crawlies were all over its eyes!"

A mad scramble ensued as the gang ran out from beneath the bushes, shuddering and dusting themselves down.

Flinky was the first to express an urgent desire. "Let's get outta 'ere, run mates! We'll keep goin' 'til it's light, then I'll pick a better spot. Keep goin', don't stop fer nothin'!"

Their sounds receded south into the distant woodlands, until everything was still and silent once more. The only things that moved were the insects crawling over the lifeless carcass of Jibsnout—lying stretched beneath the bushes where Raga Bol had flung his slain body.

Around the midnight hour, two others came along that same path. The Searats, Glimbo and Blowfly. It was the latter who searched the ground closely for signs of the fugitives.

Sceptical of ever finding them, one-eyed Glimbo complained volubly. "Wot'n the name o' Hellgates do ye expect to find in this forest at night? We ain't even got a lantern!"

Blowfly wheezed as he heaved his bulk upright. "I got good blinkers, don't need no lantern. I've tracked 'em this far, an' I'll keep on 'til I lays paws on dat scurvy liddle crew!"

He unwound a long whip from about his flabby waist and cracked it. "I'll teach 'em t'run away. They'll be lucky to 'ave a hide to their backs by the time they git back to the Abbey!"

Glimbo watched him track on a piece, then come to a halt. Blowfly inspected the ground carefully, going back and forth over the same piece, muttering and cursing.

Glimbo relaxed, leaning against a tree. He scoffed sarcastically, "Ye've lost our liddle pals, I thought ye would. Nobeast kin track anythin' at night through 'ere. Give up, mate, let's git back t'the crew. They're prob'ly inside that Abbey now, grabbin' the loot an' plunderin' the place. Yore wastin' time out in a forest when we could be back there snatchin' our share."

Blowfly gave him a surly glare. "Huh, 'tis alright fer you, I'm the one t'blame for lettin' them escape. 'Tis me who Cap'n Bol will take it out on. I can't go back empty-pawed!"

His companion did not agree. "Aw c'mon, Bol won't be frettin' over a few runaway fools. The cap'n 'as other things t'think about. A kick in the tail an' a few 'ard words is the most we'll get. Huh, we've 'ad plenny o' those afore now. Belay there, shipmate, wot are ye doin'?"

Blowfly looked up from his task of striking flint to steel. "Wot I shoulda done awhile back, makin' a torch. I'll find these runaways, just ye wait'n'see!"

Glimbo seated himself with his back against the tree trunk. "Well, ye can find 'em on yer own, 'cos I ain't goin' anywheres. When ye come back this way widout 'em, gimme a shake. I'll be right 'ere, takin' a nap."

Blowfly held up the burning torch he had fashioned. Silent and stubborn, he trudged off alone into the night.

Lonna Bowstripe saw the glow from between the trees where he sat resting. It appeared like a small floating island of light in the darkness. Silent as a wraith he arose, becoming one with the forest as he stood motionless against the elm trunk. Blowfly walked by within a paw's reach of the big badger. Staring at the ground, the Searat mumbled bloodthirsty curses as to the fate of the lost fugitives. Lonna saw his face in the torchlight, and a trigger went off in his mind. He recalled brief flashes of the night he had been attacked by the Searats. Blowfly's coarse, ugly features were instantly identifiable. Swiftly, the badger strung his bow and stole up behind the unsuspecting Searat.

Blowfly was jerked back as the tightly strung bow trapped his neck between wood and twine. The big badger managed to catch the torch before it fell.

Craning his head around painfully, the Searat caught a glimpse of his captor and spoke almost indignantly. "Yore dead!"

Lonna drew him in until they were face-to-face. Only the pressure on the bow held the Searat upright, his limbs having turned to jelly.

With torchlight flickering over his scarred features and the light glinting in his vengeful eyes, the giant badger resembled some beast straight out of a nightmare.

Blowfly's tongue suddenly ran away with him. "It was

311

Bol . . . it wasn't me . . . I wasn't nowhere near ye. I swear me oath on it, I never did nothin' . . . Gurgg!"

A sharp tug on the bowstring silenced him. Lonna's voice left the Searat in no doubt that lies would not save him. "So you never did anything, you were nowhere near, it all had nought to do with you, you are innocent of everything?

"How many times has that same excuse been made? Think of every bully, cheat, plunderer or murderer before you who has lied with those same words. Once a villain is caught with no pack around him, then everybeast is to blame, except himself, of course. He will lie, betray and cheat to save his hide. But sometimes there is justice in the world, and fate catches up with him. So speak truly to me, or you will die slowly. You have my word on it—and I never lie."

Blowfly sighed with relief. He told Lonna all he needed to know, and he spoke truly. The big badger kept his word: the Searat did not die slowly. A single, mighty jerk of the bow, and Blowfly died quicker than he had ever expected to.

Awakened by flaring torchlight, Glimbo yawned and stretched his paws. "Betcha never caught 'em, I told ye afore y . . . Ukkk!" The Searat's paw shot to his neck. Blowfly's long whip was tied around it, holding him fast to the tree he was sitting against.

A deep, forbidding voice warned him, "Be still, vermin!"

Automatically he raised his other paw, trying to free his neck. There was a hissing sound, like an angry wasp. An arrow of awesome length buried its point deep in the tree trunk, a hairbreadth from his neck. Glimbo froze.

Lonna revealed his face in the torchlight, laid another shaft on his bowstring and unhurriedly explained his purpose to the petrified Searat. "You will take me to the Abbey of Redwall. I am going to release you, but play me false, you'll wish you hadn't. Is that understood? Speak!"

Glimbo's good eye rolled about alarmingly in its socket—he was completely terrified. "Unnerstood!"

The badger drew a long knife from his arm sheath and severed the whipcoils with a swift stroke. The Searat shot off like a hare at top speed. Lonna drew back the bowstring, homing in on the fleeing figure.

"Never mind, I'll find my own way."

33

Fenna lowered her head quickly. More thin, sharp reed lances whipped viciously by. "Don't they ever run short of those things?"

Without raising himself, Bragoon hurled off a slingstone. "There's always reeds aplenty on riverbanks. They just cut 'em an' point one end—it makes a good throwin' lance, sharp an' dangerous. I've used 'em meself in the past."

Saro suddenly rolled in beside Springald. "Aye, but ye weren't much good with lances, too 'eavy pawed."

The otter scratched his rudder. "Where did you come from, mate?"

Saro smiled, secretly enjoying the surprise she had in store. "I found a bend in the river down that way, an' guess wot else I found?"

She signalled with her paw. Suddenly Springald found herself being jostled by a score of shrews who had crept out from behind trees and bushes to join them in the shelter of the log.

The otter uttered a delighted growl. "Guoraf shrews . . . Great!"

Saro pointed to Jigger. "Aye, Guoraf shrews, an' who does this 'un remind ye of, Brag?"

The otter inspected Jigger's face, noting the beard he was starting to cultivate. "Wait, don't tell me, are ye a kinbeast to Log a Log Briggy, young 'un?"

Jigger expertly caught a reed lance as it flew by. As he cast it back downhill, he was rewarded by a reptile's scream. "Briggy's me old daddy. You must be Bragoon, the mad otter. Daddy's tole me about you. Pleased t'meetcha!"

Fenna whispered to Saro. "What's a Guoraf shrew?"

The squirrel explained, "That's just the first letters of their tribename. *Gu*erilla *U*nion *o*f *R*oving *a*nd *F*ighting *Sh*rews. They're good friends an' fearsome warriors. Sometimes I think that they do all their far rangin' just lookin' for fights. Me'n Brag have battled alongside of 'em once or twice through past seasons."

When everyone was acquainted, Jigger outlined the plan. "We've got to 'old on, 'til me dad an' the others get set on the far bank. Then when we 'ears the signal, we charge an' cut loose at those reptiles on our side."

Bragoon mulled it over. "Sounds like good sense t'me, mate. This crowd down below ain't goin' anyplace. They're tryin' to outwait us, an' slay us all when we makes a move t'leave."

Jigger peered over the log and ducked a few lances. He thudded the ground with his club, chortling eagerly, "Reptiles'll stan' about waitin' fer ages in the sun. Well, I 'ope they enjoys their sunbath, 'cos we'll be givin' 'em a different kind o' tannin'. Hahaha!"

Saro spotted slight movements in the bushes on the far hillside. "Looks like ole Briggy's gettin' the lads into position. Won't be long now."

Without any prior warning, Horty came skipping blithely out from beneath the overhang. He ran by the log, speeding downhill and calling back to them, "Shrews, eh? Where'd ye meet that flippin' lot? I feel much better now, chaps. Who's for a jolly old paddle in the shallows, wot?"

When three lances came zinging at him, the young hare

stopped, but the weapons had pierced his ridiculous head-dressing. He ground to a halt, only paces from the dumb-founded reptiles.

"Great blinkin' seasons, have a flamin' care where you're chuckin' those things. A chap could get injured by them!"

Knowing that the plan had been ruined, Bragoon, Saro and Jigger, followed by their fighting force, came bounding downhill. At the bottom they found, to their shock, that the reptiles were lying prostrate, facedown in front of the young hare. Horty stood posing majestically, the three lances trans-fixing his turban.

Saro glared at him. "Wot were ye thinkin' of, ye great idiot? Lollopin' off right into the middle of the enemy like that!"

Horty gave her a scathing glance. "Hold your tongue, marm. These chaps are just showin' their respect to me. Hawhaw, they must think I'm the Great Hortyplonk, de-scended from out the bloomin' sky, wot!"

Springald scoffed in his face. "Then they must be bigger idiots than you! D'you realise you could've been killed?"

As she spoke, there was a whooping warcry from the far bank. *Logalogalogaloooooog!* Briggy had commenced at-tacking the reptiles over there.

The reptiles laid out in awe of Horty lifted their faces. When they saw the score of shrews brandishing their clubs, they rose, backing off into the shallows.

Horty took a few paces toward them. "I say there, old scaly-skinned chaps . . ."

Hissing and squeaking, the reptiles fled into the water.

The young hare turned to Jigger, who was looking rather crestfallen. "Oops, sorry about that, old lad. Were you goin' to give those bounders a good drubbin'? I didn't realise. Oh well, never mind. Come on, we'll pursue 'em into the river an' deal 'em a few severe whackin's, wot!" He trotted into the shallows but was immediately set upon and hauled back by four shrews.

Horty protested vehemently. "Wot the . . . ? I say, unpaw

me, little sirrahs, I'm not scared of a few mangy reptiles, by the left, I ain't!"

Jigger remarked caustically. "Oh, we know ye ain't, lop-ears. But it's not the reptiles that's the danger on this stretch o' the river. Watch!"

He picked up a lance and went into the shallows, holding the weapon out into the water at paw's length. Suddenly it began to shake and vibrate. When Jigger pulled it out, the tip was ripped and ragged. A small fish, which seemed to consist of only big, needlelike teeth, was clinging doggedly to it. Jigger flicked the creature back into the water.

" 'Tis the fish that are the slayers 'ere!"

The reptiles were being swept downriver, shrieking unmercifully as the water about them reddened.

Horty sat down in a collapse on the bank, looking pale about the gills.

"Oh corks, I feel quite ill all of a sudden!"

On the far bank, the reptiles were taking a colossal walloping from Briggy and his command. They had tossed a big logboat sail over their foes, capturing most of them beneath the spreading canvas. Some of the Guorafs held the ends down, while others galloped about on the sailcloth, dealing great whacks with their war clubs to any bump that appeared—be it head, tail, back or limb. Gradually the canvas subsided and was still.

Log a Log Briggy waved over to them, his stentorian bass voice booming over the waters. "Stop there, friends, I've sent a crew to git the boats. They'll pick ye up an' bring ye over!"

It was a glorious evening on the far bank. Six logboats lay prow on to the bankside, as the travellers sat among their shrewfriends.

Horty sniffed the air appreciatively, his whiskers atwitch at the aromas of cooking. "I say, old Briggathingee, is that supper I detect? Jolly nice of you chaps, wot!"

Briggy pulled a mock glare at Bragoon. "So, ye had

t'bring a starvin' hare along with ye this trip. I'll wager that lollop-lugged young famine maker can shift a tidy few platefuls, eh?"

Horty smiled primly. "Oh, I just nibble a bit here'n'there, y'know, sah. Actually I've not been feelin' too chipper of late. But if the scoff's as good as it smells, well, I might persuade myself to try it, wot."

Jigger looked askance at him. "Lissen, mate, if'n ye want to sail wid the Guorafs, ye've got t'be a big eater an' a great bragger, like Drinchy 'ere. Ain't that right, Drinch? Show the harebeast 'ow 'tis done."

A fat, powerful-looking shrew stood up, smirking, then launched into Riverbraggin, an art much admired among the longboat crews. Drinchy thumped the ground with his club and commenced roaring, "I wuz borned on a river in a thunnerstorm, an' wot did I do? I ate the bottom outta the boat an' fought six big pike who tried to eat me! Though I wuz on'y a babe, I scoffed three of 'em, an' tossed the rest on the bank an' fried 'em for me brekkist! Aye, mates, I'm Drinchy Wildgob, the roarin' son of a roarin' son who killed 'imself tryin' to feed me. I can outeat, outchew an' outswaller anybeast alive—includin' long-pawed, flop-eared, fancy bunnies!"

Finished with his mighty brag, Drinchy bowed as the shrews cheered him raucously.

Saro nodded to Horty. "I think you're bein' challenged, young 'un. Think you can do better than Drinchy?"

Horty stood up, bowing elegantly to Saro. "Marm, my dander has risen since the remarks that chap made about me. We of the Braebucks are not backward in coming forward. I shall accept this curmudgeon's braggin' challenge, forthwith!"

Without further ado, Horty bounded up, spreading his paws dramatically and yelling like a madbeast. "I'm the son of the howlin' hare! I was born on a winter's night in a gale. My parents took one look at me, chewin' on the chimney, an' left home! There ain't a cauldron big enough to hold my dinner, not one in all the land! I've ate every jolly old thing—fried frogs, toasted toads, boiled badgers, roasted reptiles, an' shrews, too! Shrew stew, shaved an' shrivelled shrews, shrew soup an' simmered shrew! I've got a stomach of iron an' a mouth like a steel trap! I'm the Horrible Hortwill Braebuck, an' nobeast steps over my line! Even little fat wretches with bellies like balloons an' spiky fur an' names like Drinchy! D'ye know what the Horrible Horty likes for supper? Daintily diced Drinchy . . . with lots o' gravy. Yaaaaaah!"

The Guoraf shrews battered the ground with their war clubs, a mark of the highest honour they could show anybeast. Then they hoisted Horty up on their shoulders, cheering him twice around the camp.

With a look of thorough humbleness, Drinchy shook the young hare's paw fervently. "Well, I more'n met me match there, mate. Ye must be the best bragger ever born, ye made me look like a beginner."

The triumphant Horty was gallant, even in victory. "No hard feelins, Drinch old lad, but mind your language in the future, wot!"

A magnificent supper was served, as befitted shrewcooks, who were renowned across the waterways for their culinary skills. Huge portions were served up to Horty. The shrews gathered round, gazing in awe as he downed one dish after another.

"Mmmm yum! This is top-hole tucker, wot wot. Pass some more o' that skilly'n'duff, please. Oh, an' lob more honey over it, I like it that way. I say, is that actually rhubarb-'n'blackberry crumble? . . . Where's me blinkin' spoon? Drinch, old scout, would y'be kind enough to fetch more shrewbeer—not that little beaker, gimme the jug!"

Bragoon chuckled. "Look at young Horty, he's in 'is element there. They'll get tired o' servin' before he does of eatin', mark my words, Briggy!"

The shrew chieftain watched Horty admiringly. "That 'un should've bin a shrew, mate. I saw 'im march straight inter that reptile crowd widout turnin' a hair. They'd already throwed three javelins an' spiked 'is hat. I tell ye, Bragoon, it takes a brave beast to do that!"

The otter poured himself another beaker of shrewbeer. "Or a ravin' idiot! I'll tell ye the truth of it all someday."

Horty was on to a wild grape and almond pudding. "Never had this before. My word, it's rather toothsome, wot. Send the old cook out, an' I'll give her a kiss!"

A small, toothless, grizzled male shrew stumped out from behind the cauldrons hanging over the fire. He grinned. "H'I'm the cook round 'ere. Wot was it ye wanted, sir?"

Horty choked on a mouthful of pudding. "Wot, er, oh nothin', granddad. Excellent scoff, wot. Top marks, well done an' all that. Back to the old fire an' keep on cookin'. Eh, wot!"

Log a Log Briggy called to his shrews. "Ye can let those reptiles free now, I reckon they've learned their lesson. If any of the slimy-skinned lot give ye any bother, give 'em another drubbin' an tell 'em you'll sling 'em in the river. That should scare 'em!"

He sat down with Bragoon and Saro, winking fondly at them. "Now then, mateys, wot brings you two t'these parts, eh?"

They explained the mission for Martha's cure and their quest for Loamhedge.

Briggy stroked his beard. "Hmm, Loamhedge eh? I've 'eard tell o' the place. But ye'd 'ave to cross the great gorge to git anywhere near where the stories say the lost Abbey o' Loamhedge lies. Did ye bring some kind o' chart along to 'elp ye find it, or are ye just trustin' to fortune?"

Bragoon produced the chart from Matthias's journal. "It's been mostly luck to date, but we do 'ave this."

Briggy rummaged a battered single eyeglass from his belt pouch and held it to his eye. "My ole peepers ain't wot they used t'be, I got to use this monocle t'see. Right, wot've we got 'ere?"

He perused the dilapidated parchment thoroughly. "Hah,

I know this country, 'tis sou'east o' where we are now. I've seen these two rocks an' all. They're called the Bell an' the Badger's 'ead, great big lumps o' stone they are. Wot's this, a large tree called the Lord o' Mossflower? Huh, that was long gone in the seasons afore my father's grandfathers. Blowed down, or collapsed more likely, when the earth trembled."

Saro looked anxiously at the shrew chieftain. "But ye do know where the two big rocks are?"

Briggy stowed his monocle away. "Ho, I knows that place sure enough. East along this river for a day or so, then cut south when ye leave the bank. Wicked country, 'tis."

Bragoon patted his swordhilt. "That don't worry us, we've travelled wicked country afore. So will ye take us up-river to the Bell an' the Badgers 'ead, me ole mate?"

Briggy held out his paw. "Course I will, 'ere's me paw an' 'ere's me heart on it. But afore ye gets to the big rocks, ye've gotta cross the great gorge. I never knew of anybeast who's done that yet."

Saro winked at him. "You leave that to us. We've done lots o' things nobeast 'as ever done, me'n my mate."

Jigger joined them, taking a great interest in Bragoon's sword. "That's a fine-lookin' blade ye carry, mate."

The otter drew the sword, holding it out to let the firelight play along its blade in the gathering twilight. It shimmered and glinted like a live thing. "Aye, a fine blade it is, young 'un. My friend, the Abbot o' Redwall, loaned it t'me for the journey. 'Tis the sword of Martin the Warrior!"

The shrews had evidently heard of Martin. As word ran through the camp, they crowded around Bragoon, straining to catch a glimpse of the legendary weapon.

"So that's the sword o' Martin. 'Tis a sight to be'old!"

"They say 'twas made at the badger mountain from a piece of a star wot fell out the sky!"

"Blood'n'fur, fancy ownin' a blade like that!"

Jokingly, Jigger drew his own short rapier and waved it. "Would ye like to challenge me to a spot o' swordplay?"

There was a twinkle in Briggy's eye as he nudged the otter. "Go on, mate, show 'im wot a real swordbeast kin do."

Bragoon rose casually, then moved like lightning. Jigger stood aghast, rooted to the spot as the sword encircled him in a streaking pattern of light. It clipped one of his whiskers and tipped the bandanna from off his forehead. The young shrew closed his eyes tightly.

Bragoon whirled the blade as he roared. "Yahaarrr, ssssss'death!"

The rapier flicked from Jigger's paw. It whipped through the air, then quivered pointfirst in the prow of his father's big logboat which was drawn up on the bank.

Jigger gasped. "Scuttle me keel! How'd ye do that, mate?"

Bragoon winked roguishly at him. "That's a secret, young 'un!"

The Guoraf shrew greatly admired the otter's prowess. "Could I see yore sword, sir, just fer a moment?"

Bragoon held the blade about a third of the way up. Raising his paw, he did a short hop and threw it. It turned once in the air, almost lazily; then, with a solid thud, buried its point into the logboat, next to the rapier.

The otter nodded. "Aye, 'elp yoreself. But take care, yon's a sharp blade."

Jigger retrieved his own rapier, but he could not budge the sword since it was too deeply imbedded in the oaken boat. Bragoon went to sit down with Briggy.

The shrew chieftain stroked his beard. "Where'd ye pick up swordtricks like that?"

The otter shrugged. "A Long Patrol hare from Salamandastron showed me some dodges with a blade one time. That 'un was wot they called a perilous beast, a real sword-fighter, no mistake!"

Horty looked up from the remnants of a huge pastie. "A Long Patrol hare, indeed! That's what I'd like to jolly well be someday, wot!"

Saro patted Horty on the stomach, knocking the wind

from him. "Then ye'll have to scoff less an' exercise more. Long Patrol hares are fightin' fit."

The young hare got quite huffy. "Fiddlesticks, marm, one's got to get the right nourishment t'grow strong first, wot?"

Briggy smiled at him. "Yore right there, Horty, an' ye need a full night's sleep, too. Go an' pick yoreself out a good berth on my vessel. We've got a journey upriver t'make at dawn. I'll put ye to the oars, that'll toughen yore muscles up a bit. You git yore rest now, an' you, too, Jigger."

Horty gathered up some bread, cheese and pear cordial. "Right y'are, Cap'n Briggathingee. I'll just take along a light snack to guard the young body against night starvation. I suffer from it terribly, y'know. I was born with the illness. I say Jigger, old lad, not takin' any rations with you? Well, suit y'self, laddie buck, but don't come pesterin' me durin' the flippin' night."

Jigger, however, was not listening. He had found a new object for his admiration. The young shrew was all smiles and attention for Springald. Carefully he helped the mouse-maid aboard the logboat that he was travelling on.

"Watch yoreself, Miz Spring, these boats are tricky craft. You take some o' my cushions an' a soft blanket. Sleep up in the prow, that's the best spot aboard!"

The pretty mousemaid played him up outrageously, fluttering her eyelashes and allowing him to make up her bed. "Oh thank you, my friend, that's so kind of you!"

Fenna scooted in and flopped down on the cushions. "Plenty of room for us both here, Spring. Thanks, Jigger mate!"

Sitting by the fire with Briggy and her otter friend, Saro watched the young ones with amusement. "Nice to see 'em gettin' on well t'gether, eh?"

Stirring the flames with his rapier, Briggy laughed. "Ha-harr, bless 'em, they're only young once. The seasons soon fly by, ain't that right, Brag, ye ole battler?"

Bragoon polished Martin's sword with a piece of damp

323

bark. "Ye never spoke a truer word, ole pal. Me'n Saro have gotten quite fond o' those three young 'uns, they're made of the right stuff. Now an' agin we gotta yell at 'em, but they learn fast. By the way, on that chart o' mine it says Long Tails an' desert beyond the river. Will that mean danger for us?"

Briggy looked scathing. "Huh, Long Tails? My ole Granpa whopped those rats seasons afore I was born. Guorafs drove 'em off into the desertlands south o' the great gorge. They shouldn't trouble ye, though the desert might. 'Tis a long dusty trek to the gorge. D'ye want us t'come with ye?"

Saro clapped the stout old shrew's shoulder. "No, mate, you git back to yore river, that's what ye know best. We've managed one desert by ourselves, another one won't make much difference. We'll be fine!"

Briggy seemed relieved. "I thankee fer that, Sarobando. I don't like bein' far from runnin' water anytime. But I'll tell ye wot I'll do. We'll bring the boats back to where we drop youse off, say in about six days. I'll pick ye up for the return journey. There's a secret route I know that'll take ye back to the flatlands below the plateau. It means shootin' a mighty waterfall to git down there. But don't fret, my crews kin do it if anybeasts can. 'Twill get ye back 'ome to Redwall much faster."

Bragoon shook the old shrew's paw heartily. "Yore a real friend, true blue'n never fail, Log a Log Briggy!"

The shrew chieftain rose from beside the fire. "Think nothin' of it, mate. I'm off t'me bed, if'n that young Horty ain't stolen it. Us old 'uns need sleep as much as the young do. Pleasant dreams, ye pair o' rips!"

The aging otter and his lifelong friend sat by the fire awhile. Bragoon stared into the flames. "We're gettin' too old for this sorta thing, Saro. I think when this adventure's over I'll settle back down at Redwall. Maybe that brother o' mine'll teach me to be a cook."

The squirrel stared levelly at him. "If'n that's wot ye

want, then fair enough, matey. I'll be by yore side wherever ye are."

The otter chuckled drily. "An' so ye will be, we been together since we was Dibbuns. I wouldn't know where to turn widout ye."

That night they slept by the fire, dreaming dreams of the sunny old days at the Abbey when they were both young tearaways together.

34

Martha was up at dawn, trying out her newfound skill—walking! At first it was painful and slow, but the progress she was making, holding on to things for support, was remarkable. With the aid of Sister Setiva's blackthorn stick, which the Infirmary nurse had parted with happily, the haremaid wandered joyfully along Great Hall.

Martha laughed inwardly at what Setiva had said: "Och, take this auld thing an' use it in good heath, ma bonny lass. Ah've only kept it tae threaten Dibbuns with—not that they ever took much notice, the wee villains!"

The young haremaid manoeuvred the stairs, pausing every few moments to revel in her newfound freedom. Walking!

Abbot Carrul came up behind her, watching Martha's progress, until she turned and noticed him.

"Good morning, Father Abbot, it's a fine morning!"

Carrul beamed back at her. " 'Tis the finest of mornings, young miss, and all the better for seeing you up and about!"

As Toran came out onto the dormitory landing, he waved down to them. "Now then, you two gabby idlers, why ain't ye bringin' brekkist up to the pore beasts on guard, eh?"

Martha started eagerly back downstairs. "Breakfast for how many, sir—one, two, ten? It'll be up there directly!"

Granmum Gurvel came trundling through Great Hall, heading a small convoy of moles who were pushing four trolleys. She brandished her best copper ladle at Martha.

"Ho no you'm woant, brekkist bee's ee cook's tarsk roun' yurr. Miz Marth', you'm 'asten oop to ee durmitrees an' set ee on a churr. Rest yore paws naow. Doo ee hurr?"

Brother Weld had joined Toran on the landing. "Best do as she says, or old Gurvel'll skelp your tail with her ladle. That's one old molecook who'll stand no nonsense."

Breakfast in the dormitory was a makeshift affair, rather inconvenient for most but huge fun for the Dibbuns. The Abbeybabes, who thought everything was a game, perched in the oddest places, singing, playing and eating together. Sister Portula was trying to coax Muggum, and several of his cohorts, down from a shelf, where they were bouncing up and down as they squabbled over hot scones and honeyed oatmeal.

In a state of despair, she turned to Martha. "Oh dear, I do wish the Searats weren't here and we were back to normal. Just look at those little ones, they're getting very wild. But with no Abbeyschool, and having to spend all day indoors, who can blame them?" Portula looked to Martha for comment, but the haremaid was not listening. Her joyous mood dispersed, she stood gazing forlornly out the window.

The kindly Sister showed concern. "Martha, dear, is something the matter, what's wrong?"

Toran was close enough to hear his young friend's reply. "I'm sorry, Sister, but I can't help feeling sad, I've just realised something. What a waste of time it all is. Bragoon and Saro, together with Horty, Springald and Fenna, have gone off questing for Loamhedge. Little do they know that I need no cure or remedy. Suddenly I can walk! My brother and good friends are far away from Redwall—who knows what deadly danger or injury may befall them? There was no real need for them to go. Oh, fate can be so cruel at times. I feel responsible and guilty about the whole thing!"

Sister Portula comforted her. "You must not blame your-self, Martha. None of this was your doing, was it, Toran?"

The ottercook had strong feelings about Martha's sup-posed dilemma, and he minced no words in telling her so. "Wot's all this nonsense, don't ye be talkin' that way, Martha! Huh, ye could go on all day, worryin' about this an' that, an' supposin'. Lissen, I'll give ye a suppose. Supposin' yore friends an' my brother an' Saro hadn't gone, eh? Things would've turned out totally diff'rent, fate would've cast other lots for everybeast. You mightn't 'ave been at that window in yore chair last night, but those Searats may've changed their plans. Then where'd ye be now, Martha? I'll tell ye, still sittin' stuck in a chair!

"So don't ye dare say that there was no point in our good friends undertakin' a mission to find a cure for ye, Martha Braebuck! An' don't talk t'me of danger or injury. If'n Brag an' Saro 'ave anythin' t'do with it, the only ones sufferin' perils an' wounds will be anybeasts who tries to stop 'em! So quit complainin' an' supposin', miss. Be grateful that ye can go runnin', on yore own footpaws, to greet the trav-ellers when they return to our Abbey!"

Martha had never heard Toran speak so forcefully, or truly. Wiping her eyes, the haremaid clasped her friend's paw fervently. "Thank you, Toran, you're right. What a silly creature I am!"

The ottercook turned away, brushing a paw across his own eyes. "No you ain't, yore our Martha. Now put a smile on that face, an' get those liddle villains down of'n that shelf afore they fall an' 'urt themselves!"

Sharpening his silver hooktip on the wall, Raga Bol lounged in the gatehouse doorway. Bright summer morn had done nothing to ease his foul mood. Dreams of the big stripedog had begun haunting him afresh, plus he was still smarting from the previous night's shameful defeat. Striving to put thoughts of the badger from his mind, he took out his mean temper on every crewrat in sight, snarling menacingly at them.

"Belay there, Wirga, ain't there any vittles left, where's me brekkist? Ahoy, you there, stop scrapin' mud off'n yoreself, an' grubbin' at yer eyes like some snotty liddle whelp. Go an' get some vittles for yore cap'n, sharpish!"

All four of the Searats, not knowing exactly whom the glaring captain was addressing, ran off to do his bidding. "Aye aye, Cap'n! Right away, Cap'n!" they chorused as they tugged their ears in salute.

Raga Bol turned his spleen upon the one called Rojin, who was sitting on the gatehouse wallsteps, poulticing a swollen eye. "Quit dabbin' at yore lamp, ye've still got a good 'un left. I never got no brekkist, 'cos Blowfly let me servants escape. They're the beasts who should be doin' the cookin'. Git yoreself after Blowfly an' Glimbo. I want t'see ye all back 'ere by noon wid the runaways in tow. 'Cos if'n ye ain't, I'll let the livin' daylights into the lotta youse wid this 'ook. Go on, gerrout o' me sight, ye laggard!"

The next to come in for a tongue lashing was the one called Rinj, who happened to stray within earshot. "Stan' by the big gate there, Rinj, ye useless mess of offal. Keep a weather eye out for Rojin an' the others comin' back. Report ter me the moment ye spot 'em!"

The Searat captain stalked back into the gatehouse, slamming the door so hard that its hinges rattled. He slumped into Old Phredd's armchair, trying to banish thoughts of the badger and concentrate instead on his plans to conquer the Abbey.

Morning rolled on into the summer noon. The crew danced attention upon their captain, but he barely glanced at the food they brought. Instead, he ordered them to bring him volumes and scrolls from the shelves. Bol rifled through them, searching vainly for some clues—a reference or a sketch, perhaps. Anything that would help him gain access to the Abbey building. After awhile he tired of this pur-

329

suit and banished the crewrats from the gatehouse. Scattering volumes and parchments over the floor, the Searat captain flung himself upon the bed and fell into a fitful slumber, the coverlet draped over his face.

On waking, Raga Bol saw that the sunlight shafts had shifted across the window. It was late afternoon, merging toward eventide. Rising, he took a mouthful of his favourite grog, swilling it around his mouth, then spat it out sourly. It was silent outside, with no sounds of activity. The Searat captain went swiftly outside.

Rinj was standing upright, propped against the gatepost, obviously sleeping. Raga Bol dealt him a savage kick, knocking Rinj flat. He continued to kick the hapless Searat, accentuating his words.

"Ye scabby-eyed, useless bilge swab! Did I tell ye to go snoozin' on duty? Wot's this door barred for, eh? Yore supposed t'be outside, watchin' for the others t'come back. If'n we was at sea now, I'd tie ye t'the anchor an' sling yore lazy carcass o'er the side!"

Dragging Rinj upright by his ears, Bol knocked the gate bars up with his hook. He hauled the gates open, still shouting. "I'll learn ye to disobey yore cap'n's orders, I'll . . . Yaaaagh!"

The gates swung inward, revealing Rojin, pinned to the timbers by a huge single arrow, head slumped and footpaws dragging in the dust. Dead as the proverbial doornail!

Beyond the outside path and ditch, out on the flatlands, Lonna Bowstripe roared as he fitted a shaft to his bowstring. "Raga Bol! Death is here! Hellgates await you, Searat! Eulaliiiiaaaaaaa!"

Bol took one glance at the avenging giant and hurled himself at the Abbey gates, slamming them and dropping the heavy baulks that served as locks. The wood shivered under the thud of the badger's massive arrow. Raga Bol leaped back from the gates, as if expecting the shaft to come right through.

Sister Setiva was prying the paws of little Yooch from the dormitory windowsill. "Och, come away from there, ye wee pestilence!" Attracted by the shouting from the gatehouse area, she peered over to see what was amiss there. Raga Bol's hoarse yells left her in no doubt.

"All paws to the walltops! Bring spears, slings an' bows. Jump to it, the stripedog's 'ere!"

Setiva caught Abbot Carrul's sleeve. "There somebeast oot there, yon Searat's howlin' like a madbeast!"

Toran was out the dormitory door, with Martha close on his heels. Carrul and Setiva followed as Toran called to them. "Up t'the floor above, mates, ye can see better from there!"

Redwallers crowded to the second-story windows, which gave them a clear view of all that was taking place. Out on the flatlands, Lonna was raising his bow again. Brother Weld transmitted an excited commentary of what was taking place, for the benefit of those few who could not see. "Great seasons of slaughter, it's a giant Badger Lord! The Searats are throwing spears, firing slingstones and arrows at him. Haha, their range is too short, their weapons can't touch him. Oh my, oh golly! Did you see that?"

Old Phredd croaked impatiently. "See what? I can't see a thing!"

Brother Weld described what he had seen. "The big badger fired off an arrow, huh, more like a spear. It struck a Searat, up on the ramparts. Got the vermin dead centre and drove him clear off the wall onto the lawn!"

Sister Setiva shook her head in disbelief. "Och, what a shot, ah've never seen aught like it!"

The Abbeybeasts set up a great cheer. Lonna caught sight of them and waved. Leaning out from the upper windows, the Redwallers waved back furiously, shouting encouragement.

"Give 'em blood'n'vinegar, well done, friend!"

"That's the stuff big feller, keep those shafts coming!"

331

"Hurr, zurr hoojbeast, you'm give ee vurmints ole bil-lyoh!"

With her eyes shining fiercely, Martha yelled at Toran, "Isn't he magnificent! Can't we do anything to help him?"

The ottercook bit his lip anxiously. "We got nothin' to throw that'd span the range twixt this Abbey an' the wall-tops, 'tis too far off for slingstones. There ain't a single bow'n'arrer in the buildin'. I'd love to 'elp the big badger, but wot kin we do, miss, wot?"

Brother Gelf, normally a quiet, inobtrusive mouse, spoke out. "Er, I may be able to help, but I'll need to be down in Great Hall. I think I'll need a long windowpole, some twine, a couple of those pepper bombs and a few stones. Er, make them slightly larger than slingstones, but not much."

His curiosity immediately piqued, the Abbot bowed to Gelf. "You shall have them, Brother. Let's go down to Great Hall. No pushing there, please, let Gelf go first."

Up on the walltops the Searats were lying low, stunned by the accuracy of the bowbeast. Raga Bol was trying to instil some confidence n his crew. "We're safe be'ind this wall, buckoes. That stripedog's got to stay out of our range. Soon as 'e moves forward we'll get 'im. Ain't been a beast born yet that spears an' arrers can't slay. All's we gotta do is stay inside these walls!"

Wirga shuffled closer to Bol. "Aye, but while we're on the inside, the stripedog has us pinned down from the outside. No Searat owns a weapon with the range an' power of that big bow, Cap'n."

Bol did not want to hear this. He stared cold-eyed at the Seer. "What would ye 'ave me do then, run out an' charge 'im?"

The loss of her three sons rankled Wirga, who now did not lose the opportunity to needle Bol. "We outnumber the bigbeast by about twoscore. I never saw a Searat cap'n back off with those odds on his side!"

Before Bol could strike out, or argue against Wirga, a

Searat further along the parapet gave out a shout. "Aaargh, wot the . . . Oooch!"

He fell sideways, slain by one of the big arrows. Raga Bol crawled swiftly along and inspected the dead crewrat. "Wot in the name o' blood'n'thunder 'appened to 'im?"

Cowering fearfully against the battlements, the rat who had been crouching beside the victim babbled out. "I saw it, Cap'n! Gornat was 'it by summat from be'ind. There 'tis, see, one o' those liddle bags o' pepper, tied on a string, wid a stone at the other end!"

Bol unwound the object from around Gornat's waist. "From be'ind, this thing got 'im—ye mean from the Abbey?"

The Searat nodded vigourously. "Aye, it came from over that way, I swear it, Cap'n. Pore Gornat got a terrible smack from it, the thing 'it 'im an' wrapped right round 'is waist. It musta cracked a rib, 'cos Gornat shouted an' jumped up. That's when the arrer took 'im, straight through the neck!"

Turning to face the Abbey building, Raga Bol saw another of the missiles come whirling through the air. It spun round and round on its twine, weighted on one end by the pepper bomb and on the other by the stone. This time it missed and struck the wallside. The pepper bomb burst, sending its load over two rats crouched directly beneath. One had the sense to stay down and do his sneezing. The other leaped up and sneezed once, then an arrow silenced him for good.

Down in Great Hall, the Redwallers had unblocked the shutters from one of the tall windows.

Toran took the windowpole from Brother Gelf. "Can I try yore new slingpole out, Brother?"

Gelf smiled quietly. "Be my guest, sir."

Laying the twine across the hooked metal end of the pole, the ottercook raised it straight up, facing out of the window. Holding the end of the pole in both paws, he let it lean back across his shoulder until it lay flat. Then he whipped it upright with swift force. The missile flew off through the high open window. There was a short interval of silence, followed by an agonized screech.

Toran grinned. "It works!"

There was no shortage of the homemade weapons. More window poles were brought, and more volunteers came forward, eager to try out the new weapons. Competition became so fierce that, owing to several of the defenders hurling the missiles at the same time, some of them missed the open window space. These projectiles struck the walls and lintels, bouncing back into Great Hall and bursting. Undeterred, the Abbeybeasts kept going, muffling their faces with towels. Soon, however, the atmosphere proved too much for the onlookers; many fled the scene, sneezing uproariously.

The Dibbuns thought the whole thing was huge fun. They chortled and giggled, dashing about and bumping into one another, shouting, "Hachoo! Blesha! Harrachoo! O blesha blesha!"

Martha helped Abbot Carrul and some of the elders to shepherd the little ones downstairs into Cavern Hole. The haremaid actually carried two Dibbuns down the steps on her back, chuckling and joking with them.

The Abbot cautioned her. "Careful, Martha, should you really be doing that? You don't want to put too much strain on those limbs!"

Martha deposited the Abbeybabes in a corner seat. "Oh fiddledeedee, Father, I feel stronger than I've ever felt. It's as if I had brand-new footpaws and legs, they're as supple as greased springs!"

Granmum Gurvel sent down some kitchen helpers to carry baskets of fresh-baked tarts and pastries and jugs of sweet elderflower cordial.

Martha lent a paw to serve the Dibbuns, then went to sit on the stairs with the Abbot. She felt very happy and carefree as they shared the food. "Oh Father, isn't it wonderful, having that giant badger on our side! I wager things will be different now."

The Abbot seemed somewhat thoughtful, though he agreed with her. "Yes, indeed, those Searats obviously fear the big badger a lot. Wouldn't it be marvellous if he were inside the Abbey with us? Things would be so much easier."

Martha sipped her cordial. "In what way?"

The Abbot warmed to the subject, propounding a theory which had been growing in his mind ever since he had first sighted Lonna standing out on the flatlands.

"Our badger fires that bow like a mighty warrior, that's for certain. If he were inside the Abbey with us, I guarantee he'd send those Searats packing in short order."

Martha thought for a moment about what the Abbot had said. "Aye, he could stand at the dormitory windows and pick the Searats off at his leisure. They're hemmed in by the outer walls, so it would make it hard for them to avoid him. The badger could use the upstairs windows on all sides."

Abbot Carrul put aside his food. "But the problem is that the badger's outside the walls at the moment. Those Searats aren't stupid, they're not likely to leave Redwall and take their chances outside. Not with that giant and his bow waiting for them."

Martha saw the wisdom in her Abbot's logic. "Hmm, that could make Raga Bol doubly dangerous to us because he'll probably try twice as hard to get inside the Abbey now. It would give him an advantage over the badger, who would have to fight his way into the grounds and take the Searats on from inside the grounds. That would place him in range of their weapons. Oh dear, I wonder what the answer is to all of this!"

Carrul had already anticipated the problem. Unfortunately, he could not hold out a great deal of hope. "We need to contact our badger friend and get him inside here, but that's not possible. The Searats are standing between him and us. We'll just have to wait our chance, though there isn't much likelihood of that at present."

Martha tried to hide the frustration in her voice. "But there won't be a much better opportunity than right now.

Most of the Searats' attention is on the badger. If only we had somebeast who could slip out unnoticed! Whoever it was could leave by the small eastwall gate. They'd be shielded from any attention by the Abbey building. It wouldn't be hard to steal through the woodlands to the corner of the northwest wall. When it got dark, it would be simple to creep out onto the flatlands and make contact with the badger. Then they could both return the same way."

The Abbot folded both paws within his wide habit sleeves. "No, 'tis far too risky at the moment, Martha. We'll wait—tomorrow, perhaps. Oh dear, all this worry and strife. I'm longing for the day when those villains are long gone from Redwall and we can all get back to a normal, peaceful life."

Martha stood up. "Don't fret, Father, it'll happen when you least expect it. Do you know, I feel restless. Think I'll exercise my new walking skills. I'll go up to the dormitory windows and see how things are going. Best steer clear of Great Hall, and all those pepper bombs bursting inside."

The Abbot smiled wearily at his young friend. "Take things easy, Martha, don't go tiring yourself out."

She paused on the stairway. "Oh, I'll go as slowly as Old Phredd. By the way, Father, could you do me a favour? Will you sit guard on these stairs and make sure those Dibbuns don't go rushing back to Great Hall?"

Abbot Carrul stretched himself lengthways across the step. "Certainly. I might doze off a little, but they won't get past me. You go on now, and remember what I said about taking things easy!"

However, taking things easy was the last thing on the young haremaid's mind. Martha had a mission: she would be the one to contact the badger. She went up to the back rooms on the east side, choosing one that was mainly used as a linen store. It was filled with blankets, sheets and tablecloths.

Knotting bedsheets together, she fashioned a makeshift

rope, reasoning aloud to herself. "Finally I can do something useful to help Redwall. Now I can walk, and run, too. After all those seasons stuck in a chair, it would be a crime to waste my new gift!"

Climbing down the rope was easier than the haremaid had imagined. She had forgotten how strong her grip had become from wheeling a chair about for most of her life.

35

Dawn light seeped over the river, casting a haze of pale green-gold mist. Saro lounged in the stern of the main logboat with Bragoon, savouring the new day, and a few scones still warm from early breakfast.

"Ah, this is the life, mate, save the wear'n'tear on me ole footpaws. There's nothin' like a nice lazy rivertrip, eh?"

The otter grinned as Horty approached them, pushing on a hefty oarpole, part of two double lines of shrews. The young hare turned and started to make his way back to the prow, where he would repeat the process of poling the craft upriver.

He glared at the otter's cheery face and stuck his tongue out insultingly at Saro. "Blinkin' idle bounders, sittin' on your bloomin' tails, wallopin' down scones, while I slave m'self into an early grave. Huh, should be blinkin' well ashamed of y'selves!"

Briggy left the prow and strode down the centre of the logboat, between both lines of polers. Exchanging a sly wink with Bragoon and Saro, he clipped Horty lightly across the ears, roaring at him in true rivercraft language, "Avast there, ye long-legged layabout, quit prattlin' an' git polin'. We gotta build those muscles up t'make a warrior of ye! Ain't it a wunnerful life, nothin' t'do but pole about all

338

day on the river, ye lucky swab! Dwingo, give us a drumbeat there. Come on, shrews, put yore backs into it. Sing
out a polin' shanty to speed us on our way. Push, ye
shrinkin' daisies. Push!"

The drumbeat rolled out, echoing around the forested
banks, with deep, gruff shrew voices singing in chorus. The
shanty was a totally untrue pack of insults about Log a Log
Briggy, but he sang along with them lustily.

"Barrum, babba, whum! Pole to the beat o' the drum!
Our Cap'n is a bad ole shrew,
I wish I'd never signed to roam.
He feeds us worms an mudpies, too,
oh ma, let me come sailin' home.
Barrum, babba, whum! Pole to the beat o' the drum!

Ole Briggy is a lazy hog,
wid a belly like a tub o' lard,
if we don't call 'im Log a Log,
he beats us bad an' treats us hard.
Barrum, babba, whum! Pole to the beat o' the drum!

One day our logboat sprang a leak,
an' I gave out an 'earty wail,
the Cap'n gave me nose a tweak,
an' plugged that leak up wid me tail.
Barrum, babba, whum! Pole to the beat o' the drum!

We ran head-on into a gale,
our Cap'n made me cry sad tears,
'cos the wind 'ad ripped right through the sail,
so he patched the canvas wid me ears.
Barrum, babba, whum! Pole to the beat o' the drum!

Ye've heard me story, messmates all,
an' if I spoke a lie to you,
may me nose swell into a fat red ball,
an' me bottom turn bright green'n'blue.
Barrum, babba, whum! Pole to the beat o' the drum!"

339

Horty was astonished; he turned to the shrew behind him. "By the left! I say, old chap, are you allowed to bandy insults like that about Briggathingee, wot?"

The shrew kept poling as he gave Horty a broad wink. "It ain't serious, mate, 'tis all done in good fun!"

Briggy saw Horty gossiping and descended upon him. "Stop jawin' an' keep pawin', rabbitchops, or I'll 'ave yore whiskers for desksweepers!"

The young hare gave Briggy a cheeky grin and launched into a barrage of insults. "Oh shut your blatherin' cakescoffer, y'great bearded windbag! You sound like a duck with beakache, hasn't anybeast ever told you? Hah, tush'n'pish for all your ilk, sah, you wobble-pawed, twinky-tailed excuse for a barrel-bummed toad. Who d'you think you're jolly well talkin' to, you wiggle-whiskered, bawlin' braggart!"

Horty turned back to the shrew he had spoken to previously. "Pretty good, wot! That told old Log-a-pudden a thing or two!"

The ashen-faced shrew hissed back at him. "We only ever does it in songs, all t'gether like. If'n you speak like that, face t'face wid a Log a Log o' Guorafs, that's mutiny, mate!"

Horty turned round to find Briggy looming over him with a face like thunder.

The force of the shrew chieftain's roars made Horty's long ears flap. "Mutiny, eh? I won't 'ave mutineers aboard my logboat! Grab 'old o' this mutinous beast, put 'im to task! No more rations for 'im while he's on this vessel!"

Four shrews frogmarched the hapless hare off to the stern where he was given a large sack of wild onions to clean and peel.

Bragoon made his way to the prow, where he had a quiet word with the shrew chieftain. "Ye were a bit 'ard on Horty there, mate. The young 'un wasn't wise to yore rules an' reg'lations, he thought 'twas all a bit of a joke. Horty didn't mean ye no real insult."

Briggy's eyes twinkled. "I know he didn't, friend, but I

said I'd toughen 'im up. If'n that young 'un ever expects t'join the Long Patrol, he's gotta learn manners an' curb his tongue. Could ye imagine one o' those hare officers from the Long Patrol lettin' a recruit speak to 'im like that? Joke or not, some stiff-eared sergeant would clap 'im on a charge an' use 'is guts fer garters!"

Bragoon agreed. "Yore right, Briggy, a bit o' discipline wouldn't 'urt 'im. All three o' them young 'uns've been livin' the soft life at Redwall fer too long. The two maids are much better be'aved than Horty, they'll lissen t'reason. But Horty's too wild an' 'eadstrong. One day he'll make a fine warrior—after he's learned a few stern lessons."

Briggy stroked his beard. "Don't fret, mate, I'll knock all the rough edges off'n Horty. My Jigger was the same 'til I showed 'im the ropes. Lookit Jigger now, commandin' his own logboat. There's a young shrew anybeast'd be proud t'call son!"

The otter went back astern and sat with Saro. Behind them Horty was weeping buckets as he peeled and chopped the pungent wild onions. He went at it with vim and vigour, though scowling and muttering about the injustices of life aboard a logboat.

"Bit flippin' thick this lot, wot? A few measly words to old Brigalog an' he treats a chap like a bloomin' vermin marauder! I mean, what did I say? The bearded old buffer should count himself jolly well lucky, wot! Oh, yes indeed, when Hortwill Braebuck Esquire starts really chuckin' insults, he could roast the flamin' ears off a milky-whiskered shrew. I could've called the chap a lot worse! Twiggle-jawed trout! Giddy-nosed toad! Pickled old pollywog! Witless water beetle! Puddle-pawed duck's bottom! Or even Skinnyforlinkee Wobblechops! Huh, I think I let him off lightly, really. Good job one can hold one's temper, wot wot!"

Log a Log Briggy came striding down between the polers. "Ahoy there, mates, is that mutineer be'avin' hisself? I might let 'im get a bite o' supper tonight, if'n I 'ears an apology."

Bragoon nudged Horty. "Did ye hear that, matey?"

The young hare turned a face, still running onion tears, to the Guoraf chieftain and declared dramatically, "Y'mean you'd restore my scoffin' privileges, sah? Merciful Logawotsyaname, I'll peel every last one of these foul fruits, I swear I will. Good Captain, I'll be the saltiest young riverbeast you ever clapped eyes on. Listen to this. Shiver me sails an' rot me timbers, fry me barnacles, scrape me keel, an' all that nautical jimjam. You, matey sah, are lookin' at a completely reformed beast!"

Briggy glanced at Saro. "Wot d'ye think, marm, is that a rogue worth feedin'?"

The aging squirrel saw the haunted look in Horty's eyes and took pity. "Aye, Cap'n, only a moment ago Horty was sayin' wot a good ole Log a Log ye are. Ain't that right, Brag?"

With difficulty, the otter kept a straight face. "Right enough, I'd give 'im another chance if 'twas up t'me."

Briggy stroked his beard a moment, before answering. "Aye, so be it then. Leave those onions now, young 'un, go amidship an' lend the cook a paw in the galley."

Horty galloped off, overjoyed at the prospect of working amid food. "Help the cook, I say, what a spiffin' job! A thousand thanks to you, Captain Briggaboat, an' you, my two chums. You have a handsome young hare's undying thanks!"

Bragoon chuckled. "Same modest Horty, eh?"

Aboard Jigger's logboat, Fenna and Springald were being treated like royalty. Fenna had also gained an admirer, a stout young shrew named Wuddle. Both he and Jigger could not do enough for the pretty Redwall maids. The shrews brought extra cushions, erected an awning to shade them from the sun and served more delicious snacks than both of them could possibly eat. Then the two creatures vanished momentarily, to reappear grinning awkwardly, carrying with them two accordionlike instruments, which they said were called shrewlodeons. Jigger and Waddle twiddled a few keys, then launched into a song. Springald and Fenna were convulsed with laughter at the faces that both shrews pulled while singing. On verses they would be scowling savagely, whilst on the choruses they adopted expressions of peaceful concern. Both had wonderful bass voices and sang in harmony.

"When I meets a beast wot ain't polite to laydeez,
I grabs 'im round the throat 'til he turns blue,
I holds him tight in check as I squeezes on his neck,
then I boots his tail three times around the deck!

'Cos be they sisters mothers aunts or daughters,
all laydeez must be treated tenderly,
they're dainty an' they're neat, an' they don't have
      much to eat,
an' they rouses gentle feelins within me.

When I'm around an' you insults a laydee,
I'll jump on yore stummick very forcibly,
then I'll punch you in the snout an' I'll prob'ly knock
      you out,
an' black both of yore eyes so you can't see!

'Cos be they sisters mothers aunts or daughters,
all laydeez must be treated tenderly,
they're dainty an' they're neat, an' they don't have
      much to eat,
an' they rouses gentle feelins within me.

So mind yore manners an' be very careful,
when in the company of laydeez sweet,
or I'll shove you in a sack, after fracturin' yore back,
an' I'll stamp upon yore paws if you gets free!"

After the final chorus, they escorted both maids on a pleasant promenade of the deck, snarling fiercely at any of the poling shrews who dared to look sideways at Fenna or Springald.

343

*

Supper on a mossy bank, overhung by weeping willows, was a total success. It was all due to Horty's onion soup. The Guorafs congratulated him on his cooking skills. He lapped up any compliments with a complete lack of modesty.

"Tut tut, nothin' to it, dear chaps—a pinch o' this, a smidgeon o' that an' a sprinklin' of the other. Plus, of course, blinkin' loads of those confounded onions. I tell you, I shed many salt tears into the recipe, wot! Wild onions? Hah, I wasn't too blinkin' pleased, havin' to tame 'em down for you lot. I'd sooner be skinned me bloomin' self than have to skin another wild onion!"

Log a Log Briggy watched the young ones cavorting, singing and playing, then lay back and stretched. "Beats me where they find the energy! Ah well, let 'em be merry while they can, 'specially those three young 'uns o' yores. I reckon we'll make our voyage end by midmorn tomorrer. That's when all the fun'n'games will finish for Horty an' the maids. I'm glad I don't have t'make the slog over desert an' gorge to Loamhedge with ye. That's country I was never fond of."

Bragoon flicked a twig into the fire. "They'll do alright, with me'n my mate to look after 'em."

Saro smiled. "Aye, but by the creakin' o' my ole bones, 'tis them who'll be lookin' after us by the time this liddle jaunt is finished!"

Next morning, they arrived on time at the spot, just as Briggy had predicted. It was indeed hard, arid country. They had been sailing upriver since the crack of dawn. Nobeast could fail to notice the difference in the terrain. Trees, bushes and grass thinned out along the banks, whilst a hot breeze wafted in dust from the wastelands.

Briggy smiled at the young creatures' downcast faces. "Cheer up, mates, it ain't good-bye just yet. We'll be moored alongside this bank when ye come back wid a cure for Horty's sister. Get goin' now, an' good fortune go with ye!"

344

"Thanks for everythin', ole friend!"

"Aye, we'd a-been in a right pickle widout you an' yore crews, matey."

"See ye in six days, eh!"

Loaded with shrew hardtack biscuits and two canteens of water apiece, the travellers set off into the unknown.

Briggy called out as the logboats pulled away. "Keep the sun on yore right cheek, ye'll see the Bell an' Badger Rocks afore dark. But y'won't be able to reach 'em until ye figure out 'ow to cross the great gorge!"

Silence reigned over the searing, dusty flatness at high noon. Bragoon led the party, with Saro bringing up the rear.

It was not long before Horty began complaining. "Phew, my ears are roasted, my tongue's parched an' my bally feet are fryin'. My word, it's even too hot to sweat! Walkin' walkin', always flamin' well walkin'. It's the story of m'life, chaps. First I was walkin' up'n'down on a blinkin' logboat, pushin' an oarpole. Now I'm walkin' again through this food'n'drink-forsaken place!"

Saro tugged the hare's tail. "We're all walkin', ole gabby gob. We're walkin' t'bring back somethin' that'll make yore sister Martha walk. So stop moanin' an' keep walkin'."

The otter glanced over his shoulder, turning his attention on Springald and Fenna. "Ahoy there, you two. Keep yore faces like that an' it'll rain afore long, ye mis'rable pair o' mopes!"

Springald dragged her paws in the dust, replying sulkily. "There's nothing at all wrong with our faces, thank you. Anyhow, you wouldn't understand."

Saro piped up from behind. "Why wouldn't we unnerstand?"

Fenna pouted. " 'Cos you just wouldn't, that's all!"

Horty could not resist smirking. "They're jolly miserable because they've been parted from old Jigger an' his pal, wotsisname, Cuddles! Oh lack a day an' woe are they! I expect your little hearts are breakin', wot?"

Kicking dust at the mocking hare, Fenna shouted, "His name isn't Cuddles, it's Wuddle, and he's far nicer than you, Horty Braebuck. So there!"

Skipping ahead of the two maids, Horty made an elegant leg and bowed with a flourish. "Fie upon you, marm, there's nobeast nicer than the charming I. Not in all the lands, or the river. Not like those two spike-headed water whompers who caterwaul songs like stricken ducks!"

This time it was Springald who kicked dust at Horty. "You vain, pompous, floppy-eared boaster!"

Horty was about to kick dust back, when Bragoon grabbed his ear and tweaked it soundly. "If'n ye value yore ear, then stop embarrassin' those maids, right now! All three of ye are startin' to try my patience. Come on, Spring, cheer up. You, too, Fenn. It won't be long afore ye see those young shrews agin. Quit bein' so mean to each other, an' no more teasin'!"

Horty rubbed at the ear that had been tweaked. "Who, me? I barely uttered a blinkin' word, it was those two who jolly well started it!"

It was Saro's shout that put an end to the bickering. "Look, mates, there's the Bell'n'Badger Rocks!"

36

Floating above the heat-shimmered distance, the tops of both stone monoliths were just about visible on the horizon.

Fenna's keen eyes confirmed Saro's discovery. "Hooray! You're right, there they are, I can see them!"

Shading her eyes, Springald stood on tippaws. "They look like one of those mirages that Old Phredd told us about. I wonder how far off they are?"

Bragoon squinted over the wasteland haze. "A fair bit yet, but if'n we press on 'til they're in plain sight, I'll call it a day an' we'll make camp. I want to look at those parchments from the Abbey. How does that sound to ye, mates?"

Bragoon and Saro watched the three young ones dashing off ahead, their quarrels all forgotten as they shouted to one another.

Saro scratched her bushy tail. "Ha, lissen to 'em, they're the best o' pals agin!"

Fenna was shouting, "I'm going to set up camp with the cloaks an' staffs. Where are you off to, Horty?"

The young hare had put on a spurt, racing ahead eagerly. "Gangway, m'dears, I'm your cook this evenin'. Had lots of valuable experience, y'know. Oh yes, a chap learns a thing or three from those shrew coves, wot!"

Springald kept pace with Fenna. "I want to help Brag and Saro to study those parchments."

Bragoon and Saro followed the young ones at a steady lope. "Looks like we've lost command o' the quest, mate. Can ye see those rocks clearly yet?"

The squirrel looked up. "Not quite, but it won't be long now."

It turned out that the three front-runners were forced to halt quicker than expected. Horty ground to a stop in a cloud of dust. "By the left, right, an' knock me blinkin' sideways! How in the name of onion soup do we get across that bloomin' thing? Looks like the end o' the flamin' earth, wot!"

Fenna and Springald joined him, gasping in disbelief at the awesome spectacle that confronted them.

"Whew! No wonder it's called the great gorge!"

"Good grief, it must be miles down to the bottom!"

Bragoon and Saro arrived on the scene. The otter ventured a glance down into the black chasm. "If'n ye fell down there, that'd be the last anybeast'd see of ye, eh mate?"

Saro, however, was more concerned with the width of the gorge. "Hmm, that's a wide ole canyon! Don't matter 'ow deep 'tis, we've got to think 'ow were goin' to cross it. Any ideas?"

Food was the only idea Horty gave priority to. "Let's get a fire goin' an' we can figure it all out over a jolly good scoff. How's that for a scheme, wot?"

The otter shook his head. "This is strange country, mate. I don't feel too easy wid the thought of a fire. Pitch the camp an' see wot ye can make from the packs, Horty. I'll go off t'the right along the rim. Spring, you come wid me. Saro, you take the left edge. Fenna'll go wid ye."

They set off, with Horty issuing dire warnings. "You chaps get back here before dusk, or I'll whomp up somethin' absolutely delicious an' eat it myself!"

Saro glanced across the gorge as she and Fenna explored

along the edge of the precipice. "Those two big rocks are plain t'see now, they mustn't be more than a couple o' slingshot distances from the other side. We're so near, yet so far, eh Fenn?"

The squirrelmaid had noticed something down in the chasm. Suddenly her voice became shrill with excitement. "There, that's how we'll get across, come and see!"

Saro lay flat on the edge, staring down at the solution to their problem. "Well spotted, young 'un. I almost walked right by an' missed that. Let's go an' tell the others!"

Horty had created a fruit salad from the rations, with elderflower and dandelion cordial to go with it.

They sat eating as Saro reported, "There's a tree trunk spannin' the gorge down that way, Fenna spotted it. About the height o' Redwall Abbey's battlement, down it lies. I don't know where it came from or whatbeast put it there, but it bridges the gap alright. 'Tis the longest trunk I've ever seen, lodged twixt a crack on one side an' a narrow ledge on the other. I think we should be able to get down to it on the rope that Cosbro, the old rabbit, gave us."

Bragoon gathered up the parchments he was about to study. "Let's go an' take a look at it."

The spot where the tree trunk lay was directly in line with the two rocks across the gorge. Bragoon was thinking hard as he gazed down at the long, old span of timber that bridged the chasm.

Springald watched him as he studied the whole thing—the twin rocks, and the tree trunk wedged inside the gorge. "You know something about this, don't you?"

The otter spread the map he had brought from Redwall. "See here, this is the Bell an' the Badger Rocks. Now this spot is where the Lord o' Mossflower once stood. Ole Briggy said that it was a large tree, which had fallen down long ago. I reckon that tree trunk down there is the one that's marked on the map. After it fell down, some creatures must've rolled it into the gorge to make a bridge. I

349

wager it took a lot o' beasts t'do the job, but they didn't know they was doin' us a favour when they took on the task. Is that rope long enough, matey?"

Saro, who had fetched Cosbro's rope along with her, dangled its length over the side. "Aye, it falls a bit short o' the trunk, but it'll do."

Satisfied, the otter issued orders. "You three young 'uns, go back an' break camp. Fetch everythin' back 'ere with ye. Make as little noise as possible. There's somethin' about this area I don't like. It might be only a feelin', but I'm takin' no chances. Saro, me'n you'll rig this rope up. Remember now, be quiet!"

Horty and the two maids did not take long to pack the gear and break camp. Returning to the spot, they found that Bragoon had broken his staff in two pieces and driven them into a crack near the rim. Saro tested the rope she had tied around the wood. Without further ado, she went silently and skilfully down, using her footpaws on the rock walls for balance. She dropped lightly onto the trunk and twirled her tail several times as a signal that everything was alright. One by one they descended into the dark quiet chasm, Bragoon being last to go.

The five travellers perched precariously on the tree trunk. Saro gave the rope a swift upward flick, bringing it down with them.

Horty peered across the gorge nervously. "I say, Brag old scout, we could do with a torch to light us over this thing, it looks jolly dangerous t'me, wot?"

The otter glared at him. "Ssshhh, don't talk, yore voice echoes off the side down 'ere!"

Saro knotted herself and the others into a line, with herself at the front and Bragoon at the rear. Getting down on all fours, the five creatures inched out onto the long trunk. It seemed like an eternity, crawling over the wide expanse with nothing beneath them but empty space and total blackness. Sometimes the big log quivered, as one of them stumbled. At moments like this, they crouched there still, until Saro moved forward again.

Bragoon emitted a hushed sigh of relief when they finally made it onto the ledge at the far side. Fenna peered into the gloom, looking fearfully at Saro. The squirrel saw three black holes, which looked like entrances, in the rock face. She nodded and placed a paw to her lips in a gesture of silence. Untying her four friends from the rope, she coiled it about her waist and began climbing up the other side of the gorge. They watched her ascending the rock face with all the grace of a born squirrel climber. Bragoon kept casting anxious glances toward the three dark, forbidding entrances, but no signs of life showed there.

Saro made it to the top in good time. Finding a convenient boulder, she tied a knot about it and lowered the rope to her companions. As they began the upward climb, the otter was still keeping a weather eye upon the dark holes.

Once all five travellers were safely together on the top of the far side, Horty laughed out loud. "Hawhawhaw! Well, chaps, that's that! I suppose it's alright for one t'make sounds now. It's almost as bad as bein' hungry, for a brilliant speaker like me not being able to flippin' well talk. Absolute torture, wot!"

Bragoon could not help smiling at the young hare. "Go on, mate, talk away, even sing if'n ye like."

Ever willing to oblige, the garrulous hare burst into song.

"Oh it ain't much fun, when you must keep mum,
an' they tell you not to speak,
standin' about with a tight-shut mouth,
an' your tongue stuck in your cheek,
'cos being silent, makes me violent,
I want to roar an' shout,
Wheehooh! Yahboo! I'm tellin' you,
I've lots to talk about!
Hello good day, how are you, say,

351

the sky went dark last night,
but it got bright this morning,
so things turned out alright.
Well there might be rain, but then again,
we'll face the storm together,
in wind or snow, oh don't y'know,
let's talk about the weather!
Wheehooh! Yahboo! I'm tellin' you,
I'll whisper, yell or shout,
I'll natter'n'blab, or chatter'n'gab,
I've lots to talk about!"

Saro cast her eyes to the darkening evening sky and sighed. "We'd better stop for supper soon. That's the only time Horty goes quiet, when he's eatin'."

Bragoon watched fondly as the young hare did some fancy high kicks and ear twiddling. "Aye, that rascal's like a weed on a wall, he grows on ye. I'll say this, though— Horty's becomin' a first-rate cook, I like 'is vittles. We'll go as far as the Bell an' the Badgers Rocks afore night comes. I think we could even risk a liddle cookin' fire. Let ole Horty create us one of his masterpieces. Come on, mate, it ain't more'n a mile or two now."

As the laughter and banter of the questers receded into the gathering eventide, a stillness fell over the wasteland.

Three faint screams echoed into the unfathomed depths of great gorge. On the ledge where the tree trunk bridged the space, several cloaked figures turned and padded silently into the three dark holes. These were passages, which led into a single hall-like cavern. The creatures from outside joined masses of others, similar to themselves. A myriad of glittering eyes were riveted on a ledge, where burned a sulphurous, yellow-green column of flame. A huge hunched beast, enveloped in a flowing cloak, stood with its back to them, facing the flame. It turned slowly. Not daring to look upon it, everybeast lay down prostrate, faces to the floor. A concerted moan arose from the masses.

"Mighty Kharanjul, Master of the Abyss! Great Slayer, in whose veins runs the blood of Wearets! Lord of Life and Death! We live only to serve thee!"

The cloak swept back to reveal Kharanjul. He was a gargantuan creature, a primitive and hideous mutation—something between a ferret and a weasel. With neither ears nor any semblance of a neck, his brutal head perched straight onto his hulking shoulders. When he spoke, his voice was a gurgling hiss, forced from between curving, discoloured fangs.

"Where are the three guards who were sleeping at their posts when strangers entered my gorge?"

One of the creatures, who had recently entered the cavern, raised his face and cried out in a reedy voice. "Lord, they are still falling into the chasm. They felt themselves too unworthy to face thy wrath, O Great Slayer!"

Kharanjul picked up a big iron trident. He ran his long misshapen claws across the weapon's three barbed points. "Nobeast has ever trespassed in my domain and lived to see the sunset that day. Ye will not fail me again, ye spawn of darkness. If those intruders set paw within a league of my gorge, to return whence they came, ye will let me know of it without fail. Double the guards both night and day. If the interlopers are caught, their suffering will be great. They will plead to be cast into the abyss of eternity. I have spoken!"

Still facedown, the masses chanted their reply. "We hear and obey, O Mighty Kharanjul, Great Wearet Lord!"

37

Martha closed the east wallgate behind her but left it unbolted. Her heart pounded wildly as she stole shakily through the night-shadowed woodlands, hugging the wall. The haremaid knew it had been an ill-advised plan, but she realised that the Abbot, or any sane Redwaller, would have forbidden her to venture on this mission alone. Her footpaws were trembling as she turned the corner to the north wall. Willing them to be still, she strove to gain control of her body. Every once in awhile, she heard weapons clanking on the parapet above. The Searats were patrolling the ramparts. The moment it went quiet, she would inch forward again.

Lonna had lit a fire out on the flatlands facing the west Abbey wall. He piled up brush and twigs into a heap, placing it so that from a distance it could be mistaken for himself, seated by the fire in the darkness. Moving off to his left he settled down, accustoming his eyes to the night. Setting a shaft to his bowstring, he watched the battlements. Soon a vermin head poked up cautiously, seeing the decoy by the fire and mistaking it for the badger. The Searat on the wall stood upright. Leaning outward, he peered toward the fire, trying to make sure that it was Lonna who was sitting crouched there. The big bow twanged, and the arrow took the Searat through his skull, sending him slamming backward onto the walkway. Hearing the resultant commotion from the walltop, the badger shifted his position, moving closer to the wall.

Raga Bol's voice was immediately recognisable as he roared directions to his confused crew. "The stripedog's somewhere out 'ere, on the far west end. Keep yore 'eads down, ye fools, or ye'll end like that 'un. Chakka, get over this way, the stripedog's over 'ere, not on the north side!"

Lonna edged closer, until he could hear Chakka's reply. "But, Cap'n, there's somebeast down here, sneakin' alongside the wall. It ain't as big as the stripedog, though. Wonder who it could be?"

Crouching, Raga Bol made his way across to the north wall. He risked a swift peek over the space between the battlements. "Gimme yore spear! 'Tis an Abbeybeast tryin' to reach the big 'un, I'll wager. Blast yore eyes, gimme the spear afore it gets away!"

Martha made a break and ran for it, out across the path. She stumbled and tripped, going headlong into the ditch, which skirted the outside path. *Thunk!* The spear quivered in the ditchside.

Raga Bol saw another Searat getting up from a crouch to pass him a second weapon. "Ye missed, Cap'n, but only just! Take my spear, 'tis me lucky one . . . Unngh!"

Bol hurled himself flat as the spear clattered to the parapet beside the slain crewrat. "Down, all of ye, down!"

Lonna was running toward the ditch, firing off arrows with amazing speed, one after another. They pinged off the stonework and shattered against the northwest wall corner, keeping the vermin down.

Martha narrowly avoided the huge bulk that crashed into the ditch beside her. She gasped, "Sir, I came from the Abbey, my name's Mar . . ."

A massive paw cut off further explanation, as she was grabbed up and tucked beneath the giant badger's quiver.

It bumped against her cheek as he rushed headlong through the ditch going northward, away from the Abbey.

A deep voice sounded close to her ear. "Time for introductions later, let's get out of range first!"

Martha felt like a Dibbun's plaything. Everything about the badger was immense—his paw, his long arrows poking from the quiver, the great bow he carried, his colossal frame. Everything! Moonlit spaces flickered past as she and the badger left the ditch and sought the shelter of Mossflower woodlands. Martha saw the badger's face. It was deeply scarred and roughly stitched, giving him a savage and fearful appearance. But his eyes were soft and gentle, friendly, the eyes of a friend.

Lonna placed her down gently. "Now, you were saying?"

The haremaid tried not to be intimidated by his size. "Thank you, sir, I was saying . . . We have need of you inside Redwall Abbey. I stole out to get you . . . Oh, my name is Martha Braebuck . . ."

The bigbeast crouched, coming level with her face. "Braebuck? I met your brother and his friends on the side of the high cliffs. Shouldn't you be in some kind of chair with wheels, miss?"

Martha found herself babbling. "You met Horty, oh, is he alright? Bragoon, Saro, all of them, are they safe? Please tell me about them. Have they been ill or injured in any way? Oh, I've been worried out of my mind . . ."

The badger's paw covered her face as he placed it over her mouth. "Hush, little Martha, your friends are fine. I'd like to stand here all night talking with you, but you say they have need of me inside your Abbey. Can you show me the way back in there? By the way, my name's Lonna Bowstripe."

Martha bobbed a small curtsy. Then she was swung up and placed upon the badger's shoulder as he moved off swiftly.

"Point me in the right direction, Martha Braebuck!" Holding on to his ear with one paw and the bowstring with the other, Martha showed him the way. "Straight ahead, Sir Lonna, you can see the belltower showing above the trees."

He chuckled. "Just call me plain old Lonna."

She whispered into his ear. "Lonna it is, you can call me Martha. I only get the full title when I'm being told off."

Raga Bol sought out Wirga. "Those poison darts, have ye got any of 'em?"

The old Searat drew a rod from her cloak. "Aye, Cap'n, there's one inside this. 'Tis the tube that I shoot 'em through."

She unplugged the ends of the rod, letting a dart show from it. "See, my little messenger of death!"

Bol murmured to her. "I'm thinkin' that the stripedog'll try t'get inside the Abbey buildin'. He's got t'be stopped. Do this for me an I'll give ye anythin' y'want!"

Wirga shuffled to the wallsteps. "My price will be high, I warn thee. I have already lost three sons."

The Searat captain spread his paws wide. "Anythin'!"

Wirga looked up from the lawn. " 'Tis as good as done!"

Abbot Carrul stood at the open window with Toran and Sister Setiva. He covered his eyes at the sight of the knotted linen rope hanging over the sill.

"I knew it, though it only occurred to me awhile after she'd been speaking with me. Oh Martha, why did you have to go and do it?"

But Toran did not stop to argue the point. He was already over the sill, clutching the linen rope and lowering himself down.

Sister Setiva leaned out of the window. "Och, ye'll get caught by yon vermin if ye go out there!"

The ottercook dropped to the ground and drew his sling. "Martha must've gone out by the east wallgate to find the badger. I'm goin' to look for her, you stay by here an' keep watch for us. Pull yoreself t'gether, Carrul!"

The Abbot stood by the window with Sister Setiva. "I should have known, I should have stopped her!"

Placing a comforting paw about him, the Infirmary Keeper shook her head. "Ah'll have a wee word wi' Martha when she returns. Ah thought it was only her brother who acted silly. Don't blame yersel', Father, yer no' a mind-reader! How were ye tae know the maid wid do sich a thing?"

Toran was stealing across the back lawn, when he saw Wirga ahead of him. He crouched low and watched her as she neared the east wallgate, then halted, obviously having heard something. Then Wirga scurried to a rhododendron bush, which grew close to the wall, hiding herself behind it.

The small door creaked on its hinges as it opened. Martha entered the Abbey grounds. Her paw lost in Lonna's grip, the haremaid turned and smiled at him. "Home at last, welcome to Redwall, Lonna!"

The badger had to stoop as he came through the gate. Toran saw Wirga slowly stand upright, placing the blowpipe to her mouth. There was no time to stop and think. He acted speedily. Bounding forward, the ottercook threw himself sideways, slamming into the Searat. Wirga's head hit the sandstone wall with a resounding crack, immediately reuniting her with her three sons.

Martha pulled on Lonna's paw as he whipped the long knife from his arm sheath. "Don't hurt him, that's my friend Toran!"

Lonna took hold of the ottercook's apron and stood him upright. Toran blinked past him at the haremaid. "Martha, is that you, matey?"

She ran forward and hugged him. "Oh Toran, that was a brave thing to do. Quick, let's get inside, there might be more Searats prowling about!"

Other Redwallers had found their way to the linen room. There were many willing paws to assist Toran and Martha back inside the Abbey. Lonna, however, was a different matter. Extra cloths and sheets had to be knotted into the makeshift rope. The badger's weight was such that no

358

amount of helpers could even raise him from the ground. Tossing his bow and quiver up to Toran, the big badger made his own way, paw over paw, up the Abbey wall to the room. At first, Martha thought Lonna would burst the window frame, but he managed to squeeze through with a certain amount of grunting and wriggling.

The haremaid beamed proudly at the Abbot as she presented her new friend to him. "Father, this is Lonna Bowstripe. He has volunteered to help us. Lonna, this is the Father Abbot Carrul of Redwall!"

There was a deal of comment from the awestruck onlookers.

"Good grief, will you look at the size of him!"

"Hurr, oi never see'd nobeast as gurt as that 'un!"

"Look, his head almost touches the ceiling!"

Without registering the least surprise, Abbot Carrul shook the badger's massive paw. "Welcome to Redwall, Lonna, and my thanks to you for returning our Martha unscathed. It was a brave deed."

Lonna immediately took a liking to the dignified old mouse. "Thank you, Father, it's a pleasure to be here. I will do all I can to rid your home of Raga Bol and his Searats."

Carrul bowed gravely, then turned his attention to the onlookers. They were still commenting on the new arrival's size, speculating as to how his face came to be so dreadfully wounded. The Abbot stared them into silence.

"It has always been our manner to welcome visitors and offer them refreshment. Have you nothing better to do than embarrass our guest with your remarks?"

Muttering apologies, the Redwallers hurried off downstairs to comply with their Abbot's wishes.

Carrul beckoned to Lonna. "Come, friend, you must be hungry and tired. Let Martha and me offer you our hospitality. You must forgive our Abbeybeasts, they meant no offence."

Lonna followed Martha and the Abbot from the linen room. "No offence taken, Father. I would be surprised if they had not mentioned the way I look. Anybeast I've ever met does."

Martha gave him a reproving look. "I never mentioned your appearance. Neither did Abbot Carrul or Toran, for that matter."

Lonna gave the haremaid one of his rare smiles. "Then I have made three good and sensible friends tonight. I think I'm going to enjoy Redwall Abbey."

Everybeast stayed up late that night, crowding into Cavern Hole to see the giant badger. Granmum Gurvel and her helpers trundled to and fro from the kitchens, bringing lots of delicious food for the guest, and for all present. Lonna sat staring at the array of fine things. Then Foremole Dwurl presented him with an outsized portion of his own personal favourite.

"Yurr zurr, this bee's deeper'n'ever turnip'n'tater'n' beet-root pie. If'n ee doant wish t'be h'offendin' ee cook, you'm best eat 'earty. Thurr bee's aplenty more whurr that cummed frumm, an' ee cook's a gurt fearsome ole villyun!"

The badger took an amused glance at the dumpy figure of Granmum Gurvel, then set to with a will. Redwallers gazed in wonder as the hungry giant satisfied his appetite.

Sister Setiva even ventured a wry wink at Lonna. "Och, there's nothin' worse than a beast with a wee flimsy appetite, pickin' away at his vittles, ah always say!"

Lonna accepted a full deep-dish apple-and-blackberry crumble from the Infirmary Keeper. He dug into it with gusto. "Aye, marm, but you must forgive me. They tell me I was a very fussy babe. It's a wonder how I survived!"

His observation broke the ice; the Redwallers burst out laughing in appreciation of their visitor's ready wit.

After the meal, they sat entranced, as Lonna related his story, which included his meeting with the travellers. The Dibbuns had infiltrated the gathering, slowly encroaching until they were sitting on Lonna's footpaws. Craning their necks, they stared in goggle-eyed admiration at the one who had confessed to being a fussy babe. Lonna gained them extra time, interceding with the elders not to send the Abbeybabes up to bed. Infants were always a source of amazement to him, he marvelled at their minute size and lack of shyness with strangers.

Having finished his narrative, Lonna asked Martha to tell him of how she came to be walking. The haremaid obliged willingly. Muggum had managed to scale the badger's footpaws and now sat upon his lap.

Tugging the badger's paw, the molebabe succeeded in gaining his attention. "You'm surpinkly a gurt creetur! Zurr Lonn', 'ow big bee's yore bed?"

Lonna looked thoughtful and adopted a serious tone. "Hmm, it's quite large, and wide, too, though I've give up carrying it around with me. Why do you ask, sir?"

Muggum waved a tiny paw generously. "You'm best take moi bed, Lonn. Oop in ee dormittees et bee's!"

The talk went back and forth, encouraged by beakers of mulled October Ale for the elders and raspberry cup for the young ones. After awhile, the old ones fell into a doze; the Dibbuns, too, no longer able to keep their eyes open, curled up and slept where they chose.

Abbot Carrul took advantage of the lull in the conversation, murmuring to Lonna, "Come up to the kitchens, there's an empty storeroom there. We'll set up a sleeping place for you. But before that, I must talk to you, friend. We'll formulate a plan to defeat the enemy and free this Abbey. Martha, Toran, Sister Portula, Brother Weld, would you come, too? I'd like you to take part in the discussion."

That night, in the quiet of the storeroom, they formulated their plans. Lonna's status as a seasoned warrior, and his expertise in the ways of his enemy Searats, earned him the main say in the discussion. His ideas made sense to his friends, although his first words were in the form of a request.

"I need more arrows, good stout shafts, and well pointed. Have you any in the building?"

Toran answered. "I'm sorry, Lonna, we haven't, but I can look for some wood and make your arrows."

Brother Weld interrupted the ottercook. "Last winter, Brother Gelf and I found an ash tree, which had collapsed outside the east wall. Skipper and his otters helped us to chop the trunk into firelogs. Gelf and I took about six sheaves of long branches from it and bundled them up. We planned on cutting them into smaller sizes to use in the orchard, for fencing and propping up berry vines. But we never got round to it. They're still piled up under the belltower stairs. Those ash branches will be well seasoned now, perfect for making arrows!"

Toran patted Weld's back. "Good work, Brother, bring them to the wine cellar. Pore Junty Cellarhog had a little forge and anvil down there. I can make arrowheads from barrel-stave iron, Junty kept a whole stock o' the stuff."

Lonna looked from one to the other enquiringly. "Flights?"

Sister Portula had an immediate answer. "There's a whole cupboardful of grey goose feathers in my room. I'll be glad to see the last of them. Two autumns back, Sister Setiva fixed the wing of a gosling, whose father was the leader of a goose skein. The geese were so grateful that they donated a load of loose feathers to me. I was supposed to cut the ends and use them as writing quills. Dearie me, they gave us enough for ten recorders to use for seven lifetimes. Please, Lonna, would you take them? If you'll relieve me of the burden, I'll recruit a team of elders to shape and bind them to your arrow shafts."

The badger agreed readily. "Thank you, Sister, there's no better flight for a shaft than a goose feather. I've been using gull feathers from the northeast shores, but they don't have the strength and firmness of good goose plumage."

Martha spoke. "You'll have a full supply of arrows, Lonna."

Stretched out on a heap of clean sacks, the big badger gazed up at the ceiling, sure now of what he was going to do. "Nobeast can live without food and water. Martha, I want you and a few others to patrol the windows all around the Abbey, where the Searats would find things to eat or drink."

The haremaid replied. "You mean the orchard and the Abbey pond? There's also a vegetable garden adjoining the orchard. Since the Searats arrived, they've taken water and fished from the pond, and as for the orchard, they're hardly ever out of there and the vegetable garden. Isn't that right, Father?"

Carrul clenched his jaw. "Correct, Martha. Those scum! I dread to think of the state our crops will be in. After all the hard work Redwallers did. Well, Lonna, you'll have a fair view of it. Orchard, vegetable patch and pond—they are all clearly visible from our south-facing windows."

Lonna reached for his bow and began running a small piece of beeswax up and down the string. "Perfect. How many arrows have I left in my quiver, Toran?"

The ottercook took a look and returned grinning. "Twenty-three . . . and a molebabe. Muggum's sleeping in there!" The little mole grumbled dozily as Sister Portula extricated him. "Oi got to stop urr. Lonn' bee's sleepin' in moi bed!"

Abbot Carrul took charge of the molebabe. "Then you can sleep in my big armchair, you rascal. In fact, I think it's time we all got a rest, there's lots to do once the day breaks. Right, Lonna?"

Bloodred tinges suffused the badger's eyes, his bowstring twanging aloud as he tested it. He gritted one word from between his clenched teeth. "Right!"

The Abbot hurriedly ushered his charges from the store-room. "We'll leave you to your sleep now, friend. Good-night."

There was no reply. Closing the door behind them, Toran the ottercook exchanged meaningful glances with the Abbot. "Did ye see that, Father? Lonna's possessed of the Bloodwrath!"

Martha looked from one to the other, perplexed. "What's the Bloodwrath, some sort of sickness?"

Toran grasped her paw so hard that she winced. "Lissen

to me, young 'un. You stay out o' that beast's way until his eyes clear up again. Badgers ain't responsible for wot they do when Bloodwrath comes upon 'em, d'ye hear?"

The haremaid managed a frightened little nod. "Lonna wouldn't hurt us, would he?"

The Abbot signalled Toran and the others to their beds. He walked through Great Hall with Martha, who was carrying the sleeping molebabe.

Carrul talked quietly with her. "Do as Toran has told you, pretty one. Only be close to Lonna when you have to. Creatures such as us know little of Bloodwrath, but grown badgers of his size can be very dangerous to anybeast when it strikes them. Take your friends tomorrow, patrol the south windows on the first and second floor. The moment you sight Searats in the grounds, report straight to Lonna. Then get out of the way. Redwallers have no business hanging around a badger who is taken by Bloodwrath. Believe me, Martha, I tell you that Lonna needs to avenge himself and his dead friend upon Raga Bol and his crew. He is here for no other reason. Go to your bed now and remember what I have said."

Carrul took the sleeping Muggum from Martha and went into his room. The haremaid looked up at the figure of Martin the Warrior on his tapestry. There was no need of visitations or dream speeches from the gallant protector of Redwall. His eyes seemed to say it all. She bowed respectfully to Martin, then went to her bed, still puzzled but obedient to her Abbot and the guiding spirit of her Abbey.

Death came to Redwall at dawn. A Searat came bursting into the gatehouse and raised Raga Bol from the bed where he had lain sprawled and twitching in broken dreams. "Cap'n, the stripedog's just kilt Cullo an' Baleclaw. They was fishin' in the pond an' 'e slayed 'em both wid one arrer!"

Bol came upright, his silver hook thrusting through the

rat's baggy shirt as he dragged him forward. "Killed 'em wid one arrer! Have ye been at the grog agin, Griml?"

The rat wailed. "I saw it meself, Cap'n. They was stannin' in the water, one afront o' the other, when a big arrer pins 'em both through their neckscruffs, like fishes on a reed!"

Bol thrust Griml roughly out the gatehouse. "Rally the crew, an' fetch Wirga t'me. Move yourself!"

Griml's mate, Deadtooth, was crouching beside the wall-steps. He, too, had witnessed the slaying of two Searats with one arrow. Deadtooth caught up with Griml. "Wot did Bol say?"

Griml shrugged unhappily. "Not much, just booted me out an' tole me t'bring the crew an' fetch Wirga."

Deadtooth persisted. "Don't the Cap'n know Wirga's dead? They found 'er just as it went light. Somebeast 'ad knocked the daylights outer 'er agin the wall. But ye knew that, didn't ye? Yew shoulda told Bol."

Griml nervously looked this way and that. "Hah, yew go an' tell 'im, if'n ye dare. I don't want no silver 'ook guttin' me. I wish we was afloat at sea, like last springtime. I tell ye, mate, we've 'ad nought but bad luck since we dropped anchor in this rotten place!"

Griml caught sight of several Searats emerging from behind a small ornamental hedge where they had been sleeping. "Ahoy, youse lot, Cap'n wants ter see ye, right now at the gate'ouse, ye best jump to it . . . ."

There was a piercing scream from the orchard as a crewrat staggered out, transfixed by an arrow. Still holding a half-ripe pear in his claws, he took one more pace and crumpled in a still heap. Griml gestured at him wildly. "See, wot did I tell ye? There's Rotpaw gone now, a good ole messmate like 'im, off to 'ellgates afore a bite o' brekkist passed 'is pore lips. I said this place is bad luck, didn't I?"

38

Having camped by the rocks and spent the night there, the travellers got their first clear view of them at sunrise next morn. Fenna found Horty, who had already risen, blowing on the embers of the previous night's fire and adding twigs to rekindle the flames. In high spirits, the young hare waved his ears at her.

"Mornin', fair Fenn'. Lots of twigs blown up against the rocks by the blinkin' wind, wot. Jolly useful to a first-class rivercook. What ho, you lazy lot, rise'n'shine, eh! So, here we are at the old Badger an' Bell. Thoughtful cove, whoever named 'em—they look just like an enormous bloomin' bell an' a blinkin' huge badger's bonce!"

Springald blinked sleep from her eyes and gave Horty a sidelong glance. "Really, have you just noticed that?"

Saro got between them. "Don't start again, you two. Horty, ole scout, ole lad, ole boy, wot's for breakfast?"

The garrulous hare giggled. "Heeheehee, would you believe fried fruit salad, marm?"

Springald came wide awake then. "Horty, you're joking?"

Bragoon had sidled up. With the tip of his sword he speared a slice of plum from the flat rock that served as a frying pan. The otter chewed it pensively. "Our cook ain't jokin', marm. Hmm, it don't taste too bad!"

366

As Saro tried a morsel, winks were exchanged all round, behind Horty's back. The aging squirrel merely nodded. "I suppose y'can't be too picky out in this country. I've ate worse an' survived."

Fenna prodded at the food with a twig. "Do we have to eat it?"

Closing her eyes, Springald gulped a piece down. "It's either that or starve. Fried fruit salad? Only a hare could think up a breakfast like that!" Horty's ears rose like flagstaffs and his cheeks bulged out. The outraged hare was about to give them a piece of his mind, when something out on the wasteland distracted his attention.

"Cads! Bounders! You rotten, ungrateful . . . I say, chaps, is that somebeast crouchin' down out there?"

Bragoon leaped up, wiping his swordblade. "Come on, let's find out!"

They spread out and made for the distant shape. Slowly and cautiously they approached the object. Then Fenna, who had the best eyesight, ran forward, calling to them. "That's no crouching beast, it's nothing but a big battered old tree stump!"

The fragmented piece of conifer stood almost as tall as Bragoon's shoulder. He tapped it with his sword.

"Y'know wot this is? All that's left o' that big tree on the map—Lord o' Mossflower. We crossed over the great gorge by walkin' across its trunk!"

Saro circled the broad base. "A shame, really. 'Twas a mighty tree in its seasons. Right, mate, 'tis time we took a look at the stuff you brought from the Abbey."

Bragoon drew out the tattered scraps of parchment he had carried since the day they left Redwall. "Let's take a look then. Loamhedge can't be too far now. Maybe we'll find some clues that'll help."

Horty was never a beast who took kindly to studying. He watched them unfolding a scrap of parchment. "Borin' old stuff, I'll go back an' break camp, wot!"

Bragoon passed the piece of paper to Springald. "Yore a

bright young 'un, read this out to us. I don't see too good for readin' lately. Think I might need those eyeglasses like Carrul an' Old Phredd wears when they reads things."

Springald studied the neat script. "Martha copied this out. It says here that it's Sister Amyl's rhyme. Listen.

"Where once I dwelt in Loamhedge,
my secret lies hid from view,
the tale of how I learned to walk,
when once I was as you.
Though you cannot go there,
look out for two who may,
travellers from out of the past,
returning home someday."

Bragoon winked at Saro. "That was us, we're the travellers from out the past. I wonder how young Martha is."

Saro folded the parchment up, returning it to the otter. "I wish she could've been fit t'make this trip with us. Now there was a young maid who had an 'ead on her shoulders. Huh, no clues there, though. Wot does that other bit say?"

Beside the map sketch, Bragoon had only one other piece of parchment. He offered it to Saro. "You read it, mate."

After unfolding it, the aging squirrel gave it to Fenna, without a second glance. "My readin' is terrible, I never payed attention at Abbeyschool. Just like you, Brag, but I ain't makin' excuses about needin' eyeglasses. You read it, Fenna. I bet you was a good learner."

The squirrelmaid straightened the creased document. "Martha tells us here that this is something which was copied by somebeast named Recorder Scrittum. The words are Sister Amyl's, but Scrittum recorded them for her.

"Beneath the flower that never grows,
Sylvaticus lies in repose.
My secret is entombed with her,

368

look and think what you see there.
A prison with four legs which moved,
yet it could walk nowhere,
whose arms lacked paws, but yet they held,
a wretched captive there."

Springald shrugged. "Well, there are clues in that rhyme.
But look around, what do you see? A broken tree stump,
two big rocks shaped like a badger's head and a bell! Besides that, all we have is a map, made so far back that
nobeast can remember. Is this all the information you
brought with you from the Abbey? Bit thin, isn't it?"

Bragoon drew patterns in the dust with his paw. Then he
and Saro cast rueful looks at each other.

Fenna spoke to them. "Wasn't there something else, a big
volume about how a party of Redwallers found Loamhedge
in bygone seasons?"

The otter explained limply. "Aye, missy, there was, but
we never took the time or the trouble to try readin' it. We
ain't no scholars, that much is plain, ain't it, mate?"

Saro nodded dolefully. "Right, we thought that, 'cos we'd
been atop o' the high cliffs an' onto the plateau one time, we
knew this country. Our mistake, I s'pose. We should've let
one of you young 'uns read the book out to us. You ain't like
us. Livin' in the Abbey all yore lives, you managed t'get
some learnin'. Me'n ole Brag, we ran away when we was
young, didn't get much schoolin'."

Fenna wanted to take them to task for going off on such
a quest without proper information, but they looked so
crestfallen. She also felt it would be unfair to berate two
creatures of such skill and craft, all of which they had
gained in the hard school of travel and experience. Scholars
they might not be, but adventurers they certainly were.

A shout interrupted her thoughts. "What ho there, you
curmudgeons! Handsome young hare approachin' with visitors! Put aside your weapons. They're friendly, an' they enjoyed my blinkin' breakfast, too!"

Bragoon thumped his rudder down in astonishment. "Horty, what'n the name o' silly seasons . . . ?"

The young hare marched up to the stump with his two new friends—a large fat dormouse, pulling a cartload of twigs and wasteland debris; and, at his side, a tiny sand lizard held by a braided lead.

Horty grinned from ear to ear. "Meet my new pal Toobledum, survivor an' hermit of the wastelands, wot! Oh, an' this other ferocious creature is Bubbub, his faithful sand-sniffer. I say, these coves really appreciate my cookin', they scoffed the bloomin' lot!"

Springald cried indignantly, "Well thanks for nothing. I scarcely took a bite of that food!"

Horty pawed his nose at her. "Serves you jolly well right, after the way you lot carried on about my fine cookin'!"

Toobledum, a cheery dormouse, wore an outrageously floppy woven grass hat, which he tipped to them. "Pleased t'meetcher, one an' all, friends o' the cook, are ye! Well, Horty's led ye this far pretty good, I'd say."

Saro glared at the young hare, paws on hips. "Led us this far, eh? I wager you've been tellin' Mister Toobledum a right ole pack o' fibs!"

Horty waffled for a moment, then changed the subject completely. "I say, chaps, here's a wheeze. Guess where Toobledum lives? Go on, tell 'em, Toob!"

The dormouse sat down and lightly scratched Bubbub's emerald-green sides. The little sand lizard arched its back with pleasure. Toobledum looked up at them from beneath the wide brim of his hat.

"Lives? Me'n likkle Bubbub lives at Loam'edge, that's where we lives. Sand lizards ain't like most reptiles, y'know. Get 'em young enough an' they're good likkle tykes."

Bragoon stared open-mouthed at the dormouse. "Y'mean to tell us you actually lives at Loamhedge?"

The floppy hat wobbled wildly as Toobeldum nodded. "All me life. Youngest o' sixteen I was, left 'ome an' came out here t'fend fer meself. Loam'edge h'aint no Redwall, like

370

the big place Horty told me that 'e rules. But 'tis 'ome, an' we like it, don't we likkle Bubbub?" The tiny sand lizard nodded and romped over to Fenna to be stroked and tickled.

Springald treated the dormouse to one of her prettiest smiles. "Could you show us the way to Loamhedge, sir?"

He flushed under his hat brim. "Ain't no sir, missy, only an ole Toobledum, but I'll show ye the way willin'ly!"

Fenna left off petting Bubbub, who nudged at her for more. "You will show us the way. Now?"

Dusting himself off, the dormouse rose with a grunt. "Now's as good a time as any, me pretty one. Long as ye let my pal Horty cook me another good mess o' vittles."

Bragoon clapped the young hare's back so heartily that he almost knocked him flat. "Well o' course, the champion quest leader an' expert cook an' ruler o' Redwall would be only too glad to cook for ye, matey!"

Toobledum passed the towing rope of his cart to Saro. "I'd be obliged if'n ye pull the ole cart fer me, marm. Me paws gets weary from luggin' it far'n'wide. Come on, likkle Bubbub, let's go 'ome."

He trundled off into the wasteland, chattering animatedly. "Nice to find somebeast t'jaw with, it gits lonely out 'ere. Likkle Bubbub don't speak, y'see. I collects useful stuff, goes far'n'wide t'find it. Firewood, nice stones, bits o' this'-n'that. Don't never waste nothin' out 'ere, I always sez. If'n ye got gear to cast off, then throw it me way!"

They journeyed on, mainly south by Bragoon's reckoning, with Toobledum talking ceaselessly, and Bubbub frisking along on his lead, moving from one to another in his efforts to find more stroking.

A camp was made out on the wastelands that evening. The dormouse donated some wood from his cart to make a fire. He was all agog in anticipation of his next meal.

"Well, Cooky, wot's fer supper? Me'n likkle Bubbub's feelin' peckish. Somethin' nice, I 'ope!"

Springald grinned pointedly at Horty. "Oh, don't worry, Cooky will turn out something delicious, I'm sure."

The young hare was beginning to tire of his role as cook. He rummaged through the dwindling supply in the ration packs. "Hmm, I expect I'll create some superb dish, but we're runnin' a bit low on the old tucker, wot. Oh, fiddlesticks! Why's it left t'me to do all the blinkin' cookin' an' slavin' round here, while you flamin' lot sit on your tails an' loll around? Huh, bit bloomin' thick, I'd say!"

Fenna joined in the teasing. "Cheer up, Mighty Ruler of Redwall, I expect you have an army of skivvies to serve you back at the Abbey. Excuse me, you're not frying another fruit salad, are you?"

Borrowing an iron pot that had been clanking along on a hook beneath Toobledum's cart, Horty answered airily. "As a matter o' fact, marm, I'm inventin' some scone soup, with a few wild onions, some sage, carrots, a leek or two an' some crumbled oatscones. Followed by fresh strawberry surprise, with dandelion tea to drink."

It was a surprisingly tasty meal. They downed it with relish. Fenna had one comment to make about the dessert. "What's in this strawberry surprise, Cooky?"

Horty grimaced. "Wish you'd stop callin' me Cooky. Oh, the strawberry surprise? I made it with some dried apple, preserved plums an' a piece o' fruitcake I found at the bottom of a ration pack. There ain't a flamin' strawberry in the whole thing—that's the surprise. Good, eh?"

Toobledum and Bubbub licked their bowls. The dormouse belched. "Parn me one an' all. We liked it. Any second 'elphins?"

Toobledum listened to the rhyme which had been dictated to Recorder Scrittum by Sister Amyl. Fenna read it out to him, but the dormouse was at a loss to cast any light on it. "Flowers wot never grows, an' four-legged prisons wid no arms? Means nought to us, does it, likkle Bubbub?"

The tiny lizard shook its head and nestled under Saro's paw. The dormouse bedded down by the fire, letting the hat brim cover his face. "I ain't clever like you beasts, I'm just an old Toobledum. No matter, ye can search for yore

372

own clues around Loam'edge in the mornin'. We'll git there afore midday. I'll bid ye 'appy dreams one an' all, g'night!"

Bragoon settled down with the sword close to paw. "I'll stay awake for first watch, mates."

Toobledum's voice came from under the hat. "You git some sleep, I've taken Bubbub off 'is lead. That likkle feller's better'n any sentry, 'e'll stand guard all night for ye."

Horty grinned with relief at Fenna. "Saves us a job, wot!"

The squirrelmaid curled up in her cloak beneath the cart. "Indeed it does. Goodnight, Cooky."

The young hare's ears shot up stiffly. "Cooky yourself, miss! Go an' boil your blinkin' heads, the bloomin' lot of you!" He closed his eyes, trying to ignore the replies.

"Nighty-night, Cooky!"

"Not staying up to plan breakfast then, Cooky?"

"I expect he has a special menu writer to do it for him back home at Redwall, don't you, Cooky?"

"A leader with stout paws, a wise ruler of an Abbey an' a cooky with a heart o' gold. Ain't we the lucky ones!"

Next day dawned on the wasteland, a warm flood of glorious colours, muted by dusty haze. The travellers ate a cold breakfast, eager to be on their way. Toobledum lingered, gossiping and trying to spin the meal out. It was only after gentle prodding that Bragoon urged the dormouse to get under way. Saro took Bubbub's lead, and Springald volunteered to pull the cart. They took up the rear, while Toobledum walked in front with Horty and Fenna. Ambling slowly along, the dormouse chatted with them.

They had been marching awhile, when Bragoon began having suspicions about the route. He called to Toobledum, who was still talking at length with Horty and Fenna, "Now then, matey, when d'ye reckon we'll be at Loamhedge?"

Without turning around, the dormouse shouted his answer. "Oh, it won't be 'til after lunch, I'm thinking. But don't ye fret, we're makin' fair progress, one an' all."

Nodding knowingly, the otter whispered to Saro. "Aye, I thought so, this ole buffer's got us on a vinegar trip."

She glanced quizzically at the otter. "Wot are ye talkin' about, mate?"

Keeping his voice low, Bragoon explained. "See those hills off to the right? We've been followin' them east instead o' south. Can ye see 'ow slow Toobledum's walkin', did ye notice how he lingered over brekkist?"

Saro was becoming impatient. "Spit it out, mate. Wot's goin' on?"

The otter conveyed his thoughts to her. "Well, we ain't exactly goin' the wrong way, the dormouse'll get us there, sooner or later. But he's stringin' the trip out so we'll feed 'im agin at lunchtime. Trouble is, the old feller loves vittles too much, an' he mightn't have much food at 'ome. So he wants to scoff our rations an' have Horty doin' all the cookin' for 'im!"

Saro looked down at Bubbub. "Is that right?"

The little sand lizard grinned and nodded as the squirrel patted him. "Well, the crafty ole grubswiper!"

Bragoon winked at her. "I'll fix that fat swindler, mate!"

He called aloud to Toobledum. "We ain't stopping fer lunch. Best press on to Loamhedge. When we arrives we'll have a big lunch an' a good rest."

The dormouse immediately altered course and speeded up, heading for the hills as he answered. "Aye, good idea. Foller me, I've just remembered a good shortcut. We'll be there afore ye know it!"

Saro whispered to Bragoon. "Lookit liddle Bubbub there, I'll swear he just sniggered."

39

In less than an hour the travellers had reached the hilltops. Below them the land took on a complete change. Gone was the arid dusty wasteland, replaced with an expansive green valley—not lush green like Mossflower woodlands but pleasant enough to appear refreshingly welcome to desert travellers. The whole area in the dip of the vale was dotted with brush, heather, grass and some stunted trees.

Toobledum whipped off his hat and made a sweeping gesture. "There 'tis, one an' all. Loam'edge!"

Halfway down the slope, Fenna stooped to pick a few daisies. She crumbled some earth in her paws and sniffed it. "This was probably rich fertile country in some bygone time."

The dormouse watched her braid the flowers into her tailbush. "Most likely it was, young missy. Mebbe those mice who lived around 'ere long ago tended the land an' farmed it t'keep it that way."

Horty stared about. "Don't see any streams or runnin' water."

Toobledum plucked a daisy stem and chewed on it. "There's underground water at the middle o' the valley. I gets it cold'n'sweet from a well down there. Once we crosses the Abbey boundary I'll take ye to it."

They carried on downhill. When the dormouse was almost on level ground he kicked aside some long grass and shrubbery. "See 'ere, that's the top o' the ole boundary wall. It must've collapsed an' been buried in the long ago, when the ground used to dance an' shake."

He exposed a line of coping stones, each one decorated with a skilful carving of a mouse. Toobledum straightened up, arching his back as he gestured around the valley bottom. "If'n ye takes the trouble, an' yore fond o' diggin', y'can follow it all around in a big square. I've never bothered meself, 'cept when I needs stones for me 'ouse. Right then, come on one an' all, don't shilly-shally, 'tis lunchtime."

They followed the old dormouse into a grove of stunted, knobbly trees, stopping as they reached a rickety hut, a rambling structure knocked together from odds and ends of stone, timber and debris.

Toobledum announced proudly, "Well, this is it, one an' all, me likkle 'ome. Me'n Bubbub wouldn't trade it fer a palace!" He set about lighting a fire beneath a rock slab oven, which stood outside the front door. Bubbub frisked happily about as the old dormouse sang.

"All round an' round the land ye well may roam,
lots o' places I 'ave rambled, far'n'near,
but there ain't no nicer nest than me ol' 'ome,
'tis so comfy an' we loves it, oh so dear.
The moment that we gets 'ere, me an' me likkle mate,
we lights a fire an' puts the kettle on,
though we ain't got much to eat, we gets along just
    great,
'cos two kin live 'ere just as well as one."

Bragoon had a quiet word with Horty. "Give 'em all we can spare from the rations. Make it a lunch to remember for the ole beast an' Bubbub."

The young hare saluted smartly. "To hear is to obey, O

376

Wise Otter, sah. I'll make it a spread that none of us'll forget!"

Fenna blew a sigh. "As long as you don't serve us fried fruit salad again!"

Horty began rummaging through their meagre supplies. "Pish tush, miss! I shall treat that remark with the blinkin' contempt it bally well deserves, wot!"

He did, however, cook a very passable meal. Drawing water from the dormouse's well, Horty produced a tasty vegetable soup and some scones and honey, with pennycress and comfrey cordial to wash it down.

Saro ate it with relish but could not resist a wry remark. "Mmm, tastes good, but I ain't even goin' to ask wot's in it."

Horty licked honey from his paws and reached for another scone. "Just as well really, marm. Wild frogs wouldn't drag the recipe from me. We cooks have our secrets, y'-know!"

Toobledum and Bubbub did the lunch full justice. Springald was astounded at the amount the little lizard ate.

The dormouse just laughed at Bubbub's appetite. "Proper likkle famine face, ain't he?"

Bragoon began questioning Toobledum, warming to the aim of their quest. "This spot we're searchin' for, it's a grave I think. Lissen to these few lines, mate, an' see if'n ye can throw any light on 'em.

"Beneath the flower that never grows,
Sylvaticus lies in repose.
My secret is entombed with her,
look and think what you see there."

"I want ye to pay attention, Toobledum. Do ye know anyplace 'ereabouts that sounds like wot I've just said?"

The dormouse pulled down his hat brim, muttering darkly, "That'll be the dead place. We never goes over there, do we, mate?"

Bubbub snuggled tight against the dormouse and shook his head.

Springald pursued the enquiry. "Whyever not? The dead never hurt anybeast, and I wager those buried there have been dead long before you were born."

Toobledum shook his head. "Say wot ye likes, miss, but there's nights when the wind blows an' I've 'eard 'em moanin'."

Horty took a light view of this sinister statement. "Maybe they get jolly hungry down there. Come on, old scout, up on your hunkers an' show us where the old graveyard is, wot!"

The dormouse refused flatly. "I ain't goin' nowheres near that place, ye can go an' see it for yoreselves. Walk south across the valley until ye see flat stones. They're all laid this way an' that, ye can't miss 'em. That's the buryin' garden. I think it was once inside the ole Abbey. I've only been there once, an' I ain't goin' there agin, nohow!"

Leaving the dormouse and his lizard, the five travellers set out, following his directions.

The ancient burying place was quiet and peaceful in the noontide sun. A few bees hummed, and grasshoppers chirruped on the still, warm air.

Saro sat down on one of the flat stones and looked about. "Nice ole spot, ain't it. Sort of a garden o' memories."

Fenna brushed the dust from a lopsided oblong of limestone. "See what this says: Sister Ethnilla, victim of the great sickness, gone to the sunny slopes and silent streams."

Bragoon traced a paw across the graven words. "Pore creature, there must be a lot of her kind buried 'ere. Sunny slopes an' quiet streams, eh? I like that."

Springald and Horty were inspecting the stones further afield.

The young hare's voice interrupted the otter's reverie. "I say, you chaps, what was the name we were lookin' for, Sivvylaticus or somesuch? I think I've found it. Yoooohaaaw!"

Bragoon sprang upright as Horty's yell disturbed the peace. "Wot's that lop-eared noisebag up to now?"

Springald was shouting. "Over here, quick, Horty's fallen down a grave!"

They dashed over to where the mousemaid was hopping about agitatedly as she pointed to a yawning dark hole. "Down there, he's fallen right through. One moment he was standing, pointing to this big stone, then something broke and he vanished!"

The otter pulled her aside. "Stand clear, miss, or ye might be the next one to disappear." He called down into the pitch-black space. "Horty, are ye alright, mate?"

There was no reply, just a faint echo of his own voice.

40

Raga Bol was at his wit's end; the Searat crew had begun to desert. He kicked out at Firzin, a rat he had posted on the main gate, screaming, "Wot'n the name o' thunder d'ye mean, nobeast has got by ye all day? Did ye unlock this gate fer anythin'?"

Firzin cringed against the gate, which he had guarded faithfully on his captain's orders. "On me oath, Cap'n, I've kept the gate tight locked!"

Bol glared this way and that, slashing at the air with his scimitar. "The walltops are too high for 'em to jump, so how've they got out? Rinj, wot d'you think?"

Rinj, who had been close to Bol all day, shrugged. "Wot about those liddle gates, Cap'n? There's one in the middle of each of the three outer walls. Bet they went through them, eh?" The Searat captain's gold fangs flashed as he snarled. "I told Argubb to post guards on those wallgates this mornin'. Go an' see if'n they're still there!"

Rinj sidled out of the scimitar's range. "They 'ad to stand in plain sight o' the winders, Cap'n. That big stripedog took the three of 'em out wid his arrers."

Raga Bol peered around the wall buttress, which was sheltering him and his two crewrats from the Abbey windows. "Get in the gate'ouse, both of ye, quick!"

The three rats crouched, swerving in a dead run around the buttress. They made it into the gatehouse and slammed the door. The timbers shook as an arrow hit the door, its barbed point showing through the wood.

Firzin wailed, "We're all deadbeasts if'n we stay in this place. There ain't nowhere to 'ide from the stripedog!"

One icy glare from his captain was sufficient to frighten the Searat into silence. Bol looked from one to the other, his face deadly calm, his voice low. "Wot's the number o' crew left d'ye reckon, Rinj?"

The rat thought for a moment. "Just over a score, Cap'n. That's countin' us three."

Since early that day, Raga Bol had been scheming furiously. His back was against the wall, but he was determined that eventually he would triumph. Then it came to his mind in a flash—he knew that he had the answer. All he had to do was convince his crew.

Slumping down in an armchair, he shook his head sadly, acting more like one of the Searat messmates than their captain. "No more'n a score left out o' fifty, eh? I tell ye, mates, 'tis a sorry day. I suppose every one of ye wants t'see the back o' this place now. Speak up, I won't harm ye."

Firzin summoned up his courage. "Aye, Cap'n, they're all sayin' we're deadbeasts if'n we stays at this Abbey. Ain't that right, Rinj?"

The other rat nodded. "Aye, mate, gettin' away from 'ere's the sensible thing to do, shore enough."

Raga Bol gave a rueful little smile, as if in agreement. "Mebbe yore right. But just think, mates, if we'd 'ave killed the stripedog an' won, eh? Redwall woulda been ours! The good life, me buckoes! Everybeast of us'd be livin' like kings now, wid slaves, loot, vittles an' a place t'call 'ome fer the winter. Strange 'ow things turn out, ain't it? Now we got to cut'n'run, all because o' one stripedog who should've been dead now by rights.

"Aye, we've got no ship, we're a season's march from saltwater an' I've lost near a score an' a half of the best

Searats a cap'n ever 'ad. Now we got nothin', we'll 'ave to tramp the land like beggars."

Rinj and Firzin had never seen their captain like this before. They shuffled their footpaws and tails awkwardly.

Then Bol dropped a single word: "Unless!"

Both crewrats were immediately curious.

"Unless wot, Cap'n?"

"Have ye got a plan, Cap'n?"

Raga Bol leaned forward, his eyes gleaming craftily. "Hoho, mates, I got a plan alright. Now 'earken t'me an' lissen!"

Abbot Carrul and Toran were sitting in the kitchens. They looked up as Martha entered. The ottercook indicated a heap of arrows, lying ready on the table.

"Does 'e want more shafts?"

The haremaid shook her head. "Not at the moment. Granmum Gurvel and I have piled arrows at every windowsill."

The Abbot poured her a beaker of cold mint tea. "What's going on out there, Martha? You and old Gurvel are the only ones who can get close to Lonna. What's he up to?"

Martha took a sip of the tea. "It's all quiet at the moment. He's roaming the upper corridors, watching from the windows. It's dreadful out there—dead Searats by the pond, on the walls and by the orchard. I think a few of them have deserted, gone through the east wallgate into the woods. Lonna is still prowling about watching the grounds, though he seems to have calmed down a little. It was frightening just to set eyes on him this morning!"

Toran brought out a stool for Martha to sit upon. "Mayhaps the Searats are gettin' ready to leave, or it might only be the calm afore the storm. Who knows wot Raga Bol's got in that evil brain—another scheme, per'aps. We'll just have t'sit an' wait. Wot d'ye think Martha?"

The haremaid rested her weary footpaws. It had not been

an easy day so far, running up and down stairs, keeping the badger supplied with arrows. "I think it's gone too quiet, Toran. But who knows how things will turn out? Like you say, we'll have to wait and see."

Sister Setiva had been listening from the kitchen doorway. "Och, all this waitin'! Everybeasts's keepin' busy, ye ken. They're all doon in Cavern Hole makin' arrows, even the Dibbuns. Ah've come tae make some food for them. Most of us have no taken a bite since breakfast!"

Toran busied himself, glad for something to do. "Leave it t'me, Sister. I'd forgotten about vittles today. Gurvel's helpin' Martha. I should've realised we 'ad no cook."

Abbot Carrul climbed down from his stool. "Here, let me help you, Toran. It's not right that my Redwallers should go hungry, even in times like these!"

Late afternoon slid into evening. Over beyond the west wall the sun set in solitary splendour. A wash of gold and purple suffused the sky, with blood red at its centre.

Lonna stood alone at the front dormitory windows. He rested against a sill, keeping watch on the gatehouse and its buttressed corner by the main gate. Now that there had been a few hours' lull from any action, the Bloodwrath had receded from him. His massive frame had relaxed. Lonna felt drained and weary, not having slept in almost two days and nights. Gradually night edged in, bringing with it a soft breeze to cool away the day's heat. Lonna began blinking a lot, nearly causing the bow to slip from his grasp. Rubbing his eyes and shaking himself, the big badger peered into the darkness, trying to keep his vision fixed on the gatehouse area. Then the voice sounded out.

Lonna came instantly alert as he identified Raga Bol's rasping tones, calling from somewhere over by the buttress where his arrows could not reach.

"Ahoy, stripedog, I see ye! Still hidin' in there be'ind the Abbot's skirts, are ye? Does yore wound still pain ye? Haharr, I should've gone for the neck an' chopped yore 'ead off! Don't worry, stripedog, Raga Bol ain't goin' nowhere. I slayed the old stripedog an' I kin finish ye, too!"

Brother Weld, who had been checking the window barricades in Great Hall, came hurrying into Cavern Hole. "There's something happening outside. I can hear the Searat captain shouting to the big badger!"

Toran bounded to the stairs. "Sister Setiva, Sister Portula, keep the little 'uns down 'ere! Anybeast who's able enough, bring a weapon an' foller me! Does anyone know where Lonna is?"

Martha seized a ladle. "He was going toward the dormitories at the front when I left him."

The ottercook wielded the big bung mallet, which had once belonged to Junty Cellarhog. "Let's see if'n he's there!"

Martha and Toran burst into the dormitory, at the head of a band of Abbeydwellers. The haremaid could see Lonna's powerful back, silhouetted in the open window frame. He was shaking with rage but silent. Raga Bol was still taunting him from somewhere outside.

"I don't slay my enemies from a distance with arrers, that ain't the way a real warrior fights! But keep yore distance if'n yore scared o' Raga Bol. Come out 'ere, ye coward, an' I'll slice the other side of yer face off afore I leaves the birds to pick over yore carcass!"

Lonna leaped up onto the windowsill, roaring, "I'll fight you any way you like, you murdering scum!"

Toran leapt forward and grabbed Lonna's footpaw. "Don't go, mate, 'tis a trap. There's still plenty o' Searats out there. Ye'll be surrounded!"

The badger dealt Toran a kick, knocking him backward. Raga Bol was visible now, standing slightly to the right on the lawn.

Paws on hips, the big Searat laughed mockingly. "Haharrharr! 'Ere I am, scarmuzzle! Come an' meet me paw't'claw widout yore bow'n'arrers fer once. Bring the magic sword an' cross blades wid Raga Bol if ye dare!"

"Eulaliiiiiaaaaaa!" Nothing could stop the giant badger now. Bellowing his warcry, Lonna jumped from the dormitory window. Luckily, the huge hill of rubble blocking the Abbey door had dried out in the sun. He landed upon it and managed to stay upright. Scrambling and rolling, he thundered down toward the ground. Without a moment's hesitation, Toran went over the sill after him, with Martha and the rest in his wake.

Raga Bol held the glittering scimitar ready to strike, the silver hook on his other pawstump whirling in readiness. He stood awaiting the badger's charge, about a spear's throw from the north wall.

Martha caught up with Toran. She pointed to the north walltop. "Quick, up there, that's where the Searats are!"

The ottercook veered, heading for the steps as he called to Martha. "Split up, take half our beasts down to the east steps. I'll go up the north stairs. Weld, Gelf, Foremole, you come with me!"

Oblivious of everything except Raga Bol waiting in his path, Lonna rushed straight at his enemy, armed only with his teeth and claws.

Bol, judging the moment when the badger was within three paces of him, dropped down, yelling out, "Spears, now!"

Lonna did not even bother to dodge the flying spears; three missed him, but one struck his left shoulder. He whipped it out and flung it aside, ignoring the wound. The Bloodwrath was upon him, his eyes red as the sunset he had watched a few hours earlier. His teeth shone from his scarred features in a savage snarl as his huge, blunt claws sought the kneeling Searat captain. Bol was halfway up when the badger grabbed his neck and swung him off the ground.

Raga Bol emitted one strangled gurgle. Then four spears,

thrown by the captain's own Searats and intended for the badger, buried their blades in Raga Bol's back instead. He died, hanging there like a rag doll in the grip of his mighty foe. The last thing he saw was Lonna Bowstripe roaring into his face.

"Go through Hellgates and burn, rat! Eulaliiiiaaaaaa!"

Holding the limp body in front of him, Lonna charged the wall, bulling up the stairs behind Toran like a juggernaut.

The ottercook shouted to his helpers. "Look out, get to the west wall, let the badger pass! Martha, back off! Git those beasts down t'the lawn!"

The haremaid, who saw what was happening, turned swiftly to the Redwallers behind her. "Get out of the way. Downstairs, now!"

Abbot Carrul confronted her, his blood roused. He waved a sweeping broom, yelling fiercely. "Let me at those rats. I'll drive them from Redwall, the filthy invaders. How dare they attack my Abbey!" He was grabbed by two stout moles and hustled down the wallsteps.

The ramparts became a scene of chaos. Using Raga Bol as a flail, Lonna swept Searats left and right. Some were knocked over the battlements, their broken bodies thudding to the woodland floor outside the walls. Any who were unfortunate enough to fall onto the lawn inside the Abbey grounds were dealt with by a horde of Redwallers, each eager to be mentioned thereafter as a beast who had taken part in the battle to win back their Abbey.

Lonna stood on the empty walkway, his chest heaving like a bellows, blood oozing from a dozen different wounds. The carcass of Raga Bol resembled a grotesque, oversized pincushion, pierced by an array of spears from Searats who had tried to fend off the badger's advance.

Cautiously, Toran and his helpers approached from the west walltop. They froze as Lonna whirled around to face them, still holding Raga Bol's slain body, the spears hanging from it rattling against the battlements. With a powerful heave, the big badger tossed his onetime enemy over the wall, listening to his body clattering through the tree limbs. Smiling like a Dibbun who had just learned a new trick, Lonna Bowstripe sat down, letting his footpaws dangle over the lawn.

"When Martha brought me to Redwall, I hoped I could be of some help to you."

The ottercook sat down beside him. "Aye, an' that ye were, mate, that ye were!"

Woodpigeons were startled from their roosts in Mossflower woodlands. They wheeled about in the night air, wondering why the bells of Redwall Abbey were pealing and booming out at such a late hour.

41

Bragoon crouched, staring down into the pit of the open grave where Horty had disappeared. Saro was fashioning a torch from twigs, grass and moss. Fenna lay flat on the edge of the hole, calling down.

"Horty, if you can hear me, then shout out!"

Springald centred the light of her chunk of rock crystal on the torchtop. Magnified sunrays produced a wisp of smoke, which grew into a small flame. Saro wafted it into a fire.

"I'm the climber, let me go first. Spring an' Fenna, ye stay up 'ere in case we need anythin'. Fetch the rope, Brag." Lowering herself over the edge, the aging squirrel dropped a bit, then landed on something solid.

"Stone steps, look!"

A dusty flight of narrow steps ran curving downward into the darkness. Bragoon coiled the rope about his shoulders and followed her carefully. "Slow down, mate—we don't want t'lose you, too!"

Springald and Fenna watched until the light vanished around the curve, down into the gloom.

The mousemaid shuddered as she sat down by the broken covering stone. "I don't like this place anymore. It looked so peaceful and sunny at first, but now there's something about it that gives me the shivers. No wonder Tooble-dum wouldn't come here. I hope Horty's alright."

Fenna was studying the big dark headstone, perched sideways at a crazy angle. "Horty's indestructible, you'll see."

Bragoon's head appeared at ground level. "Yore right there, miss. Lend a paw, you two!"

Saro was on the step behind him. Between them they carried the slumped form of Horty. Heaving and pulling, the four friends managed to lift the young hare onto solid ground, where he curled up as if asleep.

Saro patted his back. "He took a fall an' landed on the left side of his head. Pore Horty's got a fat ear, but there's no real harm done."

Fenna soaked some moss and dabbed at the swollen ear. "He's taken his share of knocks on this trip. That's a real thick ear he's got there."

The damp poultice must have worked: Horty groaned and tried to sit up but fell back, complaining miserably. "Yowch, I am awake! I say, d'you mind awfully not scrub-bin' a chap's wounded ear with that filthy wet stuff. It stings like jolly blue blazes!"

Springald took out a flask of cordial which she had brought along. "Could you manage a sip of this?"

Horty grabbed it and downed the lot in three big gulps. "Not that it'll do the noble young ear much good, but I've managed to wet my parched lips with it. Ooh, my achin' lug!"

Fenna supported his head. "Poor Horty, it must hurt ter-ribly."

The young hare put on a pitiful face. "I must be close t'death. I say Fenn, old scout, you don't happen to have a bite of scoff about you, wot?"

Bragoon stifled a laugh. "Nothin' much wrong wid that 'un! Keep an eye on 'im, you two. We're goin' back down to take a look round there. Pass me some more wood an' grass, Fenn. We got to keep the torch alight."

Fenna bundled her cloak under Horty's head. As the squirrelmaid began gathering more fuel for the torch, she shared her latest discovery with her companions.

"Now I know why Toobledum could hear moaning on windy nights from the buryin' place. See that big dark stone, it's the one that marked this grave. There's words carved on it. Listen. 'Sylvaticus. First Mother Abbot of Loamhedge Abbey. Loved by all creatures. Long in seasons and wisdom. Gone to her final rest. Forever in our thoughts.' This is the very grave we've been seeking."

Fenna indicated the beautifully carved motif at the top of the headstone. It was a lily in full bloom with a graceful stem sprouting curved and fluted leaves. The entire design was pierced right through the stonework. The squirrelmaid traced it with her paw.

"This is the flower that never dies. I'll wager that the wind sings an eerie song through this carving on windy nights. You can't blame Toobledum for steering clear of here."

Bragoon regarded her with admiration. "Yore a bright young 'un, Fenn, that was well thought out. Take care of Horty now, we'll be back afore ye know it."

For the second time, the two old friends descended the stairs.

Not one to let an injury slip by unnoticed, Horty made the most of his thick ear as the two Abbeymaids ministered to him. "Salad! Now that's the very stuff for a swollen ear, wot! Any hare'll tell you, salad's just the thing, an' lots of it. Hold hard there, Spring old gel, what's that sloppy mess? Tut tut, marm, you ain't physickin' me with that rubbish!"

Springald cradled the mixture in a dockleaf. "Don't be such a Dibbun, Horty Braebuck. It's a mud-and-moss poultice that will do your ear a power of good. Hold him, Fenn!"

Horty struggled in the squirrelmaid's firm grip. "Gerroff me, you flamin' torturesses. I'll bet you took lessons from Sister Setiva on how to persecute wounded beasts. Yugh! That dreadful gloop's gone right down me bloomin' ear.

You've done it now, I'll be deaf on one side for the rest of me short young life. Rotters!"

Springald tugged the hare's good ear sharply. "Do hold still! What can you expect if you hop about like that? Now, I'll just dress it with some dock leaves."

Horty looked blankly at her. "What rock thieves? Speak up!"

When the dressing was completed, he lay down in a sulk, while Springald cast a glance at the grave. "They've been gone an awfully long time. What d'you think, shall we go down there and check on them?"

Fenna nodded eagerly. "Yes, let's do that. You stay here, Horty. Take a nap or something."

They dropped over the edge onto the stairs, with their former patient calling after them.

"I say, what's a cap an' a dumpling? What's up, have you both gone mad?"

Holding paws, Springald and Fenna managed the steps and, placing their backs against the rough stone wall, crept forward cautiously. The ground took a curve, dipping steeply. Slowly stumbling on, in total darkness, they were relieved to see the faint glow of a torch ahead. The muted voices of their friends could be heard.

Fenna called out to them. "Saro, Brag, is that you? We've come down for a little peek."

The otter's voice, which sounded rather grumpy, echoed back at them. "I told ye t'stay on top, you should be mindin' Horty. Who knows wot that buffoon'll be up to be'ind our backs!"

Saro's voice interrupted him. "Oh, there's no harm done, mate. Let 'em come an' take a look."

It was quite a sight. The passage opened up into an underground chamber, lined with stone walls. At its centre stood a plinth, littered with old bones and a white cloth habit that had faded to the texture of a cobweb. In front of the plinth lay what had once been a chair with wheels but now was little more than a small heap of dry, insect-bored sticks. There were two more torches in wall sconces on one wall behind the plinth.

After Saro had lit them, she gestured about with her own guttering torch. "Well, this is it, mates. We've travelled long'n'far, just to find this sad ole lot. Those bones are wot's left o' pore Abbess Sylvaticus. But can ye guess wot those rotted sticks are?"

Springald picked up a piece of the timber in her paw. It crumbled to dust. "Don't tell me, this was the chair once used by Sister Amyl. Those little round black stones with holes in them must have been its wheels. Huh, they're the only things recognisable after all this time."

Crouching down, Bragoon sifted through the debris with his swordpoint. "Must've been 'ere thousands of seasons. How did the rhyme go . . .

"Beneath the flower that never grows,
Sylvaticus lies in repose.
My secret is entombed with her,
look and think what you see there.
A prison with four legs which moved,
yet it could walk nowhere,
whose arms lacked paws, but yet they held,
a wretched captive there."

Bragoon rose up and put away his blade. "Aye, that's Sister Amyl's chair, sure enough, but where's the Sister's secret?"

Saro gnawed at her lip. "Imagine pore young Martha when we get back an' tell 'er there was nought but a pile o' dust an' four black stones!"

Springald hung her head miserably. "It doesn't bear thinking about. Now I wish we'd never found it."

Fenna retrieved the four little black stone wheels. She stowed two in her belt pouch and gave the other two to Springald. "At least these'll prove we've been here. Come on, Spring, let's go back and see how Horty's doing."

Bragoon gave them one of the torches to guide them out.

"Aye, you young 'uns go an' do that. Me'n my ole mate are goin' to stay down here awhile an' search."

Fenna shrugged glumly. "Waste of time, there's nothing left to search for. Oh well, please yourselves."

The otter cautioned them. "Don't mention anythin' to Horty, wot with Miss Martha bein' 'is sister an' all that. Tell 'im we're still searchin'. Better still, take Horty back to ole Toobledum's 'ouse an' wait fer us there. We shouldn't be too long. Will ye do that for me?"

They nodded and trudged back to Horty.

Toobledum had taken the liberty of making a meal for them from the remnants of the ration packs. His little sand lizard capered about on its back paws, delighted to see the young ones returning.

The old dormouse proudly raised his floppy hat. "Sit down, one an' all, see wot I cooked up for ye. Me'n likkle Bubbub did ye a stew. 'Tis made of all things good, wid an apple crumble fer afters an' a drop o' me own special whortleberry cup brew to drink. Ho dear, wot 'appened to pore master Horty?"

Horty blinked oddly at the dormouse. "What the dickens is the old chap wafflin' about? Who's he goin' to plaster for being naughty, wot?"

Fenna roared down his good ear. "He said, What's happened to poor master Horty!"

The young hare waggled a paw in his good ear. "No need to bellow, miss!"

Then he turned to Toobledum. "Ah, well may you ask, little fat sir. I suffered a dreadful injury to the old ear, but I'm keepin' jolly brave about it. Mmmm, nothin' wrong with a chap's nose, though! That stew smells like just the ticket. Whack me out a large portion, sir dormouse, looks like a splendid cure for thickearitis!"

Toobledum humoured Horty by giving him a large bowlful. The young hare was halfway through it when he held the bowl out. "Don't stint on the stew, I always say. Never mind Brag'n'Saro, they're far too old to appreciate good scoff. I say, those two relics should be back by now. Huh, loiterin' around graveyards, bloomin' bad form, they'll go all morbid."

It was over an hour before the two searchers made an appearance. The dormouse and Bubbub welcomed them back. Springald gave them two bowls she had washed out. "Toobledum made some delicious stew, but you'd better get some fast before Horty hogs it all down."

The young hare looked up from a beaker of whortleberry cup. "I heard that, marm. Why should frogs fall down? Complete gibberish if y'ask me, wot!"

Springald waited until the two had finished eating before she enquired. "Well, did you find anything?"

Saro smiled at Bragoon, who winked back at her as he sipped his drink. "Hmm, whortleberry juice! 'Tis a while since I've tasted that. Used t'be me favourite drink at one time."

Fenna twirled her bushy tail impatiently. "You haven't answered the question. Did you find anything?"

Saro tasted her drink, still smiling secretively. "Aye, 'tis nice, a sweet taste. Mind ye, I was allus partial to a drop o' nettle beer, like those otterpals o' yores drinks, up on the north coast."

Horty looked from one to the other. "Who's seen a ghost?"

Fenna fumed. "Oh, put a cork in it, Horty! Now, Mister Bragoon, Madam Sarobando, will you answer the question. Please!"

Old Toobledum chuckled. "Heeheehee, I knows ye found somethin', yore both sittin' there lookin' like a pair o' toads eatin' trifle. Put the young 'uns out their misery an' tell 'em, mates."

The otter produced a small cylinder of parchment. He tossed it from paw to paw. "We found it—this is Sister Amyl's secret."

Springald was about to reach for it, when Saro caught the

cylinder and stowed it in her belt pouch. "No ye don't, Spring, this is for none but Martha t'read!"

Fenna pouted indignantly. "How do you know that?"

Bragoon raised his eyebrows. "Because, miss clever clogs, it sez so on the parchment. Read it to 'em, mate."

Saro took out the little scroll that had been tied with a few threads to keep it closed. On the outside was some tiny, squiggly writing. She peered at it closely, reading slow. "Only the one who needs this shall know my secret!"

Bragoon levelled a paw at them. "None of you young 'uns needs to know, only Martha, 'cos she's the one who needs it. We haven't looked at it ourselves, out o' respect to Martha. So nobeast is goin' to find out Sister Amyl's secret except that young hare back at the Abbey o' Redwall. We're bound back there at tomorrer's dawn, with all 'aste!"

Fenna, however, still had a question that needed answering. "But we saw the place, there was absolutely nothing down there but bones, powdery wood and dust. How did you come to find it?"

Bragoon paused briefly before launching into his explanation. "It was at the bottom o' that stone thing where Abbess Sylvaticus lay . . ."

Springald interrupted. "The plinth, you mean?"

Saro nodded. "Aye, the plinth, that was it. We was about to leave the place, when I took one o' those torches off'n the wall, 'cos our torch 'ad gone out. Well, I stubbed me footpaw on the bottom o' the plinth, an' one o' the stones came loose. Brag pulled it out an' there 'twas, lyin' as safe an' neat as ye like, be'ind a stone all that time."

Fenna pursued her enquiry. "But why hadn't it turned to dust like everything else down there?"

Bragoon picked something that resembled a tiny pellet from under his pawnail. "See . . . beeswax. It was wrapped tight in dock leaves covered with beeswax. I tell ye, it was difficult, separatin' that liddle roll o' paper from the beeswax, but we did it!"

Toobledum poured them more drink. "Well done, mates,

you found wot you was questin' for. I'm 'appy for ye, one an' all!"

Horty humphed. "Three scones on a wall, ridiculous, wot?"

Saro pulled Horty upright. "I've had enough o' this nonsense. Toobledum, bring me some 'ot water, not too 'ot, mind. Brag, lay Horty on one side, wid that muddy ear upwards, an sit on 'im. I couldn't put up with 'im talkin' rubbish all the way 'ome!"

Horty guffawed. "Hawhawhaw! Walkin' cabbage an' a bone? Poor old Saro's finally gone off her rocker, wot!"

Sudden panic struck as Bragoon pushed Horty down and sat on him. "What the . . . ? Gerroff me, you great plank-tailed bounder! Good grief, what's that nutty old squirrel doin' with a jug o' steamin' water? Help, somebeast, help! They're tryin' to kill me! Murderers, assassins! Boilin' me blinkin' brain, an' just 'cos I scoffed three flamin' bowls of stew? Spring, Fenna, strike the cads with rocks'n'clubs, save me!"

But no help was forthcoming. The otter held him tight whilst Saro washed out his ear with warm water. A moment later it was all over. Toobledum gently treated the young hare's cleaned-up ear.

"There there, Sir Horty, ye'll live t'cook agin. This is an ole dormouse remedy, my special ointment. I makes it wid sanicle, feverfew an' a few secret herbs. So, 'ow does that feel, young master?"

Horty relaxed, closing his eyes blissfully. "Bloomin' marvellous, old top, me ear is at peace an' very comfortable. Amazin' thing, too, I can hear again!"

Saro wiped mud and moss from her paws. "See, we never killed ye after all."

Springald muttered under her breath. "Pity."

Bragoon whispered back to her. "Shame we missed our chance."

Fenna's eyes twinkled as she chuckled along with them.

"Just think of the food we'd have saved without a hare to feed."

Horty opened one eye and fixed them with a baleful stare. "I heard all that, you rotters!"

They burst into laughter; even little Bubbub did a squeaky giggle.

Dawn of the following day saw the travellers bidding farewell to the dormouse and his lizard.

Fenna hugged the pair fondly. "Why don't you come with us to Redwall? You'd both be very welcome there."

Toobledum's hat wobbled as he shook his head. "Nay, pretty miss, me'n likkle Bubbub wouldn't ever leave Loam'edge. We ain't got much, but 'tis 'ome to us."

Saro stroked the little sand lizard one last time.

Bragoon clasped the old dormouse's paw warmly. "As ye wish, matey, take care of each other, an' live happy. Good-bye an' good fortune to ye!"

Standing on the hilltop above the valley, the five travellers looked back. Bubbub was shaking his tail as Toobledum waved his hat and shouted, "Fare ye well, one an' all, an' take our good wishes with ye!"

Fenna wiped her eyes as they marched off into the wastelands. "Those poor creatures, it must be terrible for them. Living that lonely life, and with so little to eat."

Bragoon ruffled her ears affectionately. "Aye, they're both goodbeasts, Fenn. But don't ye go believin' all that ole dormouse told ye, miss. Yore too young an' soft'earted."

Horty took a pull from his canteen, filled with fresh water from Toobledum's well. "Steady on, I liked Toob an' Bub. Bit unkind to talk about the old chap like that, wot?"

Springald agreed with him. "I think so, too. They've only got each other for company, and they shared what little they have. Why shouldn't we believe what Toobledum said?"

The otter cast a wry glance at his old friend. "That dormouse is a hermit, he likes bein' alone. As fer not havin' much in the way o' vittles . . . tell 'em, Saro."

The aging squirrel explained. "When I was swillin' Horty's ear out, I watched Toobledum goin' to fetch that special ointment. Hah, the ole fogy didn't think I could see 'im. He went into a corner an' lifted a floorstone. Do ye know wot was underneath it? A cellar, packed from wall t'wall wid vittles. Drinks, dried fruits, veggibles, nuts, enough t'feed an army fer ten seasons. That's 'ow short o' food Mister Toobledum was, mates. Brag saw it, too!"

Horty stopped in his tracks. "Well, the flamin' old fraud, wolfin' down all our grub an' tellin' whoppin' fibs about havin' none himself. What a blinkin' cheek!"

Fenna could hardly believe what she had heard. "That's a shameful thing to do, the old liar!"

Springald was about to add to their condemnation of Toobledum, when the otter cut in. "Don't be too 'ard on the ole feller. Vittles an' drink is precious in this region. If ye've got none, yore a deadbeast. Toobledum was only thinkin' of hisself an' liddle Bubbub. We were just passin' visitors. Now that we've gone, he's got to provide for 'imself an' his mate. 'Tis called survival. Ye don't go dashin' to the first beast ye see an' offerin' them a cellarful o' grub, ye takes care of yore own first."

Fenna held up her paws. "Alright, we understand, Toobledum's only doing what's best for himself and Bubbub. Please don't rub it in by telling us we're only young and we'll learn."

Saro winked knowingly at her. "Wouldn't dream of it . . . young 'un!"

A raven flew out of the great gorge. Soaring high, it hovered on the evening thermals, a dark sinister shape framed against the setting sun for a brief moment. Then it swept off southward. Down below, standing at one of the three cave entrances, a cloaked figure watched the bird's departure, then turned and went into the tunnel. Pushing through the mass of dark creatures, the cloaked one made its way to where the sulphurous flame burned constantly, a tall column of fire, giving off its acrid stench.

Kharanjul, the Great Wearet Slayer, stood waiting for the news his guard captain brought. The cloaked creature lay flat on the rocky floor and lifted its face.

"It is as ye said, Mighty Lord, the travellers are even now returning, to sully thy abyss with their presence!"

Kharanjul's hideous face stared impassively down at the captain. "Did Korvusa say when they would arrive in my domain?"

The speaker lowered his eyes from the Wearet's piercing gaze. "The bird said that they would reach the gorge rim in the second hour of darkness, Great Slayer."

Kharanjul's trident pointed at the messenger. "Take a score of my creatures across, to the other side of the long tree. Hide there and await my signal."

Accompanied by twenty spearbearers, the captain marched out, prepared to cross the tree trunk that spanned the forbidding drop.

The Wearet's harsh voice grated out, echoing around the cavern. "None of the trespassers must be slain, they are to be taken alive . . . to die at my pleasure!"

The dark masses rose, spearblades glinting as they chanted, "Blood of the Wearet runs in thy veins, O Mighty Kharanjul. Ruler of the Abyss! Lord of Life and Death!"

42

Abbot Carrul sat soaking up the warm morning sun at the orchard entrance. Folding his paws across his stomach, he smiled at Old Phredd, sitting across from him at the breakfast buffet table. The ancient hedgehog Gatekeeper was chatting away to a bumblebee, which had landed on the rim of his beaker.

"Dearie me, have you seen the mess those vermin made of my gatehouse? There's scrolls, books and parchments scattered about on the floor. One would think a herd of wild beasts had been living there. Hmm, they have really, haven't they?"

The bee buzzed, vibrating its tiny wings. Phredd pointed a bony paw at it. "Oh, that's easy for you to say, my friend. But the curtains have been ripped, the cupboards flung open and the bed linen will have to be scrubbed twice before I use it again. Thrice, even!"

Carrul reassured his old friend. "Don't worry so! Stretch your paws and enjoy being outdoors in our own Abbey again. We've time aplenty to put everything right, Phredd—the remainder of summer and all the autumn."

Foremole Dwurl and a crew of his worthies trundled up to the table. The mole tugged his snout in respectful salute. "Me'n moi moles've cleared opp all ee gurt 'eap o' rubble wot was blocken ee h'Abbey door h'entrence, zurr. Et bee's ready furr use naow, arfter they'm scrubbed ee wuddwurk daown!"

Carrul beamed gratefully at the Foremole. "Well done, Dwurl, come and have some more breakfast. There's lots of it left here, do help yourselves."

Dwurl and his molecrew, needing no second invitation, fell to with a will.

"Thankee, zurr. Much h'obliged oi'm shurr!"

Toran and Martha came running across the lawn. The ottercook called out, "Gangway, make room there, mates, two more 'ungry workers comin' in for second brekkist!"

Carrul indicated two spaces either side of himself. "Well, what have you two been up to? I haven't seen you since first serving at dawn."

Martha cut herself a slice of fruitcake. "Unblocking the windows in Great Hall, Father. Brother Gelf says he's got extra panes in the attic storeroom. The Dibbuns have gone up there to sort them out with him."

Foremole Dwurl looked up from his mushroom pastie. "Hurr, better'n sennin' they'm likkle villyuns into ee h'orchard to 'elp wid ee fruit'n'berries. Hurr hurr, they'm loike to h'eat umselfs sick afore sundaown!"

Sister Setiva was next to put in an appearance. "Och, ye should see the state o' yon dormitory, it's no fit for worms tae crawl in. Ah'm goin' tae need some bonny helpers tae make et habitable again. Martha lassie, have ye seen that braw badger taeday?"

The haremaid shook her head. "No, Sister, last beast to see him was Granmum Gurvel. He took a few scones from the kitchen and hurried off. Wonder where he's gone?"

Toran supplied the answer. "Lonna said he'd sworn to wipe out all the Searats. A few of 'em escaped yesterday by the wallgates. I saw 'im fillin' up his quiver, an' waxin' that big bow, after we left the walltop last night. I thought better of askin' 'im where he was bound."

Martha poured pennycress cordial for the ottercook. "I

don't blame you, mate. Lonna can flare up like lightning. If and when he returns, I won't be pressing him about where he's been. I pity those Searats, though. If it were me, I'd have let them go. They've learned their lesson, and a hard and bloody one it was, too!"

Old Phredd spoke to a bowl of oatmeal he was finishing. "Ah, but Martha isn't him, is she? Big badger warriors like that are different from anybeast. If he swore to wipe out all those Searats, well that's just what he'll do. Every one of them, down to the last rat!"

The last rat was, in fact, running for his life, out on the western flatlands. His tongue lolled from one side of his mouth as he looked over his shoulder at the distant figure of the avenging giant. Lonna was standing still, a long distance away. The Searat stopped as well, collapsing in a heap, his limbs wobbling and trembling uncontrollably. Then he bared his stained fangs at the sky and laughed breathlessly.

"Haharrharr . . . Done it! Can't get me now, stripedog . . . Outta yore range now . . . I escaped ye . . . stripedog!"

The big badger grunted with exertion as he leaned down on the bow, bending it so that he tightened the string by taking another loop around the end of the thick yew wood. He shed his quiver. Going through the arrows, Lonna selected one. Then, holding it to his eye, he peered down the shaft to check that it was straight and true. Spreading both footpaws, Lonna gripped the ground firmly, wetted his upper lip and raised his head to feel which way the breeze was blowing. Satisfied, he looked toward the Searat, gauging the distance. Then he placed the shaft on his bowstring and drew back. The string was resting against one scarred ear, the bow strained in a mighty arc to its full capacity. After glancing once more at the distant Searat, Lonna elevated the bow slightly skyward and let fly.

The Searat rose upright, waving his sword at the tiny figure out on the flatlands. "Outran ye, stripedog! I beat ye, didn't I?"

A distant, blood-curdling cry answered him. "Eulalilll-laaaaaa!"

The arrow came like a thunderbolt out of the blue.

Lonna strode out to view his last work of vengeance. Spread-eagled on the coarse grass, the Searat lay faceup. His eyes were wide open, staring at a sun that he would never see again, the long arrow standing out from the centre of his forehead.

The badger gazed down at the last rat of Raga Bol's once mighty crew. "Nobeast can outrun Lonna Bowstripe's arrow. Nobeast!"

Unstringing the bow, Lonna placed it lengthways across his broad shoulders, resting his paws on the weapon. Turning his back on the Searat, he strode east through the high summer midday to Redwall Abbey.

Night had fallen as the travellers neared the great gorge. They were weary after marching since early morning that day.

Bragoon called a halt within a short distance of the rim. "We'll take a breather, but without any fires. Eat'n'drink wot ye need, 'cos we'll be leavin' the rest behind."

Horty slumped down gratefully. "I say, what's the point of leavin' bloomin' good scoff here? Silly if you ask me, wot!"

The otter spoke in a low voice to the three young ones. "Keep yore voices down 'til we're on the other side o' that gorge, mates. I didn't like the place last time we crossed it, an' I likes it even less now. We've got to travel fast'n'light when we crosses that big tree trunk, so keep yore wits sharp!"

Saro had the rope. She tied a short, thick piece of wood crosswise to one end of it. "Those broken staves we stuck atop o' the other side should still be in place. If'n I throws it right, this chunk o' wood will lodge atween 'em, an' we can climb up sharpish."

Springald cast a worried glance at the pair. "You two

403

don't like that gorge one little bit, do you? Don't fret, we'll cross it as quick and quiet as you like."

Saro tested the knot she had tied around the wood. "Aye, you do that, Spring. I'll be in front of ye, an' Brag'll bring up the rear. Just do as yore told, an' everythin' will be alright. I don't like that gorge any more'n Brag does. That place has a bad feel to it!"

Fenna's voice was small and shaky as she tried to make a joke. "Don't worry about us. We're young and we've got a lot to learn, but we're willing to listen to experienced old fogies."

Grasping her paw, Bragoon smiled in the darkness. "That's the spirit, missy. Right! Up on yore hunkers, mates. Let's get ye safe back to Redwall."

Drawing the sword of Martin from behind his shoulder, the otter led them off toward the rim.

Horty took one rueful glance at the small heap of provisions on the ground, then uttered a small sigh. "What a flamin' waste. Ah well, this is it, chaps, off we jolly well go!"

The edge of the chasm loomed up, sooner than they had expected. Saro found the same boulder she had used on the previous trip. Making a wide loop in the rope's free end, she placed it about the big stone, lowering the end with the wood attached into the gorge below. Bragoon went first. Climbing carefully, he reached the ledge in front of the three cave entrances. He held the wood, so that it would not clack against the rock wall. Springald came next, followed by Horty, then Fenna. Saro was last to descend. She flipped the rope deftly, catching the end as it unlooped from the boulder and dropped down.

Before Bragoon stepped onto the tree trunk, he pressed something into Fenna's paw and whispered, "Shove this in yore belt pouch, no questions." Without a word, the squirrelmaid stuffed the object into her pouch, then followed the otter out onto the tree trunk bridge.

Total silence and engulfing dark reigned in the yawning chasm. Holding one another's paws, the five travellers edged slowly forward, step by step. They were almost across to the far side when a harsh, evil laugh sounded out from behind them.

Suddenly the lights of many smoking torches lit up the gorge. Saro turned, gasping at the incredible sight.

Kharanjul stood on the trunk, backed by an army of vermin, each holding a torch in one paw and a spear in the other. They were mainly ferrets and weasels, with a scattering of large rats among them. Everybeast's fur was thickly daubed with a sickly yellow-and-green substance, giving them a sinister, spectral appearance. But it was the horrific form of their leader that stood out.

The Wearet swung back his cloak, revealing a misshapen but powerfully bulky torso. As he gestured at them with a big, three-pronged trident, his monstrous face split into an ugly grin. "Stop where ye stand, trespasser! You belong to Kharanjul, Lord of the Abyss! I will punish you for intruding on my domain!"

Saro pushed Horty forward. "Keep goin', we're almost across!"

Bragoon was about to jump from the log onto the opposite ledge, when a score of vermin rose up in front of him.

The captain, a tall weasel, snarled in his face. "Stand still! Obey the Great Lord of Life and Death!"

The otter laughed, then slew him with a single swordthrust. Catching the captain's spear as it fell, Bragoon tossed it back to Saro. "Keep 'em busy, mate. Redwaaaaaal-lllll!"

Hurling himself from the tree trunk, Bragoon roared like a madbeast as he dealt out death and destruction with the sword of Martin the Warrior. "Heeeeeyaaaaaah! Grab some spears, young 'uns! No pack o' fancy-talkin' vermin are goin' to stop us Redwallers!"

Horty seized a long spear and was suddenly in the thick of the battle, whooping and bellowing. "Forward the buffs, give 'em blood'n'vinegar. Chaaaaarge!"

Belting a weasel flying into the abyss, the young hare stood shoulder to shoulder with the otter—cutting, thrusting and slashing. Springald and Fenna armed themselves with fallen spears. They turned to help Saro, but the aging squirrel would have none of it. Single-pawed, she held the centre of the log bridge, letting none pass. Using her spearblade, she slashed at a ferret, flaying his footpaw. He hopped off into midair and vanished screaming.

Saro yelled at the two Abbeymaids. "Take this rope an' see if ye can fix it t'the top. Then go an' help Brag an' Horty. I'm fine right 'ere, they can only come at me one at a time!"

They obeyed her immediately. As they jumped off the tree trunk, a big rat charged Springald, but he vanished over the rim with a yowl of dismay when Fenna pushed him with her spearbutt.

The squirrelmaid was momentarily stunned. "I've just slain somebeast!"

Springald shouted. "Good! Mind your back, Fenn!"

The mousemaid deflected a spear with her own. She thrust and saw the look of surprised horror on the vermin's painted face as he fell dead.

Steeling herself, Springald stood back to back with her friend. "Keep fighting or we're deadbeasts!"

Bragoon and Horty fought their way through to the side of the two maids. The otter despatched a charging weasel, then shouted, "Gimme that rope, Spring. You three, cover my back!" Grabbing the rope, he whirled it and flung it up, but it fell back. Bragoon whirled it once more, gritting his teeth against the swordblade held between them. This time his throw was good; the chunk of wood lodged between the two broken staves which they had fixed into the plateau. The otter swung his weight onto the rope, testing it. The rope held firm. He turned to the three young ones.

"Come on, mates, up y'go! Horty, take this sword, 'tis too

short for fightin' spears with. Pass me yore spear an' get climbin'!"

Horty gave him the spear and took the sword, but the hare refused to climb up. There were six vermin left to face on their side. Slaying one with a slash to the throat, Horty shook his head. "Let Spring an Fenn go, I'm stayin' here with you, sah. True blue an' never fail, that's us Braebucks, wot!"

The otter whacked a vermin over the skull with his spear, then kicked him swiftly into the abyss. Blood was flowing from a wound on his forehead as he turned on Horty furiously. "I said, git up that rope, hare. Do it now!"

Between them they faced off a vermin, who was very fancy with his spearwork.

Horty muttered rebelliously. "I ain't goin', otter! I can't leave you an' Saro here to face that flamin' lot on your own!"

Bragoon's eyes were blazing as he faced Horty. "Wot did I tell ye, I'm in charge 'ere. Obey me . . . Argh!"

The vermin's spearpoint took the otter through the footpaw. He pulled the spear from his foe's grasp, ran him through with it and booted him into oblivion. Livid with wrath, he rounded on the young hare. "Don't argue wid me, mate! Yore young, like them two maids, you got all your lives ahead o' ye. Get that sword back to Redwall! Me'n Saro knows wot we're doin'. We can't look after three young 'uns who are still wet be'ind the ears, we've lived one summer too long fer all that! Now git up that rope, Horty, or I swear I'll run ye through wid this spear! Look after the two maids, live yore life for us. Now go!"

Leaving Horty one vermin to deal with, the otter turned and limped out onto the long tree trunk to help Sarobando.

Horty downed the vermin in a perilous rage, needlessly striking at the foebeast's carcass. Springald and Fenna looked down from the top of the plateau, howling hoarsely at their young friend.

"Horty, come on, get up the rope!"

"You must obey Bragoon, do as you're told!"

Clamping the sword in his teeth, Horty ran to the rope. He took one backward look at Bragoon and Saro. Though wounded in a dozen places, they were still fighting savagely.

Reeling from a blow, Saro caught his eye and bellowed. "Get to the top an' pull the rope up, or they'll come after ye an' slay those two maids. Go! Go!"

Blinded by tears of rage and helplessness, Horty went.

Kharanjul stood on the far ledge, urging his creatures forward. Seeing so many killed by the two old battlers who were holding off the advance, the Wearet took up his trident and went out to fight.

The vermin were still coming. Bragoon and Saro were bowed with fatigue, but covered in blood and severely injured, they were still taking on all comers. They fought side by side on the narrow causeway of timber, keeping their eyes on the advancing enemy, talking to each other as they thrust and parried.

Saro panted. "The young 'uns are gone. Pity we couldn't 'ave gone with 'em."

Bragoon dislodged a foebeast with his spear. "Wot, y'mean back to Redwall? Don't think I could've stood it, mate, sittin' in the gate'ouse wid Old Phredd countin' me teeth as they fell out an' dozin' all day!"

Saro wiped blood from her eye and chuckled. "Dibbuns climbin' all over us, ole Setiva physickin' away at us, wrappin' rugs round our laps in winter!"

Bragoon caught a ferret in the throat with his spear. "Might be even worse—they could've sent us back to Abbey school. We'd 'ave Sister Portula teachin' us to readn'write'n'figger. No, that ain't fer us, pal!"

The aging squirrel caught sight of Kharanjul advancing. "Oh, look out, Brag, 'ere comes the big ugly mug. We'd better start backin' off. Blood'n'fur, lookit the size o' that monster, he must've ate some dinners with that fork!"

The vermin advanced on them as they retreated. Sorely wounded and drained of strength, the two old friends continued to hack and slash. Vastly outnumbered by their adversaries, and knowing that they would be beaten and captured by Kharanjul, they crawled down from the long bridge, with one last desperate plan in mind.

The Wearet pressed forward, holding his lethal trident ready as he taunted his victims. "The Lord of Life and Death will keep you alive. I will make your dying long and slow. Your companions escaped the Wearet, but you shall pay for them!"

Bragoon and Sarobando were not listening. Between them they had jammed a half-dozen spearbutts under the end of the tree trunk. With a last mighty effort, both beasts put their shoulders to the spears, using them as levers.

Saro gritted her teeth and growled. "One, two, three. Push!"

The long trunk moved askew, with a grating of wood on rock. Panic ensued out on the tree trunk, as vermin tried to run back to the other side. Some threw themselves flat and clung on.

Bragoon yelled above the din of wails and screams. "She's movin', mate! Again, one, two, three! Push!"

Kharanjul dropped his trident. Crouching low, he gripped the tree trunk, trying to move forward and reach his enemy. At last the mighty trunk of the tree, once called Lord of Mossflower, groaned like a living thing as it made a half-turn to one side and slid over the brink of the ledge.

With the effort of their final push, the two old warriors had fallen flat. They watched as the log seemed to hang for a split second in space, with Kharanjul's face looming in front of them. Then the whole trunk fell into the bottomless abyss. Screeches and shrieks rent the night air, swiftly fading to echoes. Down, down, into the dark gorge it all plunged—the Wearet, his vermin army and the only solid bridge that had ever spanned the awesome space.

Bragoon and Saro lay there, staring down into the void, their paws clasped. The aging squirrel closed her eyes. "Nice'n'peaceful 'ere now, mate, ain't it?"

The otter gave her paw a faint squeeze. "Aye, restful ye might say. Summer's a good time to lay down an' rest."

No longer able to keep them open, Bragoon slowly closed his eyes. "Saro, ye recall wot it said on that gravestone at Loamhedge? Young Fenna read it out to us. I said I liked the sound of it."

Saro nodded weakly. "I remember, mate. It said 'Gone to the sunny slopes an' quiet streams.' I liked it, too."

The otter's voice grew fainter as he repeated the phrase. "The sunny slopes an' quiet streams . . . I'll wait for ye there, Sarobando . . . Wouldn't go anyplace without ye." His paw went limp in the squirrel's failing grasp.

She smiled. "Wait for me, Brag ole mate, I'll be there."

Two old warriors, who had left Redwall Abbey when they were Dibbuns, paw in paw, lay on the rockledge together. They never saw the sunrise that dawn, but they went on to the land of sunny slopes and quiet streams—still holding paws.

43

Summer's days were growing short, passing gently into autumn. Redwall Abbey was restored to its former calm and grandeur. Abbot Carrul and Martha met for their early morning stroll, now a regular thing with the two friends before they took breakfast. A light mist—like golden gossamer—lay over the Abbey pond. They saw a grayling leap to catch an unsuspecting fly.

Carrul watched the ripples spread across the water. "I had a dream last night. It was a vision of Martin."

The haremaid was startled by her Abbot's revelation. "A dream of Martin the Warrior? Did he say anything, Father?"

The Abbot paused before answering. "He did, indeed, Martha. These were his very words.

"When autumn brings the harvest time,
good food you shall not lack,
when fruit lies heavy on the bough,
and travellers come back.
Look for the one who holds my sword,
these words of mine recall,
someday you will esteem that one,
as ruler of Redwall!"

Martha sat down on a log, puzzled by the rhyme. "Good grief, Father, there's a lot of information in Martin's words. Aside from the fact that there will be a fine harvest, our friends—Horty, Bragoon and the others—must be returning. Isn't that great news! But I never guessed you were thinking of retiring from being Abbot of Redwall."

Carrul sat down beside her. "The thought never crossed my mind, Martha. But Martin said someday, and someday in the future I would have to give serious thought to appointing my successor. Martin has saved me a lot of pondering, I'm grateful to him for that. However, his words are causing me a little concern. Think. Who did I give the sword to?"

The haremaid replied promptly. "You gave it to Bragoon."

Carrul nodded his agreement. "Which is why I'm worried, Martha. Bragoon is a good friend, we were Dibbuns together. But he's a rover, an adventurer. Ask Toran, Bragoon's his elder brother, he'll tell you. Bragoon's too old and too wild to be Abbot."

Martha held up a paw. "Not so fast, Father. The rhyme said ruler of Redwall, not Abbot. It may be an Abbess!"

Carrul clapped a paw to his cheek. "Fates forbid that it might be Sarobando! It would be woe to my poor Abbey."

Martha could not help laughing. "Hahaha, oh Father, think for a moment. It could be Springald, or Fenna or . . ." Now it was Martha's turn to look apprehensive. "Or Horty?"

Carrul placed a comforting paw on the haremaid's shoulder. "Oh, come on now, miss! Martin the Warrior was renowned for his wisdom. What are we thinking about? He wouldn't inflict any of those three rascals on our Abbey!"

Martha gave an audible sigh of relief. "You're right, Father. But it might be nobeast we've thought of. What if they bring somebody back with them?"

Carrul pursued this idea enthusiastically. "Of course, there may have been other creatures living at Loamhedge.

Say a sturdy young mouse, steeped in wisdom? Or a sagacious squirrel, the very model of common sense?"

Martha giggled. "Or a studious frog with the brain of an ant!"

Abbot Carrul smacked her paw playfully. "Now stop this nonsense, you young rip. Look, here comes breakfast!"

Toran had resumed his role as cook. He and Gurvel headed a procession carrying tables and benches, trolleys, dishes and food. He waved his ladle.

"Set 'em all up at the edge of the pond there, next to those two pore beasts who've been waitin' out here all night!"

Carrul chuckled. "So ends our moment of peace for the day, Martha. Besieged by breakfasters!"

The haremaid went to help the servers. "Let's join them, I'm starving!"

Setting up the tables, Brother Weld pulled a ferocious face at the Dibbuns, who were buzzing around like playful bees. "I'll toss the lot of you into the pond if you don't sit still and wait to be served. So behave yourselves!"

Muggum the molebabe clambered up on a bench, next to Buffle. "Hurr hurr, ee'm a gurt bold crittur t'be assultin' uz loike that! Wot do ee say, Buff?"

The tiny mousebabe scowled darkly. "Gurrumff um burble fink!"

Old Phredd looked over his glasses at the infant mouse. "What did he just say?"

Sister Setiva tied a bib about Buffle's neck. "Och, ah be a-feared tae repeat it. But if the wee scamp says it again, ah'll wash his mouth out with soap!"

The Dibbun squirrelbabe Shilly tugged at Martha's paw. "When izza harviss gonna be, Marth'?"

The haremaid gave the reply she had been repeating to the Abbeybabes for the past few days. "On the first morning after the night of harvest moon. Be patient, it shouldn't be too long now."

Granmum Gurvel looked up from a pan of corn and fruit slices she was doling out. "Payshunt? You'm doan't tell ee

413

Redwallers t'be payshunt when they'm a waitin' to get ee 'arvest in, Miz Marth'!"

The Dibbuns cheered Gurvel loudly, glad to have an ally on their side. Most of the babes had never been to a harvest before, so they were eager to take part in one, knowing there would be a Harvest End Feast. The little ones began clamouring for Martha to sing the Harvest Song. Knowing they would not be quiet until she did, Martha obliged by singing the lively air, which included much tapping and paw stamping.

> "Open the cupboard the bins and the stores,
> go fetch out the trolleys and carts,
> then out to the orchard the gardens and fields,
> for a harvest to gladden our hearts.
>
> Rappety tap, the Abbot'll call,
> watch out for those Dibbuns 'cos they'll eat it all!
>
> There's blackberries blueberries raspberries too
> strawberries and redcurrants bright,
> wild cherries blueberries and blaeberries ripe,
> to be all gathered in by tonight.
>
> Rappety tap, wait for the feast,
> just look at that Dibbun, the greedy wee beast!
>
> Bring basket and barrel and bucket and pail,
> pick rosehips red apples and pears,
> greengages damsons and plums big and fine,
> roll your sleeves up and banish your cares.
>
> Rappety tap, that babe's the worst,
> if he eats another I swear that he'll burst!
>
> There's almond and hazel and chestnut in bloom,
> and a crop of good acorns there'll be,
> if you hold the ladder I'll climb to the top,
> and I'll knock them all down from the tree.

Rappety tap, flat on the ground,
he's rubbing his tummy and rolling around!

Let's gather our harvest and bring it indoors,
then the Abbot'll cry out 'Well done!'
We've filled up the cupboards the bins and the stores,
in good time for the winter to come.

Rappety tap, quick close the door,
he's up on his paws and looking for more!"

As usual, Martha had to sing the whole thing again so the Dibbuns could show off their fancy paw tapping. Whilst this was going on, the Abbot took Toran aside. He related what Martin the Warrior had told him in his dream. The ottercook was overjoyed at the news.

"As soon as the 'arvest moon shows, we'll mount a watch on the walltops to welcome them back 'ome!"

Breakfast was about finished when Foremole Dwurl, who had been gatekeeper in Phredd's absence, came trundling up with Lonna in tow. He hailed Toran. "Gudday, zurr. Lookit who'm just cummed a knocken on ee gate!"

The ottercook quickly cleared a place for them both. "Sit ye down, mates, an' break yore fast. Lonna, where've ye been since yesterday? Everybeast was wonderin' where ye'd got to."

The big badger seated himself, allowing Gurvel to heap food in front of him. His fur was coated in dew, and the blood had matted on his wounds, but he looked happy. "The Searats are all accounted for—down to the last vermin. I was tired, but glad that I had ended my mission, so I lay down on the flatlands, about half a league from your Abbey. I must have slept deeply, because it was the sound of larks rising at dawn that awakened me. I was hoping there'd be a bite of breakfast left for a hungry badger. Thank you, marm!"

Granmum Gurvel piled corn and fruit slices on a platter.

"You'm eat 'earty, zurr. Oi'll cook more furr ee if'n ye be still 'ungered!"

Abbot Carrul beckoned Brother Gelf. "Draw off a pitcher of our best October Ale for Lonna. Nothing's too good for the beast who saved Redwall from the Searats. Lonna, after you've eaten, Sister Portula will find you clean robes, and Sister Setiva will care for your wounds. You must rest now, friend!"

Seating themselves around the badger, the Dibbuns watched in awe as he satisfied his appetite.

Muggum nudged Buffle. "Yurr, ee'm gurtbeast surpintly can shuv ee vikkles away!"

Stifling a smile, Martha chided the molebabe. "Really, Muggum, mind your manners!"

Lonna sat Muggum on his paw and lifted him to face-height. "Listen to me, young sir, never mess with your food. Eat it all up like I do, then someday you'll be a great warrior!"

Muggum nodded sagely. "Them bee's woise wurds, zurr!"

It was five nights hence when the harvest moon waxed fully. Most Abbeybeasts were in their beds. Toran stood watch from the ramparts on the southwest corner, where he could view both the path and woodlands. Martha and Abbot Carrul, neither of whom felt like sleeping, joined the ottercook on his vigil. The three stood there, unaware that Lonna had come up behind them. For a beast of his size and weight, the badger could move silent as a shadow. They started slightly as he spoke.

"That nice old molewife in the kitchens asked me to bring some hot vegetable soup up for you." Lonna poured the soup from a jug into four basins.

Toran sniffed it, exclaiming gratefully, "Good ole Gurvel!"

They sipped at their basins in silence, contemplating the serenity of a late summer's night.

*

Nocturnal birdsong drifted from the shadowed trees of Mossflower. The path stood out like a tranquil stream, curling southward. Galaxies of twinkling stars pinpointed the cloudless vaults of sky above. A single comet streaked through space in brief silent glory. The harvest moon ruled over all, surrounded by a soft nimbus, resplendent in its own golden solitude.

None of the others noticed Lonna fitting a shaft to his bowstring. He peered toward the foliage which fringed the pathside. Drawing back his bow, Lonna called down, "Are you friend or foe?"

Three figures stepped out onto the path. One shouted, "Ahoy the walls, we come as friends!"

Martha's good eyesight allowed her to quickly identify the caller. "It's a shrew. There's two more with him."

Lonna relaxed his bowstring. "What do you want, friends?"

The lead shrew's rapier blade flashed in the moonlight as he made a salute and offered it hilt first. "I am Jigger, son of Log a Log Briggy, Chieftain of the Guorafs crews! I carry news of your friends. My father sent me ahead to tell you of their approach!"

Toran and Lonna were already down and unbarring the gates as Martha assisted the Abbot to negotiate the wall-steps.

Old Phredd lit extra lanterns as they crowded into the gatehouse. When the introductions were completed, the young shrew made his report. It was not a happy tale that he had to relate. Martha was stunned beyond tears at the news of Bragoon's and Saro's death. Abbot Carrul hung his head and wept openly. Lonna stood by in respectful silence. Toran was the only one to speak.

"The young 'uns, are they all safe'n'well?"

Jigger nodded. "Aye, sir. Apart from a few scratches an' sore footpaws, they're fine. Miss Fenna told me that Bragoon was yore brother. 'Twas a brave thing him'n Saro did."

The ottercook drew himself up straight and spoke

417

proudly. "Aye, Bragoon an' Sarobando was true-born Redwallers! No two like 'em, they was both wild warriors. But they did their duty an' saved their friends. I wager they took a few o' those vermin with 'em, eh?"

Jigger's eyes were shining with admiration as he replied. "From wot our scouts said, they took 'em all, every last vermin, an' their chief, the Wearet. That must've been a powerful battle, I'll tell ye!"

Toran opened the gatehouse door. He took a deep breath of the fresh night air and smiled. "Funny, ain't it, some'ow I couldn't imagin' Saro an' Brag growin' old like peaceful Abbeybeasts. Not those two. They went like they wanted to, the bravest o' the brave!"

Lonna offered his paw to Toran. "True warriors have no fear of death. I only met your brother and his friend once. They were rare beasts!"

Abbot Carrul wiped at his eyes with damp habit sleeves. "Look at me, I must have forgotten my manners. Come to the Abbey, Jigger. Bring your two friends. You must be hungry after travelling so far. Lonna, will you wait by the gates and show the rest of them to the kitchens when they arrive?"

Jigger hitched up his rapier belt eagerly. "Lead on, Father. If'n the vittles at Redwall are as good as Horty tells me, I can't wait t'get at 'em!"

It was some time thereafter when Lonna herded the Guoraf shrews into the Abbey kitchens. Martha and Toran forged their way through the crowd to Horty, Fenna and Springald. They fell upon one another, hugging and shaking paws as the Abbot joined them.

"Welcome home, you weary travellers! Springald, what's up, miss, are you ill?"

The mousemaid was staring at Martha in disbelief. "Look, she's walking! Martha's walking!"

Horty held his sister at paw's length. "But how the . . . what the blinkin' flip . . . I mean, the bloomin' skin'n'blister trottin' about like . . . like? Explain y'bally self, miss. How did y'do it, wot wot?"

The haremaid stared down at her brother's bandaged right footpaw, having noticed he was sporting a gallant limp. "You'll get to know all about it later. But what happened to you, Horty, are you hurt?"

Trying to look brave and nonchalant at the same time, Horty waffled. "Oh this, line o' duty an' all that, y'know!"

Springald raised her eyebrows scathingly. "Line of duty, my tail! You great fibber, tell the truth. He was messing about with Martin's sword, showing off to the shrews, when he dropped it, tripped up and cut his footpaw on the blade!"

The Abbot exchanged a glance with Martha before he asked. "Well, who has the sword now?"

From beneath her cloak Fenna produced the sword, neatly wrapped and tied in a piece of sailcloth. "I took it off Horty and bound it up for safekeeping. Don't worry, it's in perfect condition and quite undamaged."

She looked from the Abbot to Martha. "Why, what's the matter, did I do anything wrong, should I have left the sword for Horty to fool about with?"

Both Martha and the Abbot hugged the squirrelmaid.

"No no, you did the right thing!"

"Yes, you did, Fenna, thank goodness! Please accept the gratitude of an old Abbot!"

The squirrelmaid passed the sword over to the Abbot. "Why, Father, what's this all about?"

Abbot Carrul looked over his glasses at her. "Nothing for you to worry your head about, miss. I'll tell you everything in a few seasons' time—that's, of course, providing you don't plan on leaving us to go somewhere else."

Fenna replied promptly. "Why would I go anywhere else? Redwall Abbey's my home, I'd never leave it for anything!"

Martha clasped her friend's paw. "Neither would I, Fenna. There's noplace dearer than our Abbey!"

Whilst the shrews were sampling the delights of the kitchens, the three young ones went down to Cavern Hole with Toran, Martha and the Abbot. There, away from the hubbub, they sat by the embers of a glowing fire, recounting their journey to and from Loamhedge. It was an engrossing story, vividly illustrated by the young creatures' first real experience of the outside world—enemies they had encountered, friends they had met, hardships they had undergone. Horty, Springald and Fenna each related the parts they had taken in the epic quest. Throughout the narrative it was clear that the entire thing would not have been possible without the heroism, guidance and assistance of Bragoon and Sarobando. By the time the dawn bells were tolling, the trio had reached the end of their tale. Fenna reached into her belt pouch and drew forth the slim package of parchment which Bragoon had entrusted to her. "This is Sister Amyl's secret. Take it, Martha, it's meant for you alone. I know you don't have any need for it now, but I feel you should have it."

They watched in silence as the haremaid undid the wrapping and began scanning it.

Horty leaned forward eagerly. "Well, are you goin' to jolly well read it out to us, or are you goin' to sit there bloomin' well gazin' at the blinkin' thing until next flippin' summer, wot?"

Martha hesitated. "I'm not supposed to, really. It says on the other side of this parchment that only the one who needs this shall know my secret. But I don't think it will do any harm now. Here's what it says:

"The body is ruled by the mind,
I tell you this be true,
by willpower you may find,
nought is denied to you."

Abbot Carrul took the parchment from her paws. He stared at it, turned it over, studied it a moment longer, then chuckled as he passed it to Toran. "So, that's Sister Amyl's secret, eh? Take a look at that, Toran, my friend!"

After a brief glance the ottercook burst into laughter. "Hohoho, Sister Amyl my granma's rudder! Hohoho, those rascals!"

Martha was astonished at the attitude of her friends. "Excuse me, I fail to see what's so funny. Those are the words of a young Sister who suffered the same as I did. I can see that it's written in an old-fashioned style, and the writing isn't too neat. But what's that to laugh about?"

Abbot Carrul explained. "This was never written by Sister Amyl. She was a young Sister who was well educated, her spelling was faultless and she had a neat writing paw. Remember the history of Loamhedge you were reading, the one you borrowed from Sister Portula? Amyl had written part of that, but she certainly never wrote this!"

The light of recognition dawned across Fenna's face. "I'll wager I know who did write it. I've just remembered where I've seen that parchment before. It's a piece torn from the edge of the Loamhedge map we took with us. See, there's a line on it that was the rim of the high cliffs. Bragoon or Sarobando must have written it. Everything they found in Abbess Sylvaticus's tomb had mouldered away to dust. So they invented Sister Amyl's secret themselves rather than return to Redwall empty-pawed. That's it! Either Saro or Bragoon did the writing."

Abbot Carrul patted the squirrelmaid's shoulder. "Well done, miss! Actually, Bragoon or Saro didn't write this singly, they both did! I recognise the writing on the outside, Sarobando did that. She was better at spelling but worse at writing than Bragoon. He had the neater paw but oh, dear me, that otter's spelling was dreadful, look at it!"

They examined the short rhyme closely.

"The body is rooled by the mynd,
I tell you this be troo,

421

by willpower you may fynd,
nort is denyed to you."

Toran wiped tears of laughter from his eyes. "Aye, that was
my brother, alright. Old Brag never won any prizes for his
spellin'. But he did it so ye wouldn't be let down, Martha.
So I think ye could forgive 'em both for it."

Martha stared into the fire embers. "Forgive? There's
nothing to forgive. They did it for me, undertook that whole
long quest, protected my brother and his friends, then sacrificed their lives for them."

Toran did not know whether he was smiling or weeping.
He scrubbed a paw across his eyes again. "So they did,
Martha, so they did!"

Epilogue

Ten seasons have passed since that night of the harvest moon. Fate and fortune have allowed our Abbey to prosper in peace. We had some visitors to Redwall the other day, a column of fighting hares from Salamandastron, sent by Lord Lonna Bowstripe. They were led by Captain Hortwill Longblade Braebuck, who was visiting his sister. What a change the Long Patrol has made to Horty! He went off all that time ago, with Lonna, to enlist at Salamandastron, carrying the scimitar that the badger had taken from Raga Bol. Horty is now twice as big, and twice as hungry, as he once was, a fine figure of a Long Patrol captain with a bristling military moustache. The young hares under his command admire him greatly. Abbess Fenna was delighted to see him, and so was I. We sat up until late last night, chatting about the old days, with Carrul our Gatekeeper and Cellarmole Muggum. Yes, Abbot Carrul became Gatekeeper, by his own choosing, four seasons back. He shared the task with Old Phredd until the ancient hedgehog went to his long rest last winter. Ah well, such is life, and such is its passing; not even

Phredd could live forever. Horty and his hares are staying until after the Harvest Feast. (Trust hares never to miss a chance of several days' good feeding.) Those are Ottercook Toran's words, not mine, though I share his sentiments.

On the night of the harvest moon, all our Abbeybeasts will gather on the lawn near the front wallgates. We will watch Martha climb the steps to the threshold. First she will sing the beautiful ballad, "The Rose of Redwall." Then she will carry out the promise she made to Bragoon and Sarobando. They say that, on the day they left to search for Loamhedge, she vowed that when they returned she would dance for both of them, on the walltop, right over the threshold of our Abbey. Martha has kept her promise every season since then. After singing her song, she dances— swaying, bending, curtsying and leaping—graceful as a breeze-blown flower in the golden moonlight, for the memory of her two friends. I remember then that long ago summer when we stole out of the Abbey, rebellious young creatures embarking on a great adventure. We returned at the end of that season—wiser, more obedient and more reasonable. It was the summer of growing up.

If you, too, are travelling, questing or journeying anywhere, remember this. You will always find a welcome here at Redwall Abbey, young or old. As friends come by, they often call in to enjoy Redwall hospitality. Who knows, maybe we will see you here someday. You can sit with us, rest and be refreshed and learn. Young ones have much to learn and old ones, too. Carrul said to me only the other day, we are never too old to learn. He was a wise Abbot; he is an even wiser old Gatekeeper. I hope someday I may grow as wise as him.

Springald. Recorder of Redwall Abbey in Mossflower country